BAKING ILLUSTRATED

A BEST RECIPE CLASSIC

Baking Illustrated

A BEST RECIPE CLASSIC

BY THE EDITORS OF

COOK'S ILLUSTRATED

ILLUSTRATIONS
JOHN BURGOYNE

PHOTOGRAPHY
CARL TREMBLAY
KELLER + KELLER
DANIEL VAN ACKERE

AMERICA'S TEST KITCHEN
BROOKLINE, MASSACHUSETTS

America's Test Kitchen
17 Station Street
Brookline, MA 02445

Library of Congress Cataloging-in-Publication Data
The Editors of *Cook's Illustrated*

Baking Illustrated: The Practical Kitchen Companion for the Home Baker with 350 Recipes You Can Trust
1st Edition

ISBN-13: 978-0-936184-75-3
ISBN-10: 0-936184-75-2
(hardcover): U.S. $35 CAN $45
I. Cooking. I. Title
2004

Manufactured in the United States of America

10 9 8 7 6 5 4

Distributed by America's Test Kitchen, 17 Station Street, Brookline, MA 02445.

Senior Editor: Lori Galvin
Associate Editor: Matthew Card
Recipe Development: Garth Clingingsmith, Sean Lawler, Susan Light, Meg Suzuki
Recipe Tester: Jeanne Maguire
High-Altitude Recipe Tester: Erika Bruce
Series Designer: Amy Klee
Art Director: Julia Sedykh
Graphic Designer: Nina Madjid
Photographs: Color photography copyright ©2004 by Carl Tremblay; photographs on pages iv, 281, 287 copyright ©2004 by Keller + Keller; silhouette photography copyright ©2004 by Daniel van Ackere.
Illustrations: Illustrations copyright ©2004 by John Burgoyne
Production Manager: Jessica Lindheimer Quirk
Copyeditor: Cheryl Redmond
Proofreader: Jean Rogers
Indexer: Cathy Dorsey

Contents

PREFACE

HUNTING AND FISHING ARE MORE SCIENCE than art—at least that is what I have concluded after many years of failing to bring down a large buck, land a big salmon, or net a decent-size rainbow out of our local, and famous, trout stream. And I have also concluded that it isn't just a matter of experience and familiarity with the process. I know lots of aging hunters and anglers who spend most of their time watching others do the catching. It is, I am afraid, a matter of science, a matter of knowing exactly which dry fly will produce results on a particular day in a particular hole or knowing exactly which tree to sit in during hunting season. Lack of planning, sketchy knowledge, and inattention to detail are guaranteed to produce poor results.

Much of this knowledge is simply a matter of obstinacy. One of my Vermont neighbors, Nate, sits in a tree stand in subzero temperatures for five hours at a time—I am apt to head home after a mere 90 minutes. An angler friend of mine once spent an hour watching a trout pool well populated by unsuccessful fishermen. He concluded that the fish were feeding off of mating insects, found a reasonable facsimile in his fly box, and proceeded to reel them in.

One might say that baking is much the same. Here in America's Test Kitchen, we are stubborn, baking the same recipe over and over until it comes out "right," or at least to our satisfaction. That might mean baking more than 100 yellow layer cakes over the course of two months or making pan after pan of brownies until the notion of chocolate, butter, and sugar is enough to make us green around the gills. There is no substitute for intimacy with process. It is a lifelong process of self-education, one that takes dedication to detail, an eye for the unexpected, and a love of science.

Of course, one could simply purchase *Baking Illustrated* and reap the rewards of thousands of hours of test kitchen experience. It may not be comparable to having done all of the testing oneself, but, practically speaking, it is about as good as it gets. I do the same thing when I go hunting these days. I always invite along Nate—my resident expert—who knows where to sit, where to walk, and how to make a convincing turkey call. When it comes to baking, I hope that you will let us be your well-traveled companion in the kitchen. We are eager to share what we have discovered with anyone who is kind enough to listen.

Christopher Kimball
Founder and Editor
Cook's Illustrated

WELCOME TO
AMERICA'S TEST KITCHEN

THIS BOOK HAS BEEN TESTED, WRITTEN, AND edited by the folks at America's Test Kitchen, a very real 2,500-square-foot kitchen located just outside of Boston. It is the home of *Cook's Illustrated* magazine and *Cook's Country* magazine and is the Monday-through-Friday destination for more than three dozen test cooks, editors, food scientists, tasters, and cookware specialists. Our mission is to test recipes over and over again until we understand how and why they work and until we arrive at the "best" version. We start the process of testing a recipe with a complete lack of conviction, which means that we accept no claim, no theory, no technique, and no recipe at face value. We simply assemble as many variations as possible, test a half dozen of the most promising, and taste the results blind. We then construct our own hybrid recipe and continue to test it, varying ingredients, techniques, and cooking times until we reach a consensus. The result, we hope, is the best version of a particular recipe, but we realize that only you can be the final judge of our success (or failure). As we like to say

in the test kitchen, "We make the mistakes, so you don't have to."

All of this would not be possible without a belief that good cooking, much like good music, is indeed based on a foundation of objective technique. Some people like spicy foods and others don't, but there is a right way to sauté, there is a best way to cook a pot roast, and there are measurable scientific principles involved in producing perfectly beaten, stable egg whites. This is our ultimate goal: to investigate the fundamental principles of cooking so that you become a better cook. It is as simple as that.

You can watch us work (in our actual test kitchen) by tuning in to *America's Test Kitchen* (www.americastestkitchen.com) or *Cook's Country from America's Test Kitchen* (www.cookscountrytv.com) on public television, or by subscribing to *Cook's Illustrated* magazine (www.cooksillustrated.com) or *Cook's Country* magazine (www.cookscountry.com). We welcome you into our kitchen, where you can stand by our side as we test our way to the "best" recipes in America.

Baking Ingredients
and Equipment

WITH A WELL-STOCKED PANTRY AND well-outfitted kitchen, you can tackle almost any baking project at will. Here are the ingredients and equipment we use regularly in the test kitchen when baking.

Ingredients

A NOTE ABOUT FLOUR The most elemental of baking ingredients, flour seems like a pretty simple item to choose. But a trip to the store reveals a wide variety of styles and shades of flour, not to mention all the different brands. What are the differences among them all and how do you choose the right flour for the right application?

At the simplest level, flour is classified by protein content, which is attributable to different types of wheat. For example, hard winter wheat (the season in which the wheat is grown) is about 10 percent to 13 percent protein; soft winter wheat about 8 percent to 10 percent. You can actually feel this difference with your fingers; the hard wheat flours tend to have a subtle granular feel, while soft wheat flours feel fine but starchy, much like cornstarch.

High-protein flours are generally recommended for yeasted products and other baked goods that require a lot of structural support. The reason is that the higher the protein level in a flour, the greater the potential for the formation of gluten. Gluten forms elastic sheets in dough that expand with the gas released by the yeast yet are sturdy enough to prevent that gas from escaping, so the dough doesn't deflate. Lower-protein flours, on the other hand, are recommended for chemically leavened baked goods. This is because baking powder and baking soda are quick leaveners. They lack the endurance of yeast, which can force the naturally resistant gluten sheets to expand. Gluten can overpower quick leaveners, causing the final baked product to fall flat.

Numerous factors besides protein, including milling, processing, and bleaching, play a role in how a particular flour behaves and tastes, but these factors vary according to the variety of flour and the producer. Here are the types of flours called for in the recipes in this book:

ALL-PURPOSE FLOUR A pantry staple, all-purpose flour is what most home bakers use for everything. All-purpose flour is typically made from hard red winter wheat, soft red winter wheat, or a combination of the two, yielding, on average, a flour with a relatively high protein content between 10 percent and 12 percent. Supermarkets generally carry numerous brands of all-purpose flour, ranging in price and color—many are unbleached. Does the brand really matter? Determined to get to the bottom of things, we tested nine brands of all-purpose flour (all varying slightly in protein content) in a wide variety of baked goods, from cookies and piecrusts to muffins and bread. To say it was a difficult tasting is a bit of an understatement; the differences in flavor and texture were subtle. The most obvious differences were often in appearance (white versus beige cookies, short or tall biscuits, etc.). As difficult as the tasting was, we were able to draw some conclusions.

As a general rule, the flours acted according to the basic principles regarding protein content. Brands of flour we tested with a higher protein content yielded heavier, denser biscuits than those with a lower protein content. The good news was that despite the textural differences, tasters liked all of the biscuits. Another trend we noticed was that lower-protein flours spread more in tests of chocolate chip cookies and muffins, but the flavors were fine.

As an overall category, the four bleached flours in our tests in fact did not perform as well as the unbleached flours and were regularly criticized for tasting flat or carrying "off" flavors, often described as metallic. These characteristics, however, were more difficult to detect in recipes that contained a high proportion of ingredients other than flour. Coincidentally, our tests of cake and chocolate chip cookies (both sugary recipes) were the two tests in which off flavors carried by the bleached flour went undetected or were considered faint.

Despite the variations and subtleties, we walked away with firm results. Both King Arthur and Pillsbury unbleached flours regularly produced a more consistent range of preferred products than the other seven flours in the taste tests. King Arthur has a slightly higher protein content than Pillsbury (11.7 percent as opposed to around 10 percent). Since Pillsbury and Gold Medal unbleached flour (which also performed well in tests and also contains about 10 percent protein) are more widely available, we've tested all recipes in this book with these flours. Higher-protein all-purpose flours, such as King Arthur, will work fine in most recipes, although their elevated protein content may affect texture and appearance slightly.

PROTEIN CONTENT OF UNBLEACHED ALL-PURPOSE FLOURS

All brands of all-purpose flour are not the same. If your recipe specifies a level of protein (i.e., lower protein or higher protein), we recommend you choose your flour accordingly for best results.

King Arthur	11.7	percent
Heckers/Ceresota	11.5–11.9	percent
Hodgson Mill	11.0	percent
Gold Medal	10.5	percent
Pillsbury	10.5	percent

BREAD FLOUR Flour with a protein level above 12 percent is generally sold as bread flour or labeled "made for bread machines." The high protein content ensures strong gluten development and a sturdy dough, which translates to good flavor, chewy texture, and a crisp crust. Not all styles of bread require bread flour; check the recipe before shopping.

CAKE FLOUR On the opposite end of the spectrum, cake flour is very low in protein, about 6 percent to 8 percent, which guarantees delicate, fine-crumbed cakes and light, airy biscuits. We call for cake flour only in recipes where we feel it delivers better results—usually a more tender crumb—than all-purpose flour. However, in a pinch a low-protein all-purpose flour, such as Pillsbury or Gold Medal, can be substituted with only a modest change in the finished baked good.

WHOLE-WHEAT FLOUR A wheat berry contains three elements: the outer bran layer, the germ, and the heart of the berry, the endosperm. To make traditional whole-wheat flour, the entire berry is ground (white flours are ground solely from the endosperm). Graham flour is a bit coarser and perhaps flakier than regular whole-wheat flour and provides a nuttier flavor than conventional whole wheat. It is named after its inventor, Sylvester Graham.

Because it is made from the whole wheat berry, which includes the perishable germ, whole-wheat flour does not store as well as all-purpose flour. If you don't think you will use an entire bag in a month or so, store whole-wheat flour in the freezer.

WHEAT GERM Simply the extracted germ of the wheat berry, wheat germ comes either plain (raw) or toasted. It is both highly nutritious and highly perishable; it should be stored in an airtight container in the refrigerator.

CORNMEAL We venture to guess that most people use whatever cornmeal they can find, but after testing 11 different varieties in a simple cornbread recipe, we have found major differences among them that impact the flavor, structure, and texture of baked goods.

The most obvious difference among them is color. Tasters found that yellow cornmeal has a more potent flavor than white. The way in which the cornmeal was processed, however, proved the biggest issue. Large commercial mills use huge steel rollers to grind dent corn (a hard, dry corn) into cornmeal. This is how Quaker, the leading supermarket brand, is produced. But some smaller mills scattered around the United States grind with millstones; this product is called stone-ground cornmeal. (If water is used as an energy source, the cornmeal may be labeled "water-ground.") Stone-ground cornmeal is usually a bit coarser than cornmeal processed through steel rollers.

Besides differences in milling methods, smaller millers often choose not to degerm, or remove the entire germ from, the corn. This makes their product closer to a whole-grain cornmeal. If the color is uniform, the germ has been removed. A stone-ground cornmeal with some germ will have flecks that are both lighter and darker than the predominant color, whether that's yellow or white.

In our tests, we found the texture of cornbreads made with stone-ground meals to be more interesting. More important, we found that cornbreads made with stone-ground cornmeal tasted much better than those made with the standard Quaker cornmeal. The higher moisture and oil content of stone-ground cornmeal causes it to go rancid within weeks, and thus it should be stored in the refrigerator or freezer, wrapped tightly in plastic or in a moisture-proof container. Degerminated cornmeals, such as Quaker, keep for a year if stored in a dry, cool place.

CORNSTARCH Taken from the endosperm of the corn kernel, cornstarch is exceptionally fine in texture and silky smooth. It is occasionally added to cakes, cookies, and pastries to lighten their texture, but it is primarily used in baking as a thickener for certain varieties of fruit pies. Cornstarch renders the juices clear, glossy, and smooth. We use it sparingly (primarily in lattice-top pies, where our favorite thickener, instant tapioca, cannot be effectively used), as it reheats poorly and has a tendency to "weep."

OATS All oats start out as whole oat seeds on the oat stalk. Different types of processing yield different products. Once the oat seeds are cleaned and the thick hull has been removed, they become oat groats. When rolled and steamed, groats become whole rolled oats, also known as old-fashioned oats. When neither steamed nor rolled but cut into pieces, groats become steel-cut, or Irish, oats. When these are steamed and rolled thin, they become quick oats. Quick oats generally work interchangeably with rolled oats in most baking applications. Instant oats are made from cut groats that are cooked and dried. These are not suitable for baking, as their texture quickly turns mushy.

GRANULATED SUGAR White granulated sugar is most commonly produced from either sugar cane or sugar beets (though it is rarely labeled as such and flavor differences are imperceptible). We have not detected differences among various brands of granulated sugar. Granulated sugar should be stored in an airtight container to prevent clumping.

SUPERFINE SUGAR Superfine sugar is finely processed granulated sugar that, because of its small size, dissolves more readily than conventional sugar. We rarely use it, but it is ideal for certain items, especially cookies with a delicate texture. Superfine sugar may be labeled castor sugar, depending on the country in which the sugar was produced. If superfine sugar proves difficult to find, it may be replicated at home with the aid of a food processor. Simply process granulated sugar until finely ground, about 20 to 30 seconds.

CONFECTIONERS' SUGAR The finest ground sugar is commonly referred to as either confectioners' sugar or powdered sugar and is most commonly used for dusting cakes and cookies and in making quick glazes and icings. To prevent clumping, confectioners' sugar contains a small amount of cornstarch. It may be stored indefinitely if well sealed to prevent moisture absorption.

LIGHT AND DARK BROWN SUGAR Both light and dark brown sugar are granulated sugar that has been flavored and moistened with molasses. Both light and dark brown sugar must be stored in airtight containers to prevent desiccation. If brown sugar does dry out, place it in a microwave-safe bowl with a slice of bread, wrap the bowl tightly with plastic wrap, and microwave until the sugar is once again moist, 15 to 30 seconds. If we prefer either light or dark brown sugar in a recipe, the ingredient list will indicate one or the other. If the recipe just calls for "brown sugar," use whichever type you have on hand.

MOLASSES Molasses, a byproduct of the cane sugar refining process, is the liquid that is drawn off after the cane juice has been boiled and undergone crystallization. The resultant molasses is then subjected to subsequent boilings; with each boiling, the molasses grows increasingly dark, bitter, and potent, as more sugar is extracted from it.

There are three types of molasses. Light or mild molasses comes from the first boiling, dark or robust molasses from the second, and blackstrap from the third. In the past, sulfur dioxide was often added to molasses to clarify it. Although this process made molasses more attractive, it also added an unappealing flavor. Today, most molasses, including all major brands, is unsulfured.

Most nationwide grocery store shelves offer few brands, Grandma's being the most common and Brer Rabbit a slightly rarer option. Each brand offers both light and robust, or "full," flavors. Blackstrap molasses is commonly available in natural food stores. We made cookies with the full range of both Grandma's and Brer Rabbit products, as well as with blackstrap, and tasters deemed all varieties, except for the blackstrap, acceptable. The dark, bitter tones of the blackstrap molasses overpowered all the other flavors in the cookies. So if you prefer a robust molasses flavor, use dark molasses; otherwise, stick to the lighter variety.

HONEY Honey varies in both flavor and strength according to the type of plants from which the bees have gathered pollen. As a general rule, the darker the honey, the stronger the flavor. In most cases, a mild honey, such as orange blossom or clover, should be used so as to not overpower other flavors. Honey is significantly sweeter than sugar by volume and cannot be substituted in equal amounts.

If your honey happens to crystallize, it can be easily revived either in the microwave or on the stovetop. Remove the lid and heat the jar of honey for 10-second increments in the microwave until fluid, or place the open jar in a saucepan partially filled with water and simmer over very low heat.

CORN SYRUP Used in icings for a silky smooth, glossy texture and to sweeten some cookies and pies, corn syrup is processed from cornstarch. Light corn syrup is a neutral sweetener; dark corn syrup has a slight caramel flavor. These two products are not interchangeable, but both can be stored indefinitely.

MAPLE SYRUP Pure maple syrup (not the cheap pancake syrups with little or no maple syrup or maple flavor) is available in several grades. In general, a maple syrup's grade is determined by the period during which it was made (the sugaring season lasts from February to early April). The grades of maple syrup are measured by the amount of light that can pass through the syrup. Straight from the tree, maple sap is clear, consisting of about 98 percent water and 2 percent sugar. To make maple syrup, the water has to be boiled off to a concentration of 66 percent sugar. (This means boiling about 40 gallons of water to attain just one gallon of syrup.)

Early in the season, maple syrups tend to be nearly translucent because the sugar molecules in the boiled-down sap are able to reflect much light. As temperatures warm outside, wild yeasts in the sap begin feeding on and breaking down the sugar. As a result, light can be absorbed. So as the season progresses, the syrup darkens.

The season's earliest sap flow produces Grade A light, or "Fancy," as it is called in Vermont. Honey gold and nearly translucent, it has a pronounced sweetness and a delicate flavor. The season's second syrup is Grade A medium amber. This has a warmer caramel color with a medium-strength flavor. Right on the heels of medium amber is Grade A dark amber, which is slightly deeper in color and has a more pronounced flavor. After the ambers falls Grade B, the darkest and typically least expensive of the syrups on the market. It is traditionally considered cooking grade because of its strong flavor.

After tasting nine brands of syrup (of varying grades), we concluded that most tasters prefer the stronger flavor of Grade B syrup on pancakes and waffles, although a few tasters did like the subtler flavor of the Grade A dark amber syrups. When baking, however, we think this subtlety is lost. Stick with the more flavorful Grade B syrups.

BUTTER Probably 95 percent of the recipes in this book contain butter. Most of us buy the cheapest butter in the market, figuring that there can't be too much of a difference among the brands offered. We tested numerous brands of butter in a variety of baked goods to find out.

According to U.S. Department of Agriculture standards, all butter must consist of at least 80 percent milk fat, milk solids (roughly 2 percent), and water. Most commercial butters do not exceed this minimum fat content due to economics of the marketplace (water is cheaper than butterfat), though some premium European-style butters contain between 82 percent and 88 percent milk fat. In theory, higher fat translates to more flavor, better texture, and flakier, more tender baked goods.

The results of our tests were surprising. Although the two high-fat butters in the tasting (Plugrá and Celles Sur Belle, a French brand sold in many gourmet stores) performed well in most tests, they were not runaway winners. In fact, most tasters felt that all the cakes, cookies, and pie crusts tasted pretty much the same, no matter which brand of butter was used. Even when the butters were tasted plain, the results were fairly close.

However, in a rich buttercream frosting made with softened butter, confectioners' sugar, and a little milk, the Plugrá was head and shoulders above the others for both a pleasant, delicate butter flavor and an airy texture. The other high-fat butter, Celles Sur Belle, scored well but was not judged to have as light a texture as the Plugrá. In this one instance, where the butter is such an important ingredient and the recipe is so simple, a higher-fat butter created a noticeable difference in both flavor and texture.

Overall, however, we recommend that you pay more attention to the condition in which you buy the butter and the conditions under which you store it than to particular brands. Throughout the testing, we ran across sticks of butter that were rancid or stale-tasting. We attributed these problems to improper shipping or poor storage at the market, not the manufacturer. We recommend that you purchase butter from a store you trust that has a high turnover of products.

Butter can also spoil in your refrigerator, turning rancid from the oxidation of fatty acids. Exposure to air or light is particularly damaging, which explains why some manufacturers take the precaution of using foil wrappers. We find that the best way to store butter is sealed in an airtight plastic bag in your freezer, pulling out sticks as you need them. Butter will keep in the freezer for several months and in the refrigerator for no more than two to three weeks. And skip the butter compartment; butter does better at the cooler temperatures deep within the refrigerator.

One final note about butter. We use unsalted butter in our test kitchen. We like its sweet, delicate flavor and prefer to add our own salt to recipes. We find that the quality of salted butter is often inferior and that each manufacturer adds a different amount of salt, which makes recipe writing difficult. While you can certainly get away with using salted butter in some savory recipes (as long as you adjust the total amount of salt in the recipe), we strongly recommend using unsalted butter when baking.

MILK While generally not specified, you should use whole milk in all the recipes in this book. While the slight differences in fat content among whole milk (3.5 percent), low-fat milk (1 percent or 2 percent), and skim milk (less than 0.5 percent) may seem trivial, they can impact the flavor and texture of baked goods. For example, a yellow cake prepared with skim milk instead of whole turned out tough and dry. Surprisingly, the same cake made with 1 percent milk was markedly more tender. So if whole milk is unavailable, use 1 percent or 2 percent milk and leave the skim milk for drinking.

BUTTERMILK The buttermilk sold today has little to do with the buttermilk of yesteryear, a byproduct of butter production. Modern buttermilk is cultured, not unlike yogurt; harmless bacteria are added to pasteurized milk and the combination is heated to 72 degrees. At this temperature, the bacteria convert the milk's sugar (lactose) to lactic acid, which is responsible for buttermilk's characteristic tanginess. Low-fat and nonfat buttermilk are the most commonly available types north of the Mason-Dixon line; Southerners are blessed with whole-milk buttermilk as well. Whichever style you may find, the flavors are close and each works fine in all instances.

If you don't use a whole lot of buttermilk, buying it by the quart may be a waste since recipes rarely require much more than a cup. If you fall into this category, there are a couple of good options: soured milk, made by adding 1 tablespoon white vinegar to 1 cup whole milk, and powdered buttermilk. We tasted both buttermilk biscuits and chocolate cake made with each option and found each thoroughly acceptable. Some tasters actually preferred the biscuits and cake made with the powdered buttermilk to those made with the fresh.

YOGURT Plain yogurt is an important, if not exciting ingredient in many of our quick breads and muffins. Bright and soupy or wickedly acidic and gummy, plain yogurt varies greatly from brand to brand, even style to style. Does whole-milk yogurt produce the same muffins as nonfat? Do the different bacterias employed to culture the yogurt produce different flavors?

Yogurt was probably first made by chance when milk was accidentally fermented by wild bacteria. Today, the process is controlled. Milk (whole, low-fat, or skim) is pasteurized and usually homogenized. (Some companies leave whole milk unhomogenized to produce a separate cream layer in their yogurt.) Active bacteria cultures are then added to the milk, and the milk is poured directly into cups and kept in a warm environment for several hours. The bacteria convert the milk sugar (called lactose) into lactic acid, causing the proteins in the milk to coagulate and thicken. Lactic acid also gives yogurt its characteristic tang. Finally, the yogurt is cooled and refrigerated.

We rounded up 11 leading brands of yogurt, including four made with whole milk, two with low-fat milk, and five with skim milk, and tasted them straight from the container as well as baked into muffins and quick breads. We quickly determined that the type of bacteria used to culture the milk had no discernible effect on our tasters' ratings. Fat content was more complicated. When we tasted them raw, yogurts made with low-fat milk

and whole milk took the top four spots, but they didn't produce a tremendous difference once baked (though whole-milk yogurt did yield moister muffins, and the muffins made with the nonfat yogurt were dry).

In the end, our two favorites included one low-fat yogurt and one whole-milk yogurt. They were both creamy and smooth and tangy without being sour or acidic. Some milk fat certainly proved a plus. The winners were Colombo Low-Fat Plain Yogurt, noted for its "clean taste" and "mild tang" and Brown Cow Organic Whole Milk Plain Yogurt for its "rich," "buttery" flavor.

EGGS As primal to baking as flour, butter, or sugar, eggs contribute flavor, structure, richness, and texture. Eggs are sold in a range of sizes, from small to jumbo, but for consistency, every recipe in this book uses large eggs. (Substitutions are possible if you follow the chart, below.) Eggs are also graded according to the thickness of the shells and whites, the best being AA, the worst, B. Most eggs are grade A, the middle grade.

For baking, use the freshest eggs you can find as older eggs lack the structure-lending properties of fresh eggs. Age can be gauged by reading the pack date, a three-number code stamped above or below the sell-by date. The numbers run consecutively, starting with 001 for January 1 and ending with 365 for December 31.

That said, eggs suffer more from improper storage than age. The egg tray inside the refrigerator is not the ideal storage location for two reasons: temperature and protection. The American Egg Board recommends 40 degrees for storage, but we have

EGG SIZE SUBSTITUTIONS

Use the chart on the right if you don't have large eggs, which are called for in all recipes in this book, on hand. For example, 4 jumbo eggs (2.50 ounces each) are equivalent to 5 large eggs (2.00 ounces each).

Size	Weight
Medium	1.75 ounces
Large	2.00 ounces
Extra-Large	2.25 ounces
Jumbo	2.50 ounces

found the average door temperature to be closer to 45 degrees. The interior top shelf is a better bet, as it is generally between 38 and 40 degrees. Eggs are also best stored in their cardboard carton; when removed, they absorb odors from other foods. (We've made "oniony" cakes in the test kitchen.) The carton also maintains an optimum humidity of between 70 and 80 percent.

COOKING OILS Vegetable oil is a catch-all category for oils processed from plants, nuts, seeds, etc. As a general rule, we use canola oil for its high smoke point and neutral flavor. It works equally well in recipes or as a cooking medium. For doughnuts (see page 66 and page 127), our first choice for frying is peanut oil as its slightly nutty flavor lends depth.

SHORTENING Vegetable shortening is simply vegetable oil made solid through hydrogenation (a chemical process by which extra hydrogen is added). Virtually tasteless and odorless, shortening is an integral ingredient to many pie and pastry crusts because it makes for extraordinarily flaky dough. We use some in our Basic Pie Dough, page 181, in conjunction with butter for flavor. Shortening may be stored at room temperature.

BAKING POWDER AND BAKING SODA Quick breads, muffins, and biscuits as well as cookies and cakes get their rise from chemical leaveners—baking soda and baking powder—rather than yeast. Chemical leaveners react with acids to produce carbon dioxide, the gas that causes these baked goods to rise.

To do its work, baking soda relies on acid in the recipe, provided by ingredients such as buttermilk, sour cream, yogurt, or molasses. It's important to use the right amount of baking soda in recipes. Use more baking soda than can be neutralized by the acidic ingredient and you'll end up with a metallic-tasting, coarse-crumbed quick bread or cake.

Baking powder is nothing more than baking soda (about one-quarter to one-third of the total makeup) mixed with a dry acid and double-dried cornstarch. The cornstarch absorbs moisture and keeps the baking soda and dry acid apart during storage, preventing premature production of the gas. When baking powder becomes wet, the acid comes into contact with the baking soda, producing carbon dioxide. Most commercial baking powders are "double-acting." In other words, they contain two kinds of acids—one that produces a carbon dioxide reaction at room temperature and one that responds only to heat. Baking soda reacts immediately on contact with an acid and thus is "single-acting."

We have tested and tasted the four largest national brands of baking powder and found little difference in action or flavor. (There's only one widely available brand of baking soda.) Each baking powder we tested worked well, and any differences in flavor were virtually undetectable. The only thing to keep in mind with baking powder is freshness. Old baking powder will yield squat biscuits and flat cakes. Check the date on the container or test the powder itself (to learn how, see page 54). If you find yourself without baking powder, you can make a crude approximation by replacing each teaspoon of baking powder called for in a recipe with ½ teaspoon cream of tartar and ¼ teaspoon baking soda.

CREAM OF TARTAR Cream of tartar is a white powder sold in small bottles in the spice aisle. It is a dry acid, and when mixed with baking soda and a liquid, it will produce carbon dioxide bubbles that leaven baked goods. Because of its acidic nature, cream of tartar is also used when whipping egg whites. It makes the whites more stable and allows them to obtain a greater volume.

YEAST Probably no ingredient in the baker's pantry is more misunderstood than yeast. Available in a number of forms and notoriously fickle, yeast certainly scares most novice bakers. As a general rule, we use instant yeast (also called rapid-rise yeast), as it is both faster acting and easier to use. It works in a fraction of the time of more traditional styles of yeast and can be added directly to the dry ingredients: No "proofing" of the yeast in warm water is necessary. Exhaustive side-by-side taste tests in the test kitchen have proven to us that it works and tastes as good as any other form of yeast.

Like other types of yeast, instant yeast is subject to age degradation, and expiration dates should be keenly observed. And high temperatures (in excess of 125 degrees) will kill it: Keep liquids in your recipes at 110 degrees or lower.

SALT Unless otherwise noted, all recipes in this book use regular table salt for seasoning. The fine grains of table salt dissolve and distribute more evenly than larger-grained kosher and sea salts. In some cases, like dusting the top of focaccia, we specify kosher salt. As for fancy sea salts, save those for the table; the flavor is indistinguishable from the cheap stuff in baked goods.

VANILLA EXTRACT Vanilla is a critical ingredient in baking, either as the prime flavor or serving in a supporting role for depth, roundness, and balance. Naturally, then, the quality of the vanilla that goes into those cakes and cookies will have a noticeable impact on their flavor, right? For the best possible results, it stands to reason that you should reach for expensive, high-end, pure vanilla extract. Or should you?

Vanilla has proven to be one of the most controversial taste tests we have ever conducted. On multiple occasions, spread throughout the decade-long history of the magazine, we (including an expert panel of pastry chefs and baking experts) have been unable to tell the differences between pure and imitation vanilla extract when tested in a variety of applications. So what gives?

Pure vanilla extract starts with real vanilla beans, which are notoriously expensive because of the intense manual labor necessary to grow and process them. Although more than 400 chemical compounds contribute to the overall flavor profile of vanilla, the dominant, most recognizable compound is vanillin, which is largely responsible for vanilla's trademark sweet, creamy, fruity, and floral aroma and flavor. Vanillin develops in the seed pods of the tropical climbing vine *Vanilla planifolia*, a member of the orchid family, when the pods are cured. Curing involves repeated sweating and drying of the beans, during which time they ferment and develop vanillin.

Vanillin production, however, can sidestep nature because it can be synthesized from eugenol (an essential oil in cloves), lignin (a wood pulp byproduct of the paper manufacturing process), and an ethyl coal tar derivative. On the molecular level, synthetic vanillin is indistinguishable from natural vanillin. And compared with natural vanillin, synthetic vanillin is cheap.

What does this all mean when it comes to buying vanilla extract? In essence, all of the vanilla extracts we have tried through the years have received passing grades. From high-end gourmet vanilla to a bargain bottle purchased from a local pharmacy, everything passed.

VANILLA BEANS Vanilla beans can be an invaluable addition to custards, especially pastry cream and crème anglaise. In a blind taste test of custards flavored with beans and extracts, tasters clearly preferred the bean for its fuller aroma and complex flavor. But truth be told, extract works fine as well. When shopping for vanilla beans, look for moist, plump vanilla beans that have a bit of sheen to them; avoid beans that look like dried, shriveled twigs.

UNSWEETENED CHOCOLATE Often called baking chocolate or chocolate liquor, this product is made from roasted cocoa beans and contains about 50 percent solids from the beans and 50 percent cocoa butter. It is 100 percent chocolate with nothing added. That said, we found a surprising range of flavor when we used seven different brands in brownies and chocolate sauce. If unsweetened chocolate is pure chocolate, how could one brand be so different from another?

Like coffee or wine, cacao beans vary in flavor and quality from region to region. Beans from Africa will taste decidedly different from those grown in Malaysia, and hence will yield chocolate that tastes different. Add to the mix the processing of the beans (cacao beans go through a good deal before being ground into chocolate) and the blending of different varieties of beans and you have the answer. Premium-grade chocolate is generally made from high-quality beans processed carefully and sometimes left unblended so that the unique characteristics of the bean stand out. Mass producers aim for a certain flavor profile rather than the natural flavor of one particular bean.

So what do we recommend? In our taste tests, the more expensive chocolates—Scharffen Berger, Callebaut, Ghirardelli, and Valrhona—were all well liked and received similar scores. Of the three mass-market brands (Nestlé, Baker's, and Hershey's), Nestlé received more positive comments and significantly higher scores. It's important to remember, though, that chocolate, much like coffee, is a matter of personal preference. The gamut of flavors runs from "nutty" and "cherry-like" to "smoky," "earthy," and "spicy." You may want to try different brands in order to find a chocolate that suits your palate.

BITTERSWEET AND SEMISWEET CHOCOLATE
Bittersweet and semisweet chocolates (also called dark chocolates) are made from unsweetened chocolate that is ground with sugar and then further refined. Since bittersweet and semisweet chocolates are about 50 percent sugar (the rest is chocolate liquor), they have less chocolate flavor than unsweetened, which has no added sugar. (Although individual brands may vary, bittersweet averages around 46 percent sugar by weight; semisweet is about 57 percent sugar.) The chocolate flavor they do have, however, is less bitter and more complex, features appreciated by many bakers. Their texture is also much smoother and creamier than unsweetened chocolate.

We tasted eight leading brands of bittersweet chocolate as is, in a sauce, and in a flourless chocolate cake. Tasters consistently put Ghirardelli, an American brand available in most supermarkets, at the top of the ratings. Its roasted, not-too-sweet, not-too-bitter flavor appealed to almost everyone. Callebaut, an expensive Belgian brand sold in many gourmet markets, was also well liked. Interestingly, many of the premium brands, including Valrhona, El Rey, and Scharffen Berger, drew mixed comments. A few tasters loved these complex chocolates, but many complained that they were not sweet enough. Bittersweet and unsweetened chocolate are more commonly used than semisweet chocolate when baking, though semisweet is used in some instances, like our

Thick and Chewy Double-Chocolate Cookies (page 436). When developing this recipe, we tasted four major brands head to head: Nestlé, Baker's, Ghirardelli, and Callebaut. The Baker's turned out a gritty cookie that received low marks, Nestlé had an off, somewhat fruity taste, and the Ghirardelli had a muted but pure chocolate flavor. But the Callebaut was our favorite, with a big chocolate flavor that was clean, direct, and full of punch.

MILK CHOCOLATE
Sweet and simple, milk chocolate is the first choice for a kid in a candy store but an infrequent ingredient in chocolate-flavored recipes. It can contain as little as 10 percent chocolate liquor, with sugar, milk solids, and vanilla making up the balance. Even so, we still wanted to make sure we knew the best options out there, so we conducted a typical taste test. We gathered nine brands of milk chocolate, ranging from supermarket favorites such as Hershey's and Nestlé to boutique brands such as Lindt and Perugina. We tasted them plain and in our Creamy Milk Chocolate Frosting (page 343).

Results between the two tastings did not fully align. The higher-end brands aced the raw test, but the underdog, Nestlé, scored a second place finish in the frosting. Our recommendations? For eating out of hand, purchase the good stuff, Lindt and Perugina. To save some money, go with Nestlé in baked goods: It's less than half the price.

WHITE CHOCOLATE
As most bakers know, white chocolate really isn't chocolate at all as it contains no chocolate liquor, the ingredient that lends chocolate its complex flavor and haunting aroma. White chocolate does, however, contain everything else germane to chocolate: cocoa butter (the fat from the cacao beans), sugar, milk, and flavorings. In baking, it is often used in conjunction with other, more potent ingredients, buttressing flavors rather than standing alone.

After testing many varieties, our recommended white chocolates include Barry Callebaut White Superior, Lindt Swiss White, and Peter's Snowcap. Each variety is widely available and differs in flavor and texture. Tasters noted that the Lindt possessed the strongest vanilla flavor. Each of the three contains over 30 percent cocoa butter, which contributes to a creamy mouthfeel. Avoid the inexpensive brands sold in the supermarket which do not contain any cocoa butter.

CHOCOLATE CHIPS Chips have a lower cocoa butter content than chocolate bars, which prevents them from becoming too liquidy once baked. Often the cocoa butter is replaced by sugar, an issue that became quite apparent when we tested various brands of chocolate chips. Some of the brands were surprisingly sweet. Somewhat unsurprisingly, chips we liked best straight out of the bag tasted best in cookies. Nestlé, Guittard, Ghirardelli, and Tropical Source (a brand sold in natural food stores) all received high marks. The chips that excelled were noted for a balance of bitterness, sweetness, and smoothness.

COCOA POWDER Cocoa powder is made from unsweetened chocolate. Much of the fat is removed by pressing, leaving behind the cocoa solids. These leftover solids are then fluffed up and packaged.

Cocoa is sold in two forms: regular and Dutch-processed. The difference between the two lies in acidity: Dutch-processed cocoa is less acidic (or more alkaline) than a natural cocoa such as Hershey's. The theory is that reducing the acidity of natural cocoa enhances browning reactions, which in turn results in a darker color. Because the red pigments in cocoa become more visible in a more acidic environment, the more acidic natural cocoa is supposed to produce a redder cake. Manufacturers also claim that Dutch processing results in a smoother, less bitter chocolate flavor.

To determine the veracity of these claims, we conducted a head-to-head test of three Dutch-processed cocoas—Droste, King Arthur Flour's "black" cocoa (made from beans that are roasted until they are almost burnt), and Pernigotti, a very expensive brand sold at Williams-Sonoma stores—against Hershey's natural cocoa.

All three Dutch-processed cocoas produced darker cakes with more chocolate flavor than Hershey's did, bearing out our research. Hershey's

cocoa also produced a much redder cake, just as promised. But we also noticed textural differences in the cakes. The cake made with Hershey's was dry and airy without much complexity of flavor. Among the cakes made with Dutch-processed cocoa, the cake made with the expensive Pernigotti produced a very moist, soft crumb; the one made with Droste was a bit dry with a more open crumb; and the "black" cocoa cake was very dense, almost spongy, although incredibly chocolatey as well.

So if you want a richer-tasting, darker, more velvety cake, use Dutch-processed cocoa, keeping in mind that quality matters. Those who must have a reddish color can go with regular cocoa, but the taste and texture will suffer somewhat.

Finally, because of their different pHs, Dutch-processed and natural cocoa are not interchangeable in recipes that call for either baking powder or baking soda. (In theory, these two kinds of cocoa are interchangeable in recipes without leaveners—see the baking powder and baking soda entry on page 7 for more information.)

EQUIPMENT

BAKING SHEETS Most baking sheets (also called cookie sheets) have the same basic design. They are a piece of metal that is usually slightly longer than it is wide. (A standard size is 18 inches long and 12 inches across.) Some are dark, some are light. Some have rims on all four sides. Others have rims on one or two sides but otherwise have flat edges. We tested 11 sheets in a variety of materials and came to some surprising conclusions.

First of all, shiny, light-colored sheets do a better job of evenly browning the bottoms of cookies than dark sheets. Most of the dark sheets are nonstick, and we found that these pans tend to overbrown cookies. Shiny, silver sheets heat much more evenly, and if sticking is a concern we simply use parchment paper. Parchment paper also keeps the bottom of the cookies from overbrowning.

In our testing, we also came to prefer sheets with at least one rimless edge. This way we could slide a whole sheet of parchment paper onto a cooling rack without actually touching the hot paper. (When cooled, the cookies can be peeled away from the paper.) The flat edge also makes it possible to slide cookies onto a rack, rather than lifting them and possibly dropping them. Our favorite cookie sheet is made of tinned steel and is manufactured by Kaiser. At just $7, it was also the cheapest sheet we tested.

A final note about lining baking sheets with parchment. Even when sticking is not an issue, we like to use parchment paper. It makes cleanup a snap, and we can reuse baking sheets for subsequent batches without having to wash them first. When parchment is essential, the recipes in this book call for it. Otherwise, use parchment at your discretion.

LOAF PAN A good loaf pan will evenly brown quick breads, such as banana bread, as well as yeast breads, such as sandwich bread. In addition, loaves should release cleanly, and the pans should be easy to get in and out of the oven, with little chance of sticking an oven mitt into the batter or baked bread.

We tested 10 loaf pans made from a variety of materials, including metal, glass, and stoneware. We found that dark-colored metal loaf pans browned breads more evenly than light-colored metal pans. Most of the dark metal pans were lined with a nonstick coating that also made the release of baked breads especially easy. We found that sweet breads, such as banana bread, were especially prone to burning in glass loaf pans. Sticking was also a problem in these pans. Stoneware loaf pans did a decent job of browning, but we had trouble removing loaves from these pans.

Our testers found that pans with handles at either end were easier to work with and kept us from sticking an oven mitt into the edge of a baked loaf.

We recommend that you buy metal loaf pans with a nonstick coating. Although there's no harm in spending more money on heavier pans, the cheapest, lightest pan in our testing (Baker's Secret Nonstick, $4) was the favorite. One final piece of advice: Even with the nonstick coating, we recommend greasing and flouring your loaf pan to ensure easy release.

CAKE PANS For baking any number of cakes in this book, round cake pans are a must. When shopping, make sure to buy two sets of cake pans, preferably two 8-inch pans and two 9-inch pans. The standard depth for cake pans is 1½ to 2 inches. Different pans will produce cake layers of varying sizes, and layers that are the same size are easier to assemble and frost. For this reason, buy cake pans in matched sets.

To find the best models, we baked both plain and chocolate butter cakes in 11 different pans. We found that cakes released perfectly from pans lined with nonstick or "stick-resistant" coatings. Most cakes released adequately from uncoated pans, with one exception. The flexible fiberglass pans we tested repeatedly held onto large chunks of cake. Because these pans also gave the cakes a faint rubbery flavor, they are not recommended.

When it came to browning the crust, we found dramatic differences in the pans. In general, the darker the pan, the darker the crust. Some bakers advise against using pans with dark finishes, such as nonstick coatings, because they worry about overbrowning. We found that dark pans created a darker crust but not one that was "overbrowned" or undesirable. In fact, we enjoyed the richer flavor of dark crusts when eating these cakes unfrosted, and we also found that their sturdiness and resistance to crumbling made them easier to frost.

We determined that pans with light-colored or shiny finishes could produce well-browned cakes, as long as the pans were made from aluminum. That's because aluminum conducts heat evenly and quickly. In contrast, stainless steel is a poor conductor of heat, and pans made from this material produced pale-looking cakes. In general, we prefer aluminum or tinned steel pans, preferably with a nonstick coating and/or a dark finish.

Since we preferred cakes with darker crusts, insulated pans fared poorly in our ratings—their two layers of metal separated by airspace slowed down the browning process. While we liked most of the heavier "commercial" pans, our favorite pan, the Baker's Secret Nonstick ($4), was one of the lightest. In the end, the metal used and the finish are more important than the weight.

Finally, the issue of handles proved to be

decisive in our testing. Pans with handles on either side are much easier to transfer to the oven when filled with batter and easier to rotate once in the oven. Handles make it much easier to grab the pan without landing the corner of a potholder in a finished cake. Simply put, we love handles.

BUNDT PAN Bundt pans were introduced by NordicWare (which is still in possession of the registered trademark) in the 1950s, based on the traditional cast-iron kugelhopf molds of Eastern Europe (used for a yeasted bread common to much of Europe). These fluted, turban-shaped baking pans eventually gained widespread popularity, largely thanks to a slew of Bundt cake mixes marketed by Pillsbury. We tested eight so-called nonstick Bundt pans, each with a simple ridge design and 12-cup capacity, priced from $10 to $28. We baked vanilla pound cakes in each to test for evenness and depth of browning. All of the pans performed adequately, varying slightly in cooking times (from 5 to 10 minutes) and evenness of browning (except for a flexible silicone model, which failed to brown at all). The original NordicWare pan proved the best choice, excelling on all counts—except price. At $28, it was the most expensive pan we tried, though still far from a major purchase. Our choice for "best buy" went to a pan from Baker's Secret, priced at just $12. Although it was significantly lighter than the NordicWare, it passed all of our tests with above-average results.

SPRINGFORM PAN Although infrequently used, a springform pan is essential for a variety of cakes that would be impossible to remove from a standard cake pan. To find the best model, we baked cheesecakes and chocolate mousse cakes in six pans, ranging in price from $9 to $38.

An ideal pan, we thought, would release the cakes from the sides and bottom of the pan effortlessly. All six pans tested had acceptable side release, but dislodging a cake from the pan bottom was trickier. Here, the top-performing pans possessed a rimless bottom (just two out of the six tested). These two also proved the easiest to clean.

Another valuable quality in a springform pan is its resistance to leakage when placed in a water bath. To test leakage, we baked cheesecakes in a water bath tinted with green food coloring, our theory being that the less secure the seal of the pan, the more water would seep through, the greener the cheesecake. This was a tough test. Even the best-performing pan in this test thus far showed an edge of green that traveled around one third of the cake. In the worst instances, the green made a complete circle around the outside edge of the cake. These pans were the cheapest we tested, and they were very flimsy.

In this case, price does matter as the two most expensive pans topped the testing. The Kaiser Noblesse ($20) and the Frieling Glass Bottom ($38) are both well constructed, well designed (flat bottomed and rimless as opposed to the rest tested), and worth the extra money. But because no pan demonstrated a perfect seal, we recommend wrapping the bottom of any springform pan with foil when baking in a water bath.

TART PANS Tart pans with removable bottoms are available in three types of finishes: traditional tinned steel, black steel, and nonstick. After baking tarts in each kind of pan, we found the classic tinned model sold in most cookware shops is the best choice. The black pan caused crusts to overbrown, and the nonstick finish seemed superfluous as every tart we baked slid freely from the pan. If you can find only dark tart pans, reduce the oven temperature by about 25 degrees to prevent burning. We keep two sizes in the kitchen—a 9- to 9½-inch pan for regular tarts and an 11-inch pan for large tarts.

MUFFIN TIN Muffin tins appear in a variety of shapes and sizes, from the typical light, coated aluminum models to heavy-gauge "professional" sorts and even one "air-cushioned" aluminum tin. And prices range from a reasonable $5 to a seemingly exorbitant $26. Is there much of a performance difference? We baked both corn and blueberry muffins in a diverse range of tins and found that, yes, in fact, there is a good deal of difference.

The two big issues with muffins are browning and sticking, though we found that, if liberally sprayed with nonstick cooking spray, sticking was not a problem for any of the tins we tried. Browning, however, was a different story. The best tins browned the muffins evenly; the worst browned them on the top but left them pallid and underbaked on the bottom. As we had observed in other bakeware tests, darker coated metals, which absorb heat, do the best job of browning baked goods. An air-cushioned tin produced pale muffins that were also small (the cushioning made for a smaller cup capacity, about a third of a cup rather than the standard half cup).

We found the heavier-gauged aluminum tins to have no advantage—they are much more expensive than other tins, weigh twice as much, and do not produce superior muffins. Their heft may make them durable, but unless you bake commercially, the lightweight models will last a lifetime. The $5 Baker's Secret tin took top honors, besting tins that cost five times as much. As for muffin papers, skip them. We have found that they inhibit browning, and bits of muffin inevitably stick within (though they can be helpful for cupcakes).

PIE PLATE Pie plates come in a variety of shapes and sizes as well as materials. We have tested the three main types of pie plate—glass, ceramic, and metal—and found that a Pyrex glass pie plate ($5) does the best job of browning the crust, both when filled and baked blind (the bottom crust is baked alone, filled with pie weights to hold its shape). Several metal pie plates also browned crusts quite well, but the glass pie plate has a number of other advantages. Because you can see through a glass plate, it's easy to judge just how brown the bottom crust has become during baking. With a metal pie plate, it's easy to pull the pie out of the oven too soon, when the bottom crust is still quite pale. A second feature we like about the traditional Pyrex plate is the wide rim, which makes the plate easier to take in and out of the oven and also supports fluted edges better than thin rims. Finally, because glass is nonreactive, you can store a pie filled with acidic fruit and not worry about metal giving the fruit an off flavor.

Glass pie plates do heat up more quickly than metal pie plates, so pies may be done a bit sooner than you think, especially if you are following a recipe that was tested in a metal plate. All the times in our recipes are based on baking in a glass pie plate; if baking in metal, you may need to add two to three minutes for empty crusts and five minutes for filled pies.

STANDING MIXER If you plan on serious baking, a standing mixer is virtually an essential. From mixing doughs and batters to whipping cream and egg whites, they do it all. Our test kitchen is stocked with KitchenAid mixers, which are powerful and durable. Unlike many other mixers on the market, KitchenAids mix with a "planetary action": the mixing attachment (the paddle, dough hook, or whisk) moves around a stationary bowl. It is the most effective way of blending ingredients we have seen because the paddle reaches the sides as well as the center of the bowl and gathers particles quickly. As a result, there is little need to stop the machine and scrape the sides of the bowl.

KitchenAids are sold in a variety of sizes, but for most home bakers, we recommend purchasing the smaller, 4½-quart model (around $200). Every recipe in this book will work in this size machine. We do, however, recommend picking up an extra mixing bowl—it can expedite many baking tasks and is especially helpful in recipes that call for beating egg whites in a clean bowl.

FOOD PROCESSOR A food processor can perform some of the duties of a standing mixer and vice versa, but they are not mutually exclusive. A food processor cannot knead very stiff dough, or whip egg whites, or even efficiently cream butter and sugar, but it can whip together pizza crust in a flash and make equally quick work out of numerous other doughs, batters, and crusts. Not to mention its importance for kitchen tasks outside of baking.

We have evaluated food processors for their ability to handle a wide variety of cooking jobs. After slicing, grinding, grating, pureeing, and most important in this case, kneading, our favorite two food processors came from KitchenAid and Cuisinart (around $200). Both were incredibly sturdy and stable, and worked like draft horses. If you plan on making a lot of dough in the food processor, purchase a model with a bowl capacity of at least 11 cups. A good food processor will also be heavy enough to prevent bouncing around on the counter.

HANDHELD MIXER Although we like the hands-free operation of a standing mixer, we realize that its high price tag makes it a luxury item, especially for the occasional baker. A handheld mixer will perform all the same baking tasks (minus kneading bread) and at a fraction of the cost. Although cream and egg whites may require a few extra seconds to whip, we have found that there is no real difference between cookies and cakes prepared in handheld and standing mixers. We use the KitchenAid six-speed hand mixer ($70) in the test kitchen.

DRY MEASURING CUPS Dry measuring cups are fundamental to baking; without them, even the simplest cookie recipe would be compromised. Kitchen stores offer a wide range of measuring cups, from those with rubber comfort grips on their handles to heavy-gauge aluminum and stainless steel. We wondered if one kind of cup would be easier or more efficient to use than another. To find out, we put eight readily available measuring cup sets to the test.

Across the board, measured weights were remarkably consistent. In the end, our testing boiled down to an evaluation of design and construction. A reasonably long handle proved essential for effective (and accurate) "dipping and sweeping." But a long handle proved useless if the material wasn't stiff enough. Plastic handles bent under the weight of heavy ingredients. Heavy-gauge metal was a much better option—and it cleaned up well too. After final evaluation, our nod went to a set from Amco that retails for about $13.

LIQUID MEASURING CUPS The Pyrex cup with red lines and a pour spout is the industry standard and with good reason. It is easy to use and handsome. We prefer glass models to plastic because the lines tend to wear off the latter. To read the cup properly, make sure the cup is on a flat surface and you're at eye level with the meniscus (the concave surface of the liquid); otherwise it may be too little or too much. Since liquid measuring cups cost just a few dollars, it makes sense to own at least two; we find the 2-cup and 4-cup sizes most useful.

MEASURING SPOONS Like measuring cups, measuring spoons don't usually get a lot of consideration: bought once and done. But have you ever wondered if your set of spoons is accurate? Would an expensive set do a better job? To find out, we purchased 10 different sets of measuring spoons, made from both plastic and stainless steel and ranging in price from $2 to $15.

We were prepared to find large differences in degree of accuracy but found none. All of the spoons weighed in within a few hundredths of grams of the official standard for a tablespoon of water—not enough to compromise even the most exacting recipe. But technical accuracy does not always beget accurate measurement. If a spoon cannot be leveled easily, for instance, or if it is dented, accuracy is compromised. Usability and durability are therefore the determinants of accuracy when it comes to most measuring spoons.

In terms of usability, testers preferred spoons with deeper bowls as opposed to those with narrow and elongated or wide and shallow bowls. Shallow bowls allowed more liquid to spill as the result of a slight misstep or unsteady hand. The narrow, elongated bowls made dipping and scooping into anything but a very deep container impossible. Many spoons were difficult to level cleanly. Some had bumps along the rim of the bowl, and others had handles that did not meet the bowl neatly. In terms of durability, all testers preferred stainless steel spoons; plastic models, no matter how thick, feel flimsy and are more likely to break, bend, crack, or melt. Heavier stainless steel models are sturdier and therefore less likely to become dented or scratched. In the end, we found a heavy-duty stainless steel set of spoons from Progressive International that fit the bill and cost just $4.

INSTANT-READ THERMOMETER There are two types of commonly sold handheld thermometers: digital and dial face. While they both take accurate readings, we prefer digital thermometers because they register temperatures faster and are easier to read. After testing a variety of digital thermometers, we preferred the Thermapen for its well-thought-out design (a long, folding probe and comfortable handle) and speed (just 10 seconds for a reading). Priced at around $80, it is an expensive piece of equipment, but we highly recommend the Thermapen for any serious baker or cook. At the very least, purchase an inexpensive dial face model. You can't bake without a thermometer.

OVEN THERMOMETER Unless you have your oven routinely calibrated, there is a good chance that its temperature readings may be off. We tested 16 home ovens of friends and colleagues and found many varied as much as 50 degrees in either direction. Improper temperatures can and will dramatically impact your baked goods, making all that effort for naught. To avoid such problems, we recommend purchasing an inexpensive oven thermometer and checking it once the oven is preheated. After testing a slew of models and rating them for readability and accuracy, we found that we preferred two models: the Taylor Classic Oven Guide Thermometer and the Component Design Magnet Mounted Oven Thermometer. Both are priced under $15—a small investment for such insurance.

KITCHEN SCALE Baking is an exacting art, and nothing provides accuracy more than weighing ingredients. In fact, professional bakers eschew measuring cups and spoons altogether, relying solely on weight. If you bake frequently, we strongly recommend that you purchase a scale.

There are two basic types of kitchen scales: electronic and mechanical. We tested a handful of each, and as a group, the electronic scales were vastly preferred. Their digital displays are much easier to read than the measures on most mechanical scales, where the lines on the ruler are so closely spaced it's impossible to nail down the precise weight within half an ounce. Also, many mechanical scales could weigh items only within a limited range—usually between 1 ounce and 5 pounds.

What's the point of owning a scale that can't weigh a large chicken or roast? Most electronic scales can handle items that weigh as much as 10 pounds and as little as ¼ ounce.

Among the electronic scales we tested, we found that several features make the difference between a good electronic scale and a great one. Readability is a must. The displayed numbers should be large. Also, the displayed numbers should be steeply angled and as far from the weighing platform as possible. If the display is too close to the platform, the numbers can hide beneath the rim of a dinner plate or cake pan.

An automatic shut-off feature will save battery life, but this feature can be annoying, especially if the shut-off cycle kicks in at less than two minutes. A scale that shuts off automatically after five minutes or more is easier to use. A large weighing platform that detaches for easy cleaning is another plus. Last, we preferred electronic scales that display weight increments in decimals rather than fractions. The former are more accurate and easier to work with when scaling a recipe up or down.

In the end we walked away with two favorites, the Soehnle Cyber Electronic Kitchen Scale, at $125, and the more budget-minded Salter Electronic Aquatronic The Baker's Dream, at $60.

ROLLING PIN A good rolling pin can qualify as a family heirloom. But if your grandmother's tried-and-true pin has not been passed down to your kitchen and you want to buy one, you have quite an array of choices. Should you buy a rolling pin with a nonstick coating, one that is made of marble, or one with ergonomic handles? Could any one pin really make a difference in your baking? We tested eight models readily found in kitchen and hardware stores and decided on a definite favorite.

We purchased a wide range of rolling pins, from traditional American style (rolling on bearings) to French "stick style" to a couple of real oddities (aluminum? ergonomic handles?). We tested the pins on three kinds of dough: a standard pie dough, a delicate sugar cookie dough, and a resilient yeasted coffee cake dough. We were particularly interested in the versatility of these pins—whether they could perform equally well in all tasks. For all three doughs, we were looking for a fast, easy roll—one that allowed us to feel the dough and did not require the application of too much pressure.

Almost immediately, a favorite became evident—and it wasn't one of the gimmicky pins. The French-style tapered wood rolling pin without handles took first place. Testers could easily turn and pivot the tapered pin, the classic choice for most professional bakers, and apply pressure as needed across the dough. In addition, this pin measured 20 inches long, making it suitable for any task. Many of the other wooden pins were too short (some just 10 or 11 inches in length) and could not be used to roll out large pieces of dough. And at less than $10, this rolling pin was economical to boot.

ZESTER Citrus zest is an essential flavoring in innumerable cakes, pies, and pastries. Removing that zest, however, can be a trying experience. The sharp tines of a box grater do the job but hold firmly to the zest and occasionally make for bloody knuckles. A better (and safer) option is the Microplane zester, a handheld, sharp-edged zester evolved from a wood file. The razor-sharp teeth remove zest in fine, tight curls, leaving the pith beneath intact and the fruit unharmed. They are widely available at virtually any cooking store and, at around $10, well worth it.

RUBBER SPATULAS A rubber spatula is invaluable for scraping bowls clean, stirring batters, and folding egg whites. But, as we found after exhaustive testing, not all rubber spatulas are cut from the same cloth. We put 10 spatulas of varying sizes, shapes, and materials through multiple tests, including folding egg whites into a batter and scraping down cookie dough in a bowl (as well as non-baking applications).

As a general rule, we preferred larger-bladed spatulas. Large heads minimized the amount of folding necessary—keeping batters light and fully aerated—and performed admirably through the cookie stirring tests. As for construction, a fairly stiff blade did the best job, though it needed to be flexible enough to navigate the curve of the mixing bowl. Thin, flexible edges aided in agility and scraping ability. Eight out of the 10 models tested were silicone; the outstanding two, rubber. Both materials proved reasonably heat safe, despite the supposed superiority of the silicone.

While a spatula's blade was the most important element we tested, handles also came under consideration. Made of wood, metal, hard plastic, or silicone, they came in as many shapes and sizes as the blades. In the end, we favored stiff, relatively long handles with round edges as they were the most comfortable and efficient to use.

After evaluating all the test results, our nod went to the High Heat Scraper from Rubbermaid and the Heatproof 13-inch spatula from Le Creuset. Both are priced under $15 and widely available.

OFFSET SPATULA One of our favorite tools is a flexible offset or icing spatula. Its angled blade and narrow width ideally suit it for the fickle task of frosting cakes, but it also works in any number of baking applications. From removing tarts from the pan and smoothing batters to prying loose intractable cookies, it does it all. We generally favor a 10-inch spatula, though they come in a variety of lengths. You can find a good offset spatula for around $5.

WHISKS The market is loaded with different types of whisks; long or short, narrow or balloon-shaped, thick wires or thin. So which is the best for baking? Do size and shape make all that much of a difference? After experimenting with a broad range of whisks in a variety of shapes and sizes, including a few novelty styles (involving gyroscopes and ball bearings), we found traditional models the best choice. A large balloon whisk whipped egg whites and cream the fastest, though it was awkward for emulsifying pan sauces. It's best to have at least two whisks. For adding volume to items, such as whipped cream, choose a fairly long-handled (12 inches—you can always choke up on the handle for control) balloon whisk; for whisking items in a pan, such as pastry cream, choose a smaller flat-style whisk.

BENCH SCRAPERS Invaluable for countless baking tasks, a metal bench scraper is the chef's knife of the baking world. It is nothing more than a rectangular blade with a thin edge on one side and a wood, metal, or plastic handle on the opposite side. As a general rule, look for scrapers with a fairly sharp edge and a comfortable handle. Some models come stamped with rulers on the bottom—always a bonus for accurate baking.

We also like inexpensive, flexible plastic bowl scrapers, also called dough scrapers, for certain tasks. They are ideal for working with very soft doughs like our Ciabatta (page 101) or Rustic Italian Bread (page 98) and scraping dough out of standing mixer bowls, a task difficult for some rubber spatulas. Bench scrapers can be had for under $7; bowl scrapers are even less.

WIRE RACKS Fresh from the oven, most baked goods need a cooling-down period. Left to sit directly on a countertop, a cake's bottom will overcook, a pie's crust can turn gummy, and chewy cookies will turn brittle. By resting the pans or trays on a wire cooling rack, cooling air freely circulates underneath. We recommend purchasing fairly large, sturdy wire racks. In a pinch, a cooling rack may be improvised. Rest the baking sheet on top of two empty cans of the same size or on top of four dinner knives, spaced out evenly.

PASTRY BAG For piping decorative borders on cakes and filling éclairs, a pastry bag is an essential tool. We recommend purchasing a reasonably large, sturdy bag (a small investment at about $3). One of our favorites is constructed of a flexible nylon material and lined with polyurethane to prevent leaking and for easy cleanup. The bag may be sold with a set of tips, but if not, pick up a full set and you will be prepared for all your piping needs.

In an emergency, a pastry bag can be improvised from a zipper-lock bag. Simply fill the bag and cut a hole (start small and go larger if necessary) in a bottom corner. Twist the top of the bag tight to attain maximum pressure.

PIZZA STONE Pizza stones (also called baking stones) are prized for their ability to retain heat and lessen the effects of hot spots and temperature fluctuations in home ovens. Usually made of clay or ceramics (although soapstone and composite cement stones are also available), pizza stones, when coupled with extreme heat, absorb moisture, thus producing crisper, drier pizzas, breads, and calzones. If you like to bake bread, we strongly recommend that you own a pizza stone. See page 156 for details on our testing of specific models.

PARCHMENT PAPER We use parchment paper for a variety of baking needs, everything from lining baking sheets and cake pans to organizing dry ingredients. We tested four brands—Fox Run Craftsmen (flat sheets), Beyond Gourmet (unbleached roll), Reynolds (bleached roll), and a sheet of Super Parchment (a washable and reusable product)—baking cookies and pizzas on each. In the end, all were acceptable, freely releasing cookies from their pans and enabling smooth rolling of pizza dough. Reynolds is the most widely available brand (and at 14 inches, is the widest of the lot), sold nationwide in 30-square-foot rolls for approximately $2.50.

PLASTIC WRAP Generally overlooked and always undervalued, plastic wrap is useful for many of the recipes in this book. Because of concerns over plasticizers (softening agents added to plastic wrap to promote clingability), two types of plastic wrap are commonly marketed today: those specially formulated for microwaving (they won't melt) and those designed for clinging. We purchased six varieties and put them through a few simple tests to judge their worthiness. Saran Original proved the sturdiest wrap, heavier, stiffer, and tougher than the other five we tested. Its Achilles' heel was clingability; it failed the cling tests we subjected it to. For wrapping foods, it's not the best bet. That said, it's perfect for rolling out piecrusts and cookie doughs if you don't have parchment paper. For all-around usage, Glad ClingWrap and Saran Cling Plus were better options. They both clung tenaciously, were microwave safe, and were reasonably tough.

HIGH-ALTITUDE BAKING

BAKING RECIPES DEVELOPED AT SEA LEVEL often function differently at higher elevations. Cakes and muffins may balloon up only to collapse, cookies might turn out thin and crisp instead of chewy, and breads can overproof and taste dry or gummy. The scientific explanations for these changes point to a reduction in atmospheric pressure, meaning that there is less air pressure. Less pressure means that water will boil at a lower temperature (and therefore evaporate more readily in the oven), and chemical leaveners or yeast will react with more force. Whipped eggs will expand more quickly, and sugar will become more concentrated (due to rapid water loss). Also, the typical mountain climate tends to be much drier, thus further affecting the moisture content of baked goods. Generally, it is accepted that these changes begin to emerge at around 3500 feet and amplify as the elevation increases. For this reason in particular, it is difficult to find any one set of guidelines or rules to follow when baking at high altitudes.

To learn more about baking at high altitudes, we packed our whisks and our recipes and headed to Golden, Colorado, which has an elevation of 5700 feet. We chose a selection of recipes (all developed in our Boston test kitchen, which is 50 feet above sea level and also tends to be fairly humid for at least half the year) and baked each according to the directions in this book. We compared the results with those obtained in Boston and then proceeded to test ways to solve the issues plaguing these recipes at high altitude. We based our tests on the most frequent suggestions found in our research: turning up the oven by 25 degrees, adding more liquid or eggs, underwhipping eggs, shortening rising times, and reducing the amounts of sugar, baking powder, baking soda, and yeast. Here's what we learned.

BASIC PIE DOUGH (page 181): We blind baked a pieshell so that we could analyze the results without the obstruction of a filling. The results in Colorado were almost identical to those in Boston, the only difference being a drier dough, due to the reduced moisture in the flour stored in the arid mountain climate. We added an extra tablespoon of water to make the dough a little more pliable and easier to roll out.

BUTTERMILK BISCUITS (page 55): Given the large amount of both baking powder and baking soda in this recipe, we thought for sure they would present challenges at high altitude. Surprisingly, this was not the case. The only difficulty we encountered was forming the dough into a cohesive ball (again, because the flour was so dry), but this was quickly remedied by adding an extra tablespoon of buttermilk.

CHEWY OATMEAL-RAISIN COOKIES (page 439): Much to our surprise, this was the most challenging recipe we tested at high altitude. Cookies that were moist and chewy at sea level morphed into thin, hard wafers. They also spread out too much, becoming burnt on the edges and tooth-shatteringly hard when cool. The high proportion of fat and sugar in this recipe was the culprit: The butter melted faster than the cookies could set because the water in it evaporated more readily (butter contains about 18 percent water). The loss of moisture caused the sugar to become too concentrated (the cookies tasted too sweet) and the cookies to become flat and hard. When we tried decreasing the butter, the cookies looked right but tasted and felt too dry. Decreasing the sugar by a hefty ¼ cup was more successful. Less sugar kept the cookies from spreading too much in the oven, and an extra egg yolk restored their original chew. Increasing the oven temperature 25 degrees moved the process along so the cookies didn't dry out.

CORN MUFFINS (page 49): The muffins rose high in the oven, only to have their tops collapse and flatten. When we reduced the baking powder and baking soda each by ¼ teaspoon, these muffins shaped up, but their flavor was too sweet and their texture too dry. Subtracting 1 tablespoon sugar and increasing the milk in the recipe by 1 tablespoon turned out to be the proper adjustments.

YELLOW LAYER CAKE (page 347): Drastically different at high altitude, this cake was unrecognizable with a pale, wet surface; sunken center; sweet flavor; and dry, cottony texture. The first change we made was to increase the oven temperature by 25 degrees. We reduced the baking powder by ¼ teaspoon and the sugar by 1½ table-spoons, but the cake still sank in the center and had a strange tangy flavor. Because the batter appeared wetter and shinier than before, we thought add-ing ¼ cup more flour might achieve the proper consistency. It did, and the cake also had a sturdier structure, compromised before by the high amount of butter. Still dry and bland, it needed another egg to finally become a moist, buttery, vanilla-flavored cake with a properly risen center.

FOOLPROOF SPONGE CAKE (page 357): This cake presented a different set of prob-lems. At sea level, this recipe merits the name "foolproof" because the two leaveners—the tra-ditional eggs as well as baking powder—ensure a proper rise. At high altitude, neither leavener worked properly. On our first attempt, this cake was sunken and dry, with a very large crumb. Learning from previous tests, we reduced the sugar by 1 tablespoon and the baking powder by ⅛ teaspoon and increased the oven temperature by 25 degrees. We quickly figured out that the bak-ing time needed to be shortened by at least five minutes. But these alterations were not enough to improve this cake. We also needed to underwhip both the whites and the whole eggs. We whipped the whites to very soft peaks rather than soft peaks and reduced the whipping time for the whole eggs by one minute. Underwhipping the eggs gave the cake an even top and a moist, tender crumb.

AMERICAN SANDWICH BREAD (page 74): Our first loaves were dense and gummy (not tender, as they should be), and the tops were ripped and uneven (not smooth and round). We reduced the amount of flour by 2 tablespoons,

decreased the rising time, and increased the oven temperature by 25 degrees. The loaf still suffered from the same ailments as before, and now the crust was thick and dry. Because of the short and intense rising period, we decided to decrease the yeast by ½ teaspoon instead of decreasing the rising time and revert to the original oven temperature. This version baked perfectly in the right amount of time, with a shapely, tender crust and delicate crumb.

WHAT WE LEARNED After much test-ing and trial and error, we returned to Boston with a newfound respect for bakers working at high altitudes. We also brought back some general conclusions. At high altitudes, the most sensitive recipes are those that contain leavener and/or a high proportion of sugar. Baked goods will rise more quickly, often before their structure has time to set, and then collapse, leaving the final texture too dense. In delicate baked goods, such as cakes or muffins, high amounts of fat will also compromise the structure and stability of the final product. And since water evaporates at a quicker rate, espe-cially when the climate is arid, this causes the final product to be dry and overly concentrated in sugar (which is why cookies become hard and brittle).

While many sources provide reliable-sounding formulas for reducing or increasing specific ingredients, we found this information was not terribly helpful because each recipe has its own set of problems. Unfortunately, it is impossible to write hard-and-fast rules for adjusting each and every recipe in this book. The process will require some trial and error. Our recommendations? First try each recipe as is and then make adjustments where needed, according to the specific prob-lems that arise. Note that simpler recipes, such as biscuits, will be easier to adjust than complex recipes with many variables to test, such as cakes. The chart on the following page offers possible solutions to problems you are likely to encounter when baking at high altitudes. To read more about high-altitude baking, visit our Bulletin Board at www.cooksillustrated.com. There you can share your experiences, post tips, and ask questions. Choose the high-altitude baking forum on the Cook's Chat page to continue the conversation.

TROUBLE-SHOOTING BAKING RECIPES AT HIGH ALTITUDES

WHEN YOU ARE BAKING ...	POSSIBLE PROBLEM	POSSIBLE SOLUTION
Quick Breads, Muffins, Biscuits, and Scones	Biscuit or scone dough is dry and hard to knead	Add an extra tablespoon or two of liquid
	Quick breads or muffins collapse and texture is dense	Use less baking powder and/or baking soda
	Quick breads or muffins are sweet and dry	Reduce the sugar by a tablespoon or two and/or add an extra tablespoon or two of liquid
Yeast Breads and Pastries	Dough is too dry	Hold back a small portion of the flour and add only as needed
	Top of loaf blows out and crumb is dense or gummy	Use less yeast or shorten the rising time
Pie Doughs, Tart Doughs, and Non-Yeasted Pastries	Dough is dry and hard to roll out	Add an extra tablespoon or two of ice water
Cakes	Chemically leavened cakes sink in the center	➤ Use less baking powder and/or baking soda ➤ Increase the oven temperature and decrease the baking time
	Egg-leavened cakes sink in the center	➤ Underwhip the whites and/or whole eggs ➤ Increase the oven temperature and decrease the baking time
	Cakes are dry and cottony	Use less sugar and/or add an extra egg
	Cakes are greasy	Add an extra tablespoon or two of flour
Cookies	Cookies spread too much in the oven	➤ Use less sugar ➤ Increase the oven temperature and decrease the baking time
	Cookies are too dry	Add an extra egg or yolk

1

QUICK BREADS, MUFFINS, BISCUITS, AND SCONES

Quick Breads, Muffins, Biscuits, and Scones

BANANA BREAD 23
Banana-Chocolate Bread
Banana-Coconut Bread with Macadamia Nuts
Orange-Spice Banana Bread

CRANBERRY-NUT BREAD 25

DATE-NUT BREAD 26

ZUCCHINI BREAD 28

GINGERBREAD 30
Gingerbread with Dried Fruit

BOSTON BROWN BREAD 32

GOLDEN NORTHERN CORNBREAD 35
Golden Cornbread with Cheddar Cheese
Golden Cornbread with Chiles
Golden Cornbread with Bacon

SOUTHERN CORNBREAD 37

CLASSIC IRISH SODA BREAD 41
Irish Brown Soda Bread
Oatmeal-Walnut Soda Bread
American-Style Soda Bread with Raisins and
    Caraway

BLUEBERRY MUFFINS 45
Cinnamon-Sugar-Dipped Blueberry Muffins
Ginger-Glazed Blueberry Muffins
Lemon-Glazed Blueberry Muffins

CORN MUFFINS 47
Corn and Apricot Muffins with Orange Essence
Bacon-Scallion Corn Muffins with Cheddar Cheese

COFFEECAKE MUFFINS 50
Coffeecake Muffins with Quick Confectioners' Sugar
    Icing

BUTTERMILK BISCUITS 54

CREAM BISCUITS 55
Cream Biscuits with Fresh Herbs
Cream Biscuits with Cheddar Cheese

CREAM SCONES WITH CURRANTS 57
Glazed Scones
Cakey Scones
Ginger Scones
Cranberry-Orange Scones
Lemon-Blueberry Scones

OATMEAL SCONES 59
Cinnamon-Raisin Oatmeal Scones
Apricot-Almond Oatmeal Scones
Oatmeal Scones with Dried Cherries and Hazelnuts
Glazed Maple-Pecan Oatmeal Scones

QUICK CINNAMON BUNS WITH
    BUTTERMILK ICING 61

POPOVERS 64
Muffin Tin Popovers

BUTTERMILK DOUGHNUTS 66
Powdered Sugar Buttermilk Doughnuts
Cinnamon-Sugared Buttermilk Doughnuts

QUICK BREADS ENCOMPASS LOAF BREADS like banana bread, cornbread, and Irish soda bread as well as their diminutive counterparts: muffins, biscuits, and scones. Although these breads may differ in size and shape, they have a number of elements in common. All of these baked goods can be quickly prepared (the batter or dough can usually be assembled in the time it takes to preheat the oven) and quickly baked. This sets them far apart from yeast breads, which must rise for hours on the counter. All quick breads contain chemical leaveners (baking soda and baking powder) that are speedy and reliable.

There are several methods typically used to assemble quick breads. The most common, often referred to as the quick-bread method, calls for measuring wet and dry ingredients separately, pouring wet into dry, and then mixing them together as quickly as possible, usually with a wooden spoon or spatula. A second technique, often called the creaming method and more common to cake batters, starts with creaming the butter and sugar until light and fluffy—usually with an electric mixer. Eggs and flavorings are beaten in, then the dry and liquid ingredients are alternately added. A third possibility comes from the biscuit- and pie dough–making tradition, in which cold fat is cut into the dry ingredients with fingertips, forks, a pastry blender, or the blade of a food processor. Once the mixture has achieved a cornmeal-like texture with pea-sized flecks, liquid is added and quickly mixed in.

We have tested these three mixing methods on many of the recipes in this chapter. Often we have found that the same ingredients will bake up quite differently depending on how they are combined. For instance, creaming butter and sugar together beats additional air into the batter, which generally causes the texture of the quick bread to be lighter and more cakelike. In contrast, the quick-bread method (stirring wet and dry ingredients together) yields quick breads with a denser, more springy crumb. Since each recipe has so many variables, these characteristics are really only broad guidelines and will vary from recipe to recipe.

In addition to mixing methods, it's also important to pay attention to the choice of flours and leaveners in these recipes. The protein content of the flour can greatly affect the texture in these simple baked goods. (For more information on flour, see page 1.) Chemical leaveners (that is, baking soda and baking powder) are key elements in quick bread recipes. (See page 7 for more information on these ingredients.)

BANANA BREAD

OVERRIPE BANANAS ON THE KITCHEN counter are an excellent excuse to make banana bread. However, many banana breads are flat, gritty, or heavy. Worse, some loaves taste only remotely of bananas. Good banana bread is soft and tender with plenty of banana flavor and crunchy toasted walnuts. It should be moist and light, something so delicious that you look forward to the bananas on the counter turning soft and mushy.

In our testing, we found it very important to pay close attention to the condition of the bananas. Sweet, older, darkly speckled bananas infused the bread with both moisture and flavor, which meant that the bread, whether still warm or day-old, succeeded with less butter (minus 2 tablespoons) than the amount used in most recipes (½ cup).

We also experimented with the way we prepared the banana for the batter: slightly mashed, mashed well, and pureed. Loaves with slightly mashed bananas left chunks of fruit. We preferred a smoother texture, but pureeing the bananas turned out to be a bad idea, because the batter did not rise as well. Leavener probably escaped before the thin batter developed enough structure to trap gases. Bananas well-mashed by hand kept the batter thick.

We still wanted more moisture in the bread, so we tried mixing in milk, buttermilk, sour cream, and plain yogurt. Sour cream added richness to our bread, but it also made for a heavy texture and an unattractive, pebbly crust. Milk added little flavor and created a slick crust. Buttermilk added a delightful tang, but yogurt let the banana flavor stand out. And because yogurt has more solids than buttermilk, it made for a somewhat more solid loaf, which we preferred.

While the added yogurt softened the bread's crumb, we still sought a more delicate, open grain.

So we decided to experiment with various mixing methods to see how they affected the final texture. We considered the quick-bread method (dry ingredients mixed in one bowl, liquids in another, with the two then gently stirred together) and the creaming method (butter and sugar creamed together, dry and wet ingredients then alternately mixed in).

The creaming method created a soft texture (reminiscent of butter cake) and good volume from the whipped sugar and butter. However, its lighter color looked less appetizing next to the golden-brown loaf achieved with the quick-bread method. The quick-bread method produced a delicate texture, too, and the less consistent crumb looked hearty and delicious. It also rose more than the creamed loaf. All in all, it was a better choice.

Take caution when mixing, though. When we stirred the wet and the dry ingredients into a smooth batter, the loaves turned out small and tough. Flour contains protein, and when protein mixes with water, gluten develops. The more you stir with a spoon, the more the gluten proteins form into long, orderly bundles. These bundles create an elastic batter that resists changing shape and cannot rise as well. To minimize gluten development, fold together the wet and dry ingredients gently, just until the dry ingredients are moistened. The batter should still be thick and chunky, but without any streaks of unincorporated flour.

STORING OVERRIPE BANANAS FOR BANANA BREAD

Place overripe bananas in a zipper-lock plastic bag and freeze them. As available, add more bananas to the bag. When you are ready to make bread, thaw the bananas on the counter until softened.

Banana Bread

MAKES ONE 9-INCH LOAF

For best results, be sure to use a loaf pan that measures 9 inches long, 5 inches across, and 3 inches deep.

2	cups (10 ounces) unbleached all-purpose flour, plus more for dusting the pan
1 1/4	cups walnuts, chopped coarse
3/4	cup (5 1/4 ounces) sugar
3/4	teaspoon baking soda
1/2	teaspoon salt
3	very ripe, soft, darkly speckled large bananas, mashed well (about 1 1/2 cups)
1/4	cup plain yogurt
2	large eggs, beaten lightly
6	tablespoons (3/4 stick) unsalted butter, melted and cooled
1	teaspoon vanilla extract

1. Adjust an oven rack to the lower-middle position and heat the oven to 350 degrees. Grease the bottom and sides of a 9 by 5-inch loaf pan; dust with flour, tapping out the excess.

2. Spread the walnuts on a baking sheet and toast until fragrant, 5 to 10 minutes. Set aside to cool.

3. Whisk the flour, sugar, baking soda, salt, and walnuts together in a large bowl; set aside.

4. Mix the mashed bananas, yogurt, eggs, butter, and vanilla with a wooden spoon in a medium bowl. Lightly fold the banana mixture into the dry ingredients with a rubber spatula until just combined and the batter looks thick and chunky. Scrape the batter into the prepared loaf pan.

5. Bake until the loaf is golden brown and a toothpick inserted in the center comes out clean, about 55 minutes. Cool in the pan for 5 minutes, then transfer to a wire rack. Serve warm or at room temperature. (The bread can be wrapped with plastic wrap and stored at room temperature for up to 3 days.)

➤ VARIATIONS

Banana-Chocolate Bread

Follow the recipe for Banana Bread, reducing the sugar to 10 tablespoons and mixing 2½ ounces grated bittersweet chocolate (a heaping ½ cup) into the dry ingredients.

Banana-Coconut Bread with Macadamia Nuts

Adjust the oven rack to the middle position and heat the oven to 350 degrees. Spread ½ cup flaked, sweetened coconut and 1 cup chopped macadamia nuts on a baking sheet and toast, stirring every 2 minutes, until golden brown, about 6 minutes. Follow the recipe for Banana Bread, substituting the cooled, toasted macadamias and coconut for the walnuts.

Orange-Spice Banana Bread

Follow the recipe for Banana Bread, adding 1 teaspoon ground cinnamon, ¼ teaspoon freshly grated nutmeg, and 2 tablespoons grated orange zest to the dry ingredients.

CRANBERRY-NUT BREAD

WE DON'T MAKE CRANBERRY-NUT BREAD just for ourselves. We make it for the kindergarten teacher, the mail carrier, and anyone else who deserves something homemade. The problem is that this simple bread is often sub-par, sunken in the middle, too dense, or so overly sweetened that the contrast between the tart berries and what should be a slightly sweet dough is lost. We wanted to avoid these problems, and we had some other goals in mind as well. We were looking for a crust that was golden brown and evenly thin all the way around and a texture that was somewhere between a dense breakfast bread and a light, airy cake. And, for convenience' sake, we wanted a recipe that fit easily into a standard 9 by 5-inch loaf pan. After looking at almost 60 recipes, it seemed evident that the mixing method and the leavening were the most important factors in getting the quick bread we were after.

First we tackled mixing. Some recipes called for the creaming method, others the quick-bread method. We made several loaves using each of these methods. While the creaming method did give us a marginally more tender bread, we quickly determined that it was too light and airy. We liked the denser, more compact texture produced by the

quick-bread method. An added advantage of the method is that—as its name implies—it can be put together very quickly.

Next we moved on to leavening. When we looked back at our testing, we noted that 75 percent of the recipes combined baking powder with baking soda to leaven the bread. The rest used all baking powder or all baking soda. We tried every option we could think of using these two leaveners, both alone and together. We found that baking powder seemed to enhance the flavor, while baking soda supported the structure; finding the right balance was tricky. Eventually, we came to the decision that ¼ teaspoon of baking soda combined with 1 teaspoon of baking powder gave us the bright flavor and rather dense texture we were looking for.

With our mixing and leavening methods settled, we focused on ingredients. We quickly determined that we liked the flavor that butter provided over that of oil, margarine, or shortening. More than one egg made the bread almost too rich and caused the interior to turn somewhat yellow. After testing different amounts and types of sugar, we stuck with 1 cup of granulated sugar, which provided just the right amount of sweetness. Orange zest added not only to the flavor but to the interior appearance as well, thanks to the orange flecks.

We also tinkered with the liquid component. Many recipes called for water or even boiling water, but freshly squeezed orange juice was usually mentioned and offered the best flavor. We compared fresh, home-squeezed orange juice with commercially prepared juices made both from fresh oranges and from concentrate; home-squeezed juice was the winner, hands down.

Not every recipe called for dairy, but we tested everything from heavy cream to sour cream. Both buttermilk and yogurt provided the moistness and tang we were looking for, with buttermilk edging out yogurt by a hairbreadth.

Last but not least were the cranberries. The cranberry harvest begins just after Labor Day and continues through early fall, which means that by mid- to late January, no fresh berries are available. Cranberries freeze beautifully, so grab a few extra bags to have on hand and freeze them until you're ready to use them. We found no discernible difference in the finished product whether using fresh or frozen cranberries.

Cranberry-Nut Bread

MAKES ONE 9-INCH LOAF

We prefer sweet, mild pecans in this bread, but walnuts can be substituted. Resist the urge to cut into the bread while it is hot out of the oven; the texture improves as it cools, making it easier to slice.

2	cups (10 ounces) unbleached all-purpose flour, plus more for dusting the pan
1/2	cup pecans, chopped coarse
1	tablespoon grated zest from 1 large orange
1/3	cup fresh orange juice
2/3	cup buttermilk
6	tablespoons (3/4 stick) unsalted butter, melted and cooled
1	large egg, beaten lightly
1	cup (7 ounces) sugar
1	teaspoon salt
1	teaspoon baking powder
1/4	teaspoon baking soda
1 1/2	cups cranberries (about 6 ounces), chopped coarse

1. Adjust an oven rack to the middle position and heat the oven to 375 degrees. Grease the bottom and sides of a 9 by 5-inch loaf pan; dust with flour, tapping out the excess.

2. Spread the pecans on a baking sheet and toast until fragrant, 5 to 7 minutes. Set aside.

3. Stir together the orange zest, orange juice, buttermilk, butter, and egg in a small bowl. Whisk together the flour, sugar, salt, baking powder, and baking soda in a large bowl. Stir the liquid ingredients into the dry ingredients with a rubber spatula until just moistened. Gently stir in the cranberries and pecans. Do not overmix. Scrape the batter into the prepared pan and smooth the surface with a rubber spatula.

4. Bake 20 minutes, then reduce the heat to 350 degrees; continue to bake until the loaf is golden brown and a toothpick inserted in the center comes out clean, about 45 minutes longer. Cool in the

pan 10 minutes, then transfer to a wire rack and cool at least 1 hour before serving. (The bread can be wrapped with plastic wrap and stored at room temperature for up to 3 days.)

DATE-NUT BREAD

PACKED WITH DATES AND DOTTED WITH nuts, date-nut bread brings back memories of holidays past for many of us in the test kitchen. The problem is, the date-nut bread sampled at recent holiday gatherings makes us question our recollections. Was the bread really that good, or has residual holiday goodwill colored our memories? The loaves we have sampled more recently make us suspect the latter. Heavy and sweet or dry and bland, these versions of date nut bread left us disappointed. We wanted a quick bread rich in date and nut flavor, with a moist, tender texture that is neither leaden nor light. What's more, we wanted a quick bread recipe that, true to its name, was quick to prepare. And we wanted our date-nut bread to taste so good that we would make it year round.

Our initial research unearthed no standard date-nut bread recipe. Beyond the inclusion of dates and nuts, the recipes varied widely. Some used more than one egg, others a combination of different types of flours. Some recipes called for a small amount of butter—only 1 tablespoon in one instance—while others called for 1/4 cup vegetable

CHOPPING DRIED FRUIT

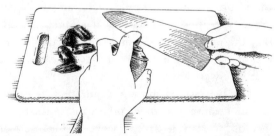

Dried fruit, especially dates, very often sticks to the knife when you try to chop it. To avoid this problem, coat the blade with a thin film of vegetable oil spray just before you begin chopping any dried fruit. The chopped fruit doesn't cling to the blade, and the knife stays relatively clean.

oil. None of the breads baked from these recipes came near our ideal date-nut bread, so we turned to other sources. Because we had such success with our Cranberry-Nut Bread (see page 26), we wondered whether it could provide the foundation for our date-nut bread. We liked the texture of the bread produced by the quick-bread method. Instead of creaming butter and sugar and then incorporating eggs and the dry ingredients, the quick-bread method simply calls for adding liquid ingredients to melted butter and then stirring into the flour. In addition to being quick—as its name implies—the quick-bread method also produces a more compact texture we found appealing.

We replaced the cranberries with dates, omitted the orange juice and increased the buttermilk to make up the difference. The rest of the recipe remained the same. The result—a golden, moist loaf whose texture was somewhere between a dense breakfast bread and a light, airy cake—was almost where we wanted to be.

While we liked the overall texture of the bread, we found the texture of the dates too firm. Some of the recipes we uncovered in our research soaked the dates in hot water and baking soda before adding them to the batter. We suspected that, in combination with the hot water, the baking soda—an alkali—would help soften the dates by breaking down their fibers. This method worked well. The dates softened significantly and had a more tender, supple texture in the baked loaf. But the soaking water in combination with the buttermilk was too much liquid and made the finished loaf a bit gummy in texture. Reluctant to discard the flavor of the dates that had leached into the soaking water, we reduced the buttermilk and added the soaking liquid to the batter along with the dates. This time the amount of liquid in the batter was just right. Although the texture of the dates was right, we felt that the loaf could support more intense date and nut flavor. We increased the dates from 1½ cups to 2 cups (1 cup hot water was still sufficient to cover the dates) and doubled the nuts from ½ cup to 1 cup. The resulting bread packed more of a date-nut punch and was richer and denser without being heavy.

One issue remained: the color. The bread's golden color was lighter than what we had in mind. Where did the deep, dark brown color of date-nut breads of yore come from? We decided to try replacing the granulated sugar with molasses and with dark brown sugar. While both made the bread much darker, we preferred the bread with the brown sugar. The molasses added too much liquid to our bread and contributed a strong flavor that tasters found out of place. Dark brown sugar, on the other hand, worked well. The dark brown sugar deepened the color of the bread and supported the bread's texture without adding too much liquid.

One unforeseen consequence of adding brown sugar, however, was the excessive darkening of the crust during baking. We discovered that after baking the bread at 375 degrees for 20 minutes and then 350 degrees for the remainder of the baking time, the bread browned too quickly and became too dark around the edges before the center was done. We found that a 350-degree oven throughout the entire baking time works best.

By now we had a tender quick bread packed with date and nut flavor. The final loaf was a deep brown and had a moist, dense texture without being leaden and a rich date-nut flavor. No longer just for the holidays, this date-nut bread would be a year-round treat.

Date-Nut Bread

MAKES ONE 9-INCH LOAF

As you chop the dates, watch for and remove pits and stems, which seem to adhere persistently even to pitted dates.

2	cups (10 ounces) unbleached all-purpose flour, plus more for dusting the pan
1	cup boiling water
1	teaspoon baking soda
2	cups (about 9 ounces) pitted whole dates, chopped coarse
1	cup pecans or walnuts, chopped coarse
²⁄₃	cup buttermilk
³⁄₄	cup packed (5¼ ounces) dark brown sugar
6	tablespoons (¾ stick) unsalted butter, melted and cooled
1	large egg
½	teaspoon salt
1	teaspoon baking powder

1. Adjust an oven rack to the middle position and heat the oven to 350 degrees. Grease a 9 by 5-inch loaf pan; dust with flour, tapping out the excess.

2. Stir together the water, baking soda, and dates in a medium bowl. Cover and set aside until the dates have softened and the water is lukewarm, about 30 minutes.

3. Meanwhile, spread the nuts on a baking sheet and toast until fragrant, 5 to 10 minutes. Set aside.

4. Stir the buttermilk and sugar together in a medium bowl. Add the melted butter and egg, and stir until combined. Stir in the date mixture until combined. In a separate medium bowl, whisk together the flour, salt, baking powder, and nuts. Stir the buttermilk mixture into the flour mixture with a rubber spatula until just moistened. Scrape the batter into the prepared pan and smooth the surface with the rubber spatula.

5. Bake until the loaf is dark brown and a skewer inserted in the center comes out clean, 55 to 60 minutes, rotating the pan halfway through baking. Cool in the pan for 10 minutes, then transfer to a wire rack and cool for at least 1 hour before serving. (The bread can be wrapped with plastic wrap and stored at room temperature for up to 3 days.)

ZUCCHINI BREAD

DURING THE SUMMER MONTHS, AMERICANS make, give, and receive zucchini bread with abandon. Rarely, however, do they actually eat the bread. Zucchini bread has become more of a symbol of neighborly affection and goodwill than a dish that people enjoy eating. Instead of the bland, leaden loaves given and received with good intentions, but wrapped and stored indefinitely in the back of the freezer, we wanted a brightly flavored, lightly sweetened quick bread with a moist crumb that was a real treat to nibble and savor.

The standard zucchini bread recipe published in countless collections of community recipes and home-style cookbooks calls for mixing dry and liquid ingredients separately and then combining them. Typically, flour, leaveners, and salt are mixed together in a large bowl. Eggs, sugar, and vegetable oil are mixed together in another bowl. The liquid ingredients and zucchini are then stirred into the flour mixture. The batter is scraped into a loaf pan and baked in a moderate oven for 50 to 60 minutes.

While we were reluctant to change the basic zucchini bread method, we were eager to find a substitute for the vegetable oil called for in every recipe we came across. We found that loaves made with vegetable oil tasted flat and bland and suspected that melted butter would complement the subtle zucchini flavor and contribute a pleasant richness. Recipes generally called for anywhere from ¼ cup to 1 cup vegetable oil in a batter that would fill a standard 9 by 5-inch loaf pan. We began our tests by replacing the vegetable oil with an equal amount of butter. After numerous tests we found that loaves with ½ to 1 cup butter tasted too rich; those with only 6 tablespoons melted butter were just right.

Although our bread no longer tasted bland, it still tasted a bit flat. We considered adding an acidic ingredient to the batter to brighten the rich buttery flavor and complement the subtle vegetal notes of the zucchini. We experimented with differing amounts of buttermilk, sour cream, and yogurt, acidic liquid ingredients we have used in other quick-bread recipes. Of the three, we preferred plain yogurt. Sour cream made the texture too heavy and the flavor too rich. While buttermilk worked well—and would be an acceptable substitute in a pinch—we preferred the texture and flavor of the bread made with plain yogurt. The slight tanginess of the yogurt complemented the zucchini flavor without adding too much liquid. A tablespoon of lemon juice added a bit more acidity as well as a pleasant citrus note. We tried lemon zest but found it to be overpowering—this recipe was for zucchini bread, not lemon-zucchini bread. In addition to increased flavor, the yogurt and lemon juice reacted with the baking soda to produce a lighter bread with more rise, which tasters preferred.

Next, we tackled the eggs, sugar, and the other ingredients added to the liquid portion of the batter. We found that two eggs worked well, adding more flavor and rise than one egg but without the slight egg flavor and texture of the bread made with three eggs. Recipes that call for granulated sugar alone tend to use at least one cup. We found these loaves to be too sweet and delicate. Just ¾ cup sugar added the right amount of sweetness without giving this almost savory bread a cakelike sweetness and texture.

We finally confronted the reason for zucchini bread: the zucchini. To this point we had been adding only 6½ ounces zucchini, the size of a small zucchini, which when shredded produced about 1½ cups lightly packed. The zucchini flavor and texture were subtle, but almost too subtle. We wondered if the bread shouldn't have a more pronounced zucchini flavor. We tried increasing the zucchini to 3 cups and found ourselves with a bread that virtually looked and tasted like mashed zucchini.

After innumerable soggy, gummy loaves packed with shredded zucchini, we finally began to re-evaluate our approach. We decided to drain the zucchini to extract as much water as possible so that we could add more than 6 ounces of the squash and still retain a texture that was more like a moist quick bread than squashed squash. We wanted more zucchini flavor without the excess zucchini moisture. We processed the zucchini in the food processor with 2 tablespoons of the sugar and placed the shredded zucchini in a fine-mesh strainer set about 2 inches over the bottom of a bowl. (You can also grate the zucchini on the large holes of a box grater and toss the shreds with 2 tablespoons sugar.) After 30 minutes the sugar had drawn nearly half a cup of liquid from 1 pound of zucchini. If you are using large zucchini—2 pounds or more—with developed internal seed structure, slice the squash in half lengthwise and use a spoon to scrape out the large seeds as you would a cucumber. Draining the zucchini turned out to be a very important step. Thirty minutes passed quickly as we prepared the pan and the remaining ingredients for the bread. The resulting bread, dotted with greens flecks of the squash, had a notably increased zucchini flavor as well as a moist, but not gummy, texture.

We tried our finished loaf with other flavorings found in various recipes: ground cinnamon, grated nutmeg, ground ginger, vanilla, nuts, and raisins. Except for the nuts, we found all of these flavoring

agents out of place in our relatively light, brightly flavored quick bread. After several tests, we found that only ½ cup chopped toasted pecans or walnuts added a pleasant textural contrast to the moist bread without making the bread compact and dense. This zucchini bread would be a welcome and delicious way to enjoy summer's bounty.

Zucchini Bread

MAKES ONE 9-INCH LOAF

If you are using large zucchini with developed internal seeds, cut each zucchini in half lengthwise and use a spoon to scrape out and discard the seeds before shredding. The test kitchen found no discernible difference in tasting loaves made with whole-milk, low-fat, or nonfat plain yogurt, so use what you have on hand.

2	cups (10 ounces) unbleached all-purpose flour, plus more for dusting the pan
1	pound zucchini, washed and dried, ends and stems removed, cut in half lengthwise and seeded if using large zucchini, each half cut into 1-inch pieces
¾	cup (5¼ ounces) sugar
½	cup pecans or walnuts, chopped coarse
1	teaspoon baking soda
1	teaspoon baking powder
½	teaspoon salt
¼	cup plain yogurt
2	large eggs, beaten lightly
1	tablespoon juice from 1 lemon
6	tablespoons (¾ stick) unsalted butter, melted and cooled

1. Adjust an oven rack to the middle position and heat the oven to 375 degrees. Grease the bottom and sides of a 9 by 5-inch loaf pan; dust with flour, tapping out the excess.

2. In the bowl of a food processor fitted with the metal blade, process the zucchini and 2 tablespoons of the sugar until the zucchini is coarsely shredded, twelve to fifteen 1-second pulses. Transfer the mixture to a fine-mesh strainer set at least 2 inches over a bowl and allow to drain for 30 minutes. Alternatively, you can shred the halved zucchini (don't cut it into 1-inch pieces) on the large holes

of a box grater, toss with the 2 tablespoons of sugar, and drain.

3. Meanwhile, spread the nuts on a baking sheet and toast until fragrant, 5 to 7 minutes. Transfer the nuts to a cooling rack and cool completely. Transfer the nuts to a large bowl; add the flour, baking soda, baking powder, and salt, and whisk until combined. Set aside.

4. Whisk together the remaining ½ cup plus 2 tablespoons sugar, yogurt, eggs, lemon juice, and melted butter in a 2-cup glass measure until combined. Set aside.

5. After the zucchini has drained, squeeze the zucchini with several layers of paper towels to absorb excess moisture. Stir the zucchini and the yogurt mixture into the flour mixture until just moistened. Scrape the batter into the prepared pan and smooth the surface with a rubber spatula.

6. Bake until the loaf is golden brown and a

SHREDDING ZUCCHINI

1. Shred trimmed zucchini on the large holes of a box grater or in a food processor fitted with the shredding disk.

2. After sugaring and draining the zucchini, wrap it in paper towels and squeeze out excess liquid. Proceed immediately with recipe.

toothpick inserted in the center comes out clean, 55 to 60 minutes, rotating the pan halfway through baking. Cool in the pan for 10 minutes, then transfer to a wire rack and cool for at least 1 hour before serving. (The bread can be wrapped with plastic wrap and stored at room temperature for up to 3 days.)

GINGERBREAD

GINGERBREAD SHOULD BE TENDER, MOIST, and several inches thick. It should be easy enough to assemble just before dinner so squares of warm gingerbread can be enjoyed for dessert. As our early tests proved, these goals are rarely met. Gingerbread has a tendency to be dry and tough, and many recipes are unnecessarily complicated. Yes, you will probably need a lot of ingredients (mostly spices already in your pantry), but the mixing method should be simple. Gingerbread is a quick bread, after all.

To start our kitchen tests, we chose a milk-based gingerbread. Many recipes call for water, but in our initial tests tasters found these breads considerably drier and less rich than those made with milk. Milk fat adds tenderness and flavor; it is a must. With that decision made, we focused next on sweeteners. Most recipes include a dry sweetener—granulated sugar, light brown sugar, or dark brown sugar—as well as a liquid sweetener—molasses most often, but sometimes honey, maple syrup, or corn syrup.

We quickly discovered that molasses is the right liquid sweetener. Honey and corn syrup were judged too bland and boring. Maple syrup had some partisans, but most tasters thought the maple flavor clashed with the spices. We preferred the gentler flavor of light or mild molasses as compared with dark or robust molasses or blackstrap molasses. (See page 4 for more information on types of molasses.)

Brown sugar is more commonly used in gingerbread recipes than white sugar. We expected to like its heartier, richer flavor. However, tasters preferred samples prepared with granulated sugar. With brown sugar added to the mix, the molasses flavor overwhelmed the spices. Granulated sugar tasted cleaner, allowing the spices to shine through.

As for the spices, tasters liked a combination of ground ginger, cinnamon, cloves, nutmeg, and allspice. We tested and liked both crystallized and grated fresh ginger, but everyone in the test kitchen agreed that regular ground ginger (something most cooks are likely to have in the pantry) delivered excellent results. If you like a stronger ginger flavor, you can replace the ground ginger with a mixture of grated fresh and crystallized ginger as directed in the note preceding our recipe. Finally, we found that a pinch of cocoa, which is sometimes added to gingerbread, added earthiness and complexity to our recipe.

In kitchen tests, butter was the hands-down favorite over vegetable oil and shortening. We found that melting the butter yielded a denser, moister cake. When we creamed the butter and sugar, the result was lighter, fluffier, and more cakelike. As for the eggs, we found that two added too much moisture to the batter, which tended to sink in the middle near the end of the baking time. A single egg ensured sufficient tenderness and proper height.

Although we had been using milk in our recipe, we were intrigued by some old-fashioned recipes that called for sour cream, yogurt, or buttermilk instead. Sour cream and yogurt gave gingerbread too much tang, and we quickly dropped them from contention. Buttermilk, however, had some nice effects on our recipe. The color was darker and the texture slightly moister. Unfortunately, buttermilk also made the crumb coarser, and the flavor was a bit too strong. By comparison, the gingerbread made with milk had a better rise and finer texture. In the end, we found that a 50-50 ratio of buttermilk and milk offered the best traits of each.

With buttermilk added to the recipe, we found that baking soda was the best leavener. We tested both cake and all-purpose flours and discovered that cake flour was too soft for this recipe—it made gingerbread with an unappealingly doughy texture. All-purpose flour gave gingerbread the proper structure.

We tested several methods for combining the wet and dry ingredients, including adding the melted fat to the dry ingredients before the liquids

as well as beating the butter, sugar, and eggs, then alternately adding wet and dry ingredients. In the end, the simplest method proved best. We combined all the dry ingredients in one bowl, all the wet ingredients (including the melted butter, egg, and sugar) in another bowl, and then beat the dry ingredients into the wet ingredients, giving ourselves gingerbread that went into the oven in less than 10 minutes and came out tasting great.

~≪

Gingerbread

SERVES 8

For a stronger ginger flavor, replace the ground ginger with 3 tablespoons grated fresh ginger and 3 tablespoons minced crystallized ginger. If you don't own an 11 by 7-inch pan, you can bake the batter in a 9-inch square pan. This gingerbread is moist and delicious on its own, but it can be served with a dollop of lightly sweetened whipped cream.

2 1/4	cups sifted (9 ounces) unbleached all-purpose flour, plus more for dusting the pan
1/2	teaspoon baking soda
1/2	teaspoon salt
2	teaspoons ground ginger
1	teaspoon ground cinnamon
1/2	teaspoon ground cloves
1/2	teaspoon freshly grated nutmeg
1/2	teaspoon ground allspice
1	teaspoon Dutch-processed cocoa
8	tablespoons (1 stick) unsalted butter, melted and cooled to room temperature
3/4	cup mild or light molasses
3/4	cup (5 1/4 ounces) sugar
1/2	cup buttermilk
1/2	cup milk
1	large egg

1. Adjust an oven rack to the middle position and heat the oven to 350 degrees. Grease the bottom and sides of an 11 by 7-inch baking dish; dust with flour, tapping out the excess.

2. Whisk together the flour, baking soda, salt, ginger, cinnamon, cloves, nutmeg, allspice, and cocoa in a medium bowl.

3. Beat the butter, molasses, sugar, buttermilk, milk, and egg in a large bowl with an electric

mixer on low speed. Add the dry ingredients and beat on medium speed until the batter is smooth and thick, about 1 minute, scraping down the sides of the bowl with a rubber spatula as needed. (Do not overmix.) Scrape the batter into the prepared pan and smooth the surface.

4. Bake until the top springs back when lightly touched and the edges have pulled away from the pan sides, about 40 minutes. Set the pan on a wire rack and cool for at least 10 minutes. Serve warm or at room temperature. (Gingerbread can be wrapped in plastic, then foil, and refrigerated up to 5 days.)

➤ VARIATION

Gingerbread with Dried Fruit

Follow the recipe for Gingerbread, folding ¾ cup raisins, dried cranberries, or chopped prunes into the finished batter.

BOSTON BROWN BREAD

RARELY EATEN MORE THAN A HUNDRED miles outside of Boston and almost never served without baked beans, Boston brown bread is a unique loaf. Characteristically steamed in an old coffee can, this chemically leavened bread is robust, dense, and strongly flavored with earthy grains and the bittersweet tang of molasses. Boston brown

bread may be a dying tradition, but, as Boston locals, we love it and wanted to come up with a perfect recipe.

Like Boston baked beans, brown bread is a study in Puritan frugality. Most of the recipes we gathered offered up a simple batter of cornmeal, whole-wheat and rye flours, molasses, raisins or currants, and baking soda for leavening. While we appreciated the simple flavors of these uncomplicated recipes, we found most of them to be unbalanced, tasting predominantly of whole wheat. We wanted a recipe in which all the ingredients were on more equal footing.

We knew that altering the basic ingredients would be akin to heresy and did not want to stray too far. We did, however, decide that changing the flour mixture—lightening the whole-wheat and rye flours with a little unbleached white flour—was a safe change. The addition of the white flour allowed the cornmeal and molasses flavors to come through more clearly. We tried substituting oat flour for part of the rye flour, but the resulting loaf was gummy and lacked any oat flavor.

We also found that the choice of cornmeal makes a real difference in this simple bread. High-quality stone-ground cornmeal was the tasters' favorite. It had a stronger corn flavor than fine-ground meal and added a pleasing texture to the loaf. If stone-ground cornmeal is difficult to find,

PREVENTING STICKY LIDS

Instead of struggling with the stuck-in-place lids of jars containing sticky contents such as jelly or molasses, try one of these tips:

A. Cover the top of the jar with plastic wrap before screwing on the lid. The plastic prevents any serious sticking, so the lid always unscrews.

B. Alternatively, dip a small piece of paper towel into a bit of vegetable oil and wipe the threads of the jar. The film of oil will prevent the lid from sticking to the jar the next time you open it.

try Goya-brand coarse cornmeal, which proved readily available and delicious.

We experimented with different kinds of molasses and were most pleased with the darker varieties, especially Grandma's robust molasses. Light, or mild, molasses was fine and provided adequate flavor, but dark molasses imparted a heartier flavor that nicely complemented the earthy whole-wheat and rye flours. Blackstrap, the dregs of sugar processing and therefore the strongest-flavored molasses, was too much, giving the loaf a bitter, one-dimensional flavor.

For cooking, there are two schools of thought: steaming and baking. In a side-by-side comparison, tasters favored the steamed loaves over the baked. Most people thought the baked loaves were closer to Irish soda bread in texture and flavor than what they knew as brown bread. While delicious, the baked bread was another species. The steamed loaves were dense, moist, and deeply satisfying.

Traditionally, Boston brown bread is steamed in a large coffee can set in a pan of simmering water on the stovetop. Because many people buy coffee in a bag, we resorted to more readily available containers: loaf pans. Small pans, about 8½ by 4 inches, proved the perfect size for even cooking in about two hours. To keep moisture (due to condensation) from seeping into the bread, we used a double layer of greased aluminum foil very tightly sealed around the lip of the pan.

We cooked the loaves in two 8-quart Dutch ovens (one loaf in each pot), with water reaching halfway up the sides of the loaf pans. With any more water, the loaves became too moist and were unevenly cooked. If you do not have two large Dutch ovens, you can use a deep roasting pan sealed with aluminum foil for one or both of the loaves. It is important to keep the water at a slow simmer which can be maintained over very low heat. It is equally important to check the water level every 30 minutes, adding more water whenever the level falls less than halfway up the side of the pan. If your pot has a tight-fitting lid, chances are you will not have to add additional water.

Two hours proved to be the best cooking time. The bread was cooked through—a skewer inserted into the middle came out clean—and had a velvety soft crumb. When we cooked the loaf any longer, it dried out and became tough.

Boston brown bread's robust flavors stand up well to baked beans and pot roasts as well as hearty soups and stews. If you have any leftover bread (an unlikely occurrence), try it toasted with butter and jam, especially marmalade. Cream cheese is good, too.

Boston Brown Bread

MAKES 2 SMALL LOAVES

Low and steady heat is the key to a tender, moist brown bread. If your burner's flame is too high to allow for a slow, barely bubbling simmer, use a heat diffuser. If you choose to go the classic route and steam the bread in coffee cans, use two 1-pound cans and make sure to liberally grease the insides of the cans. As with the loaf pans, coffee

MAKING BROWN BREAD

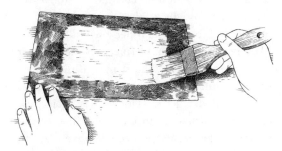

1. Fold a 16 by 12-inch piece of aluminum foil in half to yield a rectangle that measures 12 by 8 inches. Liberally grease the center portion of the foil with butter. Repeat with a second piece of foil.

2. Scrape the batter into a greased loaf pan, place the foil buttered-side down over the batter, and then seal the edges tightly. Use the second piece of foil on the second loaf pan.

cans should be tightly wrapped with buttered aluminum foil, and as with the loaf pans, the water should reach halfway up the sides. We like dark molasses, especially Grandma's Robust molasses, in this recipe. (See page 4 for more information on types of molasses.) This bread is best served warm.

2	tablespoons unsalted butter, softened
I	cup (about 5 ounces) cornmeal, preferably stone-ground
I	cup (3 1/2 ounces) rye flour
1/2	cup (2 3/4 ounces) whole-wheat flour
1/2	cup (2 1/2 ounces) unbleached all-purpose flour
2	teaspoons baking soda
I	teaspoon salt
I	cup raisins
2	cups buttermilk
3/4	cup molasses, preferably dark or robust

1. Fold two 16 by 12-inch pieces of foil in half to yield two foil rectangles, each measuring 12 by 8 inches. With the butter, liberally grease two 8½ by 4-inch loaf pans as well as the center portion of each piece of foil (see illustration 1 on page 33).

2. In the bowl of a standing mixer fitted with a paddle attachment, combine all the dry ingredients. Mix on low speed until blended, about 30 seconds. Add the raisins and mix until uniformly dispersed, about 15 seconds longer. With the machine still on low speed, slowly pour in the buttermilk and molasses and mix until fully combined, about 30 seconds. Stir the batter with a rubber spatula for several strokes, scraping the bottom of the bowl to mix in any unincorporated ingredients. (Alternatively, you can mix the batter entirely by hand in a large bowl, using a wooden spoon.) Evenly divide the batter between the greased loaf pans and wrap very tightly with the buttered foil (see illustration 2 on page 33).

3. Set each loaf pan in a large Dutch oven or a roasting pan and fill each vessel with enough water to reach halfway up the side of each loaf pan. (If your roasting pan is large enough, you may be able to fit both loaves in one pan.) Bring to a simmer over medium-high heat, reduce the heat to low, and cover. (If using a roasting pan, wrap tightly with foil.) Check the water level every 30 minutes to make sure the water still reaches halfway up the sides of the loaf pans. Cook until a skewer inserted in the middle of the loaves comes out clean, about 2 hours. Carefully remove the loaves from the loaf pans and transfer them to a cooling rack. Cool for 10 minutes. Slice and serve.

CORNBREAD

WHILE ALL CORNBREADS ARE QUICK TO make and bake, there are two very distinct types: Northern and Southern. Southerners use 100-percent white cornmeal, and they like their cornbread crumbly, dry, and flat—about one inch thick. Most Northerners prefer sweeter, lighter, and higher golden cornbreads, which they achieve by adding a little sugar and combining white flour and yellow cornmeal. Both types of cornbread sport a brown crust, although Southern cornbread crusts are also crisp and crunchy.

Since there are cooks who are attached to each style, we decided to develop recipes for both kinds of cornbread. One should be tender and fluffy but not too sweet, something akin to cake but not too rich. This Northern-style cornbread would be good enough to eat on its own. For Southern-style cornbread, we envisioned something drier and more crumbly. It would be perfect with a bowl of soup or a pot of greens. For both recipes, choosing the right cornmeal would be crucial.

Large commercial mills use huge steel rollers to grind dent corn (a hard, dry corn) into cornmeal. Smaller mills grind with millstones; this product is called stone-ground cornmeal. Stone-ground cornmeal is usually a bit coarser than cornmeal processed through steel rollers. We like Arrowhead Mills brand, which has a fine, consistent texture.

Besides the differences in milling methods, smaller millers often choose not to degerm, or remove all the germ. This makes their product closer to a whole-grain cornmeal. If the color is uniform, the germ has been removed. A stone-ground cornmeal with some germ will have flecks that are both lighter and darker than the predominant color, whether that's yellow or white.

In our tests, we found the texture of cornbreads made with stone-ground meals to be more interesting, since the cornmeals were not of a uniform grind. More important, we found that cornbreads made with stone-ground cornmeal tasted much better than those made with standard cornmeal.

The higher moisture and oil content of stone-ground cornmeal causes it to go rancid within weeks. If you buy some, wrap it tightly in plastic or put it into a moisture-proof container, then refrigerate or freeze it. Degerminated cornmeals, such as Quaker, keep for a year, if stored in a dry, cool place.

NORTHERN CORNBREAD

IN PERFECTING HOMEMADE NORTHERN cornbread, we aimed for a high-rising, moist bread, one with a rich corn taste and handsome golden color. Among other things, we wanted to find the right proportion of cornmeal to flour, the correct type and amount of chemical leavening, and the ideal amount of sugar. During our baking of 43 batches of cornbread using varying ingredients, mixing techniques, and baking temperatures and times, we uncovered some surprises.

In testing aspects of the dry ingredients, we found that the proportion of cornmeal to flour was key. The best flavor, texture, and rise resulted from a 1-1 ratio of cornmeal to all-purpose flour. If we added more cornmeal, the texture coarsened, and the cornbread baked flatter. Using more flour than cornmeal resulted in a less intense corn flavor and a cakelike texture.

Unbleached all-purpose flour easily won out over plain cake flour and whole-wheat flour. All-purpose flour yielded the tallest cornbreads. Cake flour produced a doughy cornbread that collapsed. Whole-wheat flour masked some of the corn flavor and made the cornbread too dense and gritty.

We had thought we would like a fairly sweet Northern cornbread. We changed our opinion very quickly. The amount of sugar in the recipes we examined ranged from one tablespoon to eight. We started the testing with two tablespoons and adjusted up and down. More sugar made the cornbread taste like a dessert. In test batches made without sugar, though, we missed it. In the end, 4 teaspoons of sugar was the right amount for our cornbread.

The leavener we used would depend on whether we used milk or buttermilk in the mixture, so we postponed a final decision on that dry ingredient. Finally, in tests with and without salt, we found that adding ½ teaspoon helped bring out the corn flavor and balanced the sweetness.

We had now assembled the dry ingredients. At this point, most cornbread recipes instruct the cook to add the wet ingredients—egg, milk, and fat—to the dry ones. We first tested for the number of eggs. Two eggs tasted the best. Three eggs rated as too eggy, and one left things a bit dry. The eggs added moisture and helped the cornbread rise higher; the yolks contributed to the golden interior and rich taste.

Our next set of tests focused on buttermilk and milk. Buttermilk contributed a rich, luscious taste that highlighted the corn flavor, although its use also resulted in a coarser and heavier texture. Buttermilk also placed the cornbread squarely in the bread corner—it no longer hinted at dessert. Cornbreads made with milk tasted fine but lacked richness, although the lighter texture and softer yellow color were appealing. To remedy this, we decided to use a combination of buttermilk and milk. A half-milk and half-buttermilk combination resulted in cornbread with a wonderful taste, light texture, handsome yellow-gold interior, high rise, and a brown crust with some crunch.

Next, we tested the fats. Butter outranked the other contenders. Vegetable oil, vegetable shortening, and margarine tasted boring and lackluster, and lard seemed out of place in this recipe. A couple of tasters enjoyed the flavor of bacon fat at first, but after a few more bites found it overpowering. We discovered that we liked a cornbread made with butter, but not too much. Two tablespoons per batch was enough. More butter was too heavy and started to interfere with the corn flavor. Cornbread made with less lacked richness.

Most recipes instruct the cook to add the melted butter last. Is this necessary? To find out, we tried several experiments. First we creamed the softened butter, then added the remaining ingredients. The top of this cornbread looked pebbled and not very appetizing. Next, we melted the butter, then stirred in all the other ingredients. Now the cornbread was heavy and too moist. Finally, we added the melted butter last. This method produced the best-tasting and most attractive cornbread. We detected no difference when we used hot or warm melted butter as long as we mixed it in fast.

Armed with our basic ingredients and their order into the mixing bowl, we then asked ourselves two questions. How long do we mix the batter, and with what? We learned to mix quickly, just to combine the dry and wet ingredients (if overmixed, the cornbread will be tough), and added another 10 or 12 strokes to distribute the melted butter quickly and evenly. As for the proper tool, we found that a fork left clumps of dry cornmeal at the bottom of the bowl, while a whisk, eggbeater, or electric mixer was overkill. We rated a wooden spoon as the best and easiest-to-use tool.

To obtain the light texture and high rise of Northern cornbread, some type of chemical leavening is required. As we experimented with baking soda and baking powder, the two typical leaveners for cornbread, we discovered that three or four teaspoons of baking powder produced the tallest cornbreads, but that these breads were lacking in corny taste. Cornbreads made with 100 percent baking soda sported darker, more deeply golden brown top crusts and a stronger array of interior colors: a deeper golden or yellow overall color, with flecks of deep orange and yellow.

Hoping to produce a bread with the color provided by baking soda and the high rise caused by baking powder, we combined the two chemical leavenings. After tinkering with various amounts of each, we found that 2 teaspoons of baking powder plus ½ teaspoon of baking soda yielded a tall rise, golden color, and the best taste. When we increased the baking soda, we noted a mushy, soapy taste, which meant that the available acid in the batter was not neutralizing the extra leavening, so we stuck with ½ teaspoon.

With our recipe now in hand, we looked at two final variables: the type of baking pan and oven temperature. Our goal was to produce cornbread with an evenly browned crust and a moist interior. We tried using a glass pan, but the cornbread overbaked and became hard around the edges, a common problem with glass pans, which tend to overheat. We found that metal baking pans were the best choice for making moist and light cornbread.

As for oven temperature, we found that cornbreads baked at 350 degrees and 375 degrees had very thick, heavy crusts because they took a long time to form. A 425-degree oven worked best. At this higher temperature, the crust formed more quickly and the whole cornbread baked faster, resulting in a crisper crust and lighter-textured cornbread.

Golden Northern Cornbread
MAKES 9 SERVINGS

This cornbread is moist and light, with the rich taste of corn. Use stone-ground yellow cornmeal for the best taste and texture. Stone-ground cornmeal can be recognized by its light and dark flecks. (See more about cornmeal on page 2.)

2	tablespoons unsalted butter, melted, plus more for greasing the pan
1	cup (about 5 ounces) yellow cornmeal, preferably stone-ground
1	cup (5 ounces) unbleached all-purpose flour
2	teaspoons baking powder
½	teaspoon baking soda
4	teaspoons sugar
½	teaspoon salt
2	large eggs
⅔	cup buttermilk
⅔	cup milk

1. Adjust an oven rack to the center position and heat the oven to 425 degrees. Grease a 9-inch square baking pan with butter.

2. Whisk the cornmeal, flour, baking powder, baking soda, sugar, and salt together in a large bowl. Push the dry ingredients up the sides of the bowl to make a well.

3. Crack the eggs into the well and stir lightly with a wooden spoon, then add the buttermilk and milk. Stir the wet and dry ingredients quickly until almost combined. Add the melted butter and stir until the ingredients are just combined.

4. Pour the batter into the greased pan. Bake until the top of the cornbread is golden brown and lightly cracked and the edges have pulled away from the sides of the pan, about 25 minutes.

5. Transfer the pan to a wire rack to cool slightly, 5 to 10 minutes. Cut the cornbread into squares and serve warm. (Pan can be wrapped in foil and stored at room temperature up to 1 day. Reheat cornbread in a 350-degree oven for 10 to 15 minutes.)

➤ VARIATIONS

Golden Cornbread with Cheddar Cheese

Follow the recipe for Golden Northern Cornbread, omitting the sugar. After adding the butter, quickly fold in 1 cup (4 ounces) shredded cheddar or Monterey Jack cheese.

Golden Cornbread with Chiles

Follow the recipe for Golden Northern Cornbread, omitting the sugar. After adding the butter, quickly fold in 1 small jalapeño, stemmed, seeded, and minced, for mild chile flavor. For more heat, use up to 2 jalapeños that have been stemmed and minced but not seeded.

Golden Cornbread with Bacon

To end up with the ½ cup bacon needed for this recipe, cut 8 ounces sliced bacon into small dice, then fry in a large skillet until well-browned and crisp. Drain, cool, and then set aside until ready to fold into the batter.

Follow the recipe for Golden Northern Cornbread, omitting the sugar. After adding the butter, quickly fold in ½ cup crumbled bacon bits.

SOUTHERN CORNBREAD

ALTHOUGH THE TWO INGREDIENT LISTS may look similar, the cornbreads of the North and South are as different as Boston and Birmingham. White, not yellow, is the cornmeal of choice for Southern-style cornbread. Unlike Northerners, Southerners use only trace amounts of flour, if any, and if sugar is included it is treated like salt, to be measured out in teaspoons rather than by the cup. Buttermilk moistens, bacon drippings enrich, and a combination of baking powder and soda provides lift.

Classic Southern cornbread batter is poured into a scorching hot, greased cast-iron skillet, which causes it to develop a thin, crisp crust as the bread bakes. At its best, this bread is moist and tender, with the warm fragrance of the cornfield and the subtle flavor of the dairy in every bite. It is the best possible accompaniment to soups, salads, chilis, and stews. So we set out to create a recipe for it that would be foolproof.

We began by testing 11 different cornmeals in one simple Southern cornbread recipe. Before the cornmeal tests, we would have bet that color was a regional idiosyncrasy that had little to do with flavor. But tasting proved otherwise. Cornbreads made with yellow cornmeal had a consistently more potent corn flavor than those made with white cornmeal.

Although we didn't want Southern cornbread to taste like dessert, we wondered whether a little sugar might enhance the corn flavor. So we made three batches—one with no sugar, one with 2 teaspoons, and one with a heaping tablespoon. The higher-sugar bread was really too sweet for Southern cornbread, but 2 teaspoons of sugar seemed to enhance the natural sweetness of the corn without calling attention to itself.

Most Southern-style cornbread batters are made with just buttermilk, but we found recipes calling for the full range of acidic and sweet dairy products—buttermilk, sour cream, yogurt, milk, and cream—and made batches with each of them. We still loved the pure, straightforward flavor of the buttermilk-based cornbread, but the batch made with sour cream was actually more tasty and baked into a more attractive shape.

At this point we began to feel a little uneasy about where we were taking this regional bread. A couple of teaspoons of sugar might be overlooked, but using yellow cornmeal was heresy. And sour cream was really crossing the line.

So far all of our testing had been done with a composite recipe under which most Southern cornbread recipes seemed to fall. There were two recipes, however, that didn't quite fit the mold—one very rich and one very lean—and now seemed like the right time to give them a try.

After rejecting the rich version as closer to

Measuring Techniques & Shortcuts

WHY MEASURING MATTERS

Proper measuring can make or break a recipe. Take flour, for example. In baked goods such as cakes, cookies, and breads, adding too little flour can make the end product flat, wet, or lacking in structure. Many home cooks measure flour by spooning it into a cup, then leveling it off. This method of measuring dry ingredients can yield 20 percent less flour than the method we use in the test kitchen: dip and sweep (illustrated below, at left). In helping you to measure accurately, the tips and techniques we present here will help you achieve consistently good results whenever you cook or bake.

MEASURING CUPS—WHAT'S THE DIFFERENCE?

Dry ingredients like flour and sugar should always be measured in dry measuring cups, never in liquid cups. Although liquid and dry measuring cups hold the same volume, in a liquid measuring cup, there is no way to level the surface of the contents to obtain an exact measurement.

While it is possible to measure liquids in a dry measuring cup, it's hard to fill the cup to the rim and decant it without spills. A liquid measuring cup has headroom so that it needn't be filled to the brim.

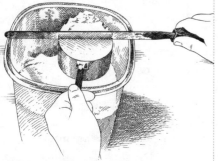

Dry Measuring (dip and sweep)
Dip a dry measuring cup into the ingredient and sweep away the excess with a straight-edged object such as an icing spatula.

Liquid Measuring
To get an accurate reading in a liquid measuring cup, set the cup on a level surface and bend down to read it at eye level. Read the measurement at the bottom of the concave arc at the liquid's surface, known as the meniscus line.

DRY MEASURING CUPS

The Good, the Bad, and the Useless
For both measuring spoons and dry measuring cups, we prefer heavy, well-constructed stainless steel models with long, sturdy, well-designed handles. Plastic spoons and cups feel flimsy, have rims prone to developing nicks and bumps, can warp in the dishwasher, and will melt if placed too close to a heat source.

OUR FAVORITE An extra-long 4-inch handle makes dipping into a bin of flour a clean endeavor.

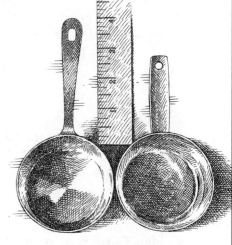

Three Problematic Handle Styles

short handle

STICKY FINGERS The short, awkward handle on this cup makes dipping and sweeping difficult. It can also be hard to keep your thumb out of the ingredients.

flexible handle

NO BACKBONE This flimsy, flexible handle bends under the slightest pressure.

heavy handle

TOPSY-TURVY This handle-heavy cup tilts when set down, increasing the chance that ingredients will spill out.

WHY AND HOW TO SIFT FLOUR

When a recipe calls for sifted flour, it is important to take the time to sift even if the flour you're using is labeled "presifted." In addition to eliminating lumps, sifting aerates the flour, making it easier to incorporate the flour into a batter. Sifted flour thus also weighs 20 to 25 percent less per cup than unsifted. We found that an additional ounce of flour caused an otherwise moist and perfectly level cake to bake up into a drier cake with a domed top.

Sift and Level

If a recipe reads "I cup sifted flour," sift the flour directly into a measuring cup (set on top of parchment paper for a hassle-free cleanup) and level off the cup.

Dip, Sweep, and Sift

If a recipe reads "I cup flour, sifted," first dip into the flour and sweep off the excess, then sift it onto a piece of parchment paper. This method yields the same amount of flour by weight as if you had simply dipped and swept, but the flour is now aerated and lump free.

MEASURING TIPS AND SHORTCUTS

Here are some ideas to help you deal with hard-to-measure ingredients.

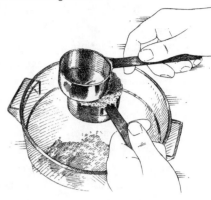

Measuring Peanut Butter

Great for measuring semisolid ingredients like sour cream and peanut butter, this push-up-style cup allows you to scoop in the ingredient, level it off, and then push it right out.

Packing Brown Sugar

Brown sugar is tacky and lumpy; packing it into a measuring cup compacts the sugar and presses out any air pockets (the difference in weight between I cup of packed brown sugar and I cup of unpacked can be as much as 2 ounces). A neat way to pack brown sugar is to use the bottom of a smaller cup to tamp and press the sugar into a larger cup.

Handling Honey and Molasses

When measuring sticky ingredients like honey and molasses, spray the measuring cup with nonstick cooking spray before filling it. When emptied, the liquid will slip right out of the cup.

Measuring Shortening

When measuring messy, malleable ingredients like shortening, line the measuring cup with plastic wrap, scoop in the shortening, and level it off. To retrieve it, simply lift out the plastic liner and the contents come with it.

MEASURING FLOUR, SIMPLIFIED

Recipe reads:	then you:	to get a weight of:
➤ I cup all-purpose flour ➤ I cup cake flour	measure flour with dip-and-sweep method	➤ about 5 ounces ➤ about 4 ounces
➤ I cup sifted all-purpose flour ➤ I cup sifted cake flour	sift flour directly into measuring cup and level off	➤ about 4 ounces ➤ about 3 ounces
➤ I cup all-purpose flour, sifted ➤ I cup cake flour, sifted	measure flour with dip-and-sweep method, then sift	➤ about 5 ounces ➤ about 4 ounces

spoonbread, a soufflé-like dish, than cornbread, we went to the other extreme. In this simple version, boiling water is stirred into the cornmeal, then modest amounts of milk, egg, butter, salt, and baking powder are stirred into the resulting cornmeal mush and the whole thing is baked. So simple, so lean, so humble, so backwater, this recipe would have been easy to pass over. But given our options at this point, we decided to give it a quick test. Just one bite completely changed the direction of our pursuit. Unlike anything we had tasted so far, the crumb of this cornbread was incredibly moist and fine and bursting with corn flavor.

We were pleased, but since the foundation of this bread was cornmeal mush, the crumb was actually more mushy than moist. In addition, the baking powder got stirred into the wet batter at the end. This just didn't feel right.

After a few unsuccessful attempts to make the cornbread less mushy, we started thinking that this great idea was a bust. In a last attempt to salvage it, we decided to make mush out of only half the cornmeal and mix the remaining cornmeal with the leavener. To our relief, the bread made this way was much improved. Decreasing the mush even further—from a half to a third of the cornmeal—gave us exactly what we were looking for. We made the new, improved cornbread with buttermilk and mixed a bit of baking soda with the baking powder, and it tasted even better. Finally our recipe was starting to feel Southern again. Although we still preferred yellow cornmeal and a touch of sugar, we had achieved a bread that was moist, tender, and rather fine-crumbed without flour, and nicely shaped without sour cream, thus avoiding two ingredients that would have interfered with the strong corn flavor we wanted.

With this new recipe in hand, we performed a few final tests. Our recipe called for 1 tablespoon of butter, but many Southern cornbreads call for no more fat than is needed to grease the pan. We tried vegetable oil, peanut oil, shortening, butter, and bacon drippings, as well as a batch with no fat at all. To our delight, the cornbread with no added fat was as moist and delicious as the other breads. Butter and bacon drippings, however, were pleasant flavor additions, so we kept a little in our recipe.

Before conducting these cornbread tests, we didn't think it was possible to bake cornbread in too hot an oven, but after tasting breads baked on the bottom rack of a 475-degree oven, we found that a dark brown crust makes bitter bread. We moved the rack up a notch, reduced the oven temperature to 450 degrees, and were thus able to bake many loaves of bread and pans of muffins to golden brown perfection.

One final question: Do you need to heat up the skillet before adding the batter? If you're not a Southerner, the answer is no. Although the bread will not be as crisp in an unheated pan, it will ultimately brown up with a longer baking time. If you are a Southerner, of course, the answer is yes. More than the color of the meal or the presence of sugar or flour, the meeting of batter and hot fat in a cast-iron skillet defines Southern cornbread.

Southern Cornbread
MAKES 8 SERVINGS

Though some styles of Southern cornbread are dry and crumbly, we favor this dense, moist, tender version. Cornmeal mush of just the right texture is essential to this bread. Make sure that the water is at a rapid boil when it is added to the cornmeal. Though we prefer to make cornbread in a preheated cast-iron skillet or heavy-bottomed oven-safe skillet, a 9-inch round cake pan or 9-inch square baking pan, greased lightly with butter and not preheated, will also produce acceptable results if you double the recipe and bake the bread for 25 minutes.

4	teaspoons bacon drippings or 1 teaspoon vegetable oil plus 1 tablespoon melted butter
1	cup (about 5 ounces) yellow cornmeal, preferably stone-ground
2	teaspoons sugar
1/2	teaspoon salt
1	teaspoon baking powder
1/4	teaspoon baking soda
1/3	cup rapidly boiling water
3/4	cup buttermilk
1	large egg, beaten lightly

1. Adjust an oven rack to the lower-middle position and heat the oven to 450 degrees. Set an

8-inch cast-iron skillet with bacon fat (or vegetable oil and butter) in the heating oven.

2. Measure ⅓ cup of the cornmeal into a medium bowl. Whisk the remaining cornmeal, sugar, salt, baking powder, and baking soda together in a small bowl; set aside.

3. Pour the boiling water all at once into the ⅓ cup cornmeal; stir to make a stiff mush. Whisk in the buttermilk gradually, breaking up lumps until smooth, then whisk in the egg. When the oven is preheated and the skillet is very hot, stir the dry ingredients into the mush mixture until just moistened. Carefully remove the skillet from the oven. Pour the hot bacon fat from the pan (or pour the melted butter) into the batter and stir to incorporate, then quickly pour the batter into the heated skillet. Bake until the bread is golden brown, about 20 minutes. Remove from the oven and instantly turn the cornbread onto a wire rack; cool for 5 minutes, then serve immediately.

IRISH SODA BREAD

AUTHENTIC IRISH SODA BREAD HAS A TENDER, dense crumb and a rough-textured, crunchy crust. It is versatile enough to be served with butter and jam at breakfast, for sandwiches at lunch, or alongside the evening meal.

As we looked over a multitude of recipes for soda bread, we found that they fell into two categories. The American versions contained eggs, butter, and sugar in varying amounts along with caraway seeds, raisins, and a multitude of other flavorings. But most Irish cookbooks combined only four ingredients: flour (white and/or whole-wheat), baking soda, salt, and buttermilk.

We decided to begin our investigations with the flour. Because of Ireland's climate, the wheat grown there is a "soft," or low-protein, variety. While not suitable for strong European-style yeast breads, this flour is perfect for chemically leavened breads. This is basically because flour with a lower protein content produces a finer crumb and more tender product, key for breads that don't have the light texture provided when yeast is used as the leavener.

After suffering through several tough, heavy loaves made with unbleached all-purpose flour, we started exploring different proportions of cake flour—a low-protein flour—as well as all-purpose flour. And, in fact, the bread did become more tender and a little lighter with the addition of some cake flour. As the ratio of cake to all-purpose exceeded 1-1, however, the bread became much more compact and heavy, with an undesirable mouthfeel: 1 cup of cake flour to 3 cups of unbleached all-purpose flour proved best.

Because the liquid-to-dry ingredient ratio is important in determining dough texture and bread moistness, we decided to test buttermilk next. (We also knew that the amount of this acidic liquid would have a direct effect on the amount of baking soda we would be able to use. As mentioned when discussing other recipes, baking soda reacts with acids such as those in buttermilk to provide leavening; however, if there is too much soda, some remains intact in the bread, giving it a slightly metallic taste.) As it turned out, bread made with 1¾ or 1⅔ cups of buttermilk produced bread that was doughy, almost gummy. With 1½ cups, the dough was firmer yet still moist—and the resulting bread was no longer doughy. (If you don't have buttermilk on hand, yogurt can be substituted for an equally delicious bread with a slightly rougher crust and lighter texture.)

With the amount of buttermilk decided upon,

SCIENCE: A Light Hand

While testing the various ingredients in our Classic Irish Soda Bread, we discovered that the way the dough is handled while you are mixing it is as crucial as the amount and type of leavener used. Because baking soda begins reacting immediately with cream of tartar and does not provide the big second rise you get with double-acting baking powder, it is important to mix the dough quickly and not too vigorously. If you mix too slowly or too enthusiastically, too much carbon dioxide will be formed and will dissipate during the mixing process; not enough will then be produced during baking to provide the proper rise. Extended kneading also overdevelops the gluten in the flour, toughening the bread. It's no wonder that in Ireland a baker who produces a superior loaf of soda bread is traditionally said to have "a light hand," a great compliment.

we were now ready to explore the amount and type of leavener used. After trying various combinations of baking soda, baking powder, and cream of tartar, we found that 1½ teaspoons of soda, combined with an equal amount of cream of tartar, provided just the right amount of lift for a bread that was light but not airy. Relying on the acidity of cream of tartar (rather than the acidity in the buttermilk) to react with the baking soda allows the tangy buttermilk flavor to come through.

Unfortunately, the flavor of these basic loaves was mediocre at best, lacking depth and dimension, and they were also a bit tough. Traditionally, very small amounts of sugar and/or butter are sometimes added to soda bread, so, starting with sugar, we baked loaves with 1 and with 2 tablespoons. Two tablespoons of sugar added just the flavor balance that was needed without making the bread sweet. It was only with the introduction of butter, though, that the loaves began to lose their toughness and become outstanding. Still, we really wanted to maintain the integrity of this basic bread and avoid making it too rich. After trying loaves with from one to four tablespoons of unsalted butter, 2 tablespoons proved a clear winner. This bread was tender but not crumbly, compact but not heavy. More than two tablespoons of butter began to shift the flavor balance of the bread and add unnecessary richness.

We were getting very close to our goal, but the crust was still too hard, thick, and crumbly. In our research, we came upon various techniques for modifying the crust. Some dealt with the way the bread was baked, while others concentrated on how the bread was treated after baking. Trying to inhibit the formation of a thick crust by covering the bread with a bowl during the first 30 minutes of baking helped some, but the resulting bread took longer to bake and was pale and uneven in color. Using a large flowerpot and clay dish to simulate a cloche (a covered earthenware dish specifically designed for baking bread) again gave us a bread that didn't color well, even when we preheated the tray and buttered the dough.

But the next test, which, by no coincidence, closely simulated historical cooking methods for Irish soda bread, was a breakthrough. Baking the loaf in a well-buttered Dutch oven or cast-iron pot, covered only for the first 30 minutes, produced a well-risen loaf with an even, golden crust that was thin and crisp yet still had a bit of chew.

We realized, however, that not everyone has a cast-iron pot available, so we explored ways of softening the crust after baking. Wrapping the bread in a clean tea towel as soon as it emerged from the oven helped soften the crust, while a slightly damp tea towel softened it even more. The best technique, though, was to brush the warm loaf with some melted butter. This gave it an attractive sheen as well as a delicious, buttery crust with just enough crunch. Although we liked the crust of the bread baked in the Dutch oven a little better, the ease of baking it on a baking sheet made the loaf brushed with butter a more practical option.

Finally, make sure that you cool the bread for at least 30 to 40 minutes before serving. If cut when too hot, the bread will be dense and slightly doughy.

Classic Irish Soda Bread

MAKES 1 LOAF

Once cooled, this bread is a great accompaniment to soups or stews, and leftovers make fine toast. With their flavorful grains and additions, the variations can stand alone.

3	cups (15 ounces) lower-protein unbleached all-purpose flour, such as Gold Medal or Pillsbury, plus more for work surface
1	cup (4 ounces) plain cake flour
2	tablespoons sugar
1½	teaspoons baking soda
1½	teaspoons cream of tartar
1½	teaspoons salt
2	tablespoons unsalted butter, softened, plus 1 tablespoon melted butter for crust
1½	cups buttermilk

1. Adjust an oven rack to the upper-middle position and heat the oven to 400 degrees. Whisk the flours, sugar, baking soda, cream of tartar, and salt together in a large bowl. Work the softened butter into the dry ingredients

with a fork or your fingertips until the texture resembles coarse crumbs.

2. Add the buttermilk and stir with a fork just until the dough begins to come together. Turn out onto a flour-coated work surface; knead just until the dough becomes cohesive and bumpy, 12 to 14 turns. (Do not knead until the dough is smooth, or the bread will be tough.)

3. Pat the dough into a round about 6 inches in diameter and 2 inches high; place on a greased or parchment-lined baking sheet. Score the dough by cutting a cross shape on the top of the loaf. (See the illustration on page 44.)

4. Bake until the loaf is golden brown and a skewer inserted into the center comes out clean, or the internal temperature reaches 180 degrees, 40 to 45 minutes. Remove the loaf from the oven and brush the surface with the melted butter; cool to room temperature, 30 to 40 minutes.

➤ VARIATIONS
Irish Brown Soda Bread
Unlike the Classic Irish Soda Bread dough, which is dry, this dough is extremely sticky.

1 3/4	cups (8 3/4 ounces) lower-protein unbleached all-purpose flour, such as Gold Medal or Pillsbury, plus more for work surface
1 1/4	cups (6 7/8 ounces) whole-wheat flour
1/2	cup (2 ounces) plain cake flour
1/2	cup toasted wheat germ
3	tablespoons brown sugar
1 1/2	teaspoons baking soda
1 1/2	teaspoons cream of tartar
1 1/2	teaspoons salt
2	tablespoons unsalted butter, softened, plus 1 tablespoon melted butter for crust
1 1/2	cups buttermilk

1. Adjust an oven rack to the upper-middle position and heat the oven to 400 degrees. Whisk the flours, wheat germ, brown sugar, baking soda, cream of tartar, and salt together in a large bowl. Work the softened butter into the dry ingredients with a fork or your fingertips until the texture resembles coarse crumbs.

2. Add the buttermilk and stir with a fork just

until the dough begins to come together. Turn out onto a flour-coated work surface; knead just until the dough becomes cohesive and bumpy, 12 to 14 turns. (Do not knead until the dough is smooth, or the bread will be tough.)

3. Pat the dough into a round about 6 inches in diameter and 2 inches high; place on a greased or parchment-lined baking sheet. Score the dough by cutting a cross shape on the top of the loaf. (See the illustration on page 44.)

4. Bake until the loaf is golden brown and a skewer inserted into the center comes out clean, or the internal temperature reaches 190 degrees, 45 to 55 minutes. Remove the loaf from the oven and brush the surface with the melted butter; cool to room temperature, 30 to 40 minutes.

Oatmeal–Walnut Soda Bread
Most of the oats should be soaked in the buttermilk for an hour before proceeding with this recipe.

2 1/2	cups (7 1/2 ounces) old-fashioned rolled oats
1 3/4	cups buttermilk
1	cup walnuts
2	cups (10 ounces) lower-protein unbleached all-purpose flour, such as Gold Medal or Pillsbury, plus more for work surface
1/2	cup (2 ounces) plain cake flour
1/2	cup (2 3/4 ounces) whole-wheat flour
1/4	cup packed (1 3/4 ounces) brown sugar
1 1/2	teaspoons baking soda
1 1/2	teaspoons cream of tartar
1 1/2	teaspoons salt
2	tablespoons unsalted butter, softened, plus 1 tablespoon melted butter for crust

1. Place 2 cups of the oats in a medium bowl. Add the buttermilk and soak for 1 hour.

2. Adjust an oven rack to the upper-middle position and heat the oven to 400 degrees. Spread the walnuts on a baking sheet and toast them until fragrant, 5 to 10 minutes. Cool and chop coarsely.

3. Whisk the flours, the remaining 1/2 cup oats, brown sugar, baking soda, cream of tartar, and salt together in a large bowl. Work the softened butter into the dry ingredients with a fork or your fingertips until the texture resembles coarse crumbs.

4. Add the buttermilk-soaked oats and nuts and stir with a fork just until the dough begins to come together. Turn out onto a flour-coated work surface; knead just until the dough becomes cohesive and bumpy, 12 to 14 turns. (Do not knead until the dough is smooth, or the bread will be tough.)

5. Pat the dough into a round about 6 inches in diameter and 2 inches high; place on a greased or parchment-lined baking sheet. Score the dough by cutting a cross shape on the top of the loaf. (See the illustration, right.)

6. Bake until the loaf is golden brown and a skewer inserted into the center comes out clean, or the internal temperature reaches 190 degrees, 45 to 55 minutes. Remove the loaf from the oven and brush the surface with the melted butter; cool to room temperature, 30 to 40 minutes.

American-Style Soda Bread with Raisins and Caraway Seeds

Additional sugar and an egg create a sweeter, richer bread.

3	cups (15 ounces) lower-protein unbleached all-purpose flour, such as Gold Medal or Pillsbury, plus more for the work surface
1	cup (4 ounces) plain cake flour
¼	cup (1 ¾ ounces) sugar
1 ½	teaspoons baking soda
1 ½	teaspoons cream of tartar
1 ½	teaspoons salt
4	tablespoons (½ stick) unsalted butter, softened, plus 1 tablespoon melted butter for crust
1 ¼	cups buttermilk
1	large egg, lightly beaten
1	cup raisins
1	tablespoon caraway seeds

1. Adjust an oven rack to the upper-middle position and heat the oven to 400 degrees. Whisk the flours, sugar, baking soda, cream of tartar, and salt together in a large bowl. Work the softened butter into the dry ingredients with a fork or your fingertips until the mixture resembles coarse crumbs.

2. Combine the buttermilk and egg with a fork. Add the buttermilk-egg mixture, raisins, and caraway seeds and stir with a fork just until the dough begins to come together. Turn out onto a flour-coated work surface; knead just until the dough becomes cohesive and bumpy, 12 to 14 turns. (Do not knead until the dough is smooth, or the bread will be tough.)

3. Pat the dough into a round about 6 inches in diameter and 2 inches high; place on a greased or parchment-lined baking sheet. Score the dough by cutting a cross shape on the top of the loaf. (See the illustration below.)

4. Bake, covering bread with aluminum foil if it is browning too much, until the loaf is golden brown and a skewer inserted into the center comes out clean, or the internal temperature reaches 170 degrees, 40 to 45 minutes. Remove the loaf from the oven and brush the surface with the melted butter; cool to room temperature, 30 to 40 minutes.

SCORING SODA BREAD

Use a serrated knife to cut a cross shape in the top of the dough. Each score should be 5 inches long and ¾ inch deep.

BLUEBERRY MUFFINS

THE OXFORD COMPANION TO FOOD DEFINES American muffins as "small, squat, round cakes," yet today's deli muffins are, by comparison, big and buxom, inflated by chemical leavening and embellished with everything from chocolate chips to sunflower seeds. We wanted a blueberry muffin with a daintier stature—a moist, delicate little cake that would support the blueberries both physically and, if we may say so, spiritually (in terms of flavor).

Despite the easy promise of a gingham-lined basket of warm, cuddly blueberry muffins, much can go wrong from kitchen to table. We made a half-dozen recipes, producing muffins that ranged from rough and tough to dense, sweet, and heavy to the typical lackluster coffee-shop cake with too few blueberries and too little flavor. It was clear that blueberry muffins came in no one style, flavor, or size, so we asked tasters to state which basic style of muffin they fancied: round tea cake or craggy biscuit. Of the 15 tasters, all but one said tea cake.

Because minor fluctuations in ingredients occasioned seismic differences in the resulting muffins, we thought it best to hold fast to a recipe whose proportions landed in between the two extremes in the original tests. That meant we would be working with 1 stick of butter, 1 cup sugar, 2 cups flour, and ½ cup milk. It was not a perfect recipe but would be a serviceable springboard for future testing.

The two principal methods available to the muffin baker are the quick-bread method and creaming. In side-by-side tests using our control recipe, we got a firsthand taste of both methods. Had we been merely licking batter off our fingers, there would have been no contest: The creamed version was like a cake batter you could suck through a straw. But the two baked muffins were nearly identical. Though the mixed muffin was slightly squatter than its creamed companion, its texture was not inferior. We were pretty sure this more-easily executed technique was one we could work with—or around.

For flour we remained true to unbleached all-purpose. Bleached flour lacked the flavor spectrum of unbleached, and cake flour produced a batter that was too light to hold the blueberries aloft. We set off next in pursuit of the perfect amount of butter

to turn out a moister, richer muffin, more like the tea cake our tasters had preferred. Increasing the butter in the control recipe simply weighed down the crumb without making the muffins any more moist. We also increased the liquid (we tested both milk and buttermilk) and added extra egg yolks. Neither approach brought improvement. When we substituted yogurt for milk, the muffins had the springiness of an old camp mattress.

Knowing that sour cream is often used in quick breads, we decided to give it a try. We also wondered if the egg white protein from two eggs might be too much of the wrong type of liquid—adding structure rather than tenderness. Our new recipe, then, called for 1 egg, 1 cup sour cream, no milk, and only half a stick of butter. It was a great success—the muffins were tender and rich, and the sour cream played up to the blueberries' flavor. An additional ¼ cup sour cream made even nicer muffins.

Through additional testing, we discovered that this rather heavy batter required a full tablespoon of baking powder to rise and shine, but tasters noted no off chemical flavor. (If too much chemical leavener is added, some of it will fail to react and will give the baked good a bitter, soapy flavor.) Next, we refined the mixing method. Hoping to get more lift, we whisked the egg and sugar together by hand until the sugar began to melt, whisked in the melted butter, then the sour cream, and poured them into the dry ingredients. This method of mixing promised to deliver more air—and lift—to the egg, sugar, and butter. We folded everything together using the gentlest strokes possible. (We found that these muffins, like most others, became tough when overmixed.) This modified technique produced lovely muffins with a nice rise and beautifully domed crowns.

Until now, the major player in this muffin had been not only offstage but out of season. Our winter testing left us with a choice between pricey fresh blueberries the size of marbles and tiny frozen wild berries. The flavor and sweetness of the frozen berries gave them a big edge over the puckery, flavorless fresh berries. In addition, the tiny wild berries distributed themselves in the batter nicely, like well-mannered guests, whereas the cultivated berries took the muffin by storm, leaving huge pockets of sour fruit pulp. So impressed were we by the superiority of these little berries that we resolved to offer them top billing in the recipe. (You shouldn't have to be vacationing in Maine to make a decent blueberry muffin.) We came across one last trick. Frozen blueberries tend to be bleeders—and gummy when tossed with flour—so we determined that they must remain completely frozen until they are stirred into the batter.

These were perfect workaday muffins, but we wanted to give them a chance to play dress-up, to be more like little cakes. With that in mind we considered a couple of options. A big fan of pebbly streusel topping dusted with confectioners' sugar, we picked up the recipe from our Dutch apple pie topping and pared it down to meet the demands of a dozen muffins. The streusel weighed heavily on the muffins and diminished their lift.

Our next topping idea came from Marion Cunningham's *Breakfast Book* (Knopf, 1987), in which she rolls whole baked muffins in melted butter and then dips them in cinnamon sugar. The concept was a winning one. The melted butter seeped into the muffin's crown, the sugar stuck, and the muffin was transformed into a tender, sugar-tufted pillow.

We also made a simple-syrup glaze with lemon juice. Brushed on the muffin tops, it made a nice adhesive for granulated sugar (which we mixed with either finely grated lemon zest or fresh ginger). Finally, muffins to take to the ball.

Blueberry Muffins
MAKES 12

When making the batter, be sure to whisk vigorously in step 2, then fold carefully in step 3. You should not see large pockets of flour in the finished batter, but small occasional sprays may remain. A large spoon sprayed with nonstick cooking spray ensures clean dispensing when transferring the dough to the cups in the muffin tin. (For results from our taste test of frozen blueberries, see page 306.)

2	cups (10 ounces) unbleached all-purpose flour
1	tablespoon baking powder
1/2	teaspoon salt
1	large egg
1	cup (7 ounces) sugar
4	tablespoons (1/2 stick) unsalted butter, melted and cooled slightly
1 1/4	cups (10 ounces) sour cream
1 1/2	cups (7 1/2 to 8 ounces) frozen or fresh blueberries, preferably wild

BLUEBERRY MUFFIN HALL OF SHAME

A lot can go wrong with blueberry muffins. Some problematic muffins we encountered in our testing: 1. Muffins made with mashed berries taste fine but look all wrong. 2. Cottony, grocery-store muffins often have sticky, clammy tops. 3. A quick packaged mix with artificial berries baked up into hockey pucks. 4. This deli muffin is dry and coarse, with mushy, marble-sized blueberries. 5. If the muffin cups are overfilled with batter, the baked muffins will have flat tops.

1. MASHED BERRIES   **2. STICKY SURFACE**   **3. ARTIFICIAL BERRIES**

4. COARSE TEXTURE   **5. FLAT TOP**

1. Adjust an oven rack to the middle position and heat the oven to 350 degrees. Grease a standard 12-cup muffin tin and set aside.

2. Whisk the flour, baking powder, and salt in a medium bowl until combined. Whisk the egg in a second medium bowl until well-combined and light-colored, about 20 seconds. Add the sugar and whisk vigorously until thick and homogenous, about 30 seconds; add the melted butter in 2 or 3 additions, whisking to combine after each addition. Add the sour cream in 2 additions, whisking just to combine.

3. Add the berries to the dry ingredients and gently toss just to combine. Add the sour cream mixture and fold with a rubber spatula until the batter comes together and the berries are evenly distributed, 25 to 30 seconds. (Small spots of flour may remain and the batter will be thick. Do not overmix.)

4. Using a large spoon sprayed with nonstick cooking spray to prevent sticking, divide the batter among the greased muffin cups. Bake until the muffins are light golden brown and a toothpick or skewer inserted into the center of a muffin comes out clean, 25 to 30 minutes, rotating the pan from front to back halfway through the baking time. Invert the muffins onto a wire rack, stand the muffins upright, and cool 5 minutes. Serve as is or use one of the toppings below.

➤ VARIATIONS

**Cinnamon-Sugar-Dipped
Blueberry Muffins**

While the muffins are cooling, mix ½ cup sugar and ½ teaspoon ground cinnamon in a small bowl and melt 4 tablespoons butter in a small saucepan. After the baked muffins have cooled 5 minutes, working one at a time, dip the top of each muffin in melted butter and then cinnamon sugar. Set the muffins upright on a wire rack; serve.

**Ginger- or Lemon-Glazed
Blueberry Muffins**

While the muffins are baking, mix 1 teaspoon grated fresh ginger or grated lemon zest and ½ cup sugar in a small bowl. Bring ¼ cup lemon juice and ¼ cup sugar to a simmer in a small saucepan over medium heat; stir to dissolve the sugar and simmer until the mixture is thick and syrupy and reduced to about 4 tablespoons. After the baked muffins have cooled 5 minutes, brush the tops with glaze; then, working one at a time, dip the tops in lemon sugar or ginger sugar. Set the muffins upright on a wire rack; serve.

CORN MUFFINS

WHETHER TOO COARSE, DRY, AND CRUMBLY, too sticky and sweet, or just too fluffy and cupcake-like, the majority of corn muffins on the market today just don't make the cut. What do we want? We want a muffin that won't set off sucrose alarms, and we want a pronounced but not overwhelming cornmeal flavor and a moist and tender crumb. And all of this goodness has to be capped off with a crunchy, golden, craggy muffin top.

We started by testing an assortment of recipes (see "Corn Muffins: The Usual Suspects," page 49) from various cookbooks. Although their ingredient lists were similar, the end results were not. Some were too chewy, too short, and too puck-shaped, while others had too little corn flavor or were just plain too sweet or savory. Two recipes, however, stood out. One recipe produced muffins that were tall and rustic; the other made muffins with a pleasant, wholesome cornmeal flavor. Working with these recipes as a starting point, we began to test variables.

For mixing the ingredients for our muffins, we tried the quick-bread method, which turned out a muffin with good height and substantial crumb. As we discovered in testing our Blueberry Muffins, page 46, the quick-bread method, in its use of melted rather than creamed butter, apparently introduced less air to the batter, and the resulting muffin was less cupcake-like. Because we wanted a sturdy muffin, not an airy confection, this suited us just fine. As an added bonus, the quick-bread method was also both easier and quicker than creaming: Just melt the butter, pour, and stir.

With the mixing method down, it was now time to focus on the choice of cornmeal. We tested three brands: Quaker, Arrowhead Mills, and Hodgson Mill. Quaker cornmeal, the most common brand in supermarkets, is degerminated. During processing, the dried corn is steel-rolled, which removes most of the germ and husk. Because the germ contains most of the flavor and natural oils, this process results in a drier, less flavorful cornmeal. When baked into a corn muffin, Quaker offered an unremarkable corn flavor and, because of its dryness, an unpleasant crunch.

Arrowhead Mills and Hodgson Mill are both whole-grain cornmeals, made from the whole corn kernel. Hodgson Mill cornmeal, which is stone-ground (ground between two stones), has a coarse, inconsistent texture, while Arrowhead Mills, which is hammer-milled (pulverized with hammers), has a fine, consistent texture. Both brands delivered a more wholesome and complex corn flavor than Quaker. However, the Hodgson Mill cornmeal made the muffins coarse, dry, and difficult to chew. Arrowhead Mills produced by far the best corn muffin, with a consistently fine texture and real cornmeal flavor. The conclusion? Use a whole-grain cornmeal in a fine grind, such as Arrowhead Mills. (See page 2 for more information on cornmeal.)

Our muffins had the right texture and good flavor, but they were too dry. Some recipes suggest mixing the cornmeal with a hot liquid before adding it to the batter. This method allows the

APPLYING COOKING SPRAY WITHOUT THE MESS

Open the dishwasher door, place the muffin tin on the door, and spray away. Any excess or overspray will be cleaned off the door the next time you run the dishwasher.

cornmeal to absorb the liquid while expanding and softening the grain. The other wet ingredients are then added to the mush and combined with the dry ingredients. This seemed like a good way to make a moister muffin—or so we thought. Unfortunately, testers found these muffins too dense and strong-tasting, more like cornbread than corn muffins, which should be lighter.

Back to square one. We made a list of the ingredients that might help produce a moist muffin: butter, milk, buttermilk, sour cream, and yogurt. We tried them all, using different amounts of each. Our initial thought was "butter, butter, butter," with enough milk added to hit the right consistency. When tested, however, these muffins were lacking in moisture. We then tried using buttermilk in place of the milk. These muffins packed more flavor into each bite, but they were still on the dry side. What finally produced a superior muffin was sour cream paired with butter and milk. These muffins were rich, light, moist, and tender, but they were certainly no dainty cupcakes. We were curious to see how a muffin made with whole-milk yogurt would stand up to the muffin made with sour cream. The difference was slight. The muffin made with whole-milk yogurt was leaner but still moist and delicious. Muffins made with low-fat yogurt, on the other hand, were too lean and dry. Based on these tests, we concluded that a moist muffin requires fat and the tenderizing effect of acidity, both of which are found in sour cream.

The leavener used in most muffins is baking powder and/or baking soda, and we found that a combination of 1½ teaspoons baking powder and 1 teaspoon baking soda delivered the ideal height. We tested oven temperatures from 325 to 425 degrees and found that 400 degrees delivered the crunchy, crispy, golden crust we were looking for.

So, with the right cornmeal and the addition of sour cream, butter, and milk, it is possible to bake a tender, moist, and delicious corn muffin. By decreasing the amount of sugar and adding a few savory ingredients, you can serve these muffins with dinner as well as for breakfast. Either way, they beat the coffee-shop variety by a country mile.

Corn Muffins

MAKES 12

Stone-ground whole-grain cornmeal has a fuller flavor than regular cornmeal milled from degerminated corn. To determine what kind of cornmeal a package contains, look closely at the label.

2	cups (10 ounces) unbleached all-purpose flour
1	cup (about 5 ounces) fine stone-ground yellow cornmeal
1½	teaspoons baking powder
1	teaspoon baking soda
½	teaspoon salt
2	large eggs
¾	cup (5¼ ounces) sugar
8	tablespoons (1 stick) unsalted butter, melted and cooled slightly
¾	cup sour cream
½	cup milk

1. Adjust an oven rack to the middle position and heat the oven to 400 degrees. Grease a standard 12-cup muffin tin and set aside.

2. Whisk the flour, cornmeal, baking powder, baking soda, and salt in a medium bowl to combine; set aside. Whisk the eggs in a second medium bowl until well-combined and light-colored, about 20 seconds. Add the sugar to the eggs; whisk vigorously until thick and homogenous, about 30 seconds; add the melted butter in 3 additions, whisking to combine after each addition. Add half the sour cream and half the milk and whisk to combine; whisk in the remaining sour cream and milk until combined. Add the wet ingredients to the dry ingredients; mix gently with a rubber spatula until the batter is just combined and evenly moistened. Do not overmix. Using a large spoon sprayed with nonstick cooking spray to prevent sticking, divide the batter evenly among the muffin cups, dropping it to form mounds. Do not level or flatten the surface of the mounds.

3. Bake until the muffins are light golden brown and a skewer inserted into the center of a muffin comes out clean, about 18 minutes, rotating muffin tin from front to back halfway through baking time. Cool the muffins in the tin 5 minutes; invert the muffins onto a wire rack, stand the muffins upright, cool 5 minutes longer, and serve warm.

➤ VARIATIONS

Corn and Apricot Muffins with Orange Essence

1. In a food processor, process ⅔ cup granulated sugar and 1½ teaspoons grated orange zest until pale orange, about 10 seconds. Transfer to a small bowl and set aside.

2. In a food processor, pulse 1½ cups (10 ounces) dried apricots for ten 2-second pulses, until chopped fine. Transfer to a medium microwave-safe bowl; add ⅔ cup orange juice to the apricots, cover the bowl tightly with plastic wrap, and microwave on high until simmering, about 1 minute. Let the apricots stand, covered, until softened and plump, about 5 minutes. Discard the plastic

CORN MUFFINS: THE USUAL SUSPECTS

Despite the simplicity of corn muffins, a lot can go wrong when making them. Here are some of the worst muffins we encountered in our testing, from left to right: 1. This flat muffin contains too much cornmeal and tastes like cornbread. 2. This pale muffin contains no butter and relies on egg whites as the leavener. 3. This hockey puck–like muffin starts with cornmeal mixed with hot water. 4. This cupcake-like muffin resembles many store-bought muffins and is made with too much sugar and leavener.

1. SQUAT AND CORNY   **2. DENSE AND DOUGHY**   **3. SMALL AND WET**   **4. FLUFFY AND CAKEY**

wrap, strain the apricots, and discard the juice.

3. Follow the recipe for Corn Muffins, substituting ¼ cup packed dark brown sugar for an equal amount of granulated sugar and stirring ½ teaspoon grated orange zest and the strained apricots into the wet ingredients before adding to the dry ingredients. Before baking, sprinkle a portion of orange sugar over each mound of batter. Do not invert the baked muffins; use the tip of a paring knife to lift the muffins from the tin one at a time and transfer to a wire rack. Cool the muffins 5 minutes; serve warm.

Bacon–Scallion Corn Muffins with Cheddar Cheese

Because these muffins contain bacon, store leftovers in the refrigerator wrapped in plastic. Bring the muffins to room temperature or rewarm them before serving.

1. Grate 8 ounces cheddar cheese (you should have 2 cups); set aside. Fry 3 slices bacon (about 3 ounces), cut into ½-inch pieces, in a small skillet over medium heat until crisp and golden brown, about 5 minutes. Add 10 to 12 medium scallions, sliced thin (about 1¼ cups), ¼ teaspoon salt, and ⅛ teaspoon ground black pepper; cook to heat through, about 1 minute. Transfer the mixture to a plate to cool while making the muffins.

2. Follow the recipe for Corn Muffins, reducing the sugar to ½ cup. Stir 1½ cups of the grated cheddar cheese and the bacon/scallion mixture into the wet ingredients, then add to the dry ingredients and combine. Before baking, sprinkle a portion of the remaining ½ cup cheddar over each mound of batter.

COFFEECAKE MUFFINS

A TRANSFORMATION OF THE ULTIMATE American breakfast treat, the perfect coffeecake muffin has the best features of coffeecake—rich, buttery cake and crunchy, sweet streusel—in an abbreviated form. The perfect coffeecake muffin should have a texture that lies somewhere between the delicate, fine crumb of coffeecake and the slightly more coarse, chewy crumb of a muffin. Too often, however, coffeecake muffins fall terribly short of their potential. Cloyingly sweet and pasty or dry and leaden, coffeecake muffins are often a disappointment. We knew we could do much better.

We began our testing by topping our Blueberry Muffins—minus the blueberries—with streusel. Rich in sour cream, the Blueberry Muffins lacked the buttery richness we wanted in our coffeecake muffins, and their texture—although delicate—was still slightly too coarse for what we had in mind. Although this attempt fell short, it did suggest a path to follow. We focused on two ingredients: butter and sour cream.

The butter was easy. Because we wanted a rich buttery flavor in our coffeecake muffins, we knew we wanted more than the 4 tablespoons called for in our blueberry muffin recipe. However, we also knew that butter tenderizes cakes and we did not want this recipe to be too cakey; after all, we were after a muffin. We increased the butter by two tablespoons at a time until we were satisfied with the buttery-rich, but not greasy, flavor that 8 tablespoons provided to the muffins.

We then moved on to the sour cream, which turned out to be the key ingredient that helped get the texture of our coffeecake muffins just right. We started by adding ½ cup sour cream and tested all the way to 1¼ cups. At ¾ cup, we found success. In addition to an appealingly tart flavor, the sour cream also added a moist richness that gave the final product a slightly chewy crumb.

Finally, we turned to the coffeecake muffin's defining feature: the streusel. Coffeecake recipes typically call for reserving a small portion of the flour, sugar, salt, and butter mixture for the streusel. The leaveners and liquid ingredients are then added to the remaining flour mixture to form the batter. We tried making the streusel with granulated sugar alone and in combination with brown sugar. Although we found that some brown sugar gave the streusel a richer depth of flavor, too much made the streusel cloyingly sweet. Just ¼ cup brown sugar worked well to flavor the streusel for 12 muffins. One teaspoon cinnamon and ½ cup finely chopped pecans added depth of flavor and an appealingly crunchy texture. In addition to topping the muffins with the streusel, we tried adding a portion of the streusel mixture back into the prepared batter so that it swirled through the finished muffin. The result was perfect. The crunchy, sweet streusel offset the rich, buttery flavor of the moist cake. We finally got what we were looking for in a coffeecake muffin. This muffin innovation is sure to be a classic.

Coffeecake Muffins

MAKES 12

We use a food processor to mix the muffin batter in this recipe because it can be used both to chop the nuts and mix the batter. If you don't have a food processor, first chop the nuts with a knife. Proceed with the recipe, mixing the ingredients in a large bowl with a wooden spoon or spatula, then use a wire whisk to cream the butter-sugar mixture.

½	cup pecans
¼	cup packed (1¾ ounces) dark brown sugar
1	teaspoon ground cinnamon
2	cups (10 ounces) unbleached all-purpose flour
1	cup (7 ounces) granulated sugar
1	teaspoon salt
8	tablespoons (1 stick) unsalted butter, cut into ½-inch pieces and softened
1½	teaspoons baking powder
½	teaspoon baking soda
¾	cup sour cream
1	large egg
1	teaspoon vanilla extract

1. Adjust an oven rack to the middle position and heat the oven to 350 degrees. Grease a standard 12-cup muffin tin and set aside.

2. In the bowl of a food processor fitted with the metal blade, process the nuts, brown sugar, and cinnamon until the nuts are the size of sesame seeds, about ten 1-second pulses. Use a rubber spatula to scrape down the sides and bottom of the food processor bowl and transfer the mixture to a medium bowl and set aside.

3. Return the bowl and metal blade to the food processor, add the flour, granulated sugar, and salt and process until combined, about five 1-second pulses. Sprinkle the butter evenly over the flour mixture and process until the butter is the size of oats, about eight 1-second pulses. Remove ½ cup of the flour-butter mixture and stir it with a fork into the reserved brown sugar mixture until combined to make the streusel. Set aside ¾ cup of the streusel for the muffin batter and the remaining portion for topping the muffins.

4. Add the baking powder and baking soda to the remaining flour mixture in the food processor bowl and process until combined, about five 1-second pulses. Whisk together the sour cream, egg, and vanilla in a 1-cup glass measuring cup and add to the flour mixture. Process until the batter is just moistened, about five 1-second pulses. Add the remaining ¾ cup of the streusel to the flour mixture and process until the streusel is just distributed throughout the batter and the batter looks crumbly, about five 1-second pulses.

5. Using a large spoon sprayed with nonstick cooking spray to prevent sticking, divide the batter among 12 muffin cups. Sprinkle a scant tablespoon of streusel on top of each muffin, pressing lightly so that the streusel sinks slightly into the batter. Bake the muffins until a toothpick inserted in the center of a muffin comes out with several crumbs clinging to it, about 18 minutes, rotating the pan from front to back halfway through the baking time. Avoid overbaking. Place the muffin tin on a wire rack and allow the muffins to cool in the tin for 2 minutes. Using the tip of a paring knife, loosen the muffins and gently transfer them from the tin to the wire rack. Cool for 5 minutes. Serve warm.

➤ VARIATION

Coffeecake Muffins with Quick Confectioners' Sugar Icing

Follow the recipe for Coffeecake Muffins. Place a sheet of parchment paper beneath the wire rack as the muffins cool. Whisk 1 cup confectioners' sugar and 2 tablespoons water in a medium bowl until smooth. Spoon about 2 teaspoons glaze over each muffin, letting the glaze run down the sides of the muffins. Serve warm.

Handling Basic Baking Tools

FOOD PROCESSORS

Keeping the Lid Clean
A food processor kneads bread dough and cuts butter into flour for pie dough in seconds. Here's how to make cleanup go just as quickly.

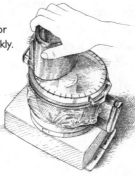

1. Place all the ingredients in the workbowl and then cover the bowl with a sheet of plastic wrap.

2. Fit the lid onto the workbowl, making sure that the plastic wrap lines the entire lid. Process as directed in the recipe. When done, simply lift off the clean lid and discard the splattered sheet of plastic.

Cleaning the Workbowl
The hole in the center of the food processor workbowl makes it impossible to soak the bowl before washing it. Here's how to plug that hole.

1. Remove the bowl cover and blade. Set an empty 35mm film canister upside down over the hole in the workbowl.

2. Fill the bowl with warm, soapy water and soak as desired.

STANDING MIXERS

Moving Heavy Mixers
Standing mixers (as well as food processors) are quite heavy and don't slide easily on the counter. Here are 2 good ways to move these heavy kitchen workhorses with ease.

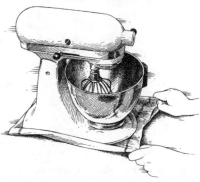

A. Place your mixer on a kitchen towel or cloth placemat, which can be pulled anywhere on the counter with little effort.

B. Stick self-adhesive floor-protector pads made of felt (normally used on furniture) to the bottom of your heavy appliances.

Keeping Mess Under Control
Dry ingredients can puff out in a cloud of fine particles when mixed, while wet ingredients, such as cream, can splatter. Here are 2 good ways to keep your counter clean when using a standing mixer.

A. Once the ingredients are in the bowl, drape a clean, very damp kitchen towel over the front of the mixer and the bowl. Draw the towel snug with one hand and then turn on the mixer. When done, simply wash the towel.

B. If you own a large KitchenAid standing mixer (the type with a crank that lifts the bowl up off the base), spread a kitchen towel out between the base and bowl to catch any ingredients that escape from the bowl.

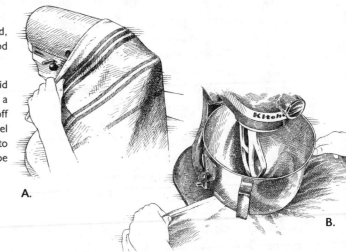

A.

B.

HANDHELD MIXERS

Keeping Mixing Bowls in Place

Many recipes (especially those for cakes) call for adding wet and dry ingredients alternately for even blending. Here's how to secure a mixing bowl so you can hold a mixer in one hand and add ingredients with the other hand.

1. Twist a damp towel to form a nest slightly larger than the base of the bowl.

2. Set the bowl into the nest, which will hold the bowl in place as you mix and add ingredients.

Splatter-Free Mixing

Handheld mixers work nearly as well as standing mixers, but they can cause excessive splashing, especially when beating thin batters or whipping cream. Using a deep, narrow mixing bowl helps, as does this trick.

1. Take a piece of parchment paper cut larger than the size of your mixing bowl and make 2 holes, spaced as far apart as the beater openings on your mixer. Insert the beater stems through the holes and into the beater base.

2. While you're mixing, the parchment will cover the bowl, preventing the contents from splattering onto the counter or walls.

THERMOMETERS

Recalibrating a Dial-Face Thermometer

Dial-face thermometers can become inaccurate with time, which is one reason we like digital thermometers (see page 14 for more information). If you own a dial-face thermometer, there's an easy way to check and adjust its accuracy. First, insert the probe into a pot of boiling water. The thermometer should register 212 degrees at sea level. (The boiling point drops about 1 degree for every 500-foot increase in elevation.) If your thermometer is inaccurate, turn it over and use a pair of pliers to adjust the nut beneath the head. Keep adjusting until the thermometer registers the correct temperature when the probe is placed in boiling water.

Protecting Hands from Pots When Measuring Temperature

Most instant-read thermometers come in a protective plastic sleeve with a metal clip (for clipping to aprons) that forms a loop at the very top. Use this clip and plastic sleeve to distance your hands from hot pots when taking a temperature. This tip is especially useful when working with caramel.

 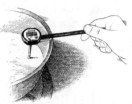 

1. Slide the probe end of the thermometer into the loop at the tip of the clip.

2. Hold the end of the plastic sleeve to keep the thermometer upright and then lower the probe into the food.

3. If you've lost the plastic sleeve that comes with your thermometer, don't despair. Insert it through a hole in a slotted spoon and hold the spoon by its handle to keep your hands away from the hot liquid as you lower the thermometer into it.

Measuring Temperature in Shallow Liquid

Recipes for curds and pastry cream are temperature-sensitive but often involve small quantities, which can make it hard to get an accurate reading. Tilt the pan so that the liquid collects on one side, creating enough depth to get an accurate reading.

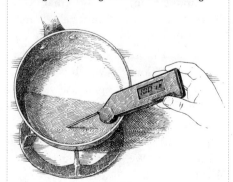

Retrieving Fallen Oven Thermometer

Oven thermometers are apt to fall off the rack and onto the oven floor. Retrieval can be difficult, especially with a hand protected by a bulky oven mitt. In the test kitchen, we use a pair of tongs to retrieve and reposition an oven thermometer. Tongs keep your hands away from the hot rack and enable dexterity that's not possible with your hand clad in an oven mitt.

TESTING BAKING POWDER FOR FRESHNESS

Baking powder will lose its leavening ability with time. We suggest writing the date the can was opened on a piece of tape affixed to the can. After 6 months, the baking powder should be tested to see if it's still good. Mix 2 teaspoons of baking powder with 1 cup of hot tap water. If there's an immediate reaction of fizzing and foaming (right), the baking powder is fine. If the reaction is delayed or weak (left), throw the baking powder away and buy a fresh can. A can of baking powder that has been opened for a year or more should be replaced.

BUTTERMILK BISCUITS

BISCUITS SHARE WITH MUFFINS THE distinction of being among the simplest of all breads. They are made from a mixture of flour, leavener (baking powder or soda), salt, fat (usually butter or vegetable shortening), and liquid (milk, buttermilk, sour milk, yogurt, or cream). To make them, the fat is cut into the dry ingredients and the liquid is then stirred in until a dough forms. Biscuits are usually rolled out and cut, although they can also be shaped by hand or dropped onto a baking sheet by the spoonful.

We began our testing by focusing on the flour. We found that the kind of flour you choose has a great effect on the biscuit you end up with. The main factor here is the level of protein in the flour. Low-protein, or "soft," flour (such as cake flour or White Lily, a favored brand in the South) encourages a tender, cake-like texture as well as a more moist crumb. Higher-protein, or "strong," flour (such as all-purpose flour) promotes a crispier crust and a drier, denser crumb.

Tasters liked the crispier crust of the biscuits made with all-purpose flour and the tender, airy crumb of the biscuits made with cake flour. We found that a combination of half cake flour and half all-purpose flour delivered the best results—a crisp crust and a tender crumb. If you don't have cake flour, all-purpose flour makes a fine biscuit as long as you add more liquid to the batter.

Fat makes biscuits (and other pastries) tender, moist, smooth, and tasty. Butter, of course, delivers the best flavor, while vegetable shortening makes a slightly flakier biscuit with better holding powers. However, we don't think this gain in shelf life is worth the loss in flavor. Stick with unsalted butter when making biscuits.

We discovered that a proportion of ½ cup fat to 2 cups flour provides the best balance of tenderness and richness with structure. The way in which the fat and flour are combined is nearly as important as their proportions. The fat must be "rubbed" into the dry ingredients, making a dry, coarse mixture akin to large bread crumbs or rolled oats, with some slightly bigger lumps mixed in. This rubbing may seem unimportant, but in fact it is crucial to the proper rising of the biscuits. Gas released by the leavener during baking must have a space in which to collect; if the texture of the dough is homogeneous, the gas will simply dissipate. Melting fat particles create convenient spaces in which the gas can collect, form bubbles, and produce a rise. Proper rubbing breaks the fat into tiny bits and disperses it throughout the dough. As the fat melts during baking, its place is taken up by gas and steam, which expand and push the dough up. The wider the dispersal of the fat, the more even the rising of the dough.

If, however, the fat softens and binds with the dry ingredients during rubbing, it forms a pasty goo, the spaces collapse, and the biscuits become leaden. To produce light, airy biscuits, the fat must remain cold and firm, which means rubbing must be deft and quick. Traditionally, biscuit makers pinch the cut-up fat into the dry ingredients, using only their fingertips—never the whole hand, which is too warm—and they pinch hard and fast, practically flinging the little bits of flour and fat into the bowl after each pinch. Less experienced cooks sometimes cut in the fat by scraping two knives in opposite directions or by using a bow-shaped pastry blender. We found, however, that the easiest way to go about this task is with the help of a food processor. Pulsing the dry ingredients and the fat is fast and almost foolproof.

After cutting in the fat, liquid is added and the dough is stirred just until the ingredients are bound, using a light hand so the gluten will not become activated. We found that buttermilk (or plain yogurt) gives biscuits the best flavor. It also creates a lighter, airier texture than regular milk. That's because the acid in the buttermilk reacts with the leaveners to increase the rise.

Biscuits are best formed by gently patting gobs of dough between your hands. If the work surface, the dough, and the cutter are generously floured, fluffy biscuits can be rolled and cut; but the softness of the dough makes this a tricky procedure, and the extra flour and handling will make the biscuits heavier and somewhat dense.

Because they need quick heat, biscuits are best baked in the middle of the oven. Placed too close to the bottom, they burn on the underside and remain pale on top; set too near the oven roof, they do not rise well because the outside hardens into a shell before the inside has had a chance to rise properly. As soon as they are light brown, they are done. Be careful, as overcooking will dry them out. Biscuits are always at their best as soon as they come out of the oven. The dough, however, may be made some hours in advance and baked when needed; the biscuits will still rise well.

Buttermilk Biscuits

MAKES 12

Mixing the butter and dry ingredients quickly so the butter remains cold and firm is crucial to producing light, tender biscuits. The easiest and most reliable approach is to use a food processor fitted with the metal blade. Expect a soft and slightly sticky dough. The wet dough creates steam when the biscuits bake and promotes the light airy texture. If the dough is too wet for you to shape the biscuits by hand, lightly flour your hands and then shape the biscuits.

If you don't have cake flour on hand, substitute an extra cup of all-purpose flour and increase the buttermilk and yogurt by 2 tablespoons.

1	cup (5 ounces) unbleached all-purpose flour
1	cup (4 ounces) plain cake flour
2	teaspoons baking powder
1/2	teaspoon baking soda
1	teaspoon sugar
1/2	teaspoon salt
8	tablespoons (1 stick) cold unsalted butter, cut into 1/4-inch cubes
3/4	cup cold buttermilk, or 3/4 cup plus 2 tablespoons plain yogurt

1. Adjust an oven rack to the middle position and heat the oven to 450 degrees.

2. Place the flours, baking powder, baking soda, sugar, and salt in a large bowl or the workbowl of a food processor fitted with the metal blade. Whisk together or process with six 1-second pulses.

3. If making by hand, use two knives, a pastry blender, or your fingertips to quickly cut in the butter until the mixture resembles coarse meal with a few slightly larger butter lumps. If using a food processor, remove the cover and distribute the butter evenly over the dry ingredients. Cover and process with twelve 1-second pulses.

4. If making by hand, stir in the buttermilk with a rubber spatula or fork until the mixture forms a soft, slightly sticky ball. If using a food processor, remove the cover and pour the buttermilk evenly over the dough. Process until the dough gathers into moist clumps, about eight 1-second pulses.

5. Transfer the dough to a lightly floured surface and quickly form into a rough ball. Be careful not to overmix. Using a sharp knife or dough cutter, divide the dough in quarters and then cut each quarter into thirds. Quickly and gently shape each piece into a rough ball (see illustration on page 137), and place on an ungreased cookie sheet. (The baking sheet can be wrapped in plastic and refrigerated for up to 2 hours.)

6. Bake until the biscuit tops are light brown, 10 to 12 minutes. Serve immediately.

CREAM BISCUITS

OUR BUTTERMILK BISCUITS ARE EASY TO prepare; you can have biscuits on the table in 20 minutes. But many cooks are intimidated by this kind of biscuit because they are not comfortable with the traditional process of cutting butter into flour. We wondered if we could come up with a recipe for homemade biscuits that could be made quickly and easily and that would not require cutting fat into flour. In short, was it possible to take the guesswork out of making biscuits to create a foolproof recipe?

First, we tried varying the dairy. The biscuits made with yogurt and sour cream were a bit sodden in texture, those with a milk and milk-and-butter combination were tough and lifeless, and a whipped cream biscuit was too light. This last approach also required whipping the cream, which seemed like too much trouble for a simple recipe. So we tried using plain heavy cream, without whipping, and this biscuit was the best of the lot.

Next we decided to do a blind tasting, pitting the cream biscuits against our conventional buttermilk biscuit recipe, which requires cutting butter into the flour. The result? Both biscuits had their partisans. The cream biscuits were lighter and more tender. They were also richer tasting. The buttermilk biscuits were flakier and had the distinctive tang that many people associate with good biscuits. Although neither biscuit was sweet, the buttermilk version seemed more savory.

At this point, we decided that cream biscuits were a worthy (and easier) alternative to traditional buttermilk biscuits. Still, we were running into a problem with the shape of the biscuits, as they were spreading far too much during baking; they needed more structure. When making biscuits, we have always followed the conventional advice about not overworking the dough. Kneading the dough encourages the development of gluten, a protein that gives baked products structure but that when overdeveloped can also make them tough. In our experience, the best biscuits are generally made from dough that is handled lightly. This is certainly true of buttermilk biscuits. But cream biscuits, being less sturdy than those made with butter, become soft and "melt" during baking. In this case, we thought, a little more structure produced by a little more handling might not be such a bad thing. So we baked up two batches. The first dough we patted out gingerly; the second dough we kneaded for 30 seconds until it was smooth and uniform in appearance. The results

were remarkable. The more heavily worked dough produced much higher, fluffier biscuits than those made from the lightly handled dough, which looked short and bedraggled.

We ran into a problem, though, when one batch of biscuits had to sit for a few minutes while we waited for the oven to heat up. During baking, the dough spread, resulting in biscuits with bottoms that were too wide and tops that were too narrow. Clearly, the biscuits had to be popped into the oven immediately after cutting. As for dough thickness, we found that 1 inch provides a remarkably high rise, more appealing than biscuits that start out ½ inch thick. We also discovered that it was best to add just enough cream to hold the dough together. A wet dough does not hold its shape as well during baking.

Although we found it easy enough to quickly roll out this dough and then cut it into rounds with a biscuit cutter, you can simply shape the dough with your hands or push it into the bottom of an 8-inch cake pan. The dough can then be flipped onto the work surface and cut into wedges with a knife or dough scraper.

Now we had the simplest of biscuit recipes: Whisk together the dry ingredients, add heavy cream, form the dough, knead it, cut it, and bake it. Serve these biscuits with a savory bowl of soup or stew. The rich reward will surprise you.

Cream Biscuits
MAKES 8

Bake the biscuits immediately after cutting them; letting them stand for any length of time can decrease the leavening power and prevent the biscuits from rising in the oven.

2	cups (10 ounces) unbleached all-purpose flour
2	teaspoons sugar
2	teaspoons baking powder
½	teaspoon salt
1½	cups heavy cream

1. Adjust the oven rack to the upper-middle position and heat the oven to 425 degrees. Line a rimmed baking sheet with parchment paper.

2. Whisk together the flour, sugar, baking

powder, and salt in a medium bowl. Add 1¼ cups of the cream and stir with a wooden spoon until the dough forms, about 30 seconds. Transfer the dough to the countertop, leaving all dry, floury bits behind in the bowl. In 1 tablespoon increments, add up to ¼ cup cream to the dry bits in the bowl, mixing with a wooden spoon after each addition, until moistened. Add these moistened bits to the rest of the dough and knead by hand just until smooth, about 30 seconds.

3. Following the illustrations on page 137, cut the biscuits into rounds or wedges. Place the biscuits on the parchment-lined baking sheet and bake until golden brown, about 15 minutes. Serve immediately.

➤ VARIATIONS

Cream Biscuits with Fresh Herbs

Follow the recipe for Cream Biscuits, whisking 2 tablespoons minced fresh herbs into the flour along with the sugar, baking powder, and salt.

Cream Biscuits with Cheddar Cheese

Follow the recipe for Cream Biscuits, stirring ½ cup (2 ounces) cheddar cheese cut into ¼-inch pieces into the flour along with the sugar, baking powder, and salt. Increase the baking time to 18 minutes.

SCONES

SCONES IN AMERICA—UNLIKE THEIR MORE diminutive British counterparts—have the reputation of being thick, heavy, dry bricks. To enhance their appeal, they are often disguised under a sugary shellac of achingly sweet glaze or filled with chopped ginger, chopped fruit, or chocolate chips. Despite these feeble attempts to dress them up, it is no secret that today's coffeehouse confections are a far cry from what a scone should be: tender and flaky, like a slightly sweetened biscuit.

We started our testing by focusing on the flour. We made a composite recipe with bread flour, with all-purpose flour, and with cake flour. The differences in outcome were astonishing. The scones made with bread flour were heavy and tough. The scones made with all-purpose flour

were lighter and much more flavorful. Cake flour produced scones that were doughy in the center, with a raw taste and poor texture. Subsequent tests revealed that a lower-protein all-purpose flour, such as Gold Medal or Pillsbury, is better than a higher-protein flour, such as King Arthur.

After trying scones made with butter and with lard, we decided we preferred the rich flavor of butter. (If we made scones commercially, we might reconsider, because day-old scones made with lard hold up better. The preservative effects of different fats, along with lower cost, may be why store-bought scones are often made with margarine or other hydrogenated fats.) Although the amount of solid fat can be varied, we found 5 tablespoons of butter to 2 cups flour to be just right. More butter and the scones will almost melt in the oven. Less butter and the baked scones will be dry and tough.

The choice of liquid can also profoundly affect the flavor of a scone. We tested various liquids and found that cream made the best scones that were tender yet still light. Scones made with milk were bland and dry. Buttermilk gave scones plenty of flavor, but the scone was too flaky and biscuit-like. Scones made with cream were moister and more flavorful than the others.

We tried adding an egg to the dough. We found that it made the scones very cakey. Many tasters liked the effect of the egg. Since the addition of egg helps the scone hold onto moisture and remain fresher longer, we decided to use the egg in a variation called Cakey Scones.

In traditional recipes, one to two tablespoons of sugar is enough to sweeten an entire batch of scones. American scones tend to be far sweeter than the British versions, which are usually served with sweet toppings such as jam. Americans seem to eat their scones like muffins, without anything more than a smear of butter, so the sweetness is baked in. We prefer the British approach but decided to increase the sugar slightly to three tablespoons.

Finally, scones are often glazed to enhance their appearance and add sweetness. We tried brushing the dough with a beaten egg as well as with heavy cream just before baking. Scones brushed with egg can become too dark in the oven. We preferred the more delicate look of scones brushed with cream and then dusted with a little granulated sugar.

Scones can be mixed by hand or with a food processor. (The processor is used to cut fat into flour; minimal hand mixing is required afterward.) We found the food processor to be more reliable than mixing entirely by hand, which can overheat the butter and cause it to soften. Once the dough comes together, we prefer to pat it into a cake pan, gently pull it out onto a floured surface, and then cut it into eight wedges. We find this method easier than using a rolling pin.

Cream Scones with Currants

MAKES 8

The most traditional sweet biscuit-like texture is obtained by using both butter and heavy cream. If you prefer a more cake-like texture, or want the scones to stay fresher longer, try the Cakey Scones variation. The easiest and most reliable approach to mixing the butter into the dry ingredients is to use a food processor fitted with the metal blade. Resist the urge to eat the scones hot out of the oven. Letting them cool for at least 10 minutes firms them up and improves their texture.

2	cups (10 ounces) unbleached all-purpose flour, preferably a lower-protein brand such as Gold Medal or Pillsbury
1	tablespoon baking powder
3	tablespoons sugar
1/2	teaspoon salt
5	tablespoons cold unsalted butter, cut into 1/4-inch cubes
1/2	cup currants
1	cup heavy cream

1. Adjust an oven rack to the middle position and heat the oven to 425 degrees.

2. Place the flour, baking powder, sugar, and salt in a large bowl or the workbowl of a food processor fitted with the metal blade. Whisk together or process with six 1-second pulses.

3. If making by hand, use two knives, a pastry blender, or your fingertips and quickly cut in the butter until the mixture resembles coarse meal with a few slightly larger butter lumps. If using a food processor, remove the cover and distribute the butter evenly over the dry ingredients. Cover and process with twelve 1-second pulses. Add the currants and quickly mix in or pulse one more time. Transfer the dough to a large bowl.

4. Stir in the heavy cream with a rubber spatula or fork until the dough begins to form, about 30 seconds.

5. Transfer the dough and all dry flour bits to a countertop and knead the dough by hand just until it comes together into a rough, slightly sticky ball, 5 to 10 seconds. Following the illustrations on page 137, cut the scones into 8 wedges. Place the wedges on an ungreased baking sheet. (The baking sheet can be wrapped in plastic and refrigerated for up to 2 hours.)

6. Bake until the scone tops are light brown, 12 to 15 minutes. Cool on a wire rack for at least 10 minutes. Serve warm or at room temperature.

VARIATIONS

Glazed Scones

A light cream and sugar glaze gives these scones an attractive sheen and a sweeter flavor. If baking the scones immediately after making the dough, brush the dough just before cutting it into wedges.

Follow the recipe for Cream Scones, brushing the tops of the scones with 1 tablespoon heavy cream and then sprinkling them with 1 tablespoon sugar just before baking them.

Cakey Scones

An egg changes the texture and color and helps these scones stay fresher longer, up to 2 days in an airtight container.

Follow the recipe for Cream Scones, reducing the butter to 4 tablespoons and the cream to ¾ cup. Add 1 large egg, lightly beaten, to the dough along with the cream.

Ginger Scones

Follow the recipe for Cream Scones, substituting ½ cup chopped crystallized ginger for the currants.

Cranberry-Orange Scones

Follow the recipe for Cream Scones, adding 1 teaspoon grated orange zest with the butter and substituting ¾ cup dried cranberries for the currants.

Lemon–Blueberry Scones

Mix the dough by hand after adding the blueberries to keep them plump and whole.

Follow the recipe for Cream Scones, adding 1 teaspoon grated lemon zest with the butter and substituting ½ cup fresh or frozen (not thawed) blueberries for the currants.

OATMEAL SCONES

AFTER TACKLING TRADITIONAL SCONES, WE were ready to revamp the heaviest, densest, driest variation of them all: the oatmeal scone. The first few recipes we tried confirmed our worst fears about oatmeal scones. There was the lean, mean, whole-wheat-flour oatmeal scone, which was gritty and dense, and the dried-fruit-laden oatmeal scone, which was thick like a cookie. Although tasters had different preferences when it came to texture, all agreed on the need for a stronger oat flavor. Our goal, then, was to pack the chewy nuttiness of oats into a moist and tender breakfast pastry, one that wouldn't require a fire hose to wash down the crumbs.

The first hurdle was deciding what type of oats to use (for explanations of the different types, see page 3). Because they take at least 30 minutes to cook, we quickly ruled out steel-cut oats for this recipe—the baking time of these scones would not be long enough to cook them through. The most familiar type seemed to be rolled oats, but we still had two choices: whole (old-fashioned) and quick. This was not such an easy decision, as each had qualities to recommend it. The flavor of the whole rolled oats was deeper and nuttier (a few tasters even asked if there was peanut butter in the scones), and the smaller flaked quick oats had a softer texture, which was considered more palatable by some. We finally decided that either would do.

Next we had to figure out how to pack in the most oat flavor without sacrificing the texture of the scone. We were sure we could achieve this by simply processing the oats into the flour. But instead, the texture was horrible, very gluey and dense. We even tried adding real oat flour (found mostly in health food stores) along with the all-purpose flour, but the same gumminess resulted. Waving our white flag, we attributed this failure to the fact that oat flour does not have any gluten. Without gluten, it had nothing to contribute to the structure of our scones, adding only dead weight and a leaden texture. Leaving the oats intact, we found that equal parts oats to flour provided good flavor and a decent texture. (Most of the test recipes called for much smaller proportions of oats, thus their wimpy oat flavor.) But we were still yearning for a nuttier taste, so we took a hint from one of the test recipes and toasted the oats before mixing them with the flour.

We kept the sugar content to a minimum—just enough to tenderize the scones while enhancing the oat flavor. We tried all white sugar, all light brown sugar, and a combination of the two. Some tasters liked the deep robust flavor of brown sugar, but most preferred the lighter texture and cleaner flavor created by white sugar alone.

We settled on just 2 teaspoons of baking powder, a teaspoon less than we used in our cream scones, which contain more flour.

Moving on to the butter, we quickly realized why so many oatmeal scones are so dry: They don't have nearly enough fat. A lean oatmeal scone is simply not worth eating, so we used 10 tablespoons of butter, which adds flavor as well as tenderness. We used a mixture of milk and heavy cream for a rich oatmeal scone that doesn't double as a paperweight. (Using all half-and-half works just as well.) And, as in our recipe for cakey scones, an egg gives these oatmeal scones a nice richness and airy crumb. As with any biscuit or scone recipe, we found it important not to overwork the dough. It should be mixed just until the ingredients come together.

We baked the scones at temperatures ranging from 350 degrees all the way up to 425 degrees—and every 25-degree increment in between. The best of the lot were those baked at 425 degrees, but they were not ideal. We tried pushing the oven temperature to 450 degrees (a bit of a gamble, as the sugar in the recipe might burn) and were rewarded. These scones had a dramatic rise and a deep golden brown crust. In such high heat, the cold butter melted quickly and produced steam, which created the light texture we were looking for. The intensity of the rise also gave the scones a cracked, craggy, rustic look that was enhanced when we added a sugar topping. The higher temperature also meant that the scones spent less time in the oven, which kept them from drying out. Finally, we had an oatmeal scone that was hearty and flavorful from toasty whole oats, yet light enough to be consumed in one sitting without having to drink a super-size latte to wash it down.

Oatmeal Scones

MAKES 8

This recipe was developed using Gold Medal unbleached all-purpose flour; best results will be achieved if you use the same or a similar flour, such as Pillsbury unbleached. King Arthur flour has more protein; if you use it, add an additional 1 to 2 tablespoons milk.

Half-and-half is a suitable substitute for the milk-cream combination if you happen to have some on hand.

Once baked, these scones will keep for up to 3 days in an airtight container at room temperature.

1 1/2	cups (4 1/2 ounces) old-fashioned rolled oats or quick oats
1/4	cup whole milk
1/4	cup heavy cream
1	large egg
1 1/2	cups (7 1/2 ounces) lower-protein unbleached all-purpose flour, such as Gold Medal or Pillsbury
1/3	cup (2 1/3 ounces) sugar, plus 1 tablespoon for sprinkling
2	teaspoons baking powder
1/2	teaspoon salt
10	tablespoons (1 1/4 sticks) cold unsalted butter, cut into 1/4-inch cubes

1. Adjust an oven rack to the middle position and heat the oven to 375 degrees. Spread the oats evenly on a baking sheet and toast them in the oven until they are fragrant and lightly browned, 7 to 9 minutes; cool on a wire rack. Increase the oven temperature to 450 degrees. Line a second baking sheet with parchment paper. When the oats are cooled, measure out 2 tablespoons (for dusting the work surface) and set aside.

2. Whisk the milk, cream, and egg in a large measuring cup until incorporated; remove 1 tablespoon to a small bowl and reserve for glazing.

3. Place the flour, sugar, baking powder, and salt in the workbowl of a food processor fitted with the metal blade and process until combined, about four 1-second pulses. Scatter the cold butter evenly over the dry ingredients and process until the mixture resembles coarse cornmeal, twelve to fourteen 1-second pulses. Transfer the mixture to a medium bowl; stir in the cooled oats. Using a rubber spatula, fold in the liquid ingredients until large clumps form. Using your hands, gently knead the mixture in the bowl until the dough forms a cohesive mass.

4. Dust the work surface with half of the reserved oats, turn the dough out onto the work surface, and dust the top with the remaining oats. Gently pat the dough into a 7-inch circle about 1 inch thick. Using a bench scraper or chef's knife, cut the dough into 8 wedges and set on the parchment-lined baking sheet, spacing them about 2 inches apart. Brush the surfaces with the reserved milk-and-egg mixture and sprinkle with 1 tablespoon sugar. Bake until golden brown, 12 to 14 minutes; cool scones on the baking sheet on a wire rack 5 minutes, then remove scones to a wire rack and cool to room temperature, about 30 minutes. Serve.

ACHIEVING GOOD RISE AND A WELL-BROWNED CRUST

The scone on the left was baked in a moderate oven and did not rise as much as the scone baked in a very hot oven, which quickly turns the moisture in the dough into steam. Scones baked in a hot oven rise dramatically and have a craggy, well-browned top.

BAKED AT 350 DEGREES　　　**BAKED AT 450 DEGREES**

QUICK BREADS, MUFFINS, BISCUITS, AND SCONES

➤ VARIATIONS

Cinnamon-Raisin Oatmeal Scones

Follow the recipe for Oatmeal Scones, adding ¼ teaspoon ground cinnamon to the dry ingredients and ½ cup golden raisins to the flour/butter mixture along with the toasted oats.

Apricot-Almond Oatmeal Scones

Follow the recipe for Oatmeal Scones, reducing the oats to 1 cup (3 ounces), toasting ½ cup slivered almonds along with the oats, and adding ½ cup chopped dried apricots to the flour/butter mixture along with the toasted oats and almonds.

Oatmeal Scones with Dried Cherries and Hazelnuts

Follow the recipe for Oatmeal Scones, reducing the oats to 1¼ cups (3¾ ounces), toasting ¼ cup coarsely chopped skinned hazelnuts along with the oats, and adding ½ cup chopped dried sour cherries to the flour/butter mixture along with the toasted oats and nuts.

Glazed Maple-Pecan Oatmeal Scones

Follow the recipe for Oatmeal Scones, toasting ½ cup coarsely chopped pecans along with the oats, whisking ¼ cup maple syrup into the milk/cream/egg mixture (before removing 1 tablespoon for brushing the scones), and omitting the sugar. When the scones are cool, whisk 3 tablespoons maple syrup and ½ cup confectioners' sugar in a small bowl until combined; drizzle the glaze over the scones.

QUICK CINNAMON BUNS

CINNAMON BUNS ARE QUICK TO PLEASE. The bun is tender and fluffy, the filling is sweet and spicy, and the glaze is sinful, encouraging even the well-bred to lick the gooey remnants from their fingers. It's a shame, then, that making cinnamon buns at home can try the patience of the most devoted cook. Most recipes call for yeast, which means they also call for a lot of time and skill as well as a standing mixer (or powerful biceps). The alternative is to make cinnamon buns from a tube or a box, options that produce inferior buns whose flavor lies somewhere between chemicals and cardboard. Our aim was to put cinnamon buns back in the home kitchen in good time, sacrificing neither flavor nor fluffiness for speed.

We started with a tasting of our favorite yeasted cinnamon buns on page 118. With a soft and resilient texture and a bready, open crumb, the texture of these buns was top-notch, and the combination of cinnamon and yeast produced a grown-up flavor. Unfortunately, the start-to-finish time was hours long. We knew what we wanted from cinnamon buns. Now we just wanted it quicker and easier.

Toward this end, the first decision we made was to work from recipes leavened with baking powder rather than yeast. The next step was to determine the best method for incorporating the fat into the other ingredients. First we tried the classic mixing method of cutting cold butter into dry ingredients. Unfortunately, this method turned out cinnamon buns that were dense, flaky, and craggy rather than tender, light, and fluffy.

The next mixing method we tried called for combining melted butter with the liquid ingredients in a food processor, then adding the dry ingredients. While we hoped that the food processor would make the mixing process easier, the dough was very sticky, making it difficult to work with, and the finished buns weren't worth the effort.

The last method we tried was a quick cream biscuit method, in which heavy cream is added to flour, sugar, baking powder, and salt. What makes this dough unique is its complete lack of butter. The dough relies entirely on the heavy cream for tenderness and flavor. Better still, the dough can be mixed in a minute using just one bowl. This process was by far the fastest and easiest, and we wanted to go with it, but a few refinements would be required before it produced really good cinnamon buns.

To make the dough more tender, our first thought was to replace the all-purpose flour with more delicate cake flour. But cake flour turned the dough into a sticky mess that was hard to roll out.

Our next inclination was to test whole or skim milk in place of heavy cream, but whole milk made the buns too heavy, and skim milk made them tough and bland. We increased the amount of baking powder to achieve lightness but ended up with metallic-tasting buns. We then tested buttermilk, a common ingredient in biscuit doughs, and had some success. We also added ½ teaspoon of baking soda to balance the acidity of the buttermilk. Baking soda reacts with the acid in buttermilk to produce carbon dioxide gas, which causes lift. The acid in the buttermilk gave the buns a more complex flavor and tenderized the gluten in the dough, making the interior airy and light.

But now the dough was too lean for our taste, owing to the buttermilk, most of which is made by adding acidic cultures to skim or low-fat milk. (To read more about buttermilk, see page 5.) We arrived at the solution when we added 2 tablespoons of melted butter to the buttermilk. Just as we had hoped, the dough was tender, complex, and rich.

Whereas most recipes instruct bakers to roll out the dough, we found it easier to pat the dough into a rough-shaped rectangle, thus making the recipe even simpler. For the cinnamon-sugar filling we decided on a union of brown sugar, white sugar, cinnamon, cloves, and salt. Before sprinkling the filling on the dough, we brushed the dough with 2 tablespoons of melted butter to help the filling cling to it. Because the cinnamon mixture was loose and dry, however, it was still apt to fall away from the dough when the buns were cut and transferred to the baking pan. The easy solution was to add 1 tablespoon of melted butter to the dry ingredients, which made the mixture the consistency of wet sand, allowing us to press it into the dough easily. This time the filling stayed put.

Next we addressed the look of our rolls. Instead of rising to the occasion in the oven, they were slouching in their seats. We reviewed the quick cream biscuit recipe to see if we might find the source of the problem there. Sure enough, the

MAKING CINNAMON BUNS

1. Pat the dough into a 12 by 9-inch rectangle and brush it with melted butter. Sprinkle the filling evenly over the dough, leaving a ½-inch border. Press the filling firmly into the dough.

2. Using a bench scraper or metal spatula, loosen the dough from the work surface. Starting at a long side, roll the dough, pressing lightly, to form a tight log. Pinch the seam to seal.

3. Roll the log seam-side down and cut it evenly into 8 pieces. With your hand, slightly flatten each piece of dough to seal the open edges and keep the filling in place.

4. Place 1 roll in the center of the prepared nonstick pan and place the remaining 7 rolls around the perimeter of the pan.

recipe stated that if the dough wasn't kneaded before being shaped, it didn't rise nicely in the oven. We made two batches of dough, kneading one and not the other, and were surprised to find that just a quick 30-second knead solved the problem. Contrary to what one might think, the short knead didn't toughen the buns; it just provided the dough with enough strength to take in a big breath and hold it.

To finish the buns, we tried a host of different glazes, all based on a quick confectioners' sugar and water glaze, which is inherently pasty and grainy. After a few trials, we found a way to sufficiently mask the graininess and pasty flavor by combining buttermilk and cream cheese, then sifting the confectioners' sugar over the paste. (If the sugar is not sifted, the glaze will be lumpy.) This glaze was smooth, thick, and pleasantly tangy, although it does add one more ingredient to the shopping list for the buns: cream cheese.

As for what to bake the buns in, we tried muffin tins, pie plates, baking sheets, springform pans, glass baking dishes, and cake pans. With its straight sides, round shape, and perfect size, a 9-inch nonstick cake pan was the perfect choice. We started baking at 425 degrees and got lucky the first time out. The buns baked in 25 minutes, rose and browned nicely, and were cooked all the way through.

Now the moment of truth had come. It was time for a blind tasting of our quick cinnamon buns head-to-head with our yeasted version. The quick buns got a quick nod of approval, with many tasters even preferring them to the more sophisticated and elegantly flavored yeasted buns. Best of all, these shortcut cinnamon buns can be on the table in an hour—a fact you may very well choose to keep to yourself.

Quick Cinnamon Buns with Buttermilk Icing

MAKES 8

Melted butter is used in both the filling and the dough and to grease the pan; melt the total amount (8 tablespoons) at once and measure it out as you need it. The buns are best eaten warm, but they hold up well for up to 2 hours.

1   tablespoon unsalted butter, melted, for greasing the pan

CINNAMON-SUGAR FILLING
3/4   cup packed (5 1/4 ounces) dark brown sugar
1/4   cup (1 3/4 ounces) granulated sugar
2   teaspoons ground cinnamon
1/8   teaspoon ground cloves
1/8   teaspoon salt
1   tablespoon unsalted butter, melted

BISCUIT DOUGH
2 1/2   cups (12 1/2 ounces) unbleached all-purpose flour, plus additional flour for work surface
2   tablespoons granulated sugar
1 1/4   teaspoons baking powder
1/2   teaspoon baking soda
1/2   teaspoon salt
1 1/4   cups buttermilk
6   tablespoons (3/4 stick) unsalted butter, melted and cooled

ICING
2   tablespoons cream cheese, softened
2   tablespoons buttermilk
1   cup (4 ounces) confectioners' sugar

1. Adjust an oven rack to the upper-middle position and heat the oven to 425 degrees. Pour 1 tablespoon of the melted butter into a 9-inch nonstick cake pan; brush to coat the pan. Spray a wire cooling rack with nonstick cooking spray; set aside.

2. FOR THE CINNAMON-SUGAR FILLING: Combine the sugars, spices, and salt in a small bowl. Add 1 tablespoon of the melted butter and stir with a fork until the mixture resembles wet sand; set the filling mixture aside.

3. FOR THE BISCUIT DOUGH: Whisk the flour, sugar, baking powder, baking soda, and salt in a large bowl. Whisk the buttermilk and 2 tablespoons of the melted butter in a measuring cup or small bowl. Add the liquid to the dry ingredients and stir with a wooden spoon until the liquid is absorbed (the dough will look very shaggy), about 30 seconds. Transfer the dough to a lightly floured work surface and knead until just smooth and no longer shaggy.

4. Pat the dough with your hands into a 12 by 9-inch rectangle. Brush the dough with 2 tablespoons of the melted butter. Sprinkle evenly with the filling, leaving a ½-inch border of plain dough around the edges. Following the illustrations on page 62, press the filling firmly into the dough. Using a bench scraper or metal spatula, loosen the dough from the work surface. Starting at the long side, roll the dough, pressing lightly, to form a tight log. Pinch the seam to seal. Roll the log seam-side down and cut it evenly into 8 pieces. With your hand, slightly flatten each piece of dough to seal the open edges and keep the filling in place. Place 1 roll in the center of the prepared nonstick pan, then place the remaining 7 rolls around the perimeter of the pan. Brush with the remaining 2 tablespoons melted butter.

5. Bake until the edges of the buns are golden brown, 23 to 25 minutes. Use an offset metal spatula to loosen the buns from the pan. Wearing oven mitts, place a large plate over the pan and invert the buns onto the plate. Place a greased cooling rack over the plate and invert the buns onto the rack. Cool about 5 minutes before icing.

6. For the icing and to finish the buns: While the buns are cooling, line a rimmed baking sheet with parchment paper (for easy cleanup); set the rack with the buns over the baking sheet. Whisk the cream cheese and buttermilk in a large nonreactive bowl until thick and smooth (the mixture will look like cottage cheese at first). Sift the confectioners' sugar over the mixture; whisk until a smooth glaze forms, about 30 seconds. Spoon the glaze evenly over the buns; serve immediately.

Popovers

POPOVERS ARE IMPRESSIVE BECAUSE THEIR few humble ingredients—eggs, milk, flour, salt, and butter—are transformed by the heat of the oven into the culinary equivalent of hot air balloons. The goal in developing the batter is to create a framework that, like a balloon, can expand and stretch without breaking as pressure is applied from within. We were after the biggest, best-tasting popovers we could make, with huge crowns, lightly crisp, golden brown exteriors, and tender, moist, airy interiors crisscrossed with custardy webs of dough.

The recipes we looked at during our research were remarkably consistent in terms of the ingredients and their proportions. We soon arrived at a list that would stand by us throughout testing: 2 eggs, 1 cup milk, 1 cup flour, ½ teaspoon salt, and 1 tablespoon butter. The variables we needed to test revolved around technique: Could we use a muffin tin, or would a popover pan be necessary? How should we mix the batter? How much should each individual muffin or popover pan cup be filled—that is, would the volume of the batter affect the rise? How hot should the oven be? Should the heat be lowered partway through cooking, as most recipes suggested? Should the popovers go into a hot oven or a cold oven? Was it necessary to preheat the pan and the fat used to grease it?

Our first efforts were baked in a muffin tin, and they failed to impress. Short and squat, with tops that looked something like overstuffed commas, these popovers were far from our ideal. Would the popover pan make a difference? The logic behind the pan design suggested that it would. Whereas the cups in a muffin tin are wider than they are tall, those in a popover pan are narrow and deep. Without much room to spread out, the batter has nowhere to go but up. We tried a popover pan and the shape of the popovers was improved—they were taller and puffier—but they still didn't have that beautiful crown we were looking for, and their texture was wrong, more like a dinner roll crossed with a muffin than a popover.

The popovers' resemblance to muffins got us thinking about the way we had been mixing the batter. Most recipes came with the following warning: Do not overmix the batter. In general, the more a batter or dough is mixed or kneaded, the more gluten is created. Gluten, which forms when the proteins in flour are combined with liquid, helps to create an elastic network that gives most baked goods the support they need to stand up. When mixing muffins, which should be tender, the goal is to develop only enough gluten to hold things together, and this is usually accomplished by gently folding the ingredients. So this is what we had been doing with our popover batter; leaving the mixture a little lumpy so as not to overdevelop the gluten. One or two recipes had different advice: Whisk the ingredients until smooth. We tried this, and the popovers rose a bit higher and their texture began to improve, becoming slightly more airy.

Next we tried letting the batter rest for 30 minutes before putting it in the oven, a common practice with pancake and waffle batter, the idea being to give the gluten a chance to relax. When it relaxes, the gluten becomes more pliable and better able to expand and stretch rather than breaking like a rubber band pulled too tight. If the gluten had more give, we reasoned, the popovers should rise still higher. We decided to let the batter rest on the countertop so that the chilled ingredients could get closer to room temperature before baking. This common baker's practice gives the batter a bit of a head start when it enters the oven. This test, too, was a success. Our popovers were growing slowly but surely over the rim of the popover tin, and their interior texture was becoming feathered with eggy layers of dough.

We were finally ready to experiment with oven temperature. The rationale for starting with a hot oven (450 degrees in most recipes) and lowering the heat about halfway through baking (to 350 degrees) is to give the popovers the intense heat they need to turn the moisture in the batter to steam. The popovers expand, brown, and set their shape at 450, and the heat is then lowered to let the interior cook through without overcooking the shell. We tried starting the popovers in a cold oven, and we tried baking them at a constant 375 degrees, as recommended in a couple of recipes. The popovers did rise under these conditions, but not as dramatically as when we started at 450 degrees.

Following through on the idea that an initial blast of heat is good for popovers, we also tried preheating the greased pan. The problem was that the butter we had been using to grease the pan burned before the pan had a chance to heat up fully. Our thoughts turned to clarified butter, which is made by slowly heating butter to let the milk proteins—the source of butter's sensitivity to heat—separate from the fat. This worked, but clarifying butter can be time-consuming. We tried preheating the pan

with simple vegetable oil, and the results were every bit as good. Relying on condition and technique, we were able to turn simple ingredients like eggs, milk, flour, salt, and butter into huge and flavorful hot air balloons.

Popovers

MAKES 6

Unlike most popover batters, this one is smooth, not lumpy. High heat is crucial to the speedy, high rise of the popovers. When it's time to fill the popover pan with batter, get the pan out of and back into the oven as quickly as possible, making sure to close the oven door while you pour the batter into the pan. Popovers made in a 12-cup muffin tin won't rise nearly as high as those made in a popover pan, but they can still be quite good. See the variation that follows if you can't locate a popover pan.

2	large eggs
1	cup whole milk
1	cup (5 ounces) unbleached all-purpose flour
1/2	teaspoon salt
1	tablespoon unsalted butter, melted
1	tablespoon vegetable oil

1. In a large bowl, whisk the eggs and milk until well combined, about 20 seconds. Whisk the flour and salt in a medium bowl and add to the egg mixture; stir with a wooden spoon or spatula just until the flour is incorporated; the mixture will still be lumpy. Add the melted butter. Whisk until the batter is bubbly and smooth, about 30 seconds. Let the batter rest at room temperature for 30 minutes.

2. While the batter is resting, measure ½ teaspoon vegetable oil into each cup of the popover pan. Adjust the oven rack to the lowest position, place the popover pan in the oven, and heat to 450 degrees. After the batter has rested, pour it into a 4-cup liquid measuring cup or another container with a spout (you will have about 2 cups batter). Working quickly, remove the pan from the oven and distribute the batter evenly among the 6 cups in the pan. Return the pan to the oven and bake for 20 minutes, without opening the oven door. Lower the heat to 350 degrees and bake until golden brown all over, 15 to 18

minutes more. Invert the pan onto a wire rack to remove popovers and cool for 2 or 3 minutes. Serve immediately.

➤ VARIATION
Muffin Tin Popovers
MAKES 10

Proceed as above, using a 12-cup muffin tin in place of a popover pan and using only the 10 outer cups of the tin. You will need an extra 2 teaspoons of vegetable oil to grease the muffin tin.

BUTTERMILK DOUGHNUTS

WITH NO RISING REQUIRED, BUTTERMILK doughnuts are what you want if you're tight on time but crave a tasty, old-fashioned accompaniment to your morning coffee or mug of apple cider. In just 45 minutes, you can fry up two dozen robust country doughnuts with great crunch and flavor.

We proceeded to test half a dozen different recipes for nonyeast fried doughnuts, choosing methods that seemed as different as possible so that we could judge a wide range of outcomes. And this is exactly what we got: everything from flat, greasy rounds of dough to high-rise cakey rings. After a fair amount of discussion, we agreed that the ideal doughnut would be crispy on the outside and tender on the inside, which meant we would steer clear of recipes that were extra crunchy and therefore extra greasy. (Although many factors affect greasiness in fried foods, we discovered that the deeper the oil penetrated into the doughnut, the crispier the exterior. In general, the wetter doughs allowed more oil penetration and were therefore all-crunch.) Our final recipe, therefore, needed to give us a doughnut with good crunch and a minimum of grease, a true country doughnut, rather than an airy Dunkin' Donuts confection.

As a starting point, we cobbled together a master recipe using buttermilk, eggs, flour, sugar, baking powder, baking soda, melted butter, salt, and grated nutmeg. We made up a batch of dough and fried it in generic vegetable oil. The resulting doughnuts were good but needed improvement.

So we set out to test each ingredient, starting with the buttermilk.

As is often the case with baking, buttermilk proved superior to regular milk; the doughnuts made with milk were denser, firmer, and less crisp.

Our master recipe used both baking powder and baking soda for lift, so in an attempt to simplify things, we left out the baking powder altogether and increased the baking soda to a full teaspoon. The doughnuts made with this formula were far too dense. We also tried decreasing the amounts of both leaveners but found that the master recipe had a slightly better chew.

Next we tried increasing the amount of butter in the recipe, but it did not improve the flavor. Likewise, bumping the sugar up ¼ cup (from 1 cup to 1¼ cups) simply made the doughnuts brown up more readily, which was not necessarily an improvement. Besides, they were sweet enough already. At first we thought we liked the addition of vanilla, but after a few tastings it became clear that this extra flavor overpowered the delicate taste of nutmeg, our spice of choice. When bread flour was substituted for all-purpose, the dough was firmer and drier; this resulted in a doughnut that was less crisp on the outside, not what we were looking for. Bleached flour made no noticeable difference.

So far none of our testing had yielded improvements in the master recipe, but we had some luck when we added one extra egg yolk. This made a moister dough, and the extra fat also created a more tender doughnut. Additionally, we tried boosting the flour by ¼ cup and determined that this drier dough does make a less crispy, but also less greasy, product. It is also a bit firmer and more chewy inside, but the lack of crackle on the outside placed this variation in second place.

With the recipe set, we were ready to begin our most important set of tests, involving the frying oil. First, though, we had to settle on the proper pot for frying. We found the best implement by far to be a cast-iron kettle; it retains heat extremely well, so the oil stays at the right temperature even when the doughnuts go in. This is crucial in getting nongreasy doughnuts. We found that the 12-inch-diameter model was superior to the 10-inch because it maintains a nice, steady heat, keeping the oil at the proper temperature without our having to adjust the burner. We also tested anodized aluminum pots, but they were a disappointment because they really do not retain heat well. An enameled cast-iron pan works fine but is much more expensive, retailing for about $130 versus $45 or so for a simple cast-iron kettle.

The first fats we tried were soybean oil, corn oil, and canola oil, all of which were given mediocre grades by the tasters. However, we went on to test peanut oil and safflower oil, both of which were well liked. We then did a head-to-head taste-off

DOUGHNUT TIPS

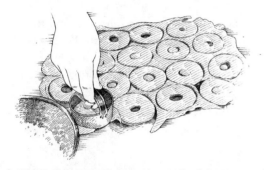

1. When rolling out the dough, make sure that it is no more or less than ½ inch thick, about the width of the last joint of your little finger. Thinner doughs make doughnuts that are squat, with insufficient height to provide contrast between the exterior and interior. Dough that is rolled out to ⅝ inch or more will produce a bloated orb that is undercooked inside because of its excessive corpulence. Roll the dough out on a heavily floured surface, then stamp out rounds as close together as possible. Gather the scraps, press into a disk, and repeat rolling and stamping.

2. As the doughnuts rise to the surface of the hot oil, flip them over with a Chinese skimmer, slotted spoon, or tongs.

between the two favorites, and peanut oil came in first, producing doughnuts with a rich flavor as well as a good texture.

The doughnuts were still on the greasy side, though, so we tried Crisco, a hydrogenated vegetable oil. To our surprise, these doughnuts were very good, absorbing much less oil than ones cooked in the peanut oil, our previous favorite. We also found that doughnuts fried in the vegetable shortening held up better than those fried in oil.

In the past we have found that a combination of lard and oil works very well for most fried foods. But lard has changed over the years. In the old days, the lard used in cooking was "leaf" lard, the fat around a pig's kidneys. This superior lard has no strong flavor. Today, lard consists simply of pork fat, which may come from any portion of a pig. Generally speaking, it is much stronger and of lower quality than the lard of yesteryear.

Even knowing this, though, we pressed on with our tests. We started off by using all lard, but it was much too meaty-tasting. We then cut back and used 5 ounces of lard with 5 cups of Crisco. This was good, very similar to what we were seeking, but little different from doughnuts fried in Crisco alone. We then increased the lard to 2 ounces per cup of shortening. This resulted in a nice boost of flavor. However, because many people want to avoid lard for health reasons and because doughnuts made without lard are very satisfactory, this is purely an optional ingredient.

In terms of cooking temperature, we found that with the oil at 350 degrees the dough absorbs too much oil, while at 385 degrees the outside starts to burn before the inside can cook through. A temperature of 360 seemed the ideal. We discovered, though, that it works best to start out with the oil at 375 degrees because the temperature will fall back to between 360 and 365 as soon as the doughnuts are put in. Also, be sure to bring the shortening back up to temperature between batches.

We also wanted to find out if the shortening was reusable. Although we had been successful when reusing peanut oil, Crisco just didn't hold well; a batch of doughnuts made the next day using the same shortening suffered a good deal in terms of flavor.

Many recipes call for cooking doughnuts for 1½

minutes per side, a time that we found to be much too long. Once the doughnuts had been placed in the hot shortening and flipped, we tested 40 seconds, 50 seconds, 60 seconds, and 70 seconds and found that 50 seconds was ideal. The center was just cooked, and the doughnut did not take on that dry, catch-in-your-throat texture. The big surprise, however, was that doughnuts cooked longer were also greasier. The shorter the frying time, the less chance the shortening had to penetrate the dough.

Buttermilk Doughnuts

MAKES 15 TO 17

For a bit more flavor, add 2 ounces of lard to every cup of shortening. You can also add ¼ cup of flour to the recipe for a chewier doughnut with a less crisp exterior. Regardless, these doughnuts are best eaten very warm, as soon out of the pot as possible. The dough can be made by hand, using a large bowl with a wooden spoon, or in a mixer as directed.

3½	cups (17½ ounces) unbleached all-purpose flour, plus extra for work surfaces
1	cup (7 ounces) sugar
½	teaspoon baking soda
2	teaspoons baking powder
1	teaspoon salt
1½	teaspoons freshly grated nutmeg
¾	cup buttermilk
4	tablespoons (½ stick) unsalted butter, melted
2	large eggs, plus 1 yolk
6	cups (40 ounces) vegetable shortening for frying

1. Mix 1 cup of the flour, the sugar, baking soda, baking powder, salt, and nutmeg in the bowl of a standing mixer fitted with the paddle attachment.

2. Mix the buttermilk, butter, and eggs including the yolk in a 2-cup liquid measuring cup. Add the wet ingredients to the dry; beat on medium speed until smooth, about 30 seconds. Decrease the speed to low, add the remaining 2½ cups flour, and mix until just combined, about 30 seconds. Stir the batter once or twice with a wooden spoon or

rubber spatula to ensure that all the liquid is incorporated. (The dough will be moist and tacky, like a cross between cake batter and cookie dough.)

3. Fit a candy thermometer to the side of a cast-iron kettle or large, heavy-bottomed Dutch oven; gradually heat the shortening over medium-high heat to 375 degrees. Meanwhile, turn the dough onto a floured work surface. Roll with a heavily floured rolling pin to ½-inch thick. Following the illustration on page 67, stamp out the dough rings with a heavily floured doughnut cutter, reflouring between cuts. Transfer the dough rounds to a baking sheet or large wire rack. Gather the scraps and gently press them into a disk; repeat the rolling and stamping process until all the dough is used. (Cut doughnuts can be covered with plastic wrap and stored at room temperature up to 2 hours.)

4. Carefully drop the dough rings into the hot fat 4 or 5 at a time, depending on the kettle size. As they rise to the surface, turn the doughnuts with tongs, a Chinese skimmer, or a slotted spoon. Fry the doughnuts until golden brown, about 50 seconds per side. Drain on a paper towel–lined baking sheet or wire rack. Repeat frying, returning the fat to temperature between batches.

➤ VARIATIONS

Powdered Sugar Buttermilk Doughnuts

Regular confectioners' sugar breaks down into a gummy glaze on the doughnuts, but Snow White Non-Melting Sugar makes a long-lasting coating. Snow White Non-Melting Sugar can be ordered through The Baker's Catalogue (P.O. Box 876, Norwich, Vermont 05055; 800-827-6836; www.kingarthurflour.com).

Follow the recipe for Buttermilk Doughnuts, tossing doughnuts in nonmelting sugar to coat (about 1 cup) after cooling for 1 minute.

Cinnamon-Sugared Buttermilk Doughnuts

Follow the recipe for Buttermilk Doughnuts. Mix 1 cup sugar with 1½ tablespoons ground cinnamon in a small bowl. Cool the doughnuts about 1 minute and toss with cinnamon sugar to coat.

2

YEAST BREADS AND ROLLS

Yeast Breads and Rolls

WHY MAKE BREAD AT HOME? THERE ARE many reasons. Depending on where you live, it's not always easy to find good bread at your local bakery. And, if you like to bake, it is a uniquely challenging and therefore uniquely satisfying experience. This chapter covers American favorites such as sandwich bread, bagels, and yeasted doughnuts along with European classics like French baguettes, Italian ciabatta, and yeasted coffeecakes. Although ingredients vary among these recipes, there are two constants. All of these favorite baked goods are made with yeast, and all the doughs must be kneaded.

INGREDIENTS Starting with the correct ingredients is part of the puzzle when making good breads, because essentially, bread contains no more than water, yeast, flour, and salt, so each ingredient counts.

WATER Our rule in the test kitchen is, if you don't drink your tap water, you do not want to use it in your bread, especially if your tap water has an "off" flavor. Don't get us wrong, we are not suggesting that you seek out fancy bottled waters—any good-quality bottled spring water or filtered tap water will work fine. Of course, if your tap water tastes fine, use it in bread recipes.

YEAST Several kinds of yeast are available to home cooks. We prefer instant yeast because it is reliable and works quickly, and we call for it in our recipes. Instant yeast (sometimes labeled as "rapid-rise" yeast) is usually sold in packages of three envelopes. Each envelope contains about 2¼ teaspoons of yeast. For more about yeast, see page 7.

FLOUR Most of our recipes call for unbleached all-purpose flour and some recipes call for bread flour. Do not substitute one for the other or your results will be unsatisfactory. To read more about flour, see page 1.

SALT Salt lends flavor to bread. Don't omit this ingredient, even from sweet breads—salt-free breads generally don't taste right. We use table salt

in the test kitchen, because it dissolves evenly and is easy to measure.

TECHNIQUE Proper technique is equally important. Our experience in the test kitchen has revealed the importance of several issues.

MEASURING The ratio of flour to water is key in bread recipes and if you have too little or too much of either ingredient, the loaf will suffer or perhaps fail altogether. For this reason, we recommend weighing flour, especially when baking bread. When measuring water, use a glass or plastic liquid measuring cup with a pour spout (not a dry measure) and make sure to place the cup on a flat surface and bend down so the water level is at eye level.

KNEADING Most bread doughs do not require lengthy kneading. In fact, we have found that kneading bread for 10 to 15 minutes can often produce an inferior loaf because the action of the electric mixer beats air throughout the dough, eventually stripping it of valuable flavor, color, and aroma. Often, simply kneading for a few minutes in a standing electric mixer or a few seconds in a food processor, coupled with a minute or two on a floured surface to bring the dough together in a ball, will suffice.

If you are kneading by hand, resist the temptation to add too much flour to the dough or you risk a dry texture. (This temptation is one reason why we prefer to knead bread dough in a standing mixer or food processor when possible.) In many recipes, the dough will at first seem very sticky, as if it needs more flour. However, as it rises, the dough hydrates—that is, the water becomes more evenly distributed as the flour absorbs it—and the texture becomes very soft and smooth. So do not add more flour unless the dough seems much too wet. One way to avoid adding more flour is to slightly moisten your hands to prevent sticking.

RISING On rare occasions, you may find that a loaf does not rise properly. Check to make sure that the expiration date on your yeast has not passed. Another possibility is that the water was too hot and killed the yeast. Water at about 110 degrees is a safe bet. A poor rise may also mean that you have added too much flour or placed the bread in a cool, drafty spot. To remedy the latter situation, heat your oven for 10 minutes at 200 degrees and turn it off; the oven can now be used as a proofing box—an enclosed draft-free space conducive to rising bread. A microwave oven can also be used as a proofing box. All that's involved is to nearly fill a 2-cup liquid measuring cup with water, place it in the microwave, and bring the water to a boil, then place the dough (which should be in a bowl covered with plastic wrap) in the microwave oven with the measuring cup. The preheated water will keep the microwave oven at the proper temperature for rising.

ACHIEVING A CRISP CRUST Many bread bakers add moisture to the oven as loaves bake to promote crispness in the crust. There are several ways to add moisture, including spraying the loaf with water, throwing water or ice cubes directly onto the floor of the oven during baking, or placing a roasting pan with hot water on a separate rack in the oven. We prefer the last method because it supplies a steady (and sizable) amount of moisture during the entire baking time. After blowing out the lights in several of the test kitchen ovens, we don't recommend throwing water or ice cubes into a hot oven. Spraying loaves with water before they go into the oven is safe but is not terribly effective with all types of bread.

TESTING FOR DONENESS It should also be noted that the length of time the bread is in the oven has a tremendous effect on its texture and quality. Most cookbooks tell you to tap the bottom of a loaf of bread to see if it is done. (Supposedly, a loaf will sound hollow when done.) This is, at best, an inexact method. We find it is much better to use an instant-read thermometer. For bread baked in a loaf pan, insert the thermometer into one end of the loaf, angling it down toward the middle. This method produces the same reading as poking through the bottom of the loaf without having to remove the bread from the pan. Note that different types of bread should be baked to different internal temperatures. Cooling bread before slicing is equally important. Bread sliced before it has cooled will be gummy.

STORAGE Most breads, unless otherwise specified, will go stale in a day or two. There is however an option for longer storage. In the test kitchen, we have had great success with freezing most of our breads. Wrapped first in aluminum foil and then in a large, plastic zipper-lock bag, the bread will keep for several months. When you're ready to eat the bread, just remove it from the freezer, slip the foil-wrapped bread out of the zipper-lock bag, and place it on the center rack of a 450-degree oven for 10 to 15 minutes, depending on the size of the loaf. After the allotted time, carefully remove the foil (watch out for steam) and return the loaf to the oven for a few minutes to give the crust a chance to crisp.

Most bread recipes don't require much in the way of equipment. As mentioned, we recommend kneading dough in a standing mixer or food processor and we think that an instant-read thermometer is the best way to judge the temperature of the water as well as doneness. You will want sturdy loaf pans for some recipes (see page 11 for our recommendations) as well as a baker's peel and a baking stone for free-form breads (see page 156 for more information on these items).

AMERICAN SANDWICH BREAD

AMERICAN LOAF BREADS ARE QUITE DIFFERENT from their European cousins, primarily because they contain fat in the form of milk and melted butter, as well as a touch of sweetener. This produces softer, more tender-crumbed loaves that are particularly well-suited to sandwiches. These home-style sandwich loaves are baked in metal loaf pans, and their crusts are thin. As we discovered during the testing process, this is not just an exercise in convenience. American sandwich bread is every bit as inspiring as those toothier imports. There is nothing like a fresh-from-the-oven loaf cut into slabs and slathered with butter and honey.

These days, many home cooks might choose to use a bread machine to make this type of bread. In our experience, bread machines produce a crust that is mediocre at best and an interior of unpredictable quality that is all too often cake-like. As for purchasing good American sandwich bread, it's actually not that easy. Most bakeries don't carry a basic sandwich bread. Of course, many people who might enjoy making terrific sandwich bread at home don't even try it because they think it takes most of a day. We set out to develop a good, solid recipe that could be done in two hours, start to finish, including baking time.

For many home cooks, the other great impediment to making bread at home is the notion of kneading by hand. To find out if this was essential, we used a standard American loaf bread recipe and tested hand-kneaded bread against bread kneaded by machine—both in a standing mixer and a food processor—to find out if hand kneading makes better bread. The results were eye-opening. The hand-kneaded loaf was not as good as the two loaves kneaded by machine. It was denser and did not rise as well, and the flavor lacked the pleasant yeastiness found in the other loaves. After some additional testing and discussion, we hit on a reasonable explanation: When kneading by hand, most home cooks cannot resist adding too much flour, because bread dough is notoriously sticky. In a machine, however, you need no additional flour, and the resulting bread has the correct proportion of liquid to flour.

Now that we knew that kneading this kind of bread by machine was actually preferable to doing it by hand, we set out to refine the techniques. We wanted to include separate recipes for a standing mixer and a food processor, given that many home kitchens have one or the other, but not both.

Starting with the standing mixer, we tested the dough hook versus the paddle attachment. (Some recipes use the paddle for part or all of the kneading process.) The hook turned out to be vastly preferable, as dough quickly got caught in the paddle, requiring frequent starting and stopping to free it. We also found that a medium-speed setting is better than a slow setting. Although the hook appears to move at an alarming rate, the resulting centrifugal force throws the dough off the hook, resulting in a more thorough kneading. At slower speeds, the dough has a tendency to cling to the hook like a child on a tire swing.

Next we turned to the food processor. This method, to our surprise, was very successful, although the dough did require about four minutes of hand kneading at the finish. (A food processor does not knead as thoroughly as a standing mixer.) Using a metal blade, we pulsed the dry ingredients to combine them. Then, with the machine running, we added the liquid ingredients through the feed tube and processed the dough until it formed a rough ball. After a rest of two minutes, we processed the dough a second time, for about 30 seconds, and then removed it to a lightly floured counter to knead it by hand. We also tested the recipe without

SCIENCE: Yeast and Gluten

Yeast is a microorganism that is maintained in pure culture. Under proper conditions in liquid, it can multiply continuously until the growth medium is exhausted. Yeast in liquid medium is sold by the tanker-full to commercial food manufacturers. For bakeries, yeast companies remove some of the moisture to create a product called crumbled yeast, which is sold in 50-pound bags. The next processing step extrudes the yeast to make a product that remains fully hydrated yet is fine enough to press into the small cakes you see for sale in supermarkets, labeled cake yeast. Further drying yields dried, powdered yeast, called active dry yeast. The same process is used to make other dry yeasts, including instant yeast, although this product starts with a different strain of yeast. (For more information on instant yeast, see page 7.)

Although yeast does provide the gas (in the form of carbon dioxide) that gives bread lift, it needs long sheets of gluten to trap the gas. What exactly is gluten? When water is mixed with wheat flour, proteins, most importantly the proteins glutenin and gliadin, bind to each other and to the water and become pliable. Gluten is the name given to this combination of proteins. Kneading stretches the gluten into elastic sheets that trap and hold the gases produced by the yeast, which allows the bread to rise.

any hand kneading and found the resulting bread inferior—coarser in texture, with less rise.

We noted that the action of the food processor was quite different from that of the standing mixer. A relatively dry dough had worked well in the mixer because it was less likely to stick to the dough hook. However, in the food processor a slightly wetter dough seemed preferable, as the metal blade stretched and pulled it better than a dry dough, which ended up simply being cut into pieces. Therefore, to improve the performance of the food processor, we added 2 tablespoons of water to the dough.

With our dough and kneading methods set, we turned to oven temperatures and baking times. When we baked our bread at oven temperatures of 350, 375, and 400 degrees, the two higher temperatures overcooked the crust by the time the inside of the loaf was done. Again, unlike most European breads, this American loaf is prone to quick browning because it contains milk, butter, and honey.

To determine the proper baking time, you have to figure out how to decide when your bread is done. After testing bread taken from the oven at internal temperatures of 190, 195, and 200 degrees, the loaf producing a reading of 195 degrees was clearly the winner. The lower temperature produced dense bread, and the higher temperature produced dry, overcooked bread.

As stated above, one of our objectives in developing this recipe was to produce bread as quickly as possible. Therefore we chose instant yeast. Not only did the instant yeast greatly reduce rising times, but, in a blind tasting, the bread tasted better than loaves made with regular active dry yeast.

To further speed the rising process, we preheated the oven to 200 degrees for 10 minutes, turned it off, then used it as our proofing box, allowing the dough to rise in a very warm, draft-free environment. Next we tried heating the milk and water to jump-start the yeast. When the liquids were too hot, well above 130 degrees, we had some failures because the yeast was killed by the excessive heat. We did find, however, that when we warmed the liquids to about 110 degrees, the rising times were reduced by 5 to 10 minutes. These three changes brought the first rise down to 40 minutes and the

second rise to a mere 20. Now we could make homemade bread in two hours, including kneading, both risings, and the baking time, which for this bread took no more than 40 minutes.

American Sandwich Bread
MAKES ONE 9-INCH LOAF

This recipe uses a standing electric mixer; a variation on page 75 gives instructions for using a food processor. You can hand-knead the dough, but we found it's easy to add too much flour during this stage, resulting in a somewhat tougher loaf. To promote a crisp crust, we found it best to place a loaf pan filled with boiling water in the oven as the bread bakes.

3¾	cups (18¾ ounces) unbleached all-purpose flour, plus more for dusting the work surface
2	teaspoons salt
1	cup warm whole milk (about 110 degrees)
⅓	cup warm water (about 110 degrees)
2	tablespoons unsalted butter, melted
3	tablespoons honey
1	envelope (about 2¼ teaspoons) instant yeast

1. Adjust an oven rack to the lowest position and heat the oven to 200 degrees. Once the oven temperature reaches 200 degrees, maintain the heat for 10 minutes, then turn off the oven.

2. Mix 3½ cups of the flour and the salt in the bowl of a standing mixer fitted with the dough hook. Mix the milk, water, butter, honey, and yeast in a 4-cup liquid measuring cup. Turn the machine to low and slowly add the liquid. When the dough comes together, increase the speed to medium and mix until the dough is smooth and satiny, stopping the machine two or three times to scrape dough from the hook, if necessary, about 10 minutes. (After 5 minutes of kneading, if the dough is still sticking to the sides of the bowl, add flour, 1 tablespoon at a time and up to ¼ cup total, until the dough is no longer sticky.) Turn the dough onto a lightly floured work surface; knead to form a smooth, round ball, about 15 seconds.

3. Place the dough in a very lightly oiled large bowl, rubbing the dough around the bowl to coat lightly. Cover the bowl with plastic wrap and place

in the warmed oven until the dough doubles in size, 40 to 50 minutes.

4. Gently press the dough into a rectangle 1 inch thick and no longer than 9 inches. With a long side facing you, roll the dough firmly into a cylinder, pressing with your fingers to make sure the dough sticks to itself. Turn the dough seam-side up and pinch it closed. Place the dough seam-side down in a greased 9 by 5-inch loaf pan and press it gently so it touches all four sides of the pan. Cover with plastic wrap; set aside in a warm spot until the dough almost doubles in size, 20 to 30 minutes.

5. Keep one oven rack at the lowest position and place the other at the middle position and heat the oven to 350 degrees. Place an empty baking pan on the bottom rack. Bring 2 cups of water to a boil in a small saucepan. Pour the boiling water into the empty pan on the bottom rack and set the loaf onto the middle rack. Bake until an instant-read thermometer inserted at an angle from the short end just above the pan rim into the center of the loaf reads 195 degrees, 40 to 50 minutes. Remove the bread from the pan, transfer to a wire rack, and cool to room temperature. Slice and serve.

➤ VARIATIONS

Sandwich Bread Kneaded in a Food Processor

Add an extra 2 tablespoons of water so the food processor blade can knead the dough more effectively. During the hand-kneading phase, you may need to add a little flour to make a workable dough. To ensure a tender bread, however, add as little as possible.

Follow the recipe for American Sandwich Bread, increasing the warm water by 2 tablespoons. Mix the flour and salt in a food processor. Add the liquid ingredients; process until a rough ball forms. Let the dough rest 2 minutes. Process 35 seconds. Turn the dough onto a lightly floured work surface and knead by hand until the dough is smooth and satiny, 4 to 5 minutes. Proceed as directed.

Slow-Rise Sandwich Bread

If you do not have instant yeast on hand, try this slow-rise variation.

Follow the recipe for American Sandwich Bread, substituting an equal amount of active dry yeast for the instant yeast. Let the dough rise at room temperature, instead of in the warm oven, until almost doubled (about 2 hours for the first rise and 45 to 60 minutes for the second rise).

Buttermilk Sandwich Bread

Buttermilk gives the bread a slight tang.

Follow the recipe for American Sandwich Bread, bringing the water to a boil rather than to 110 degrees. Substitute cold buttermilk for the warm milk, adding it to the hot water. (The mixing of hot water and cold buttermilk should bring the liquid to the right temperature, about 110 degrees, for adding the yeast.) Increase the first rise to 50 to 60 minutes.

Oatmeal Sandwich Bread

To turn this loaf into oatmeal-raisin bread, simply knead ¾ cup raisins, tossed with 1 tablespoon flour, into the dough after it comes out of the food processor or mixer.

Bring ¾ cup water to a boil in a small saucepan. Add ¾ cup (2¼ ounces) old-fashioned rolled oats; cook to soften slightly, about 90 seconds. Follow the recipe for American Sandwich Bread, decreasing the flour from 3½ cups to 2¾ cups, adding the cooked oatmeal to the flour, and omitting the warm water from the wet ingredients.

TAKING THE TEMPERATURE OF LOAF PAN BREAD

Internal temperature is a good way to gauge whether or not a loaf of bread is done. Don't be tempted to pierce the top crust in the center, which will leave a conspicuous hole. Insert the thermometer from the side, just above the edge of the loaf pan, directing it at a downward angle toward the center of the loaf.

ANADAMA BREAD

ANADAMA IS AN ECCENTRIC NAME FOR what amounts to sandwich bread enriched with cornmeal and molasses. Most sources attribute the unique name to an ornery New England farmer "damning" his wife "Anna" for the unwavering diet of cornmeal mush she provided for him. Whatever the case, anadama bread has deep roots in rustic New England cookery. As we found, however, this bread can suffer from a variety of ills, including gritty texture, denseness, and saccharine sweetness. We hoped to overcome these problems and make a great loaf, ideal for toasting and sandwiches.

Because anadama is similar to a basic loaf bread, we started off by trying to manipulate our sandwich loaf into anadama bread. We quickly learned that we would have to make some major adjustments. Incorporating the cornmeal into the dough was the first step. Adding raw cornmeal to the dough resulted in gritty bread without much corn flavor. Soaking the cornmeal in the lukewarm milk and water also produced a gritty loaf. We realized that the cornmeal had to be cooked to soften it, but what was the best method? The amount of water in our sandwich bread recipe (⅓ cup) was too little; the cornmeal solidified into a thick paste punctuated with lumps that remained hard in the dough. Simmering the cornmeal in the milk in our sandwich bread recipe (1 cup) worked much better. After a mere minute of cooking, the cornmeal softened and developed the texture of soft polenta. We decided to melt the butter in the milk to save a step.

We tried various methods to mix the dough. Adding everything together—flour, water, yeast, molasses, and cornmeal mush—yielded unevenly combined dough flecked with lumps of cornmeal mush. The mush had to be combined with the flour prior to adding the other ingredients for the best integration. As little as a minute of mixing adequately blended the cornmeal mush and flour. With the cornmeal mush incorporated, the water, yeast, and molasses were easily added to form a uniform dough.

We found that it was tricky gauging when and if the dough needed more flour during kneading.

The molasses made the dough quite sticky, and it looked as if it needed more flour, but when we felt the dough, it rarely needed any flour. Feeling the dough is the best way to tell; if you can touch the dough without it tenaciously sticking to your hands, the dough probably does not need any more flour. When it did stick, we added flour a tablespoon at a time until it reached the right texture. Occasionally scraping the dough off the dough hook and the sides of the workbowl during kneading helped as well. After 10 minutes of machine kneading and a quick turn by hand, the dough was smooth, shiny, and elastic.

Because this dough is sticky, we had trouble kneading it by hand or in a food processor. When we tried to knead it by hand, the dough stuck to our hands and the counter unless we added more flour, which made the finished loaf tough. As for the food processor, the dough stuck to the blade and could not be properly kneaded. The larger bowl of a standing mixer and the dough hook are the best tools for kneading this dough.

Unfortunately, we found that this dough rose quite a bit more slowly than the dough in our sandwich bread recipe. Even in a warmed oven, it took a full hour and a half to double in bulk. We figured that the heavy cornmeal and molasses weighed down the dough. Adding more yeast

JUDGING WHEN DOUGH HAS ENOUGH FLOUR

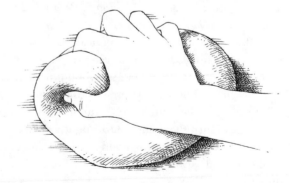

Many bakers add too much flour to bread dough, which results in dry loaves. To gauge whether your dough has enough flour, squeeze the dough gently with your entire hand. Even with especially soft, sticky doughs, your hand will pull away cleanly once the dough has enough flour.

made the dough rise faster, but the flavor was adversely affected. After shaping, the dough took another hour and a half to double in bulk—a small inconvenience but well worth it for the flavor.

We baked the risen loaf according to the sandwich bread recipe, with a pan of water underneath. In a slight alteration, we brushed the top of the loaf with butter and sprinkled a little cornmeal across it to emphasize the nutty corn flavor. The resulting loaf was everything we hoped for: an appealing dark and chewy crust yielding to a moist and dense crumb.

Anadama Bread

MAKES ONE 9-INCH LOAF

We think it is worth searching out high-quality, stone-ground cornmeal for this hearty bread; the deep corn flavor is well worth the effort. If you cannot find stone-ground cornmeal, use the coarsest meal you can find. We were pleased with Goya coarse cornmeal, which is readily available in most markets, often in the Latin foods section. (See page 2 for more information on cornmeal.) We liked Grandma's robust molasses in this recipe, but any dark molasses will do the job. Just stay away from blackstrap; its dark, bitter flavor is overpowering. (See page 4 for information on molasses.)

1	cup whole milk
4	tablespoons (1/2 stick) unsalted butter
1/2	cup (2 3/4 ounces) plus 2 teaspoons stone-ground cornmeal
3–3 1/4	cups (15 to 16 1/4 ounces) unbleached all-purpose flour, plus more for dusting the work surface
2	teaspoons salt
1/3	cup warm water (about 110 degrees)
1	envelope (about 2 1/4 teaspoons) instant yeast
5	tablespoons dark molasses (not blackstrap)

1. Adjust an oven rack to the lowest position and heat the oven to 200 degrees. Once the oven reaches 200 degrees, maintain the heat for 10 minutes, then turn off the heat.

2. Combine the milk and 2 tablespoons of the butter in a small saucepan and bring almost to a simmer over medium heat. Whisk in 1/2 cup of the cornmeal and continue to stir for 1 minute.

Transfer the mixture to a small bowl and cool until lukewarm (about 100 degrees).

3. Mix 3 cups of the flour and the salt in the bowl of a standing mixer fitted with the dough hook. Mix the water, yeast, and molasses in a liquid measuring cup. Briefly mix together the flour and salt at low speed, then add the cornmeal mush, mixing at low speed until roughly incorporated, about 1 minute. Still at low speed, gradually add the liquid, and once the dough comes together, increase the speed to medium and knead until the dough is smooth and satiny, stopping the machine two or three times to scrape the dough from the hook and the sides of the bowl if necessary, about 10 minutes. (After 5 minutes of kneading, if the dough is still sticking to the sides of the bowl, add the remaining flour, 1 tablespoon at a time and up to 1/4 cup total, until the dough is no longer sticky.) Turn the dough out onto a lightly floured work surface and knead to form a smooth, round ball, 15 to 30 seconds.

4. Place the dough in a very lightly oiled large bowl, rubbing the dough around the bowl to coat lightly with the oil. Cover the bowl with plastic wrap and place in the warmed oven until the dough doubles in size, about 1 1/2 hours.

5. Gently press the dough into a rectangle 1 inch thick and no longer than 9 inches. With a long side facing you, roll the dough firmly into a cylinder, pressing with your fingers to make sure the dough sticks to itself. Place the dough seam-side down in a greased 9 by 5-inch loaf pan and press gently so it touches all four sides of the pan. Loosely cover with plastic wrap and set aside in a warm place until the dough almost doubles in size, about 1 1/2 hours.

6. Keep one oven rack at the lowest position and place the other at the middle position and heat the oven to 350 degrees. Place an empty loaf pan on the bottom rack. Bring 2 cups of water to a boil in a small saucepan.

7. Melt the remaining 2 tablespoons butter in a small saucepan. Remove the plastic wrap from the loaf and carefully brush the top with the melted butter and evenly sprinkle the remaining 2 teaspoons cornmeal across the top. Pour the boiling water into the empty loaf pan in the oven

and set the loaf onto the middle rack. Bake until an instant-read thermometer inserted at an angle from the short end just above the pan rim into the center of the loaf reads 195 degrees, 40 to 45 minutes. Remove the bread from the pan, transfer to a wire rack, and cool to room temperature. Slice and serve.

CINNAMON SWIRL BREAD

MUCH TOO OFTEN, THE BEST PART OF cinnamon swirl bread is the heavenly aroma emanating from the oven. Once the loaf is removed from the oven, there are unsightly gaps between the swirls of cinnamon filling and bread, and the filling has leaked out and burned in the pan.

We wanted to solve these problems when developing our recipe. We also wanted the baked texture to be moist and light, yet firm enough to be sliced fresh the first day and toasted for a few days after. To achieve the best texture and crust, we knew we needed to perfect the baking time and temperature as well as fine-tune the ingredients.

To get our bearings, we tried a range of yeast bread recipes, from rich brioche-type formulas with a high proportion of eggs, butter, and sugar to recipes for lean, white sandwich-style bread. When these first breads were tasted, everyone was drawn to the richer versions, as expected. However, for a more versatile bread that could be cut into thin or thick slices and toasted, we decided on a formula that was a compromise between the two.

We began our tests by focusing on milk, eggs, and sugar—the ingredients that most affect richness and texture. We tested loaves using all milk, all water, and a combination. Milk yielded a denser texture than we wanted; water had the opposite effect, producing a loaf that was too lean. An equal combination of milk and water was the answer. To lighten the texture a little bit more, we increased the eggs in our original recipe to two. Eggs contribute to the evenness of the crumb as well as to color and flavor, but using more than two produced a crumb that was too light and airy for this type of bread.

Our final measurements of sugar and butter resulted in a crumb that was tender and soft the first day and retained some moisture for two to three days. We found that ⅓ cup sugar per loaf was enough to add flavor to the bread without competing with the filling. As for the butter, since it also contributes color and richness, we knew that to some extent the amount was a personal preference. For the everyday loaf we were after, we tested from 2 to 8 tablespoons per loaf and settled on 4; using more than that resulted in a loaf that was fattier than we wanted.

We had no problem settling on unbleached all-purpose flour in our recipe, but as with many breads, we did face challenges in determining the total amount used. Depending on a number of factors, including the humidity of the air, the exact size of the eggs, and how precisely the liquids are measured, the dough will take anywhere from 3¼ to 3¾ cups of flour. Any of the doughs we made could have taken the greater amount (or more), but when we used it, the resulting loaves were dry. We had the best results when we reserved the last half cup of flour to use only as necessary, adding it little by little at the end of kneading (either by hand or machine). To test the dough to determine if the flour level is correct, squeeze it using your entire hand (completely clean with no dough clinging to it) and release it. When the dough does not stick to your hand, the kneading is complete. Even if the dough still feels soft, resist the temptation to add more flour.

Now that we had perfected the dough, we were ready to tackle filling, rolling, and shaping the loaf. For the filling, we tried both brown and granulated sugar mixed with cinnamon. Although we like the taste of brown sugar, we finally had to rule it out because it melted readily and leaked through the dough in places during baking.

The amount of filling was determined by one factor besides taste. We discovered that using much more than ¼ cup of the cinnamon-sugar mixture resulted in small separations between the filling and the bread because the excess sugar prevented the dough from cohering. We eventually discovered that ¼ cup of sugar mixed with 5 teaspoons of cinnamon resulted in a tasty bread with no gaps.

Rolling and shaping the dough into a loaf are crucial steps. To create swirls in the finished bread and end up with a loaf that would fit into a 9-inch loaf pan, we rolled the dough out evenly into a rectangle 18 inches long and 8 inches wide. When we rolled the dough out longer than this, it was so thin that the filling popped through the edges in some places. Rolling the dough up evenly and closely was also important. When we rolled the dough too tightly, the filling popped through; rolling too loosely produced an uneven loaf and gaps between the swirls and the bread. Finally, we found that we could prevent the filling from leaking and burning in the pan while baking if we pinched the edges of the bottom seam and the ends of the roll together very tightly.

Getting the dough mixed, filled, and shaped still doesn't guarantee great bread. Rising time is also crucial. In fact, finding the proper rising time entirely solved the problem of gaps in the bread. When we allowed the shaped loaf to rise just to the top of the pan, the baked bread was dense and did not have a fully risen, attractive shape. But when we allowed the unbaked loaf to rise too much, 1½ inches or more above the pan, we ended up with those unwanted gaps between dough and filling. Our overrisen loaves also collapsed in the oven. Allowing the dough to rise just 1 inch above the top of a 9-inch loaf pan before baking resulted in a perfectly shaped loaf with no gaps.

To determine the best baking temperature, we first tested the bread in a slow oven (300 to 325 degrees). Because this allowed the unbaked loaf too long a time to continue to rise before the yeast died (at an internal temperature of 140 degrees), the bread rose too much and lost its shape. A hotter oven (375 to 425 degrees) resulted in a loaf that was too brown on the outside before it was baked through. Since our bread formula contained milk, eggs, and sugar, all browning agents, we found that a moderate oven (350 degrees) baked the most evenly.

We tested final internal temperatures between 180 and 210 degrees and found 185 to 190 to be the ideal range. Technically, bread is not finished baking until all the steam has evaporated and it has cooled completely on a rack, so resist the temptation to cut the bread while it's hot. The pressure of the knife will compress the loaf and you'll end up with a doughy slice.

Cinnamon Swirl Bread
MAKES ONE 9-INCH LOAF

If you like, you can make the dough one day, refrigerate it overnight, then shape it, allow it to rise, and bake it the next day. This recipe also doubles easily.

ENRICHED BREAD DOUGH
½ cup whole milk
4 tablespoons (½ stick) unsalted butter, cut into ½-inch pieces
1 envelope (about 2¼ teaspoons) instant yeast
½ cup warm water (about 110 degrees)
⅓ cup (2⅓ ounces) sugar
2 large eggs
1½ teaspoons salt
3¼–3¾ cups (16¼ to 18¾ ounces) unbleached all-purpose flour, plus more for dusting the work surface

FILLING
¼ cup (1¾ ounces) sugar
5 teaspoons ground cinnamon
Milk for brushing

GLAZE
1 large egg
2 teaspoons milk

1. FOR THE DOUGH: Heat the milk and butter in a small saucepan or in the microwave until the butter melts. Cool until warm (about 110 degrees).

2. Meanwhile, sprinkle the yeast over the warm water in the bowl of a standing mixer fitted with the paddle. Beat in the sugar and eggs and mix at low speed to blend. Add the salt, lukewarm milk mixture, and 2 cups of the flour; mix at medium speed until thoroughly blended, about 1 minute. Switch to the dough hook. Add 1¼ cups more flour and knead at medium-low speed, adding more flour sparingly if the dough sticks to the sides of the bowl, until the dough is smooth and comes away from the sides of the bowl, about 10 minutes.

3. Turn the dough onto a work surface. Squeeze the dough with a clean dry hand. If the dough is sticky, knead in up to ½ cup more flour to form a smooth, soft, elastic dough. Transfer the dough to a very lightly oiled large bowl. Cover the bowl with plastic wrap and let the dough rise until doubled in size, 2 to 2½ hours. (The ideal rising temperature for this bread is 75 degrees.) After the rise, punch down the center of the dough once. (The dough can be refrigerated, covered, up to 18 hours.) Making sure not to fold the dough, turn it onto an unfloured work surface; let the dough rest about 10 minutes.

4. FOR THE FILLING: Grease the bottom and sides of a 9 by 5-inch loaf pan. Mix the sugar and cinnamon in a small bowl.

5. Press the dough neatly into an evenly shaped 8 by 6-inch rectangle. With a short side of the dough facing you, roll the dough with a rolling pin into an evenly shaped 18 by 8-inch rectangle (flour the work surface lightly if the dough sticks). Brush the dough liberally with the milk. Sprinkle the filling evenly over the dough, leaving a ½-inch border on the far side. Starting at the side closest to you, roll up the dough, pinching the dough gently with your fingertips to make sure it is tightly sealed. To keep the loaf from stretching beyond 9 inches, push the ends in occasionally with your hands as you roll the dough. When you finish rolling, pinch the seam tightly to secure it. With the seam-side facing up, push in the center of both ends. Firmly pinch the dough at either end together to seal the sides of the loaf.

6. Place the loaf, seam-side down, into the prepared pan; press lightly to flatten. Cover the top of the pan loosely with plastic wrap and set aside to rise. Let rise until the dough is 1 inch above the top of the pan, about 1½ hours, or about 1 hour longer if the dough has been refrigerated. As the dough nears the top of the pan, adjust an oven rack to the center position and heat the oven to 350 degrees.

7. FOR THE GLAZE: Meanwhile, in a small bowl, whisk together the egg and milk. Gently brush the top of the loaf with the egg mixture.

8. Bake until the loaf is golden brown and an instant-read thermometer inserted at an angle from the short end just above the pan rim into the center of the loaf reads 185 to 190 degrees, 30 to 35 minutes. Remove the bread from the pan and cool on its side on a wire rack until room temperature, at least 45 minutes. (The bread can be double-wrapped in plastic wrap and stored at room temperature for 4 days or frozen up to 3 months.)

➤ VARIATION

Hand–Kneaded Cinnamon Swirl Bread
Follow the recipe for Cinnamon Swirl Bread, sprinkling the yeast over the water in a large bowl in step 2. Use a wooden spoon to incorporate the other ingredients as directed. When the dough comes together, turn it onto a lightly floured surface and knead until smooth and elastic, 12 to 15 minutes, adding more flour if necessary. Transfer the dough to a lightly oiled bowl and follow the rising instructions.

WHOLE–WHEAT BREAD

IF ASKED TO DESCRIBE THE PERFECT LOAF of distinctly American whole-wheat bread, you might say that it should be wheaty but not grainy, chewy but not tough, dense but not heavy, and full-flavored but not overpowering.

We decided to make a few loaves from various cookbooks just to explore the range of possibilities, starting with recipes from five of our favorite bread books. A recipe for an Italian walnut bread was terrific but clearly a rustic European loaf, not the distinctly American whole-wheat bread we were looking for. Other recipes were bitter, had odd flavors, or had too many other grains or flours to qualify as whole-wheat. Still others were too dense, too salty, or not sweet enough, an important element because a little sweetness enhances the rich flavor of the wheat flour.

We went back to the drawing board to create a master recipe that had the elements we liked best from each of the test breads. The recipe we started with contained 1 tablespoon of yeast, 2⅓ cups of warm water, 4 cups of whole-wheat flour, 1¼ cups of all-purpose flour, ¼ cup of rye flour (to add complexity of flavor), 1 teaspoon of salt, and 2 tablespoons of honey.

The initial results from this recipe were good, but not great. The bread was too dense, and it needed a boost of both salt and honey for flavor. So we made a new loaf in which we doubled the amount of both yeast and honey and punched up the salt to 2 teaspoons. The taste-test results were encouraging, and the loaf was even better when we tried making it again, using ½ tablespoon less yeast and adding ¼ cup of melted butter for flavor. But some problems remained. The texture was still too dense for our taste, and the flavor was a bit generic, reminiscent of what one might find at a diner served with two individually wrapped pats of butter.

Having already tested a higher amount of yeast, we suspected that the texture might be improved by using a drier dough, which tends to produce a lighter bread. We therefore increased the total amount of flour from 5½ cups to 6 cups. We then varied the proportion of whole-wheat flour to white to rye. The loaf with slightly more whole-wheat than white flour and with some rye flour was the best of the lot and actually quite good.

Now we were close, but the bread still lacked the proper texture and wheatiness we expected from a whole-wheat loaf. So we turned to one of our favorite bread books, *The Book of Bread* (HarperPerennial, 1982) by Evan and Judith Jones, and discovered that one of their whole-wheat bread recipes contained wheat germ. As it turned out, this simple addition—a mere ¼ cup of wheat germ—made a terrific difference in our loaf, producing a nutty flavor and slightly more complex texture. We liked it so much that we tried a loaf with ½ cup of wheat germ, which turned out to be the ideal amount.

Into our thirtieth loaf at this point, we decided to press on with the issue of sweeteners. We tend to use honey in bread doughs, but we also made loaves with a variety of other sweeteners, including ¼ cup of each of the following: granulated sugar, dark brown sugar, maple syrup, barley malt, and molasses. We also tested half quantities of malt and molasses paired with an equal amount of honey. Oddly, it was hard to differentiate the flavors added by the sweeteners. That said, though, the honey version was generally picked by our tasters as number one,

with a nice, clean, sweet flavor and moist texture.

We went on to try different fats. We sampled loaves made with vegetable oil (a noticeable lack of flavor), melted lard (a strong flavor but unwelcome in this recipe), melted butter (by far the best: good texture, sweet flavor), cold butter (denser, not as moist), and a whole egg (grainy, gritty texture—almost cottony).

Having found the dough recipe we wanted, we proceeded to test the variables of kneading, rising, and baking. One of the most interesting tests involved kneading times. Using a standing mixer, we kneaded for eight, 12, and 16 minutes, respectively, with no discernible difference in the finished loaves. Because whole-wheat flour contains so much protein, a reasonable amount of gluten is formed as long as the ingredients are quite thoroughly mixed together. With this recipe, it matters little whether the kneading is done by machine or by hand, for a short time or a long time.

Our final recipe calls for an initial rising of just under one hour (a relatively short rising time owing to the relatively high amount of yeast). We tested a shorter rising time of only 30 minutes, but the resulting loaf was dense and dry. For the second rise, after the dough has been shaped, we found that 20 to 30 minutes was best. When left to rise for longer than this, the dough baked up into a light loaf with a dry, cottony texture and a crust that had separated from the rest of the loaf.

Although we were confident about oven temperatures and baking times, we tested them to be sure. As we had expected, a 375-degree oven worked best. A 350-degree oven turned out doughy bread, while a 400-degree oven produced a loaf with a slightly burned bottom. To determine when a loaf is properly baked, we used an instant-read thermometer inserted from one end into the middle of the loaf (for a free-form loaf, simply insert the thermometer from the bottom to the middle of the loaf). An internal temperature of 205 degrees proved ideal; at lower temperatures the bread was underbaked.

It did occur to us that perhaps the brand of whole-wheat flour might make a difference. We had performed all of our tests to this point with King Arthur flour. So we tried Arrowhead Mills

Stone Ground Whole Wheat Flour. This flour produced a loaf with a nice wheat flavor, but it was lighter in both color and texture. Next we made a loaf using Hodgson Mill Whole Wheat Graham Flour, which produced a wonderful loaf with a terrific, nutty flavor. Graham flour is a bit coarser and perhaps flakier than regular whole-wheat flour and, as we noted in our testing, provides a nuttier flavor. It is named after its inventor, Sylvester Graham. Although the King Arthur was also very good, we felt that the Hodgson flour was best suited for this recipe.

Whole-Wheat Bread with Wheat Germ and Rye

MAKES TWO 9-INCH LOAVES

Because kneading this wet, sticky dough can cause damage to lower-horsepower mixers, it's best to use a heavy-duty standing mixer and be sure to use the low speed during kneading. Follow the instructions for hand kneading if you don't own a heavy-duty standing mixer. This recipe makes too much dough to knead in a food processor.

2⅓	cups warm water (about 110 degrees)
1½	tablespoons instant yeast
¼	cup honey
4	tablespoons (½ stick) unsalted butter, melted
2½	teaspoons salt
¼	cup (⅞ ounce) rye flour
½	cup toasted wheat germ
3	cups (16½ ounces) whole-wheat flour, preferably Hodgson Mill Whole Wheat Graham Flour
2¾	cups (13¾ ounces) unbleached all-purpose flour, plus more for dusting the work surface

1. In the bowl of a standing mixer, mix the water, yeast, honey, butter, and salt with a rubber spatula. Mix in the rye flour, wheat germ, and 1 cup each of the whole-wheat and all-purpose flours.

2. Add the remaining whole-wheat and all-purpose flours, attach the dough hook, and knead at low speed until the dough is smooth and elastic, about 8 minutes. Transfer the dough to a lightly floured work surface. Knead just long enough to make sure that the dough is soft and smooth, about 30 seconds.

3. Place the dough in a very lightly oiled large bowl; cover with plastic wrap. Let rise in a warm, draft-free area until the dough has doubled in volume, about 1 hour.

4. Heat the oven to 375 degrees. Gently press down the dough and divide into two equal pieces. Gently press each piece into a rectangle, about 1 inch thick and no longer than 9 inches. With a long side of the dough facing you, roll the dough firmly into a cylinder, pressing down to make sure that the dough sticks to itself. Turn the dough seam-side up and pinch it closed. Place each cylinder of dough in a greased 9 by 5-inch loaf pan, seam-side down and pressing the dough gently so it touches all four sides of the pan. Cover the shaped dough; let rise until almost doubled in volume, 20 to 30 minutes.

5. Bake until an instant-read thermometer inserted at an angle from the short end just above the pan rim reads 205 degrees, 35 to 45 minutes. Transfer the bread immediately from the baking pans to wire racks; cool to room temperature.

➤ VARIATION
Hand-Kneaded Whole-Wheat Bread
Follow the recipe for Whole-Wheat Bread with Wheat Germ and Rye, mixing the water, yeast,

NO-FUSS FLOURING

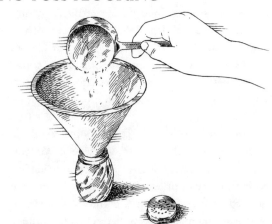

Hauling out a large container can be a nuisance when all you have to do is dust a cake pan or work surface with some flour. Instead, set a funnel in an empty glass salt shaker and scoop a little flour into the funnel. When the shaker has been filled, seal it and store it in the pantry. These small shakers are easy to reach and do an excellent job of lightly coating a surface with flour. Use this tip for confectioners' sugar as well.

honey, butter, salt, rye flour, and wheat germ in a large mixing bowl. Mix 2¾ cups of the whole-wheat flour and the all-purpose flour in a separate bowl, reserving ¼ cup of the whole-wheat flour. Add 4 cups of the flour mixture to the wet ingredients; beat with a wooden spoon 5 minutes. Beat in another 1½ cups of the flour mixture to make a thick dough. Turn the dough onto a work surface that has been sprinkled with some of the reserved flour. Knead, adding only as much of the remaining flour as necessary to form a soft, elastic dough, about 5 minutes. Continue with step 3.

Deli-Style Rye Bread

JEWISH RYE, A.K.A. NEW YORK RYE, IS ONE of our favorite breads: We love its tang and chew. Unfortunately, it's difficult to find good Jewish rye these days. The mass-produced varieties in supermarkets (and even the loaves at our local Jewish bakery in Boston) are too refined, fluffy, and soft, with only a hint of rye flavor. The rye bread we hanker for is slightly moist and chewy but not too dense. It has a tight, uneven crumb, a hard, thin, almost brittle crust, and a tangy rye flavor. Perhaps most important, the bread doesn't become soggy or limp when stacked with a pile of pastrami.

We discovered a myriad of rye bread recipes during our research; not just the Jewish varieties but Old World recipes containing buttermilk, sour cream, mashed potato, molasses, ginger, and even sauerkraut. Intriguing as these variations were, we stuck to the basics: rye and white flours, water, a sweetener, salt, fat, and caraway seeds. Working with these ingredients, we identified three variables that we thought would affect the texture and flavor of the bread: the method of leavening, the type of rye flour, and the ratio of rye to white flour.

We focused first on two basic methods for leavening the dough, both of which are practical for home cooks. The sponge method, which we use in our European loaves later in this chapter, involves first mixing a small amount of flour, water, and yeast, then leaving this sponge to ferment for a defined period of time. More flour and water

are then added to make the dough. In the second method, yeast and water are mixed and when the yeast dissolves, the mixture is added directly to make the dough.

Using a variety of cookbook rye bread recipes, we did side-by-side testing of the sponge and direct methods. We found the sponge method clearly preferable. Because the slow rise allows time for the creation of fermentation byproducts that add flavor, this method produced a bread with strong, tangy flavor and a chewy, pleasantly uneven texture. We also liked the way the bread made using the sponge method maintained its moistness during storage. The bread made with the direct method had a tighter web of holes and a more even crumb.

We also tested different sponge fermentation times, including a half hour, 2½ hours, and overnight. As we increased the fermentation time, the rise was faster, the bread baked higher, the crumb was more uneven, the bread was chewier, and the flavor was stronger. The sponge fermentation time can, therefore, be varied to taste, with 2½ hours being the minimum. We prefer an overnight sponge fermentation, and we find that the initial intense and slightly sour rye flavor improves with cooling and storage. However, we were looking for more chew and a sharper tang than even the longest fermentation time could give. In search of this, we turned to the choice and ratio of different flours.

We suspected that different rye flours might affect the texture and flavor of the rye bread. However, many rye bread recipes don't specify the type of rye flour to use. Up to this point, all of our testing had been done using a whole-grain rye flour. We now proceeded to round up the rest of the nationally available rye flours: light rye, medium rye, and pumpernickel. The breads they produced were dramatically different. We preferred the breads made with light rye or medium rye, both of which had an earthy, tangy flavor with a slight springiness.

Following our successes with these two flours, we moved on to test different ratios of rye to white flour. Rye flour alone does not contain enough gluten-forming proteins to make the bread rise adequately, so some protein-rich wheat flour must be used as well.

Our test recipe had 3 cups of rye flour and 4½ cups of unbleached all-purpose flour. As we reduced the rye flour (increasing the all-purpose flour proportionally), the breads became significantly lighter, softer, and less chewy. As one tester said, they were too "bready." With 4 cups of rye flour and 3½ cups of all-purpose flour, the bread was too heavy and dense. We settled on 3½ cups of rye flour to 4½ cups of all-purpose flour. This produced a rye bread with a perfect balance of tang, chew, and moistness.

After baking 20 or so loaves (some with caraway seeds and some without), it became clear that rye bread just isn't rye bread without caraway seeds. We have to admit that before this testing, we had confused the flavor of caraway with rye. Rye gives the bread its earthy, tangy, and fruity character, while caraway adds pepper and spice. Too much caraway is overpowering. Too little caraway and the bread seems incomplete. Two tablespoons is just about right.

We tried substituting honey, molasses, and malt syrup in place of the two tablespoons of sugar in our test recipe. The malt and molasses added a bitter flavor, but we did prefer the honey over the sugar. The bread made with honey was slightly moister. When we tried increasing the amount of sweetener, the bread tasted too sweet, and this obscured the other flavors.

We also experimented with several different types of fat in the bread, including butter, Crisco, and oil. With such a small amount of fat in the recipe, the differences were barely discernible, so we opted to stick with vegetable oil. We even tried using no fat at all, but it was not a good idea—a relatively small amount of fat, about two tablespoons per loaf, goes a long way to soften and moisten the bread.

Finally, we decided to try adding rye flakes (rye kernels that are steamed and then rolled flat to form flakes similar to rolled oats) to the bread dough. The flakes added a nice boost of rye flavor and a bit of extra chew, but they had an unattractive raw appearance. We then tried adding them to the sponge, rather than the dough. This was just the trick: The rye flakes softened up during the rise and lost their rough appearance.

Throughout the testing, we noticed that working with rye dough is different from working with wheat dough. The most obvious differences are the rye dough's slimy tackiness and its lack of elasticity. It bears more resemblance to molding clay slightly puffed up with air than to a stretchy and springy bread dough. The visual and textural cues that guide the wheat bread baker don't hold true with rye bread. Because rye dough is so sticky, the temptation is to add more flour, but we found that this makes the bread dry and coarse. Using wet hands makes it easier to remove the dough from the bowl and dough hook. We use a tablespoon or two of flour to help us shape the dough into a ball, which is then placed in an oiled container to rise. From there on, it is more manageable.

Rye dough's lack of elasticity results from the low gluten content of rye flour. Some references claim that because it has so little gluten the dough should be kneaded longer to allow the gluten to develop. So we tested kneading the dough for five, 10, 15, and 20 minutes. At five minutes the dough was very sticky, soft, and inelastic, yet the bread rose the highest and had the strongest, springiest, and most moist texture. As we increased the kneading time, the bread became more fluffy and soft, characteristics we did not want in a rye bread. So we found that, contrary to conventional wisdom, five minutes of kneading produced the best results.

Like most doughs, rye dough is given two rises. Most recipes suggest letting the dough double in volume during both the first and second rises. It is easy to gauge the first rise in a straight-sided container, as the dough doubles in height. After the first rise, the dough should be gently punched down and shaped into loaves. The second rise is more difficult to gauge, since the dough is on a baking sheet and a doubling in volume is less apparent. During the second rise, we found that the dough develops a bloated appearance and tends to spread out rather than up. This spread is actually a crucial indicator of proper rising; if the dough hasn't started to spread out, it's not ready.

Underrisen rye dough does not bake as high and can have a "blowout" in which the soft inner dough of the partially baked loaf oozes out from the developing crust. As soon as the dough has that bloated look and starts to spread, get it into the oven—overrising reduces oven rise.

As a final touch, we wanted to develop the shiny, brittle crust that is the hallmark of Jewish rye. In our research, we found numerous glaze mixtures designed to achieve this, including egg yolks on their own, egg whites on their own or mixed with water or milk, a mixture of cornstarch and water, and a mixture of potato starch and water. The most interesting (and authentic) approach is to apply a potato starch and water mixture to the loaf as it is removed from the oven. We found, however, that this liquid gave the bread a milky white coating rather than a clear sheen. All the other recommended methods involve glazing the dough before it is baked. After trying them all, we found that preglazing with one egg white mixed with 1 tablespoon of milk worked best.

Deli-Style Rye Bread

MAKES 1 LARGE LOAF OR
2 SMALLER LOAVES

Because this dough requires so much flour (a whopping 8 cups), it is best kneaded in a heavy-duty standing mixer. The rye flakes should be toasted for best flavor. Although the rye flakes intensify the bread's flavor, if unavailable, they can be omitted from the recipe.

SPONGE
2/3	cup rye flakes (optional)
2 3/4	cups water, at room temperature
1 1/2	teaspoons instant yeast
2	tablespoons honey
3	cups (15 ounces) unbleached all-purpose flour

DOUGH
1 1/2	cups (7 1/2 ounces) unbleached all-purpose flour, plus more for dusting the work surface
3 1/2	cups (12 1/8 ounces) medium or light rye flour
2	tablespoons caraway seeds
2	tablespoons vegetable oil

1	tablespoon salt
	Cornmeal for sprinkling on the baking sheet

GLAZE
1	egg white
1	tablespoon milk

1. FOR THE SPONGE: Heat the oven to 350 degrees; toast the rye flakes, if using, on a small baking sheet until fragrant and golden brown, 10 to 12 minutes. Cool to room temperature. Mix the water, yeast, honey, rye flakes, and flour in the mixing bowl of a standing mixer to form a thick batter. Cover with plastic wrap and let sit until bubbles form over the entire surface, at least 2½ hours. (The sponge can stand at cool room temperature overnight.)

2. FOR THE DOUGH: Stir the all-purpose flour, 3¼ cups of the rye flour, the caraway seeds, oil, and salt into the sponge. Attach the dough hook and knead the dough at low speed, adding the remaining ¼ cup rye flour once the dough becomes cohesive; knead until smooth yet sticky, about 5 minutes. With moistened hands, transfer the dough to a well-floured work surface, knead it into a smooth ball, then place it in a very lightly oiled large bowl or straight-sided container. Cover with plastic wrap and let rise at warm room temperature until doubled in size, 1¼ to 2 hours.

3. Generously sprinkle the cornmeal on a large baking sheet. Turn the dough onto a lightly floured work surface and press it into a 12 by 9-inch rectangle. (For two smaller loaves, halve the dough, pressing each portion into a 9 by 6½-inch rectangle.) With one of the long sides facing you, roll the dough into a 12-inch log (or two 9-inch logs), seam-side up. Pinch the seam with your fingertips to seal. Turn the dough seam-side down, and with your fingertips, seal the ends by tucking them into the loaf. Carefully transfer the shaped loaf to the prepared baking sheet, cover loosely with oiled plastic wrap, and let rise until the dough looks bloated and dimply and starts to spread out, 60 to 75 minutes. Adjust an oven rack to the lower-middle position and heat the oven to 425 degrees.

4. FOR THE GLAZE: Whisk the egg white and

milk together and brush over the sides and top of the loaf. Right before baking, make 6 or 7 slashes, ½ inch deep, on the top of the dough with a single-edge razor blade or very sharp knife. Bake for 15 minutes, then lower the oven temperature to 400 degrees and bake until golden brown and an instant-read thermometer inserted in the center of the loaf reads 200 degrees, 25 to 30 minutes (or 15 to 20 minutes for smaller loaves). Transfer to a wire rack and cool to room temperature.

BAGUETTES

IN THE TEST KITCHEN, THE TOPIC OF FRENCH baguettes had long been contemplated as promising but risky. Everyone agreed that a great baguette is made from just four ingredients—flour, water, yeast, and salt—and that it must express excellence in its chief characteristics: crust, crumb, flavor, and color. We agreed that it should have a thin, shattering crust of the deepest golden brown; an open, airy texture; a light, moist crumb; and fully developed flavor. Where we parted ways was on the question of whether you could actually create an outstanding baguette at home in a regular oven. Some were skeptical, but those of us who have spent some time as professional bakers dismissed their skepticism.

The first problem we had to figure out was, as bakers say, "rising" the dough. Modern French bread uses a direct-rise method, in which flour and water are mixed with commercial yeast, given a rise, punched down, shaped, allowed to rise again, and baked. But we found that an older method, one that prevailed before commercial yeast became affordable, appealed to us more. This method, known as a pre-ferment, uses a small amount of yeast to rise a portion of the dough for several hours or overnight. The pre-ferment becomes a dough when it is refreshed with additional flour, yeast, and water, given some salt as well, mixed, and set to rise again.

We tried a number of apparently authentic French baguette recipes, using the pre-ferment method. Although none of these baguettes bowled us over, the flavor and texture of the breads made were definitely very good. Among the two or three types of pre-ferments, we chose the sponge method, which basically calls for a thinnish mixture of flour and water and a small amount of yeast. These ingredients are easily stirred together, and the resulting relatively liquid structure encounters little physical resistance to fermentation, so it rises fully (or ripens) in hours, not days.

Any given bread type has a correct proportion of ingredients. In a system known as the "baker's percentage," these proportions are based on the weight of the flour, which is judged to be 100 percent, with the other ingredients lining up behind. A correct baguette dough, for instance, is said to have a hydration of 62 to 65 percent. This means that for every 1 pound of flour, there will be between 0.62 and 0.65 pound of water. We found it necessary to weigh both flour and water to make sure the sponge had the correct consistency when we were ready to mix the dough. We settled on 6 ounces of both flour and water for the pre-ferment stage; this gave us a sponge that was soft but still firm enough to require additional water when we mixed the dough.

As for the yeast, we knew that we wanted to use as little as possible for greatest flavor development (using a lot of yeast results in bread that tastes more of yeast than of the flavorful byproducts of fermentation), but we weren't sure just how little. While we also knew the sponge should have doubled in volume and be pitted with small bubbles

ACHIEVING WINDOWPANE

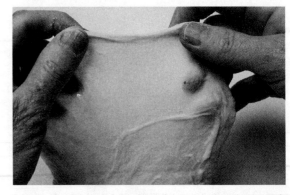

A piece of well-kneaded dough can be stretched until it is nearly translucent.

when ripe, we didn't know exactly how long this might take—it could reach this stage in as little as three hours or take as many as eight. Finally, we determined that a pinch of instant yeast was equal to the task of rising the sponge and ½ teaspoon was enough to refresh the body of the dough. But we remained in a quandary about fermentation time until we came across Daniel Wing's exemplary book *The Bread Builders* (Chelsea Green, 1999) and his explanation of "the drop." This term refers to a sponge rising and then falling under its own weight. Far from representing deflation or exhaustion of the yeast, which seems logical and which we had previously supposed, the drop revitalizes the sponge and is a sign that the sponge is ready for action. The drop is a critical visual cue. By using warm water and a pinch of yeast, we got a sponge that rose and dropped in about six hours in a 75-degree kitchen.

The second phase of bread making is kneading, or mixing. Mixing unites wet and dry ingredients and transforms them from a shaggy ball of dough to a satiny orb. Our preferred partner was a standing mixer outfitted with the dough hook. However, for the dough hook to engage our small amount of dough, we had to mix at high speed. The sticky blob we ended up with once or twice was a direct result of overheating—the dough was irreparably damaged and the character of the bread destroyed. By kneading with a dough hook instead of by hand, we had unwittingly distanced ourselves from some important tactile permutations

that were taking place: the dough's temperature, its increasing elasticity and stretchiness, and its surface tackiness. At this point, we switched to hand kneading and began to experience the dough's transformation in a measured and controlled way. The process was pleasurable as well.

We never supposed we would be sprinkling a dough with water instead of flour. We had often made wet doughs, thinking the resulting crumb would be more open and moist, only to throw flour on them near the end. But this is a poor approach because, as Wing cautions, rather than working its way into the dough, the flour slides around on the surface. Real friction must be generated for proper gluten development. A relatively dry dough, vigorously hand-kneaded, on the other hand, welcomes incremental additions of water to bring it to the correct hydration. We discovered that a method of kneading used in Germany for strudel dough known as "crashing," in which the dough is picked up and flung repeatedly against the counter, worked beautifully to incorporate water. The doughs we produced using this technique had a texture far more satiny than did the wet doughs to which we added flour, and the bread had a far nicer crumb as well.

But perhaps the single most important contribution to our understanding of mixing came from Peter Reinhart's book *Crust and Crumb* (Ten Speed, 1998), in which he describes a technique known as "windowpaning." In windowpaning, when you think the dough is fully kneaded, you stretch

THE RISE AND FALL OF A PRE-FERMENT

In the beginning stages, a pre-ferment shows no evidence of rising or bubbling (left). Its middle phase is characterized by substantial swelling and surface bubbling (center). The final stage, or "drop," is characterized by a slight sinking of the sponge, leaving a higher edge around the circumference of the bowl (right). At this point, the sponge is ready to use.

a small amount between your fingers. If it can be stretched until it is very thin, almost translucent, the dough has been adequately kneaded and can be set to rise (see the photo on page 86). Should it tear while being stretched, more kneading is required. With the baker's percentage and the windowpane technique now firmly part of the plan, our testing began to show significant improvement.

The next steps in bread making, which precede the final rise, are punching down and shaping. A fully risen dough should feel puffy and will not long bear the imprint of a finger. But punching down, experts agree, is a misleading term, inviting more force than is desirable. A gentle fist to the center of the dough does the trick. It is now ready to be scaled or divided and given a rough shape. We knew from experience that a covered rest of about 20 minutes is necessary to relax the dough again, giving it some workability. Attempts to shape long thin baguettes from freshly punched-down dough are frustrating because the dough feels tough and uncooperative and snaps back at you.

ROUNDING THE DOUGH

Rounding relies on the friction created between the moisture in the dough and the work surface. (As you drag the dough with cupped palms, its tackiness will pull on the work surface, causing the top to scroll down and to the back to create a smooth, taut surface.) Rounding the dough rids the dough's interior of air pockets and encourages a uniform crumb.

Divide the dough into two 12-ounce pieces. Cover one piece with plastic wrap while you shape the first loaf. Place one piece of dough on a work surface and cup your hands stiffly around the dough as you drag it in half-circular motions toward the edge of the counter. Repeat with the second piece of dough. The pieces of dough should be in a rough torpedo shape. Drape plastic wrap over the dough and allow to relax, 15 to 20 minutes.

Having gotten this far, we had no idea that our most exciting discovery was right around the corner—in the refrigerator. Traditional wisdom holds that the second rise takes place in a warm, draft-free spot to encourage rapid rising and is accomplished in about half the time required for primary fermentation. So we were intrigued when we read about cool fermentation in Reinhart's book. Cool fermentation retards, or slows down, the second rise—the formed loaves go into the refrigerator overnight and are baked the following day. With this method, the dough is thought to become better hydrated, to develop more flavor, and to achieve greater volume. Refrigeration also maintains humidity around the loaves, which keeps a skin from forming on the surface and inhibiting the rise. But surely the most dramatic contribution cold fermentation makes is to the crust.

The first baguettes we baked using overnight fermentation were beyond anything we had yet experienced. The surface of the crust was pitted with tiny bubbles and gave a sharp, thrilling crackle when torn. Shards of crust sprayed the counter to reveal a creamy interior. But it was the flavor of the crust that rocketed this bread to stardom: It was incomparable. Though the French, Reinhart told us, believe a baguette's surface should be smooth and unblistered, we were untroubled by this breach of tradition. To us, this bread was the ultimate.

The final step in bread making is, of course, baking. Home baking is plagued by the problems that attend home ovens, which can neither deliver nor maintain heat in the way that stone or brick does. We tried a number of baguette pans, both perforated and black (thought to improve browning), but by far the best means of conducting heat to the bread proved to be a large pizza or baking stone, preheated for a full 45 minutes in a hot oven. A stone is the closest home ovens can get to hearth ovens. Precise placement is crucial: Once dough meets stone, there is no turning back—or over, as it were. We tried different approaches with calamitous results. Ultimately, the best approach proved to be letting the baguettes rise on an inverted sheet pan covered with parchment paper, then sliding the baguettes—paper and all—from the sheet pan onto the stone.

Realizing that the goal of baking baguettes is to get a deep, golden brown crust in the short period of time it takes to finish the bread, we began experimenting with oven temperatures. Temperatures below 500 degrees browned the crust inadequately or overbaked the interior. Even an initial temperature of 500 degrees accompanied by temperature reduction after a few minutes did not produce the color we wanted. Some recipes suggest leaving the bread in the oven for a few minutes after baking with the oven turned off to help set the crust, but our 12-ounce baguettes needed full, steady heat all along. In the end, 15 minutes at 500 degrees produced the crust and color we desired as well as a moist interior. The final temperature of the bread was around 208 degrees.

Bakery-Style French Baguettes

MAKES TWO 15 BY 3-INCH BAGUETTES

For the sponge, the ideal ambient temperature is 75 degrees; if it is cooler, fermentation will take longer. This recipe will yield baguettes for breakfast; the following version uses altered rising times so that the baguettes are baked in time for dinner. In either case, begin the recipe the day before you intend to serve the bread; the baguettes will emerge from the oven 20 to 24 hours after you start the sponge. Do not add flour while kneading or shaping the dough. You will need a spray bottle for misting the loaves. The baguettes are best served within 2 hours after baking.

SPONGE

1/8   teaspoon instant yeast
3/4   cup warm water (about 110 degrees)
6   ounces (1 cup plus 3 tablespoons) lower-protein unbleached all-purpose flour, such as Gold Medal or Pillsbury

DOUGH

1/2   teaspoon instant yeast
1/2   cup water (at 75 degrees) plus 2 teaspoons water if needed
10   ounces (2 cups) lower-protein unbleached all-purpose flour, such as Gold Medal or Pillsbury
1   teaspoon salt

GLAZE

1   large egg white
1   tablespoon water

1. FOR THE SPONGE: Combine the yeast, water, and flour in a medium bowl and stir together with a wooden spoon to form a thick batter. Scrape down the bowl with a rubber spatula. Cover the bowl with plastic wrap and punch a couple of holes in the plastic wrap with a paring knife; let stand at room temperature. After 4 or 5 hours, the sponge should be almost doubled in size and pitted with tiny bubbles. Let stand at room temperature until the surface shows a slight depression in the center, indicating the drop, 2 to 3 hours longer. (See the photo on page 87.) The sponge now is ready to use.

2. FOR THE DOUGH: Add the yeast and 6 tablespoons of the water to the sponge. Stir briskly with a wooden spoon until the water is incorporated, about 30 seconds. Stir in the flour and continue mixing with a wooden spoon until a scrappy ball forms. Turn the dough onto a work surface and knead by hand, adding drops of water if necessary, until the dry bits are absorbed into the dough, about 2 minutes. (The dough will feel dry and tough.) Stretch the dough into a rough 8 by 6-inch rectangle, make indentations in the dough

SLASHING A PROOFED LOAF NEATLY

A proofed loaf of bread should be slashed across the top to allow some of the trapped air to escape, but the knife used for this purpose often snags and drags the loaf out of shape. For clean, neat slashes, spray the knife blade lightly with nonstick cooking spray before slashing the loaf.

with your fingertips, sprinkle with 1 tablespoon of the water, fold the edges of the dough up toward the center to enclose the water, and pinch the edges to seal. Knead the dough lightly, about 30 seconds. (The dough will feel slippery as some water escapes but will become increasingly pliant as the water is absorbed.) Begin "crashing" the dough by flinging it against the work surface several times. (This process helps the dough absorb the water more readily.) Knead and crash the dough alternately until it is soft and supple and the surface is almost powdery smooth, about 7 minutes. Stretch the dough again into a rough 8 by 6-inch rectangle and make indentations with your fingertips; sprinkle the dough with the salt and the remaining 1 tablespoon water. Repeat folding and sealing the edges and crashing and kneading until the dough is once again soft and supple and the surface is almost powdery smooth, about 7 minutes. If the dough still feels tough and nonpliant, knead in the 2 additional teaspoons water.

3. Determine if the dough is adequately kneaded by performing a windowpane test (see photo on page 86). If the dough tears before stretching thin, knead 5 minutes longer and test again. Gather the dough into a ball, place it in a large lightly oiled bowl, and cover with plastic wrap. Let stand 30 minutes, then remove the dough from the bowl and knead gently to deflate, about 10 seconds; gather into a ball, return to the bowl, and replace the plastic wrap. Let rise until doubled in bulk, about 1½ hours.

4. Decompress the dough by gently pushing a fist in the center of the dough toward the bottom of the bowl; turn the dough onto a work surface. With a dough scraper, divide the dough into two 12-ounce pieces. Working with one piece of dough at a time, covering the second piece with plastic wrap, cup your hands stiffly around the dough and drag it in short half-circular motions toward the edge of the work surface (see the illustration for rounding the dough on page 88) until the dough forms a rough torpedo shape with a taut, rounded surface, about 6½ inches long. (As you drag the dough, its tackiness will pull on the work surface, causing the top to scroll down and to the back to create a smooth, taut surface.) Repeat with the second piece of dough. Drape the plastic wrap over the dough on the work surface; let rest 15 to 20 minutes.

5. Meanwhile, cover an inverted rimmed baking sheet with parchment paper. Working with one piece of dough at a time, keeping the second piece covered in plastic wrap, follow illustrations 1 through 4 below to shape the dough. Place seam-side down on the prepared baking sheet. Repeat

SHAPING A BAGUETTE

1. Working with one piece of dough at a time (and keeping the other covered in plastic wrap), make an indentation along the length of the dough, with the side of an outstretched hand.

2. Working along the length of the dough, press the thumb of one hand against the dough while folding and rolling the upper edge of the dough down with the other hand to enclose the thumb. Repeat this process 4 or 5 times until the upper edge meets the lower edge and creates a deep seam.

3. Using your fingertips, press the seam to seal. At this point, the dough will have formed a cylinder about 12 inches long.

4. Roll the dough cylinder seam-side down; gently and evenly roll and stretch the dough until it measures 15 inches long by 2½ inches wide. Place seam-side down on the prepared baking sheet. Repeat with the second piece of dough.

with the second dough piece. Space the shaped dough pieces about 6 inches apart on the baking sheet. Drape a clean dry kitchen towel over the dough and slide the baking sheet into a large clean plastic bag; seal to close. Refrigerate until the dough has risen moderately, at least 12 but no longer than 16 hours.

6. To GLAZE AND BAKE: Adjust one oven rack to the lower-middle position and place a baking stone on the rack. Adjust the other rack to the lowest position and place a small empty baking pan on it. Heat the oven to 500 degrees. Remove the baking sheet with the baguettes from the refrigerator and let the baguettes stand covered at room temperature 45 minutes; remove the plastic bag and towel to let the surface of the dough dry, then let stand 15 minutes longer. The dough should have risen to almost double in bulk and feel springy to the touch. Meanwhile, bring 1 cup water to a simmer in a small saucepan on the stovetop. Make the glaze by beating the egg white with the water.

7. With a single-edge razor blade or very sharp knife, make five ¼-inch-deep diagonal slashes on each baguette. Brush the baguettes with the egg white glaze and mist with water. Working quickly, slide the parchment paper with the baguettes off the baking sheet and onto the hot baking stone. Pour the simmering water into the pan on the bottom rack, being careful to avoid the steam. Bake,

TESTING FOR DONENESS

To check the doneness of free-form bread, tip the loaf up with a hand shielded by an oven mitt or potholder and insert the probe of an instant-read thermometer through the bottom crust into the center of the loaf.

rotating the loaves front to back and side to side after 10 minutes, until a deep golden brown and an instant-read thermometer inserted into the center of the loaves through the bottom crust reads 205 to 210 degrees, about 5 minutes longer. Transfer to a wire rack; cool 30 minutes.

➤ VARIATION
Dinner Baguettes
The altered rising times in this version help you get the baguettes on the table at the same time as dinner.

Follow the recipe for Bakery-Style French Baguettes, starting the sponge at about noon and using 75-degree water; let the sponge rise 5 to 6 hours, then refrigerate overnight, 12 to 14 hours. In step 2, make the dough using 110-degree water. Continue to knead, rise, and shape as directed in the recipe. Place the shaped and covered dough in the refrigerator until slightly risen, 7 to 10 hours. Continue with the recipe from step 6.

HEARTY COUNTRY BREAD

FLOUR, WATER, YEAST, AND SALT. THAT'S about as simple as it gets in the kitchen, or so we thought when we set out to develop a reliable home recipe for a crusty, full-textured, European-style country bread. This is the kind of bread that is a main course all by itself; the first bite hits you with a heady burst of crackle and chew, an inspired whiff of yeast, and a hint of sourness.

We expected that a sponge starter (a "sponge" of flour, water, and yeast is left to ferment, then additional flour, water, and other ingredients are added in) would produce more flavor than a quick rise using a greater amount of yeast, and this turned out to be true. In fact, we used only ½ teaspoon of instant yeast for 6 cups of flour (most recipes call for up to a tablespoon). We also varied the sponge recipe by using equal amounts of whole-wheat and white flour for added flavor and texture.

The next element to consider was water. Professional bakers know that a high water content produces more texture. To figure out the amount of water in a bread recipe as a percentage of the flour weight, you divide the weight of the water by the weight of the flour. After some research, we figured that a water content of 68 percent would be about right. The theory was that the higher percentage of water—most bread recipes run around 60 percent—would improve the chew. We tried this formula and got mediocre results. It was good bread, but without the big-league chew we wanted.

We then visited Iggy's Bakery just outside of Boston. The bread made there has a big crust, wonderful texture, and big flavor. The chief baker told us we needed to push the water level even higher. He pointed to the plastic vats filled with rising dough—a sticky mass that would just about pour. This was a breakthrough. Our idea of bread dough had been a nonstick satin ball, easy to handle and more solid than liquid. But this stuff puddled and pulled, shimmered and shook. At Iggy's, they use a mixture of three flours—high-gluten, whole-wheat, and rye—for optimum flavor and texture, and these flours absorb more water than all-purpose flour does.

Back in the test kitchen, we increased the water percentage to near-dangerous levels. The revised recipe now had 2½ cups of water to 6 cups of flour, which brought the level of water up to a whopping 76 percent, a percentage so high it borders on heresy. However, this high amount of water was slightly counteracted by the fact that almost 30 percent of the total flour we used was whole-wheat and rye.

Professional bakers use giant mixers and special shaping machines that handle moist dough easily. In our test kitchen we use the same equipment that home cooks use, and the bread stuck to our hands, the wooden countertop, the mixer bowl, the damp dish towel, and even the heavily floured peel (the shovel-like tool used to get breads in and out of the oven). We tried to knead the dough by hand, but this was almost impossible without adding lots of flour. Still, at the end of the day, the bread was vastly improved. Although a bit sticky, the inside had cavernous air holes and some real chew.

We now turned our attention more closely to the flour. Up until now, we had been using a professional baker's bread flour, which has a

very high level of protein (about 14 percent). We decided to try both a regular bread flour and an all-purpose flour to see if protein content would have a noticeable effect on the finished product. The all-purpose flour yielded an extremely wet, unworkable dough; the dough made with regular bread flour was wetter than the high-protein loaf but still workable. Of most interest, however, was the fact that these lower-protein flours produced a chewier, crustier loaf, although we felt that the loaf made with all-purpose flour was a little too tough. After additional testing, it became clear that we had to adjust the recipe to accommodate the lower-protein flours, which can't absorb as much water as higher-protein flour. When we reduced the amount of water used in our regular bread flour dough to 2⅓ cups, the results were even better. Since this flour is sold in supermarkets, we decided to use it in our recipe.

We also wanted to try varying the amount of the other ingredients we were using: salt and honey. Most recipes with 6 cups of flour use 2 teaspoons of salt, and this amount was just right. Honey is often added to both boost flavor and promote browning of the crust. When we added 2 tablespoons of honey, the flavor was a bit deeper, and the crust turned a rich nut-brown.

Kneading by hand was not our first choice (it can be done, however). We tried using a food processor with a metal blade, which worked fine except that our $250 machine sounded like a lawnmower in a dense patch of weeds; all that was missing was a curl of blue smoke and the smell of burning rubber. The machine simply could not handle 6 cups of quicksand. We tried the recipe in two half-batches, which worked pretty well. We found that leaving the metal blade in the processor between batches is best (you won't get absolutely all of the first batch out of the processor bowl); otherwise your hands will get sticky and dough may ooze out around the center core of the bowl when the second batch is mixed. We recommend that you process for no more than 30 seconds, which is enough time to knead the dough, and we recommend this method only for home cooks with a good heavy-duty processor.

The best solution was a heavy-duty standing

mixer with a dough hook. We simply threw in the ingredients, mixed them briefly with a large, stiff rubber spatula, and then turned the machine on at the lowest setting for 15 minutes. We then transferred the dough to an oiled bowl to rise for about 2 hours, or until tripled in volume. Allowing the dough to triple in volume both improves flavor and helps the dough to develop more "muscle," which helps the bread maintain its shape when baked.

Even after 15 minutes of kneading, the dough was difficult to handle. After a few tries with various methods, we came up with the following, which was the least messy: For the first rise, simply use a rubber spatula to transfer the wet dough to an oiled bowl (a plastic tub is fine, too). After letting the bread rise for about 2 hours, use the same spatula to transfer the dough onto a lightly floured surface. Now flour both your hands and the dough (the latter lightly). Press the dough very gently into a round and then fold it into a ball. Note that you should handle the dough as little as possible at this point both because it is still a little sticky (you'll be tempted to add extra flour) and because excessive handling is bad for rustic bread—you want an irregular texture with lots of air holes. This point goes for all bread making: Strong kneading after the first rise will harm the delicate structure of the dough.

The best way to move the dough from here on is to use a large dough scraper, two wide metal spatulas, or a thin floured baking sheet. Transfer the dough, smooth-side down, into a colander or a basket that has been lined with a well-floured piece of muslin or linen. The flour should be rubbed into the fabric so the dough will not stick. A banneton is a cloth-lined woven basket designed just for this purpose. You can purchase one or make your own, as we did. Muslin, which is cheaper than linen, works well and comes in different grades, from fine (the most expensive) to coarse (the least expensive). Use the cheaper variety to line your basket and make sure that it is 100 percent unbleached cotton. A real banneton has the linen or muslin sewn right into the basket, an optional refinement. The basket we used was 4 inches high, 7 inches wide across the bottom, and 12 inches wide across the top. A colander is also a perfectly good option. It works well because it allows for air flow (the

dough is more likely to stick to the muslin when sitting in a bowl).

For its second rise, the dough needs to be covered directly. We tried a damp dish towel, but it stuck to the dough. It was like unwrapping a piece of saltwater taffy on a hot day. Aluminum foil proved much more effective because the dough is less likely to stick to it and it allows the dough to breathe, thus keeping the dough from rising too much. If the dough rises too much at this point, you will end up with a fluffy texture (plastic wrap, for example, will cause too much rising). The foil gives the dough shape and allows you to transfer it easily to the peel when the second rise is completed.

The last major issue was the crust. Steam is often identified as the key to a good crust, and after baking one loaf with no steam (which yielded a paper-thin crust), we agreed. We tested ways to introduce the steam: spritzing the bread with water, adding ice cubes to the oven, and adding a pan of hot water to the oven. Of the three, we found that the hot pan of water worked, but only if the pan was preheated. Two cups of water generates both instant steam and enough residual water to maintain a steamy atmosphere throughout baking. It is important, though, to use caution when working with steam. Use thick oven mitts and a long-sleeved shirt when pouring the hot water into the pan.

Most recipes state that bread should be baked to an internal temperature of 190 degrees, but our bread was undercooked at this temperature. We found that a temperature of 210 degrees was perfect. An undercooked loaf will be sticky inside and will not have developed the very dark brown crust we prefer.

We also tested starting oven temperatures. We began testing with a 500-degree oven, which we turned down to 400 degrees when the dough went in, working under the assumption that the higher temperature would offset the drop in temperature caused by opening the oven door and adding the dough (the dough absorbs a great deal of heat quickly). The resulting crust was thin and disappointing. Next we tried baking the bread at 500 degrees for the first 15 minutes and then reducing the temperature to 400. The crust on this loaf was scorched. The exterior cooked so fast that the interior of the bread had no time to cook properly. The best baking temperature turned out to be a constant 450 degrees.

Hearty Country Bread

MAKES 1 LARGE ROUND LOAF

Whole-wheat and rye flours contribute to this bread's full flavor, and extra oven time gives the bread its thick crust. Because of its high water content, the bread will be gummy if pulled from the oven too soon. To ensure the bread's doneness, make sure its internal temperature reads 210 degrees by inserting an instant-read thermometer into the bottom of the loaf. Also look at the crust—it should be very dark brown, almost black. Because the dough is so sticky, a heavy-duty standing mixer is best for kneading, but food processor and hand-kneading instructions are provided for this recipe. Keep in mind that rising times vary depending on kitchen temperature (the times listed below are minimums). For the second rising, we used a round basket that was 4 inches high, 7 inches wide across the bottom, and 12 inches wide across the top. A colander of similar proportions works equally well. For a coarser, chewier bread, decrease the bread flour by ¼ cup. You will need muslin or linen as well as a baking stone for this recipe. A baker's peel is helpful but not essential.

SPONGE

½	teaspoon instant yeast
1	cup water, at room temperature
1	cup (5 ounces) bread flour
1	cup (5½ ounces) whole-wheat flour

DOUGH

3½	cups (17½ ounces) bread flour, plus more to lightly dust the work surface, hands, and dough
½	cup (1¾ ounces) rye flour
1⅓	cups water, at room temperature, plus more as needed
2	tablespoons honey
2	teaspoons salt

1. FOR THE SPONGE: Stir the yeast into the water in a medium bowl until dissolved. Mix in the flours with a rubber spatula to create a stiff, wet dough. Cover with plastic wrap; let sit at room temperature for at least 5 hours, preferably overnight. (The sponge can be refrigerated up to 24 hours; return to room temperature before continuing with the recipe.)

2. FOR THE DOUGH: Mix the flours, water, honey, and sponge in the bowl of a standing mixer with a rubber spatula. Attach the dough hook and knead the dough at the lowest speed until the dough is smooth, about 15 minutes, adding the salt during the final 3 minutes. If the dough looks dry after the salt is added, add water in 1-tablespoon increments every 30 seconds until a smooth consistency is reached. Transfer the dough to a very lightly oiled large bowl. Cover with plastic wrap; let rise until tripled in size, at least 2 hours.

3. Turn the dough onto a lightly floured work surface. Dust the top of the dough and your hands with flour. Lightly press the dough into a round by folding the edges of the dough into the middle from the top, right, bottom, and left, sequentially, then gathering it loosely together. Transfer the dough, smooth-side down, to a colander or basket lined with heavily floured muslin or linen. Cover loosely with a large sheet of aluminum foil; let the dough rise until almost doubled in size, at least 45 minutes.

4. Meanwhile, adjust an oven rack to the lower-middle position and place a large baking stone on the rack. Adjust the other rack to the lowest position and place a small empty baking pan on it. Heat the oven to 450 degrees.

5. Cover a peel or the back of a large baking sheet with a large piece of parchment paper. Invert the dough onto the peel and remove the muslin. Use a single-edge razor blade or very sharp knife to cut a large X about ½ inch deep into the top of the dough. With scissors, trim the excess parchment around the dough.

6. Slide the dough, still on the parchment, from the peel onto the stone; remove the peel with a quick backward jerk. Pour 2 cups hot tap water into the heated pan on the bottom rack, being careful to avoid the steam. Bake until an instant-read thermometer inserted in the bottom of the bread reads 210 degrees and the crust is very dark brown, 35 to 40 minutes, turning the bread around after 25 minutes if it is not browning evenly. Turn the oven off, open the door, and let the bread remain in the oven 10 minutes longer. Remove, then cool

to room temperature before slicing, about 2 hours. To crisp the crust, place the cooled bread in a 450-degree oven for 10 minutes.

➤ VARIATIONS

Hearty Country Bread Kneaded in a Food Processor

Make the sponge as directed in the recipe for Hearty Country Bread. Place half of the sponge, 1¾ cups of the bread flour, ¼ cup of the rye flour, and 1 tablespoon of the honey in a food processor. Pulse until roughly blended, three to four 1-second pulses. With the machine running, add ⅔ cup of the water slowly through the feed tube; process until the dough forms a ball. Let sit for 3 minutes, then add 1 teaspoon of the salt and process to form a smooth dough, about 30 seconds longer. Transfer the dough to a large lightly oiled container or bowl, leaving the metal blade in the processor (some dough will remain under the blade). Repeat the process with the remaining half of the ingredients.

Hand-Kneaded Hearty Country Bread

Make the sponge as directed in the recipe for Hearty Country Bread. Place the sponge and all the dough ingredients, except 2 cups of the bread flour, in a large bowl. Stir the mixture with a wooden spoon until smooth, about 5 minutes. Work in the reserved flour and then turn out onto a floured work surface. Knead by hand for 5 minutes, incorporating no more than an additional ¼ cup flour as you work. The dough will be very wet and sticky. Proceed with the recipe.

RUSTIC ITALIAN BREAD

IN ITALY, RUSTIC BREAD IS SERIOUSLY crusty, with a toothsome crumb and a clean, strong flavor that lends itself readily to a variety of recipes and is so hearty and satisfying, it's almost a meal in itself. Because this common bread has only four ingredients—flour, water, yeast, and salt—we wondered how hard it could be to make an authentic loaf at home.

We quickly discovered that "rustic Italian bread" describes several different loaf styles, from flat and chewy (like our Ciabatta on page 100) to soft, enriched, and thinly crusted. We wanted a loaf that fell between these two extremes—chewy yet tender, crusty but not too tough. Although supermarket Italian loaves are undoubtedly shabby, their classic football shape does make it easy to slice uniform pieces for sandwiches even after half the loaf has been consumed; this was the shape we wanted.

Next we brushed up on some elementary bread-baking procedures and confirmed the following: First, good bread bakers don't measure their ingredients by volume, which is too imprecise. Instead,

---

SCIENCE: How Autolyse Works

Developed by French bread-making authority Raymond Calvel in the 1970s, autolyse (pronounced AUTO-lees) is a technique in which flour and water are briefly mixed together and allowed to rest before being kneaded. Finding that autolyse made a significant difference in both the flavor and structure of our Rustic Italian Bread and other European breads, we wanted to understand the magic behind this 20-minute power nap.

To understand autolyse, however, we first found it necessary to learn how gluten develops. Gluten gives baked goods structure. When water and flour first mix, gluten forms in a random, disorganized matrix that is very weak.

As this matrix is kneaded, the disorganized bonds are pulled apart and reattached into straight, strong, orderly sheets (see below). Autolyse occurs after the random matrix has come together but before the sheets of gluten have formed and aligned. While the mixture rests, naturally occurring enzymes break down the disorganized bonds of gluten. When this rested dough is then kneaded, the gluten is positioned to form a stronger, more organized network more quickly.

When the water and flour are first combined, the gluten is like a random pile of pencils (left). Autolyse ensures that the gluten becomes orderly and strong (right) with minimal kneading.

they weigh them. Second, to help manage the ratio of ingredients they use something called a baker's percentage, which lists the ingredients as a percentage of the total amount of flour (which is always calculated at 100 percent). Our plan was simple. We would nail down the proportions of the four ingredients, then figure out the mixing, kneading, and shaping techniques.

We started with a common baker's percentage for white bread: 100 percent flour, 65 percent water, 2 percent salt, and 0.5 percent instant yeast (roughly 6 cups flour, 2½ to 2⅔ cups water, 2¼ teaspoons salt, and 1½ teaspoons instant yeast). For our first test, we wanted to compare the effects of all-purpose flour and bread flour. The all-purpose flour turned out shorter loaves with thinner crusts and gentler crumbs, while the bread flour produced heartier loaves with better height and thicker crusts. These differences can be attributed to different levels of protein: all-purpose flour is 10 to 12 percent protein, while bread flour is above 12 percent. A higher percentage of protein generally translates into baked goods with a sturdier crust and crumb, making bread flour the right choice for many breads. The two brands of bread flour we repeatedly found at the store, Gold Medal Better for Bread Flour and King Arthur Bread Flour, performed similarly, as their protein levels are quite

THE ROLE OF WATER

The loaf on the top was made with too much water, which caused large holes to form in the crumb. This dough was difficult to work with, and the loaf turned out squat. The nicely shaped loaf on the bottom was made with the right amount of water and is chewy but not overly so.

close (12.6 percent and 12.7 percent, respectively).

We tried making the bread with varying amounts of water, including 65, 70, 75, and 80 percent. As the amount of water increased, the doughs became almost pourable, producing loaves that were flat and wide. The crumb texture also changed from tight and even to bubblegum-chewy, with gaping, erratic holes. Tasters preferred the bread made with 70 percent water. It had an uneven crumb, with most holes about the size of a grain of rice, and a hearty chew (see photos below).

As for the salt and yeast, we found that the original ratios worked best. The bread was perfectly seasoned with 2 percent table salt, and 0.5 percent instant yeast struck the perfect balance between a fairly speedy rise and a bread that wasn't overly yeasty. Wanting to produce a large loaf that would serve four to six people for dinner with an ample amount left over, we took these percentages and scaled them into variously sized loaves. When made with 22 ounces (4 cups) of flour, the loaves were simply too small to survive more than one sitting at the table. Loaves made with 6 cups or more, however, were comically gigantic and barely fit inside the oven. We found that 27.5 ounces (five cups) of bread flour was just right. All we had to do now was scale the other ingredients to match our final baker's percentages: 100 percent flour, 70 percent water, 2 percent salt, and 0.5 percent yeast.

The next issue was whether or not to use a sponge. Made the day before the bread itself is made, the sponge is said to build flavor in the final loaf. We made loaves with and without a sponge, and tasters noted that the loaves made with a sponge tasted impressive, with wheaty, multidimensional flavors. To figure out how much sponge was needed, we baked loaves with varying amounts, making sure to keep the total amounts of ingredients the same. Finding that too much sponge turned the dough incredibly elastic and gave it an off, sour flavor, we determined that a little less than half of the final dough should consist of sponge.

Despite all our work thus far, the loaf remained far from perfect and the results were inconsistent; on any given day the bread would turn out either shapely and golden or squat and pale. Taking a closer look at the last few loaves, we found that they all tended to spread sideways rather than upward and that the dough itself appeared weak. Not wanting to lose the chewy crumb we had achieved by using 70 percent water, we turned our attention to making the dough stronger by extending the kneading (20 to 25 minutes instead of the more customary 15 minutes). Unfortunately, these doughs merely became warm and turned from a wheaty tan to a grayish white, producing loaves with sickly pale crumbs and expired flavors. As it turned out, we had overmixed and overheated these doughs. Although nearly impossible to do by hand, overmixing and overheating are quite easy to do when using a standing mixer. The action of the dough hook creates heat through friction and also kneads excessive air into the dough, sapping it of flavor and color in a process known as oxidation.

We then consulted several bakers, who turned us onto a technique called "autolyse." Setting the sponge aside, we mixed the remaining flour, water, and instant yeast for two minutes to form a scrappy dough, then set it aside for 20 minutes. Then, we combined the rested dough with the sponge and salt and kneaded it in the mixer for 10 minutes. As a result, the loaves made using this technique turned out taller, with a more definite shape and a clean, strong flavor. What happened? That 20-minute rest resulted in a stronger network of proteins and allowed us to cut down on the kneading time. (For a more detailed explanation, see "How Autolyse Works," on page 95.)

Right off the bat, we noticed that the more this rustic Italian dough was handled, the denser the final loaf turned out. Minimal handling was key so as not to disrupt any air pockets that had developed, yet if the shaped loaf wasn't taut it would sag rather than rise in the oven. We finally found it easiest to gently push the dough into a square, fold the top corners down as if making a paper airplane, and then roll the loaf up. This produced a floppy, loosely shaped piece of dough that we were able to transfer to a piece of parchment and finally tuck into the classic football shape.

Now we were ready to bake the bread. Here we were guided by three techniques from prior test kitchen investigations: a blast of high heat right at the beginning to maximize loaf height; a shot of steam at the outset to help the loaf rise and the crust develop; and a hot baking stone to provide an even, sustainable heat. We tried baking the loaf entirely at 500 degrees but found we needed to turn the oven down to 450 degrees after 10 minutes to keep the crust from burning. We were baffled, though, when the crisp crust that emerged from the oven turned soft within minutes. After much trial and error, we discovered that the bread, which cooked through in just 25 minutes, was being baked too fast. By turning the oven down to 400 degrees after the first 10 minutes, we extended the total baking time to about 45 minutes, which resulted in a fantastically crisp crust with staying power.

As for getting steam into the oven, we found

TURNING THE DOUGH

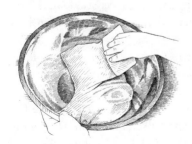  

1. Slide a plastic bench scraper under one side of the dough; gently lift and fold a third of the dough toward the center.

2. Repeat step 1 with the opposite side of the dough.

3. Finally, fold the dough in half, perpendicular to the first folds. The dough shape should be a rough square.

that for this recipe spritzing the loaf with water (from a plastic spray bottle) was both easy and effective. The spray of water kept the crust from setting too early, thus maximizing the bread's initial oven spring (or growth spurt), and it helped to gelatinize the starches on the surface of the loaf, turning the crust shatteringly crisp.

We were now turning out excellent loaves, but they were inconsistently shaped, and the crumb and crust varied somewhat, too. We turned to Didier Rosada, head instructor at the San Francisco Baking Institute, who convinced us to try something called turning. A variation on the idea of punching down the dough after it has risen, turning involves delicately folding the dough over several times as it rises. The theory behind turning is that the dough is stretched gently, building strength as any wayward sheets of gluten—the protein that gives baked goods structure—are brought into alignment. Rosada said that turning the dough twice during its first rise would help iron out any inconsistencies as well as reduce the kneading time. He was right on both counts; we were able to reduce kneading time to just five minutes. Best of all, we found that turning could be done right in the bowl and was nearly effortless. Now our loaves not only

PERFECT SLICES FROM CRUSTY LOAVES

Artisanal breads, like Rustic Italian Bread and Hearty Country Bread, have heavy crusts that can be difficult to slice neatly. Often the bread knife fails to cut all the way through the thick bottom crust. The result is that you must yank the slice free from the loaf, often tearing it in the process. To slice a crusty loaf neatly, turn the loaf on its side and cut through the top and bottom crusts simultaneously. The crust on the side of the bread, which is now facing down, is often thinner and easier to slice.

looked and tasted nearly identical but were perfect in height, crust, and crumb, with an unbelievably authentic flavor.

Rustic Italian Bread

MAKES 1 LARGE LOAF

This recipe requires a bit of patience—the sponge, which gives the bread flavor, must be made 11 to 27 hours before the dough is made. We find it makes the most sense to prepare the sponge (which requires just 5 minutes of hands-on work) the day before you want to bake the bread. On the second day, remove the sponge from the refrigerator and begin step 2 at least 7 hours before you want to serve the bread. If you own two standing mixer bowls, in step 1 you can refrigerate the sponge in the bowl in which it was made. Use the second bowl to make the dough in step 2. Have ready a spray bottle filled with water for misting the loaves.

SPONGE

2	cups (11 ounces) bread flour
1/4	teaspoon instant yeast
1	cup water, at room temperature

DOUGH

3	cups (16 1/2 ounces) bread flour, plus more for dusting the work surface and hands
1	teaspoon instant yeast
1 1/3	cups water, at room temperature
2	teaspoons salt

1. FOR THE SPONGE: Combine the flour, yeast, and water in the bowl of a standing mixer fitted with the dough hook. Knead at the lowest speed until the ingredients form a shaggy dough, 2 to 3 minutes. Transfer the sponge to a medium bowl, cover tightly with plastic wrap, and let stand at room temperature until it begins to bubble and rise, about 3 hours. Refrigerate the sponge at least 8 hours or up to 24 hours.

2. FOR THE DOUGH: Remove the sponge from the refrigerator and let stand at room temperature while making the dough. Combine the flour, yeast, and water in the bowl of a standing mixer fitted with the dough hook; knead at the lowest speed until a rough dough is formed, about 3

minutes. Turn the mixer off and, without removing the dough hook or bowl from the mixer, cover the bowl loosely with plastic wrap; let the dough rest 20 minutes.

3. Remove the plastic wrap, add the sponge and salt to the bowl, and continue to knead at the lowest speed until the ingredients are incorporated and the dough is formed (the dough should clear the sides of the bowl but stick to the bottom), about 4 minutes. Increase the mixer speed to medium low and continue to knead until the dough forms a more cohesive ball, about 1 minute. Transfer the dough to a large lightly oiled bowl (at least 3 times the dough's size) and cover tightly with plastic wrap. Let the dough rise in a cool, draft-free spot until slightly risen and puffy, about 1 hour.

4. Remove the plastic wrap and, following the illustrations for turning the dough on page 97, turn the dough. Replace the plastic wrap; let the dough rise 1 hour. Turn the dough again, replace the plastic wrap, and let the dough rise 1 hour longer.

5. To SHAPE THE DOUGH: Dust a work surface liberally with flour. Gently scrape the dough from the bowl and invert onto the work surface (the side of dough that was against the bowl should now be facing up). Dust the dough and your hands liberally with flour and, using minimal pressure, push the dough into a rough 8- to 10-inch square. Following the illustrations below, shape the dough and transfer to a large sheet of parchment paper. Dust the loaf liberally with flour and cover loosely with plastic wrap; let the loaf rise until doubled in size, about 1 hour. Meanwhile, adjust an oven rack to the lower-middle position, place a baking stone on the rack, and heat the oven to 500 degrees.

6. To BAKE: Using a single-edge razor blade or sharp chef's knife, cut a slit ½ inch deep lengthwise along the top of the loaf, starting and stopping about 1½ inches from the ends; spray the loaf lightly with water. Slide the parchment sheet with

SHAPING THE LOAF

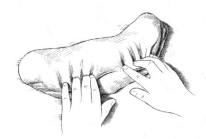

1. After delicately pushing the dough into an 8- to 10-inch square, fold the top right corner diagonally to the middle.

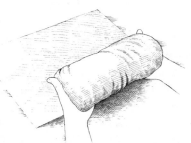

2. Repeat step 1 with the top left corner.

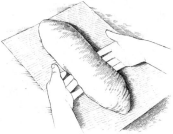

3. Begin to gently roll the dough from top to bottom.

4. Continue rolling until the dough forms a rough log.

5. Roll the dough onto its seam and, sliding your hands under each end, transfer the dough to a sheet of parchment paper.

6. Gently shape the dough into a 16-inch football shape by tucking the bottom edges underneath.

the loaf onto a peel or inverted rimmed baking sheet, then slide the parchment with the loaf onto the hot baking stone in the oven. Bake 10 minutes, then reduce the oven temperature to 400 degrees and quickly rotate the loaf from front to back using the edges of the parchment; continue to bake until deep golden brown and an instant-read thermometer inserted into the center of the loaf reads 210 degrees, about 35 minutes longer. Transfer to a wire rack, discard the parchment, and cool the loaf to room temperature, about 2 hours.

CIABATTA

ALTHOUGH NOW COMMONLY SERVED IN swank Italian eateries, ciabatta is a flattened, flour-streaked loaf whose rough appearance reveals its rustic roots. The name, which translates as "slipper," is an apt description, as long as you envision a threadbare bedroom scuff, not a dainty silk number. Despite its unappetizing name, ciabatta is a delicious bread characterized by a crisp, full-flavored crust and a spongy, tart crumb punctuated by irregular bubbles. As we quickly found out, achieving this distinctive texture and flavor requires an eccentric dough and a leap of faith.

Our preliminary attempts at baking ciabatta revealed that ciabatta dough is unlike anything we had ever worked with. First, it is stunningly wet. We thought we were making grave mistakes in measuring the flour and water, but every recipe we tried produced dough closer in texture to thick cake batter than bread dough. Confused by this inexplicably gooey dough, we dug deeper and started our research from the ground up.

Ciabatta dough starts off with a sponge (called a biga in Italian). A sponge is nothing more than a mixture of flour, water, and yeast that is allowed to ferment overnight. The fermentation develops the wheat's character and gluten, which in turn add flavor, leavening, and structure to the bread. Sponges were traditionally used in Italy to contribute structure to the notoriously low-protein flour available there. Therefore, bread made with a sponge often does not need high-protein bread flour for structure. In fact, we found that ciabatta

should be made with all-purpose flour so that the crumb remains springy and soft. The sponge also contributes sourness, as a result of lactic and acetic acid buildup, a byproduct of fermentation. Because ciabatta is characteristically sour, a large amount of sponge is used. Milder-tasting loaves, like Olive-Rosemary Bread (page 103), use smaller amounts.

While the recipes we consulted urged strict guidelines for making and fermenting the sponge, we found that much of the fuss was unnecessary. We mixed everything together with the aid of a standing mixer, then covered the bowl and left it out on the counter overnight. By morning, 12 hours later, it bubbled with activity and smelled sour. We found that as long as the ambient temperature was between 65 and 70 degrees it was okay to leave the sponge unrefrigerated. Higher temperatures yielded an overly fermented sponge that tasted too sour and produced a poorly leavened loaf. Lower temperatures fermented too slowly, and the sponge was not ready for use the following morning.

Unlike most bread doughs, ciabatta dough is barely kneaded—just enough to activate the flour's gluten and make a smooth, elastic dough, albeit a very wet one. Anything longer than five minutes in a standing mixer made for a uniform crumb, which is not desirable in a ciabatta.

Because of its short knead, ciabatta dough is often turned (gently folded onto itself) as it rises to increase flavor and gluten development. We were initially skeptical of the technique but were surprised by the results; unturned dough paled in comparison, producing a loaf with a milder flavor and a less interesting crumb than dough that had been turned.

Turning is a simple technique. During the first rise, the dough is typically emptied onto a floured work surface and folded onto itself gently so that the dough's pent-up gases are not expressed. Our ciabatta dough was so sticky that this resulted in a gummy mess. However, we found we could turn the dough in the bowl with the aid of a large rubber spatula or dough scraper. The technique felt similar to folding egg whites into a batter, requiring a similar gentle touch and circular motion.

After several turns and tripling in bulk, the

dough was ready to be shaped, the step we feared the most. Because of its high moisture content, ciabatta dough cannot be shaped using conventional methods. Instead, it is stretched and folded with quick, decisive movements and liberal amounts of flour. There are two distinct ways to shape ciabatta: a simple stretch and a more complicated trifold, which starts with a stretch but also involves folding the ends of the dough over each other. Both shapes produced ungainly-looking loaves, but we preferred the trifold as it lent more structure to the loaf, making it slightly taller. Traditional bakers employ clouches, flour-infused heavy muslin cloths, for shaping and proofing the dough, but we found that parchment paper served well too. Further, the dough can be baked directly on the parchment, avoiding more tricky maneuvers.

After experimenting with oven temperature, we found that the higher the temperature, the better the bread's crust and crumb. We baked ciabatta at temperatures ranging from 400 to 500 degrees, and 500 degrees yielded superior bread. The crust was darker in color (like a dark caramel), crisper, and more flavorful. The crumb was more uneven— liberally pockmarked with big air bubbles. Placing a pan of water in the oven improved the crumb and assisted in oven spring, the quick expansion of the loaf during the first moments of baking.

While the top crust was ideal, the bottom crust was lacking. The parchment paper—essential for moving the fragile dough into the oven—blocked the evaporation of moisture and prevented the crust from browning. We found that once the dough had firmed, the loaf could be flipped over and the parchment paper removed. Finishing the loaf upside down colored the bottom to the desired brown, just a shade lighter than the top.

Ciabatta

MAKES 2 LOAVES

The sponge for ciabatta must be made a day ahead, so plan accordingly. As you make this bread, keep in mind that the dough is unique; it is wet and very, very sticky. The key to manipulating it is working quickly and gently; rough handling will result in flat, tough bread. Use a large rubber spatula and a dough scraper rather than your hands to move the dough. Make sure to keep the uncooked loaf well covered as the other loaf bakes. Ciabattas are best eaten within a day or two. Because of the amount of flour, this dough must be prepared in a standing mixer.

SPONGE
2½ cups (12½ ounces) unbleached all-purpose flour
¼ teaspoon instant yeast
1½ cups water, at room temperature

DOUGH
4 cups (20 ounces) unbleached all-purpose flour, plus more for dusting the work surface, hands, and dough
1 teaspoon instant yeast
2 teaspoons salt
1½ cups water, at room temperature

1. FOR THE SPONGE: Place the flour, yeast, and water in the bowl of a standing mixer fitted with the paddle. Mix at the lowest speed until the ingredients form a uniform, sticky mass, about 1 minute. Scrape down the sides of the bowl with a rubber spatula and turn the mixer to the second-lowest speed. Mix until the sponge becomes a glutinous mass, about 4 minutes. Remove the bowl from the mixer, cover it tightly with plastic wrap, and allow it to sit at cool room temperature (60 to 70 degrees) overnight.

2. FOR THE DOUGH: Add all of the ingredients to the bowl with the sponge. Place the bowl in a standing mixer fitted with the paddle. Mix at the lowest speed until a roughly combined, shaggy dough forms, about 1 minute; scrape down the sides of the bowl as necessary. Continue mixing at low speed until the dough becomes shiny and uniform (unlike most bread dough, this dough will never clear the sides of the bowl), about 5 minutes. Turn the dough into a large lightly oiled bowl, cover tightly with plastic wrap, and keep at room temperature.

3. After 1 hour, uncover the dough, liberally dust the top with flour, and slide a rubber spatula between the bowl and the dough, about 3 inches straight down the side of the bowl, and following

the illustrations on page 97, gently lift and fold the edge of the dough toward the middle. Repeat the process around the dough's circumference until all of it has been turned. Tightly re-cover the bowl with plastic wrap. Repeat the process in 1 hour.

4. Within 2½ to 3 hours, the dough should have roughly tripled in volume. Heavily dust a work surface with flour and, using a rubber spatula, gently turn the dough out onto the work surface. Liberally dust the top of the dough with flour. Using a bench scraper dipped in water, cut the dough into 2 roughly equal pieces. With one fluid motion, grasp the end of one piece of dough with the bench scraper and the other end with your free hand (well dusted with flour) and lift the dough over a large sheet of parchment paper. Allow the middle of the dough to drop onto the parchment paper and fold the ends of the dough over like a business letter (see the illustration below). With well-floured hands, gently stretch the dough to approximately 10 by 5 inches. Repeat with the remaining dough and a second sheet of parchment. Cover each loaf loosely with plastic wrap and allow to rest until roughly doubled in bulk and the dough feels relatively firm to the touch, about 1 hour.

5. Meanwhile, adjust an oven rack to the middle position and place a large baking stone on the rack.

SHAPING CIABATTA

With one fluid motion, grasp the end of one piece of dough with the bench scraper and the other end with your free hand (well dusted with flour) and lift the dough over a large sheet of parchment paper. Allow the middle of the dough to drop onto the parchment paper and fold the ends of the dough over like a business letter.

Adjust the other rack to the lowest position, and place a small empty baking pan on it. Heat the oven to 500 degrees.

6. Gently transfer one shaped loaf (still on the parchment) to a peel or the back of a baking sheet. Remove the plastic wrap and slide the dough into the center of the baking stone. Pour 2 cups hot tap water into the heated pan on the bottom rack, being careful of the steam. Bake for 20 minutes, then remove the bread from the oven and remove the parchment paper from the bottom of the loaf. Return the bread to the oven, bottom-side up. Bake until the crust is dark golden brown, 15 to 20 minutes longer. Remove the bread from the oven, set it right-side up on a wire rack, and cool for at least 1 hour. Repeat the process with the remaining loaf and 2 more cups of hot tap water. Before serving, brush any excess flour off the loaf with a pastry brush.

OLIVE AND ROSEMARY BREAD

OLIVE AND ROSEMARY BREAD SHOULD BE A hefty, rustic country loaf. Armored with the thickest of crusts and full of incredible chew, this bread at its best is pure substance. After making a few recipes for olive and rosemary bread, however, we found the same problems again and again. Flimsy, anemic crusts, fluffy, tasteless interiors with little sign of olive or rosemary—this bread needed help.

We wanted to develop a loaf with a substantial crust that would challenge the sturdiest bread knife. This bread would have a fabulous tug-and-pull texture that made us want to rip it apart with our hands. We also wanted it to be brimming with the flavor of olives and perfumed with rosemary, a whiff of yeast, and a hint of sourness.

After several rounds of less-than-satisfying testing, we had a thought. Could our Hearty Country Bread (page 94), which has the chew and heft we wanted, be transformed into Olive and Rosemary Bread? With one minor modification, we found that the answer is yes. We decided to replace the rye flour, which tasters felt competed with the flavor of the olives, with an equal amount of bread flour. Otherwise, the loaves are identical, except for the addition of the olives and rosemary.

Determining the type of olives to add was next on our list, and a quick testing of green and black varieties led tasters to choose the latter, mostly for their piquant flavor and dramatic color. When it came to brined versus oil-cured, there was no debate. Tasters overwhelmingly preferred the oil-cured olives. Their potent flavor brought olive impact to every bite.

Getting the olives into the dough begat a new set of problems. Adding them to the dough in the mixer turned the dough an unattractive shade of gray. We found it better to gently knead the olives in by hand. We also found that it was important not to chop the olives. Cut into pieces, the olives leached their black liquid into the dough. Tasters wanted distinct pieces of olives, so unless they were extremely large (bigger than 1 inch), we left them alone once pitted.

The other main flavor ingredient in this bread is rosemary, and here we found that more is definitely better. Tasting after tasting, tasters asked that the rosemary level be increased. Finally, we found that ¼ cup of chopped fresh rosemary sufficiently filled the loaf with its potent flavor.

Olive and Rosemary Bread

MAKES 1 LARGE ROUND LOAF

Because of its high water content, this bread will be gummy if pulled from the oven too soon. To ensure the bread's doneness, make sure its internal temperature reads 210 degrees by inserting an instant-read thermometer into the bottom of the loaf. Also look at the crust—it should be very dark brown, almost black. Because the dough is so sticky, a heavy-duty standing mixer is best for kneading. Keep in mind that rising times vary depending on kitchen temperature (the times listed here are minimums). For the second rising, we used a basket that was 4 inches high, 7 inches wide across the bottom, and 12 inches wide across the top. A colander of similar proportions works equally well. For a coarser, chewier bread, decrease the bread flour by ¼ cup. You will need muslin or linen as well as a baking stone for this recipe. A baker's peel is helpful but not essential.

SPONGE

½	teaspoon instant yeast
1	cup water, at room temperature
1	cup (5½ ounces) bread flour
1	cup (5½ ounces) whole-wheat flour

DOUGH

4	cups (22 ounces) bread flour, plus more for dusting the work surface, hands, and dough
1⅓	cups water, at room temperature, or more as needed
2	tablespoons honey
¼	cup chopped fresh rosemary leaves
2	teaspoons salt
12	ounces oil-cured black olives, pitted and cut in half widthwise if larger than 1 inch
1	tablespoon coarse sea salt for sprinkling into the dough (optional)

1. FOR THE SPONGE: Stir the yeast into the water in a medium bowl until dissolved. Mix in the flours with a rubber spatula to create a stiff, wet dough. Cover with plastic wrap; let sit at room temperature for at least 5 hours, preferably overnight. (The sponge can be refrigerated up to 24 hours; return to room temperature before continuing with the recipe.)

2. FOR THE DOUGH: Mix the flour, water, honey, rosemary, and the sponge in the bowl of a standing mixer with a rubber spatula. Attach the dough hook and knead the dough at the lowest speed until smooth, about 15 minutes, adding the salt during the final 3 minutes. If the dough looks dry after the salt is added, add water in 1-tablespoon increments every 30 seconds until a smooth consistency is reached. Transfer the dough to a lightly floured surface. Lightly flour your hands and, working quickly but gently, knead in the olives in 3 batches, making sure to handle the dough as little as possible. Transfer the dough to a very lightly oiled large bowl. Cover with plastic wrap; let rise until tripled in size, at least 2 hours.

3. Turn the dough onto a lightly floured surface. Dust the top of the dough and your hands with flour. Lightly press the dough into a round by folding the edges of the dough into the middle

from the top, right, bottom, and left, sequentially, then gathering it loosely together. Transfer the dough, smooth-side down, to a colander or basket lined with heavily floured muslin or linen (or a dish towel). Cover loosely with a large sheet of aluminum foil; let the dough rise until almost doubled in size, at least 45 minutes.

4. Meanwhile, adjust an oven rack to the lower-middle position and place a large baking stone on the rack. Adjust the other rack to the lowest position and place a small empty baking pan on it. Heat the oven to 450 degrees.

5. Cover a peel or the back of a large baking sheet with a large piece of parchment. Invert the dough onto the peel and remove the muslin. Use a single-edge razor blade or very sharp knife to cut a large X about ½ inch deep into the top of the dough. Sprinkle the coarse salt, if using, into the X. With scissors, trim the excess parchment around the dough.

6. Slide the dough, still on the parchment, from the peel onto the stone; remove the peel with a quick backward jerk. Pour 2 cups hot tap water into the heated pan on the bottom rack, being careful to avoid the steam. Bake until an instant-read thermometer inserted in the bottom of the bread reads 210 degrees and the crust is very dark brown, 35 to 40 minutes, turning the bread around after 25 minutes if it is not browning evenly. Turn the oven off, open the door, and let the bread remain in the oven 10 minutes longer. Remove, then let cool to room temperature before slicing, about 2 hours. To crisp the crust, place the cooled bread in a 450-degree oven for 10 minutes.

PITTING OLIVES

Removing the pits from olives is not an easy job. We found the following method to be the most expedient. Cover a cutting board with a clean kitchen towel and spread the olives on top, spacing them about 1 inch apart. Place a second clean towel over the olives. Using a mallet, pound all of the olives firmly for 10 to 15 seconds, being careful not to split the pits. Remove the top towel and, using your fingers, press the pit out of each olive.

CHALLAH

CHALLAH IS A BRAIDED BREAD THAT IS traditionally made for the Jewish Sabbath. The best challah is rich with eggs and lightly sweetened, with a dark, shiny crust and a firm but light and tender texture. The mass-produced challah found in grocery stores can be dry, disappointingly bland, and disconcertingly fluffy. We wanted ours to be at once tender but substantial, with a rich, eggy flavor.

The ingredients for challah are flour, yeast, eggs, water or milk, sugar, salt, and butter or oil. During our initial research, we found some recipes that called for starter or sponge instead of yeast, which turned the challah-making process into a complicated and lengthy affair. Since we knew we wanted to use instant yeast, any versions requiring starter were eliminated at the outset.

We began by pitting all-purpose flour against bread flour. There was no significant difference, so we decided to stick with the more readily available all-purpose flour. One envelope (2¼ teaspoons) of instant yeast gave the challah the right amount of lift.

Next, we experimented with egg amounts. A combination of two whole eggs and one yolk proved to be the best, making a loaf with good egg flavor and a tender texture. Instead of throwing away the remaining egg white, we used it for the egg wash. We found that most recipes called for water, although a few used milk. We tried both. The challah made with milk was slightly more dense and heavy. We preferred the lighter texture of the challah made with water.

We tried granulated sugar, brown sugar, and honey in our working recipe. Differences were minimal, but we found that granulated sugar made challah with the cleanest flavor. Amounts ranging from 1 tablespoon to ½ cup were used. Because we wanted a lightly sweetened loaf, ½ cup was too much, resulting in a challah that tasted more like dessert than bread. One-quarter cup of sugar was perfect, giving the challah just the right degree of sweetness.

Would butter or oil make a better challah? Differences in flavor were minimal, but the challah made with butter had a more tender texture.

Next, we compared a loaf made with melted butter versus one made with softened butter (like Brioche on page 108). Because challah requires much less butter than brioche, we found that it didn't matter if the butter was melted or softened; both produced identical results. We decided to go with the melted butter, which could simply be added along with the eggs and water.

What was the best mixing method? We made the dough in a standing mixer, in a food processor, and by hand. The dough worked well in both the processor and standing mixer. Making the dough by hand required quite a bit of muscle power, but because the challah dough was somewhat soft and pliable, it didn't prove to be an impossible feat. Unlike brioche, which is loaded with softened butter and best kept away from warm hands, challah dough is more forgiving. Once the dough was formed and baked, there was little difference in the finished products made with the three methods.

Now that the ingredients and the mixing method were set, we needed to find the best way of shaping the loaf. We began with a simple braid, the recommended shaping method found in most cookbooks, but we ran into a problem. After being braided, the loaf rose out but not up. A flat loaf simply would not do. After trying complicated braids that involved braiding together as many as six strands of dough (and required a degree in macramé), we came up with a much simpler solution. By making two braids, one large and one small, and placing the smaller braid on top of the larger one, we made a loaf that not only appeared to be braided in a complicated manner but also achieved the height of those breads composed of more complicated braids.

Up to this point, we had been using the leftover egg white for the egg wash. Was an egg wash really necessary? We made one loaf and baked it with no egg wash. The result was surprising: Not only was the loaf pale and dull-looking, but the braids had lost their definition, almost melting into each other. An egg wash was clearly needed to get the challah's characteristic dark, shiny crust. We tried a challah brushed with a whole-egg wash instead of just the egg white. There was little difference. We decided to be frugal and stick with the egg-white wash. Challah is sometimes sprinkled with poppy or sesame seeds, and the egg-white wash helps the seeds adhere to the bread—we leave their inclusion up to you.

The last thing to tackle was the oven temperature. We tested oven temperatures from 350 to 450 degrees. Because this dough contains butter, eggs, and a fair amount of sugar (all browning agents), 450 degrees was far too high. Higher temperatures are better suited for lean breads. A more moderate 375 degrees was ideal.

Challah

MAKES 1 LARGE LOAF

We prefer to knead this dough in a standing mixer, but a food processor or your hands can do the job. If using a food processor, place the flour mixture in a processor fitted with the dough blade. Mix together the eggs, yolk, butter, and water in a large measuring cup, and with the processor running, add the egg mixture in a steady stream. Process until a ball of dough forms, about 1 minute. Remove the dough to a lightly floured surface and knead by hand for an additional minute, or until the dough becomes smooth and elastic. Alternatively, you can mix the dough by hand in a large bowl with a wooden spoon, until the dough comes together. Then transfer the dough to a lightly floured surface and knead until the dough forms a smooth ball. If the dough remains tacky, add more flour 1 tablespoon at a time. This method will take longer than using a standing mixer, but you will get the same results.

3–3¼	cups (15 to 16¼ ounces) unbleached all-purpose flour, plus more for dusting the work surface
1	envelope (about 2¼ teaspoons) instant yeast
¼	cup (1¾ ounces) sugar
1¼	teaspoons salt
2	large eggs plus 1 egg separated (reserve the white for the egg wash)
4	tablespoons (½ stick) unsalted butter, melted
½	cup plus 1 tablespoon water, at room temperature
1	teaspoon poppy or sesame seeds (optional)

1. In a medium bowl, whisk together 3 cups of the flour, the yeast, sugar, and salt; set aside. In the bowl of a standing mixer, mix together the

2 eggs, egg yolk, melted butter, and ½ cup of the water. Add the flour mixture; using the dough hook, knead at low speed until a ball of dough forms, about 5 minutes, adding the remaining ¼ cup flour, 1 tablespoon at a time, if necessary. In a small bowl, whisk the reserved egg white together with the remaining 1 tablespoon water. Cover the bowl with plastic wrap and refrigerate the egg wash until ready to use.

2. Place the dough in a very lightly oiled large bowl, turning the dough over to coat with the oil. Cover with plastic wrap and let rise in a warm place until doubled in size, 1½ to 2 hours. Gently press the dough to deflate it, cover with plastic wrap, and let rise until doubled in size again, 40 to 60 minutes.

3. Transfer the dough to a lightly floured surface. Divide the dough into 2 pieces, one roughly half the size of the other. (The small one will weigh about 9 ounces, and the large one will weigh about 18 ounces.) Divide the large piece into 3 equal pieces. Roll each piece into a 16-inch-long rope, about 1 inch in diameter. Line up the ropes of dough side by side and braid them together, pinching the ends of the braid to seal them (see the illustrations below). Place the braid on a lightly greased baking sheet. Divide the smaller piece of dough into 3 equal pieces. Roll each piece into a 16-inch-long rope, about ½ inch in diameter. Braid together, pinching the ends to seal. Brush some of the egg wash on the top of the large loaf and place the small braid on the larger braid. Loosely drape the loaf with plastic wrap and let it rise in a warm place for 30 to 45 minutes, or until the loaf becomes puffy and increases in size by a third.

BRAIDING CHALLAH

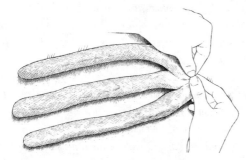

1. Divide the dough into 2 pieces—one weighing 18 ounces, the other weighing 9 ounces. Shape the large piece of dough into 3 ropes, each 16 inches long and 1 inch thick. Line up the three ropes of dough side by side. Pinch the top ends together.

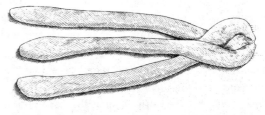

2. Take the dough rope on the right and lay it over the center rope. Take the dough rope on the left and lay it over the center rope.

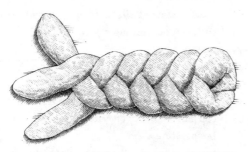

3. Repeat this process until the ropes of dough are entirely braided. Pinch the ends together, tuck both ends under the braid, and transfer the braid to a lightly greased baking sheet. Divide the smaller piece of dough into 3 equal ropes about 16 inches long and ½ inch thick and repeat the braiding process.

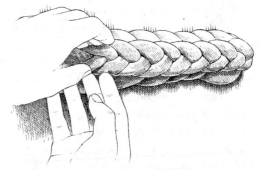

4. Brush the larger braid with some of the egg wash and place the smaller braid on top. Cover loosely with plastic wrap. Once the dough has become puffy (this will take 30 to 45 minutes), brush the top of the loaf with the remaining egg wash and bake.

4. Adjust an oven rack to the lower-middle position and heat the oven to 375 degrees. Brush the loaf with the remaining egg wash and sprinkle with the poppy seeds (if using). Bake the loaf for 30 to 40 minutes, or until it is golden brown and an instant-read thermometer inserted into the side of the loaf reads 190 degrees. Place the baking sheet on a wire rack. Let the loaf cool completely before slicing.

BRIOCHE

BRIOCHE IS A RICH AND DECADENT BREAD made with eggs, sugar, and butter. This French bakery staple is characterized by its golden color, butter-rich flavor, and fine crumb that can sometimes resemble cake more than bread. Eaten on its own, used in French toast, spread with preserves, or soaked in a rum-flavored sugar syrup (as in Babas au Rhum, page 110), good brioche is one of our favorite breads. Bad brioche is truly bad: greasy and leaden as well as overly eggy and dense. We set out to develop a brioche rich in flavor, tender in texture, and worth every calorie.

The first ingredient up for examination was the flour. We tried both all-purpose flour and bread flour. All-purpose flour was the clear winner, giving the brioche a fluffier, more tender crumb. The brioche made with bread flour was heavy and dense. Tasters quickly settled on 3 tablespoons

of sugar as the right amount for this loaf, which should have only a hint of sweetness.

One of the hallmarks of brioche is its eggy flavor. Because we wanted our brioche to be tender and rich, we started by using just yolks. To our surprise, the all-egg-yolk brioche was dry and heavy. We tried various yolk and whole-egg combinations and found that the lightest, most tender brioche was made with three whole eggs.

As for liquids, we tried water, milk, and half-and-half. Water produced the best results, giving the brioche a lighter texture than either milk or half-and-half. Ice water, rather than the more typical room temperature water, helps keep this dough (and the butter) cool. As for yeast, we tried amounts ranging from 1 teaspoon to 1½ tablespoons and got the best results with 1 tablespoon of yeast. Because of the high egg and butter content, we found that a significant amount of yeast was necessary to help the dough rise properly.

Brioche just wouldn't be brioche without butter. But how much? We tried amounts as little as 4 tablespoons and as much as a whopping 16. As we expected, more butter made the bread taste better and gave it a richer texture. However, there was a limit. We thought that if 16 tablespoons did the trick, then more would be even better. However, as the butter increased beyond 16 tablespoons, the loaves became leaden and greasy.

Now that the butter amount was set, we needed

QUICK RELEASE FOR BREAD

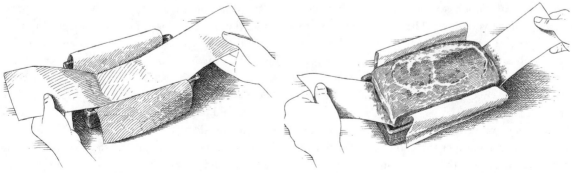

1. Make a sling for the loaf by laying long wide strips of parchment paper across the length and width of the pan so that the paper overlaps the edges.

2. Use the overlap as a handy grip when it's time to remove the loaf from the pan.

to find the best way to incorporate it. Traditionally, the butter is softened and kneaded into the dough. We wanted to know what would happen if we added melted butter instead. Adding the butter in its liquid form made the dough greasy and wet, necessitating the addition of more flour, which resulted in a drier, tougher brioche. Softened butter was a must.

On to the mixing method. Because there was so much butter in the dough, we found that kneading by hand was difficult. By the time the dough was fully kneaded, the heat from our hands had melted some of the butter, resulting in a heavy, greasy loaf. The food processor failed to totally incorporate the butter, making it necessary to finish kneading the dough by hand (again, not the answer). We needed to find a method that would knead the dough thoroughly while allowing it to remain cool. The answer was to use a standing mixer with the dough hook and a chilled mixer bowl. (It takes only about 15 minutes in the freezer for the bowl to become thoroughly chilled.) This combination evenly incorporated the butter while keeping the dough cool.

Brioche is traditionally allowed to ferment in a cool place overnight. What would happen if the dough were allowed to rise in a warm place? We let one dough rise at room temperature for two hours and put it up against one that had risen in the refrigerator overnight. The room-temperature brioche had a strong yeasty flavor, oily texture, and uneven crumb; the refrigerator brioche had a clean, mild flavor with a delicate, even texture. Allowing the dough to rise in the refrigerator accomplishes two things: The lower temperature keeps the butter from melting, and it lets the yeast develop slowly, resulting in a fine, tender crumb. After experimenting with fermentation times, we found that a stay of at least 10 hours in the refrigerator was necessary.

We knew we wanted an initial blast of high heat to give the loaf a proper rise and a nicely browned crust. To determine the best baking temperature, we tried baking the brioche at temperatures ranging from 300 to 425 degrees. After much testing, we determined that placing the loaf in a 450-degree oven, then immediately turning the

temperature down to 350 degrees for the duration of the baking gave us an evenly baked bread with a uniformly browned exterior.

Brioche

MAKES 1 LARGE LOAF

Because of all the butter in this dough, we don't recommend kneading this by hand or in a food processor. We found that a standing mixer did the best job of keeping this dough cool, especially if we chilled the mixer bowl in the freezer for 15 minutes before adding any ingredients. This recipe is best prepared over 2 days so that the dough can rise overnight in the refrigerator.

3¼–3¾	cups (16¼ to 18¾ ounces) unbleached all-purpose flour
1	tablespoon instant yeast
3	tablespoons sugar
1	teaspoon salt
3	large eggs plus 1 egg for the egg wash
½	cup ice water, plus 1 tablespoon water at room temperature for the egg wash
16	tablespoons (2 sticks) unsalted butter, cut into 16 pieces, softened but still cool

1. Make a sling for the loaf by laying long, wide strips of parchment paper across the length and width of the pan so that the paper overlaps the edges (see the illustrations on page 107). Set aside.

2. In a medium bowl, whisk together 3¼ cups of the flour and the yeast; set aside. In the chilled bowl of a standing mixer, mix together the sugar, salt, 3 eggs, and ice water. Add the flour mixture; using the dough hook, knead at low speed until a ball of dough forms, about 3 minutes. Raise the speed to medium-low and continue kneading, scraping down the sides of the bowl with a rubber spatula occasionally, until the dough becomes smooth and elastic, about 8 minutes longer (it will stick to the sides of the bowl). Add the butter, 1 piece at a time, waiting about 15 seconds between additions and scraping the sides of the bowl as necessary. Continue to knead until a very soft ball of dough forms, about 15 minutes longer, adding the remaining flour 1 tablespoon at a time as needed. Place the dough in a very lightly oiled large bowl.

Cover with plastic wrap and place in the refrigerator for 10 to 24 hours. (Because of the high butter content, the dough will rise only slightly.)

3. Flatten the dough into an 8-inch square about 1 inch thick. Roll the dough into a log and place in the parchment-lined loaf pan. Loosely cover the dough with plastic wrap and let rise at room temperature until doubled in size (it should rise slightly above the rim), 2 to 2½ hours.

4. Adjust an oven rack to the lower-middle position and heat the oven to 450 degrees. Beat the remaining egg with 1 tablespoon water and brush the loaf gently with the egg mixture. Place the loaf pan in the oven and turn the temperature down to 350 degrees. Bake the loaf until browned and an instant-read thermometer inserted into the side of the loaf reads 190 degrees, 50 to 60 minutes, rotating it from front to back halfway through the baking time. Place the loaf pan on a wire rack and cool for 15 minutes. Remove the brioche from the loaf pan by using the parchment overlaps as a grip. Place the loaf on a wire rack. Let the brioche cool completely before slicing.

BABAS AU RHUM

DESSERT HAS BEEN FASHIONED FROM LEFT-over bread for centuries. Legend has it that the baba au rhum was invented in the 1600s by an exiled Polish king who improved his stale bread by soaking it in rum. The king named his invention after his favorite folk hero, Ali Baba. Today, babas are usually individual buttery and sweet baked goods that are a cross between cake and bread. Bad babas can be soggy, dense, and cloyingly sweet, like bad fruitcake drowned in rum. We wanted babas with subtly sweet fruit flavors and a light texture, imbued by a flavorful rum syrup.

Looking at various baba recipes, we found that the ingredient list was similar to that of brioche: flour, eggs, sugar, salt, yeast, and a copious amount of softened butter. Two things set it apart from brioche: a much shorter rising time and the addition of dried fruit and rum syrup. We began by simply making our standard brioche recipe, adding raisins, and baking it in baba molds, which are specially made cylindrical molds. What we got were babas that were bready with a tight crumb, miniature versions of our brioche loaves. Not bad, but we wanted the babas to have a lighter texture and more open crumb—less bread-like and more like a cake.

The first ingredient we examined was the flour. We wanted a crumb that was delicate, yet sturdy enough to stand up to a rum-syrup soaking. Babas made with cake flour never rose high enough and fell apart when dunked in the syrup. Bread flour made the interior too dense and chewy. All-purpose flour was the best choice. It had enough gluten to handle the butter and yeast, and it still produced a baba with a light interior.

Next, we experimented with different types and amounts of liquid. Milk, water, and half-and-half were used. The fluffiest babas were made using water; both the milk and half-and-half contributed to a heavier texture. In fact, the more water we used, the lighter the babas became. Several doughs were made, varying in consistency from kneadable bread dough to loose cake batter. The babas made from the looser batter had a light, airy interior. Four whole eggs and 1 cup of butter added just the right amount of richness. Because most of the sweetness would be coming from the rum syrup, we didn't want the babas themselves to be too sugary. One-quarter cup of sugar did the trick. Granulated sugar was preferred over both light and dark brown sugars for its clean flavor. Like brioche, this butter-laden batter needed a fair amount of yeast. One envelope of yeast (2¼ teaspoons) provided the right amount of leavening.

Along the way, we had seen recipes that called for raisins, currants, citrus zest, candied fruit, and spices such as clove, cinnamon, and nutmeg. After testing all of them, we found that a simple combination of orange zest and currants had the best flavor and complemented the rum syrup nicely. Spices and candied fruit overwhelmed the babas and didn't go well with the rum.

Up until now, we had been making the batter using a standing mixer with the paddle attachment. Because of the batter's consistency, we wondered if it would be possible to mix it together by hand or in a food processor. (The processor's fast action makes it a better tool for batter than for stiff dough.) We made babas using all three methods and were surprised by the outcome. After letting the batter rise for two hours, the difference became clear. Neither the ones made the old-fashioned way (with a bowl and wooden spoon) nor those made with the processor rose as high as the ones made using the standing mixer. Once the babas were baked, we saw even more differences. The batch made by hand had an uneven texture, and the ones made in the processor were dense and had a craggy surface. The standing mixer was clearly the best choice. It incorporated the softened butter more thoroughly than the wooden spoon and more gently than the processor.

Our next problem was finding the right baking pan. Individual baba molds are available at specialty stores, but we wondered if there was another, more widely available, pan we could use. Babas made in muffin tins were squat and lacked the characteristic tall, cylindrical shape. Popover pans did the trick. The pan's shape was almost identical to that of baba molds.

Next we tried baking the babas at temperatures ranging from 350 to 450 degrees. Higher temperatures were not the answer here. The quantity of browning agents in the batter (eggs, sugar, butter) meant that a more moderate temperature would be required. The babas baked at 375 degrees achieved the best rise, the right amount of browning, and the most tender texture.

The last item to test was the rum syrup. Although dark rum is traditionally used, we tried light rum as well. Our palates agreed with tradition; the dark rum had a much richer, deeper flavor that gave the babas a spicy character. Although we found recipes that used other flavorings in the syrup, we preferred syrup made simply with rum, water, and sugar. The addition of spices and citrus zest got in the way of the rum's flavor. We came across some recipes that called for glazing babas. We liked the sheen that a glaze gave these buns, and with a brush of apple or apricot jelly, we had found the babas we were looking for.

Babas au Rhum
MAKES 12

The babas can be baked in advance. Keep them in an airtight container at room temperature for up to 2 days, or wrapped well and frozen for up to 2 weeks. Bring them to room temperature, soak them in the syrup, and glaze them just before or up to 2 hours before serving. The babas will absorb the syrup more readily if the syrup is warm. If desired, serve with lightly sweetened whipped cream.

BATTER

3	cups (15 ounces) unbleached all-purpose flour
I	envelope (about 2 1/4 teaspoons) instant yeast
1/4	cup (1 3/4 ounces) sugar
1/2	teaspoon salt
1/2	cup water, at room temperature
4	large eggs, beaten
2	teaspoons grated zest from I orange
16	tablespoons (2 sticks) unsalted butter, cut into 16 pieces and softened
1/4	cup currants

SYRUP

1 1/4	cups water
1/2	cup (3 1/2 ounces) sugar
1/2	cup dark rum

GLAZE

1/2	cup apple or apricot jelly, heated

1. FOR THE BATTER: In a medium bowl, whisk together the flour, yeast, sugar, and salt. In the bowl of a standing mixer fitted with the paddle, mix together the water, eggs, and orange zest. Add the flour mixture and mix at low speed until a very loose dough forms and no dry spots remain, scraping the sides of the bowl as necessary, about 2 minutes. With the mixer running at low speed, add the softened butter, one piece at a time. Continue to beat until the batter is smooth, about 2 minutes. Add the currants and beat until incorporated, about 15 seconds longer.

2. Place the batter into 2 lightly greased popover pans, filling each cup halfway. Loosely cover with plastic wrap and let rise at warm room temperature until the batter reaches the tops of the

popover pans, about 2 hours.

3. Adjust the oven rack to the lower-middle position and heat the oven to 375 degrees. Bake until the babas are golden brown, rotating the pans halfway through, 14 to 17 minutes. When the babas have cooled slightly, remove them from the pans and place them on wire racks to cool.

4. FOR THE SYRUP: Stir the water and sugar together in a small saucepan. Place over medium heat and bring to a simmer, stirring occasionally. When the sugar has dissolved, turn off the heat and add the rum. Stir to combine.

5. Using tongs, take a cooled baba and dip it into the warm rum syrup, turning to coat, leaving the baba in the syrup for no more than 5 seconds. Place the soaked baba back on the rack. Repeat with the remaining babas. Brush the melted apple jelly onto the top of each baba. If desired, serve with lightly sweetened whipped cream.

CRESCENT ROLLS

PERHAPS THE MOST POPULAR DINNER ROLL served at holiday tables is the crescent roll. What's a shame is that the crescent rolls most Americans serve come from the supermarket refrigerator case—those diminutive arcs of prefab dough that taste artificial and go stale in minutes. We wanted to make rolls that were tender, rich, and easy enough to accommodate in an already jam-packed holiday schedule.

Our first few attempts turned out rolls that were paunchy and flat-flavored. They were hard to handle, stuck to the countertop, and had much too much yeast. Many bread recipes try to speed up the rising time of a dough by using an excessive amount of yeast—sometimes as much as 2 tablespoons for 3 or 4 cups of flour. What you get besides speed is a cheesy-flavored, lackluster roll that goes stale quickly. So a more modest quantity of yeast was going to be key.

For flour, our options included all-purpose and bread flour. Because crescent rolls should be soft and supple, bread flour, with a high protein content that makes for strong gluten development, would give the rolls more chew and a crustier

crust than we wanted. We stuck with our kitchen workhorse, unbleached all-purpose flour. We particularly like a lower-protein all-purpose flour like Gold Medal in this recipe.

The next variable was the eggs. The working version of our recipe called for one. We compared batches made with one, two, and three eggs, and the last batch was the winner. These rolls were soft and pillowy, with a lovely golden crumb.

Although we had been using whole milk in our testing, we wanted to compare three liquids side by side: water, skim milk, and whole milk. The whole-milk rolls tasted the richest but were also the densest. The rolls made with water lacked flavor and tenderness. The rolls made with skim milk were just right—flavorful and rich.

Up until now, we had been adding 8 tablespoons of softened butter in 1-tablespoon increments while the bread dough was kneaded in a standing mixer. Could these rolls absorb more fat without becoming heavy or greasy? We increased the butter in the next two batches by 4 and 8 tablespoons, respectively. It was clear that these rolls liked their fat; they took to 16 tablespoons of butter (two whole sticks) with aplomb. However, adding the softened butter incrementally to the mixing dough was a messy and drawn-out process. To simplify things, we decided to melt the butter and add it to the dough along with the other ingredients. This worked perfectly.

So far, we had developed a better-than-average crescent roll recipe, but the crust was not sufficiently flaky, and we were having difficulty rolling out and shaping the sticky dough. The easiest way to handle a butter-laden, sticky dough is to let it rest in the refrigerator before rolling it out. This combats two problems. First, the gluten in the dough relaxes, allowing the dough to be rolled without "bucking," or snapping back into shape after rolling. Second, the butter in the dough solidifies, making the dough easier to roll and less sticky to handle.

We had intended to refrigerate the risen and punched-down dough for a couple of hours, but we forgot about it until the next morning. Panic-stricken, we took the dough out of the refrigerator and easily rolled it into a long sheet, cut it, and shaped the pieces into little bundles. After allowing the rolls to rise at room temperature for about an hour, we popped them into the oven. When they were done, we noticed the difference immediately—blisters! When we bit into a roll, the crust snapped and flaked. This was the kind of crescent roll we had been trying to achieve all along, with rich flavor and a flaky crust.

To find out why an overnight chill had paid off, we called Maggie Glezer, a baker certified by the American Institute of Baking. She explained that when dough is chilled for a long time—a process bakers call retarding—acetic acid builds up in the dough, giving it a richer flavor as well as a blistered crust. Carl Hoseney, professor emeritus in the department of grain science and industry at Kansas State University, added that blisters are also caused by gases escaping from the dough during retardation.

With these points in mind, we set out to see if a longer stay in the refrigerator would be even better. We made another batch of dough, let it rise at room temperature, punched it down, and put it in the fridge. The next morning, we formed the dough into crescents, then, instead of letting the rolls rise for an hour and baking them, we put them back in the fridge. The following day, we let the rolls lose their chill at room temperature, then baked them. The crust was even more blistered than before. Next we tried chilling the rolls for three nights; these were better still, with an excellent flavor and a stunning, crackled crust. What we also liked about these rolls is that all you need do on the day they are served is to let them rise one last time and bake them, creating no dirty dishes and taking up no precious workspace.

All we had to do now was tweak the baking method. Up until this point, we had been baking the rolls at 375 degrees from start to finish. But during our research on retarding dough, we learned that boosting the oven temperature to 425 degrees for the initial bake, then lowering it to 350 degrees when the rolls were just starting to color, would improve their oven spring. (Oven spring, a term used by professional bakers, defines the dramatic increase in size caused when bread gets that initial blast of heat from the oven.) This temperature combination worked, making the rolls pleasantly larger and loftier.

We wondered if adding steam to the baking bread would help with oven spring and encourage formation of a thin and delicate crust. After placing the rolls on the lower-middle rack, we poured a cup of hot tap water into a preheated pan on the lowest rack. The burst of steam, combined with the high oven temperature, gave the rolls an even higher rise and turned the crust into a thin and still-flakier shell. Now we had a dramatic-looking roll with great flavor, a lovely, tender crumb, and a delicate crust. We bit into these crescent rolls with the satisfaction of knowing that making them would be just as easy to fit into a busy holiday schedule as popping open a can.

Crescent Rolls

MAKES 16

You can make the dough up to 4 days ahead of time or even partially bake the rolls and freeze them for longer storage. To do this, begin baking the rolls as instructed, but let them bake at 350 degrees for only 4 minutes, or until the tops and bottoms brown slightly. Remove them from the oven and let cool. Place the partially baked rolls in a single layer inside a zipper-lock bag and freeze. When you're ready to serve them, defrost at room temperature and place them in a preheated 350-degree oven for 12 to 16 minutes. You can freeze the rolls for up to 1 month.

DOUGH

- ³/₄ cup skim milk
- 16 tablespoons (2 sticks) unsalted butter, cut into 16 pieces
- ¹/₄ cup (1 ³/₄ ounces) sugar
- 3 large eggs
- 4 cups (20 ounces) lower-protein unbleached all-purpose flour (such as Gold Medal or Pillsbury), plus more for dusting the work surface and dough
- 1 teaspoon instant yeast
- 1 ¹/₂ teaspoons salt

EGG WASH

- 1 egg white
- 1 teaspoon water

1. FOR THE DOUGH: Heat the milk, butter, and sugar in a small saucepan or in the microwave until the butter is mostly melted and the mixture is warm (about 110 degrees), about 1½ minutes. Whisk to dissolve the sugar. Beat the eggs lightly in a medium bowl; add about a third of the warm milk mixture to the eggs, whisking to combine. When the bottom of the bowl feels warm, add the remaining milk mixture, whisking to combine.

2. Combine the flour and yeast in the bowl of a standing mixer fitted with the paddle; mix at the lowest speed to blend, about 15 seconds. With the mixer running, add the milk and egg mixture in a steady stream; mix at low speed until a loose, shiny dough forms (you may also see satiny webs as the dough moves in the bowl), about 1 minute. Increase the speed to medium and beat 1 minute; add the salt slowly and continue beating until stronger webs form, about 3 minutes longer. (The dough will remain loose rather than forming a neat, cohesive mass.) Transfer the dough to a large lightly oiled bowl, cover the bowl with plastic wrap, and place in a warm, draft-free spot until the dough doubles in bulk and the surface feels tacky, about 3 hours.

3. Line a rimmed baking sheet with plastic wrap. Sprinkle the dough with flour (no more than 2 tablespoons) to prevent sticking and press down. Turn the dough onto a floured work surface and form into a rough rectangle. Transfer the rectangle to the lined baking sheet, cover with plastic wrap, and refrigerate overnight.

4. Line a rimmed baking sheet with parchment paper. Turn the dough rectangle onto a lightly floured work surface and, following the illustrations below, roll and shape. Arrange the crescents in 4 rows on the parchment-lined baking sheet; wrap the baking sheet with plastic wrap and refrigerate at least 2 hours or up to 3 days.

5. Remove the baking sheet with the chilled rolls from the refrigerator, unwrap, and cover with an overturned large disposable roasting pan. (Alternatively, place the baking sheet inside a large plastic bag.) Let rise until the crescents feel slightly tacky and soft and have lost their chill, 45 to 60 minutes. Meanwhile, adjust an oven rack to the lower-middle position. Adjust the other rack to the lowest position and place an empty baking pan on it. Heat the oven to 425 degrees.

6. FOR THE EGG WASH: Whisk the egg white with the water in a small bowl until well combined. With a pastry brush, lightly dab the risen crescent rolls with the egg wash. Transfer the baking sheet with the rolls to the lower-middle oven rack and, working quickly, pour 1 cup hot tap water into the hot baking pan on the bottom rack. Close the door immediately and bake 10 minutes; reduce the oven temperature to 350 degrees and continue baking until the tops and bottoms of the rolls are deep golden brown, 12 to 16 minutes longer. Transfer the rolls to a wire rack, cool for 5 minutes, and serve warm.

SHAPING CRESCENT ROLLS

1. Roll the dough to a 20 by 13-inch rectangle; use a pizza wheel to trim the edges. Cut the dough in half lengthwise, then cut 16 triangles, as illustrated.

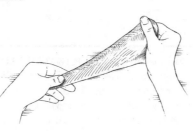

2. Before rolling the crescents, elongate each triangle of dough, stretching it an additional 2 to 3 inches in length.

3. Starting at the wide end, gently roll up each crescent, ending with the pointed tip on the bottom, and push the ends toward each other to form a crescent shape.

Handling Basic Baking Ingredients

STORING CAKE FLOUR

Most bakers keep all-purpose flour in a covered container to prolong freshness and facilitate measuring. However, most bakers don't bother to treat cake flour this way. In the test kitchen, we like to store cake flour in a large, heavy-duty zipper-lock bag, which is sealed and stored in the original box. The bag protects the flour from humidity (and bugs), and it's easy to dip a measuring cup right into the bag and level off the excess back into the bag.

SOFTENING BUTTER IN A HURRY

It can take a long time (sometimes an hour) for chilled butter to soften on the counter. The microwave is a quick but sometimes imperfect solution (see box below). We like to cut the butter into tablespoon-size pieces, which should soften in just 15 minutes—the time it takes to gather other ingredients and heat the oven. If, despite all precautions, your butter is still too cool when you start to cream it, a quick remedy is to wrap the mixing bowl with a warm, damp towel and continue creaming.

MELTING CHOCOLATE

Melting chocolate in a heatproof bowl set over a pot of simmering water is a classic technique. This method works well but is a bit of a bother. In the test kitchen, we often handle this chore in the microwave (see box below). If you need to melt a relatively small amount of chocolate and don't own a microwave, you can use the gentle heat from an electric coffee maker. Place the chopped chocolate in a small heatproof bowl and cover the bowl with plastic wrap, being careful not to bring the plastic too far down the sides of the bowl. Place the bowl on the burner plate of an electric drip coffee machine and turn on the coffee machine. Whatever you do, don't melt chocolate in a pan set directly on the stovetop—it will likely burn.

MELTING CHOCOLATE IN A MICROWAVE

Place the chopped chocolate in a microwave-safe bowl and microwave at 50 percent power for 2 minutes. Stir and continue heating until melted. If melting butter with chocolate, add the butter at the 2-minute mark when stirring the chocolate. The timing will vary based on the amount of chocolate being melted and the strength of your microwave.

CUTTING BUTTER INTO FINE DICE

Many recipes call for chilled butter cut into small dice. Although this sounds easy enough, the butter can soften if you just start chopping away with abandon. Here's how we handle the task, quickly and efficiently, so the butter doesn't warm up.

1. Cut the butter lengthwise into 3 even strips.

2. Separate the strips and then cut each lengthwise into thirds.

3. Stack the strips on top of each other, then cut them crosswise into 1/4-inch dice—a size that works well in most biscuit and pie doughs.

SOFTENING BUTTER IN A MICROWAVE

Using the microwave to soften butter can be risky business. A few seconds too long and the butter can melt and your cakes or cookies might not rise properly. If you're going to soften butter in the microwave, here's how to keep it from melting.

Place 4 tablespoons of butter in one piece on a small plate and microwave for 1 minute at 10 percent power. Press on the butter with your finger to see if it has softened sufficiently; if not, heat for an additional 20 seconds at 10 percent power. This method also works for whole sticks (or even two sticks). Just increase the second microwave time by 10 seconds for each additional 2 tablespoons of butter. For example, a whole stick should be microwaved for 1 minute, checked, and then microwaved for 40 seconds more. These times work in newer, 1100-watt microwaves. If you own an older, 800-watt microwave, times will be longer.

PARKER HOUSE ROLLS

WE HAVE A SOFT SPOT FOR PARKER HOUSE rolls. The epitome of thin-crusted, fluffy-crumbed American rolls, they're pillowy soft, a little sweet, and packed with butter. They owe their name to Boston's famed Parker House, a hotel that has been a bastion of Brahmin hospitality since the middle of the nineteenth century. Truth be told, the Parker House roll is pretty much a standard dinner roll; it's the shape that matters. It starts off as a round roll that is flattened, buttered, and folded in half. For our version, we wanted a simple, rich roll that would be ready in the least time possible.

Almost all of the recipes we gathered had the same ingredients in varying proportions. They were fairly rich, loaded with milk, eggs, butter, and a fair amount of sugar. Each recipe also employed a healthy amount of yeast for a quick rise and big yeast flavor. We tinkered with proportions until we arrived at a roll that was buttery but not too rich and very tender-crumbed from the large amount of milk and egg.

Selecting the ideal kneading time took some testing. With a soft, billowy, tender crumb as our goal, we knew a reasonably short knead was in order, but how short was short? We tried times of four to 10 minutes (in a standing mixer at medium speed) and were most pleased with a six-minute knead, followed by a scant minute of hand kneading. With 10 minutes of kneading, the dough's gluten was overdeveloped and too elastic—its texture more like that of a chewy sandwich. With four minutes, the dough lacked structure and collapsed during baking. Six minutes built just enough gluten for support but not enough to detract from the airy crumb.

With a full envelope of yeast to a scant 4 cups of flour, we knew a quick rise would not be a problem. We also decided to hasten the first rise by setting the dough in a preheated oven. We found that an oven heated to 200 degrees for 10 minutes and then turned off retained just enough heat to speed along the rising dough without having a detrimental effect on the yeast. Within 45 minutes, the dough had doubled in volume.

After we divided the dough, we rounded the individual portions on the countertop until they developed a smooth, tight skin and perfect globe shape. Rounding relies on the friction created between the moisture in the dough and the work surface, and this process helps the dough rise by redistributing the yeast and sugars and expunging the carbon dioxide.

By the time we rounded all 24 balls of dough, the first to be rounded had relaxed enough to be shaped. We found that the best way to shape the dough was to lightly flatten it with our palms and then roll it into an oval shape with a small French-style rolling pin or short dowel. We found out the hard way that it is important to keep the edges thicker than the center so that they will adhere to each other when the dough is folded and not puff open during baking.

After folding and spacing the rolls on a baking sheet, we gave them a light brushing of butter. They were now ready for their second rise, this time outside of the oven. Traditional recipes suggest dunking the formed rolls in melted butter, but we thought this would be too much of a good thing.

We tried baking the rolls in baking dishes and on baking sheets and were most pleased with the sheets. While we liked the height of the rolls baked in a dish, the rolls in the middle were gummy long after the outer rolls were perfectly baked. A metal baking sheet delivered even heat and got the rolls out of the oven in about 20 minutes. Parker House rolls must be eaten warm. After a 10-minute rest once out of the oven, they are ready to serve, preferably with a roast and plenty of gravy.

Parker House Rolls

MAKES 24

When rounding the dough and shaping the rolls, it is important to keep the remaining dough covered, otherwise it will quickly dry out and develop a "skin." Rolling the dough into symmetrical rounds takes a little practice, but you will quickly get the hang of it. A dry, unfloured work surface helps because the dough will stick a little. Although we like using a French-style rolling pin for flattening the rolls, a more traditional option is a thin dowel or the handle of a wooden spoon. Whatever your choice, lightly flour it or the dough will stick to it.

115

1¼ cups whole milk

2 tablespoons sugar

1 envelope (about 2¼ teaspoons) instant yeast

1 large egg, lightly beaten

4–4¼ cups (20 to 21¼ ounces) unbleached all-purpose flour, plus more for dusting the work surface

1½ teaspoons salt

14 tablespoons (1¾ sticks) unsalted butter, 8 tablespoons cut into 8 pieces and softened

1. Adjust an oven rack to the lowest position and heat the oven to 200 degrees. Once the oven reaches 200 degrees, maintain the oven temperature for 10 minutes and then turn off the heat.

2. Heat the milk and sugar together in a small saucepan or in the microwave until the mixture is lukewarm (about 100 degrees). Whisk in the yeast and the egg and set aside. Combine 4 cups of the flour and the salt in the bowl of a standing mixer fitted with the paddle and mix at the lowest speed to blend, about 15 seconds. With the mixer running at low speed, add the liquid mixture in a steady stream and mix until the flour is moistened, about 1 minute. With the mixer still running, slowly begin to add the 8 tablespoons of softened butter, 1 piece at a time, until incorporated into the dough. Increase the speed to medium and beat until the dough is thoroughly combined and scrappy, about 2 minutes longer. Replace the paddle with a dough hook and knead the dough at medium speed until smooth but still sticky, about 6 minutes, adding more flour in 1-tablespoon increments, if necessary for the dough to clear the sides of the bowl. Scrape the dough out of the mixing bowl and onto a lightly floured work surface and knead by hand until very smooth and soft, but no longer sticky, about 1 minute. Transfer the dough to a very lightly oiled large bowl, cover with plastic wrap, and place in the warmed oven until the dough doubles in bulk, about 45 minutes.

3. Once the dough has doubled, press it down,

SHAPING PARKER HOUSE ROLLS

1. Divide the relaxed dough into two equal pieces and, with your hands, pull and shape each piece until it is 18 inches long and about 1½ inches across.

2. With a bench scraper, cut each length of dough into twelve 1½-inch-square pieces (each piece will weigh about 1½ ounces). Loosely cover all 24 pieces with plastic wrap.

3. With a cupped palm, roll each piece of dough into a smooth, tight ball and then loosely cover it with plastic wrap.

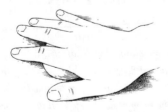  

4. Beginning with the ball rounded first (because the dough has relaxed), use the palm of your hand to flatten the ball of dough into a ½-inch-thick circle.

5. With a small rolling pin or thick dowel, floured to prevent sticking, flatten out the center of the dough until the circle becomes a rough oval. Make sure to keep the edges thicker than the middle.

6. Lightly brush the dough with melted butter, then fold in half and gently seal the edges. Place the roll on the prepared baking sheet. Repeat steps 4 through 6 with the remaining balls of dough, making sure to space the rolls evenly on the baking sheet.

replace the plastic wrap, and allow the dough to rest for 5 minutes. Meanwhile, melt the remaining 6 tablespoons butter and, with a pastry brush, liberally butter the bottom and sides of a large rimmed baking sheet with 3 tablespoons of the melted butter. Follow the illustrations on page 116 to shape the dough into rolls and place them on the baking sheet. Lightly brush the tops of the rolls with the remaining 3 tablespoons melted butter and loosely cover with plastic wrap. Set the rolls in a warm place and let rise until almost doubled, about 45 minutes.

4. When the rolls are almost fully risen, adjust an oven rack to the middle position and heat the oven to 375 degrees. Bake the rolls until the tops are dark golden brown, 20 to 22 minutes. Transfer the rolls to a wire rack and cool for 10 minutes. Serve warm.

GLAZED CINNAMON ROLLS

A PUFFY CINNAMON ROLL COATED WITH thick white icing brings out the child in all of us, encouraging even the most mature person to greedily uncoil its tight swirls and dig in. Some of us in the test kitchen have been known to drop by the local mall just to worship at that shrine to calorie-laden cinnamon rolls (which shall remain nameless). As delicious as those artery-clogging rolls can be, they are too much for all but the rarest hedonistic fit. They are so sweet and so rich that it's nearly impossible to finish one roll.

Our ideal cinnamon roll is a little more reserved. The dough should be soft and rich but not greasy. The filling should be slightly sweet, rather than sugary sweet, and potent with cinnamon. The icing should be creamy and thick and boast a tang sufficient to balance the richness and sweetness elsewhere in the roll.

With our ideal cinnamon roll in mind, we collected recipes and started testing. The recipes we found used a variety of dough types, from lean sandwich bread dough to buttery brioche dough (a very rich French dough made with huge amounts of egg yolks and butter). While we were inclined toward recipes using the rich brioche-style dough because they would undoubtedly taste better, after further thought we realized that combining such a rich dough with cinnamon filling and glaze would be gilding the lily.

We decided to start with our recipe for basic American sandwich bread made with milk and a modest amount of butter (just 2 tablespoons). To develop richness, we tried adding varying amounts of eggs, butter, and cream. With too many whole eggs, the dough turned hard, dry, and almost cakey, though it did have an appealing golden hue. More butter gave the dough more flavor and a softer texture. However, with too much butter, the dough practically oozed off the counter and was difficult to work with. Cream, surprisingly, did little at all. Milk was just fine for this dough.

After many attempts, we settled on a soft dough enriched with a good amount of butter (8 tablespoons) as well as a single whole egg and two egg yolks. When baked, this dough had a tender crumb, buttery richness, slight golden color, and enough gluten development for a little resiliency. (Gluten is the protein formed when flour is mixed with water and the mixture is kneaded; it gives bread its structure.) The recipe also allowed us to add the butter melted rather than in softened pieces, as for brioche.

With our dough ready, we turned our attention to the filling, which came together easily. Our tasters preferred cinnamon mixed with just enough sugar to temper the cinnamon's bitterness. Tasters liked rolls with a whopping 3 tablespoons of cinnamon.

We tested granulated sugar as well as light and dark brown sugar in the filling. Granulated sugar was too dry and added little flavor. Dark brown sugar proved too wet and turned syrupy, like the filling for a sticky bun. And the strong molasses flavor detracted from the cinnamon. Light brown sugar proved the best sweetener, adding moisture and a lighter molasses flavor that complemented the cinnamon. Salt mixed with the cinnamon and sugar helped marry the flavors and sharpen the sugar's sweetness.

Shaping the dough into pinwheel spirals could not have been any easier. The soft dough gracefully yielded to a light touch under the rolling pin as we rolled it out. We then sprinkled it with the filling and rolled it up slowly and tightly so that the rolls would not uncoil while cooking. The best tool for cutting the soft dough into rounds turned out to be dental floss. Eccentric as it seems, using dental floss (make sure it's unflavored) lets you smoothly cut through soft dough without squeezing the filling out of place.

Although a few tasters liked a thin, drizzled powdered sugar and cream glaze, most tasters preferred a thick, tangy cream cheese icing. We altered a standard cream cheese icing by omitting the butter and adding corn syrup for glossiness and smoothness. A judicious smear of icing (rather than a heavy, thick coating) was appropriate on these civilized rolls.

Glazed Cinnamon Rolls

MAKES 12

Because cinnamon is the predominant flavor in these rolls, make sure to have good-quality, fresh cinnamon on hand. While we rarely grind our own cinnamon, we try to make sure that our ground cinnamon is less than 6 months old and from a reputable source, like Penzeys or McCormick/ Schilling. This dough should be very tender and soft, so be stingy with additions of flour. Only a very light dusting is necessary to prevent the dough from sticking to the work surface while rolling it.

DOUGH

1/2	cup milk
8	tablespoons (1 stick) unsalted butter
1/2	cup warm water (about 110 degrees)
1	envelope (about 2 1/4 teaspoons) instant yeast
1/4	cup (1 3/4 ounces) sugar
1	large egg plus 2 large egg yolks
1 1/2	teaspoons salt
4–4 1/4	cups (20 to 21 1/4 ounces) unbleached all-purpose flour, plus more for dusting the work surface

ICING

8	ounces cream cheese, softened but still cool
2	tablespoons corn syrup
2	tablespoons heavy cream
1	cup (4 ounces) confectioners' sugar, sifted to remove any lumps
1	teaspoon vanilla extract
	Pinch salt

FILLING

3/4	cup packed (5 1/4 ounces) light brown sugar
3	tablespoons ground cinnamon
1/8	teaspoon salt

1. FOR THE DOUGH: Heat the milk and butter in a small saucepan or in the microwave until the butter melts. Remove the pan from the heat and set aside until the mixture is lukewarm (about 100 degrees).

2. In the bowl of a standing mixer fitted with the paddle, mix together the water, yeast, sugar, egg, and yolks at low speed until well mixed. Add the salt, warm milk mixture, and 2 cups of the flour and mix at medium speed until thoroughly blended, about 1 minute. Switch to the dough hook, add another 2 cups of the flour, and knead at medium speed (adding up to 1/4 cup more flour, 1 tablespoon at a time, if necessary) until the dough is smooth and freely clears the sides of the bowl, about 10 minutes. Scrape the dough onto a lightly floured work surface. Shape the dough into a round, place it in a very lightly oiled large bowl, and cover the bowl with plastic wrap. Leave in a warm, draft-free spot until doubled in bulk, 1½ to 2 hours.

3. FOR THE ICING: While the dough rises, combine all of the icing ingredients in the bowl of a standing mixer and blend together at low speed until roughly combined, about 1 minute. Increase the speed to high and mix until the icing is uniformly smooth and free of cream cheese lumps, about 2 minutes. Transfer the icing to a small bowl, cover with plastic wrap, and refrigerate.

4. TO ROLL AND FILL THE DOUGH: After the dough has doubled, press it down and turn it out onto a lightly floured work surface. Using a rolling pin, shape the dough into a 16 by 12-inch rectangle, with a long side facing you. Mix together the filling ingredients in a small bowl and sprinkle the filling evenly over the dough, leaving a ½-inch border at the far edge. Following the illustrations on page 120, roll the dough, beginning with the long edge

closest to you and using both hands to pinch the dough with your fingertips as you roll. Moisten the top border with water and seal the roll. Lightly dust the roll with flour and press on the ends if necessary to make a uniform 16-inch cylinder. Grease a 13 by 9-inch baking dish. Cut the roll into 12 equal pieces using dental floss and place the rolls, cut-side up, evenly in the prepared baking dish. Cover with plastic wrap and place in a warm, draft-free spot until doubled in bulk, 1½ to 2 hours.

5. TO BAKE THE ROLLS: When the rolls are almost fully risen, adjust an oven rack to the middle position and heat the oven to 350 degrees. Bake the rolls until golden brown and an instant-read thermometer inserted into the center of one reads 185 to 188 degrees, 25 to 30 minutes. Invert the rolls onto a wire rack and cool for 10 minutes. Turn the rolls upright on a large serving plate and use a rubber spatula to spread the icing on them. Serve immediately.

STICKY BUNS

ALTHOUGH BETTER KNOWN FOR CHEESESTEAKS and Rocky films, Philadelphia's best export, in our humble opinion, is the sticky bun. These rich, tender rolls are swirled with sugar and spices and liberally coated with a sticky caramel and pecan glaze. Sticky buns should be over-the-top and sinfully rich. There's no such thing as a "slightly rich" sticky bun.

For the base of our sticky bun dough, we hoped to adapt the dough from our cinnamon roll recipe (the cinnamon roll being the polite, uptown relative of the sticky bun). While not quite as rich as brioche dough, which many recipes appear to use for sticky buns, our cinnamon roll dough was buttery and chewy and much easier to make than brioche. Our intuition proved right: The rich, soft dough was perfectly suited to the job and was as delicious with pecans and caramel as with cinnamon and cream cheese icing. Our only alterations to the dough were the addition of a little extra sugar to make the dough moister (and more decadent) and a healthy dose of vanilla to complement the caramel glaze.

Most of the flavor in sticky buns comes from the topping, so the filling should be simple and must complement both the caramel and the pecans. A thick smear of butter was a given, as was a coating of sugar. Granulated sugar lent little flavor, so we chose dark brown sugar for its deep, earthy notes. We found a few traditional sticky bun recipes flavored with cardamom (reflecting the once substantial Scandinavian population in the Philadelphia area), and we loved the slightly exotic flavor and aroma of this spice. A little cinnamon added complexity, and salt tied all the flavors together.

The sticky-sweet sauce is certainly the most important element of a proper sticky bun. We found most recipes make a quick "caramel" sauce by combining brown sugar, corn syrup, and butter. When we tried this sort of sauce, the flavors were one-dimensional and the color was unappealing—sort of thin and transparent. We decided that if we were going to go to all the trouble of making sticky buns, it was worth making a real caramel sauce.

While a lot of home cooks are hesitant to make caramel sauce because of the perceived dangers of molten sugar, there is really nothing to fear. We came up with a foolproof technique that could not be any easier or safer. To prevent unmelted sugar clumps from marring the sauce's supple texture, we dissolved the sugar in water and then brought the mixture to a boil. In a separate pot, we heated the remaining ingredients—cream, butter, vanilla, corn syrup, and salt. (The liquid being added to the caramelized sugar must be quite hot to prevent the caramel from clumping and to reduce spattering.) As we boiled the sugar syrup, we monitored it with a candy thermometer; when it reached the dark amber hue we desired, it registered about 350 degrees. As soon as it reached 350 degrees, we removed the caramel from the heat to prevent further darkening and added the hot cream mixture. A brief stir combined everything, and our sauce was done.

With our method perfected, we focused on the ratio of ingredients in our caramel sauce. Traditional caramel sauces have almost equal amounts of cream and sugar. We reduced the amount of cream so that the sauce would better adhere to the buns. We also wanted the sauce to harden and turn sticky as it cooled, a must for any self-respecting sticky bun. Adding more butter accomplished this goal and improved the sheen of our sauce.

As for the pecans, toasted and coarsely chopped was the way to go, according to all of our tasters. Untoasted nuts tasted bland and steamed. A mere five minutes in a skillet over medium heat dramatically improved their flavor. Whole pecans looked inviting on top of our sticky buns, but they proved difficult to eat. A coarse chop allowed the nuts to coat the buns evenly and fall into all the nooks and crannies.

Sticky Buns

MAKES 12

The only tricky part of this recipe is turning out the baked buns from the baking dish; the caramel coating is very hot and gooey. We like the convenient handles on a Pyrex baking dish, which allow for a firm grasp out of harm's way. Cardamom is extremely volatile and quickly loses its flavor once ground. If you have a spice grinder, buy whole cardamom pods, remove the seeds, and simply pulse the seeds until reduced to a fine powder.

DOUGH

Dough from Glazed Cinnamon Rolls (page 118), with sugar increased to 1/2 cup and 2 teaspoons vanilla extract beaten with water-yeast mixture in step 2

1 **tablespoon unsalted butter, softened, for greasing baking dish**

CARAMEL SAUCE

2 **cups (14 ounces) sugar**
1 **cup water**
3/4 **cup heavy cream**
4 **tablespoons (1/2 stick) unsalted butter**
1 **teaspoon vanilla extract**
Pinch salt
2 **tablespoons corn syrup**
2 **cups whole pecans, lightly toasted and chopped very coarse**

FILLING

4 **tablespoons (1/2 stick) butter, cut into 1/4-inch pieces and softened**
3/4 **cup packed (5 1/4 ounces) light brown sugar**
1 **teaspoon ground cardamom**
1 **teaspoon ground cinnamon**
1/4 **teaspoon salt**

1. FOR THE DOUGH: Prepare as directed through step 2 of the recipe for Glazed Cinnamon Rolls. Butter a 13 by 9-inch baking dish with handles.

2. FOR THE CARAMEL SAUCE: While the dough rises, combine the sugar and water in a heavy-bottomed 2-quart saucepan, pouring the sugar into the center of the pan to prevent the sugar crystals from adhering to the sides of the pan. Cover and bring the mixture to a boil over high heat. Once boiling, uncover and continue to boil until the syrup is thick and straw-colored, about 7 minutes (it will register 300 degrees on a candy thermometer). Reduce the heat to medium and continue to

---

SHAPING CINNAMON ROLLS AND STICKY BUNS

1. Sprinkle the filling evenly over the dough, leaving a border of 1/2 inch on the far end. Roll up the dough, pinching it gently with your fingertips to keep it tightly rolled.

2. Moisten the top border with water and then pinch the dough ends together to form a secure seam.

3. With dental floss, cut the formed roll in half, cut each in half again, and then cut each piece into 3 rolls for a total of 12 rolls.

cook until the sugar syrup is golden and begins to smoke, 1 to 2 minutes (it will be 350 degrees).

3. Meanwhile, bring the cream, butter, vanilla, salt, and corn syrup to a simmer over high heat in a small saucepan. (If the cream mixture reaches a simmer before the syrup reaches the proper stage, remove from the heat and set aside.)

4. As soon as the sugar syrup reaches 350 degrees, remove it from the heat, pour about a quarter of the cream mixture into it, and let the bubbling subside. Add the remaining cream mixture and whisk until the sauce is smooth. While still hot, pour the caramel sauce into the prepared baking dish. Sprinkle the pecans over the caramel and set the pan aside.

5. TO ROLL AND FILL THE DOUGH: After the dough has doubled in size, punch it down and turn it out onto a lightly floured work surface. Using a rolling pin, shape the dough into a 16 by 12-inch rectangle with a long side facing you. Combine the filling ingredients in a small bowl and sprinkle the filling evenly over the dough, leaving a ½-inch border at the far edge. Following the illustrations on page 120, roll the dough, beginning with the long edge closest to you and using both hands to pinch the dough with your fingertips as you roll. Moisten the top border with water and seal the roll. Lightly dust the roll with flour and press on the ends if necessary to make a uniform 16-inch cylinder. Cut the roll into 12 pieces using dental floss and evenly distribute the rolls, cut-side up, in the prepared baking dish. Cover with plastic wrap and place in a warm, draft-free spot until doubled in bulk, 1½ to 2 hours.

6. TO BAKE THE BUNS: When the buns are almost fully risen, adjust an oven rack to the middle position and heat the oven to 350 degrees. Bake the buns until golden brown and an instant-read thermometer inserted into the center of one reads 185 to 188 degrees, 25 to 30 minutes. Cool in the pan for 5 minutes. Very carefully, holding the baking dish by the handles, invert the buns onto a large serving plate. With a rubber spatula, scrape out any caramel remaining in the dish and spread it over the buns. Cool for 10 minutes; serve warm.

BAGELS

IF YOU LIVE IN NEW YORK OR ANOTHER large city (although some bagel fans would argue that good bagels don't exist outside of New York), you can get great bagels. But what about everyone who lives in the rest of the country? We decided there was a need for a simple way to bake delicious, attractive, authentic bagels at home.

Looking at all the recipes we could get our hands on, we developed a fairly typical one. We used bread flour, salt, sugar, yeast, and water, reasoning that the bread flour would give the bagels the chewy texture we were looking for. Following the procedure outlined in all the recipes, we kneaded the dough and then allowed it to rise for about an hour. Next, we shaped it into rings, let them rise, boiled them, and finally baked the bagels. Rather than plump, smooth, golden brown bagels, we ended up with small, dense hockey pucks, with crusts that were dull, wrinkled, and mottled brown. The flavor was bland and unappealing. We had our work cut out for us.

We decided that the first issue we needed to address was appearance. One problem we had encountered in forming the bagels was that after the first rise, the dough was somewhat grainy and loose. Instead of stretching easily, it was more inclined to tear. Forming bagels at this stage, as all the recipes we came across advocated, tended to produce a lumpy, uneven crust.

To overcome this difficulty, we tried forming the bagels immediately after we kneaded the dough, letting the rings rise until puffy, then boiling and baking as before. This approach turned out to be an improvement in terms of handling the dough and also in the appearance of the bagels. However, they were still small and tough.

We began to question our choice of flour. We had chosen bread flour, with about 13 percent protein, over all-purpose flour, which has 10 to 12 percent protein. We knew that the higher protein level would lead to the formation of more gluten, that network of elastic protein strands that traps the carbon dioxide released by the activity of the yeast, allowing bread to rise. It stood to reason, then, that an even higher-protein flour would rise better, yielding a bagel that was plumper and had a finer, chewier texture.

The next flour up the protein scale is high-gluten flour, which is produced by milling high-protein wheat. High-gluten flour has the highest protein content of any flour, usually around 14 percent, and is the flour of choice at most professional bagel bakeries and pizza parlors. We made our next batch of bagels using high-gluten flour and saw a difference the moment we removed the dough from the mixer. This dough was satiny smooth and much more elastic than the dough made with bread flour. And the bagels made with high-gluten flour were larger and rose higher. In addition, their crust was smoother and more attractive. The interior structure of these bagels was also better—lighter and chewier.

We were getting close now, but the bagels were still a bit flat on the bottom. A little fiddling around with the water-to-flour ratio quickly solved that problem. Initially, we were treating the bagel dough like any other bread dough, trying to achieve a smooth, slightly tacky consistency. A few test batches using less water in relation to flour revealed that a stiffer, drier dough produces a firmer-textured, chewier bagel. "Dry," however, may not be the most appropriate word to use in describing the correct consistency. A dough with the right consistency will be smooth and elastic, though somewhat firm. After the dough has come

together in the first five minutes of mixing, it should not stick to your fingers when pressed. And when you have completely kneaded the dough, a piece about the size of a golf ball should hold its shape and should not sag.

With the shape and texture of the bagels very much improved, we turned to the issue of flavor. Traditionally, bagels are placed in a specially designed refrigerator, called a retarder, for several hours or overnight after being formed. This practice allows for a slower, more natural fermentation. It is during this retarding process that bagels develop most of their flavor. We wanted to test the impact of retarding, so after mixing and forming a batch of bagels, we placed them in a refrigerator overnight. The results were both dramatic and surprising.

The most obvious change in the bagels was in their size. What had gone into the refrigerator as tight, shapely rings of dough came out as flaccid blobs. The yeast fermentation had continued unabated, and the bagels had overrisen. We finished the boiling and baking process anyway.

In spite of being overlarge and flat-bottomed, these overrisen bagels were a vast improvement over our previous attempts. When we sliced one open, we were greeted by a heavenly aroma. This was more than just flour, salt, and yeast! The long, slow fermentation process the bagels had undergone yielded the complex flavor and aroma we

SHAPING BAGELS

1. Form each dough ball into a rope 11 inches long by rolling it under your outstretched palms. Do not taper the ends of the rope. Overlap the ends of the rope about 1 1/2 inches and pinch the entire overlapped area firmly together. If the ends of the rope do not want to stick together, you can dampen them slightly.

2. Place the loop of dough around the base of your fingers and, with the overlap under your palm, roll the rope several times, applying firm pressure to seal the seam. The bagel should be roughly the same thickness all the way around.

were seeking. So retarding really was crucial for great bagel flavor. We were even more surprised by the other effects of retarding: The crust of these bagels had taken on a dark, reddish sheen, and the surface was covered in crispy "fish eyes."

So what was actually happening to the bagels during retarding? The primary mechanism involved is bacterial fermentation. At lower temperatures, yeast fermentation is suppressed, and the lactobacilli bacteria naturally present on grains and in yeast begin to produce a variety of organic acids, primarily lactic acid and acetic acid. These organic acids, the same acids present in a healthy sourdough culture, give the dough a more complex flavor. The fish eyes are a result of the same bacterial reaction, which breaks down some of the gluten in the dough. The weakened gluten structure on the surface of the bagels allows the formation of fermentation bubbles. The richer, reddish brown color of the crust was the result of another chemical process, called the Maillard, or browning, reaction. During the retarding process, enzymes produced by the bacteria convert wheat starch into simple sugar, which during baking produces a rich, toasty color and flavor.

In subsequent tests, we lowered the yeast level in our recipe by half. We also lowered the temperature of the water we used in the dough, to control the activity of the yeast. Initially, we had been proofing the yeast in 110-degree water as recommended on the envelope. We ultimately decided against dissolving the yeast before adding it to the flour in favor of using 80-degree water.

Experimenting with different retarding times, we eventually concluded that a period of 13 to 18 hours is best for a balance between flavor and crust development. Less time and the flavor did not develop as fully, although a short retarding time is better than none. More than 18 hours and we began to notice some adverse effects on the bagels, such as an excessive darkening of the crust, the formation of large bubbles inside the bagels, and the development of too many fermentation bubbles on the surface.

Boiling the dough, which is the most unusual step in the bagel-making process, is responsible for the bagel's unique characteristics—its shiny crust and its chewy texture. Boiling a bagel before baking it serves three purposes. Most important, it sets the shape of the bagel by cooking the surface and killing off some of the yeast in the outer layer of dough. This helps to limit the expansion of the bagel when it is baked. A bagel that is not boiled, we discovered, will expand into a round ball in the heat of the oven. The second function of the boiling process is to give the bagel its characteristic shine. When you boil the bagel, starches on the surface become gelatinized. These starches then cook to a crispy, shiny coating in the oven. The third purpose of boiling is to activate the yeast in the inner layers of dough, which has been made sluggish by the retarding process.

All of the home recipes we reviewed recommended boiling the bagels for a period of one to four minutes. We tried the whole range of suggested times and found, surprisingly, that a shorter boil of only 30 seconds yielded the best results. Bagels boiled for four minutes had noticeably less shine and were not as plump as those we had boiled for 30 seconds. We surmised that the bagels boiled for four minutes had developed such a thick crust that they were unable to expand fully in the oven.

Plain Bagels

MAKES 8

Because bagel dough is much drier and stiffer than bread dough, it takes longer for the ingredients to cohere during mixing. For this reason, we recommend that you neither double this recipe nor try to knead the dough by hand. Most natural food stores carry barley malt syrup. High-gluten flour might be more difficult to find. You can order both the syrup and the flour from The Baker's Catalogue at King Arthur Flour: www.kingarthurflour.com.

4	cups (22 ounces) high-gluten flour
2	teaspoons salt
1	tablespoon barley malt syrup
1 1/2	teaspoons instant yeast
1 1/4	cups water (at 80 degrees)
3	tablespoons cornmeal, for dusting the baking sheet

1. Mix the flour, salt, and barley malt in the bowl of a standing mixer fitted with the dough hook. Add the yeast and water; mix at the lowest speed until the dough looks scrappy, like shreds just beginning to come together, about 4 minutes. Increase the speed to medium-low; continue mixing until the dough is cohesive, smooth, and stiff, 8 to 10 minutes.

2. Turn the dough onto a work surface; divide into 8 portions, about 4 ounces each. Roll the pieces into smooth balls and cover with a towel or plastic wrap to rest for 5 minutes.

3. Form each dough ball into a rope 11 inches long by rolling it under your outstretched palms. Do not taper the ends of the rope. Shape the rope into a circle, overlapping the ends of the rope about 1½ inches (see illustration 1 on page 122). Pinch the overlapped area firmly together, dampening it slightly if the ends won't stick. Place the ring of dough around your hand at the base of your fingers and, with the overlap under your palm, roll the dough ring several times, applying firm pressure to seal the seam (illustration 2). The dough ring should be roughly the same thickness all the way around. Dust a large baking sheet with the cornmeal, place the dough rings on the sheet, cover tightly with plastic wrap, and refrigerate overnight (12 to 18 hours).

4. About 20 minutes before baking, remove the dough rings from the refrigerator. Adjust an oven rack to the middle position and heat the oven to 450 degrees. Pour water into a large stockpot to a depth of 3 inches and bring the water to a rapid boil.

5. Working 4 at a time, drop the dough rings into the boiling water, stirring and submerging them with a Chinese skimmer or slotted spoon, until very slightly puffed, 30 to 35 seconds. Remove the dough rings from the water and transfer them to a wire rack, bottom-side down, to drain.

6. Transfer the boiled rings, rough-side down, to a baking sheet lined with parchment paper. Bake until deep golden brown and crisp, about 14 minutes. Use tongs to transfer to a wire rack to cool. Serve warm or at room temperature.

> VARIATIONS

Topped Bagels

Follow the recipe for Plain Bagels, dunking the dough rings into one of the following: ½ cup raw sesame seeds, poppy or caraway seeds, dehydrated onion or garlic flakes, or sea or kosher salt while they are still wet and sticky (at the end of step 5, after draining).

Everything Bagels

Follow the recipe for Topped Bagels, dunking the dough rings into a mixture of 2 tablespoons each sesame and poppy seeds and 1 tablespoon each caraway seeds, sea or kosher salt, dehydrated onion flakes, and dehydrated garlic flakes.

Cinnamon-Raisin Bagels

Follow the recipe for Plain Bagels, mixing 1 teaspoon vanilla extract, 1 tablespoon ground cinnamon, and ½ cup raisins into the flour, salt, and barley malt in step 1.

SOFT PRETZELS

TIED INTO A KNOT, SPRINKLED WITH coarse salt, and slathered with mustard, soft pretzels are a quintessential American snack. But the pale, tasteless versions sold in shopping mall food courts and hawked by street vendors just don't cut it, and homemade pretzels are scarce. We set out to change that.

It takes just a few ingredients to make a pretzel: flour, yeast, sugar, salt, and water. The first ingredient to examine was the flour. Which would be better, all-purpose or bread flour? Pretzels made with all-purpose flour had a fluffy interior, which resembled dinner rolls more than pretzels. The ones made using bread flour had the chewiness we were looking for. Bread flour has a higher gluten content than all-purpose flour. Gluten helps to form an elastic structure that holds in the bubbles of air that are produced by the yeast. The bread flour gave the pretzels just the right texture. As for yeast, we found that just one teaspoon of instant yeast (for three cups of bread flour) gave the dough the perfect amount of lift.

To give our pretzels just a hint of sweetness, we experimented with brown sugar, granulated sugar, and honey. Both sugars made an acceptable pretzel, but the ones made with honey had a more subtle, balanced sweetness.

Now that the ingredients were set, we needed to find the best mixing method. We first tried kneading the dough by hand. Because pretzel dough is stiff, we found that the manual method not only took a long time but also resulted in sore muscles and a less flavorful pretzel. We were pleased to find that both the standing mixer and the food processor were better alternatives. The standing mixer produced the best results, but the processor worked well, too. However, because the processor didn't knead the dough as thoroughly as the standing mixer, the dough required some resting time and a little hand kneading at the end.

Like bagels, pretzels are briefly cooked in boiling water before baking to give them their chewy texture. However, unlike bagels, pretzels are traditionally boiled in a combination of baking soda and water. But was this extra step really necessary? We found other recipes that had eliminated this step entirely or used a shortcut in its place. We tried several variations: The first batch was boiled in a baking soda solution, the second was boiled in plain water, the third was simply brushed with a baking soda solution, and the fourth was baked as is. The pretzels that were baked as is turned out puffy and pale. They were just pretzel-shaped buns with none of the characteristic texture or color. The ones that had been brushed with baking soda and water were slightly browner, but they, too, lacked the chewiness we wanted. The pretzels boiled in plain water had that ideal texture but were pale in color and flavor. Clearly, the only way to get both the ideal texture and the dark brown color (along with the flavor that went with it) was to boil the pretzels in the baking soda solution.

Baking soda is primarily used as a leavening agent (though not in this case), but it also aids in browning. The alkaline baking soda helps to give the pretzels their characteristic crisp, mahogany-brown exterior. When the pretzels are boiled, the heat and moisture combine with the starch on the surface of the pretzel and gelatinize. The starch gel serves two purposes: It hardens to form the chewy exterior, and it sets the surface, limiting the amount of expansion. The starchy surface also helps the coarse salt stick to the pretzel, eliminating the need for an egg wash.

Our final tests were with oven temperatures. We tried temperatures ranging from 350 to 450 degrees. Pretzels baked at 350 degrees didn't brown enough. Higher temperatures produced the most well-browned and evenly baked pretzels. We had the best results with an oven set at 450 degrees.

Soft Pretzels
MAKES 12

A 12-inch skillet is the best pan for blanching the pretzels. The pan is wide enough to fit 3 or 4 pretzels at a time, and the shallow sides make it easy to add and remove the pretzels from the water. Any wide pot or Dutch oven may be substituted if a skillet is not handy. Coarse salt is best (as well as traditional), but if it is unavailable, kosher salt may be substituted. The pretzels are best eaten the day they are baked but will keep at room temperature in an airtight container for 2 days or in the freezer, wrapped well, for 2 weeks.

1	teaspoon instant yeast
1/4	cup honey
1	teaspoon salt
3	cups (16 1/2 ounces) bread flour, plus more for dusting the work surface
1	cup warm water (about 110 degrees)
3	tablespoons baking soda
2	tablespoons coarse salt, poppy seeds, or sesame seeds (optional)

1. Mix together the yeast, honey, salt, flour, and water in the bowl of a standing mixer. Using the dough hook, knead at low speed until a smooth, elastic ball of dough forms (the dough will be quite stiff), 5 to 7 minutes.

2. Place the dough in a lightly oiled large bowl and turn the dough to coat with the oil. Cover with plastic wrap and let rise at warm room temperature until doubled in size, 1 to 1½ hours. Deflate the dough, cover, and let rise until nearly doubled in size again, 30 to 40 minutes.

3. Meanwhile, adjust an oven rack to the middle position and heat the oven to 450 degrees. Pour 6 cups water into a 12-inch skillet, add the baking soda, stir, cover, and bring to a boil over high heat. Line a baking sheet with aluminum foil and spray generously with vegetable cooking spray. Set aside.

4. Divide the dough into 12 equal pieces (about 2 ounces each). Roll each piece into a 20-inch-long, ½-inch-wide rope. Following the illustrations below, shape each rope into a pretzel and place on the prepared baking sheet.

5. Using a wire skimmer or slotted spoon, gently place the pretzels into the boiling water, top-side down (you should be able to fit 3 or 4 pretzels at a time), for 30 seconds. Using tongs, carefully flip the pretzels over and boil for 30 seconds longer. Remove the pretzels with a slotted spoon, drain

well, and place back onto the prepared baking sheet (because the pretzels will not rise much in the oven, you should be able to fit all 12 pretzels on one baking sheet). Sprinkle with coarse salt or sesame or poppy seeds (if using) and bake for 12 to 16 minutes, or until the pretzels are well-browned, turning the baking sheet halfway through the baking time. Remove the pretzels from the baking sheet to a wire rack. Serve warm or at room temperature.

➤ VARIATIONS

Soft Pretzels Kneaded in a Food Processor

Place the yeast, salt, and flour in a food processor. Stir the water and honey together in a liquid measuring cup. With the processor running, add the honey mixture in a slow, steady stream (this should take about 30 seconds). Process the dough for another 40 to 60 seconds, or until a ball of dough forms. Remove the dough from the processor, place it onto a lightly floured surface, and loosely cover with plastic wrap. After letting the dough rest for 2 minutes, knead by hand to form a smooth ball, about 30 seconds.

SHAPING PRETZELS

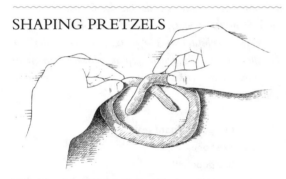

1. Working one at a time, pick up the ends of the 20-inch dough rope and cross them over to form an oval with about 1½ inches of the ends overlapping.

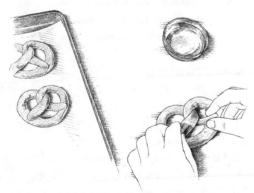

2. Twist the top end of the overlapping end over the bottom end and bring the ends down to form a pretzel shape. Lightly moisten the ends with water and firmly press the ends onto the dough at about the 5 o'clock position and the 7 o'clock position.

Cinnamon-Sugared Pretzels

Although these flavors are not traditionally found on pretzels, we found that these cinnamon-sugared pretzels were a test kitchen favorite.

Follow the recipe for Soft Pretzels, but do not salt them after blanching. In a shallow plate or pie pan, mix together ⅓ cup sugar and ½ teaspoon ground cinnamon. After the pretzels are baked and cool enough to handle (but still quite warm), generously brush the tops of the pretzels with 3 tablespoons melted unsalted butter. One at a time, press the buttered side of each pretzel into the cinnamon sugar and place the sugared pretzel (sugared-side up) on a wire rack to cool. Serve warm or at room temperature.

Cheese Pretzels

Follow the recipe for Soft Pretzels, sprinkling the blanched pretzels with 1 cup (4 ounces) shredded cheddar, Monterey Jack, or pepperjack cheese instead of coarse salt or seeds. Bake as directed. Serve warm or at room temperature.

YEASTED DOUGHNUTS

THE DOUGHNUTS FOUND IN CHAIN SHOPS always seem to look more impressive than they taste, and the flavor always seems to fall short. Although some of us in the test kitchen might be tempted to overlook the shortcomings of chain doughnuts, it's those killer calories that stop us in our tracks. In our mind, if something contains excessive calories, it just ups the ante on the flavor factor. We set out to develop the ultimate yeasted doughnut and to make every calorie count.

What we wanted was a lightly sweetened doughnut that was tender on the inside and lightly crisp on the outside. Yeasted doughnuts are simply enriched bread dough, rolled and cut into circles and fried. We examined the ingredients: flour, yeast, sugar, eggs, butter, and milk. The first item up for scrutiny was the flour. When we compared bread flour with all-purpose, we found that bread flour made the doughnut too dense and chewy, almost like a deep-fried bagel. All-purpose flour was the better choice, making a doughnut with a lighter interior. What about amounts? Would a soft dough or a stiff dough produce the best results? We tried amounts of flour ranging from 3 to more than 4 cups. Adding more flour to the dough did nothing to improve the doughnuts; it just made them tough. The ones made from the softer dough had the tender, light texture we were looking for, and 2¼ teaspoons of instant yeast gave the doughnuts just the right amount of lift.

After experimenting with various egg amounts and yolk-to-white combinations, we settled on two whole eggs. As for liquids, we found recipes that called for milk, water, and even apple cider. Among the three, there wasn't much difference in flavor, but the doughnuts made with milk had the most tender texture.

Next, we looked at the amount of sugar. Because we wanted the doughnut to complement fillings and glazes, we didn't want the doughnut itself to be excessively sweet. We tried amounts ranging from 1 to 12 tablespoons. Six tablespoons was the right amount, adding just the right amount of sweetness. Doughnuts made with more sugar not only tasted too sweet but browned too quickly in the hot oil. The same tests were done with butter. Again, 6 tablespoons was the ideal amount. Any less and the dough was too lean, and more butter made a doughnut that was heavy and overly rich.

Now that we had found the right ingredients and ratios, we needed to find the best mixing method. As with brioche, doughnut dough is made with softened butter. Mixing and kneading the dough by hand made the dough wet and greasy, a result of warm hands melting the butter. A food processor failed to knead this soft dough properly. The best results were achieved with a standing mixer, which thoroughly kneaded the dough while allowing it to remain cool.

In order to find the best oil for frying the doughnuts, we tried peanut, canola, safflower, vegetable, soybean, and corn oil. Peanut oil was the front-runner, making doughnuts with the cleanest flavor and good crunch—albeit a tad greasy. We then pitted the peanut oil against lard and vegetable shortening (Crisco). The doughnuts fried in lard had a light, crunchy texture but tasted faintly of meat. Not bad for french fries, perhaps, but not what we wanted in a doughnut. Vegetable shortening was the clear winner; it made doughnuts with a clean flavor and perfectly crunchy exterior. Our biggest surprise was to find that the doughnuts fried in shortening were not only less greasy than the ones cooked in peanut oil but also remained crisp longer.

Next, we needed to determine the best cooking temperatures. We tried temperatures ranging from 350 to 390 degrees. At 350 degrees, the doughnuts soaked up too much oil and became greasy; the doughnuts fried at 390 degrees burned on the outside before the insides were done. We found that 360 degrees was the perfect temperature. However, when we added the doughnuts to the oil, the temperature dropped 10 to 15 degrees. Starting with the oil at 375 degrees solved that problem, making it easier to maintain 360 degrees while frying.

Yeasted Doughnuts

MAKES ABOUT 16 DOUGHNUTS AND HOLES, OR 16 FILLED DOUGHNUTS

If you don't have a doughnut cutter, you can improvise with 2 biscuit cutters: a standard size cutter (about 2½ inches) for cutting out the doughnuts and a smaller one (about 1¼ inches) for cutting out the holes. For those adept with chopsticks, long-handled cooking chopsticks are the best tool for removing the doughnuts with holes from the hot fat. Otherwise, use a slotted spoon, tongs, or Chinese skimmer. Don't try to make this dough by hand or in a food processor; your hands or the metal blade will heat the butter too much and make the dough greasy. These doughnuts are best eaten the day they are made.

3–3¼	cups (15 to 16¼ ounces) unbleached all-purpose flour
1	envelope (about 2¼ teaspoons) instant yeast
6	tablespoons sugar (about 2½ ounces), plus 1 cup for rolling
½	teaspoon salt
⅔	cup whole milk, at room temperature
2	large eggs, beaten lightly
6	tablespoons (¾ stick) unsalted butter, cut into 6 pieces, softened but still cool
6	cups (40 ounces) vegetable shortening, such as Crisco, for frying

1. In a medium bowl, whisk together 3 cups of the flour, the yeast, 6 tablespoons sugar, and the salt. Set aside.

2. Place the milk and eggs in the bowl of a standing mixer fitted with the dough hook. Add the flour mixture and mix on low speed for 3 to 4 minutes, or until a ball of dough forms.

3. Add the softened butter one piece at a time, waiting about 15 seconds after each addition. Continue mixing for about 3 minutes longer, adding the remaining flour 1 tablespoon at a time if necessary, until the dough forms a soft ball.

4. Place the dough in a lightly oiled medium bowl and cover with plastic wrap. Let the dough rise at room temperature until nearly doubled in size, 2 to 2½ hours. Place the dough onto a floured surface and, using a rolling pin, roll it out to a thickness of ½ inch. Cut the dough using a 2½- or 3-inch doughnut cutter, gathering the scraps and rerolling them as necessary. Place the doughnut rings and holes onto a floured baking sheet. Loosely cover with plastic wrap and let rise at room temperature until slightly puffy, 30 to 45 minutes.

5. Meanwhile, fit a candy thermometer to the side of a large Dutch oven. Add the shortening to the pot and gradually heat the shortening over medium-high heat to 375 degrees. Place the rings and holes carefully into the hot fat 4 or 5 at a time. Fry until golden brown, about 30 seconds per side for the holes and 45 to 60 seconds per side for the doughnuts. Remove the doughnuts from the hot oil and drain on a paper towel–lined rimmed baking sheet or wire rack. Repeat with the remaining doughnuts, returning the fat to temperature between batches. Cool the doughnuts for about 10 minutes, or until cool enough to handle. Roll the warm doughnuts in the remaining 1 cup sugar. Serve warm or at room temperature.

➤ VARIATIONS

Cinnamon-Sugared Doughnuts

Follow the recipe for Yeasted Doughnuts. Mix 1 cup sugar with 1 tablespoon ground cinnamon in a medium bowl or pie pan. In step 5, roll the doughnuts in the cinnamon sugar (rather than plain sugar) to coat.

Vanilla-Glazed Doughnuts

Follow the recipe for Yeasted Doughnuts, omitting the 1 cup sugar for rolling. While the doughnuts are cooling, whisk together ½ cup half-and-half, 3 cups confectioners' sugar, sifted, and ⅛ teaspoon vanilla extract in a medium bowl until combined. When the doughnuts have cooled, dip both sides of each doughnut into the glaze, shake off any excess glaze, and transfer to a wire rack to set the glaze.

Chocolate-Glazed Doughnuts

Follow the recipe for Yeasted Doughnuts, omitting the 1 cup sugar for rolling. While the doughnuts are cooling, place 4 ounces finely chopped semisweet or bittersweet chocolate in a small bowl. Add ½ cup hot half-and-half and whisk together to melt the chocolate. Add 2 cups confectioners' sugar, sifted, and whisk until no lumps remain. When the doughnuts have cooled, dip one side of each doughnut into the glaze, shake off any excess glaze, and transfer to a wire rack to set the glaze.

YEASTED COFFEECAKE

UNLIKE CHEMICALLY LEAVENED COFFEECAKES (made with baking powder or soda), which are quick to put together and have a texture that resembles cake, yeasted coffeecakes have a bread-like texture—in fact, they are sometimes called coffee breads. When we decided to create our recipe, we knew what was most important: a flavorful, rich crumb that did not suffer from the dryness that is a common problem with this type of coffeecake. We also wanted to avoid developing the hard, dark crust typical of rich coffeecakes because of their sugar and egg content. We wanted to create a dough that could be shaped and filled in a variety of ways and that was not overwhelming to make.

We began by exploring the relative proportions of the primary ingredients—eggs, butter, sugar, flour, and yeast. Since the coffeecake we wanted was very light yet rich, with a golden finish and a brioche-type texture, we knew that it would require a high proportion of eggs. Keeping the other ingredients constant, we tried the recipe with from one to six eggs. Six eggs added so much liquid that we had to increase the amount of flour, which resulted in a texture that tasters found a bit heavy and dry. One egg also threw off the proportions, requiring so much less flour that the baked dough was greasy and rather coarse. Two or three eggs produced a decent crumb, but we still wanted a bit more lightness, so we settled on four eggs.

Next we tested amounts of butter, ranging from ¼ cup to 1½ cups. One-half cup or less produced breads that were not rich enough for our coffeecake; amounts over 1¼ cups produced doughs that had a slightly heavy quality. One cup of butter resulted in a soft texture that yielded a good buttery taste and aroma, a rich crumb, and a melt-in-your-mouth quality.

Sugar is an interesting ingredient because it is a flavor enhancer as well as a sweetener. Without a certain level of sugar, our baked doughs tasted flat; not bad, just not as flavorful as we wanted. Most of our testing was done with ⅓ cup of sugar (an average amount for this type of recipe), but when we made a few batches with ½ cup, they tasted better.

When it came to flour, we understood that the amount, and not the type, would be the crucial factor. For the soft, moist texture that we wanted, 4¼ cups of all-purpose flour turned out to be the correct amount. When we added more than this, the coffeecake was slightly dry.

With yeast, as with flour, we were more concerned with the amount than with the type. Working with instant yeast, we tried amounts ranging from 1 teaspoon to 6 teaspoons per recipe. Since rich doughs like this one take longer to rise than lean doughs, less than 3 teaspoons of yeast prolonged the rising time and did not produce good oven spring (the last burst of yeast growth in the heat of the oven). Two envelopes of yeast, about 4½ teaspoons, produced the best results.

In the process of working out the ingredient proportions, we realized that the mixing and rising times were also crucial to developing the desired texture. This rich dough requires a lot of beating; the eggs must be well incorporated, the butter has to be evenly combined into the mixture, and a great deal of gluten is needed for structure and strength. What worked superbly was a standing mixer equipped with the paddle first, to thoroughly combine the ingredients, and then the dough hook, for kneading. We perfected the times and speeds for adding the eggs, most of the flour, and then the butter. Doughs that were not beaten for long enough did not rise well, and the baked structure was heavy and gummy.

We tried mixing and kneading the dough by hand, but because it was so soft we had to add flour to prevent it from sticking to our fingers and to the work surface. We also tried a food processor, but the metal blade heated up the dough and tended to melt the butter into the dough. For this recipe, we strongly recommend using a standing mixer.

The two rising or resting times, the first at room temperature and the second in the refrigerator, turned out to be important for both texture and flavor. When we tried working with dough that had no initial rise, the baked texture was coarse and the taste not very interesting. During the second rise in the refrigerator, which is actually more of a resting period, the dough develops further and, most importantly, it becomes firm, with a very smooth, luxurious texture that makes it easy to shape and fill.

After shaping, the coffeecake must rise again to

achieve a light texture and an attractive, full look. After rising, the dough is ready for baking, or it can be refrigerated overnight and placed directly in a preheated oven to bake the next morning. Brushing with an egg wash (egg mixed with a little milk or cream) added a beautiful luster to the baked cake. When we omitted this step, the baked crust was dull and very unattractive.

One final technique that we had read about but not tried before these tests was freezing the dough raw. We froze some of the dough for a week and then baked it, but had no success because very rich dough will not rise again after defrosting. If you have extra dough, it is best to shape and bake it before freezing.

Rich Coffeecake with Sweet Cheese Filling

MAKES 2 CAKES, EACH SERVING 8 TO 10

The finished cakes freeze beautifully, so we like to make the full amount of dough, bake two smaller cakes (as the smaller pieces of dough are easier to work with), and freeze one for later. You can use the full quantity of dough to make one large cake if you prefer (increase the baking time to 35 to 40 minutes), or the recipe can be halved. Between rising, shaping, and proofing, preparing these cakes is time-consuming, though not at all labor-intensive. An early morning start will let you make, rise, shape, proof, and bake the dough all in one day. Alternatively, you can refrigerate the shaped, proofed loaf overnight and bake it the next morning for breakfast. For variety and color, equal proportions of cheese and fruit fillings (see the variations) can be used together in a single cake.

RICH COFFEECAKE DOUGH

2	envelopes (about 4¹/₂ teaspoons) instant yeast
¹/₄	cup warm water (about 110 degrees)
¹/₂	cup (3¹/₂ ounces) granulated sugar
4	large eggs
2	tablespoons milk
I	teaspoon vanilla extract
4¹/₄	cups (21¹/₄ ounces) unbleached all-purpose flour
1¹/₂	teaspoons salt
16	tablespoons (2 sticks) unsalted butter, cut into 1-inch pieces and softened but still cool

SWEET CHEESE FILLING

8	ounces cream cheese, softened but still cool
¹/₄	cup (1³/₄ ounces) granulated sugar
2¹/₂	tablespoons unbleached all-purpose flour
	Pinch salt
2	teaspoons finely grated zest from 1 lemon
I	large egg
¹/₂	teaspoon vanilla extract

STREUSEL TOPPING (OPTIONAL)

¹/₃	cup packed (2¹/₃ ounces) light or dark brown sugar
I	tablespoon granulated sugar
¹/₂	cup (2¹/₂ ounces) unbleached all-purpose flour
¹/₂	teaspoon ground cinnamon
¹/₄	teaspoon salt
5	tablespoons cold unsalted butter, cut into 8 pieces

COFFEECAKE ICING (OPTIONAL)

³/₄	cup (3 ounces) confectioners' sugar, sifted
3¹/₂	teaspoons milk
¹/₂	teaspoon vanilla extract

EGG WASH

I	large egg
I	teaspoon heavy cream (preferably) or whole milk

1. FOR THE DOUGH: Sprinkle the yeast over the warm water in the bowl of a standing mixer; stir to dissolve. Add the sugar, eggs, milk, and vanilla; attach the paddle and mix at the lowest speed until well combined. Add 3¼ cups of the flour and the salt, mixing at low speed until the flour is incorporated, about 1 minute. Increase the speed to medium-low and add the butter pieces 1 at a time, beating until incorporated, about 20 seconds after each addition (total mixing time should be about 5 minutes). Replace the paddle with the dough hook and add the remaining 1 cup flour; knead at medium-low speed until soft and smooth, about 5 minutes longer. Increase the speed to medium and knead until the dough tightens up slightly, about 2 minutes longer.

2. Scrape the dough (which will be too soft to pick up with your hands) into a straight-sided

lightly oiled plastic container or bowl using a plastic dough scraper. Cover the container tightly with plastic wrap and let the dough rise at warm room temperature until doubled in size, 3 to 4 hours. Press down the dough, replace the plastic, and refrigerate until thoroughly chilled, at least 4 or up to 24 hours. Alternatively, for a quick chill, spread the dough about 1 inch thick on a baking sheet, cover with plastic, and refrigerate until thoroughly chilled, about 2 hours.

3. FOR THE FILLING: Meanwhile, beat the cream cheese, sugar, flour, and salt in the bowl of a standing mixer at high speed until smooth, 2 to 4 minutes. Add the lemon zest, egg, and vanilla. Reduce the speed to medium and continue beating, scraping down the sides of the bowl at least once, until incorporated, about 1 minute. Scrape the mixture into a small bowl and chill thoroughly before using. (The filling can be refrigerated in an airtight container up to 3 days.)

4. FOR THE STREUSEL: Mix the brown and granulated sugars, flour, cinnamon, and salt in a small bowl. Add the butter and toss to coat. Pinch the butter chunks and dry mixture between your fingertips until the mixture is crumbly. Chill thoroughly before using. (The streusel can be refrigerated in an airtight container up to 2 weeks.)

5. FOR THE ICING: Whisk all the ingredients in a medium bowl until smooth. (The icing can be refrigerated in an airtight container up to 1 week. Thin with a few drops of milk before using.)

6. When you are ready to shape the coffeecakes, remove the chilled dough from the refrigerator and turn it out onto a lightly floured work surface, scraping the container sides with a rubber spatula if necessary. Divide the dough in half for 2 cakes. Roll, shape, and top or fill, following the illustrations for Lattice Top or Twisted Coil cakes, pages 132 and 133 (the cheese filling is too soft to use the Horseshoe shape).

7. Cover loosely with plastic wrap on a parchment-covered baking sheet and let the cakes rise until slightly puffed (they will not increase in volume as dramatically as a leaner bread dough), about 1½ to 2 hours. (After this final rise, the unbaked cakes can be refrigerated overnight and baked the next morning.)

8. FOR THE EGG WASH: Beat the egg and cream in a small bowl until combined.

9. Adjust an oven rack to the middle position and heat the oven to 350 degrees. Working with and baking one coffeecake at a time, brush the egg wash evenly on the exposed dough. Sprinkle evenly with half the streusel topping, if using. Slide the baking sheet onto a second baking sheet to prevent the bottom crust from overbrowning and bake until deep golden brown and/or an instant-read thermometer inserted in the center of the cake reads 190 degrees, 25 to 30 minutes. Slide the parchment with the coffeecake onto a wire rack and cool at least 20 minutes. Drizzle the cake with half the icing, if using, and serve.

➤ VARIATIONS

Rich Coffeecake with Apricot-Orange Filling

MAKES 2 SMALL CAKES, EACH SERVING 8 TO 10

Because of the stiff consistency of the Apricot-Orange filling, the Horseshoe shape is particularly nice for this cake. (Omit the streusel topping if making the Horseshoe shape.) This cake can be made in the Lattice Top and Twisted Coil shapes as well.

APRICOT-ORANGE FILLING

2　cups dried apricots
3　tablespoons sugar
1　tablespoon finely grated zest and
　　3 tablespoons juice from 1 medium orange
2　tablespoons rum (optional)

CAKE

1　recipe Rich Coffeecake Dough (page 130)
1　recipe Streusel Topping (optional; page 130)
1　recipe Coffeecake Icing (optional; page 130)
1　recipe Egg Wash (page 130)

1. FOR THE FILLING: Bring the apricots, sugar, and 1 cup water to a boil in a medium saucepan over medium-high heat. Reduce the heat to medium and, stirring occasionally, boil gently until the apricots are soft and the water has nearly evaporated, 16 to 18 minutes. Off heat, add the orange zest and juice and rum (if using); transfer the mixture to a food processor and process until smooth,

SHAPING YEASTED COFFEECAKES

The dough can be formed into a variety of shapes after filling. By following the step-by-step directions below, you will be able to make 3 of our favorite shapes—the Horseshoe, the Lattice Top, and the Twisted Coil. Note that this dough is rather sturdy, so you can roll it in any direction, and lift and turn it if necessary. When the coffeecakes are shaped and proofed, bake them according to the instructions on page 131. You will need a separate baking sheet for each cake.

HORSESHOE

1. Working with a half recipe of cold dough at a time, use your fingertips to shape the dough evenly into a 6 by 5-inch rectangle.

2. Roll the dough evenly into a 15 by 9-inch rectangle (the dough should be about $1/4$ inch thick). As you roll, straighten the dough occasionally with a pastry scraper, as shown.

3. Spread the Apricot-Orange Filling (page 131) evenly over the dough, leaving a $1/2$-inch border on one long side. Straighten the sides again with a pastry scraper to keep the rectangle even.

4. Using both hands, roll the dough up evenly lengthwise.

5. Pinch the dough securely to seal the seam. Do not seal the ends of the roll.

6. Place the roll in a semicircle on a parchment paper–lined baking sheet. Using scissors, cut $2/3$ of the way into the dough at 2-inch intervals.

7. Gently lift and separate the cut sections and flatten them slightly. Cover with plastic wrap and proof until slightly puffed, $1 1/2$ to 2 hours. Brush uncut surfaces with egg wash and bake as directed.

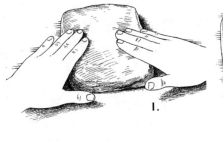
1.

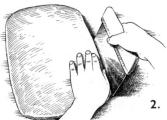
2.

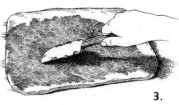

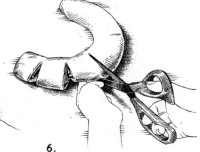
3.

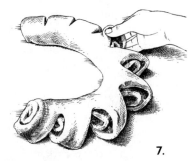
4.

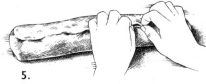
5.

6.

7.

LATTICE TOP

1. Working with a half recipe of cold dough at a time, shape dough into a 6 by 5-inch rectangle, then roll into a 12 by 8-inch rectangle (the dough should be about $1/3$ inch thick). Straighten with a bench scraper to keep the sides even.

2. Place the dough rectangle on a parchment paper–lined baking sheet. Spread a 3-inch-wide strip of filling down the center of the dough, leaving a $1 1/2$-inch border at each short end.

3. Using a knife, cut a $1 1/2$-inch square out of each corner of the dough.

LATTICE TOP (CONTINUED)

4. Using scissors, cut a triangle with 1½-inch sides in the center of one long side of the dough. Cut 2 more triangles (leaving a 1-inch strip of dough between triangles) to the right and 2 to the left of the center triangle. Set aside the dough scraps. Repeat with the other long side.

5. Fold the ends over the filling, pinching the corner edges together to seal.

6. Bring the flaps of dough from the long sides together in the center, overlapping the ends and pinching tightly to secure.

7. Cover lightly with plastic and proof until slightly puffed, 1½ to 2 hours. Brush with the egg wash and sprinkle the streusel topping down the center, leaving a 1-inch border.

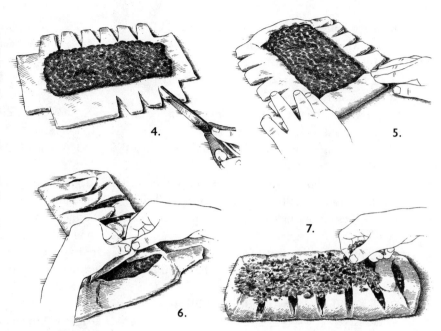

TWISTED COIL

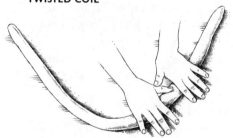

1. Working with a half recipe of cold dough at a time, shape the dough into a log about 8 inches long and 2 inches in diameter. Using your outstretched hands, roll the log evenly into a 40-inch rope about 1 inch in diameter.

2. With your fingers together, gently press the log to flatten slightly into a 1½-inch-wide strip.

3. Using both hands, twist the rope.

4. Loosely coil the rope in a spiral pattern, leaving a ¼-inch space between coils. Tuck the end under and pinch to secure. Place the coil on a parchment paper–lined baking sheet and cover with plastic wrap.

5. Proof until slightly puffed, 1½ to 2 hours. Brush with egg wash and place the filling over the center of the top, leaving a 1½-inch border around the perimeter. If desired, sprinkle the top with streusel. Bake as directed.

6. After baking, dip a spoon into the white icing and drizzle it over the cooled cake.

133

about 1 minute, stopping to scrape the sides of the workbowl at least once. Scrape the mixture into a small bowl and cool to room temperature before using. (The filling can be refrigerated in an airtight container up to 3 days.)

2. FOR THE CAKE: Make the dough as directed in steps 1 and 2 of Rich Coffeecake with Sweet Cheese Filling. Turn the chilled dough onto a lightly floured work surface, scraping the container sides with a rubber spatula if necessary; divide in half for 2 cakes. Roll, shape, and top or fill following illustrations for Horseshoe, Lattice Top, or Twisted Coil cakes, pages 132 and 133.

3. Complete the cakes following steps 7, 8, and 9 of Rich Coffeecake with Sweet Cheese Filling.

Rich Coffeecake with Berry Filling

MAKES 2 SMALL CAKES, EACH SERVING 8 TO 10
The Lattice Top and Twisted Coil shapes are best for this juicy, berry-filled cake.

BERRY FILLING
2 1/2   cups fresh or frozen raspberries or
         blueberries
3   tablespoons sugar
2   tablespoons juice from 1 lemon
         Pinch salt
         Pinch ground cinnamon

1 1/2   tablespoons cornstarch dissolved in
         2 tablespoons water

CAKE
1   recipe Rich Coffeecake Dough (page 130)
1   recipe Streusel Topping (page 130)
1   recipe Coffeecake Icing (optional; page 130)
1   recipe Egg Wash (page 130)

1. FOR THE FILLING: Place the berries, sugar, lemon juice, salt, cinnamon, cornstarch, and water in a medium saucepan and bring the mixture to a boil, stirring occasionally, over medium heat. Continue boiling, stirring constantly, until the mixture is thick and shiny, 1½ to 2 minutes. Scrape the mixture into a small bowl, cover, and chill thoroughly before using. (The filling can be refrigerated in an airtight container up to 3 days.)

2. FOR THE CAKE: Make the dough as directed in steps 1 and 2 of Rich Coffeecake with Sweet Cheese Filling. Turn the chilled dough onto a lightly floured work surface, scraping the container sides with a rubber spatula if necessary; divide in half for 2 cakes. Roll, shape, and top or fill following illustrations for Lattice Top or Twisted Coil cakes, pages 132 and 133.

3. Complete the cakes following steps 7, 8, and 9 of Rich Coffeecake with Sweet Cheese Filling.

COFFEECAKE SHAPES

LATTICE TOP

HORSESHOE

TWISTED COIL

Common Baking Problems and How to Avoid Them

Over the years, we have made our share of baking blunders in the test kitchen. Of course, our testing process is designed so we can learn from these mistakes. In fact, some of our most important baking discoveries have occurred by accident. At home, however, a mistake is a mistake, and few cooks take pleasure in preparing an unattractive pie or squat biscuits. So how do you avoid the common pitfalls associated with baking? Let our test cooks make the mistakes, so you don't have to. In the pages that follow, we have assembled some common problems that bakers encounter every day and our solutions for avoiding them.

Before we address specific baking issues, there are some general mistakes that are at the root of many baking problems. Follow the suggestions below and your kitchen skills (as well as the quality of your baked goods) will improve markedly.

Before You Bake

1. Turn on the oven. It takes at least 15 minutes for a standard oven to reach the desired temperature. Baked goods, especially biscuits, scones, and pizzas, need that immediate blast of high heat in order to rise and develop a crisp exterior. Also, make sure the oven racks are set to the correct position. A pie crust that browns properly on the lower rack will emerge pale and unappealing if baked on the middle rack.

2. Pay attention to temperature. An oven that is not calibrated properly will ruin many baked goods. It pays to use an oven thermometer. In addition, ingredients at the wrong temperature will often cause problems in baked goods. Butter that is too cold or too warm can result in a flat, dense cake. Water that is too warm can kill yeast and prevent dough from rising. Use an instant-read thermometer to avoid these kinds of problems. For more about thermometers, including brand recommendations, see pages 14 and 15.

3. Choose the right measuring cups. Liquids must be measured in liquid measures (glass or plastic cups with pour spouts and handles), and dry ingredients must be measured in dry measures (handled cups with straight edges so ingredients can be leveled off). For more about measuring, see page 14.

4. Use good ingredients. Old eggs don't have the rising properties of fresh eggs. After six months, baking powder can lose its punch. Butter can pick up off flavors after a few weeks in the refrigerator. A gritty, low-quality chocolate can ruin a flourless chocolate cake. See pages 1 through 10 for information about buying and handling essential ingredients.

5. Use the right equipment. If you bake cake layers in 8-inch pans but the recipe calls for 9-inch pans, the batter is likely to rise right out of the pans (and onto the floor of your oven). See pages 10 through 18 for information about outfitting your kitchen with essential baking equipment.

6. Don't make substitutions. Cooking at the stovetop or the grill allows for plenty of creativity and improvisation. Baking is as much science as art. Recipes are often complex chemical formulas, and if you change one ingredient, the formula no longer works. Read the recipe through before you begin baking and make sure that you have all the ingredients and equipment on hand.

7. Watch the mixing bowl or oven, not the clock. Most baking recipes, including those in this book, are filled with times for mixing and baking. However, good baking recipes, including all those in this book, also offer visual cues. The times are merely guidelines. In many cases, cream may be "at soft peaks" well before a recipe says so. Likewise, a toothpick may emerge from brownies "with just a few moist crumbs" well before the stated baking time. Don't slavishly follow times in recipes. Rely on the visual cues.

8. Time your kitchen work properly. Many baking recipes contain multiple components that must come together in a specific order. For instance, pastry cream must be well chilled before being spread in a tart shell, so it makes sense to prepare the pastry cream first. Many recipes are also best served at specific temperatures. Pay heed to this information when choosing a recipe. For instance, don't start a cheesecake at four in the afternoon and hope to serve it that night. Even though the cheesecake might be assembled and baked in two hours, it needs at least four hours to firm up in the refrigerator.

Mixing Quick Breads

DENSE BANANA BREAD

TENDER BANANA BREAD

Quick breads and muffins are the fast food of the baking world, but like most fast food, they can suffer from a variety of ills. They can be notoriously tough, squat, and rubbery. Overmixing the batter encourages gluten development, which in turn inhibits proper rise. The solution is simple: Blend the wet and dry ingredients separately and combine the two with a gentle hand using a rubber spatula or wooden spoon. Occasional sprays of visible flour punctuating the batter are ideal. The dense, squat banana bread on the left was mixed until thoroughly blended with an electric mixer, and its crumb is quite tough. The tall, domed loaf on the right was mixed lightly by hand, and its crumb is tender.

1. Whisk together all of the dry ingredients — sugar, flour, leavener, and spices — in a bowl until evenly combined.

2. In another bowl, whisk together all of the wet ingredients — dairy, melted butter, eggs, extracts, and pureed fruit — until evenly combined.

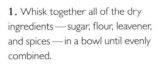

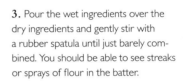

3. Pour the wet ingredients over the dry ingredients and gently stir with a rubber spatula until just barely combined. You should be able to see streaks or sprays of flour in the batter.

Portioning Muffin Batter and Removing from the Tin

MESSY MUFFINS

NEAT MUFFINS

Like quick breads, muffin batter should be mixed very lightly (see above). Once the batter is prepared correctly, dividing it evenly and cleanly is the next challenge. Unevenly portioned batter leads to irregular cooking; peewee muffins will brown long before gargantuan muffins have even set, as shown with the muffins on the left. And batter dribbled around the top of the muffin tin will burn and can make removing the muffins neatly from their cups nearly impossible, as is also the case with the tray of blueberry muffins on the left. To solve both problems, we used a large serving spoon slicked with nonstick cooking spray to evenly and neatly divide the batter for the muffins on the right. Muffins are best removed from the tin when they are still quite warm. An unlikely tool—a grapefruit knife—facilitates this process.

1. Spray a large serving spoon with nonstick cooking spray and spoon even amounts of batter into each cup of the muffin tin. Batter will slide easily from the spoon into holes in the muffin tin.

2. The thin, slightly curved blade of a grapefruit knife is particularly well suited to getting under a stubborn muffin with little risk of tearing the muffin apart.

Mixing Buttermilk Biscuit Dough

TOUGH BISCUITS

FLUFFY BISCUITS

Despite a short ingredient list and seemingly simple mixing method, biscuits pose a problem for many cooks. Dense and doughy biscuits, like those on the left, are all too common, yet easily avoided. For tall, fluffy biscuits, like those on the right, there are two key points to keep in mind: The butter must be well chilled and the dough only minimally handled. We recommend using a food processor to cut the butter into the flour. If working by hand, follow steps 2 and 3 to work the butter into the flour. To prevent overworking our very wet buttermilk biscuit dough, we recommend shaping it quickly and gently by hand. That way, the biscuits will not become tough.

1. Cut a chilled stick of butter into $1/4$-inch cubes. Place the butter cubes on a plate and chill briefly in the freezer. With a spatula, add the butter cubes to the food processor with the dry ingredients and pulse until the butter is evenly mixed into the dry ingredients.

3. With two butter knives, work the grated butter into the dry ingredients. By not using your fingertips, you reduce the chance that the butter will melt.

2. If you don't have a food processor, combine the dry ingredients in a bowl. Rub a frozen stick of butter against the large holes of a regular box grater over the bowl with the dry ingredients.

4. Once the butter has been cut into the dry ingredients, add the buttermilk. Our biscuit dough is too soft to roll and cut. Using a sharp knife, divide the dough into quarters and then cut each quarter into thirds. With cupped hands, gently shape each piece into a ball.

Shaping Cream Biscuits and Scones

MISSHAPEN BISCUITS

TALL, NEAT BISCUITS

Proper shaping and baking of cream biscuit and scone dough is key. Many cooks grab the closest glass or butter knife to cut circles or trim wedges, which, as the photo on the left illustrates, leads to poorly risen biscuits and scones with sloping shoulders. A dull cutting implement compresses the biscuit's edges, limiting rise. We suggest using either a biscuit cutter or sharp-edged bench scraper. And crank that oven, too: High heat contributes to proper rise. The butter's moisture rapidly evaporates, and steam lifts the dough upward. Make sure your oven is fully heated before baking.

FOR ROUNDS
1. Pat the dough on a lightly floured work surface into a $3/4$-inch-thick circle.

FOR WEDGES
1. Press the dough into an 8-inch cake pan, then turn the dough out onto a lightly floured work surface.

2. Punch out the dough rounds with a biscuit cutter. Push together the remaining pieces of dough, pat into a $3/4$-inch-thick round, and punch out several more dough rounds. Discard the remaining scraps.

2. With a sharp knife or bench scraper, cut the dough into 8 wedges.

Shaping Pizza Dough

TORN PIZZA DOUGH

ROUND PIZZA DOUGH

Pizza dough is very easy to prepare, but shaping that dough into a perfect circle can intimidate even the most experienced cook. Many cooks resort to the rolling pin and roll the dough like a pie crust, but that forces out the air bubbles trapped in the dough and makes for a flat, tough-crusted pizza. Others yank the dough to and fro, yielding the pizza shown on the left: thick on one end and paper-thin and ripped open on the other—not to mention its ungainly amoeba-like shape. The experts fling the dough skyward and use centrifugal force for their perfect rounds, but this technique takes lots of practice and steely nerves. We prefer a simpler way: gently stretching the dough with our hands on a flour-dusted work surface.

1. Working with one ball of dough at a time and keeping the rest covered with a damp cloth, flatten the dough ball into a disk using the palms of your hands.

2. Starting at the center of the disk and working outward, use your fingertips to press the dough until it is about 1/2 inch thick.

3. Holding the center in place, stretch the dough outward. Rotate the dough a quarter turn and stretch again. Repeat until the dough reaches a diameter of 12 inches.

4. Use your palm to press down and flatten the thick edge of the dough.

Topping Pizza Dough

SLOPPY PIZZA

PERFECT PIZZA

Overloading a pizza crust with sauce and toppings is a surefire recipe for disaster. Once in the oven—if you can manage to successfully transfer the sloppy pizza onto the stone—sauce and cheese are liable to flow off the crust and affix the pizza permanently to the stone, as seen on the left. Trying to scrub a wickedly hot baking stone free of melted cheese will quickly drive you to the phone for take-out. For successful pizza at home, keep the toppings limited—a slick of sauce, a sprinkling of cheese, and a scattering of toppings. And make sure to leave a ½-inch border around the rim to contain the toppings.

1. Carefully lift the dough round and transfer it to a peel dusted with semolina or cornmeal.

2. If the dough loses its round shape, adjust it on the peel to return it to the original shape.

3. Brush the entire dough round with a little olive oil. Add the toppings. To make it easier to hold pizza slices when eating, leave a 1/2-inch border of dough uncovered.

4. Use a quick jerking action to slide the topped dough off the peel and onto the hot tiles or stone. Make sure that the pizza lands far enough back so that the front edge does not hang off the tiles or stone.

Assembling Calzones

LEAKY CALZONE   SEALED CALZONE

More than simply folded-over pizzas, calzones suffer their own problems. At the top of the list are burst seams and leaking cheese, as shown in the amorphous mess on the left. Both problems are attributable to internal moisture accumulation. Properly sealing the seams shut and cutting vents into the top solve the problem.

1. Turn the risen dough out onto an unfloured work surface. With a bench scraper or knife, divide the dough in half, then cut each half into thirds to form a total of six pieces.

2. With your hand, gently reshape each piece of dough into a ball. Transfer the dough balls to a baking sheet, cover with oiled plastic wrap, and let rest 15 to 30 minutes.

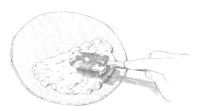

3. With your fingertips, press the dough ball into a 5-inch circle. With a floured rolling pin, roll outward from the center in all directions until the dough forms a 9-inch circle. If the dough sticks, dust the work surface underneath with flour.

4. Place a scant 1/2 cup of the filling in the center of the bottom half of the dough round. Using a small spatula, spread or press the filling in an even layer across the bottom half of the dough round, leaving a 1-inch border uncovered.

5. Fold the top half of the dough over the cheese-covered bottom half, leaving a 1/2-inch border of the bottom layer uncovered.

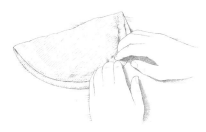

6. With your fingertips, lightly press around the silhouette of the filling and out to the edge to lightly seal the dough shut.

7. Beginning at one end of the seam, place your index finger diagonally across the edge and gently pull the bottom layer of the dough over the tip of your index finger; press into the dough to seal. Repeat the process until the calzone is fully sealed.

8. With a very sharp paring knife or razor blade, cut 5 slits, about 1 1/2 inches long, diagonally across the top of the calzone, making sure to cut through only the top layer of dough and not completely through the calzone.

Gauging Softened Butter for Cookies

FLAT COOKIES

THICK, CHEWY COOKIES

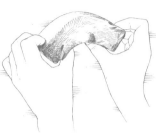

Proper butter temperature is as crucial in a simple sugar cookie as it is in the fanciest cake. The cookies on the left were made with butter that was too warm; consequently, they spread too much in the oven and are very flat. The cookies on the right were made with butter at the proper temperature and baked up thick and chewy. Most cookies (unless the butter is melted) specify softened butter, which is between 65 and 70 degrees, or roughly room temperature. If the butter is much cooler, the dough may curdle; if any warmer (as often happens when the butter has been softened in the microwave), the cookies will spread as pictured. We have found a few helpful hints that take the guesswork out of gauging temperature. The simplest method, of course, is to use a thermometer.

1. When you unwrap the butter, the wrapper should have a creamy residue on the inside. If there's no residue, the butter is probably too cold.

2. The stick of butter should bend with little resistance and without cracking or breaking.

3. The butter should give slightly when pressed but still hold its shape.

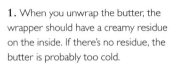

Shaping and Baking Cookies

UNEVENLY BAKED COOKIES

FUSED COOKIES

PERFECT COOKIES

Accurate measuring doesn't stop once the batter is prepared. Uneven portioning of dough can ruin a batch of cookies as fast as too much flour, since they will cook unevenly, as the photo on the left shows. Cookies that are all the same size will bake at the same rate, as in the photo on the right. Make sure to arrange the dough properly on the baking sheet so the cookies don't fuse together in the oven, as in the middle photo. Finally, if baking the cookies on two racks, it's imperative to rotate them midway through the baking time for even baking.

1. Set the ruler on top of the bowl. Rather than placing the ball of dough on top of the ruler (where it's hard to measure the diameter), bring the ball up alongside of the ruler.

2. Instead of placing the dough in neat rows of three or four so that all the cookies line up, alternate the rows. For example, three cookies in the first row, two in the second, three in the third, two in the fourth, and so on.

3. Line the cookie sheets with parchment paper and mark the front edge of the paper, indicating which pans start on the top and the bottom. This will help you keep track of which edge goes where when you reverse the pans' positions.

Baking Multiple Batches of Cookies

BURNT, IRREGULAR COOKIES

GOOD COOKIES

Few cooks own enough baking sheets for large batches of cookies and inevitably load dough onto baking sheets hot from the oven. Haste makes waste in this instance because the dough melts on the hot tray long before it reaches the oven. Consequently, the cookies are rimmed with hard, brittle edges or, worse, they've burnt as shown in the photo to the left. To avoid such disasters, arrange the shaped dough on parchment paper and cool the trays in between batches with a quick rinse in cool water.

1. Load up a sheet of parchment with balls of dough, slide the paper onto the baking sheet, and place the cookies in the oven.

2. While the first batch is baking, load up a second piece of parchment paper with balls of dough.

3. When the baked cookies come out of the oven, whisk the parchment and its cargo onto a wire rack. After cooling the baking sheet with a quick rinse and dry, it's ready for the next prepared batch.

Removing Bar Cookies from the Pan

CRUMBLY BROWNIES

NEAT BROWNIES

With their gooey fillings and high sugar content, it's nearly impossible to remove some bar cookies from their baking pan. No matter how well the pan is greased, the corners are generally fixed fast, the sides need trimming, and the bars are a crumbly mess. And there's always a bar or two sacrificed when wiggling a spatula underneath the bars for extraction. Such casualties are easily prevented by lining the pan with an aluminum foil or parchment paper "sling" before baking. Once cooled, the bar cookies may be lifted en masse from the pan and cut into neat portions.

1. Place two sheets of aluminum foil (or parchment paper) perpendicular to each other in the pan, pushing the foil (or paper) into the corners.

2. After the brownies or bars have baked and cooled, use the foil (or paper) to transfer them to a cutting board, then slice into individual portions.

Rising Dough for Sandwich Bread

SQUAT SANDWICH BREAD

TALL SANDWICH BREAD

Proper rising is as important to bread's success as proper mixing and kneading. That said, most cooks leave their dough out to "double" in any old bowl loosely covered with a dish towel, thereby subjecting it to the whims of the kitchen's ambient conditions. A drafty or cold room can wreak havoc with rise times, slowing yeast's growth down to a snail's pace. That loaf planned for dinner might serve for breakfast the following morning. And "doubled" only means something when you know how much you had to start with. Most cooks eyeball their dough and guess when it's ready, which can lead to under- or overproofing. The photo on the left illustrates underrisen dough, which is dense and tastes largely of yeast. The photo on the right shows the benefits of letting the dough double before shaping it.

1. Ideally, let the dough rise in a straight-sided container and mark its initial height by placing a rubber band around the container. It will be easy to gauge the dough's growth.

2. Whether the dough rises in a straight-sided container or round bowl, tightly seal the vessel with plastic wrap to keep out drafts and trap moisture. Do not use a dish towel instead.

3. For doughs that rise a second time in the loaf pan, slip the pan into an empty plastic bag. Blow air into the bag to inflate it, then seal it securely with a twist tie.

4. Place the bagged loaf pan into another loaf pan so that the air inside the bag is pushed up, providing room for the dough to expand.

Shaping Dough for Sandwich Bread

DENSE SANDWICH BREAD

TENDER SANDWICH BREAD

All the hard work of mixing and kneading bread is for naught if the dough is not properly shaped into a loaf. The loaf on the left shows what happens when the dough is simply dumped into the pan: no structure and a dense crumb. Successful loaves, such as the one on the right, must be flattened to a rectangle, rolled tightly, and sealed shut.

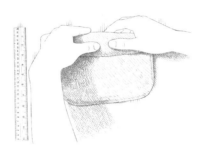

1. Flatten the dough into a square measuring 8 inches by 8 inches. Starting with the side farthest from you, roll the dough toward you into a log.

2. Seal the seams shut with your fingertips.

Preventing Unsightly Cracks in Cheesecakes

CRACKED CHEESECAKE

SMOOTH CHEESECAKE

A cheesecake with a deep fissure across the top, like the one on the left, is nothing new to most bakers, but it is easily avoided. The crack is indicative of overbaking: The eggs in the batter coagulate too much and pull the cooked cake apart. Taking the cheesecake's temperature is the only foolproof method for ascertaining doneness, a job we like to do with an instant-read thermometer. Freeing the edges of the baked cheesecake from the sides of the springform pan with a paring knife is another preventative measure we take. If the sides are not released, the surface tension on the cooling top can prompt cracking.

1. Puncturing the surface of a cheese-cake multiple times with an instant-read thermometer can weaken the structure of the surface and cause cracking. If you must take the temperature more than once, use the same hole you made on your first attempt. Or eliminate the problem altogether by inserting the thermometer through the part of the cheesecake that rises above the pan.

2. As a cheesecake cools, its surface contracts. If the edges are stuck to the pan, the surface can crack as it attempts to contract. Once the baked cheesecake emerges from the oven, run a paring knife around the inside edge to loosen the cheesecake before it cools.

Baking Layer Cakes

MISMATCHED CAKE LAYERS

EVEN CAKE LAYERS

While a thick coat of frosting can hide many of a cake's problems, it can't make up for uneven layers of cake or uneven baking. As soon as the cake is sliced, the problems will become self-evident. The cakes on the left clearly illustrate the problems. One layer is scrawny and overbrowned, while the other layer is quite large and only halfway browned. To portion evenly, we rely on a scale: no eyeballing for us. And no matter how accurate your oven is, rotating the pans from side to side is crucial for even browning. Knowing when the cake layers are ready to come out of the oven is also imperative.

1. To ensure that you put equal amounts of batter in each cake pan, use a kitchen scale to measure the weight of each filled pan.

2. When baking more than one cake layer at a time, leave some space between the pans and between the pans and the oven walls. Also, stagger their placement in the oven so air can circulate. Halfway through the baking time, use tongs to rotate the cake pans 180 degrees.

3. Telling when cakes are done can be tricky. A cake tester or skewer inserted into the center should come out clean. If batter clings to the skewer, the cake needs more time in the oven.

4. Fully baked cakes should feel springy and resilient when the center is gently pressed with your fingers. If an impression is left in the surface, the cake is not done.

Frosting Layer Cakes

UGLY CAKE

PERFECT CAKE

Most cooks think a bakery-smooth frosted cake is well beyond their ability and make do with a decidedly "homemade" looking cake. The cake on the left illustrates the most common problems: uneven frosting, including holes and thick patches; weak transitions from the sides to the top; and crumbs caught in the frosting. With the directions that follow, these problems are easily avoided. Although a professional rotating cake stand makes icing a cake easy, you can also improvise with a Lazy Susan (see step 9).

1. To anchor the cake, spread a dab of frosting in the center of a cardboard round cut slightly larger than the cake. Center the first layer of cake on the cardboard round. If using a split layer, place it crust-side up; if using a whole layer, place it bottom-side down. Set the cardboard round with the cake on the stand.

2. Place a large blob of frosting in the center of the cake and spread it to the edges with an icing spatula. Imagine that you are pushing the filling into place rather than scraping it on as if it were peanut butter on toast. Don't worry if crumbs are visible; the filling will be sandwiched between layers.

3. To level the frosting and remove any excess, hold the spatula at a 45-degree angle to the cake and, starting at the edge farthest away from you, gently drag the spatula toward you. Turn the cake slightly and repeat. It will take a few sweeps to level the frosting.

4. Using a second cardboard round, slide the next cake layer, crust-side up, on top of the frosted bottom layer, making sure that the layers are aligned. Press the cake firmly into place. If making a three- or four-layer cake, add some filling (as directed in steps 2 and 3) and repeat this process with the remaining layers.

5. A thin base coat of frosting helps seal in crumbs. To coat the top, place a blob of frosting in the center of the cake and spread it out to the edges, letting any excess hang over the edge. Don't worry if it is imperfect. Smooth the frosting as in step 3.

6. Scoop a large dab of frosting on the spatula's tip. Holding the spatula parallel to the cake stand, spread the frosting on the side of the cake with short side-to-side strokes. Repeat until the entire side is covered with a thin coat of frosting. Refrigerate the cake until the frosting sets, about 10 minutes.

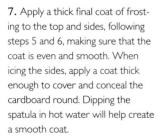

7. Apply a thick final coat of frosting to the top and sides, following steps 5 and 6, making sure that the coat is even and smooth. When icing the sides, apply a coat thick enough to cover and conceal the cardboard round. Dipping the spatula in hot water will help create a smooth coat.

8. As you ice the top and sides, a ridge will form along the edge where they meet. After you've finished icing, hold the spatula at an angle, and, with a very light hand, starting at the farthest edge of the cake, smooth the ridge toward the center. Rotate the cake and repeat until the ridge no longer exists.

9. If you don't own a rotating cake stand, you can perform steps 1 through 8 on a Lazy Susan. Just set the cardboard round on the Lazy Susan and spin slowly.

Beating Egg Whites

CURDLED EGG WHITES   SMOOTH EGG WHITES

Whipped egg whites can be finicky and require a keen eye and close attention for the best results. If improperly handled, they won't have the structure to properly support batter. The batch of whites illustrated on the left is overwhipped and has curdled (while it may look firm, it will rapidly collapse). For perfect whipped whites every time, start with slightly warmed whites and a low mixer speed. Only add the cream of tartar and a little sugar once the whites have developed some structure. Soft peaks will droop slightly downward from the tip of the whisk; stiff peaks, as seen in the photo on the right, will stand tall.

1. Beat the egg whites at medium-low speed until frothy, about 30 seconds. Raise the speed and add the cream of tartar to help stabilize the egg foam. Slowly add the sugar and continue to beat.

2. Just before the whites reach the proper consistency, turn off the mixer. Detach the whisk attachment and remove the bowl from the mixer. Use the whisk attachment to make the last few strokes by hand. Be sure to scrape along the bottom of the bowl. This technique works well with cream, too, and helps prevent overmixing.

Folding Egg Whites

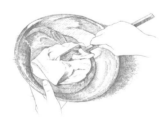

TOO MUCH FOLDING   JUST ENOUGH FOLDING

Whipped egg whites are the sole leavener for many baked goods, so it is imperative to preserve as much of their volume as possible. Folding, the judicious blending of the whites into the batter, is a commonly misunderstood baking technique. Cooks either mix too little, failing to effectively incorporate the whites into the batter, or mix too much, deflating the batter as seen in the photo on the left. A dense batter will of course yield a flat, dense cake. The best tool for folding is a large-bladed spatula, as it efficiently blends whites and batter together, but a balloon whisk will do in a pinch. A small portion of the whites is stirred into the batter to lighten it before adding the rest of the whites. When you are done, the batter will still have a few streaks of whites.

1. Gently stir a quarter of the whites into the batter to lighten it. Scrape the remaining whites onto the lightened batter. Cut through the center of the two mixtures down to the bottom of the bowl.

2. Pull the spatula toward you, scraping along the bottom and up the side of the bowl.

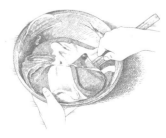

3. Once the spatula is out of the mixture, rotate the spatula so any mixture clinging to it falls back onto the surface of the batter.

4. Spin the bowl a quarter turn and repeat this process until the beaten whites are just incorporated and no large streaks of whites remain visible.

Making Pie Dough

CRUMBLY DOUGH   STICKY DOUGH   GOOD DOUGH

Despite its "difficult" reputation, perfect pie dough is a whole lot easier than most bakers think. The secret is in the details, including the temperature of the fat and water (icy cold) as well as the amount of liquid. Most pie dough disasters arise from too much or too little moisture. The doughs on the left exhibit both extremes: One is crumbly dry and unworkable, the other overhydrated and equally unrollable. To keep the butter cold, we like to use the food processor, but when adding water, we do it by hand.

1. Pulse the flour, salt, and sugar in a food processor. Add the cold butter and vegetable shortening in small pieces and then pulse until the butter pieces are no longer clearly visible. The mixture will be slightly yellow, mealy in texture, and ride up the sides of the workbowl.

2. Transfer the mixture to a bowl and add the ice water bit by bit, tossing and pressing the dry ingredients against the sides of the bowl with a rubber spatula.

3. Too much water is better than too little — a dry dough cannot be rolled out, but you can flour the work surface if the dough is a bit too wet. Ideally, the dough will clear the sides of the bowl and be wet to the touch. Form the dough into a ball, flatten it into a 6-inch disk, wrap in plastic, and refrigerate for at least one hour.

Rolling and Fitting Pie Dough

TORN DOUGH   SMOOTH DOUGH

Even perfect pie dough can cause headaches if improperly handled, as the photo on the left illustrates. This dough warmed up too much and consequently became sticky and ripped. Keeping the dough cool is the first step for success, but equally important is a judicious use of flour for dusting the work surface and a bench scraper to loosen and maneuver the dough. We favor a French-style rolling pin (with tapered ends) for accurate rolling and methodical turning to keep the crust even in thickness and uniformly round.

1. Using a tapered pin, roll a quarter turn, from about 2 o'clock to 5 o'clock, keeping your left hand stationary and moving the pin with your right hand.

2. Turn the dough a quarter turn and roll again as in step 1. Continue rolling until the dough is 8 or 9 inches in diameter. If necessary, lightly reflour the work surface.

3. Using a bench scraper, lift the dough onto the rolling pin, pick it up, reflour the counter, and replace the dough upside down. Keep rolling until the diameter of the dough is 4 inches wider than the pie plate.

4. Roll the dough over the pin and unroll it evenly onto the pie plate.

5. After draping the dough evenly over the pie plate, lift up the edges of the dough and ease it down into the lower creases of the pan. Press lightly to adhere the dough to the sides of the pan.

Making a Decorative Edge on Single-Crust Pies

FAILED PIE SHELL

FLUTED PIE SHELL

1. Use scissors to trim the dough overhang to within 1/2 inch of the outer lip of the pie plate.

2. Roll the trimmed overhang under so that it is even with the lip of the pan.

An attractively crimped border is window dressing on a pie, but it's a step many bakers have real problems with. The pie dough on the left was improperly trimmed and, consequently, has made for a messy, uneven border. The most important thing to keep in mind is having enough dough for a proper border. Tucked under itself along the pan's top edge, it is then quick work to add a decorative border.

3. Use the index finger of one hand and the thumb and index finger of the other to create fluted edges. The edge of the dough should be perpendicular to the edge of the pie plate.

4. Another option is to simply press the tines of a fork against the dough to flatten it against the rim of the pie plate.

Assembling Double-Crust Pies

UGLY PIE

ATTRACTIVE PIE

1. Unroll the dough over the filled pie, making sure to center the piece of dough on the pie plate.

2. Use scissors to trim the overhanging edges of the top and bottom crusts to about 1/2 inch.

A double-crust apple pie is the quintessential American pie, but rarely do its looks match its flavor. Too often, the pie is marred by crumbling edges, a cracked top, and uneven borders, even before it goes into the oven, as shown on the left. For an attractive pie, the top crust should be draped, not stretched across the top, and the bottom and top crusts must be sealed together to prevent juices from escaping. A clean crimping of the edge is the finishing touch. Nice straight slits, evenly spaced across the top crust, allow steam to escape and prevent a soupy filling; they also provide an attractive decoration. The pie on the right will bake up beautifully.

3. For a neat edge that stays sealed, press the edges of the top and bottom crusts together. The folded edge should be flush with the lip of the pie plate.

4. Use the index finger of one hand and the thumb and index finger of the other to create evenly spaced fluted edges. The edge of the dough should be perpendicular to the edge of the pie plate.

5. Use a sharp knife to cut vents in the top crust.

Weaving a Lattice Top

LUMPY LATTICE TOP

EVEN LATTICE TOP

De rigueur for brightly colored fruit pies like peach and cherry, a lattice top is stunningly attractive. Beauty is more than skin deep though: The open weave allows excess moisture to evaporate, preventing a soupy filling. Most bakers have had disastrous results with lattice, probably not dissimilar to that shown on the left. Melted together, lumpy, and pale, the dough was too warm to work with and the strips too thick to cook before the rest of the pie browned. A successful lattice top requires dough that is chilled to prevent it from melting. The strips must also be narrow enough—1¼ inches—to brown in the time that the rest of the pie cooks. Using a ruler to cut the strips helps keep things neat and tidy. We weave the strips together off the pie and transfer the lattice to the pie only after freezing until very firm.

1. To make the lattice, lay out 4 strips of dough on parchment paper. Fold the first and third strips back, then place a long strip of dough slightly to the right of the center as shown.

2. Unfold the first and third strips over the perpendicular strip and fold the second and fourth strips back. Add a second perpendicular strip. Now unfold the second and fourth strips

3. Repeat this process with 2 more perpendicular strips (you will have a total of 8 strips of dough, 4 running in each direction). Freeze the finished lattice until very firm and then slide it over the filling.

4. Trim off the excess lattice ends, fold the rim of the shell up over the lattice strips, and crimp.

Whipping Cream

CURDLED CREAM

BILLOWY CREAM

Whipped cream is as much about texture as flavor. Soft and billowy, properly whipped cream is the perfect foil to a dense cake or rich tart. Overwhipped cream, as seen on the left, looks unappealingly stiff and chunky and has a greasy mouthfeel to boot. Most cooks whip cream at a breakneck pace and fail to catch the cream at its peak. To prevent this mistake, there are simple rules to follow. Equipment and cream should be well chilled in the freezer; the cream should be started at a low speed, gradually increasing the speed; and it should be finished by hand to prevent overwhipping.

1. At least 15 minutes before whipping the cream, fill the mixing bowl with ice cubes and cold water and place the whisk or beaters in the ice water.

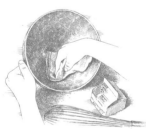

2. Dump out the ice water, dry the bowl and whisk or beaters, and add the cream. The cold bowl ensures that the cream will whip up beautifully.

3. Many recipes instruct the cook to whip cream to either soft or stiff peaks. Cream whipped to soft peaks will droop from the ends of the beaters.

4. Cream whipped to stiff peaks will cling tightly to the ends of the beaters. (To prevent overwhipping, switch to a whisk during this crucial stage, even if using an electric mixer.)

Fitting Tart Dough into the Pan

TORN TART DOUGH

NEAT TART DOUGH

1. Ease the dough over the rolling pin and roll it up loosely. Unroll the dough on top of the tart pan.

2. Lift the edge of the dough with one hand and ease it into the corners of the pan with the other.

3. Press the dough into the fluted sides of the pan, forming a distinct seam around the pan's circumference.

4. If parts of the edge are too thin, reinforce them by folding the dough back on itself.

U nlike the gentle sloping shoulders of a pie pan, a tart pan has steep, sharp edges that can and will tear holes in tender tart dough. The photo on the left illustrates dough that had a run-in with the pan: torn edges, cracked bottom, and uneven sides. A properly lined tart shell requires cool dough and a gentle touch, as shown in the steps at right. And, unlike pie dough, which toughens if overhandled, tart dough can be patched and reworked without adverse effects. If the sides are thin, follow step 4.

5. Run the rolling pin over the top of the tart pan to remove any excess dough.

6. The finished edge should be $1/4$-inch thick. If it is not, press the dough up over the edge and trim the excess.

Blind Baking Pies and Tarts

SHRUNKEN PIE SHELL

GOOD PIE SHELL

1. There are several easy ways to work with pie weights. We like to store them in a doubled-up ovenproof cooking bag, which you can simply lift in and out of the pie plate or tart pan and use over and over again, eliminating the extra step of lining the crust with foil.

2. If you don't own metal or ceramic pie weights, pennies conduct heat beautifully (far better than dried beans). Line the pie plate or tart pan with foil and place the pennies in the foil to hold the crust in place.

T he crusts for most cream and custard-filled pies and tarts are baked before filling so that they are golden brown, crisp, and flaky. The step is called blind baking and confuses many bakers. Baking the fitted dough as is leads to the photo on the left: The sides have slid down toward the pan's bottom. For success, the dough must be lined with pie weights to keep it in place. In addition, refrigerating the shaped dough before baking will help prevent shrinkage. A short stay in the freezer—after refrigeration but before baking—will improve flakiness in the finished product.

3. Once the crust has set, it is important to let it brown. To do this, remove the foil and weights and continue to bake the pie or tart shell until nicely browned.

Making and Turning Puff Pastry

FLAT PUFF PASTRY

FLAKY PUFF PASTRY

While we leave classic puff pastry to the experts, "rough" puff pastry—a perfectly proper approximation—is easy to make at home. Not much more labor intensive than a standard pie crust, the dough serves well in everything from homey apple turnovers (page 276) to upscale Napoleons (page 277). As with pie dough, the best results are achieved by keeping the butter cold. If the butter begins to melt, the puff pastry won't rise properly, as in the photo on the left.

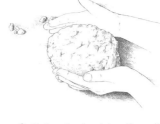

1. Turn the shaggy dough onto the work surface and fraisage it by bracing the heel of one hand against the work surface and dragging small portions of the dough forward in short, brisk strokes.

2. Gather the dough together with a bench scraper and repeat the fraisage a second time. Press the dough into an 8 by 4-inch rectangle, wrap in plastic, and refrigerate at least 30 minutes.

3. Place the dough on a lightly floured large piece of parchment and roll into a 15 by 10-inch rectangle. Fold the dough lengthwise into thirds.

4. Starting from the narrow end, loosely roll up the dough as illustrated. Press it to form a 6 by 5-inch rectangle. Repeat steps 3 and 4, first chilling the dough if it is soft and sticky.

Preparing Pastry Cream

LUMPY PASTRY CREAM

SMOOTH PASTRY CREAM

Pastry cream is a common filling, used for innumerable pies, tarts, and pastries, but it never fails to intimidate bakers. The very real fear of curdled hot eggs and milk, as shown in the photo on the left, is enough to send some running for the goof-proof box of instant pudding to fill their baked goods. Pastry cream is easier than it appears, and with a minimum of fuss and attention, a silky smooth rendition is possible. Tempering the yolks (adding a small amount of hot liquid to warm them) and straining the hot cream through a fine-mesh strainer are keys to success, as is constant stirring. Unattended pastry cream will quickly turn chunky.

1. Add ½ cup of simmering cream to the egg yolk–cornstarch mixture, stirring well to temper the yolk and scraping down the sides of the bowl.

2. Add the tempered yolk mixture back to the simmering cream all at once, whisking vigorously. Bring the cream quickly back to a simmer, whisking constantly.

3. Off heat, whisk in the cold butter, one piece at a time.

4. For an absolutely smooth texture, pass the pastry cream through a fine-mesh strainer, using a rubber spatula to push the cream into a bowl set under the strainer.

3

PIZZA, FOCACCIA, AND FLATBREAD

Pizza, Focaccia, and Flatbread

THIS CHAPTER COVERS PIZZA, CALZONES, focaccia, grissini (breadsticks), and flatbread—all thin yeast-raised breads that are much quicker to bake than the thick loaf breads in Chapter 2. Classically, pizza is thin and crisp and baked directly on a pizza stone. Deep-dish pizza (also known as Chicago-style or pan pizza) is, as the name implies, thicker, crustier, and baked in a round deep-dish pan. Both styles of pizza are topped with cheese, tomato sauce, and cooked vegetables and/or meat.

Calzones are similar to pizza in that the dough contains the same ingredients—in slightly different proportions—and the "toppings" are enveloped in the dough, thus becoming the filling. Focaccia is thicker, softer, and more lightly topped than pizza, often with nothing more than coarse salt, olive oil, and herbs. Although pizza and calzones are often served as a meal, focaccia is reserved as an accompaniment to soups or salads or, cut into small pieces, as a light hors d'oeuvre. Grissini also make nice hors d'oeuvres. Long, elegant, and easy to make, these rustic breadsticks are made using pizza dough and are much better than what you can find on your supermarket shelves. Pan-grilled flatbreads are generally served like focaccia, as an accompaniment to meals.

PIZZA

THE DOUGH IS PROBABLY THE TRICKIEST part of making pizza at home. While pizza dough is nothing more than bread dough with oil added for softness and suppleness, we found in our testing that minor changes in the ingredient list can yield dramatically different results.

Our goal in testing was threefold. The recipe had to be simple to put together; the dough had to be easy to shape and stretch thin; and the crust needed to bake up crisp and chewy, not tough and leathery.

After initial tests, it was clear that bread flour delivers the best texture. Bread flour makes pizza crust that is chewy and crisp. All-purpose flour can be used in a pinch, but the resulting crust is less crisp.

The second key to perfect crust is water. We found that using more water makes the dough softer and more elastic. Soft dough stretches more easily than a stiffer, harder dough with less water. We prefer to jump-start the yeast in a little warm water for five minutes. We then add more water, at room temperature, along with oil.

For combining the dry ingredients (flour and salt) with the wet ingredients, the food processor is our first choice. The liquid is evenly incorporated into the dry ingredients, and the blade kneads the dough in just 30 seconds. Of course, the dough can be kneaded by hand or with a standing mixer. If you make the dough by hand, resist the temptation to add a lot of flour as you knead.

We use plastic wrap to cover the oiled bowl that holds the rising dough. We found that the tight seal offered by plastic wrap keeps the dough moist and protects it from drafts better than the standard damp cloth. We reserve the damp cloth for use when the dough has been divided into balls and is waiting to be stretched.

To stretch dough to its maximum diameter, let it rest once or twice during the shaping process. Once you feel some resistance, cover the dough with a damp cloth and wait five minutes before going at it again. Fingertips and hands generally do a better job of stretching dough than a rolling pin, which presses air out of the risen dough and makes it tough. This low-tech method is also superior to flipping dough into the air and other frivolous techniques that may work in a pizza parlor but can lead to disaster at home. For illustrations of shaping pizza dough, see page 138.

Even if you're baking just one medium pizza, make a full dough recipe. After the dough has risen and been divided, place the extra pieces of dough in separate airtight containers and freeze them for up to several weeks. Defrost and stretch the dough when desired.

Pizza Dough

MAKES ENOUGH FOR 3 MEDIUM PIZZAS

We find that the food processor is the best tool for making pizza dough. However, only a food processor with a capacity of at least 11 cups can handle this much dough. You can also knead this dough by hand or in a standing mixer (see the variations that follow). Unbleached all-purpose flour can be used in a pinch, but the resulting crust will be less crisp. If you want to make pizza dough in the morning and let it rise on the counter all day, decrease the yeast to ½ teaspoon and let the covered dough rise at cool room temperature (about 68 degrees) until doubled in size, about 8 hours. You can prolong the rising time even further by refrigerating the covered dough for up to 16 hours and then letting it rise on the counter until doubled in size, which will take 6 to 8 hours. See the illustrations below for more tips on making pizza dough.

½	cup warm water (about 110 degrees)
1	envelope (about 2¼ teaspoons) instant yeast
1¼	cups water, at room temperature
2	tablespoons extra-virgin olive oil
4	cups (22 ounces) bread flour, plus more for dusting work surface and hands
1½	teaspoons salt
	Olive oil or nonstick cooking spray for oiling the bowl

1. Measure the warm water into a 2-cup liquid measuring cup. Sprinkle in the yeast and let stand until the yeast dissolves and swells, about 5 minutes. Add the room-temperature water and oil and stir to combine.

2. Process the flour and salt in a large food processor, pulsing to combine. Continue pulsing while pouring the liquid ingredients (holding back a few tablespoons) through the feed tube. If the dough does not readily form into a ball, add the remaining liquid and continue to pulse until a ball forms. Process until the dough is smooth and elastic, about 30 seconds longer.

MIXING THE PIZZA DOUGH

1. Measure ½ cup warm water at about 110 degrees into a 2-cup measuring cup. Sprinkle the yeast over the water and let it stand until swollen, about 5 minutes. Add enough room-temperature water to equal 1¾ cups and then add the oil.

2. The food processor is the easiest place to make pizza dough. Pulse the flour and salt to combine them. Then pour the liquid ingredients through the feed tube while continuing to pulse.

3. Once the dough comes together, process it until it is smooth and elastic, about 30 seconds.

4. Turn the dough onto a lightly floured work surface and shape it into a smooth, round ball.

5. If kneading the dough by hand, don't worry about overworking the dough. You can't be too rough. Use your palms for maximum leverage against the dough.

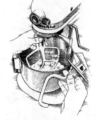

6. If kneading dough in a standing mixer, use the paddle to combine the dry and wet ingredients. When the dough forms a cohesive mass, stop the mixer and switch to the dough hook for kneading.

7. Plastic wrap forms a tighter seal than a damp towel and keeps the dough moister. Place the kneaded dough in a deep oiled bowl and cover the bowl tightly with the wrap.

8. After the dough has doubled in size (about 2 hours), deflate it by pressing down on it with your fist. Divide and shape the punched-down dough as directed in the pizza recipes in this chapter.

3. The dough will be a bit tacky, so use a rubber spatula to turn it out onto a lightly floured work surface. Knead by hand for a few strokes to form a smooth, round ball. Put the dough into a deep oiled bowl and cover with plastic wrap. Let rise until doubled in size, 1½ to 2 hours. Press the dough to deflate it.

➤ VARIATIONS

Pizza Dough Kneaded by Hand

Follow the recipe for Pizza Dough through step 1. Omit step 2 and instead combine the salt and half the flour in a deep bowl. Add the liquid ingredients and use a wooden spoon to combine. Add the remaining flour, stirring until a cohesive mass forms. Turn the dough onto a lightly floured work surface and knead until smooth and elastic, 7 to 8 minutes, using as little dusting flour as possible while kneading. Form the dough into a ball, put it in a deep oiled bowl, cover with plastic wrap, and proceed with the recipe.

Pizza Dough Kneaded in a Standing Mixer

Follow the recipe for Pizza Dough through step 1. Omit step 2 and instead place the flour and salt in the bowl of a standing mixer fitted with the paddle. Briefly combine the dry ingredients at low speed. Slowly add the liquid ingredients and continue to mix at low speed until a cohesive mass forms. Stop the mixer and replace the paddle with the dough hook. Knead until the dough is smooth and elastic, about 5 minutes. Form the dough into a ball, put it in a deep oiled bowl, cover with plastic wrap, and proceed with the recipe.

Pizza Dough with Garlic and Herbs

This dough is especially good when you want a pizza with a minimum of toppings but big flavor. The dough also makes excellent Grissini (Italian breadsticks) on page 174.

Heat 2 tablespoons extra-virgin olive oil in a small skillet. Add 4 medium minced garlic cloves and 1 teaspoon minced fresh thyme, oregano, or rosemary leaves. Sauté until the garlic is golden, 2 to 3 minutes. Cool the mixture and use in place of the oil in the recipe for Pizza Dough.

Whole-Wheat Pizza Dough

Whole-wheat flour gives the dough a hearty flavor but slows down the rising process a bit.

Follow the recipe for Pizza Dough, replacing 2 cups of the bread flour with an equal amount of whole-wheat flour. The dough may require an extra 30 minutes to double in size while rising.

～✦～

Pizza Bianca with Garlic and Rosemary

MAKES 3 MEDIUM PIZZAS, SERVING 6

Pizza bianca translates as "white pizza," referring to the fact that there are no tomatoes—just garlic, oil, rosemary, and salt—in this recipe. See the illustrations on page 138 for tips on shaping and topping pizza dough.

1	recipe Pizza Dough (page 153)
¼	cup extra-virgin olive oil, plus more for brushing on the stretched dough
6	medium garlic cloves, minced or pressed through a garlic press
4	teaspoons minced fresh rosemary leaves
	Salt and ground black pepper
	Semolina or cornmeal for dusting the pizza peel

1. Prepare the dough as directed in the Pizza Dough recipe. Place a pizza stone on a rack in the lower third of the oven. Heat the oven to 500 degrees for at least 30 minutes. Turn the dough out onto a lightly floured work surface. Use a chef's knife or dough scraper to divide the dough into three pieces. Form each piece of dough into a smooth, round ball and cover it with a damp cloth. Let the dough relax for at least 10 minutes but no more than 30 minutes.

2. While preparing the dough, combine the oil, garlic, rosemary, and salt and pepper to taste in a small bowl. Set the herb oil aside.

3. Working with one piece of dough at a time and keeping the others covered, shape the dough as directed in the illustrations on page 138, then transfer it to a pizza peel that has been lightly dusted with semolina.

4. Lightly brush the dough round with plain olive oil. Prick the dough all over with a fork to prevent ballooning in the oven (see the illustration on page 157).

PIZZA BASICS

Unless you build a brick oven in your kitchen, it's not possible to duplicate pizzeria-style pies at home. Commercial pizza ovens can reach 800 degrees; home ovens just can't compete. That said, homemade pizza is delicious even if different from the pies you get when you eat out: The crust is chewier, crisper, and not nearly as greasy. To ensure good homemade pizza, here are a few things to know:

USE TILES OR A PIZZA STONE In our testing, we found that baking pizza on tiles or a pizza stone is a must because crusts baked on a pizza screen (a perforated pan) or a baking sheet were not as crisp and chewy. Unglazed quarry tiles made of terra cotta are porous and absorb heat better than a metal baking sheet; thus, they transfer more heat to whatever food is cooked on them. Pizza crust becomes especially crisp and well browned on the bottom when cooked on tiles. (In our test kitchen, we have found that these tiles are good for most bread as well.) Look for $\frac{1}{2}$-inch-thick tiles—they come in 6-inch squares and can be cut at a tile store to fit your oven rack perfectly. If using tiles, simply line the bottom rack of your oven with them—you will need six or eight, depending on the size of your oven. But if you don't want to bother with tiles (they can chip and we have "lost" one on occasion in the test kitchen), consider a pizza stone.

Pizza stones (also called baking stones) are prized for their ability to retain heat and lessen the effects of temperature fluctuations in home ovens. Pizza stones are usually made of clay or ceramic (although soapstone and composite cement stones are also available). When coupled with extreme heat, they absorb moisture, producing crisper, drier pizzas, breads, and calzones. In a recent testing of pizza stones, we looked at two main criteria: design (including ease of use, installation, and storage) and performance (including heat conductivity, evenness of browning, and crispness of baked goods). There was little issue with heat conductivity. We took the surface temperature of each stone, and each one exceeded 500 degrees after 60 minutes of heating. With little variation, all seven stones also produced evenly colored and crisp crusts in pizzas and calzones.

Although performance was similar in all models tested, some designs were much easier to work with. Lipped edges inhibited easy placement and removal of food from a peel, and stones with this feature were downgraded, as were stones that were extremely heavy (one weighed a whopping 19 pounds). Stones that were either too big to fit in most home ovens or too small to handle a large pizza received low marks. Our recommendation: Choose a good-sized stone (about 14 by 16 inches is ideal) with smooth edges and don't equate a higher price with a better stone. In terms of whether to buy tiles or a stone, we think a stone is easier to store, but if you already own tiles, use them—they work very well.

PREHEAT THE OVEN Our testing revealed that an oven temperature of 500 degrees is your best bet. When cooked at a lower temperature, the crust was not as crisp. Remember to heat the oven (and stone or tiles) for at least 30 minutes.

USE A PEEL We find that a pizza peel is the best tool for getting topped pizza dough onto a heated stone. The long handle on the peel makes it easy to slide the dough onto tiles or a stone in a hot oven. Although a rimless metal baking sheet can be used in this fashion, the lack of a handle means your hands are that much closer to the oven heat, so use caution. When shopping for a pizza peel, note that there are two choices. Aluminum peels with heat-resistant wooden handles are probably the better bet because they can be washed and cleaned easily. Peels made entirely of wood can mildew when washed, so it's best just to wipe them clean. Either way, make sure your peel measures at least 16 inches across so that it can accommodate a large pizza with room left around the edges.

PREVENT THE DOUGH FROM STICKING Pizza dough is sticky. There are a few options for preventing your dough from sticking to the peel. With its fine, sandy texture, semolina does a good job at helping pizza dough slide off the peel. Cornmeal can also be used, as can flour. Alternatively, if parchment paper is handy, you can simply stretch out the dough onto the parchment and slide the pizza, paper and all, directly onto the stone. Although this method works well, we like the crunch and flavor the semolina or cornmeal gives to the bottom of our crusts. We leave the choice up to you.

BAKE FULLY Depending on your oven, the type of stone or tiles used, and the amount of topping, pizza may be done in as little as 6 minutes or may take as long as 12 minutes. Don't pull a pizza out of the oven until the edge of the crust is golden brown and the toppings are sizzling.

THE BEST PIZZA STONE
We found the Baker's Catalogue Baking Stone (manufactured by Old Stone Oven) to be our favorite. It is modestly priced at $35.00.

5. Slide the dough onto the heated stone. Bake until the crust begins to brown in spots, 6 to 10 minutes. Brush the crust with a third of the herb oil and continue baking until the garlic is fragrant, 1 to 2 minutes. Remove the pizza from the oven, cut into wedges, and serve immediately. Repeat steps 3, 4, and 5 with the remaining two pieces of dough and the remaining herb oil.

➤ VARIATIONS

Pesto Pizza

Follow the recipe for Pizza Bianca with Garlic and Rosemary through step 4, omitting the herb oil in step 2. Bake the dough as directed until golden brown in spots, 8 to 10 minutes. Remove the crust from the oven and spread with ¼ cup Classic Pesto (recipe at right), leaving a ½-inch border. Cut into wedges and serve.

Lemon–Sea Salt Pizza

Follow the recipe for Pizza Bianca with Garlic and Rosemary through step 3. Brush the dough round with plain olive oil as directed in step 4. Arrange 1 small lemon, sliced paper-thin, over the dough round, leaving a ½-inch border uncovered. Sprinkle with coarse sea salt to taste. (Do not prick the dough.) Bake and brush with the herb oil as directed in step 5.

PREVENTING PIZZA DOUGH FROM BALLOONING IN THE OVEN

Some pizzas are baked without toppings. To keep the dough from ballooning in the oven, prick the dough all over with a fork before it goes into the oven. If bubbles form during baking, prick them before they become too large.

Classic Pesto

MAKES ABOUT ¾ CUP

Basil often darkens in pesto, but you can boost the color by adding parsley. For a sharper flavor, substitute 1 tablespoon finely grated pecorino cheese for 1 tablespoon of the Parmesan.

¼	cup pine nuts, walnuts, or almonds
3	medium garlic cloves, unpeeled
2	cups packed fresh basil leaves
2	tablespoons packed fresh parsley leaves (optional)
7	tablespoons extra-virgin olive oil
	Salt
¼	cup finely grated Parmesan cheese

1. Toast the nuts in a small, heavy skillet over medium heat, stirring frequently, until just golden and fragrant, 4 to 5 minutes. Transfer the nuts to a plate.

2. Add the garlic to the empty pan. Toast, shaking the pan occasionally, until the cloves are fragrant and their color deepens slightly, about 7 minutes. Transfer the garlic to a cutting board; cool, peel, and chop.

3. Place the basil and parsley (if using) in a heavy-duty gallon-sized zipper-lock plastic bag. Pound the bag with the flat side of a meat pounder or a rolling pin until all the leaves are bruised.

4. Place the nuts, garlic, herbs, oil, and ½ teaspoon salt in a food processor and process until smooth, stopping as necessary to scrape down the sides of the bowl. Transfer the mixture to a small bowl, stir in the Parmesan cheese, and adjust the salt to taste. (The surface of the pesto can be covered with a sheet of plastic wrap or a thin film of oil and the pesto can be refrigerated for up to 3 days.)

White Pizza with Spinach and Ricotta

MAKES 3 MEDIUM PIZZAS, SERVING 6

Ricotta cheese and garlicky sautéed spinach flavor this tomatoless pizza. Be sure to squeeze the cooked spinach of any liquid to prevent a soggy crust. See the illustrations on page 138 for tips on shaping and topping pizza dough.

I	recipe Pizza Dough (page 153)
2	tablespoons extra-virgin olive oil, plus more for brushing on the stretched dough
4	medium garlic cloves, minced or pressed through a garlic press
¼	teaspoon hot red pepper flakes
1½	pounds spinach, stemmed, washed, shaken to remove excess water, and chopped coarse
	Salt and ground black pepper
	Semolina or cornmeal for dusting the pizza peel
I	(15-ounce) container whole-milk ricotta cheese
6	tablespoons grated Parmesan cheese

1. Prepare the dough as directed in the Pizza Dough recipe. Place a pizza stone on a rack in the lower third of the oven. Heat the oven to 500 degrees for at least 30 minutes. Turn the dough out onto a lightly floured work surface. Use a chef's knife or dough scraper to divide the dough into three pieces. Form each piece of dough into a smooth, round ball and cover it with a damp cloth. Let the dough relax for at least 10 minutes but no more than 30 minutes.

2. While preparing the dough, heat the oil in a Dutch oven set over medium heat. Add the garlic and hot red pepper flakes and cook until fragrant, about 1 minute. Add the damp spinach, cover, and cook, stirring occasionally, until just wilted, about 3 minutes. Season with salt and pepper to taste. Transfer the spinach to a medium bowl, squeezing out any liquid with the back of a spoon and leaving the liquid behind in the pot. Set the spinach aside; discard the liquid.

3. Working with one piece of dough at a time and keeping the others covered, shape the dough as directed in the illustrations on page 138, then transfer it to a pizza peel that has been lightly dusted with semolina.

4. Lightly brush the dough round with olive oil. Arrange a third of the spinach mixture over the dough round, leaving a ½-inch border uncovered. Dot with ⅔ cup ricotta cheese.

5. Slide the dough onto the heated stone. Bake until the crust edges brown in spots, 8 to 12 minutes. Remove the pizza from the oven, sprinkle with 2 tablespoons Parmesan, cut into wedges, and serve immediately. Repeat steps 3, 4, and 5 with the remaining two pieces of dough and the remaining toppings.

GRATING MOZZARELLA

Mozzarella and other semisoft cheeses can stick to a box grater and cause a real mess. Here's how to keep the holes on the grater from becoming clogged.

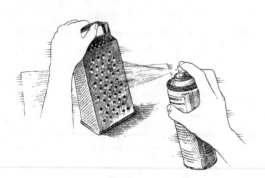

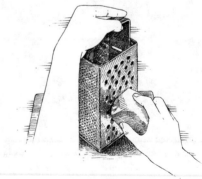

1. Use nonstick cooking spray to lightly coat the side of the box grater that has large holes.

2. Shred the cheese as usual. The cooking spray will keep the cheese from sticking to the surface of the grater.

Three-Cheese Pizza

MAKES 3 MEDIUM PIZZAS, SERVING 6

This classic combination of mozzarella, Parmesan, and Gorgonzola is not a study in excess, as the name might imply. A little of each cheese contributes to a rich, complex flavor. We also recommend adding garlic and olives, although these ingredients are optional. See the illustrations on page 138 for tips on shaping and topping pizza dough.

I   recipe Pizza Dough (page 153)
    Semolina or cornmeal for dusting the pizza
    peel
    Extra-virgin olive oil for brushing on the
    stretched dough
4   ounces mozzarella cheese, shredded
    (about I cup)
8   ounces Gorgonzola cheese, crumbled
    (about 2 cups)
3   medium garlic cloves, sliced thin (optional)
6   tablespoons pitted and quartered
    oil-cured black olives (optional)
6   tablespoons grated Parmesan cheese

1. Prepare the dough as directed in the Pizza Dough recipe. Place a pizza stone on a rack in the lower third of the oven. Heat the oven to 500 degrees for at least 30 minutes. Turn the dough out onto a lightly floured work surface. Use a chef's knife or dough scraper to divide the dough into three pieces. Form each piece of dough into a smooth, round ball and cover it with a damp cloth. Let the dough relax for at least 10 minutes but no more than 30 minutes.

2. Working with one piece of dough at a time and keeping the others covered, shape the dough as directed in the illustrations on page 138, then transfer it to a pizza peel that has been lightly dusted with semolina.

3. Lightly brush the dough round with olive oil. Sprinkle evenly with ⅓ cup mozzarella, leaving a ½-inch border uncovered. Dot with ⅔ cup Gorgonzola cheese and sprinkle with a third of the garlic and olives, if using.

4. Slide the dough onto the heated stone. Bake until the crust edges brown and the cheeses are golden and bubbling, 8 to 12 minutes. Remove the pizza from the oven, sprinkle with 2 tablespoons Parmesan, cut into wedges, and serve immediately. Repeat steps 2, 3, and 4 with the remaining two pieces of dough and the remaining toppings.

Classic Tomato Pizza with Mozzarella and Basil

MAKES 3 MEDIUM PIZZAS, SERVING 6

Known as pizza Margherita, this Neapolitan specialty is Italian cooking at its simplest and best. See the illustrations on page 138 for tips on shaping and topping pizza dough.

I   recipe Pizza Dough (page 153)
    Semolina or cornmeal for dusting the pizza
    peel
    Extra-virgin olive oil for brushing on the
    stretched dough
3   cups Quick Tomato Sauce for Pizza (recipe
    follows)
12 ounces mozzarella cheese, shredded
    (about 3 cups)
3   tablespoons grated Parmesan cheese
½   cup packed fresh basil leaves

1. Prepare the dough as directed in the Pizza Dough recipe. Place a pizza stone on a rack in the lower third of the oven. Heat the oven to 500 degrees for at least 30 minutes. Turn the dough out onto a lightly floured work surface. Use a chef's knife or dough scraper to divide the dough into three pieces. Form each piece of dough into a smooth, round ball and cover it with a damp cloth. Let the dough relax for at least 10 minutes but no more than 30 minutes.

2. Working with one piece of dough at a time and keeping the others covered, shape the dough as directed in the illustrations on page 138, then transfer it to a pizza peel that has been lightly dusted with semolina

3. Lightly brush the dough round with olive oil. Spread 1 cup tomato sauce evenly over the dough round, leaving a ½-inch border uncovered. Sprinkle with 1 cup mozzarella.

4. Slide the dough onto the heated stone. Bake

until the crust edges brown and the cheese is golden brown in spots, 8 to 12 minutes. Remove the pizza from the oven and sprinkle with 1 tablespoon Parmesan. Tear a third of the basil leaves and scatter them over the pizza. Cut the pizza into wedges and serve immediately. Repeat steps 2, 3, and 4 with the remaining two pieces of dough and the remaining toppings.

Quick Tomato Sauce for Pizza

MAKES ABOUT 3 CUPS

1   (28-ounce) can diced tomatoes
2   tablespoons extra-virgin olive oil
2   large garlic cloves, minced or pressed through a garlic press
    Salt and ground black pepper

1. Place the tomatoes in a food processor and process until smooth, about five 1-second pulses.
2. Heat the oil and garlic in a medium saucepan over medium heat until the garlic is sizzling, about 40 seconds. Stir in the tomatoes. Bring to a simmer and cook, uncovered, until the sauce thickens enough to coat a wooden spoon, about 15 minutes. Season with salt and pepper to taste.

Fresh Tomato Pizza with Arugula and Prosciutto

MAKES 3 MEDIUM PIZZAS, SERVING 6

The arugula for this pizza is tossed with a little oil to keep it moist and then sprinkled over the baked pizza as soon as it comes out of the oven. The heat from the pizza wilts the arugula without causing it to dry out. See the illustrations on page 138 for tips on shaping and topping pizza dough.

1   recipe Pizza Dough (page 153)
    Semolina or cornmeal for dusting the pizza peel
2   tablespoons extra-virgin olive oil, plus more for brushing on the stretched dough
3   medium ripe tomatoes (about 1 pound), cored and sliced crosswise into thin rounds
    Salt and ground black pepper

4   ounces thin-sliced prosciutto
6   ounces mozzarella cheese, shredded (about 1 1/2 cups)
3   cups stemmed arugula leaves, washed and thoroughly dried

1. Prepare the dough as directed in the Pizza Dough recipe. Place a pizza stone on a rack in the lower third of the oven. Heat the oven to 500 degrees for at least 30 minutes. Turn the dough out onto a lightly floured work surface. Use a chef's knife or dough scraper to divide the dough into three pieces. Form each piece of dough into a smooth, round ball and cover it with a damp cloth. Let the dough relax for at least 10 minutes but no more than 30 minutes.
2. Working with one piece of dough at a time and keeping the others covered, shape the dough as directed in the illustrations on page 138, then

INGREDIENTS:
Supermarket Mozzarella Cheese

We selected five widely available brands of "supermarket," or low-moisture, mozzarella cheese and sampled those made with part-skim or whole milk. Because the most common use for this type of cheese is quick and convenient melting, we decided to include both preshredded and block forms. Fifteen *Cook's Illustrated* staff members tasted these cheeses both raw (all block cheeses were tasted shredded) and melted on pizza. Separate tests were performed in this manner, one for the category of shredded cheeses and the other for block cheeses. Based on the combined scores of the raw and the

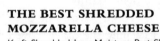

pizza tests, here are the two that came out on top:

THE BEST SHREDDED MOZZARELLA CHEESE
Kraft Shredded Low Moisture Part-Skim Mozzarella was described by tasters as "rich," "tangy," and "fresh."

THE BEST BLOCK MOZZARELLA CHEESE
Dragone Low Moisture Mozzarella Cheese (Whole Milk) was described by tasters as "rich and creamy" and "tangy and briny."

transfer it to a pizza peel that has been lightly dusted with semolina.

3. Lightly brush the dough round with olive oil. Arrange a third of the tomato slices in concentric circles over the dough round, leaving a ½-inch border uncovered. Season with salt and pepper to taste and drizzle with 1 teaspoon oil.

4. Slide the dough onto the heated stone. Bake until the crust edges start to brown, 6 to 10 minutes. Lay a third of the prosciutto slices over the tomatoes and sprinkle with ½ cup mozzarella. Continue baking until the cheese melts, 2 to 3 minutes more. Toss 1 cup arugula with 1 teaspoon oil in a small bowl. Remove the pizza from the oven and top with the arugula. Cut the pizza into wedges and serve immediately. Repeat steps 2, 3, and 4 with the remaining two pieces of dough and the remaining toppings.

Mushroom Pizza with Sage, Fontina, and Parmesan

MAKES 3 MEDIUM PIZZAS, SERVING 6

Any fresh mushrooms will work in this recipe, but cremini are especially good. See the illustrations on page 138 for tips on shaping and topping pizza dough.

1	recipe Pizza Dough (page 153)
2	large garlic cloves, minced or pressed through a garlic press
2	tablespoons extra-virgin olive oil, plus more for brushing on the stretched dough
1	pound fresh mushrooms, stem ends trimmed, sliced thin
1	teaspoon minced fresh sage leaves
	Salt and ground black pepper
	Semolina or cornmeal for dusting the pizza peel
3	cups Quick Tomato Sauce for Pizza (page 160)
6	ounces fontina cheese, shredded (about 1 ½ cups)
6	tablespoons grated Parmesan cheese

1. Prepare the dough as directed in the Pizza Dough recipe. Place a pizza stone on a rack in the lower third of the oven. Heat the oven to 500 degrees for at least 30 minutes. Turn the dough

out onto a lightly floured work surface. Use a chef's knife or dough scraper to divide the dough into three pieces. Form each piece of dough into a smooth, round ball and cover it with a damp cloth. Let the dough relax for at least 10 minutes but no more than 30 minutes.

2. While preparing the dough, heat the garlic and oil in a large skillet set over medium-high heat. When the garlic begins to sizzle, add the mushrooms and sauté until the mushrooms are golden brown and the juices they release have evaporated, about 7 minutes. Stir in the sage and salt and pepper to taste. Set the mushrooms aside.

3. Working with one piece of dough at a time and keeping the others covered, shape the dough as directed in the illustrations on page 138, then transfer it to a pizza peel that has been lightly dusted with semolina.

4. Lightly brush the dough round with olive oil. Spread 1 cup tomato sauce over the dough round, leaving a ½-inch border uncovered. Scatter a third of the mushrooms and then ½ cup fontina cheese over the sauce.

5. Slide the dough onto the heated stone. Bake until the crust edges brown and the cheese is golden brown in spots, 8 to 12 minutes. Remove the pizza from the oven, sprinkle with 2 tablespoons Parmesan, cut into wedges, and serve immediately. Repeat steps 3, 4, and 5 with the remaining two pieces of dough and the remaining toppings.

SLICING BUTTON MUSHROOMS THINLY

Slicing button mushrooms thin takes some patience. To slice them quickly, use an egg slicer. Place the stem-trimmed mushrooms, one at a time, into the egg slicer. The pieces will be even and thin.

Caramelized Onion Pizza with Oil-Cured Olives and Parmesan

MAKES 3 MEDIUM PIZZAS, SERVING 6

See the illustrations on page 138 for tips on shaping and topping pizza dough.

1	recipe Pizza Dough (page 153)
2	tablespoons extra-virgin olive oil, plus more for brushing on the stretched dough
2	medium yellow onions, halved and sliced thin
1	teaspoon fresh thyme leaves
	Salt and ground black pepper
	Semolina or cornmeal for dusting the pizza peel
1 1/2	cups Quick Tomato Sauce for Pizza (page 160)
1/4	cup pitted and quartered oil-cured black olives
6	anchovies, chopped coarse (optional)
1/4	cup grated Parmesan cheese

1. Prepare the dough as directed in the Pizza Dough recipe. Place a pizza stone on a rack in the lower third of the oven. Heat the oven to 500 degrees for at least 30 minutes. Turn the dough out onto a lightly floured work surface. Use a chef's knife or dough scraper to divide the dough into three pieces. Form each piece of dough into a smooth, round ball and cover it with a damp cloth. Let the dough relax for at least 10 minutes but no more than 30 minutes.

2. While preparing the dough, heat the oil in a large skillet set over medium-high heat. Add the onions and sauté until softened and somewhat caramelized, about 10 minutes. Stir in the thyme; season with salt and pepper to taste. Set the onions aside.

3. Working with one piece of dough at a time and keeping the others covered, shape the dough as directed in the illustrations on page 138, then transfer it to a pizza peel that has been lightly dusted with semolina.

4. Lightly brush the dough round with olive oil. Spread ½ cup of the tomato sauce over the dough round, leaving a ½-inch border uncovered. Scatter a third of the onions over the sauce onto the dough round and sprinkle with a third of the olives and

anchovies, if using.

5. Slide the dough onto the heated stone. Bake until the crust edges start to brown, 6 to 12 minutes. Sprinkle with a third of the Parmesan and continue baking until the cheese melts, 2 to 3 minutes more. Remove the pizza from the oven, cut into wedges, and serve immediately. Repeat steps 3, 4, and 5 with the remaining two pieces of dough and the remaining toppings.

Pepperoni Pizza

MAKES 3 MEDIUM PIZZAS, SERVING 6

This classic pizzeria favorite is especially easy to prepare. See the illustrations on page 138 for tips on shaping and topping pizza dough.

1	recipe Pizza Dough (page 153)
	Semolina or cornmeal for dusting the pizza peel
	Extra-virgin olive oil for brushing on the stretched dough
1 1/2	cups Quick Tomato Sauce for Pizza (page 160)
8	ounces pepperoni, peeled and sliced thin
4	ounces mozzarella cheese, shredded (about 1 cup)
1/4	cup grated Parmesan cheese

1. Prepare the dough as directed in the Pizza Dough recipe. Place a pizza stone on a rack in the lower third of the oven. Heat the oven to 500 degrees for at least 30 minutes. Turn the dough out onto a lightly floured work surface. Use a chef's knife or dough scraper to divide the dough into three pieces. Form each piece of dough into a smooth, round ball and cover it with a damp cloth. Let the dough relax for at least 10 minutes but no more than 30 minutes.

2. Working with one piece of dough at a time and keeping the others covered, shape the dough as directed in the illustrations on page 138, then transfer it to a pizza peel that has been lightly dusted with semolina.

3. Lightly brush the dough round with olive oil. Spread ½ cup of the tomato sauce over the dough round, leaving a ½-inch border uncovered. Scatter a third of the pepperoni slices over the sauce.

4. Slide the dough onto the heated stone. Bake the pizza until the crust edges start to brown, 6 to 12 minutes. Sprinkle with ⅓ cup mozzarella and a third of the Parmesan and continue baking until the cheeses melt, 2 to 3 minutes more. Remove the pizza from the oven, cut into wedges, and serve immediately. Repeat steps 2, 3, and 4 with the remaining two pieces of dough and the remaining toppings.

Sausage and Bell Pepper Pizza with Basil and Mozzarella

MAKES 3 MEDIUM PIZZAS, SERVING 6

If bulk sausage is not available, buy link sausage, remove the meat from the casings, and then break it into bite-size pieces. See the illustrations on page 138 for tips on shaping and topping pizza dough.

I	recipe Pizza Dough (page 153)
³/₄	pound bulk sweet Italian sausage, broken into bite-size pieces
I ¹/₂	teaspoons extra-virgin olive oil (approximately), plus more for brushing on the stretched dough
I	red or yellow bell pepper, cored, halved, seeded, and cut into thin strips
	Salt and ground black pepper
	Semolina or cornmeal for dusting the pizza peel
I ¹/₂	cups Quick Tomato Sauce for Pizza (page 160) combined with 2 tablespoons minced fresh basil leaves
4	ounces mozzarella cheese, shredded (about I cup)

1. Prepare the dough as directed in the Pizza Dough recipe. Place a pizza stone on a rack in the lower third of the oven. Heat the oven to 500 degrees for at least 30 minutes. Turn the dough out onto a lightly floured work surface. Use a chef's knife or dough scraper to divide the dough into three pieces. Form each piece of dough into a smooth, round ball and cover it with a damp cloth. Let the dough relax for at least 10 minutes but no more than 30 minutes.

2. While preparing the dough, put the sausage and ¼ cup water in a large skillet. Cook over medium-high heat until the water evaporates and the sausage cooks through and browns, about 10 minutes. Remove the sausage with a slotted spoon and set aside. Add enough oil so that the amount of fat in the skillet equals 1 tablespoon. Add the bell pepper and sauté until softened slightly, about 5 minutes. Season the bell pepper with salt and pepper to taste. Set the bell pepper aside.

3. Working with one piece of dough at a time and keeping the others covered, shape the dough as directed in the illustrations on page 138, then transfer it to a pizza peel that has been lightly dusted with semolina.

4. Lightly brush the dough round with olive oil. Spread ½ cup of the tomato sauce over the dough round, leaving a ½-inch border uncovered. Scatter a third of the sausage and a third of the bell pepper over the sauce.

5. Slide the dough onto the heated stone. Bake until the crust edges start to brown, 6 to 12 minutes. Sprinkle with ⅓ cup of the cheese and continue baking until the cheese melts, 2 to 3 minutes more. Remove the pizza from the oven, cut into wedges, and serve immediately. Repeat steps 3, 4, and 5 with the remaining two pieces of dough and the remaining toppings.

DEEP-DISH PIZZA

DEEP-DISH PIZZA (ALSO KNOWN AS Chicago-style or pan pizza) may have its roots in Italy, but this recipe is as American as apple pie. In fact, Italians would not recognize this creation—it has no counterpart in Italy.

Deep-dish pizza is about 75 percent crust, so the crust must be great. We wanted it to be rich, substantial, and moist, with a tender, yet slightly chewy crumb and a well-developed flavor, like that of a good loaf of bread. We also thought the crust should be crisp and nicely browned without being dry or tough. Finally, knowing how time-consuming pizza making can be, we wanted a pizza dough that could be made in as little time as possible without sacrificing quality.

After scouring various cookbooks, we made

five different pizza doughs and baked them in deep-dish pans. To our disappointment, none delivered the flavorful, crisp brown crust that we felt was needed.

After these initial tests, we tried dozens of variations. We played around with the ratio of water to flour, the amount of oil, the type of flour, and just about every other variable we could think of. But we weren't satisfied until we finally widened the field and tried a recipe for focaccia that used boiled, riced potatoes to add moisture and flavor to the dough. This dough was just what we were hoping for: very wet and yet easy to handle, light, and smooth. When baked, it was soft and moist, yet with a bit of chew, and had a sturdiness and structure that was not present in the previous doughs. (For more information on this somewhat unusual use of potatoes, see above.)

Now that we had found a dough that we liked, the challenge was to come up with a rising and baking method suited to deep-dish pizza. We placed the pizza dough in a barely warmed oven for the first rise, reducing the initial rising time from 1 hour to 35 minutes and producing dough that tasted no different from the dough that rose at room temperature for a full hour.

Next we tried reducing—even eliminating—

the amount of time allowed for the second rise. The dough given a full 30 minutes for the second rise was vastly better than doughs given only 15 minutes or no second rise at all. The flavor was more complex, and the texture of the pizza crust was softer and lighter, making the second rise too important to pass up or shorten.

After some testing, we discovered that a crust baked at 425 degrees on a baking stone was almost perfect—the bottom and sides of the pizza were well-browned, and the interior crumb was moist, light, and evenly cooked through. The exterior of this crust was, however, slightly tough. To combat this, we tried coating the pizza pan with oil. After some experimentation, we found that the pizzas made with a generous amount of oil coating the pan (¼ cup was optimal) had a far more desirable crust than those made with little or no oil in the pan. Lightly "frying" the dough in the pan made for a rich, caramelized exterior; this added a good amount of flavor and a secondary texture to the crust, without drying it out or making it tough.

Now it was time for the toppings. On most pizzas, the toppings can simply be placed on raw dough and baked, since the crust bakes in about the same amount of time as the toppings. But we found that the weight of the toppings prevented the crust from rising in the oven, resulting in a dense, heavy crust, especially in the center of the pie. So we tried prebaking crusts from 5 minutes up to 15 minutes to develop some structure before adding the toppings. The pizza that we prebaked for 15 minutes, then topped, was perfect. The crust had a chance to rise in the oven without the weight or moisture of the toppings, and the toppings had just enough time to melt and brown.

DEEP-DISH PIZZA: POTATOES ARE THE SECRET INGREDIENT

Dough with potato (right) produced a much springier, chewier, and softer crust than the same dough without potato (left).

Deep-Dish Pizza

MAKES ONE 14-INCH PIZZA, SERVING 4 TO 6

Prepare the topping while the dough is rising so it will be ready when the dough is ready. Baking the pizza in a deep-dish pan on a hot pizza stone will help produce a crisp, well-browned bottom crust. Otherwise, a heavy rimless baking sheet (do not use an insulated cookie sheet) will work almost as well. If you've got only a rimmed baking sheet, turn it upside down and bake the pizza on the flat side. The amount of oil used to grease the pan may seem excessive, but in addition to preventing sticking, the oil helps the crust brown nicely.

1	medium russet (baking) potato (about 9 ounces), peeled and quartered
3½	cups (17½ ounces) unbleached all-purpose flour
1½	teaspoons instant yeast
1¾	teaspoons salt
1	cup warm water (about 110 degrees)
6	tablespoons extra-virgin olive oil, plus more for oiling the bowl
1	recipe topping (recipes follow)

1. Bring 1 quart water and the potato to a boil in a small saucepan over medium-high heat; cook until the potato is tender, 10 to 15 minutes. Drain the potato and cool until it can be handled comfortably; press through the fine disk on a potato ricer or grate through the large holes on a box grater. Measure 1⅓ cups lightly packed potato; discard the remaining potato.

2. Adjust one oven rack to the highest position and the other rack to the lowest position; heat the oven to 200 degrees. Once the temperature reaches 200 degrees, maintain the heat for 10 minutes, then turn off the heat.

3. Combine the flour, yeast, and salt in a food processor. With the motor running, add the water and process until the dough comes together in a shaggy ball. Add the potato and process for several seconds, then add 2 tablespoons of the oil and process several more seconds, until the dough is smooth and slightly sticky. Transfer the dough to a lightly oiled medium bowl, turn to coat with oil, and cover the bowl tightly with plastic wrap. Place in the warmed oven until the dough is soft and

spongy and doubled in size, 30 to 35 minutes.

4. Oil the bottom of a 14-inch deep-dish pizza pan with the remaining 4 tablespoons olive oil. Remove the dough from the oven and gently punch down; turn the dough onto a clean, dry work surface and pat into a 12-inch round. Transfer the round to the oiled pan, cover with plastic wrap, and let rest until the dough no longer resists shaping, about 10 minutes.

5. Place a pizza stone or rimless baking sheet on the lowest oven rack (do not use an insulated cookie sheet; see note above) and preheat the oven to 500 degrees. Uncover the dough and pull it into the edges and up the sides of the pan to form a 1-inch-high lip. Cover with plastic wrap; let rise in a warm draft-free spot until doubled in size, about 30 minutes. Uncover the dough and prick generously with a fork. Reduce the oven temperature to 425 degrees and bake on the heated stone or baking sheet until the crust is dry and lightly browned, about 15 minutes. Add the desired toppings; bake on the stone or baking sheet until the cheese melts, 10 to 15 minutes. Move the pizza to the top rack and bake until the cheese is golden brown in spots, about 5 minutes longer. To make sure the crust is done, use a spatula to lift up the crust—it should be nicely browned underneath (see illustration below). Let cool 5 minutes, then, holding the pizza pan at an angle with one hand, use a wide spatula to slide the pizza from the pan to a cutting board. Cut into wedges and serve.

DETERMINING WHEN DEEP-DISH PIZZA IS DONE

Use a spatula to lift up the pizza slightly. If the bottom crust is nicely browned, the pizza is done.

➤ VARIATIONS

10-Inch Deep-Dish Pizzas

If you don't own a 14-inch deep-dish pizza pan, divide the dough between two 10-inch cake pans.

Follow the recipe for Deep-Dish Pizza through step 3. Grease the bottom of two 10-inch cake pans with 2 tablespoons olive oil each. Turn the dough onto a clean, dry work surface and divide it in half. Pat each half into a 9-inch round; continue with recipe, reducing the initial baking time on the lowest rack to 5 to 10 minutes and dividing the topping evenly in half between the pizzas.

Fresh Tomato Topping with Mozzarella and Basil

4	medium ripe tomatoes (about 1 1/2 pounds), cored, seeded, and cut into 1-inch pieces
2	medium garlic cloves, minced
	Salt and ground black pepper
6	ounces mozzarella cheese, shredded (about 1 1/2 cups)
1 1/4	ounces Parmesan cheese, grated (about 1/2 cup)
3	tablespoons shredded fresh basil leaves

1. Mix together the tomatoes and garlic in a medium bowl; season to taste with salt and pepper and set aside.

2. Spread the partially baked crust with the tomato mixture; sprinkle with the mozzarella, then the Parmesan. Bake as directed in step 5 of the recipe for Deep-Dish Pizza. Scatter the basil over the fully baked pizza before cutting it into wedges.

Four-Cheese Topping with Pesto

1/2	cup Classic Pesto, page 157
6	ounces mozzarella cheese, shredded (about 1 1/2 cups)
4	ounces provolone cheese, shredded (about 1 cup)
1 1/4	ounces Parmesan cheese, grated (about 1/2 cup)
1 1/4	ounces blue cheese, crumbled (about 1/4 cup)

Spread the partially baked crust evenly with the pesto; sprinkle with the mozzarella, followed by the provolone, Parmesan, and blue cheese. Bake as directed in step 5 of the recipe for Deep-Dish Pizza.

RICOTTA CALZONES

WITH SOGGY FILLINGS AND BREADY CRUSTS, bad calzones are a dime a dozen. We tested a host of modern calzone recipes and came up with specimens that even the most fast food–deadened palate would reject. These calzones were pale and blond, soggy and limp, and they tended to hover at one of two extremes—too bready and rubbery or too thin and cracker-like. One domed calzone required serious sawing with a serrated knife, only to reveal a cavernous interior with a thin smear of filling. Another hollow calzone was the result of a faulty seal that caused the cheese to end up on the baking stone. These scant fillings were no match for the calzone shell; time after time, we were left with a mouthful of dry bread. After this first tasting, we knew what we wanted: a crisp crust that had plenty of chew, with a healthy proportion of rich, creamy, flavorful filling.

We started with the dough, thinking it would be easy; after all, the test kitchen had already developed pizza dough recipes (thin crust and deep dish), and we made the seemingly logical assumption that calzone dough and pizza dough were one and the same. Well, perhaps at your local pizzeria, but after trying several pizza doughs (including our own recipe), we can safely say that the best pizza dough will not necessarily make a good calzone. Why? Most pizza dough is wet and puffy, and the calzones made using pizza dough turned out misshapen and bloated. The excess moisture in pizza dough vaporizes at high temperatures, leaving air bubbles that may be acceptable in a pizza crust but not in our calzones.

To get a crispy, chewy crust, we started with the flour, pitting bread and all-purpose flours against each other. As expected, the dough made with higher-protein bread flour gave the crust the qualities we were looking for; the calzones made with all-purpose flour were too tender and soft. Even with bread flour, however, the crust was a little too fluffy; instead of a cleanly defined half-moon shape, we had a blurry, amorphous grin. We knew that yeast was what made the dough rise, so we assumed that by decreasing the yeast in the dough we could reduce the rise and therefore the puffiness of the dough. We were wrong. Yeast does of course cause dough to rise, but a smaller amount of yeast does not necessarily translate to a smaller rise. Rather, it simply takes longer for the dough to achieve that rise.

The key to a hearty, more substantial crust, we discovered, resided in the water, not the yeast. We used as much as 2 cups of water (with 4 cups of flour), which gave us a loose, wet dough, and as little as 1 cup, which gave us a dry, tight dough that was difficult to work with. A happy medium of 1½ cups—just ¼ cup less than our pizza dough—yielded a dough that was slightly tacky but not too hard to handle and that baked up with good definition, chew, and flavor—and much less fluff.

At this point, our dough was a bit lean, so we added oil and found that 1 tablespoon improved the dough but 2 tablespoons made it even better, giving us an easy-to-handle dough that was also richer in flavor. We experimented with mixing times and found five minutes (the amount recommended by many recipes) to be acceptable, but we wondered if extending the mixing time might make for a chewier crust. Ten minutes proved to be ideal to fully develop the gluten in the dough and give the crust good chew.

With our crust in good shape, we turned our attention to the filling. It was difficult to find recipes for calzones with a simple ricotta filling. Most were adulterated with an odd-flavored ingredient such as blue cheese or used wet ingredients such as tomatoes, fresh mozzarella, and mushrooms, all of which delivered a soggy crust.

We started by pitting whole-milk ricotta against part-skim ricotta. Not surprisingly, whole milk ricotta had a richer, fuller flavor that tasters preferred. We also tasted tried-and-true mozzarella alongside some other meltable cheeses, including fontina (both high- and low-end), Muenster, Monterey Jack, and Havarti. Mozzarella barely eked out a win over the runner-up, Muenster.

Our master recipe called for a high proportion of ricotta paired with lesser quantities of mozzarella as well as Parmesan to balance the flavor. Tasters panned this filling for being too grainy. We tried a different mixing method, using a food processor to smooth out the ricotta. The result was a smooth but overly aerated, fluffy filling (likened to an "oozy omelet" by one taster).

In the end, the solution came in two parts. First, the quantities of the three cheeses had to be just right, with more mozzarella to improve the texture. We ended up reducing the ricotta to 15 ounces, increasing the mozzarella to 8 ounces, and holding the Parmesan at 1½ ounces. The second step was to add an egg yolk (two yolks were too eggy) to the filling, which provided cohesiveness as well as improved texture. Now we had a smooth cheese filling that wouldn't run.

But we still had something to figure out. Why were so many of the calzones exploding during baking? Steam turned out to be the culprit; it forced holes in the crust during baking, and it made for a damp dough. The solution seemed simple enough: Drain the ricotta before mixing it with the other ingredients. To our dismay, the filling made with drained ricotta was like overchewed bubble gum. On top of that, some of the calzones still burst open. One solution was to cut a few vents in the top crust before putting the calzones in the oven, allowing the steam from the ricotta to escape and preventing any explosions in the oven. The vents, unfortunately, did nothing for the bottom crust, which came out of the oven crisp but turned soggy within minutes. Borrowing a method from the pastry world, we

CALZONE CATASTROPHES

We encountered plenty of problems in our early tests. One calzone (left) was nicely domed but nearly empty inside. Another (right) leaked in the oven because the dough was not properly sealed.

cooled the calzones on a rack. This kept the bottoms crusty as they cooled.

All that was left was to flavor our cheesy filling. Tasters preferred the earthy Italian flavor of oregano to other herbs, with just a few red pepper flakes to impart a feisty kick. We tried garlic raw, toasted, roasted, and cooked in a generous amount of oil and found that garlic oil added the smoothest flavor, with no overtly sharp (as in the raw garlic) or sweet (as in the roasted garlic) overtones.

Although we'd tackled how to prevent our calzones from bursting open, we still needed to address why the filling sometimes oozed out of the crust. We tried moistening the edges with water or egg, and we tried pressing the edges with the tines of a fork and with our fingers. No technique was completely effective. We then tried roping the edge, folding it up onto itself in a decorative design. To do this we left a ½-inch rim on the bottom layer, which we then pulled up and over the top layer as we formed a rope design. It cooked through and looked great. (Be sure not to leave more than a ½-inch rim, otherwise the edges won't cook through.) A final brush of olive oil and a sprinkle of coarse salt before going into the oven gave our calzones a crisp texture, a salty flavor, and a beautifully rustic appearance.

Ricotta Calzones

MAKES 6

To make this recipe, you will need a standing mixer or food processor, parchment paper, and a pizza stone. The stone must heat for an additional 30 minutes once the oven has come up to temperature; if your oven heats slowly, begin heating it about an hour into the dough's first rise. Leftover calzones must be refrigerated; to reheat, heat the oven with the pizza stone just as you did when making the recipe, then set the calzones on the hot pizza stone for about 10 minutes. A simple tomato sauce like the Quick Tomato Sauce on page 160 is a nice accompaniment to the calzones. See the illustrations on page 139 for tips on shaping and filling calzones.

DOUGH

- 4 cups (22 ounces) bread flour, plus more for dusting work surface
- 1 envelope (about 2¼ teaspoons) instant yeast
- 1½ teaspoons table salt
- 2 tablespoons extra-virgin olive oil
- 1½ cups plus 1 tablespoon warm water (about 110 degrees)

FILLING

- 3 medium garlic cloves, pressed through a garlic press or minced (about 1 tablespoon)
- 2 tablespoons extra-virgin olive oil
- ¼ teaspoon hot red pepper flakes
- 1 (15-ounce) container whole-milk ricotta cheese
- 8 ounces mozzarella cheese, shredded (2 cups)
- 1½ ounces finely grated Parmesan cheese (about ¾ cup)
- 1 large egg yolk
- 1 tablespoon chopped fresh oregano leaves
- ¼ teaspoon table salt
- ⅛ teaspoon ground black pepper

Extra-virgin olive oil for brushing on the shaped calzones
Kosher salt for sprinkling the calzones

1. FOR THE DOUGH: In the bowl of a standing mixer, whisk the flour, yeast, and salt to combine. Attach the bowl and dough hook to the mixer; with the mixer running at medium-low speed, add the olive oil, then gradually add the water, continuing to mix until the mixture comes together and a smooth, elastic dough forms, about 10 minutes. Lightly spray a large bowl with nonstick cooking spray; form the dough into a ball, transfer it to the bowl, cover the bowl with plastic wrap lightly sprayed with nonstick cooking spray, and let rise in a warm spot until doubled in size, 1½ to 2 hours.

2. FOR THE FILLING: While the dough rises, stir together the garlic, olive oil, and red pepper flakes in an 8-inch skillet over medium heat until the garlic is fragrant and sizzling and the mixture registers 200 degrees on an instant-read thermometer, 1½ to 2 minutes. Transfer to a small bowl and cool until warm, stirring occasionally, about 10 minutes.

3. In a medium bowl, stir together the cheeses, egg yolk, oregano, salt, black pepper, and cooled garlic-pepper oil until combined; cover with plastic wrap and refrigerate until needed.

4. Adjust the oven rack to the lowest position, set a pizza stone on the oven rack, and heat the oven to 500 degrees for at least 30 minutes. Line a baking sheet with parchment paper and spray the parchment lightly with nonstick cooking spray. Turn the risen dough out onto an unfloured work surface. Divide the dough in half, then cut each half into thirds. Gently reshape each piece of dough into a ball. Transfer to the baking sheet and cover with plastic wrap lightly sprayed with nonstick cooking spray. Let the dough rest at least 15 minutes but no more than 30 minutes.

5. Cut eight 9-inch squares of parchment paper. Working with one piece of dough at a time and keeping the other pieces covered, roll the dough into a 9-inch round. Set the dough round onto a parchment square and cover it with another parchment square; roll out another dough ball, set second dough round on top of first, and cover with a parchment square. Repeat to form a stack of 3 dough rounds, covering the top round with a parchment square. Form a second stack of 3 with the remaining dough balls and parchment squares.

6. Remove the top parchment square from the first stack of dough rounds and place the rounds with parchment beneath on the work surface; if the dough rounds have shrunk, gently and evenly roll them out again to 9-inch rounds. Following the illustrations on page 139, form the calzones. With a pastry brush, brush the tops and sides of the calzones with olive oil and lightly sprinkle with kosher salt. Trim the excess parchment paper; slide the calzones on the parchment onto a pizza peel or rimless baking sheet, then slide the calzones with parchment onto the hot pizza stone, spacing them evenly apart. Bake until the calzones are golden brown, about 11 minutes; use a pizza peel or rimless baking sheet to remove the calzones with the parchment to a wire rack. Remove the calzones from the parchment, cool 5 minutes, and serve. While the first batch of calzones bakes, form the second batch and bake them after removing the first batch from the oven.

➤ VARIATIONS

Food Processor Method

The calzone dough can be made in an 11-cup food processor, although it bakes up with slightly less chew than we like.

Place the flour, yeast, and salt in an 11-cup food processor and process to combine, about five 1-second pulses. While pulsing, add the olive oil through the feed tube, then gradually add the water; continue pulsing until the dough forms a ball, then process until smooth and elastic, about 30 seconds. Turn the dough out onto a lightly floured work surface and knead it by hand a few turns to form a smooth, round ball. Transfer the dough to a lightly oiled bowl and proceed as directed.

Ricotta Calzones with Sausage and Broccoli Rabe

1. Follow the recipe for Ricotta Calzones through step 1 to make the dough; while the dough rises, combine the cheeses, egg yolk, oregano, salt, and black pepper in a medium bowl, cover with plastic wrap, and refrigerate until needed. Omit the step for making the garlic oil.

2. Remove the casing from 8 ounces of hot or sweet Italian sausage. Wash and dry 12 ounces broccoli rabe and trim the stalks to about 1 inch below leaves; cut the broccoli rabe crosswise into 1-inch pieces. Cook the sausage in a 12-inch nonstick skillet over high heat, stirring constantly with a wooden spoon and breaking the sausage into ½-inch pieces, until no longer pink, about 4 minutes; stir in 1 tablespoon pressed or minced garlic and ¼ teaspoon red pepper flakes and cook until fragrant, about 10 seconds. Stir in the broccoli rabe, 1 tablespoon water, and ⅛ teaspoon salt; cook, stirring constantly, until the broccoli rabe is crisp-tender and the water has evaporated, about 4 minutes. Transfer the mixture to a large paper towel–lined plate and cool to room temperature; once cooled, pat it with paper towels to absorb excess moisture and set aside until needed.

3. Continue with the recipe from step 4. To fill the calzones, divide the sausage mixture evenly into 6 portions on the plate; place 1 portion of the sausage mixture on top of the cheese filling on each dough round and continue with the recipe to seal and bake the calzones.

Ricotta Calzones with Red Peppers, Spinach, and Goat Cheese

This variation calls for only 10 ounces of ricotta.

1. Follow the recipe for Ricotta Calzones through step 1 to make the dough; while the dough rises, combine 10 ounces (1¼ cups) whole-milk ricotta, with the mozzarella, Parmesan, egg yolk, oregano, salt, and black pepper in a medium bowl, cover with plastic wrap, and refrigerate until needed. Cut 2 medium red bell peppers into ½-inch by 2-inch strips; wash, dry, and trim stems off 1 pound spinach (you should have about 4 cups). Heat 1 tablespoon extra-virgin olive oil in a 10-inch nonstick skillet over high heat until the oil begins to smoke. Stir in the bell peppers and ⅛ teaspoon salt; cook until slightly softened and spotty brown, about 5 minutes, stirring only 2 or 3 times. Clear the center of the pan; add 1 tablespoon extra-virgin olive oil, 1 tablespoon minced or pressed garlic, and ¼ teaspoon red pepper flakes to the clear space and mash with the back of a spoon until fragrant, about 10 seconds, then stir into the red peppers. Remove from the heat and immediately stir in the spinach and ⅛ teaspoon salt; continue to stir until the spinach is wilted, about 1 minute. Transfer the mixture to a paper towel–lined plate and cool to room temperature; once cooled, pat with paper towels to absorb excess moisture and set aside until needed.

2. Continue with the recipe from step 4. To fill the calzones, divide 6 ounces goat cheese evenly into 6 portions and divide the pepper mixture evenly into 6 portions on the plate. Place 1 portion pepper mixture on top of the ricotta cheese filling on each dough round, then crumble 1 portion goat cheese over the pepper mixture and continue with the recipe to seal and bake the calzones.

FOCACCIA

MANY OF THE FOCACCIA RECIPES WE have tried in the past produced a crusty, crisp bread that was only slightly thicker than pizza. These dense, hard breads were often loaded down with toppings. They were more like a meal than a snack or an accompaniment to dinner.

We wanted something quite different. Good focaccia should have a soft, chewy texture and high rise. The crumb should be filled with small to medium-sized air pockets, which will give the bread a good rise and create an overall impression of lightness and chewiness. As for the toppings, they should be minimal. Focaccia is a bread, not a meal.

We began our investigations with a composite recipe of yeast, warm water, olive oil, flour, and salt that was similar to our pizza dough. After more than a dozen initial tests, we were not much closer to a solution. We tried reducing the salt because it can inhibit the action of the yeast and ended up with a better rise but bland bread. We tried bread flour, all-purpose flour, whole-wheat flour, and all possible combinations of these three. Bread flour makes focaccia chewy but also dry and tough. Whole-wheat flour works at cross-purposes with our stated goal of a soft texture and high rise. Unbleached all-purpose flour turned out to be the right choice, but we still had a lot of work to do.

We tried milk instead of water and got better browning and a softer dough, but the bread was kind of flat. Increasing the yeast produced a high focaccia, but the flavor of the yeast was too dominant. We tried letting the dough ferment in the refrigerator for a day. This lightened the texture and produced larger holes in the dough but seemed like a lot of work for a relatively small improvement. We wanted to be able to make and enjoy focaccia on the same day.

In our research we ran across two recipes from southern Italy that added riced potatoes to the dough. When we tried a recipe from Carol Field's *The Italian Baker* (Harper & Row, 1985), we liked the moistness, high rise, and soft texture of this bread. However, the crumb was fairly dense and compact, like a cake. This bread had several appealing traits but still was not quite what we wanted.

We knew that sponges (relatively thin mixtures of yeast, water, and flour that are allowed to ferment briefly) are often used to lend flavor and create air holes in breads. We were not terribly concerned about flavor. With olive oil, salt, and herbs, we were sure that any flavor boost from a sponge would be hard to detect. But we did want those air holes, so we tried a quick sponge.

We stirred the yeast, half the water, and a small

portion of the flour together in a small bowl, covered the bowl with plastic wrap, and let the sponge rest before adding the remaining water, flour, oil, and salt. The difference was quite remarkable. The extra half-hour of fermentation produced wonderfully large bubbles. The result was a bread that rose very high but still had a nice, light texture. We tried longer resting times and found that 30 minutes was enough for the yeast to work its magic.

With the sponge having been successful in our basic recipe, we now tried it with Carol Field's potato focaccia, which we had liked so much. The result was perfect. The sponge transformed the crumb from dense and cake-like to chewy and airy. The bread rose higher than the version made with just flour, and the crumb was softer and more moist.

A couple of notes about working with this dough. The moisture from the potatoes helps keep the crumb soft but also makes the dough very sticky. Adding extra flour makes the dough easier to handle, but the results are not as good because the wet dough helps produce bread with air pockets and chewiness. Sticky doughs are best kneaded in a standing mixer or a food processor. You can make the dough by hand, but you will probably end up incorporating slightly more flour.

When it comes time to shape the dough, moisten your hands with a little water. This will prevent the dough from sticking to your fingers. If you're trying to stretch the dough into a rectangular pan, you may need to let it rest before completing the final shaping. The dough is quite elastic and will put up a good fight without this rest.

An easier method is to divide the dough in half and shape it into two 8-inch disks on a large oiled baking sheet. These free-form disks rise and bake on the same pan, thus eliminating the tricky task of transferring such a sticky dough. You may also form each disk on a wooden peel that has been liberally coated with cornmeal, then slide it onto a pizza stone. The bottom crust is especially thick and chewy when the focaccia is cooked on a stone.

The problem with using a peel is that the focaccia dough often sticks, even when the peel is well dusted with cornmeal. When we were able to get the dough onto the stone without incident, however, the results were excellent. For the sake of simplicity,

we opted to rise and bake the dough in an oiled metal pan, as described in the recipe below.

An oven temperature of 425 degrees bakes the focaccia quickly without any burning. Higher temperatures can cause the bottom to burn, and lower temperatures produce an inferior crust. Be sure to keep the focaccia away from the bottom of the oven to prevent the crust from scorching. Once the bread is golden brown, transfer it immediately to a cooling rack to keep the bottom crust from becoming soggy. Focaccia tastes best warm, so wait about 20 minutes and then serve.

Rosemary Focaccia

MAKES ONE 15 1/2 BY 10 1/2-INCH
RECTANGLE OR TWO 8-INCH ROUNDS

Our focaccia dough is made with potato, as is our deep-dish pizza. For information on how potatoes give bread flavor and crust, see "The Role of Potatoes in Pizza and Focaccia" on page 164.

DOUGH

1	medium baking potato (about 9 ounces), peeled and quartered
1 1/2	teaspoons instant yeast
3 1/2	cups (17 1/2 ounces) unbleached all-purpose flour
1	cup warm water (about 110 degrees)
2	tablespoons extra-virgin olive oil, plus more for oiling the bowl and pan
1 1/4	teaspoons salt

TOPPING

2	tablespoons extra-virgin olive oil
2	tablespoons fresh rosemary leaves
3/4	teaspoon coarse sea salt (or 1 1/4 teaspoons kosher salt)

1. FOR THE DOUGH: Bring 1 quart water to a boil in a small saucepan; add the potato and simmer until tender, about 25 minutes. Drain the potato well; cool until it can be handled comfortably; press it through the fine disk on a ricer or grate through the large holes on a box grater. Reserve 1⅓ cups lightly packed potato.

2. Meanwhile, using a standing mixer or a food processor, mix or process the yeast, ½ cup flour, and

½ cup warm water until combined. Cover tightly with plastic wrap (or put the workbowl lid on) and set aside until bubbly, about 20 minutes. Add the remaining dough ingredients, including reserved potato. If using the mixer, attach the paddle and mix on low speed until the dough comes together. Switch to the dough hook and increase the speed to medium; continue kneading until the dough is smooth and elastic, about 5 minutes. For the food processor, process until the dough is smooth and elastic, about 40 seconds.

3. Transfer the dough to a lightly oiled bowl, turn to coat with oil, and cover tightly with plastic wrap. Let rise in a warm, draft-free area until the dough is puffy and doubled in volume, about 1 hour.

4. With wet hands (to prevent sticking), press the dough flat into a generously oiled 15½ by 10½-inch rimmed baking sheet. If the dough resists going into the corners (and it probably will), cover it with a damp cloth and let it relax for 15 minutes before trying to stretch again. Or, if making rounds, halve the dough and flatten each piece into an 8-inch round on a large (at least 18 inches long), generously oiled baking sheet. Either way, cover the dough with lightly greased or oil-sprayed plastic wrap; let rise in a warm, draft-free area until the dough is puffy and doubled in volume, 45 minutes to 1 hour.

5. Meanwhile, adjust the oven rack to the lower-middle position and heat the oven to 425 degrees. With two wet fingers, dimple the risen dough at regular intervals. The dimples (there should be about 2 dozen) should be deep enough to hold small pieces of topping, herbs, and pools of olive oil.

6. FOR THE TOPPING: Drizzle the dough with the oil and sprinkle evenly with the rosemary and coarse salt, landing some in pools of oil.

7. Bake until the bottom crust is golden brown and crisp, 23 to 25 minutes. Transfer to a wire rack to cool slightly. Cut rectangular focaccia into squares or round focaccia into wedges; serve warm. (Focaccia can be kept at room temperature for several hours and reheated just before serving. Or wrap cooled focaccia in plastic and then foil, and freeze for up to 1 month; unwrap and defrost in a 325-degree oven until soft, about 15 minutes.)

➤ VARIATIONS

Hand-Kneaded Focaccia

Follow the recipe for Rosemary Focaccia through step 1. In step 2, mix the starter ingredients with a wooden spoon in a large bowl; cover and let stand 20 minutes. Add 1½ cups of the flour to the starter, then beat with a wooden spoon for 5 minutes. Add 1¼ cups flour along with the remaining dough ingredients; continue beating until the dough comes together. Turn the dough onto a floured surface; knead in the remaining ¼ cup flour until the dough is elastic and sticky, 4 to 5 minutes. Transfer the dough to an oiled bowl as in step 3 and follow the remaining instructions.

Sage Focaccia

Follow the recipe for Rosemary Focaccia, adding 1 tablespoon chopped fresh sage leaves with the other dough ingredients in step 2 and substituting 24 whole fresh sage leaves for the rosemary. Place one sage leaf in each oil-filled dimple.

Parmesan Focaccia

Follow the recipe for Rosemary Focaccia, substituting ⅔ cup grated Parmesan cheese for the rosemary and coarse sea salt.

Focaccia with Black Olives and Thyme

Follow the recipe for Rosemary Focaccia, substituting 1 teaspoon fresh thyme leaves and 24 pitted large black olives for the rosemary. Place one olive in each oil-filled dimple.

DIMPLING FOCACCIA DOUGH

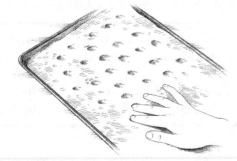

After the dough has risen a second time, wet two fingers and use them to make indentations at regular intervals.

GRISSINI

IN ITALY, GRISSINI ARE A TABLETOP FIXTURE at most trattorias. Long, rail-thin, and precariously brittle, they take the edge off your hunger and whet your appetite for the meal to come. Made from the simplest of doughs, they are intensely crisp and taste of little but browned wheat and salt, with perhaps a hint of yeast and olive oil as well. By no means are they the puffy, over-leavened logs of dough peddled by chain restaurants and pizza joints so familiar these days, nor are they the dusty, cellophane-wrapped, sesame-studded rods that often accompany takeout. Grissini are the real deal, authentically Italian from tip to tip. They seem simple enough to make, but we wondered what it would take to prepare such authentic fare at home.

After some basic research into grissini, we knew we could set some parameters from the start. From the recipes we found, we realized that grissini dough is essentially identical to pizza dough: a simple, oil-enriched bread flour dough that does not require much kneading for structural development or flavor. For that reason, we opted to use our basic Pizza Dough recipe (page 153) instead of developing a discrete (though nearly identical) grissini dough. With a dough recipe in hand, testing was predominantly limited to shaping the grissini and uncovering the perfect oven temperature.

Craggy and uneven, part of the charm of grissini is their rustic, hand-shaped form. So how's it done? Most recipes we found provided sketchy instruction, so we approached shaping in our own way. We started off by rolling out the dough—one quarter of the pizza dough recipe, as any more proved unmanageable—into a thin rectangle, roughly ¼ inch thick. Then we sliced the dough into thin strips. The pizza dough recipe yields very wet dough, which translates to a crisp crust and good oven spring (the quick expansion of the dough during the initial few moments in the oven), so we found it important to use a fair amount of additional flour when handling to prevent it from sticking to the work surface or our hands. It was easy to gently stretch the thin slices of dough to the length of a rimmed baking sheet, about 18 inches. Extremely thin, slightly rectangular, and pudgy at the ends, our breadsticks weren't aesthetically ideal, but we knew we could finesse the shape. But that would come later—first we wanted to find the perfect oven temperature.

Despite being made from pizza dough, which is best cooked in blistering heat, the grissini did not bake well at high temperatures. At 500 degrees, their thin midsections were burnt long before their thick ends were even brown. Even in an oven 100 degrees cooler, the results were similar. At 375 degrees, the breadsticks fared better, and 350 degrees proved perfect: Lightly browned from tip to tip, they were crisp, brittle, and flavorful.

With an ideal oven temperature established, we revisited our basic shaping technique. Looking for something a little rounder, we tried rolling

SHAPING GRISSINI

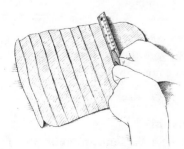

1. Using a pizza cutter or very sharp chef's knife and ruler, slice the dough into 3/4-inch-wide strips.

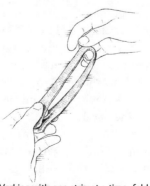

2. Working with one strip at a time, fold the strip in half lengthwise.

3. On a slightly damp work surface, roll it out into a cylinder slightly longer than the baking sheet (the dough will contract after it is placed in the pan). Transfer to a parchment paper–lined rimmed baking sheet and repeat the process with the remaining dough, spacing the breadsticks about 1/3 inch apart.

the strips into thin cylinders once they had been stretched. With a floured work surface, this proved nearly impossible as the strips slid back and forth on the countertop. A barely moistened work surface, however, worked well, as the dough adhered slightly to the tacky surface and thus rolled into a fairly even cylinder. On occasion, the dough would tear, and we would have to rejoin the strips into nubby breadsticks deemed too "rustic" for our finicky tasters.

But these broken strips actually led us to our chosen method (as our mistakes often do). Instead of discarding the broken pieces, we tried doubling them up and rerolling them. The two pieces rolled together into a double helix and formed a stronger, more even cylinder than a single piece of dough. They were less fragile and more pliant—the gluten was more developed and thus easier to manipulate. They could be stretched farther and with less risk of breaking. In fact, it was necessary to roll the dough into a cylinder slightly longer than our pan (about 20 inches). After the breadsticks are shaped, the gluten in the dough relaxes, causing them to contract to just the right size. If you roll the dough to just fit the pan, you'll end up with thicker, unevenly baked breadsticks.

Well shaped and perfectly crisp, the breadsticks lacked only seasoning. Traditionally, grissini flavorings are kept pretty simple, little but salt, pepper, and maybe a sprinkling of Parmesan or a spice or two. Tasters preferred the rougher texture of kosher salt to fine grains of table salt, and relatively coarse-ground black pepper beat out fine-ground. We also tried adding ground fennel seed to the mix, which most tasters liked, but some felt it unnecessarily complicated the grissini's clean flavors. We leave that choice to you. Spraying the breadsticks with nonstick cooking spray prior to seasoning helped the salt and pepper stick to the dough. Brushing the breadsticks with oil accomplished the same goal, but the thicker coating of oil made for slightly greasier grissini.

For a quick variation, we tried adding a dusting of finely grated Parmesan cheese. When it was added at the beginning of baking, it browned long before the breadsticks did. A better option is to sprinkle it on midway through the baking.

Grissini
(Ultra-Thin Italian Breadsticks)
MAKES ABOUT 5 DOZEN

Because this recipe yields a lot breadsticks (and leftover grissini tend to lose their crispness after a day), use half the dough for pizza or freeze for future use. If you have an oil-pump sprayer, you can spray the breadsticks with extra-virgin olive oil. And if you prefer simpler seasoning, sprinkle the breadsticks only with salt.

I	recipe Pizza Dough (page 153)
I	tablespoon coarse salt (kosher)
2	teaspoons coarse-ground black pepper
I	teaspoon fennel seeds, chopped fine (optional)

1. Prepare the dough as directed. Adjust an oven rack to the middle position and heat the oven to 350 degrees. Line a large rimmed baking sheet (17½ by 12 inches) with parchment paper.

2. Combine the salt, pepper, and fennel (if using) in a small bowl; set aside. Divide the pizza dough into four equal pieces (9 to 10 ounces each). Work with one piece of dough at a time (and keep the others covered with plastic wrap to protect them from drying out). Roll out the dough on a heavily floured work surface to a 12 by 8-inch rectangle. Follow illustrations 1 through 3 on page 173 to shape the breadsticks, transferring each one to the prepared baking sheet. You should be able to fit about 20 breadsticks on the baking sheet.

3. Liberally spray the breadsticks with nonstick cooking spray (or extra-virgin olive oil from a pump) and sprinkle some of the seasoning mixture evenly over the tops. Bake the breadsticks until golden brown, 25 to 30 minutes. Slide the breadsticks, still on parchment paper, onto a wire cooling rack and allow them to cool completely before serving. Repeat the process with the remaining dough. The grissini are best eaten the same day they are made.

➤ VARIATION
Parmesan Grissini

Follow the recipe for Grissini, sprinkling ¼ cup finely grated Parmesan cheese over each batch of the breadsticks halfway through the baking time (1 cup Parmesan total).

FLATBREAD

SEVERAL SOUTH AND CENTRAL ASIAN CUISINES— from Afghanistan down through Pakistan and India—prepare breads far different in style than American and European loaf breads. Generally flat or lightly puffed and round in shape, they are soft and chewy—more suited to ripping and dipping into stews and sauces than making into sandwiches or toast. And best of all, flatbreads of this style can be prepared quickly with a modicum of effort; their flavor and texture are not dependent on a long, slow rise. While not out for authenticity per se, we sought to replicate the flavor and texture of an Asian-style flatbread in a recipe that could be easily prepared at home.

After researching and experimenting with many different kinds of flatbreads, we knew what we wanted: a bread that was soft and tender yet chewy, and with a slightly wheaty, mellow flavor. And we wanted a bread easy enough for home cooks to make while dinner is cooking.

Our criteria made it easy to dismiss whole categories of flatbreads right from the beginning. First, we eliminated doughs that used starters (because of the time element), unleavened doughs (which were paper thin and very good but not the style we wanted), and doughs that used hard-to-find ingredients. We also knew the bit of tang and moistness we desired would come from yogurt.

Flour was the main ingredient in all the bread recipes we tested, so it was our starting point. We tried a range of flour mixtures, from all wholewheat to all white, from all-purpose to bread flour. We found the combination of whole-wheat and bread flour to be the best. In our research, we found some recipes that called for "chapati flour," a finely milled whole-wheat flour that contributes a more delicate texture. In our last round of testing, we passed supermarket whole-wheat flour through a fine sieve, which removed some of the rougher bran flakes. To our surprise, this step resulted in a more tender texture, meaning we could take advantage of the flavor of whole-wheat flour without the heaviness.

Because we wanted a simple bread that didn't take hours to prepare, we were pleased to discover that 45 minutes to 1 hour was sufficient rising time. Because the bread is rolled or stretched rather thin, it does not require a long time to develop the complex structure necessary to produce the large holes and crunchy, crisp crust that are important in many loaf-style breads. The yeast and minimum rising time still create the tiny air pockets and the structure necessary to deliver a tender, chewy texture. After shaping, the breads need only a brief rest, instead of a long proofing stage, which saves even more time.

Another great discovery we made along the way was that the dough will keep in the refrigerator for a couple of days, so you can pinch off a piece whenever you want fresh bread. Let the dough come to room temperature and then proceed with the rolling and cooking.

We found that dividing the dough into eight pieces, shaping each piece into a ball, and then rolling and stretching it was the best way to manipulate the dough. A few minutes of rest between these steps helped to prevent the dough from shrinking back and wrinkling. The dough is also very forgiving—if the stretched dough is thinner in spots or a little uneven, it simply adds an interesting dimension to the cooked bread.

Next, we moved on to pan-grilling our bread on the stovetop. We found it best to heat the pan for five minutes over medium-high heat before cooking the bread. Cast iron is the best choice because of its ability to retain heat and cook evenly without burning, although any heavy-bottomed pan will do the job.

We discovered that when we fully cooked the bread on one side first, large, unwieldy bubbles formed on the surface. When we turned the bread over to cook the second side, it was "suspended" on the bubbles and didn't lie flat in the pan. As a result, the bread did not cook evenly. To solve that problem, we cooked the first side for 30 seconds, until small bubbles appeared. At that point, we flipped the bread, cooked the other side for a couple of minutes, and then flipped it back to the first side to finish cooking. The result was an evenly cooked and evenly colored bread.

Pan-Grilled Flatbread

MAKES EIGHT 6- TO 7-INCH BREADS

This type of flatbread is akin to naan, a soft and chewy Indian flatbread used to sop up curries. Don't use a food processor to mix this very sticky dough because you may burn out the motor. Instead, mix the dough with a standing mixer. If you want to mix the dough by hand (the method is provided), be aware that the mixing and kneading times will increase substantially. Only one flatbread will fit in a skillet, but you can speed up the cooking process by using two skillets.

1	package (about 2¼ teaspoons) instant yeast
2	teaspoons sugar
1½	teaspoons salt, plus more for sprinkling
¼	cup (1⅜ ounces) whole-wheat flour, sieved before measuring to remove coarse flakes of bran
2½	cups (13¾ ounces) bread flour, plus more for dusting work surface
1	cup water, at room temperature
¼	cup plain yogurt
1	tablespoon olive oil, plus more for oiling the bowl
2	tablespoons sesame seeds (optional)
4	tablespoons (½ stick) unsalted butter for brushing on flatbreads

1. IN A STANDING MIXER: Combine the yeast, sugar, salt, whole-wheat flour, and bread flour in the bowl of a standing mixer and mix with the paddle attachment until blended, about 15 seconds. Add the water, yogurt, and olive oil and mix on low speed until a shaggy dough forms, about 30 seconds. Replace the paddle with the dough hook and knead the dough on medium speed until smooth and glossy, about 8 minutes, adding more flour in 1-tablespoon increments if necessary for the dough to clear the sides of the bowl (the dough will stick to the bottom of the bowl). Scrape down the sides of the bowl with a rubber spatula as necessary.

2. BY HAND: Mix the yeast, sugar, salt, flours, water, yogurt, and oil in a large bowl with a wooden spoon until the flour is incorporated, about 3 minutes. Turn the dough out of the mixing bowl onto a very lightly floured work surface and knead until smooth and elastic, 12 to 15 minutes. Squeeze the dough gently; if the dough is sticky, sprinkle with flour and knead just to combine.

3. Transfer the dough to a lightly oiled large bowl, cover with plastic wrap, and place in a draft-free spot until the dough has doubled in bulk, about 45 minutes to 1 hour. (At this point, the dough can be punched down, wrapped tightly in plastic wrap, and refrigerated up to 2 days.)

4. Turn the dough onto a lightly floured work surface and, if it is sticky, sprinkle very lightly with flour. Use a chef's knife to cut the dough into 8 equal portions. Roll each portion on the work surface to form a round ball. Roll each ball into a 4-inch circle, let rest for 10 minutes, then roll into a 6-inch circle. If using the sesame seeds, brush the tops lightly with water, sprinkle each round with ¾ teaspoon seeds, and gently roll over with a rolling pin once or twice so the seeds adhere to the dough.

5. Five to 10 minutes before cooking the flatbreads, heat a large, heavy skillet (preferably cast iron) over medium-high heat until hot. Working one at a time, lift the dough circles, gently stretch about 1 inch larger, and place in the skillet. Cook until small bubbles appear on the surface of the dough, about 30 seconds. With tongs, flip the bread and cook until the bottom is speckled and deep golden brown in spots, about 2 minutes. Flip the bread over again; cook until the bottom is speckled and deep golden brown in spots, 1 to 2 minutes longer.

6. Transfer the bread to a wire rack and cool for about 5 minutes (brush the bread lightly with the butter and sprinkle with salt to taste, if desired). Wrap the breads loosely in a clean kitchen towel and serve warm. Or, wrap the breads tightly in foil and store at room temperature up to 2 days; reheat in a 300-degree oven until warm, about 15 minutes.

4

PIES AND TARTS

Pies and Tarts

IF THERE IS ONE TASK THAT STRIKES FEAR into the hearts of novice bakers, it is pie making, but it need not be a vexing endeavor. The key is to use the right recipe and the right technique. We promise you that any of the pies in this chapter will be far superior to anything you could order through the mail, pick up from a supermarket bakery, or fashion from a prefab piecrust. This chapter includes all our favorite pies: fruit pies such as apple, blueberry, and peach as well as custard and cream pies such as pumpkin, chocolate cream, and lemon meringue.

Tarts are similar to pies in that they contain crust and filling, but the dough is usually sweeter than pie dough and the amount of filling is reduced. The overall effect is generally more sophisticated. Most tarts are baked in a shallow ring pan with a removable bottom. Some tarts are baked free-form on a baking sheet, with the crust folded up and over the edges of the filling. Recipes for fresh fruit tarts (both free-form and classic patisserie tarts baked in a pan) are included, as well as our favorites such as lemon tart, chocolate truffle tart, Italian fig-walnut tart, and linzertorte (an Austrian almond and jam tart). The chapter ends with recipes for savory tarts, quiches, and phyllo pies.

PIE TIPS

Why is it that some cooks produce piecrusts that are consistently tender and flaky, while others, despite their best intentions, repeatedly deliver tough or crumbly crusts? Essentially, pie dough is a simple affair with a short ingredient list consisting of flour, salt, sugar, fat (such as butter or vegetable shortening), and water. The two areas most crucial to making pie dough are the temperature of the fat and water and the method by which the dough is mixed. Rolling the dough, which most people mistake as the onerous part of pie making, is a cinch once you have the right dough. Here are tips for making pastry successfully.

USE COLD BUTTER AND SHORTENING

Cold butter and shortening make a big contribution to the flakiness of our piecrust, and it is important that the shortening remain cold and not melt until it enters the oven. As the butter heats during baking, steam is produced. The steam

creates pockets in the dough that help to make it flaky. (It is important to use cold water as well, to maintain the butter's chilled temperature.)

CUT, DON'T MIX THE BUTTER AND SHORTENING INTO THE FLOUR

When dough is overprocessed and the butter is dispersed too evenly, it coats the flour and prevents it from absorbing liquid; the same thing happens when dough is made with oil. The result is a crumbly dough rather than a flaky one. Underprocessing, however, will create a tough dough, because the fat has failed to coat the flour enough. We recommend a two-step method for mixing pie dough: First cut the shortening and butter into the dough in a food processor until the mixture is sandy, with butter bits no larger than the size of a pea. Then, transfer the mixture to a bowl, add the ice water, and fold it in using a rubber spatula. This method exposes all of the dough to moisture without overworking it, something that can happen if the dough is left in the food processor and the water is pulsed in. Using a spatula to incorporate the water allows for the smallest amount of water to be used (less water means a more tender dough) and reduces the likelihood of overworking the dough.

Refer to the illustrations and photos on pages 146 through 149, which detail all the major points in preparing and rolling out pie dough. In addition, see the illustrations on page 190 for pie baking tips and tricks that the test kitchen has picked up over the years.

TART TIPS

Although tart dough is often a little bit sturdier than pie dough and thus more forgiving, the baker faces similar issues when it comes to mixing, rolling, and if necessary, fitting the tart dough into the pan. The illustrations and photos on page 149 explain all you need to know about these issues. It's also very important to use the size tart pan specified in recipes. If you use a pan that is too small, the crust will be too thick and the filling will overflow. If you use a pan that is too large, the crust will be thin (it can even rip) and the filling will seem too skimpy. See the illustrations on page 190 for more tips on tarts.

USE COLD BUTTER Cold fat makes all dough, including tart dough, easier to handle and roll out. Sweet pastry dough typically requires at least an hour of refrigerated resting time for the liquid ingredients to hydrate the dough fully and make it more manageable. In fact, a two-hour rest is even better. The butter gives the dough a nice plasticity if the dough is cold enough and makes rolling relatively easy.

ROLL BETWEEN PARCHMENT Because it contains high amounts of butter and sugar, tart dough can be a challenge to roll out on the counter. The best results are obtained by rolling the dough out between two layers of wide parchment paper or plastic wrap. See the illustration on page 190 for details.

CHILL BEFORE BAKING AND THEN BAKE UNTIL WELL BROWNED We found that a half hour in the freezer sets the dough nicely to prepare it for blind baking (baking the shell without any filling). A baking sheet placed directly beneath the tart shell (to conduct heat evenly to the crust bottom) browns the tart beautifully. Because of the crust's delicate nature, the metal weights used to blind bake the tart are best left in place until the crust's edges are distinctly brown, about 30 minutes, at which point the weights can be removed and the top side of the crust allowed to brown.

Pie Dough

SIMPLE AS IT CAN BE, PIECRUST—ESSENTIALLY a combination of flour, water, and fat—raises numerous questions: What are the ideal proportions of the main ingredients? What else should be added for character? What methods should be used to combine these ingredients?

The most controversial ingredient in pastry is fat. We've found that all-butter crusts taste good, but they are not as flaky and fine-textured as those made with some shortening, which are our favorites. All-shortening crusts have great texture but lack flavor; oil-based crusts are flat and entirely

unappealing; and those made with lard are not only heavy and strongly flavored but out of favor owing to concerns about the effects of animal fat on health. After experimenting with a variety of combinations, we ultimately settled on a proportion of 3 parts butter to 2 parts shortening as optimal for both flavor and texture.

Vegetable shortenings such as Crisco are made from vegetable oil that has been hydrogenated, a process in which hydrogen gas is pumped into vegetable oil to incorporate air and to raise its melting point above room temperature. Unhydrogenated (or regular) vegetable oil holds no more air than water and so makes for poor pie doughs. Crisco, on the other hand, is about 10 percent gas and does a good job of lightening and tenderizing. The way the fat is incorporated into the flour also contributes to flakiness.

We experimented with the relative proportions of fat and flour and finally settled on a ratio of 2 parts flour to 1 part fat, which produces crusts that are easy to work with and, when baked, more tender and flavorful than any other.

Piecrusts are usually made with all-purpose flour. No matter what we've tried—substituting cornstarch for part of the all-purpose flour (a cookie-baking trick that increases tenderness), adding ¼ teaspoon baking powder to increase rise and flakiness, and mixing cake flour or pastry flour with the all-purpose flour (again, to increase tenderness)—we always come back to plain old all-purpose flour.

We also tackled the proportions of salt and sugar, which were much easier to resolve. After testing amounts ranging from ¼ teaspoon to as much as 2 tablespoons, we settled on 1 teaspoon salt and 2 tablespoons sugar for a double-crust pie, amounts that enhance the flavor of the dough without shouting out their presence.

We experimented with a variety of liquid ingredients, such as buttermilk, milk, and cider vinegar, a common ingredient in many pastry recipes. No liquid additions improved our basic recipe, so we recommend that you stick with ice water.

Pie dough can be made by hand, but we've found that a food processor is faster and easier and does the best job of cutting the fat into the flour.

Proper mixing is important. If you undermix, the crust will shrink when baked and become hard and crackly. If you overprocess, you'll get a crumbly, rather than flaky, dough. The shortening should be pulsed with the flour until the mixture is sandy; butter is then pulsed in until the mixture looks like coarse crumbs, with butter bits no larger than the size of a pea.

Once the flour and fat have been combined, the dough can be transferred to a bowl, and the ice water can be added and mixed in. We recommend a rubber spatula and a folding motion to mix in the water. Use the flat side of the spatula to press the mixture until the dough sticks together. Incorporating the water in this manner allows for the least amount of water to be used (less water means a more tender dough) and reduces the likelihood of overworking the dough. Still, we've also learned that it doesn't pay to be too stingy with the water. If there isn't enough, the dough will be crumbly and hard to roll.

Finally, we found that pie dough need not be difficult to roll out if you remember two basic guidelines: Make sure the dough is well chilled before rolling, and add a minimum of flour to the work surface. Flour added during rolling will be absorbed by the dough, and too much flour will cause the dough to toughen. If the dough seems too soft to roll, it's best to refrigerate it rather than add more flour.

Basic Pie Dough

FOR 1 DOUBLE-CRUST 9-INCH PIE

See the photos and illustrations on page 146 for tips on rolling out pie dough.

2½	cups (12½ ounces) unbleached all-purpose flour, plus more for dusting the work surface
1	teaspoon salt
2	tablespoons sugar
½	cup vegetable shortening, chilled
12	tablespoons (1½ sticks) cold unsalted butter, cut into ¼-inch pieces
6–8	tablespoons ice water

1. Process the flour, salt, and sugar in a food processor until combined. Add the shortening and process until the mixture has the texture of coarse sand, about 10 seconds. Scatter the butter pieces over the flour mixture; cut the butter into the flour until the mixture is pale yellow and resembles coarse crumbs, with butter bits no larger than small peas, about ten 1-second pulses. Turn the mixture into a medium bowl.

2. Sprinkle 6 tablespoons of the ice water over the mixture. With a rubber spatula, use a folding motion to mix. Press down on the dough with the broad side of the spatula until the dough sticks together, adding up to 2 tablespoons more ice water if the dough will not come together. Divide the dough into 2 balls and flatten each into a 4-inch disk. Wrap each in plastic and refrigerate at least 1 hour, or up to 2 days, before rolling.

➤ VARIATION

Pie Dough for Lattice-Top Pie

This crust has a firmer texture than the basic recipe, making it easier to work with when creating a lattice top. This leaner dough also keeps its shape better in the oven so the lattice looks more attractive.

Follow the recipe for Basic Pie Dough, increasing the flour to 3 cups (15 ounces), reducing the shortening to 7 tablespoons, reducing the butter to 10 tablespoons, and increasing the ice water to 10 tablespoons. Divide the dough into 2 pieces, one slightly larger than the other. (If possible, weigh the pieces; they should weigh 16 ounces and 14 ounces.) Flatten the larger piece into a rough 5-inch square and the smaller piece into a 4-inch disk; wrap separately in plastic and chill as directed.

PIE DOUGH FOR PREBAKED PIE SHELL

BAKING AN UNFILLED PIE PASTRY, COMMONLY called blind baking, can turn out to be the ultimate culinary nightmare. Without the weight of a filling, a pastry shell set into a hot oven can shrink dramatically, fill with air pockets, and puff up like a linoleum floor after a flood. The result? A shrunken, uneven shell that can hold only part of the filling intended for it.

We started with our basic pie dough recipe and began to investigate the effects of resting the dough in the refrigerator or the freezer, docking it (pricking the dough before it bakes), and weighting the crust as it bakes to keep it anchored in place. All three tricks are used by professional bakers to prevent common problems encountered when baking a crust blind.

We found that refrigeration does the best job of preventing shrinkage. Pastry shrinkage is caused by gluten. Simply put, when you add water to the proteins in flour, elastic strands of gluten are formed. The strands of gluten in the dough get stretched during the rolling process, and if they are not allowed to relax after rolling, the pastry will snap back like a rubber band when baked, resulting in a shrunken, misshapen shell. Resting allows the tension in the taut strands of dough to ease so that they remain stretched and do not shrink back when heated.

This process does not occur, however, when the dough is placed in the freezer immediately after rolling. When the water in the crust freezes, the gluten is held in place so it is not free to relax. As a result, when you bake the dough, the tense, stretched strands of gluten snap back, causing the crust to shrink.

We might have concluded that pie dough should be refrigerated and not frozen if we hadn't noticed that the frozen crusts, although shrunken, were much flakier than the refrigerated crusts. Pastry is made up of layers of dough (protein and starch from the flour combined with water) and fat. Dough and fat have different heat tolerances. When you place the pastry in the oven after freezing it (rather than just refrigerating it), the dough heats up and starts to set relatively quickly in comparison with the time it takes for the butter to melt and then vaporize, as the butter has a much higher proportion of water than the dough. As a result, by the time the water in the butter starts to turn to steam, the dough is well into its setting phase. The air spaces occupied by the frozen butter, now that it has largely turned to steam, hold their shape because the dough has started to set.

Dough that you have refrigerated, on the other hand, is not as well set by the time the butter vaporizes; hence the air pockets disappear, the soft dough simply sinking into the spaces left by the butter. We came to a simple conclusion: first refrigerate the pie shell to relax the gluten, thus solving the problem of shrinkage during baking, then pop the dough into the freezer to improve flakiness.

While this combination chilling method prevents shrinkage, ballooning can occur when air pockets form beneath the crust. Typically, bakers dock the dough with the tines of a fork before it goes into the oven. However, we found that docking is not necessary as long as the dough is weighted. Since weighting is a must—it not only prevents ballooning but keeps the shell, especially the sides, in place as it bakes—we do not bother to dock pastry dough. Some professional bakers swear by "official" pie weights, made of metal or ceramic, while others make do with rice or dried beans. We found that metal or ceramic pie weights do a better job than rice or beans. They are heavier and therefore more effective at preventing the pastry from puffing. Metal and ceramic are also better heat conductors and promote more thorough browning of the pastry.

We got the most consistent results and even browning by baking on the middle rack at a constant 375 degrees. At higher temperatures, the pastry was prone to overbrowning and burned in spots, while lower temperatures caused the edges to brown well before the bottom did. More important than temperature and placement, though, was cooking time.

There are two stages in baking blind. In the first stage, the dough is baked with a lining and weights. This stage usually takes about 25 minutes; the objective is to cook the dough until it sets, at which point it can hold its shape without assistance. When the dough loses its wet look, turns from its original pale yellow to off-white, and the edges just start to take on a very light brown color, the dough is set. If you have any doubts, carefully (the dough is hot) touch the side of the shell to make sure that the crust is firm. If you remove the pie weights too soon, the sides of the dough will slip down, ruining the pie shell.

For the second stage, the foil and weights are removed, and the baking continues. At this point, if you are going to fill the pie shell and then bake it again, as for pumpkin or pecan pie or quiche, you should bake it until it is just lightly browned, about 5 minutes. Pie shells destined for fillings that require little or no further cooking, such as cream and lemon meringue pies, should be baked for about 12 more minutes.

Pie Dough for Prebaked Pie Shell

FOR 1 SINGLE-CRUST 9-INCH PIE

See the photos and illustrations on page 146 for tips on rolling out pie dough. We prefer ceramic or metal pie weights for prebaking the pie shell. If you don't own any weights, rice or dried beans can stand in, but since they're lighter than pie weights, be sure to fill up the foil-lined pie shell completely. Better yet, improvise with pennies (see page 149).

1¼	cups (6¼ ounces) unbleached all-purpose flour, plus more for rolling out the dough
½	teaspoon salt
1	tablespoon sugar
3	tablespoons vegetable shortening, chilled
4	tablespoons (½ stick) cold unsalted butter, cut into ¼-inch pieces
4–5	tablespoons ice water

1. Process the flour, salt, and sugar in a food processor until combined. Add the shortening and process until the mixture has the texture of coarse sand, about 10 seconds. Scatter the butter pieces over the flour mixture; cut the butter into the flour until the mixture is pale yellow and resembles coarse crumbs, with butter bits no larger than small peas, about ten 1-second pulses. Turn the mixture into a medium bowl.

2. Sprinkle 4 tablespoons of the ice water over the mixture. With a rubber spatula, use a folding motion to mix. Press down on the dough with the broad side of the spatula until the dough sticks together, adding up to 1 tablespoon more ice water if the dough will not come together. Flatten the dough into a 4-inch disk. Wrap in plastic and refrigerate at least 1 hour, or up to 2 days, before rolling.

3. Remove the dough from the refrigerator (if refrigerated longer than 1 hour, let stand at room temperature until malleable). Following the illustrations on page 146, roll the dough on a lightly floured work surface or between 2 sheets of parchment paper or plastic wrap to a 12-inch circle. Transfer the dough to a 9-inch pie plate by rolling the dough around the rolling pin and unrolling over the pan. Working around the circumference of the pie plate, ease the dough into the pan corners by gently lifting the edge of the dough with one hand while gently pressing into the pan bottom with the other hand. Trim the dough edges to extend about ½ inch beyond the rim of the pan. Fold the overhang under itself; flute the dough or press the tines of a fork against the dough to flatten it against the rim of the pie plate. Refrigerate the dough-lined pie plate until firm, about 40 minutes, then freeze until very cold, about 20 minutes.

4. Adjust an oven rack to the lower-middle position and heat the oven to 375 degrees. Remove the dough-lined pie plate from the freezer, press a doubled 12-inch piece of heavy-duty foil inside the pie shell, and fold the edges of the foil to shield the fluted edge; distribute 2 cups ceramic or metal pie weights over the foil. Bake, leaving the foil and weights in place until the dough looks dry and is light in color, 25 to 30 minutes. Carefully remove the foil and weights by gathering the corners of the foil and pulling up and out. For a partially baked crust, continue baking until light golden brown, 5 to 6 minutes; for a fully baked crust, continue baking until deep golden brown, about 12 minutes more. Transfer to a wire rack.

➤ VARIATION

Prebaked Pie Dough Coated with Graham Cracker Crumbs

Custard fillings, such as those used in lemon meringue pie and cream pies, are tough on crisp crusts. After much experimentation, we found that rolling out the pie dough in graham cracker crumbs promotes browning and crisps the crust. It also adds a wonderful graham flavor that complements the lemon and cream pie fillings without masking the character of the dough itself.

Follow the recipe for Pie Dough for Prebaked Pie Shell, sprinkling the work surface with 2 tablespoons graham cracker crumbs when rolling out the dough. Sprinkle more crumbs over the dough itself. Continue sprinkling additional crumbs underneath and on top of the dough as it is rolled, coating the dough heavily with crumbs. You will use a total of about ½ cup crumbs. Fit the graham cracker–coated dough into a pie plate as directed and bake fully.

APPLE PIE

COOKS WHO SLATHER THE APPLES IN THEIR pies with butter, cinnamon, and sugar do themselves and the apples a disservice; we set out to make a pie in which the apples would take center stage. We started by examining the choice of apples for the filling, by testing the nine best-selling apples to come up with a recipe that would work with apples commonly available in supermarkets throughout the year.

We determined that Granny Smith and McIntosh apples both have excellent qualities; the former is tart with a good texture, and the latter has excellent flavor. But each also has its drawbacks. A pie made with Grannies alone was too sour and a bit dull in flavor, while an all-McIntosh pie was too soft, more like applesauce in a crust than apple pie. A pie made with both varieties, however, was outstanding. The Grannies hold up well during cooking, and the Macs add flavor. The mushy texture of the Macs becomes a virtue in this setting, providing a nice base for the firmer Grannies and soaking up some of the juice.

We also tested a dozen not-so-common apple varieties, the kinds you may see in local markets during the fall, especially if you live near an apple orchard. We found that Macoun, Royal Gala, Empire, Winesap, Rhode Island Greening, and Cortland apples all make excellent pies. Unlike Granny Smiths, these well-balanced apples work well on their own without thickeners or the addition of McIntosh.

We have always used butter in our pies. In fact, we used to use up to 6 tablespoons in a deep-dish pie, cutting this back to a more modest 2 tablespoons over the years. But when we taste-tested pies with and without butter, the leaner pies won hands down. Butter simply dulls the fresh taste of apples, so now we do without it altogether. Lemon juice, however, is absolutely crucial to a good apple pie, heightening the flavor of the apples rather than dulling or masking it. In the end, we settled on 1 tablespoon of lemon juice and 1 teaspoon of zest.

In our opinion, many recipes call for too much thickener (usually flour), and the result is a lifeless filling. A bit of tart, thin juice gives the pie a breath of the orchard, whereas a thick, syrupy texture is dull. We prefer to thicken the filling for our apple pie very lightly, with just 2 tablespoons flour.

Many cookbooks claim that letting apples sit in a bowl with the sugar, lemon juice, and spices, otherwise known as macerating, is key in developing flavors and juice. We found, however, that this simply caused the apples to dry out, making them rubbery and unpleasant. In addition, the apples themselves lose flavor, having exuded all of their fruitiness into the juice. So macerating, a common step in apple pie recipes, was clearly out.

In many apple pies, the top crust sets up quickly, leaving an air space between it and the apples, which reduce in volume as they cook. With our crust recipe, however, this is not an issue. Sufficient shortening is cut into the flour so that the crust sinks down onto the apples as they cook. We did notice, however, that this high ratio of shortening produces a very flaky crust, one that is not easily cut into perfect slices. In addition, because there is still a fair amount of juice, which we find essential for good flavor, the filling may spread slightly once the pie is cut into individual slices. The trade-off for less-than-perfect presentation is excellent flavor.

Classic Apple Pie

SERVES 8

When all of the apples have been sliced, you should have a total of about 8 cups. The pie is best eaten when cooled to room temperature, or even the next day. See the illustrations on page 146 for rolling and fitting pie dough.

1 recipe Basic Pie Dough (page 181)

2 tablespoons unbleached all-purpose flour, plus more for dusting the work surface

3 large Granny Smith apples (about 1 1/2 pounds)

4 large McIntosh apples (about 2 pounds)

1 tablespoon juice and 1 teaspoon grated zest from 1 lemon

3/4 cup (5 1/4 ounces) plus 1 tablespoon sugar

1/4 teaspoon freshly grated nutmeg

1/4 teaspoon ground cinnamon

1/8 teaspoon ground allspice

1/4 teaspoon salt

1 egg white, beaten lightly

1. Adjust an oven rack to the lowest position, place a rimmed baking sheet on it, and heat the oven to 500 degrees. Remove one piece of dough from the refrigerator (if refrigerated longer than 1 hour, let stand at room temperature until malleable).

2. Roll the dough on a lightly floured work surface or between 2 large sheets of parchment paper or plastic wrap to a 12-inch circle. Transfer the dough to a 9-inch pie plate by rolling the dough around the rolling pin and unrolling over the pan. Working around the circumference of the pan, ease the dough into the pan corners by gently lifting the edge of the dough with one hand while pressing into the pan bottom with the other hand. Leave any dough that overhangs the lip of the pie plate in place; refrigerate the dough-lined pie plate.

3. Peel, core, and quarter the apples; cut the quarters into 1/4-inch slices and toss with the lemon juice and zest. In a medium bowl, mix 3/4 cup of the sugar, the flour, spices, and salt. Toss the dry ingredients with the apples. Turn the fruit mixture, including juices, into the chilled pie shell and mound it slightly in the center.

4. Roll out the second piece of dough to a 12-inch circle; place it over the filling. Trim the edges of the top and bottom dough layers to 1/2 inch beyond the pan lip. Tuck this rim of dough underneath itself so that the folded edge is flush with the pan lip. Flute the edge or press with fork tines to seal. (See the illustrations on page 147 for tips on trimming and crimping pie dough.) Cut 4 slits in the dough top. If the pie dough is very soft, place the pie in the freezer for 10 minutes. Brush the egg white on the top crust and sprinkle evenly with the remaining 1 tablespoon sugar.

5. Place the pie on the baking sheet and lower the oven temperature to 425 degrees. Bake the pie until the top crust is golden, about 25 minutes. Rotate the pie from front to back and reduce the oven temperature to 375 degrees; continue baking until the juices bubble and the crust is deep golden brown, 30 to 35 minutes longer.

6. Transfer the pie to a wire rack; cool to room temperature, at least 4 hours.

➤ VARIATIONS

Apple Pie with Crystallized Ginger

Follow the recipe for Classic Apple Pie, adding 3 tablespoons chopped crystallized ginger to the apple mixture.

Apple Pie with Dried Fruit

Macerate 1 cup raisins, dried sweet cherries, or dried cranberries in the lemon juice, adding 1 tablespoon applejack, brandy, or cognac. Follow the recipe for Classic Apple Pie, adding the macerated dried fruit and liquid to the apple mixture.

Apple Pie with Fresh Cranberries

Follow the recipe for Classic Apple Pie, increasing the sugar to 1 cup (7 ounces) and adding 1 cup fresh or frozen cranberries to the apple mixture.

DUTCH APPLE PIE

AS MUCH AS WE LOVE CLASSIC APPLE PIE, life would indeed be boring if we did not venture further afield into apple pie territory. Dutch apple pie is composed of tender, creamy apple filling, flaky piecrust, and buttery mounds of streusel—a decidedly decadent apple pie. To get our bearings, we began by making five Dutch apple pies, each with a different recipe and technique. Surely one had to come close to our ideal. Not so. Each pie was a miserable failure. Variously soupy and void of crust, filled with undercooked apples or dotted with greasy, melted pools of butter, these pies were bad enough to induce laughter in the test kitchen. But we were stymied—why had they failed? What makes baking a Dutch apple pie any different from baking a standard American-style apple pie?

Before we could begin to solve the problems of Dutch apple pie, we needed to define just what it is. As it turns out, there are three components and one major omission that convert an ordinary apple pie into a Dutch apple pie. The additions consist of dried fruit (such as currants or raisins), dairy in the filling, and a streusel topping in lieu of the standard top crust. The major omission is lemon juice.

This omission was far from incidental, as it turned out. A standard apple pie is baked from start to finish with lemon juice, which helps to break down the apples and allows them to release their juices, making for a juicy as well as tender pie filling. But most of the recipes for Dutch apple pie that we had unearthed called for the addition of only one liquid ingredient—usually heavy cream—five minutes before the pie was done baking. When we sliced into these pies, we noticed two things. First, the interior was not creamy and golden; it was greasy and runny. Second, the apples didn't seem to have cooked through, despite the 45-minute-plus baking times.

So what went wrong? We eventually figured out that when the cream came into contact with the hot, acidic apples, the fat and water in the cream separated, giving the pies their lumpy, greasy, runny interiors. In addition, because these pies were undergoing dry-heat cooking (since there was no liquid, such as lemon juice, providing the apples with moisture), a much slower process than wet-heat cooking, the apples were remaining too crunchy. While a few recipes call for adding the dairy at the beginning of the baking sequence, they, too, produced pies with a coagulated filling.

At first we thought we might doctor the situation by heating the cream before adding it to the almost-finished pie. But even if the cream didn't separate, five minutes in the oven wouldn't provide enough baking time for the cream to set amidst the layers of apples, and we would still be stuck with unevenly distributed amounts of cream in the pie. Our next thought was to try adding some lemon juice and zest to the pie prior to adding the cream.

But the lemon-cream combination sent tasters running for cover. The quickest fix we came up with was to reduce the amount of water in the cream by cooking it, thereby preventing the fat from separating when it encountered the hot pie filling. This remedied our dairy dilemma, but the apples were still too crunchy.

It occurred to us that sautéing the apples with some butter and sugar before they went into the pie might solve the crunch problem. So we prepared for a new experiment: precooking the apples as well as prebaking the pie shell.

Choosing a Dutch oven for its size (as well as apropos name), we sautéed the apples until they were tender throughout and some of the softer pieces began to break down. We strained the apples of their juices, packed them into the prebaked pie shell, and reduced ½ cup of heavy cream with the remaining apple juices (to give the cream reduction a flavor boost). The cream reduction was thick, glossy, and redolent with apple undertones. We spooned the sauce over the filling and topped

TESTING FOR DONENESS

You'll know your pie filling is ready when the McIntosh apples just start to break down, as shown in the middle spoon. The filling shown in the top spoon is about halfway cooked; the filling in the bottom spoon is overcooked.

the pie with streusel. After a mere 10 minutes in the oven, the filling was just right, and we had a perfectly crisp and flaky piecrust to boot.

Now that the filling and crust met our expectations, we moved on to the streusel. We wanted it to be just crunchy enough on the outside to allow for some textural deviation from the plush and tender filling, but it also had to have enough fat to create a melt-in-your-mouth sensation. After trying almost all possible combinations of dark brown sugar, light brown sugar, granulated sugar, honey, cornmeal, baking powder, flour, salt, spices, and butter, we found the perfect streusel to be composed of melted butter with a touch of salt, just enough cornmeal to give it some crunch, a combination of light brown sugar and granulated sugar, and enough flour to bind everything together. By tossing the melted butter into the dry ingredients with a fork, we were able to create large chunks of streusel surrounded by smaller pea-sized morsels.

Now the only thing standing between us and a real Dutch apple pie was the dried fruit. The earliest recipe we found was published in 1667 and included currants. While currants far surpassed shriveled black raisins in terms of beauty, they did not contribute much flavor or chew. Dried cherries and cranberries were too tart and too bold a shade of red for the subtle, wheaty hue of the pie interior. We finally found solace in golden raisins, sweet and plump, yet not too showy.

Dutch Apple Pie

SERVES 8

The most efficient way to make this pie is to use the dough's chill times to peel and core the apples and prepare the streusel, then cook the apples while the dough prebakes. For a finished look, dust the pie with confectioners' sugar just before serving.

1	recipe Pie Dough for Prebaked Pie Shell (page 183)

APPLE FILLING

5	large Granny Smith apples (about 2 1/2 pounds)
4	large McIntosh apples (about 2 pounds)
1/4	cup (1 3/4 ounces) granulated sugar

1/2	teaspoon ground cinnamon
1/8	teaspoon salt
2	tablespoons unsalted butter
3/4	cup golden raisins
1/2	cup heavy cream

STREUSEL TOPPING

1 1/4	cups (6 1/4 ounces) unbleached all-purpose flour
1/3	cup packed (2 1/3 ounces) light brown sugar
1/3	cup (2 1/3 ounces) granulated sugar
1	tablespoon cornmeal
7	tablespoons unsalted butter, melted

1. FOR THE PIE SHELL: Follow the directions for fully baking the crust until deep golden brown. Remove the baked pie shell from the oven and increase the oven temperature to 425 degrees.

2. FOR THE APPLE FILLING: Meanwhile, peel, quarter, and core the apples; slice each quarter crosswise into pieces 1/4 inch thick. Toss the apples, sugar, cinnamon, and salt in a large bowl to combine. Heat the butter in a large Dutch oven over high heat until foaming subsides; add the apples and toss to coat. Reduce the heat to medium-high and cook, covered, stirring occasionally, until the apples are softened, about 5 minutes. Stir in the raisins; cook, covered, stirring occasionally, until the Granny Smith apple slices are tender and the McIntosh apple slices are softened and beginning to break down, about 5 minutes longer (see the photographs on page 186).

3. Set a large colander over a large bowl; transfer the cooked apples to the colander. Shake the colander and toss the apples to drain off as much juice as possible. Bring the drained juice and the cream to a boil in the now-empty Dutch oven over high heat; cook, stirring occasionally, until thickened and a wooden spoon leaves a trail in the mixture, about 5 minutes. Transfer the apples to the prebaked pie shell; pour the reduced juice mixture over and smooth with a rubber spatula.

4. FOR THE STREUSEL TOPPING: Combine the flour, sugars, and cornmeal in a medium bowl; drizzle with the melted butter and toss with a fork until evenly moistened and the mixture forms many large chunks with pea-sized pieces mixed

throughout. Line a rimmed baking sheet with parchment paper and spread the streusel in an even layer on the paper. Bake the streusel until golden brown, about 5 minutes; cool the baking sheet with the streusel on a wire rack until cool enough to handle, about 5 minutes.

5. To FINISH THE PIE: Sprinkle the streusel evenly over the pie filling. Set the pie plate on the now-empty baking sheet and bake until the streusel topping is deep golden brown, about 10 minutes. Cool on a wire rack to room temperature and serve.

➤ VARIATION

Quick Dutch Apple Crisp

This quick variation on our Dutch apple pie eliminates the piecrust, allowing you to have dessert on the table in less than an hour.

Follow the recipe for Dutch Apple Pie, omitting the pie dough and beginning with step 2. In step 3, pack the cooked apples into an 8-inch square baking dish and pour the reduced juice mixture over. Continue with the recipe at step 4.

STRAWBERRY RHUBARB PIE

IF YOU VISIT ANY NEW ENGLAND FARMSTAND in the late spring, you're liable to see a table groaning under the weight of strawberry rhubarb pies for sale. With a crusty golden brown top stained pink by rivulets of escaping juice, the pies are irresistible—a welcome harbinger of warm weather. But those homespun looks can be deceiving; too often, that crispy crust covers a soupy, bland filling, more fruit soup than fruit pie. Or the crust may mask the other extreme: a filling so loaded with thickener that it's gummy. So what's the secret to a juicy, but not watery, full-flavored strawberry rhubarb pie?

Both strawberries and rhubarb have a high moisture content, especially when it's been a wet spring. And if you've ever cooked rhubarb, you know how quickly rhubarb transforms from firm stalk to soupy sauce—mere moments. Now imagine all that liquid contained within a pie. Where is it all supposed to go? Most recipes we found load the pie up with a thickener like cornstarch or flour, but this yields an unpleasantly starchy pie with a muddied flavor. Our goal, then, was to reduce the pie's moisture content and use as little thickener (and the most flavorless one) we could for the freshest, brightest-tasting pie.

There are two approaches to eradicating excess moisture in fruit pies: cooking the fruit prior to assembling the pie and preparing the pie in such a way that excess moisture can escape, as with an open-faced or lattice-topped pie. Strawberry rhubarb pie is almost always covered (rhubarb can take on a muddy-brown color once cooked), and we weren't out to buck tradition, so we opted to try precooking the fruit. Slowly stewing the rhubarb until it was completely broken down before mixing it with the strawberries yielded a flat-tasting filling as the rhubarb was overcooked and had lost its characteristic brightness. But on a promising note, the filling was much drier. Borrowing from a savory rhubarb recipe we found, we sautéed chopped rhubarb in a smoking-hot skillet until the juices were exuded but the pieces of rhubarb were still on the firm side. Once the rhubarb had cooled, we tossed it with the strawberries and assembled the pie. The baked pie tasted bright and clean and was much less soupy than before. Clearly we were on the right track.

But the moisture was only partially tamed: We still needed to pick a thickener. We have tested all the standard thickeners in previous recipes and have a pretty good idea of what we like and don't like. As a general rule of thumb, we avoid flour and cornstarch because they turn gummy when cooked and tend to muddy the fruit's flavor. We do like the properties of tapioca, potato starch, and arrowroot because they thicken without turning gummy and never alter the fruit's flavor. Thickeners produced from roots, as these three are, thicken more effectively than flour or cornstarch because they are composed of longer chains of amylose (a starch), which means that less is needed to thicken the fruit's juices. For many of our fruit pie recipes, we favor instant or minute tapioca, as it is inexpensive and widely available, but tasters disliked it in this case: The combination of tapioca and rhubarb yielded an unpleasant viscous texture. Even when we reduced the tapioca to a bare minimum, tasters found fault with the filling's texture. Revisiting the other starches, tasters most preferred arrowroot for its non-gummy, non-viscous texture. A scant three tablespoons proved perfect.

Since the filling was still on the moist side, we opted to add a few more vents to the top crust. We made a total of eight slits radiating outward from the center, four more than we usually add to covered pies. The difference was slight but noticeable: The pie's interior was definitely drier. So with a few tweaks, we finally had a gorgeous (and not soupy) strawberry rhubarb pie well worth the effort.

Strawberry Rhubarb Pie

SERVES 8

If any leaves remain attached to the rhubarb, be sure to trim them; they are toxic. Try to find bright red rhubarb as it has the best flavor. Arrowroot, a very fine white powder, is found in the spice aisle of most supermarkets. See the illustrations on page 146 for rolling and fitting pie dough.

2	teaspoons vegetable oil
1 ½	pounds rhubarb, ends trimmed, peeled if the outer layer is especially fibrous, and cut into 1-inch pieces (5 to 6 cups)
1	cup (7 ounces) plus 1 tablespoon sugar
1	recipe Basic Pie Dough (page 181) Flour for dusting the work surface
3	tablespoons arrowroot Pinch salt
1 ½	pounds strawberries, hulled and quartered (about 5 cups)
½	teaspoon vanilla extract
2	teaspoons grated zest from 1 orange (optional)
1	egg white, lightly beaten

1. Heat the oil in a large skillet over medium-high heat until smoking. Add the rhubarb and ¼ cup of the sugar and cook, stirring frequently, until the rhubarb has shed most of its liquid but is still firm, about 5 minutes. Transfer to a large plate and refrigerate until cool.

2. Remove one piece of dough from the refrigerator (if refrigerated longer than 1 hour, let stand at room temperature until malleable). Roll the dough on a lightly floured work surface or between 2 large sheets of parchment paper or plastic wrap to a 12-inch circle. Transfer the dough to a 9-inch pie plate by rolling the dough around the rolling pin and unrolling over the pan. Working around the circumference of the pan, ease the dough into the pan corners by gently lifting the edge of the dough with one hand while gently pressing into the pan bottom with the other hand. Leave the dough that overhangs the lip of the pie plate in place; refrigerate until needed.

3. Adjust an oven rack to the lowest position, place a rimmed baking sheet on it, and heat the oven to 500 degrees.

4. In a small bowl, mix together ¾ cup of the sugar, the arrowroot, and salt. In a large bowl, toss together the strawberries, cooled rhubarb, vanilla, and orange zest (if using). Sprinkle the sugar mixture over the top and stir to combine. Spoon the fruit evenly into the pie shell and pack lightly. Roll out the second piece of dough to a 12-inch circle; place it over the filling. Trim the edges of the top and bottom dough layers to ½ inch beyond the pan lip. Tuck this rim underneath itself so that the folded edge is flush with the pan lip. Flute the edge or press with fork tines to seal. (See the illustrations on page 147 for tips on trimming and crimping pie dough.) Cut 8 slits in the dough top. If the pie dough is very soft, place in the freezer for 10 minutes. Brush the top of the crust with the egg white and sprinkle evenly with the remaining 1 tablespoon of sugar.

5. Place the pie on the hot baking sheet and lower the oven temperature to 425 degrees. Bake until the top crust is golden, about 25 minutes. Rotate the pie from front to back and reduce the oven temperature to 375 degrees; continue baking until the juices bubble and the crust is deep golden brown, 30 to 35 minutes longer. Cool the pie on a wire rack until room temperature, 3 to 4 hours, before serving.

Tips for Better Pies and Tarts

PRESSING CRUMBS INTO PLACE

Pressing graham cracker crumbs into a pie plate can be messy, especially when the buttered and sugared crumbs stick to your hands. Keep the crumbs where they belong by sheathing your hand in a plastic sandwich bag and pressing the crumbs firmly but neatly.

MAKESHIFT ROLLING PIN

We prefer a tapered French rolling pin for rolling out pie and tart dough. But if you're stuck in a kitchen without a rolling pin, an unopened bottle of wine has the right weight and shape for rolling out dough. If possible, use white wine (the square shoulders on most white wine bottles are preferable to the sloping shoulders on red wine bottles) and chill the bottle. The cold temperature of the bottle will help keep the fat in the dough chilled.

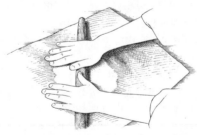

USING PARCHMENT TO ROLL OUT DOUGH

If you have trouble rolling out pie dough or tart dough, even when the work surface has been floured, we suggest sandwiching the dough between two sheets of parchment paper. The parchment ensures that the dough won't stick and eliminates the temptation to add too much flour to the dough as it is being rolled—a danger because excess flour will make the dough dry and tough.

PROTECTING PIE EDGES FROM BURNING

The fluted edge on a pie can burn before the filling or bottom crust is fully cooked. Many recipes suggest piecing together strips of foil to fashion a protective cover for the edge. Instead of trying to twist pieces of foil together, we prefer to use a single sheet of foil to cover the pie edge.

1. Lay out a square of foil slightly larger than the pie. Fold the square in half to form a rectangle. Cut an arc that is roughly half the size of the pie.

2. When you unfold the foil, you will have cut out a circle from the middle of the sheet. This open circle exposes the filling, while the surrounding foil covers the crust and protects it from coloring further.

A NEATER FIRST SLICE

Extracting the first slice of pie (or tart or cake) is a challenge for even the most accomplished server. To increase your chances of removing a neat first slice, try this method. After making the first two cuts (to form the first slice), make a third cut as if to form the second slice. This third cut makes it easier to slide out the first piece intact.

PROTECTING TART EDGES FROM BURNING

Sometimes the edges of a tart shell can burn before the bottom is cooked through and nicely browned. Instead of trying to fashion together strips of foil, we invert the ring from a second, larger tart pan over the endangered crust. The tart can continue to bake without further coloring of the edges.

TART UNMOLDING MADE EASY

Lifting up the removable pan bottom with your hand causes the ring to slide down your arm like a Hula-Hoop. To remove the ring easily, place a wide can, such as a 28-ounce tomato can, on a work surface and set the cooled tart pan on top of the can. Hold the pan ring and gently pull it downward.

IMPROVISED COVER FOR TARTS

A footed cake stand might be the best plate for serving a pretty tart, but it won't fit in the refrigerator to protect leftovers. For that job, we use an inverted springform pan. Place the tart, still on the removable pan bottom, on a shelf in the refrigerator and cover with an inverted springform pan. You can even stack light items on top of the springform pan.

BLUEBERRY PIE

BLUEBERRY PIES TRADITIONALLY RELY ON flour or cornstarch to thicken the fresh fruit filling. We sometimes find these thickeners problematic. We thickened our blueberry cobbler with cornstarch with good results (see page 307), but a pie requires a firmer filling than a cobbler and hence more cornstarch. If you use enough cornstarch, it will thicken a blueberry pie quite well. But in our tests, such a large amount of cornstarch dulled the fruit flavor and made it noticeably less tart.

Using flour resulted in fruit filling that was similarly unsatisfying in appearance and taste, and it also had another failing—2 tablespoons was not enough to firm up the fruit sufficiently. To give flour another chance, we ran a test using 4 tablespoons. This time, the fruit was gummy and almost inedible. As it turns out, this is because flour, unlike the other thickeners, contains proteins and other components as well as starch. As a result, it takes at least twice as much flour by volume to create the same degree of thickening as cornstarch. This amount of flour will adversely affect your blueberry pie—you can taste it.

Given our experience with peach pie (see page 192), we expected tapioca and potato starch to perform much better, and they did. Tasters slightly preferred the potato starch; however, the tapioca, when pulverized in a food processor, did an admirable job.

During additional testing, we found that the amount of potato starch or tapioca should be adjusted depending on the juiciness of the berries. If you like a juicier pie, 3 tablespoons of potato starch or tapioca is an adequate amount for 6 cups of fresh blueberries. If you like a really firm pie with no juices, 4 tablespoons is the correct amount.

Blueberries and lemon are a natural combination, and a little zest and juice enhanced the flavor of the berries. Allspice and nutmeg were a welcome change of pace from the traditional cinnamon, which can overwhelm the delicate flavor of the berries. Finally, we found that 2 tablespoons of butter, cut into small bits and scattered over the filling just before the top crust was put in place, gave the berry filling a lush mouthfeel that everyone enjoyed.

With our filling done, the rest of this pie went together quickly. The double crust produced by our Basic Pie Dough (page 181) worked perfectly with blueberries. Tasters liked the effect of brushing the top crust with egg white and sprinkling it with sugar just before the pie went into the oven.

Unlike other fruit pies, for which the fruit must be peeled and sliced, blueberry pie goes together rather quickly, especially if you have the dough on hand in the refrigerator or freezer. Even with the rolling steps, you can have a blueberry pie in the oven in about 20 minutes.

~

Blueberry Pie

SERVES 8

You will want to vary the amount of sugar and potato starch depending on personal taste and the quality of the fruit. If you prefer a less sweet pie or if the fruit is especially sweet, use the lower sugar amount. (Save the 1 tablespoon sugar for sprinkling on the pie just before it goes into the oven.) If you like your pie juices fairly thick or if the fruit is really juicy, then opt for the higher amount of starch. Potato starch is sold in the baking aisle. If you don't have or can't find it, substitute an equal amount of pulverized Minute tapioca, ground for about 1 minute in a food processor or spice grinder. See the illustrations on page 146 for rolling and fitting pie dough.

I	recipe Basic Pie Dough (page 181)
	Flour for dusting the work surface
6	cups (30 ounces) blueberries, rinsed and picked over
³/₄–I	cup (5¼ to 7 ounces) plus I tablespoon sugar
2	teaspoons juice and I teaspoon grated zest from I lemon
¼	teaspoon ground allspice
	Pinch freshly grated nutmeg
3–4	tablespoons potato starch or Minute tapioca (see note)
2	tablespoons unsalted butter, cut into small pieces
I	egg white, lightly beaten

1. Adjust an oven rack to the lowest position, place a rimmed baking sheet on it, and heat the oven to 500 degrees. Remove one piece of dough from the refrigerator (if refrigerated longer than 1 hour, let stand at room temperature until malleable).

2. Roll the dough on a lightly floured work surface or between 2 large sheets of parchment paper or plastic wrap to a 12-inch circle. Transfer the dough to a 9-inch pie plate by rolling the dough around a rolling pin and unrolling over the pan. Working around the circumference of the pan, ease the dough into the pan corners by gently lifting the edge of the dough with one hand while pressing into the pan bottom with the other hand. Leave the dough that overhangs the lip of the pie plate in place; refrigerate the dough-lined pie plate.

3. Toss the berries, ¾ to 1 cup sugar, lemon juice and zest, spices, and potato starch in a medium bowl; let stand for 15 minutes.

4. Roll out the second piece of dough to a 12-inch circle. Spoon the berries into the pie shell and scatter the butter pieces over the filling. Place the second piece of dough over the filling. Trim the top and bottom edges to ½ inch beyond the pan lip. Tuck this rim of dough underneath itself so that the folded edge is flush with the pan lip. Flute the edge or press with fork tines to seal. (See the illustrations on page 147 for tips on trimming and crimping pie dough.) Cut 4 slits in the dough top. If the pie dough is very soft, place in the freezer for 10 minutes. Brush the egg white onto the top of the crust and sprinkle evenly with the remaining 1 tablespoon sugar.

5. Place the pie on the baking sheet and lower the oven temperature to 425 degrees. Bake until the top crust is golden, about 25 minutes. Rotate the pie and reduce the oven temperature to 375 degrees; continue baking until the juices bubble and the crust is deep golden brown, 30 to 35 minutes longer.

6. Transfer the pie to a wire rack; cool to room temperature, at least 4 hours.

PEACH PIE

OUR OCCASIONAL DISAPPOINTMENT WITH peach pies in the past has taught us to wait for peach season and then buy only intoxicatingly fragrant peaches, ripe enough when squeezed to make you swoon. But even ripe peaches vary in juiciness from season to season and from peach to peach, making it difficult to know just how much thickener or sweetener a pie will need. Because fresh peaches are so welcome, we are inclined to forgive them if the pie they make is soupy or overly sweet or has a bottom crust that didn't bake properly.

But we wanted to remove the guesswork from this anthem to summer. We wanted to create a filling that was juicy but not swimming in liquid, its flavors neither muscled out by spices nor overwhelmed by thickeners. The crust would be buttery, flaky, and well browned on the bottom, with a handsome, peekaboo lattice on the top.

Our first challenge was to find a thickener that would leave the fruit's color and flavor uncompromised. A fruit pie should appear to be self-thickening, producing clear, syrupy juices. Early tests demonstrated that flour and cornstarch were both too noticeable; what's wanted is a thickener that does the job without calling attention to itself. Other options we though might work were tapioca and potato starch.

We conducted side-by-side tests with flour, cornstarch, Minute tapioca (pulverized so no undissolved beads would remain in the baked pie), and potato starch. Flour and cornstarch fared no better than expected. The ground tapioca performed admirably, having no lumps. The potato starch scored big: Its clarity outshone flour but was less cosmetically glossy than cornstarch; its thickening qualities rivaled tapioca in strength and neutrality; and, still better, there was no need for pulverizing.

Next we turned our attention to the peaches themselves. After attempting to shave a ripe peach with a vegetable peeler, we resorted to traditional blanching and found that two full minutes in boiling water were necessary to loosen the skins of even the ripest of peaches. A quick dip in an ice bath stabilized the temperature of the fruit and got the peels moving.

Experimenting with different sugars, we were surprised to discover that both light and dark brown sugar bullied the peaches, while granulated sugar complemented them. As in most fruit pies, lemon juice brightened the flavor of the peaches; it also kept the peach slices from browning before they went into the pan. A whisper of ground cinnamon and nutmeg and a dash of salt upped the peach flavor and added a note of complexity.

Trying different oven rack levels and temperatures to satisfy the browning requirements of both the top and bottom crust, we found that baking the pie on a low rack at an initial height heat of 425 degrees and a moderately high heat of 375 degrees worked best. We also found that a glass pie dish and preheated baking sheet gave us a pleasantly firm and browned bottom crust. A quick prebaking spritz of the lattice top with water and a sprinkle of sugar brought this pie home.

Lattice-Top Peach Pie

SERVES 8

If your peaches are larger than tennis balls, you will probably need 5 or 6; if they're smaller, you will need 7 or 8. Cling and freestone peaches look identical; try to buy freestones, because the flesh will fall away from the pits easily. See page 308 for tips on peeling the peaches. Use the higher amount of potato starch if the peaches are very juicy, less if they are not terribly juicy. If you don't have or can't find potato starch, substitute an equal amount of Minute tapioca ground for about 1 minute in a food processor or spice grinder.

1	recipe Pie Dough for Lattice-Top Pie (page 181)
	Flour for dusting the work surface
6–7	ripe, medium-sized peaches (about 7 cups when sliced)
1	tablespoon juice from 1 lemon
1	cup (7 ounces) plus 1 tablespoon sugar
	Pinch ground cinnamon
	Pinch freshly grated nutmeg
	Pinch salt
3–5	tablespoons potato starch or Minute tapioca (see note)

1. Remove the dough from the refrigerator (if refrigerated longer than 1 hour, let stand at room temperature until malleable). Roll the larger piece of dough to a 15 by 11-inch rectangle, about ⅛ inch thick; transfer the dough rectangle to a baking sheet lined with parchment paper. With a pizza wheel, fluted pastry wheel, or paring knife, trim the long sides of the rectangle to make them straight, then cut the rectangle lengthwise into 8 strips, 15 inches long by 1¼ inches wide. Freeze the strips on the baking sheet until firm, about 30 minutes.

2. Following the illustrations on page 146, roll the smaller piece of dough on a lightly floured work surface or between 2 large sheets of parchment paper or plastic wrap to a 12-inch circle. Transfer the dough to a 9-inch pie plate by rolling the dough around a rolling pin and unrolling over the pan. Working around the circumference of the pan, ease the dough into the pan corners by gently lifting the edge of the dough with one hand while pressing into the pan bottom with the other hand. Leave the dough that overhangs the lip of the pie plate in place; refrigerate the dough-lined pie plate.

3. Remove the dough strips from the freezer; if they are too stiff to be workable, let them stand at room temperature until malleable and softened slightly but still very cold. Following the illustrations on page 148, form the lattice top and place in the freezer until firm, about 15 minutes.

4. Meanwhile, adjust an oven rack to the lowest position, place a rimmed baking sheet on it, and heat the oven to 500 degrees. Bring 3 quarts water to a boil in a large saucepan and fill a large bowl with 2 quarts cold water and 2 trays ice cubes. Peel the peaches according to the illustrations on page 308. Halve, pit, and cut each peeled peach into ⅜-inch slices.

5. Toss the peach slices, lemon juice, 1 cup sugar, cinnamon, nutmeg, salt, and potato starch in a medium bowl.

6. Turn the peach mixture into the dough-lined pie plate. Remove the lattice from the freezer and place on top of the filled pie. Trim the lattice strips and crimp the pie edges (see illustration on page 148). Lightly brush or spray the lattice top with 1 tablespoon water and sprinkle with the remaining 1 tablespoon sugar.

7. Lower the oven temperature to 425 degrees. Place the pie on the baking sheet and bake until the crust is set and begins to brown, 25 to 30 minutes. Rotate the pie and reduce the oven temperature to 375 degrees; continue baking until the crust is deep golden brown and juices bubble, 25 to 30 minutes longer. Cool the pie on a wire rack for at least 2 hours before serving.

CHERRY PIE

WITH ITS GLOSSY CRIMSON CHERRIES peeking from beneath a golden lattice top, a cherry pie is irresistible—the prima donna of fruit pies. But looks can be deceiving, and often the first bite of pie reveals its true character: a weak fruit flavor and lip-sealing sticky sweetness. Cherry pies never fail to please the eyes better than the palate. What's the secret to making a cherry pie as flavorful as it is attractive?

Few cherries are actually fit for pie. Sweet cherries, like the glossy maroon Bing or lighter Rainier, are best eaten out of hand. Once cooked, their flavor is dissipated and their texture compromised. Tart sour cherries are the best bet for baking, but it's rare to find them fresh outside of Michigan, the Pacific Northwest, and pockets of New England. So if this excludes you (as it does us), what to do? We put the lessons we learned from cherry cobbler (page 310) to use and employed jarred Morello cherries for filling. Earthy, bright, and firm textured, jarred Morello cherries are the best alternative we have found to fresh. But this product is generally available at specialty markets (not regular supermarkets) and somewhat spottily at that. Revisiting more mainstream options to fresh cherries, we retried frozen cherries and canned cherries. The former were mushy and bland once cooked, and the latter, for the most part, were sticky sweet and thick with cornstarch. There was an exception, however, that proved almost perfect. Canned sour cherries from Oregon Fruit Products were tart, fully flavored, and firm—in fact rivaling the quality of the jarred Morellos. The one hitch was the stiff price, about five dollars a can. But for the sake of a perfect cherry pie, we found the price well worth it.

With the cherry issue sorted out, we revisited the crust, thickening agent, and flavorings. An open-weave lattice top is the classic choice, both for aesthetics and function. The vibrant cherry color paired with the golden crust is inviting, and the open top allows for excess moisture to escape, preventing a soupy filling and soggy crust. That said, we knew the standard issues with thickening—type and amount of thickener—would be less of an issue than with a double-crust pie, in which all the moisture is sealed within. For our lattice-top peach pie (page 193) and blueberry pie (page 191), we used either potato starch or pulverized tapioca, but tasters disliked both thickeners when paired with the cherries. Peaches break down more than cherries during baking and hence require stronger thickeners. We moved on to flour and cornstarch and the latter won the tasting. The cornstarch added the minor binding required and gave a glossy coat to the cherries. Four tablespoons or a little less yielded the best texture.

And to accent the cherries' bright flavor, we stayed close to tradition with flavorings. Tasters liked a hint of cinnamon, as well as a splash of almond extract. But anything fancier, say brandy, allspice, or citrus, only unnecessarily complicated matters and displeased tasters. With cherry pie, we found it is best to keep things simple and let the fruit speak for itself.

Lattice-Top Cherry Pie

SERVES 8

If you are lucky and have access to fresh sour cherries, by all means, use them. Otherwise we favor jarred Morello cherries (we particularly like those carried by Trader Joe's markets) or canned Morello cherries from Oregon Fruit Products. Always taste fruit before adding sugar: If it is particularly tart, add the higher amount of sugar listed. While a lattice top is the classic cover to the pie, a solid top is arguably faster and easier to prepare. If you prefer this route, use Basic Pie Dough (page 181) and follow the double-crust instructions in Classic Apple Pie on page 184. If using fresh cherries, toss the filling ingredients together and allow to sit for 20 minutes before assembling the pie.

1	recipe Pie Dough for Lattice-Top Pie (page 181)
	Flour for dusting the work surface
¼	cup (1 ounce) cornstarch
1-1¼	cups (7 to 8¾ ounces) plus 1 tablespoon sugar
¼	teaspoon ground cinnamon
	Pinch salt
3	(24-ounce) jars Morello cherries, drained (about 6 cups), or fresh or canned sour cherries, pitted or drained (see note)
¼	teaspoon almond extract

1. Remove the dough from the refrigerator (if refrigerated longer than 1 hour, let stand at room temperature until malleable). Roll the larger piece of dough to a 15 by 11-inch rectangle, about ⅛ inch thick; transfer the dough rectangle to a baking sheet lined with parchment paper. With a pizza wheel, fluted pastry wheel, or paring knife, trim the long sides of the rectangle to make them straight, then cut the rectangle lengthwise into 8 strips, 15 inches long by 1¼ inches wide. Freeze the strips on the baking sheet until firm, about 30 minutes.

2. Following the illustrations on page 146, roll the smaller piece of dough on a lightly floured work surface or between 2 large sheets of parchment paper or plastic wrap to a 12-inch circle. Transfer the dough to a 9-inch pie plate by rolling the dough around a rolling pin and unrolling over the pan. Working around the circumference of the pan, ease the dough into the pan corners by gently lifting the edge of the dough with one hand while pressing into the pan bottom with the other hand. Leave the dough that overhangs the lip of the pie plate in place; refrigerate the dough-lined pie plate.

3. Remove the dough strips from the freezer; if they are too stiff to be workable, let stand at room temperature until malleable and softened slightly but still very cold. Following the illustrations on page 148, form the lattice top and place in the freezer until firm, about 15 minutes.

4. Meanwhile, adjust an oven rack to the lowest position, place a rimmed baking sheet on it, and heat the oven to 500 degrees.

5. Mix together the cornstarch, 1 to 1¼ cups sugar (taste fruit and adjust amount as desired), cinnamon, and salt in a medium bowl. Stir in the cherries and almond extract.

6. Turn the cherry mixture into the dough-lined pie plate. Remove the lattice from the freezer and place on top of the filled pie. Trim the lattice strips and crimp the pie edges (see the illustration on page 148). Lightly brush or spray the lattice top with 1 tablespoon water and sprinkle with the remaining 1 tablespoon sugar.

7. Lower the oven temperature to 425 degrees. Place the pie on the baking sheet and bake until the crust is set and begins to brown, 25 to 30 minutes.

Rotate the pie and reduce the oven temperature to 375 degrees; continue baking until the crust is deep golden brown and the juices bubble, 25 to 30 minutes longer. Cool the pie on a wire rack for at least 2 hours before serving.

MINCEMEAT PIE

MINCEMEAT WAS ONCE A COMMON ITEM PUT up every fall along with tomatoes and pickles. Rich, jam-like mincemeat takes on many forms but is commonly a mixture of apples, dried fruits, spices, alcohol, suet, and minced meat. Mincemeat originated in the Middle Ages, when the mixing of sweet and savory flavors was much more common. Meatless versions date back at least a century and make more sense to the modern cook not accustomed to the combination of sweet and savory.

Our first challenge was to replace the suet with butter. This was easy enough. The filling has a lighter flavor with butter but is still rich and delicious. We also found that a combination of soft McIntosh apples and firmer Granny Smiths works best. The tart Granny Smiths hold their shape during the long cooking process, while the sweeter McIntosh apples fall apart and help thicken the filling.

As for the dried fruits, we like the combination of golden raisins, currants, and candied orange peel. Dark brown sugar gives the filling a rich molasses flavor, and modest amounts of spice add depth without overpowering the fruits.

Long cooking is essential when making mincemeat. The ingredients need time to cook down and meld into a thick, rich mixture. However, we found that by the time we had cooked the fruit down into a soft mass with concentrated flavors, the pot was dry and there was not enough syrup to moisten the crust.

Many recipes add a lot of rum, brandy, or other spirits, but we felt that more than ⅓ cup was overpowering. After several missteps, we hit upon an easy solution. We added apple cider, which reinforces the apple flavor and keeps the mincemeat moist but does not stand out. Some of the cider goes into the pot at the start of the cooking time, the rest when the fruit has cooked down (after about three hours) along with the alcohol. We then simmer the mincemeat for another 10 minutes or so, just until this liquid reduces to a dense syrup.

Modern Mincemeat Pie

SERVES 10 TO 12

This recipe uses fresh and dried fruit (but no meat) in the filling. Serve with whipped cream or vanilla ice cream. See the illustrations on page 146 for rolling and fitting pie dough.

MINCEMEAT FILLING

3	large Granny Smith apples (about 1 1/2 pounds), peeled, cored, and cut into 1/4-inch dice
3	large McIntosh apples (about 1 1/2 pounds), peeled, cored, and cut into 1/4-inch dice
1	cup golden raisins
1	cup currants
	Grated zest and juice from 1 orange
	Grated zest and juice from 1 lemon
1/4	cup diced candied orange peel (optional)
3/4	cup packed (5 1/4 ounces) dark brown sugar
1	teaspoon ground cinnamon
1/2	teaspoon ground allspice
1/2	teaspoon ground ginger
1/4	teaspoon ground cloves
1/4	teaspoon salt
8	tablespoons (1 stick) unsalted butter
1 1/2	cups apple cider, plus more as needed
1/3	cup rum or brandy
1	recipe Basic Pie Dough (page 181)
	Flour for dusting the work surface
1	beaten egg white for glazing the pie dough
1	tablespoon sugar for sprinkling over the pie dough

1. FOR THE FILLING: Place all the ingredients except 1/2 cup of the cider and the rum in a large, heavy saucepan set over medium-low heat. Bring to a boil and simmer gently, stirring occasionally to prevent scorching, until the mixture thickens and darkens in color, about 3 hours, adding more cider as necessary to prevent scorching. Continue cooking, stirring every minute or two, until the mixture has a jam-like consistency, about 20 minutes. Stir in the remaining 1/2 cup apple cider and the rum and cook until the liquid in the pan is thick and syrupy, about 10 minutes. Cool the mixture. (The mincemeat can be refrigerated for several days.)

2. When the mincemeat filling is almost done, remove the dough from the refrigerator. If the dough is stiff and very cold, let it stand until it is cool but malleable. Adjust an oven rack to the middle position and heat the oven to 400 degrees.

3. Following the illustrations on page 146, roll the dough on a lightly floured work surface or between 2 large sheets of parchment paper or plastic wrap to a 12-inch circle. Transfer the dough to a 9-inch pie plate by rolling the dough around the rolling pin and unrolling over the pan. Working around the circumference of the pan, ease the dough into the pan corners by gently lifting the edge of the dough with one hand while gently pressing into the pan bottom with the other hand. Leave the dough that overhangs the lip of the pie plate in place; refrigerate until needed.

4. Roll out the second piece of dough to a 12-inch circle. Spoon the mincemeat into the pie shell. Place the second piece of dough over the filling. Trim the edges of the top and bottom dough layers to 1/2 inch beyond the pan lip. Tuck this rim of dough underneath itself so that the folded edge is flush with the pan lip. Flute the edge or press with fork tines to seal. (See the illustrations on page 147 for tips on trimming and crimping pie dough.) Cut 4 slits in the dough top. If the pie dough is very soft, place it in the freezer for 10 minutes. Brush the egg white on the top crust and sprinkle evenly with the sugar.

5. Place the pie on the middle rack of the oven. Bake until the crust is light golden brown, 25 minutes. Rotate the pie and reduce the oven temperature to 350 degrees; continue to bake until the juices bubble and the crust is deep golden brown, about 35 minutes. The bottom crust should also be golden.

6. Transfer the pie to a wire rack and cool to room temperature before serving.

SUMMER BERRY PIE

WE LOVE SUMMER FRUIT PIES, BUT THE prospect of wrestling with buttery pie dough in a 90-degree kitchen is unappealing. In addition, we find that berries (as opposed to peaches, apples, and cherries) are spectacular when eaten fresh, not baked. But the alternatives to baked pies hardly inspired us—quick "no-bake" pies consisting mainly of rubbery Jell-O or viscous instant pudding garnished with Cool Whip. Our idea of this summer dessert was closer to the bright flavors of a berry tart, but in the more substantial form of a pie.

Our first round of tests with no-bake pies was disheartening. The first recipe called for "red" flavored gelatin and a cornstarch-thickened syrup that were poured over fresh berries in a premade crust. It had only one redeeming quality: neat slices. Other attempts that utilized cornstarch as a thickener left us with a soupy, cinnamon-laden blueberry "icebox" pie and an overly sweet mixed-berry mash in soggy pastry dough. The best recipe called for merely tossing the mixed berries in melted raspberry jam and then pouring them into a prebaked graham cracker crust. The problem with this method became readily apparent: Once the pie was sliced, the berries spilled out, making it impossible to serve neatly and difficult to eat. Exasperated, we set out to find a technique for making a fresh, flavorful pie with good texture and neat slices.

We did learn one thing from these initial tests: A graham cracker crust is not only easy to make but pairs nicely with tangy sweet berries. Some recipes call for simply pressing and chilling the crust before filling it, but we found that prebaking dramatically improved the flavor of the crust and gave it more structure by fusing the butter and sugar together. As we continued our testing, it became clear that a careful balance of the three ingredients—crumbs, butter, and sugar—would also be crucial to texture and flavor. If we added too much butter, the sides of the crust slid down as it baked, and the crust pooled in the center of the pan. If we added too much sugar, the crust became too hard and exceedingly sweet. The right proportions were 5 tablespoons of butter and 2 tablespoons of sugar to 1 cup of crumbs. We found it was much easier to press the crumbs into the pan when the butter was melted and still very warm.

Having created a recipe for the crust, we could now focus on the mound of berries that would top it. Because strawberry season peaks in early summer, we decided to limit our selection to raspberries, blackberries, and blueberries, all of which ripen in midsummer.

The biggest issue before us was figuring out how to hold the berries together. We needed a binder that would give the pie enough structure to stand up to slicing without interfering with the pure flavor of the fruit.

Early on, we found that combining a berry puree with whole berries was best for optimal flavor; using Jell-O or some other commercial filler resulted in poor flavor and less-than-ideal texture. But we still needed to thicken the puree somehow.

ASSEMBLING SUMMER BERRY PIE

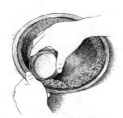  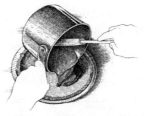 

1. Press the crumb mixture into the pie plate. Use a thumb and measuring cup to square off the top of the crust. Bake the crust.

2. Drizzle the melted jelly over the whole berries and gently toss them together until the berries are glazed.

3. Pour the slightly cooled berry puree into the cooled crust and smooth the top with a rubber spatula.

4. Distribute the glazed berries evenly over the puree and gently press into the surface.

In the summer, our goal is to keep things simple, so we wanted to see if any of the convenient ready-to-use graham cracker piecrusts found in the supermarket were worth their weight in pie tins. All you have to do is fill, chill, and serve. We purchased three different brands—Nabisco Honey Maid Graham Pie Crust, Keebler Graham Cracker Ready Crust, and the local supermarket brand, and tasters unanimously rejected all three, describing them as pale in color, with a "chalky," "sandy" texture, and a "bland," "artificial" flavor. This could be attributed to the fact that all are made with vegetable shortening (already present in the graham crackers themselves but in a much lower amount). It became obvious that adding real butter to ground graham crackers was the best way to get a good-flavored crust and well worth the extra few minutes.

An early test recipe called for cornstarch, which seemed like a good idea, but that recipe also added orange juice, which made the pie soupy. Our plan was simple: lose the juice but keep the cornstarch (or another thickener). We would briefly cook the puree with the thickener, sugar, and salt and then season with lemon juice at the end. After cooling this mixture slightly, we would pour it over the whole berries in the prebaked crust. The pie would then go into the refrigerator to set up.

But which thickener would be best? We started our tests with tapioca, which, because of the short stovetop cooking time, turned out an unpleasantly grainy filling. (We wanted to keep the cooking time as short as possible to retain the fresh berry flavor.) Potato starch produced a gummy filling. In the end, cornstarch worked just fine, producing a good texture without adding any "off" flavors. But we still had some kinks to work out; namely, the seeds that kept sticking between our teeth. The obvious solution was to strain the filling before cooking, a step that took only a couple of minutes and made a huge difference. Now that we had all of our components, we were ready for assembly.

So far, so good, but we had found that pouring the puree over the sun-sweetened whole berries made the filling dark and murky looking. And merely tossing the berries on top of the thickened puree was no way to turn heads either. This pie needed some gloss. So we borrowed a trick from tart making: glazing the fresh whole berries with a thin layer of melted seedless jam. Because we weren't interested in a precise arrangement of berries (we wanted a fast and unfussy pie), gently tossing them with the glaze, rather than painting them with it, as is often done when making tarts, was a quick solution. We had managed to gussy them up and enhance their flavor at the same time. Now when we poured the glazed berries over the puree, the result was a truly attractive berry pie. Better yet, it tasted fresh, sliced well, and was a whole lot easier to make than a traditional baked fruit pie.

Summer Berry Pie

SERVES 8 TO 10

Berries are not sold in standard half-pint containers. When shopping for ingredients, use the weights on the containers as a guideline, but make sure to measure the berries (gently, to avoid bruising). If you wind up short on one type of berry but have extras of another type, make up the difference with the extras. If blackberries are not available, use 3 cups each of raspberries and blueberries. When pureeing the berries, be sure to process them for a full minute; otherwise, the yield on the puree may be too small. Apple jelly can be substituted if red currant jelly is unavailable.

GRAHAM CRACKER CRUST

9	graham crackers (5 ounces), broken into rough pieces
2	tablespoons sugar
5	tablespoons unsalted butter, melted and warm

BERRY FILLING

2	cups raspberries (about 9 ounces)
2	cups blackberries (about 11 ounces)
2	cups blueberries (about 10 ounces)
1/2	cup (3 1/2 ounces) sugar
3	tablespoons cornstarch
1/8	teaspoon salt
1	tablespoon juice from 1 lemon
2	tablespoons red currant jelly
2	cups Whipped Cream (page 500)

1. FOR THE CRUST: Adjust an oven rack to the middle position and heat the oven to 325 degrees.

2. In a food processor, process the graham crackers until evenly fine, about 30 seconds (you should have 1 cup crumbs). Add the sugar and pulse to combine. Continue to pulse while adding warm melted butter in a steady stream; pulse until the mixture resembles wet sand. Transfer the crumbs to 9-inch glass pie plate; following illustration 1 on page 197, use the bottom of a ramekin or measuring cup to press the crumbs evenly into the bottom and up the sides, forming a crust. Bake the crust until it is fragrant and beginning to brown, 15 to 18 minutes; transfer to a wire rack and cool completely while making the filling.

3. FOR THE FILLING: Combine the berries in a large colander and gently rinse (taking care not to bruise them); spread the berries on a paper towel–lined rimmed baking sheet and gently pat dry with additional paper towels.

4. In a food processor, puree 2½ cups of the mixed berries until smooth and fully pureed, about 1 minute. Strain the puree through a mesh strainer into a small nonreactive saucepan, scraping and pressing on the seeds to extract as much puree as possible (you should have 1¼ to 1½ cups). Whisk the sugar, cornstarch, and salt in a small bowl to combine, then whisk the mixture into the puree. Bring the puree to a boil over medium heat, stirring constantly with a wooden spoon; when the mixture reaches a boil and is thickened to the consistency of pudding, remove from the heat, stir in the lemon juice, and set aside to cool slightly.

5. While the puree is cooling, place the remaining berries in a medium bowl. Heat the jelly in a second small saucepan over low heat until fully melted. Follow illustrations 2 through 4 on page 197 to combine the jelly with the berries, to pour the berry puree into the cooled crust, and to distribute the glazed berries over the puree. Loosely cover the pie with plastic wrap; refrigerate until chilled and the puree has set, about 3 hours (or up to 1 day). Cut the pie into wedges and serve with whipped cream.

CUSTARD PIE

AN OLD-FASHIONED CUSTARD PIE IS MADE with fresh cream, sugar, nutmeg, and eggs. The custard should be extraordinarily delicate and light, with a rich cream flavor. But when we baked up a sampling of custard pies in our test kitchen, we were quickly reminded of their shortcomings. Many had a tough, overbaked outer ring of custard (the perimeter overbaked by the time the center was set); a soggy, milk-soaked piecrust; and an eggy taste that was less than delightful for a dessert.

Although this dessert was relatively simple to make, clearly it was not foolproof. After these early tests, we were clear about what we wanted—a custard pie recipe with a crisp crust, a tender yet flavorful filling, and a relatively foolproof cooking method.

The first question was, which type of liquid is best? We tried, in order of ascending cholesterol count, skim milk, whole milk, half-and-half, light cream, and heavy cream. The skim milk gave the custard a hollow taste and a thin texture; the whole milk provided good flavor but did not set up well; the half-and-half was good; the light cream was a bit fatty; and the heavy cream was much too much of a good thing. We played a bit more with proportions and settled on 2 cups milk to 1 cup heavy cream.

Before we pursued this recipe any further, however, we had to deal with the issue of the crust. When making other custard-based pies, such as pumpkin, the test kitchen has found the best method is to prebake the crust, add a hot filling, and then finish the baking in the oven as quickly as possible. Since we wanted to completely prebake the crust (to prevent sogginess), we had to get the filled pie in and out of the oven fast (so the fully baked crust wouldn't color further). So the question became, how could we speed up the thickening process?

We naturally turned to the issue of the thickener itself. After some reflection, we thought that a combination of cornstarch and eggs might be best. The reason for this pairing lies in understanding the science of thickeners. When cornstarch is added to an egg custard mixture, the viscosity is greater—in other words, the mixture becomes thicker. This causes heat to be transmitted more evenly throughout the custard, which neatly solves the problem of the overcooked perimeter. At the same time, eggs add flavor and provide emulsification, which ensures a longer-lasting custard mixture less likely to "weep" the next day. Finally, it is a well-known fact among bakers that cornstarch helps prevent eggs from curdling. One theory is that swelling starch granules make it more difficult for egg proteins to bond, the immediate cause of curdling. A good balance between cornstarch and eggs should therefore produce the best and most foolproof custard pie.

Having thought this through, we started a new round of tests using cornstarch along with the eggs. (We later discovered that custard pies that use both eggs and cornstarch do exist; most often from the South, they are referred to simply as custard pies or sometimes silk pies.) At first, we added 2 tablespoons of cornstarch to 2 cups of milk, 1 cup of cream, and 3 whole eggs. The pie had difficulty setting up properly, so we increased the cornstarch to 3 tablespoons, which worked fine. The pie was evenly cooked throughout, including the edges, and had a delicate, light texture, a major improvement on a standard eggs-only custard pie. We also tried 4 tablespoons of cornstarch, which produced a gloppy, Jell-O–like product.

Now the issue was finding the best way to assemble the filling. We thought that preheating the milk and cream mixture made a lot of sense since it could be done quickly without fear of overcooking the eggs. The hot milk and cream mixture could be slowly whisked into the eggs, and the custard could then be heated until thick. We used a medium-low heat until the custard reached 155 degrees. We stirred occasionally but not constantly. Once the mixture reached that temperature, we stirred constantly but gently with a wooden spoon. At 170 degrees, the custard on the edge of our wooden spoon thickened to a loose paste; this meant that the custard in contact with the bottom of the saucepan was starting to set up. At this point, we noticed that the custard looked a bit clumpy, with small curds in the mix. At first we thought that the mixture had curdled, but this in

fact was not a problem. The pie came out just fine. We poured the hot, thickening custard into the hot prebaked pie shell and found that it took only 12 to 15 minutes at 375 degrees to finish cooking. We removed the pie from the oven when the custard still wobbled a bit when lightly shaken but felt mostly set, not very loose.

To finish off the testing, we fiddled with the sugar and settled on ⅔ cup; this was enough to add flavor but less than the ¾ cup or more called for in most recipes. We liked the addition of nutmeg, but only ¼ teaspoon. After experimenting to find the best lemon and orange variations, we were done.

Custard Pie

SERVES 8

The prebaked pie shell can be made ahead, but it should be heated in a 375-degree oven until hot, about 5 minutes, before the custard filling is poured into it. Or, if you prefer to prebake the pie shell and make the pie in one continuous process, begin heating the milk and cream for the custard when the foil and pie weights are removed; the filling should be ready at the same time that the shell is ready to be filled. (The oven rack position and temperature for prebaking the pie shell remain the same for the filled pie.)

I	recipe Pie Dough for Prebaked Pie Shell (page 183)

	CUSTARD FILLING
2	cups whole milk
I	cup heavy cream
3	large eggs
²/₃	cup (4²/₃ ounces) sugar
3	tablespoons cornstarch
2	teaspoons vanilla extract
¼	teaspoon freshly grated nutmeg
⅛	teaspoon salt

1. FOR THE PIE SHELL: Follow the directions for fully baking the pie crust until deep golden brown. Remove the baked crust from the oven and leave the oven on.

2. FOR THE CUSTARD FILLING: While the crust is baking, heat the milk and cream in a medium saucepan over medium-low heat until steaming, about 6

minutes. Meanwhile, whisk together the eggs, sugar, cornstarch, vanilla, nutmeg, and salt in a medium bowl until thoroughly combined and smooth.

3. Whisk the steaming milk and cream into the egg and cornstarch mixture in a slow, steady stream. Return the egg and milk mixture to the saucepan and cook over medium-low heat, stirring constantly with a wooden spoon and occasionally scraping the bottom of the pan, until the custard begins to thicken and forms a ridge on the tip of the spoon when the bottom of the pan is scraped and the spoon is lifted, 6 to 8 minutes. (If using a thermometer, stir occasionally until the custard reaches 155 degrees, then constantly until the custard reaches 170 degrees.)

4. To FINISH AND BAKE THE PIE: Pour the custard into the hot pie shell. Bake in a 375-degree oven until the custard has set around the edges but jiggles slightly in the center when shaken, 12 to 15 minutes. Cool to room temperature, about 2 hours.

➤ VARIATIONS

Lemon Custard Pie

Follow the recipe for Custard Pie, decreasing the vanilla to 1 teaspoon, substituting 1½ tablespoons grated lemon zest for the nutmeg, and whisking 1½ tablespoons lemon juice into the egg and cornstarch mixture.

Orange Custard Pie

Follow the recipe for Custard Pie, decreasing the vanilla to 1 teaspoon, substituting 1½ tablespoons grated orange zest for the nutmeg, and whisking 1½ tablespoons orange juice into the egg and cornstarch mixture.

PUMPKIN PIE

A PUMPKIN PIE IS NO MORE THAN A VARIATION on custard pie, and it presents the baker with the same challenge—making the crust crisp while developing a filling that is firm but still tender. After baking countless pumpkin pies, we found it necessary to take a threefold approach.

First, we began baking our crusts almost completely before filling them; that way we knew they started out crisp. Next, we made sure that both shell and filling were hot when we assembled the pie, so the custard could begin to firm up almost immediately rather than soaking into the pastry. Finally, we baked the pie quickly, in the bottom of the oven, where the bottom of the crust is exposed to the most intense heat. (Baking in the top of the oven exposes the rim of the crust to the most intense heat, while baking in the middle fails to expose the crust to intense heat from any source.)

Because it sets the filling quickly, high oven heat works to the advantage of all custard pies; the quicker the pie gets out of the oven, the less likely the filling is to soak into the crust and make it soggy. But baking at high heat also has its perils—when overbaked, custard will curdle, becoming grainy and watery. No matter what the heat level, however, curdling can be averted if the pie is taken out of the oven immediately once the center thickens to the point where it no longer sloshes but instead wiggles like gelatin when the pan is gently shaken. Residual heat will finish the cooking outside the oven. Because the presence of the pumpkin dilutes the egg proteins and therefore interferes with curdling, you have a window of about five minutes between "set" and "curdled," considerably longer than with most other custards.

Two other features of our recipe provide further insurance against curdling. First, because the filling is hot when it is put into the shell, the center cooks quickly; this means that the edges, which receive the most direct heat, are less likely to become overcooked. Second, as with many older recipes, this recipe calls for heavy cream as well as milk and a goodly quantity of sugar. These ingredients not only improve the flavor but also protect the texture, since both fat and sugar serve to block the curdling reaction.

Fresh pumpkin is so difficult to use that few modern cooks go down this road. Canned pumpkin is surprisingly good, and, given a little special treatment, it can be as tasty as fresh. One problem with canned pumpkin is its fibrous nature, which is easily corrected by pureeing it in a food processor. You can freshen the taste of canned pumpkin by cooking it with the sugar and spices before combining it with the custard ingredients.

As the pumpkin simmers, you can actually smell the unwelcome canned odor give way to the sweet scent of fresh squash. This is a small but delightful culinary miracle.

Pumpkin Pie
SERVES 8

The key to this recipe is timing. Start preparing the filling when you put the pie shell in the oven. The filling should be ready when the pie shell has partially baked. The pie may be served slightly warm, chilled, or at room temperature, which is our preference.

I	recipe Pie Dough for Prebaked Pie Shell (page 183)

PUMPKIN FILLING

2	cups (16 ounces) plain canned pumpkin puree
I	cup packed (7 ounces) dark brown sugar
2	teaspoons ground ginger
2	teaspoons ground cinnamon
1/2	teaspoon freshly grated nutmeg
1/4	teaspoon ground cloves
1/2	teaspoon salt
2/3	cup heavy cream
2/3	cup milk
4	large eggs

BRANDIED WHIPPED CREAM

I 1/3	cups heavy cream, chilled
2	tablespoons sugar
I	tablespoon brandy

1. FOR THE PIE SHELL: Follow the directions for partially baking the crust until light golden brown.

2. FOR THE FILLING: Meanwhile, process the pumpkin puree, brown sugar, spices, and salt in a food processor for 1 minute until combined. Transfer the pumpkin mixture to a 3-quart heavy-bottomed saucepan; bring it to a sputtering simmer over medium-high heat. Cook the pumpkin, stirring constantly, until thick and shiny, about 5 minutes.

3. As soon as the pie shell comes out of the oven, adjust an oven rack to the lowest position and increase the oven temperature to 400 degrees. Whisk the heavy cream and milk into the pumpkin and bring to a bare simmer. Process the eggs in a food processor until the whites and yolks are combined, about 5 seconds. With the motor running, slowly pour about half of the hot pumpkin mixture through the feed tube. Stop the machine and add the remaining pumpkin mixture. Process 30 seconds longer.

4. Immediately pour the warm filling into the hot pie shell. (Ladle any excess filling into the pie after it has baked for 5 minutes or so—by this time the filling will have settled.) Bake the pie until the filling is puffed, dry-looking, and lightly cracked around edges, and the center wiggles like gelatin when the pie is gently shaken, about 25 minutes. Cool on a wire rack for at least 1 hour.

5. FOR THE WHIPPED CREAM: When ready to serve the pie, beat the cream and sugar in the chilled bowl of an electric mixer at medium speed to soft peaks; add the brandy. Beat to stiff peaks. Accompany each wedge of pie with a dollop of the whipped cream.

SWEET POTATO PIE
THERE ARE TWO KINDS OF SOUTHERN cooking: lady food and down-home food. In the former category are such treats as Coconut Layer Cake (page 353). Sweet potato pie was from the start in the latter category, since sweet potatoes have always been cheap and available and the recipes for this dessert are traditionally short on eggs, milk, and white sugar. Instead of scarce granulated sugar, country cooks relied more heavily on the natural sweetness and texture of the sweet potatoes themselves, combined with sorghum syrup or molasses. This resulted not in the custard-like pie we know today but in a toothier pie, something more akin to a delicate version of mashed sweet potatoes.

But all that is history. The question for our test kitchen was how to create a distinctive sweet potato pie, a recipe that honored the texture and flavor of sweet potatoes while being sufficiently recognizable as a dessert. Neither a custardy, pumpkin-style pie nor a mashed-potatoes-in-a-crust pie would do.

A review of more than 30 recipes led us to five distinctive approaches to this dish, ranging from mashed sweet potatoes with a modicum of milk and eggs to Paul Prudhomme's syrup-soaked Sweet Potato Pecan Pie to a typical pumpkin pie, with sweet potatoes substituted for the pumpkin. Some recipes separated the eggs and whipped the whites, some used evaporated or condensed milk, others used a combination of white and sweet potatoes, and most of them used a profusion of spices. To our surprise, all of them had abandoned molasses or sorghum for either granulated or brown sugar.

Although the classic pumpkin-pie style was good, our tasters were drawn to more authentic recipes, especially one published in *Dori Sanders's Country Cooking* (Algonquin Books of Chapel Hill, 1995), which had more sweet potato flavor. One problem with all such recipes, however, was their mashed-potatoes-in-a-crust quality. We wanted a recipe that would work as a dessert, not a savory side dish to a turkey dinner. This would require fiddling with the amount of milk, eggs, and sugar as well as with the method of preparing the potatoes.

The first step was to determine the best method of preparing the sweet potatoes. One group of tasters was keen on slicing cooked potatoes and then layering them in the pie shell. This method was quickly discarded, since its product bore little resemblance to a dessert. We also gave up on using a food processor to beat the cooked potatoes; this resulted in a very smooth, custardy texture. We finally settled on coarsely mashing the potatoes, leaving a few small lumps. This also simplified the recipe, precluding the need to pass the potatoes through a sieve to remove fibrous strings, a step called for in some of the more refined recipes. We also decided on microwaving as the easiest method of precooking the sweet potatoes. It took just 10 minutes, without having to first boil water or heat an oven.

Next, we discarded the notion of using a bit of white potato in the recipe (a technique often used by traditional Southern cooks to lighten the texture). This made the pie more complicated and a bit grainy as well. Separating the eggs and whipping the whites, another common procedure, produced an anemic, fluffy dessert lacking in moisture and flavor. Sweetened condensed milk did not improve the flavor, and we ended up preferring regular milk to half-and-half. We added two yolks to three whole eggs to properly moisten the filling. Orange zest and lemon juice were tried and discarded because they detracted from the delicate flavor of the sweet potato itself, but a bit of bourbon helped to accentuate the flavor.

A major problem with modern sweet potato pies is that they call for the usual pumpkin pie spices, which overwhelm the taste of the sweet potato. The solution was to use only a modest amount of nutmeg. Granulated sugar was fine, but since older recipes often call for molasses (or sorghum syrup, cane syrup, dark corn syrup, and even maple syrup), we decided to test it. The results were mixed, so we settled on 1 tablespoon of molasses as optional. This boosts flavor without overpowering the pie with the distinctive malt taste of molasses. (Even 2 tablespoons of molasses were too many.)

At this point we had a pie that we liked a lot, with real sweet potato flavor and enough custardy richness to place it firmly in the dessert category. But something was still lacking. The pie tasted a bit vegetal; it needed more oomph. Borrowing from Paul Prudhomme's notion of adding pecan pie flavorings to the mix, we made a few pies to see if we could create two layers—one of sweet potato filling and one similar to the sweet filling in a pecan pie—to jazz things up. Creating two separate layers presented a challenge until we came upon the idea of baking the pecan pie filling first, until it set in the shell, about 20 minutes, and then adding the sweet potato filling on top. This worked like a charm and made a stupendous pie. Even so, many tasters found the process a little unwieldy. After more experiments, we came up with an easy-as-pie technique for adding a separate bottom layer: We simply sprinkled the bottom of the crust with brown sugar before adding the filling.

Now we had something really special, a pie with an intense, thick, pure-sweet-potato filling, perfectly complemented by a layer of melted brown sugar just beneath. Its unique nature is reflected in the color of the filling, which is a fantastic orange rather than the dull brown that results from the use of too much molasses and too many spices. This is a sweet potato pie that any Southern cook would be proud of.

Sweet Potato Pie

SERVES 8 TO 10

Prepare the sweet potato filling while the crust is baking so that it will be ready soon after the pie shell comes out of the oven. (The crust should still be warm when you add the brown sugar layer and sweet potato filling.) The sweet potatoes cook quickly in the microwave, but they can also be pricked with a fork and baked uncovered in a 400-degree oven until tender, 40 to 50 minutes. Some tasters preferred a stronger bourbon flavor in the filling, so we give a range below. If you like molasses, use the optional tablespoon; a few tasters felt it deepened the sweet potato flavor. Serve the pie with Whipped Cream, page 500.

1	recipe Pie Dough for Prebaked Pie Shell (page 183)

SWEET POTATO FILLING

2	pounds sweet potatoes (about 5 small to medium)
2	tablespoons unsalted butter, softened
3	large eggs plus 2 yolks
1	cup (7 ounces) sugar
1/2	teaspoon freshly grated nutmeg
1/4	teaspoon salt
2–3	tablespoons bourbon
1	tablespoon molasses (optional)
1	teaspoon vanilla extract
2/3	cup whole milk
1/4	cup packed (1 3/4 ounces) dark brown sugar

1. FOR THE PIE SHELL: Follow the directions for partially baking the crust until light golden brown. Remove the baked crust from the oven and reduce the oven temperature to 350 degrees.

2. FOR THE SWEET POTATO FILLING: Meanwhile, prick the sweet potatoes several times with a fork and place them on a double layer of paper towels in a microwave. Cook at full power for 5 minutes; turn each potato over and continue to cook at full power until tender, but not mushy, about 5 minutes longer. Cool 10 minutes. Halve a potato crosswise, insert a small spoon between the skin and flesh, and scoop the flesh into a medium bowl; discard the skin. (If the potato is too hot to handle comfortably, fold a double layer of paper towels into quarters and use this to hold each potato half.) Repeat with the remaining sweet potatoes; you should have about 2 cups. While the potatoes are still hot, add the butter and mash with a fork or wooden spoon; small lumps of potato should remain.

3. Whisk together the eggs, yolks, sugar, nutmeg, and salt in a medium bowl; stir in the bourbon, molasses (if using), and vanilla, then whisk in the milk. Gradually add the egg mixture to the sweet potatoes, whisking gently to combine.

4. TO FINISH AND BAKE THE PIE: Sprinkle the bottom of the warm pie shell evenly with the brown sugar. Pour the sweet potato mixture into the pie shell over the brown sugar layer. Bake on the lower-middle rack until the filling is set around the edges but the center jiggles slightly when shaken, about 45 minutes. Transfer the pie to a wire rack; cool to room temperature, about 2 hours, and serve.

PECAN PIE

PECAN PIE TYPICALLY PRESENTS A COUPLE of problems. First, this pie is often too sweet, both in an absolute sense and in relation to its other flavors, which are overwhelmed by the sugariness. This problem is easily remedied by lowering the amount of sugar.

The other major complaint has to do with texture. Pecan pies too often turn out to be curdled and separated, and the weepy filling turns the crust soggy and leathery. The fact that the crust usually seems underbaked to begin with doesn't help matters.

Pecan pie should be wonderfully soft and smooth, almost like a cream pie. Taking the pie out of the oven before it is completely set helps achieve this texture. The pie continues to cook after being removed from the oven, as the heat travels from the edges to the middle by conduction. And since pecan pies are composed largely of sugar and butter, cooling serves to make them still more solid.

A hot oven spells disaster for pecan pie. At 375 degrees and above, the edges of the filling solidified before the center had even thickened. A moderate oven (325 to 350 degrees) is better, but a slow oven (250 to 300 degrees) turned out the best pie filling, with a nicely thickened center and no hardened edges.

There was a problem, however. Pies baked at very low temperatures took so long to firm up that the crusts turned soggy, even when the shells were thoroughly prebaked. Furthermore, the filling tended to separate into a jelly-like layer on the bottom with a frothy cap on top. To solve this problem, we tried adding hot filling to a hot, partially baked crust. When we tried this, we cut the baking time by close to half and fixed the problems of soggy crust and separated filling.

We tested pies made with whole pecan halves, chopped pecans, and a combination of chopped and whole nuts. We had no problem deciding our preference. We found whole pecans too much of a mouthful, and we had difficulty cutting through them with a fork as we consumed a slice. Chopped nuts are easier to slice through and eat.

Toasting the nuts beforehand is a major improvement. We toasted the nuts in the oven while it was heating in preparation for baking the crust. Toasting takes about seven minutes, but the nuts should be watched carefully and stirred from time to time to prevent burning. Be sure to let them cool to lukewarm before chopping them or they will crumble. Use a knife rather than a food processor, which tends to cut the nuts too fine.

Pecan Pie

SERVES 8

If you want warm pie, cool the pie thoroughly so that it sets completely, then warm it in a 250-degree oven for about 15 minutes and slice. Serve with lightly sweetened Whipped Cream (page 500) or vanilla ice cream.

| 1 | recipe Pie Dough for Prebaked Pie Shell (page 183) |

PECAN FILLING

6	tablespoons ($3/4$ stick) unsalted butter, cut into 1-inch pieces
1	cup packed (7 ounces) dark brown sugar
$1/2$	teaspoon salt
3	large eggs
$3/4$	cup light corn syrup
1	tablespoon vanilla extract
2	cups pecans, toasted and chopped into small pieces

1. FOR THE PIE SHELL: Follow the directions for partially baking the crust until light golden brown.

2. FOR THE FILLING: Meanwhile, melt the butter in a medium heatproof bowl set in a skillet of water maintained at just below a simmer. Remove the bowl from the skillet; stir in the sugar and salt with a wooden spoon until the butter is absorbed. Beat in the eggs, then the corn syrup and vanilla. Return the bowl to hot water; stir until the mixture is shiny and hot to the touch, about 130 degrees on an instant-read thermometer. Remove from the heat; stir in the pecans.

3. As soon as the pie shell comes out of the oven, decrease the oven temperature to 275 degrees. Pour the pecan mixture into the hot pie shell.

4. Bake on the middle rack until the pie looks set and yet soft, like gelatin, when gently pressed with the back of a spoon, 50 to 60 minutes. Transfer the pie to a rack; cool completely, at least 4 hours.

➤ VARIATIONS

Triple Chocolate Chunk Pecan Pie

To accommodate the richness and sweetness of the chocolate, you must reduce the amount of the other filling ingredients. The pie may need to bake an extra five minutes.

Cut 2 ounces each semisweet, milk, and white chocolate into ¼-inch pieces and set aside. Follow the recipe for Pecan Pie, reducing the butter to 3 tablespoons, the brown sugar to ¾ cup, the eggs to 2, the corn syrup to ½ cup, the vanilla to 1 teaspoon, and the pecans to 1 cup. Prepare the filling and pour it into the hot pie shell as directed. Scatter the chocolate pieces over the filling and press the pieces into the filling with the back of a spoon. Proceed as directed.

Maple Pecan Pie

More liquid than corn syrup, maple syrup yields a softer, more custard-like pie. Toasted walnuts can be substituted for pecans.

Follow the recipe for Pecan Pie, reducing the butter to 4 tablespoons, replacing the brown sugar with ½ cup granulated sugar, replacing the corn syrup with 1 cup maple syrup, omitting the vanilla, and reducing the pecans to 1½ cups. Proceed as directed.

LEMON MERINGUE PIE

THE IDEAL LEMON MERINGUE PIE HAS A RICH filling that balances the airy meringue without detracting from the flavor of lemon. The lemon filling should be soft but not runny, firm enough to cut but not stiff and gelatinous. Finally, the meringue itself should not break down and puddle on the bottom or "weep" on top—not even on rainy days.

The ingredients in lemon meringue pie have remained constant for some time: sugar, water (or sometimes milk), cornstarch (sometimes mixed with flour), egg yolks, lemon juice (and usually zest), and a little butter. To our tastes, the straight-forward lemon flavor of the water-based filling is pleasant, but it is also one-dimensional and lacking depth. Milk, however, subdues the lemon flavor.

The solution is to rely primarily on water and a lot of egg yolks (we use six rather than the usual three), eliminating the milk altogether. This has another benefit: The addition of egg yolks allows you to cut back on both sugar (which acts as a softener at a certain level) and cornstarch and still achieve a firm yet tender filling.

The meringue is much more tricky. On any given day it can shrink, bead, puddle, deflate, burn, sweat, break down, or turn rubbery. Most cookbooks don't even attempt to deal with the problems of meringue. They follow the standard recipe—granulated sugar and cream of tartar beaten slowly into the egg whites—assuming, apparently, that there is no way around the flaws. After making 30-something lemon meringue pies, we're not sure we blame anyone for skirting the issue. For as easy as it was to figure out the perfect lemon filling, the meringue turned into a vexing proposition. We could not simply spread the meringue used in Meringue Cookies (page 479) or Pavlova (page 317). This meringue faced an extra challenge: cooking on top of the filling without remaining raw on its underside or weepy on top.

The puddling underneath the meringue is from undercooking. Undercooked whites break down and return to their liquid state. The beading on top of the pie is from overcooking. This near-the-surface overcooking of the meringue causes the proteins in the egg white to coagulate, squeezing out moisture,

APPLYING A MERINGUE TOPPING

1. Start by placing dabs of meringue evenly around the edge of the pie. Once the edge of the pie is covered with meringue, fill in the center of the pie with the remaining meringue.

2. Use a rubber spatula to anchor the meringue to the edge of the crust or it may pull away and shrink in the oven.

which then surfaces as tears or beads.

This double dilemma might seem insurmountable, but we hit upon a solution. If the filling is piping hot when the meringue is applied, the underside of the meringue will not undercook; if the oven temperature is relatively low, the top of the meringue won't overcook. A relatively cool oven also produces the best-looking, most evenly browned meringue. To further stabilize the meringue, we like to beat in a some cornstarch; if you do this, the meringue will not weep, even on hot, humid days.

Lemon Meringue Pie

SERVES 8

As soon as the filling is made, cover it with plastic wrap to keep it hot and then start working on the meringue topping. You want to add hot filling to the pie shell, apply the meringue topping, and then quickly get the pie into the oven.

LEMON FILLING

1	cup (7 ounces) sugar
1/4	cup (1 ounce) cornstarch
1/8	teaspoon salt
1 1/2	cups cold water
6	large egg yolks
1	tablespoon grated zest and 1/2 cup juice from 2 or 3 lemons
2	tablespoons unsalted butter

MERINGUE

1	tablespoon cornstarch
1/3	cup water
1/4	teaspoon cream of tartar
1/2	cup (3 1/2 ounces) sugar
4	large egg whites
1/2	teaspoon vanilla extract

1	recipe Prebaked Pie Dough Coated with Graham Cracker Crumbs (page 183), fully baked and cooled completely

1. FOR THE FILLING: Mix the sugar, cornstarch, salt, and water in a large, nonreactive saucepan. Bring the mixture to a simmer over medium heat, whisking occasionally at the beginning of the process and more frequently as the mixture begins to thicken. When the mixture starts to simmer and turns translucent, whisk in the egg yolks, 2 at a time. Whisk in the zest, then the lemon juice, and finally the butter. Bring the mixture to a good simmer, whisking constantly. Remove from the heat; place plastic wrap directly on the surface of the filling to keep it hot and prevent a skin from forming.

2. FOR THE MERINGUE: Mix the cornstarch with the water in a small saucepan; bring to a simmer, whisking occasionally at the beginning and more frequently as the mixture thickens. When the mixture starts to simmer and turns translucent, remove from the heat.

3. Adjust an oven rack to the middle position and heat the oven to 325 degrees. Mix the cream of tartar and sugar together. Beat the egg whites and vanilla until frothy. Beat in the sugar mixture, 1 tablespoon at a time, until the sugar is incorporated and the mixture forms soft peaks. Add the cornstarch mixture, 1 tablespoon at a time; continue to beat the meringue to stiff peaks. Remove the plastic from the lemon filling and return to very low heat during last minute or so of beating the meringue (to ensure that the filling is hot).

4. Pour the hot filling into the pie shell. Using a rubber spatula, immediately distribute the meringue evenly around the edge and then the center of the pie to keep it from sinking into the filling (see illustration 1 on page 206). Make sure the meringue attaches to the piecrust to prevent shrinking (see illustration 2 on page 206). Use the back of a spoon to create peaks all over the meringue. Bake the pie until the meringue is golden brown, about 20 minutes. Transfer to a wire rack and cool to room temperature. Serve that day.

KEY LIME PIE

THE STANDARD RECIPE FOR CONDENSED milk Key lime pie is incredibly short and simple: beat four egg yolks, add a 14-ounce can of sweetened condensed milk, and then stir in a half cup of lime juice and a tablespoon of grated lime zest. Pour it all into a graham cracker crust and chill

True Key limes, *Citrus aurantifolia*, have not been a significant commercial crop in this country since storms destroyed the Florida groves early in the 20th century. However, a few growers have recently begun to revive the crop, and Key limes occasionally show up in supermarkets. Most food writers seem to like Key lime juice much better than Persian lime juice, but they give wildly divergent reasons for their preference. One book describes Key limes as "sourer and more complex" than their supermarket cousins. But another writer holds that Key limes differ from Persian limes in being more "mild" and "delicate."

We'd love to be able to say that Key lime juice made all the difference in the world, but it didn't. To our testers, it tasted pretty much the same as the juice of supermarket limes. Key limes are a nuisance to zest and squeeze, for they are thin-skinned, full of seeds, and generally little bigger than walnuts. You need only three or four Persian limes to make a Key lime pie, but you will need up to a dozen Key limes. So despite the name of the pie, we actually find the juice of Persian limes preferable as an ingredient.

it until firm, about two hours. Top the pie with sweetened whipped cream and serve.

It would be lovely if this recipe worked, but we found that it doesn't. Although the filling does set firm enough to yield clean-cut slices, it has a loose, "slurpy" consistency. We tried to fix the consistency by beating the yolks until thick, as some recipes direct, but this did not help. Nor did it help to dribble in the lime juice rather than adding it all at once, as other recipes suggest. We also made the filling with only two yolks and with no yolks at all (such "eggless" versions of the recipe do exist), but this yielded even thinner fillings.

Still, the time we spent mixing Key lime pie fillings in various ways was not a total loss. While in the heat of experimenting, we inadvertently threw the lime zest into a bowl in which we had already placed the egg yolks. When we whisked up the yolks, they turned green, and the whole filling ended up tinted a lovely shade of pale lime.

Having found the mix-and-chill method wanting, we decided to try baking the pie, as some recipes suggest. We used the same ingredients as we had before and simply baked the pie until the filling stiffened slightly, about 15 minutes in a moderate oven. The difference between the baked pie (which was really a custard) and the unbaked pie (which had merely been a clabber) was remarkable. The baked filling was thick, creamy, and unctuous, reminiscent of cream pie. It also tasted more pungent and complex than the raw fillings had, perhaps because the heat of the oven released the flavorful oils in the lime zest.

The filling is fairly tart and must be offset by whipped cream that has been generously sweetened. Since granulated sugar can cause graininess at high concentration, we opt for confectioners' sugar in the whipped cream topping for this pie.

Key Lime Pie

SERVES 8

Prepare the filling for the pie first, so it can thicken during the time it takes to prepare the crust. If you prefer, you can use the Prebaked Pie Dough Coated with Graham Cracker Crumbs (see page 183), but we like the simple graham cracker crust in this recipe.

LIME FILLING

- 4 teaspoons grated zest plus ½ cup strained juice from 3 or 4 limes
- 4 large egg yolks
- 1 (14-ounce) can sweetened condensed milk

GRAHAM CRACKER CRUST

- 9 graham crackers (5 ounces), broken into rough pieces
- 2 tablespoons granulated sugar
- 5 tablespoons unsalted butter, melted and warm

WHIPPED CREAM TOPPING

- ¾ cup heavy cream, chilled
- ¼ cup (1 ounce) confectioners' sugar
- ½ lime, sliced paper thin and dipped in sugar (optional)

1. FOR THE FILLING: Whisk the zest and yolks in a medium nonreactive bowl until tinted light green, about 2 minutes. Beat in the milk, then juice; set aside at room temperature to thicken (about 30 minutes).

2. FOR THE CRUST: Adjust an oven rack to the middle position and heat the oven to 325 degrees.

3. In a food processor, process the graham crackers until evenly fine, about 30 seconds (you should have 1 cup crumbs). Add the sugar and pulse to combine. Continue to pulse while adding the warm melted butter in a steady stream; pulse until the mixture resembles wet sand. Transfer the crumbs to a 9-inch glass pie plate and, following illustration 1 on page 197, evenly press the crumbs into the pie plate, using your thumb and a ½ cup measuring cup to square off the top of the crust. Bake the crust until it is fragrant and beginning to brown, 15 to 18 minutes; transfer to a wire rack and cool completely.

4. Pour the lime filling into the crust; bake until the center is set, yet wiggly when jiggled, 15 to 17 minutes. Return the pie to a wire rack; cool to room temperature. Refrigerate until well chilled, at least 3 hours. (The pie can be covered directly with lightly oiled or oil-sprayed plastic wrap and refrigerated up to 1 day.)

5. FOR THE WHIPPED CREAM: Up to 2 hours before serving, whip the cream in the chilled bowl of an electric mixer to very soft peaks. Adding the confectioners' sugar 1 tablespoon at a time, continue whipping to just-stiff peaks. Decoratively pipe the whipped cream over the filling or spread the whipped cream evenly with a rubber spatula. Garnish with optional sugared lime slices and serve.

➤ VARIATION
Key Lime Pie with Meringue Topping
We prefer to top Key lime pie with whipped cream, but meringue is another option.

Follow the recipe for Key Lime Pie, replacing the Whipped Cream Topping with the Meringue from the recipe for Lemon Meringue Pie on page 207. Bake the pie only 7 minutes, then apply the meringue gently, first spreading a ring around the outer edge to attach the meringue to the crust, then filling in the center. Return the pie to the oven and bake 20 minutes more.

VANILLA CREAM PIE

CREAM PIE HAS ALMOST UNIVERSAL appeal, with enough flavoring options—vanilla, chocolate, banana, coconut, and butterscotch—to satisfy almost everyone. The key is to create a filling that is soft and creamy yet stiff enough to be cut cleanly. It's not as easy as it sounds.

In our tests, adding flour left us with a filling that was too soft. Gelatin made for a rubbery filling, and tapioca, which works well in fruit pies, produced a filling with the texture of stewed okra. Only cornstarch coupled with egg yolks (whole eggs yielded a grainy texture) gave us the proper results.

The dairy component is also vital. Cream is simply too rich for a pie that already contains butter and eggs. Skim milk tastes thin and lacks the

---

SCIENCE: How Key Lime Pie Thickens

The extraordinarily high acid content of limes and the unique properties of sweetened condensed milk are responsible for the fact that lime pie filling will thicken without cooking.

The acid in the lime juice does its work by causing the proteins in both the egg yolks and the condensed milk to coil up and bond together. This effect is similar to that of heat. The same process can be observed in the Latin American–style dish seviche, in which raw fish is "cooked" simply by being pickled in lime juice.

But this process does not work well with just any kind of milk; it requires both the sweetness and the thickness of sweetened condensed milk. This canned product is made by boiling most of the water out of fresh milk and then adding sugar. Because the milk has

a lower moisture content, it is thick enough to stiffen into a sliceable filling when clabbered with lime juice. The sugar, meanwhile, plays the crucial role of separating, or "greasing," the protein strands so that they do not bond too tightly. If they did, the result would be a grainy or curdled filling rather than a smooth and creamy one. Of course, a liquidy, curdly filling is exactly what one would get if one tried to use fresh milk instead of canned.

We discovered that cream is not a viable substitute for sweetened condensed milk either. It does not curdle the way milk does because its fat, like the sugar in condensed milk, acts as a buffer to the lime juice. Cream is roughly 50 percent liquid, however, and thus it will only thicken, not stiffen, when clabbered.

creamy texture we wanted. Both 2 percent and whole milk work well, but they are even better when combined with a bit of evaporated milk, which adds a rich, round, caramel flavor. The basic vanilla cream filling also benefits greatly from the use of a vanilla bean in place of extract.

When making a cream filling for a pie, some cooks heat the sugar, cornstarch, and milk to a simmer, gradually add some of this mixture to the yolks to stabilize them, and then add the stabilized yolks to the rest of the simmering milk. We found that this process, called tempering, is not necessary in this recipe. You can dump everything except the flavorings and butter into a saucepan and cook, stirring often, until the mixture begins to bubble. This method is simpler, and because the cornstarch prevents the eggs from curdling, it isn't that risky.

Developing a filling with great body as well as flavor is important, as is preventing that filling from turning the prebaked crust soggy. Unlike most pies, cream pie filling does not bake in the crust. The moist, fluid filling is simply poured into the crust and chilled. We found two procedures that help to keep the crust crisp.

Coating the dough with graham cracker crumbs as it is rolled out produces an especially crisp, browned pie shell. It also helps to pour filling into the crust while the filling is warm but not quite hot. Hot filling keeps the crust crisp, but because it is still quite liquid when poured into the crust, it settles compactly and falls apart when sliced. Warm filling, having had a chance to set a bit, mounds when poured into the crust and slices beautifully. What's more, it won't make the crust soggy.

Whatever you do, don't wait until the filling has cooled to scrape it into the pie shell. Cooled filling turned soupy and moistened our once-crisp crust. You can't disturb the filling once the starch bonds have completely set. If you break the starch bonds, you destroy the filling's structure. Those who have tried stirring liqueur into a chilled pastry cream may have been confronted with similar results. When we stirred the cold filling to put it into the crust, we broke the starch bonds so that the filling went from stiff to runny. We learned a major lesson. You can cool the filling to warm, but once it has set, don't stir it.

Vanilla Cream Pie

SERVES 8

For this pie, warm (but not hot) filling is poured into a fully baked, cooled crust. The filled pie is then refrigerated until thoroughly chilled and topped with whipped cream.

CREAM FILLING

½	cup plus 2 tablespoons (4 ⅞ ounces) sugar
¼	cup (1 ounce) cornstarch
⅛	teaspoon salt
5	large egg yolks, lightly beaten
2	cups 2 percent or whole milk
½	cup evaporated milk
½	vanilla bean, about 3 inches long, split lengthwise, or 1 teaspoon vanilla extract
2	tablespoons unsalted butter
1–2	teaspoons brandy
1	recipe Prebaked Pie Dough Coated with Graham Cracker Crumbs (page 183), fully baked and cooled completely

WHIPPED CREAM TOPPING

1	cup heavy cream, chilled
1	tablespoon sugar
1	teaspoon vanilla extract

1. FOR THE FILLING: Whisk the sugar, cornstarch, and salt together in a medium saucepan. Add the yolks, then immediately but gradually whisk in the milk and evaporated milk. Drop in the vanilla bean (if using). Cook over medium heat, stirring frequently at first, then constantly, as the mixture starts to thicken and begins to simmer, 8 to 10 minutes. Once the mixture simmers, continue to cook, stirring constantly, for 1 minute longer. Remove the pan from the heat; whisk in the butter, vanilla extract (if using), and brandy. Remove the vanilla bean, scrape out the seeds, and whisk them back into the filling.

2. Pour the filling into a shallow pan (another pie pan works well). Put plastic wrap directly on the filling surface to prevent a skin from forming; cool until warm, 20 to 30 minutes. Pour the warm filling into the pie shell and, once again, place a sheet of plastic wrap directly on the filling surface. Refrigerate the

pie until completely chilled, at least 3 hours.

3. FOR THE TOPPING: When ready to serve, beat the cream and sugar in the chilled bowl of an electric mixer at medium speed to soft peaks; add the vanilla. Continue to beat to barely stiff peaks. Spread over the filling and serve immediately.

> VARIATIONS

Banana Cream Pie

The best place for the banana slices is sandwiched between two layers of filling. If sliced over the pie shell, the bananas tend to moisten the crust; if sliced over the filling top or mashed and folded into the filling, they turn brown faster.

Follow the recipe for Vanilla Cream Pie, spooning half the warm filling into the baked and cooled pie shell. Peel 2 medium bananas and slice them over the filling. Top with the remaining filling.

Butterscotch Cream Pie

Whisking the milk slowly into the brown sugar mixture keeps the sugar from lumping. Don't worry if the sugar does lump—it will dissolve as the milk heats—but make sure not to add the egg and cornstarch mixture until the sugar completely dissolves.

BUTTERSCOTCH FILLING

1/4	cup (1 ounce) cornstarch
1/4	teaspoon salt
1/2	cup evaporated milk
5	large egg yolks
6	tablespoons (3/4 stick) unsalted butter
1	cup packed (7 ounces) light brown sugar
2	cups whole milk
1 1/2	teaspoons vanilla extract
1	recipe Prebaked Pie Dough Coated with Graham Cracker Crumbs (page 183), fully baked and cooled completely

WHIPPED CREAM TOPPING

1	cup heavy cream, chilled
1	tablespoon sugar
1	teaspoon vanilla extract

1. FOR THE FILLING: Dissolve the cornstarch and salt in the evaporated milk; whisk in the egg yolks and set aside.

2. Meanwhile, heat the butter and brown sugar in a medium saucepan over medium heat until an instant-read thermometer reads 220 degrees, about 5 minutes. Gradually whisk in the milk. Once the sugar dissolves, gradually whisk in the cornstarch mixture. Continue cooking until the mixture comes to a boil; cook 1 minute longer. Turn off the heat, then stir in the vanilla. Pour the filling into a shallow pan (another pie pan works well). Put plastic wrap directly on the filling surface to prevent a skin from forming; cool until warm, 20 to 30 minutes. Pour the filling into the pie shell and, once again, place a sheet of plastic wrap on the filling surface. Refrigerate until completely chilled, at least 3 hours.

3. FOR THE TOPPING: When ready to serve, beat the cream and sugar in the chilled bowl of an electric mixer at medium speed to soft peaks; add the vanilla. Continue to beat to barely stiff peaks. Spread the whipped cream over the filling and serve immediately.

CHOCOLATE CREAM PIE

DESPITE ITS GRAND FLOURISHES AND snowcapped peaks, a chocolate cream pie is essentially pastry cream whose substance has been given form. Comprising very basic ingredients—milk or cream, eggs, sugar, flour or cornstarch, butter, vanilla, and chocolate—it is cooked on the stovetop in a matter of minutes, chilled in a baked pie shell for a couple of hours, then topped with whipped cream. This pie, while looking superb, can be gluey or gummy, too sweet, even acrid.

We started our tests by using our basic Pastry Cream (page 227) and concluded that the texture of chocolate cream filling benefits immeasurably when fats are used as thickeners and basic starch is minimized. Butter, egg yolks, and half-and-half render a silky texture and provide most of the requisite thickening with greater finesse than cornstarch.

We had three chocolate options: semisweet (or bittersweet, which is quite similar), unsweetened, or a mixture of the two. Tasters felt that fillings made exclusively with semisweet or bittersweet chocolate lacked depth of flavor, while those made with unsweetened chocolate alone hit a sour note. Without exception, tasters wanted the filling to land on the dark, intense bittersweet side and the cream topping to be sweet and pure.

The roundest, most upfront chocolate flavor, with lingering intensity at the finish, came in the form of 6 ounces semisweet and 1 ounce unsweetened chocolate. The seemingly negligible amount of unsweetened chocolate contributed hugely to the flavor. Unsweetened chocolate, which does not undergo the kneading, grinding, and smoothing process known as conching, retains all of its strong and sometimes bitter flavors, which translate well in small amounts.

This was not the only advantage of using a small amount of unsweetened chocolate. Because it further thickened the cream (see "Chocolate as a Thickener" at right), we were able to reduce the cornstarch from 3 tablespoons to 2.

Next we moved on to compare fancy imported chocolates with domestic grocery store brands. The first test, pitting the widely available Baker's unsweetened chocolate against several unsweetened chocolates with European pedigrees, confirmed our fears that the supermarket stuff would be no match for its European competition. Of the imported chocolates, all tasters preferred Callebaut. Even at 1 ounce, the Baker's chocolate contributed an "off" flavor and rubberiness of texture that everyone noticed. But the next round of testing brought unexpected good news: Hershey's Special Dark chocolate was a consistent winner in the semisweet category, beating out not only a premium American semisweet entry but also its European competitors—and you can buy it in a drugstore! Hershey's unsweetened chocolate, while not as refined in flavor and texture as Callebaut unsweetened, placed a respectable second to Callebaut and was miles ahead of Baker's.

Because the filling is three standing inches of pure chocolate, a texture less than faultlessly smooth will deliver an experience less than ethereal. Temperature, timing, and technique are important.

As for the crust, tasters swooned over a crumb crust made with chocolate cookie crumbs to the exclusion of all others. Although easier to make

SCIENCE: Chocolate as a Thickener

Everyone knows that bittersweet and unsweetened chocolates have different flavors and levels of sweetness. But their dissimilarities do not end there. As we developed our chocolate cream pie recipe, we discovered that, ounce for ounce, unsweetened chocolate has more thickening power. We were aware of chocolate's starchy properties (cocoa solids are rich in starches), but we were not prepared for the dramatic differences in texture revealed in side-by-side pie fillings made with each type. Though both fillings had roughly the same amount of cocoa solids by volume, the unsweetened chocolate filling was significantly stiffer and had a viscous, gummy quality. Its counterpart made only with bittersweet chocolate had a smooth and creamy texture.

than rolled pastry dough and arguably better suited to chilled pudding fillings, crumb crusts are not altogether seamless enterprises. Sandy and insubstantial at one extreme, tough and intractable at the other, they can be a serving nightmare. While no one expects a slice of cream pie to hold up like a slab of marble, it shouldn't collapse on a bed of grit or lacerate a cornea with airborne shrapnel, either. It's got to slice.

The standard cookie used to make a chocolate crumb crust is Nabisco Famous Chocolate Wafers, but we didn't care for the flavor of these crusts unbaked and found them somewhat tough (if sliceable) baked. After trying without much success to soften the crust with a percentage of fresh white bread crumbs, we made a leap of faith to Oreo cookies pulverized straight up with their filling. We hoped that the creaminess of the centers would lend flavor and softness to the finished crust. The Oreo flavor came through loud and clear, and the creamy centers, along with a bit of butter, prevented the baked crumbs from becoming tough. No additional sugar or even salt was required. Ten minutes in a 350-degree oven set the crust nicely; higher temperatures burned the cocoa. The crisp salty-sweet chocolate crumbs gave the rich filling voice and definition. Cloaked with whipped cream, this pie is a masterpiece.

Chocolate Cream Pie

SERVES 8 TO 10

For the best chocolate flavor and texture, we recommend either Callebaut semisweet and unsweetened chocolates or Hershey's Special Dark and Hershey's unsweetened chocolates. Do not combine the yolks and sugar in advance of making the filling—the sugar will begin to break down the yolks, and the finished cream will be pitted.

CHOCOLATE COOKIE CRUMB CRUST

16	Oreo cookies with filling, broken into rough pieces (about 2 1/2 cups)
2	tablespoons unsalted butter, melted and cooled

CHOCOLATE CREAM FILLING

2 1/2	cups half-and-half
	Pinch salt
1/3	cup (2 1/3 ounces) sugar
2	tablespoons cornstarch
6	large egg yolks, at room temperature
6	tablespoons (3/4 stick) cold unsalted butter, cut into 6 pieces
6	ounces semisweet or bittersweet chocolate, finely chopped
1	ounce unsweetened chocolate, finely chopped
1	teaspoon vanilla extract

WHIPPED CREAM TOPPING

1 1/2	cups heavy cream, chilled
1 1/2	tablespoons sugar
1/2	teaspoon vanilla extract

1. FOR THE CRUST: Adjust an oven rack to the middle position and heat the oven to 350 degrees. In a food processor, process the cookies with fifteen 1-second pulses, then let the machine run until the crumbs are uniformly fine, about 15 seconds. (Alternatively, place the cookies in a large zipper-lock plastic bag and crush with a rolling pin.) Transfer the crumbs to a medium bowl, drizzle with the butter, and use your fingers to combine until the butter is evenly distributed.

2. Transfer the crumbs to a 9-inch glass pie plate. Following illustration 1 on page 197, use the bottom of a 1/2 cup measuring cup to press the crumbs evenly into the bottom and up the sides, forming a crust. Refrigerate the lined pie plate 20 minutes to firm the crumbs, then bake until the crumbs are fragrant and set, about 10 minutes. Cool on a wire rack while preparing the filling.

3. FOR THE FILLING: Bring the half-and-half, salt, and about 3 tablespoons of the sugar to a simmer in a medium saucepan over medium-high heat, stirring occasionally with a wooden spoon to dissolve the sugar. Stir together the remaining sugar and the cornstarch in a small bowl. Whisk the yolks thoroughly in a medium bowl until slightly thickened, about 30 seconds. Sprinkle the cornstarch mixture over the yolks and whisk, scraping down the sides of the bowl, if necessary, until the mixture is glossy and the sugar has begun to dissolve, about 1 minute. When the half-and-half reaches a full simmer, drizzle about 1/2 cup hot half-and-half over the yolks, whisking constantly to temper; then whisk the egg yolk mixture into the simmering half-and-half (the mixture should thicken in about 30 seconds). Return to a simmer, whisking constantly, until 3 or 4 bubbles burst on the surface and the mixture is thickened and glossy, about 15 seconds longer.

4. Off the heat, whisk in the butter until incorporated; add the chocolates and whisk until melted, scraping the pan bottom with a rubber spatula to fully incorporate. Stir in the vanilla, then immediately pour the filling through a fine-mesh sieve set over a bowl. Using a spatula, scrape the strained filling into the baked and cooled crust. Press plastic wrap directly on the surface of the filling and refrigerate the pie until the filling is cold and firm, about 3 hours.

5. FOR THE TOPPING: When ready to serve, beat the cream and sugar in the chilled bowl of an electric mixer at medium speed to soft peaks; add the vanilla. Continue to beat to barely stiff peaks. Spread or pipe the whipped cream over the chilled filling. Serve immediately.

COCONUT CREAM PIE

COCONUT CREAM PIE SHOULD BE A FLUFFY cloud of a dessert, a sweet finish to a satisfying home-cooked meal. But to imagine the taste of a coconut cream pie and to taste one on the plate in front of you are likely to be discordant experiences. We discovered this firsthand when we whipped up a few recipes. These coconut cream pies were not the dreamily soft, smooth and satiny, delicately perfumed, luscious cream pie fillings floating in crisp crusts we had hoped for. Instead, they were disappointingly heavy, leaden, pasty, noxiously sweet, bland vanilla puddings in soggy pie shells.

First we went to work on the crust. Though a plain pastry crust is typical of a coconut cream pie, we were not the least bit wowed—the crust was fully prebaked and started out perfectly crisp, but when the filling went in, it quickly became soggy. It was a graham cracker crust—a somewhat unorthodox but not completely odd option—that was the crowd-pleaser. Its crisp, sandy texture, sturdy build, and substantial presence were the perfect contrast to the creamy smooth filling. Its sweet, toasty flavor also complemented the filling's gentle flavors.

It occurred to us, though, that the flavor of the graham cracker crust could be heightened and made to better fit its role by adding some coconut to it. In our next attempts, we toasted some shredded coconut until it was golden brown, then processed it along with the graham crackers so that it could be broken down into the finest bits. The coconut was a welcome addition; though it offered only a little flavor, a quarter cup of it dispersed throughout the cracker crumbs gave the crust that characteristic fibrous, nubby coconut crunch.

Many recipes for coconut cream pie fillings are boring and domesticated. They consist of no more than eggs, sugar, cornstarch or flour, and cream or milk. In a nutshell, they are vanilla cream pies garnished with a spray of toasted shredded coconut. We wanted to breathe some life into this downtrodden pie by pumping the filling full of true coconut flavor.

The first thing we needed to do was find the right kind of cream or "milk" to use. We made versions with half-and-half, milk, and coconut milk. As we expected, the first two were boring, bland puddings. The coconut milk filling had a delicate coconut flavor and aroma, but it was far too rich to be palatable. We pulled back on the coconut milk and tried a filling made with one 14-ounce can of coconut milk cut with a cup of whole milk. Much better, but still we felt we needed to work in more coconut flavor.

We stirred some toasted shredded coconut into the filling, but the long stringy shreds suspended in the otherwise smooth filling were unappealing. Next, we took the advice of a recipe that suggested steeping unsweetened shredded coconut (which comes shredded in fine flecks and is available in natural food and Asian grocery stores) in the milk to extract some of its flavor; the coconut was then strained out and pressed to remove any liquid that it was withholding. Though this technique didn't yield the results expected—the steeped mixture didn't have much more flavor and was a nuisance to boot—we did make the fortuitous discovery that the unsweetened shredded coconut itself had good, pure coconut flavor. We captured this delicate coconut flavor by leaving the tiny bits in the filling. One-half cup of coconut in the filling was good; any more and it overran the smoothness of the filling.

Next, we tasted a filling thickened with cornstarch and one with flour. The cornstarch, as we expected, made a filling with a lighter, more natural feel; the flour made a heavy, starchy goo. One-quarter cup of cornstarch was just the right amount to allow the filling to set up into a firm texture. When chilled, the pie sliced neatly and cleanly. The filling had just enough resistance to keep it from slipping and sliding onto the plate.

As for eggs, some recipes called for whole eggs, some for just yolks, and a few for both. The number called for ranged from two to six. Our preference was for five yolks. This number made a filling with a smooth, lush, supple mouthfeel and a full, deep flavor. By comparison, fillings with whole eggs—even with whole eggs plus yolks—had a leaner, gummier texture and a hollow flavor. In addition, their color wasn't as appealing as an all-yolk filling.

We were now very close to a final recipe. The last adjustments were to add some salt and vanilla to heighten and round out the flavors. Some butter whisked into the hot filling just before pouring it into its shell was the finale that smoothed out any rough edges and made the coconut cream feel and taste superbly creamy, rich, and silky, but not so unctuous as to make one slice—topped with a puff of whipped cream—a challenge to eat.

Coconut Cream Pie

SERVES 8 TO 10

Unsweetened shredded coconut is available in natural food stores as well as in Asian grocery stores. When toasting the coconut, keep a close eye on it because it burns quite easily.

CRUST

5	tablespoons unsweetened shredded coconut
9	graham crackers (about 5 ounces), broken into rough pieces
2	tablespoons sugar
5	tablespoons unsalted butter, melted

FILLING

1	(14-ounce) can coconut milk, well stirred (*not* cream of coconut)
1	cup whole milk
1/2	cup (1 1/4 ounces) unsweetened shredded coconut
2/3	cup (4 2/3 ounces) sugar
1/4	teaspoon salt
5	large egg yolks
1/4	cup (1 ounce) cornstarch
1 1/2	teaspoons vanilla extract
2	tablespoons unsalted butter, cut into 4 pieces

WHIPPED CREAM TOPPING

1 1/2	cups heavy cream, chilled
1 1/2	tablespoons sugar
1/2	teaspoon vanilla extract
1 1/2	teaspoons dark rum (optional)

1. FOR THE CRUST: Adjust an oven rack to the middle position and heat the oven to 325 degrees. Spread the 5 tablespoons coconut in a 9-inch glass pie plate and toast in the oven until golden brown, about 9 minutes, stirring 2 or 3 times. When cool enough to handle, reserve 1 tablespoon for garnishing the finished pie.

2. Pulse the graham crackers and the remaining 4 tablespoons toasted coconut in a food processor until the crackers are broken down into coarse crumbs, about ten 1-second pulses. Process the mixture to evenly fine crumbs, about 12 seconds more. Transfer the crumbs to a medium bowl and stir in the sugar to combine; add the melted butter and toss with a fork until the crumbs are evenly moistened. Wipe out the now-empty pie plate and empty the crumb mixture into it. Following illustration 1 on page 197, use the bottom of a 1/2 cup measuring cup to press the crumbs evenly into the bottom and up the sides, forming a crust. Bake the crust until deep golden brown and fragrant, about 22 minutes. Cool the crust on a wire rack while making the filling.

3. FOR THE FILLING: Bring the coconut milk, milk, shredded coconut, 1/3 cup sugar, and the salt to a simmer in a medium saucepan over medium-high heat, stirring occasionally with a wooden spoon to dissolve the sugar. When the mixture reaches a simmer, whisk the egg yolks in a medium bowl to break them up, then whisk in the remaining 1/3 cup sugar and cornstarch until well combined and no lumps remain. Gradually whisk the simmering liquid into the yolk mixture to temper it, then return the mixture to the saucepan, scraping the bowl with a rubber spatula. Bring the mixture to a simmer over medium heat, whisking constantly, until 3 or 4 bubbles burst on the surface and the mixture is thickened, about 30 seconds. Off the heat, whisk in the vanilla and butter. Pour the filling into the cooled crust, press a sheet of plastic wrap directly on the surface of the filling, and refrigerate until the filling is cold and firm, at least 3 hours.

4. FOR THE TOPPING: When ready to serve, beat the cream and sugar in the chilled bowl of an electric mixer at medium speed to soft peaks; add the vanilla and rum, if using. Continue to beat to barely stiff peaks. Spread or pipe the whipped cream over the chilled filling. Sprinkle the reserved 1 tablespoon toasted coconut over the whipped cream. Serve.

TARTE TATIN

TARTE TATIN, A FRENCH DESSERT SAID
to have been invented by two sisters named Tatin
at their hotel in the Loire Valley, is basically an
apple tart. The apples, however, are caramelized,
and the tart is served upside down; therefore, the
dessert looks and tastes much more special.

The first step in the making of tarte Tatin takes
place on the stove, not in the oven. The apples,
neatly arranged in a tarte Tatin pan or a skillet, are
boiled in a buttery caramel sauce over ferociously
high heat until they absorb the syrup and become
virtually candied. These syrup-soaked apples are
then covered with a circle of pastry, and the tart
is baked. After baking, the tart is flipped over,
revealing concentric circles of apples glazed with
a golden caramel. It can be served with whipped
cream or vanilla ice cream or with a tangy topping that offsets the sweetness of the caramel, such
as crème fraîche or a mixture of cream and sour
cream whipped together. A good tarte Tatin is one
that tastes like caramelized apples, not like apples
coated with caramel or, worse, an unidentifiable
caramel glop.

When tarte Tatin first came to this country, all
sorts of different recipes for it appeared. Some were
based on traditional French formulas, but others
were highly Americanized. The latter, generally
speaking, simply do not work. The unsuccessful

recipes vary, but most of them exhibit one of two
serious flaws. One of these mistakes is using sliced
or chopped apples, which makes a wet, loose tart
that sprawls and collapses when inverted. The
second common error in Americanized recipes
is the decision to caramelize the apples on top of
the stove after the tart has been completely baked.
Caramelizing a fully baked tart is simply impossible. If the tart turns out juicy, it will not caramelize at all, and if it bakes up dry, it will burn. And
you won't even know which disaster is about to
befall you because you cannot see what the apples
are doing underneath the crust.

Tarte Tatin is typically made with apple quarters. Some recipes, however, call for apple halves,
and we found this idea intriguing. When made
with apple quarters, tarte Tatin can sometimes
seem a little light on fruit because the apples lose
juice and shrink when caramelized. When we
tried using halved apples, though, we encountered
a new set of problems.

In our first experiments, we had trouble getting
the caramel to penetrate all the way through such
large pieces of apple. While we eventually resolved
this problem simply by cooking the apples longer,
we still were not enthralled by the results. Our
tarte Tatin now struck us as pulpy and mushy, and
there seemed to be too much fruit in relation to
crust. Worse, we found that if the skillet was just a

PREPARING TARTE TATIN

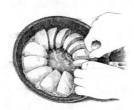

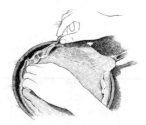

1. Place the first apple quarter
cut-side down and with an end
touching the skillet wall. As you
continue to arrange the apples,
lift each quarter on its edge while
placing the next apple quarter on
its edge, so that the apples stand
straight up. Fill the skillet middle
with the remaining quarters.

2. Return the skillet to high heat;
cook until the juices turn from
butterscotch to a rich amber
color, 10 to 12 minutes. Remove
the skillet from the heat and,
using a fork or the tip of a paring
knife, turn the apples onto the
uncaramelized sides.

3. Slide the prepared dough off
the baking sheet over the skillet
and, taking care not to burn your
fingers, tuck the dough edges
gently up against the skillet wall.
Bake and cool as directed.

4. Place a heatproof serving platter over the skillet and hold it
tightly against the skillet. Invert
the skillet and platter and set the
platter on the counter. Lift the
skillet up from the platter, leaving
the tart behind.

tad too small—or the apples unusually juicy—the caramel overflowed the pan during the caramelization process, making a horrible mess.

In the end, we abandoned the apple halves, but these experiments nonetheless proved useful since they gave us an idea of how to refine the original method using quarters. When you make a tarte Tatin with halved apples, the apples rest on the outer peeled surface so that the full cut side faces up. Apple quarters, by contrast, tend to flop over onto a cut side, but we reasoned that if we tipped each apple quarter onto its cut edge and held it there while we laid the next quarter in place, we could fit more fruit in the skillet. It turned out that we were able to cram an entire extra apple into the skillet this way, with very good results. The tart looked fuller and tasted fruitier, but it did not suffer from apple overload or overflow onto the stove.

The only problem now was that the apples, because they were almost perpendicular to the skillet, caramelized only on the skillet side, leaving the other side pale and sour. One recipe solved this problem by flipping the apples over during the caramelization process. This maneuver sounded tricky to us, but, as the recipe promised, it was easily accomplished by spearing the quarters with a table fork or the tip of a paring knife. Even though the caramelized side of the apples is very soft, the side facing up remains firm enough not to tear when the apples are speared and flipped. Furthermore, even if the skillet doesn't have a nonstick coating, the apple quarters never stick.

We have always used Granny Smith apples for tarte Tatin, but many recipes recommend Golden Delicious, and one recipe that we had on hand specified, of all things, Red Delicious, which, it was claimed, gave the tart a pretty look because of the elongated shape. We tested both Golden and Red Delicious as well as Gala and Fuji apples.

The results were surprising. We had expected most of the apples—certainly the Red Delicious—to fall apart, but all held their shape quite well. Flavor, however, was another story. The Golden Delicious apples were acceptable, if barely, but the rest were tasteless. We tried adding lemon juice to augment the flavor of the insipid apples, but did not find this to be an effective remedy. Lemon

juice did cut the sweetness of the caramel, but it did nothing to boost apple flavor. You need to start with apples that are flavorful to begin with, and if supermarket apples are your only option, we think it is safest to stick with Granny Smiths.

Finally, there is the matter of the crust. A crust for tarte Tatin needs extra durability and strength, and so bakers of tarte Tatin usually make the crust with an egg. Egg pastry does not have to be sweetened, but it is indisputably more delicious when it is, and therein lies the problem. Sugar makes pastry dough sticky, crumbly, and generally difficult to handle, and it also tends to fuse the spacers—the little bits of butter that make pastry flaky—leaving the baked crust crunchy, cookie-like, and a little hard. After struggling with these problems for years, we finally discovered that the solution was to use confectioners' sugar rather than regular granulated. Granulated sugar is too coarse to dissolve well in dough. It remains in individual grains, then melts into tiny droplets of sticky syrup that wreak havoc. Confectioners' sugar, by contrast, simply disappears, sweetening the dough without causing any problems. It makes a superbly flaky egg pastry, worthy of the dessert masterpiece called tarte Tatin.

Tarte Tatin

SERVES 8

If the caramel isn't cooked to a rich amber color, the apples will look pale and dull rather than shiny and appealingly caramelized.

FLAKY EGG PASTRY

1 1/3	cups (6 7/8 ounces) unbleached all-purpose flour, plus more for dusting the work surface
1/4	cup (1 ounce) confectioners' sugar
1/2	teaspoon salt
8	tablespoons (1 stick) cold unsalted butter, cut into 1/4-inch pieces
1	large egg, cold, beaten

CARAMELIZED APPLES

8	tablespoons (1 stick) unsalted butter
3/4	cup (5 1/4 ounces) plus 1 tablespoon sugar
6	large Granny Smith apples (about 3 pounds), peeled, quartered, and cored

TANGY CREAM TOPPING

1	cup heavy cream, cold
½	cup sour cream, cold

1. FOR THE PASTRY: Pulse the flour, sugar, and salt in a food processor until combined. Scatter the butter over the dry ingredients; process until the mixture resembles cornmeal, 7 to 12 seconds. Turn the mixture into a medium bowl; add the egg and stir with a fork until little balls form. Press the balls together with the back of the fork, then gather the dough into a ball. Wrap the dough in plastic, then flatten it into a 4-inch disk. Refrigerate at least 30 minutes. (The dough can be refrigerated overnight; let stand at room temperature to warm slightly before rolling it out.)

2. Unwrap the dough and turn out onto a well-floured work surface. Sprinkle with additional flour. Starting from the disk center outward, roll the dough into a 12-inch circle, strewing flour underneath to prevent sticking. Slide a lightly floured, rimless baking sheet or pizza peel under the crust, cover with plastic, and refrigerate while preparing the apples. Adjust an oven rack to the upper-middle position and heat the oven to 375 degrees.

3. FOR THE FILLING: Melt the butter in a 9-inch ovenproof skillet; remove from the heat and sprinkle evenly with the sugar. Following the illustrations on page 216, arrange the apples in the skillet by placing the first apple quarter, cut-side down and with an end touching the skillet wall. As you continue to arrange the apples, lift each quarter on its edge while placing the next apple quarter on its edge, so that the apple quarters stand straight up. Fill the skillet middle with the remaining quarters, placing them cut-side down.

4. Return the skillet to high heat; cook until the juices turn from butterscotch to a rich amber color, 10 to 12 minutes. Remove the skillet from the heat and, using a fork or the tip of a paring knife, turn the apples onto their uncaramelized sides. Return the skillet to the highest heat; boil to cook the uncaramelized sides of the apples, about 5 minutes longer.

5. Remove the skillet from the heat. Slide the prepared dough from the baking sheet onto the apple filling and, taking care not to burn your fingers, tuck the dough edges gently up against the skillet wall.

6. Bake until the crust is golden brown, 25 to 30 minutes. Set the skillet on a wire rack; cool about 20 minutes. Loosen the edges with a knife, place a serving plate on top of the skillet, and, holding the plate and skillet together firmly, invert the tart onto the serving plate. Scrape out any apples that stick to the skillet and put them back into place. (The tart can be kept for several hours at room temperature, but unmold it onto a dish that can withstand mild heat. Before serving, warm the tart for 10 minutes in 200-degree oven.)

7. FOR THE TOPPING: Beat the heavy cream and sour cream at medium-high speed in the bowl of an electric mixer until the mixture thickens and holds soft but definite peaks. (The topping can be made a day ahead; cover and refrigerate.) Accompany each wedge of the tart with a generous dollop of topping.

FREE-FORM SUMMER FRUIT TART

THE MOST FLAVORFUL DESSERTS ARE OFTEN the simplest ones. Such is the case with this free-form tart made with summer fruit at the height of its season. Given the simplicity of the dessert—fresh fruit placed unceremoniously on top of pastry—we wanted to make this rustic dessert with an easy-to-work-with pastry that would be tender, flaky, and flavorful.

We began our testing by making a variety of doughs, all of which we found too firm or too bland. We wanted a relatively soft dough that would be easy to roll out and would provide a delicate, but flavorful contrast to the fruit, so we tested different liquid and fat ingredients. Although vegetable shortening made the dough tender, it added no flavor and therefore was rejected. Butter alone worked best. We tried adding eggs—whole eggs and egg yolks, alone or in combination—and found that although the eggs contributed to the tenderness of the dough, they did not add as much flavor as we wanted. We then tried heavy cream, buttermilk, yogurt, sour cream, and cream cheese.

The heavy cream made the dough too tender, the cream cheese was too overpowering, but the buttermilk, yogurt, and sour cream worked well. Of the three, our favorite was sour cream in combination with a couple tablespoons of water. The sour cream added just the right amount of richness and tang without detracting from the fruit flavors. We found that 2 teaspoons of sugar was ideal. Any more produced a dough too delicate and tender for our purposes. Any less and the dough was too firm.

At this point, tasters gave high marks to our tart dough. But something was missing. Following the lead of a similar tart dough recipe we found, we replaced ¼ cup of the flour with cornmeal and were pleased with the results. The cornmeal played a supporting, not dominant, role that made the dough even more flaky and tender. It also added a subtle earthy component to the buttery flavor of the tart pastry. We were surprised that although tasters much preferred this pastry to the one without the cornmeal, they could not immediately identify the difference in ingredients.

We tried our tart dough with a variety of fruit fillings and found that 3 cups of prepared fruit worked best. We liked tarts made with a mixture of berries, such as strawberries, blueberries, blackberries, and raspberries, or with pitted, sliced stone fruit, such as peaches, nectarines, plums, and apricots. Tasting the fruit before assembling the tart helped us determine how much sugar to sprinkle over the fruit. We found that 3 teaspoons sugar sprinkled over the fruit and 2 tablespoons butter slivered on top generally gave the right amount of sweetness and flavor. If, however, the fruit you are using is especially tart or underripe, add up to 2 additional teaspoons of sugar to the fruit.

Shaping the tart couldn't be easier. Once the dough is rolled into a 13-inch circle, 3 cups of fresh fruit is placed on top, leaving a 2½-inch border. Once sprinkled with sugar and dotted with slivers of butter, the fruit is partially covered by the tart pastry as you lift up and fold over the edges of the dough. As you pick up an edge of the circle of dough and place it over the fruit, the dough will pleat naturally. There is no need to force the dough into a particular shape. The pastry will cover the edges of the fruit and leave the center exposed. Brush the edges of the pastry with water and then sprinkle them with sugar to create a crisp, sweet surface once the tart is baked. Tasters liked the tart served warm or at room temperature.

Free-Form Summer Fruit Tart
SERVES 6

This is a very easy dough to work with. If, however, it becomes too sticky and soft when rolling, slide the dough and parchment paper onto a baking sheet and refrigerate until firm, about 20 minutes. Choose a mixture of fresh berries: blueberries, blackberries, raspberries, and strawberries or a mixture of pitted and sliced stone fruit: peaches,

SHAPING A FREE-FORM TART

1. Place the fruit in the center of the rolled-out dough, leaving a 2½-inch border.

2. Fold the dough border up over the filling, using the underlying parchment to lift and pleat the dough to fit snugly.

nectarines, plums, and apricots. Before assembling the tart, taste the fruit to determine its level of sweetness. If the fruit is underripe or tart, sprinkle up to 2 additional teaspoons sugar over the fruit when assembling the tart.

FREE-FORM TART PASTRY

- 2 tablespoons sour cream
- 2 tablespoons ice water
- 1 cup (5 ounces) unbleached all-purpose flour
- 1/4 cup (about 1 1/3 ounces) fine stone-ground yellow cornmeal
- 2 teaspoons sugar
- 1/2 teaspoon salt
- 7 tablespoons cold unsalted butter, cut into 1/2-inch pieces

FILLING

- 3 cups fresh mixed berries or pitted stone fruit cut into 1/4-inch slices (about 1 pound)
- 5 teaspoons sugar, plus more if necessary
- 2 tablespoons unsalted butter, cut into small slivers

1. FOR THE PASTRY: Stir together the sour cream and water in a small liquid measuring cup. Set aside in the refrigerator.

2. In a food processor, process the flour, cornmeal, sugar, and salt until combined, four 1-second pulses. Scatter half of the butter pieces over the flour mixture and process to cut the butter into the flour mixture until the butter is the size of small peas, about four 1-second pulses. Scatter the remaining butter over the flour mixture and pulse to cut the butter into the flour mixture until most of the butter is incorporated and some pea-size bits remain. While processing, pour the sour cream mixture through the feed tube until the dough just comes together around the blade, about five 1-second pulses. Turn the dough onto a sheet of plastic wrap, flatten into a 6-inch disk, wrap tightly, and refrigerate at least 2 hours or up to 2 days before rolling.

3. When ready to roll and bake the tart, adjust an oven rack to the middle position and heat the oven to 400 degrees.

4. Remove the dough from the refrigerator. Unwrap and roll the dough between 2 large sheets of parchment paper into a 13-inch round. Slide the dough, still between the sheets of parchment paper, onto a baking sheet and refrigerate until firm, about 20 minutes.

5. TO ASSEMBLE THE TART: Remove the dough and baking sheet from the refrigerator and peel off the top sheet of parchment paper. Pile the fruit in the center of the dough, leaving a 2 1/2-inch border of dough. Sprinkle 3 teaspoons of the sugar over the fruit (or more if necessary) and dot with the slivers of butter. Fold the edges of the dough over the fruit following illustration 2 on page 219. (If the dough is sticking to the parchment, run a bench scraper or thin metal spatula under the pastry to loosen it from the paper.) Using a pastry brush, brush the edges of the dough with water and sprinkle with the remaining 2 teaspoons sugar.

6. Bake until the crust is golden brown and crisp and the fruit is bubbling, about 40 minutes. Place the baking sheet on a wire rack and allow the tart to cool for 10 minutes. Using a large offset spatula, transfer the tart to the wire rack to cool an additional 10 minutes. The tart may be served warm or at room temperature.

> VARIATION

Individual Summer Fruit Tartlets

Follow the instructions for Free-Form Summer Fruit Tart and, instead of rolling the dough into a 13-inch round, divide the chilled 6-inch disk of dough into 6 equal pieces. Roll each piece between 2 half sheets of parchment paper into a 6-inch round. Trim the parchment under each round of dough, leaving a 1 1/2-inch border around the edges. Chill each round until ready to assemble the tartlets. Remove the top sheet of parchment from each round of dough. Place the dough rounds and bottom parchment on a large baking sheet. Pile 1/2 cup fruit in the center of each round, leaving a 1 1/2-inch border of dough. Divide the 3 teaspoons sugar (or more if necessary) and 2 tablespoons butter among the tartlets. Lift the borders of dough over the fruit in folds, brush the edges with water, and sprinkle the edges of the tartlets with the 2 teaspoons sugar. Bake as instructed until the crusts are golden brown, about 30 minutes. Cool as instructed in step 6.

Free-Form Apple Tart

BECAUSE A FREE-FORM APPLE TART HAS no top crust to seal in moisture, the filling can dry out during baking. Obviously, the variety of apple used would be key. And the method used to prepare and cook the apples would affect their taste and texture. Should they be sliced thick or thin when placed in the tart? Should they be precooked or raw?

To answer these questions, we gathered some of the most commonly available apple varieties: Granny Smith, Gala, McIntosh, Braeburn, Fuji, and Red and Golden Delicious. We tested each type in a tart. In every case but one, the apples cooked up tough, dry, and leathery. The exception was the McIntosh, which baked to the other extreme; they were so moist that they turned to mush. Of the varieties tested, we found that Granny Smiths, Galas, and McIntosh had the most distinct flavor after being baked. It looked like the solution that had worked in our Classic Apple Pie recipe (to combine Grannies with Macs) would here, too. We tested Macs with both Granny Smiths and Galas and, sure enough, tasters preferred the Granny-Mac combo. The apple filling had good apple flavor and a decent texture, but it was still a bit dry.

Next, we attempted to cook the apples before placing them in the tart, hoping this would make the filling more moist. We sautéed the apples, reduced their cooking juices, and added the liquid to the tart. This was not a success: The apples turned mushy, and the pure apple flavor we had wanted to preserve was lost during precooking.

We returned to our original method—layering raw apple slices into the tart—but this time sliced them thinner and increased the oven temperature. These thinner slices were more moist but still not perfect. A colleague suggested that we sprinkle the apples with sugar as they cooked. This turned out to be a great idea—the sugar prevented the apples from drying out in the oven and the filling was moist but not runny. When sugar is sprinkled on top of fruit during baking, it combines with some of the moisture the fruit has released and forms a syrup. This syrup doesn't give up water easily, so the syrup doesn't evaporate and thus keeps the filling moist.

Free-Form Apple Tart
SERVES 6

When all of the apples have been sliced, you should have a total of about 4½ cups. Serve slices of the warm tart with a scoop of ice cream or lightly sweetened Whipped Cream (page 500).

- 1   recipe Free-Form Tart Pastry (page 220)
- 2   large Granny Smith apples (about 1 pound)
- 2   large McIntosh apples (about 1 pound)
- 1   tablespoon juice from 1 lemon
- 3   tablespoons sugar, plus 1 tablespoon for sprinkling on the crust
- ⅛   teaspoon ground cinnamon

1. Prepare the pastry as directed through step 4.
2. While the rolled dough is chilling, peel, core, and cut the apples into ¼-inch-thick slices and toss with the lemon juice, 3 tablespoons sugar, and cinnamon in a large bowl.
3. Remove the dough on the baking sheet from the refrigerator and peel off the top sheet of parchment paper. Pile the fruit in the center of the dough, leaving a 2½-inch border of dough. Fold the edges of the dough over the fruit following illustration 2 on page 219. (If the dough is sticking to the parchment, run a bench scraper or thin bladed knife under the pastry to loosen it from the paper.) With cupped hands, gently press the dough toward the filling, reinforcing the shape of the tart and compacting the apples. Chill the formed tart on the pan for 30 minutes.
4. Adjust an oven rack to the lower-middle position and heat the oven to 375 degrees. Using a pastry brush, brush the edges of the dough with water and sprinkle with the remaining 1 tablespoon sugar. Bake until the crust is deep golden brown and crisp and the apples are tender, about 60 minutes. Place the baking sheet on a wire rack and allow the tart to cool for 10 minutes. Using a large offset spatula, transfer the tart to the wire rack to cool an additional 10 minutes. The tart may be served warm or at room temperature.

> VARIATION
Individual Apple Tartlets
The individual tartlets can withstand a slightly higher oven temperature of 400 degrees.

Follow the instructions for Free-Form Apple Tart and, instead of rolling out the dough into a 13-inch round, divide the chilled 6-inch disk of dough into 6 equal pieces. Roll each piece between 2 half sheets of parchment paper into a 6-inch round. Trim the parchment under each round of dough, leaving a 1½-inch border around the edges. Chill each round while the apple filling is being prepared, about 20 minutes. Remove the top sheet of parchment from each round of dough. Place the dough and parchment on a large baking sheet. Pile ¾ cup fruit in the center of each round, leaving a 1½-inch border of dough. Lift the borders of dough over the fruit in folds. With cupped hands, gently press the dough toward the filling, reinforcing the shape of the tartlets and compacting the apples. Chill the formed tartlets on the pan for 30 minutes. Brush the dough edges with water and sprinkle with 1 tablespoon sugar. Bake on the middle rack in a 400-degree oven until the crusts are deep golden brown and the apples are tender, about 30 minutes. Cool as instructed in step 4.

SWEET TART PASTRY

OVER THE YEARS WE HAVE COME TO APPRECIATE traditional American pie dough as well as its European cousin, pâte sucrée (literally, "sugar dough"). But many American pie bakers have yet to discover the virtues of sweet pastry dough. While regular pie dough is tender and flaky, sweet pastry dough is tender and crisp. Fine-textured, buttery rich, and crumbly, it is often described as cookie-like. In fact, cookies are actually descendants of sweet pastry dough—a dough deemed so delicious by the French that it was considered worth eating on its own. There are also differences in the dough's relationship to the filling. Rather than encasing a deep hearty filling, a tart shell shares the stage with its filling. Traditional tart fillings—caramel, frangipane, pastry cream, or even jam, often adorned with glazed fresh fruits or nuts—would seem excessive if housed in a deeper pie. But these intense flavors and textures are perfect in thin layers balanced by a crisp, thin pastry.

Though you can make sweet pastry as you would cookie dough, by creaming the butter and sugar together, then adding flour and finally egg, we found this technique too time-consuming. Like pie pastries, most sweet pastry recipes direct the cook to cut butter into flour by hand or food processor and then add liquid. Knowing cold butter and minimal handling to be critical to the success of this method, we headed straight for the food processor. Pulsing very cold butter with dry ingredients to obtain a fine, pebbly consistency took all of 15 seconds. The addition of liquid ingredients with the food processor took about 25 seconds. Armed with this quick, no-fuss technique, we wanted to tweak the major players in the dough to tease out the most tender, tastiest pastry imaginable.

The first ingredients to come under scrutiny were the butter and sugar. The higher the proportion of butter in a pâte sucrée, the more delicate its crumb. We experimented with the amount and found 8 tablespoons to be the maximum allowable for ease of handling. More butter simply made the dough too soft and did not improve its flavor or texture. As for the sugar, the traditional half cup did not seem overly sweet, and any less than that produced a dough lacking in flavor and tenderness. Most recipes recommend the use of superfine sugar (thought to be important for dissolving in a dough with so little liquid), but because few people have it in their pantry, we tried confectioners' sugar, an ingredient most people have on hand. We found that ⅔ cup confectioners' sugar gave us a crisper dough than the one made with granulated sugar.

Next up for examination were the liquid ingredients. Though most recipes call for a whole egg, some call for a combination of egg yolk and cream. (As in any cookie dough, the egg lends structure to a dough that would otherwise be completely crumbly.) Testing these side by side, we discovered that the yolk and cream combination (1 yolk and 1 tablespoon of cream) created a lovely crust with a degree of flakiness, a quality we value over the slightly firmer dough produced when using a whole egg alone.

The last major player to be manipulated was the flour. Perfectly happy with our tests using all-purpose, we nevertheless performed a couple of tests using half all-purpose and half pastry flour, as well as half all-purpose and half cake flour. Our reasoning was this: Low-protein flours, such as pastry and cake flours, tend to develop less gluten, thus yielding a more tender dough. We were surprised to learn that pastry and cake flours are identical in composition; cake flour is simply bleached. (Bleached flour improves the rise of high-sugar batters like cake batter; pastry flour is used in pie doughs where rise isn't so important.) To be honest, we liked the dough made with half pastry flour. It was a bit more tender and delicate than the one made with all-purpose and no more difficult to work with. But the improvement was not impressive enough for us to recommend using pastry flour, particularly since it's not as readily available as all-purpose. The dough made with half cake flour had a pleasing texture as well, but a less-pleasing flavor; bleaching can impart a slightly metallic taste to flour, which can be detected in such a simple recipe.

Sweet pastry dough typically requires at least an hour of refrigerated resting time for the liquid ingredients to hydrate the dough fully and make it more manageable. In fact, a two-hour rest is even better. The butter gives the dough a nice plasticity if the dough is cold enough and makes rolling relatively easy. We knew it would be a challenge to roll out the dough directly on the counter. The best results were obtained with minimal flouring and by rolling the dough out between two layers of wide parchment paper or plastic wrap without letting it become warm. Though many recipes suggest that a sweet pastry dough can simply be pressed into a pan, our tests did not support this recommendation. The patchwork technique made the crucial "even thickness" all but unattainable, and the imperfectly fused pieces did not have the same structural integrity as a correctly fitted, single sheath of dough. The patched crust crumbled along the fault lines as it was unmolded or cut.

A half hour in the freezer "set" the dough nicely to prepare it for blind baking (baking the shell without any filling). A baking sheet placed directly beneath the tart shell (to conduct heat evenly to the crust bottom) browned the tart beautifully. Because of the crust's delicate nature, the metal weights used to blind-bake the tart are best left in place until the crust's edges are distinctly brown, about 30 minutes, at which point the weights can be removed and the top side of the crust allowed to brown.

Sweet Tart Pastry for Prebaked Tart Shell

MAKES ONE 9- TO 9½-INCH TART SHELL

If the dough becomes soft and sticky while rolling, chill it again until it becomes easier to work with. This is preferable to adding more flour, which will damage the delicate, crisp texture of the dough. We find a tapered French rolling pin to be the most precise instrument for rolling tart pastry. Bake the tart shell in a 9- to 9½-inch tart pan with a removable bottom and fluted sides about 1 to 1⅛ inches high. See the illustrations on page 149 for tips on working with this dough.

1	large egg yolk
1	tablespoon heavy cream
½	teaspoon vanilla extract
1¼	cups (6¼ ounces) unbleached all-purpose flour, plus more for dusting the work surface
⅔	cup (2⅔ ounces) confectioners' sugar
¼	teaspoon salt
8	tablespoons (1 stick) cold unsalted butter, cut into ½-inch cubes

1. Whisk together the yolk, cream, and vanilla in a small bowl; set aside. Place the flour, sugar, and salt in a food processor and process briefly to combine. Scatter the butter pieces over the flour mixture; process to cut the butter into the flour until the mixture resembles coarse meal, about fifteen 1-second pulses. With the machine running, add the egg mixture and process until the dough just comes together, about 12 seconds. Turn the dough onto a sheet of plastic wrap and press into a 6-inch disk. Wrap in plastic and refrigerate at least 1 hour or up to 48 hours.

2. Remove the dough from the refrigerator (if refrigerated longer than 1 hour, let stand at room

temperature until malleable). Unwrap and roll out between 2 lightly floured large sheets of parchment paper or plastic wrap to a 13-inch round. (If the dough is soft and sticky, slip it onto a baking sheet and refrigerate until workable, 20 to 30 minutes.) Transfer the dough to a tart pan by rolling the dough loosely around the rolling pin and unrolling over a 9- to 9½-inch tart pan with a removable bottom. Working around the circumference of the pan, ease the dough into the pan corners by gently lifting the edge with one hand while pressing it into the corners with the other hand. Press the dough against the fluted sides of the pan. (If some sections of the edge are too thin, reinforce them by folding the excess dough back on itself.) Run the rolling pin over the top of the tart pan to remove the excess dough. Set the dough-lined tart pan on a large plate and freeze 30 minutes. (The dough-lined tart pan can be sealed in a gallon-size zipper-lock plastic bag and frozen up to 1 month.)

3. Meanwhile, adjust an oven rack to the middle position and heat the oven to 375 degrees. Set the dough-lined tart pan on a baking sheet, press a 12-inch square of foil into the frozen tart shell and over the edge, and fill with metal or ceramic pie weights. Bake for 30 minutes, rotating halfway through the baking time. Remove from the oven and carefully remove the foil and weights by gathering the edges of the foil and pulling up and out. Continue to bake until deep golden brown, 5 to 8 minutes longer. Set the baking sheet with the tart shell on a wire rack.

TIPS FOR PERFECT TARTS

FOR STRAWBERRY TART
To fill the gaps between the whole berries, begin at the center of the tart and place quartered berries between them, pointed-side up and skin-side out, leaning the quartered berries toward the center.

FOR MIXED BERRY TART
Place the berries in a large plastic bag. Hold the bag closed with one hand and use the other to gently jostle the berries about to combine them. Empty the mixed berries into the tart.

FRESH FRUIT TART WITH PASTRY CREAM

THE PERFECT FRESH FRUIT TART HAS SEVERAL components working in concert to produce complementary textures and flavors. Its crust is buttery, sweet, and crisp like a sugar cookie, not flaky like a pie pastry. The pastry cream filling is creamy and lithe, just sweet enough to counter the tartness of fresh fruits and just firm enough to support their weight. A finish of jellied glaze makes the fruits sparkle and keeps them from drying out. With each forkful, you experience the buttery crumbling of crust; the chill of cool, rich, silky pastry cream; and the juicy explosion of luscious ripe fruit.

We would be using our baked sweet tart pastry but what about the filling? We gathered and prepared a number of recipes for pastry cream and even included a couple of atypical fruit tart fillings—whipped cream and crème anglaise (stirred custard), both stabilized with gelatin. These anomalies were quickly and unanimously rejected by tasters for being uninteresting and Jell-O–like, respectively. We also included basic pastry creams stabilized with gelatin and lightened with egg whites or whipped cream (both often called *crème chiboust* in the French pastry vernacular), but these more labor-intensive preparations turned out not to be worth the effort. It was evident from this tasting that a simple, basic pastry cream (see page

226) was the one to pursue.

As for timing, we found it best to prepare the pastry cream before beginning the pastry shell. In fact, it can be made a day or two in advance. This gives the cream adequate time to chill, and we found a fruit tart with filling that is cool on the tongue much more thrilling to eat. And since it is best to fill the pastry fairly close to serving time lest it become soggy, the cream must be cold when it goes into the shell and is topped with fruit.

Small, soft, whole fruits—in other words, berries—are ideal atop fresh fruit tarts. Raspberries, blackberries, and blueberries require no paring and no slicing. That means no breaking of fruit skin to release juices that can ruin a tart. Strawberries are certainly acceptable, although they do need to be hulled. Sliced strawberries can make an attractive display if arranged, glazed, and served swiftly. While fruits like mangoes and papayas, with their juicy, soft, creamy textures, might seem inviting, they aren't good candidates for a tart because they quickly send their juices flowing. What's more, their irregular and awkward shapes can be difficult to slice and arrange attractively. Kiwis, however, work well and their brilliant green is a gorgeous counterpoint to the berry reds and blues. But use kiwis sparingly, as they, too, can water things down. We do not wash berries that are destined to grace a fruit tart. They need to be utterly dry and completely bruise- and blemish-free. Any excess water can cause the tart to weep, which ultimately results in a soggy bottom.

In the test kitchen, the tarts that met with the most flattery were simple ones that showed restraint, not overdesigned ones with lots of fanfare. Bear in mind that one goal is to arrange the fruit in a tight design so that very little to none of the ivory-toned pastry cream peeks out of the spaces between the fruit (see the illustration on page 224). Also, the nicest designs are those in which the tallest points are at the center of the tart, with a gradual and graceful descent to the edges.

The finishing touch on a fruit tart is the glaze. For tarts that are covered only with berries of red and blue hues, garnet-colored red currant jelly is perfect. For tarts covered with kiwi and other fair-colored fruits (for instance, golden raspberries), apricot jam

is the norm because of its neutral tones, but we took to using apple jelly because it eliminated the need to strain out chunks of fruit and then reheat.

Fresh fruit tarts are often shellacked with an armor of glaze. After glazing dozens of tarts, we know all too well that sticky brush bristles can ensnare and dislodge bits of fruit, wrecking a design. Instead, we dab, drizzle, and flick the glaze onto the tart with a pastry brush. The result is not a smooth, even coat but something more dazzling—a sheath of droplets that catch the light and glisten like dewdrops. The caveat is that the glaze must have the correct consistency. Too thin and the glaze will run off the fruit and pool in valleys; too thick and it falls from the brush in heavy globules. We found it helpful to bring the jelly to a boil, stirring it occasionally to ensure that it melts entirely, then use it straight off the stove.

Fresh Fruit Tart with Pastry Cream
SERVES 8 TO 10

The pastry cream can be made a day or two in advance, but do not fill the prebaked tart shell until just before serving. Once filled, the tart should be topped with fruit, glazed, and served within half an hour or so. See the specific variations for tips on matching the type of jelly with the fruit.

- 1 recipe Pastry Cream (page 227), thoroughly chilled
- 1 recipe Sweet Tart Pastry for Prebaked Tart Shell (page 223), fully baked and cooled to room temperature
  Fruit, unwashed (see variations that follow for specific ideas)
- ½ cup red currant or apple jelly

1. Spread the cold pastry cream over the bottom of the tart shell, using an offset spatula or large spoon. (You can press plastic wrap directly on the surface of the pastry cream and refrigerate it up to 30 minutes.) Arrange the fruit on top of the pastry cream, following a method on page 226.

2. Bring the jelly to a boil in a small saucepan over medium-high heat, stirring occasionally to smooth

out any lumps. When boiling and completely melted, apply by dabbing and flicking onto fruit with a pastry brush; add 1 teaspoon water and return the jelly to a boil if it becomes too thick to drizzle. (The tart can be refrigerated, uncovered, up to 30 minutes.) Remove the outer ring of the tart pan, slide a thin metal spatula between the bottom of the crust and the tart pan bottom to release, then slip the tart onto a cardboard round or serving platter; serve.

➤ VARIATIONS

Kiwi, Raspberry, and Blueberry Tart

Peel 2 large kiwis, halve lengthwise, and cut into half-circles about ⅜ inch thick. Arrange them in an overlapping circle propped up against the inside edge of the pastry. Sort two cups (about 9 ounces) raspberries by height, and arrange them in three tight rings just inside the kiwi, using the tallest berries to form the inner ring. Mound 1 cup (about 5 ounces) blueberries in the center. Use apple jelly to glaze this tart.

Strawberry Tart

Brush the dirt from 3 quarts (about 2½ pounds) of ripe strawberries of medium, uniform size and slice off the stem ends. Sort the berries by height and place the tallest strawberry, pointed end up, in the center of the tart. Arrange the nicest and most evenly shaped berries in tight rings around the center, placing them in order of descending height to the edge of the pastry. Quarter the remaining berries lengthwise and use them to fill gaps between the whole berries (see illustration on page 224). Use red currant jelly to glaze this tart.

Mixed Berry Tart

Sort 1 cup (about 5 ounces) blueberries, 1 cup (about 5½ ounces) blackberries, and 2 cups (about 9 ounces) raspberries, discarding any blemished fruit. Place all the berries in a large plastic bag, then very gently shake the bag to combine them (see the illustration on page 224). Empty the berries on top of the tart, distributing them in an even layer. Then, using your fingers, adjust the berries as necessary so that they cover the entire surface and the colors are evenly distributed. Use red currant jelly to glaze this tart.

PASTRY CREAM

PASTRY CREAM IS AN ESSENTIAL COMPONENT in fruit tarts, Boston cream pie, and éclairs. It is cooked in a saucepan on the stovetop like a homemade pudding. Making it is not necessarily difficult, but making it just right, we knew, would mean finding the perfect balance of ingredients— milk (or cream), eggs, sugar, and starch (usually either cornstarch or flour).

We first sought to determine which was preferable: milk, half-and-half, or heavy cream. The milk was lean on flavor, and the cream had a superfluous amount of fat. Half-and-half was the dairy of choice; the pastry cream made with it was silky in texture and agreeably, not overly, rich. To fill a 9- to 9½-inch tart shell, we needed 2 cups, sweetened with only ½ cup of sugar.

Egg yolks and sometimes whole eggs help thicken and enrich pastry cream. A whole-egg pastry cream was too light and flimsy. An all-yolk cream was richer, fuller flavored, and altogether more serious. Three yolks were too few to do the job, four (a very common proportion of yolks to dairy) were fine, but with five yolks the pastry cream was sensational—it was like smooth, edible silk, with a remarkable glossy translucency much like that of mayonnaise.

Thickener was up next. We made four batches of pastry cream, using 3 or 4 tablespoons of cornstarch or flour in each one. Four tablespoons of either starch made gummy, chewy, gluey messes of the pastry creams. Three tablespoons was the correct amount; any less would have resulted in soup. In equal amounts, cornstarch and flour were extremely close in flavor and texture, but cornstarch inched out in front with a slightly lighter, more ethereal texture and a cleaner and purer flavor; flour gave the pastry cream a trace of graininess and gumminess. That the cornstarch pastry cream was marginally easier to cook than one made with flour was a bonus. Once a cornstarch cream reaches a boil, it is done. A pastry cream with flour must remain on the heat for a few minutes to allow the raw flour flavor to cook off and the cream to reach maximum viscosity.

Most pastry cream recipes finish by whisking butter into the just-made cream. As fine-grained sandpaper removes the smallest burrs and gives wood a velveteen finish, so butter rounds out the flavor of pastry cream and endows it with a smooth, silken texture. We found that a relatively generous amount of butter (4 tablespoons) also helped the chilled cream behave better when it came time to slice a tart; it resisted sliding and slipping much more than one made without the extra butter. When the well-chilled tart was served, the pastry cream held its own.

Pastry Cream

MAKES ABOUT 3 CUPS

Don't whisk the egg yolks and sugar together until the half-and-half is already heating. Straining the finished pastry cream through a fine-mesh sieve ensures a perfectly silky texture. See page 150 for more information about preparing pastry cream.

2	cups half-and-half
1/2	cup (3 1/2 ounces) sugar
	Pinch salt
5	large egg yolks
3	tablespoons cornstarch
4	tablespoons (1/2 stick) cold unsalted butter, cut into 4 pieces
1 1/2	teaspoons vanilla extract

1. Heat the half-and-half, 6 tablespoons of the sugar, and the salt in a medium heavy-bottomed saucepan over medium heat until simmering, stirring occasionally to dissolve the sugar.

2. Meanwhile, whisk the egg yolks in a medium bowl until thoroughly combined. Whisk in the remaining 2 tablespoons sugar and whisk until the sugar has begun to dissolve and the mixture is creamy, about 15 seconds. Whisk in the cornstarch until combined and the mixture is pale yellow and thick, about 30 seconds.

3. When the half-and-half mixture reaches a full simmer, gradually whisk the simmering half-and-half into the yolk mixture to temper. Return the mixture to the saucepan, scraping the bowl with a rubber spatula; return to a simmer over medium heat, whisking constantly, until a few bubbles burst on the surface and the mixture is thickened and glossy, about 30 seconds. Off the heat, whisk in the butter and vanilla. Strain the pastry cream through a fine-mesh sieve set over a medium bowl. Press plastic wrap directly on the surface to prevent a skin from forming and refrigerate until cold and set, at least 3 hours or up to 2 days.

➤ VARIATION

Pastry Cream for Éclairs and Napoleons
Our recipes for Éclairs and Napoleons require just 2 cups of pastry cream rather than a full recipe.

Follow the recipe for Pastry Cream, adjusting the following ingredients: 1½ cups half-and-half, 5 tablespoons plus 1 teaspoon sugar (use 4 tablespoons for step 1 and 1 tablespoon plus 1 teaspoon for step 2), a pinch of salt, 3 egg yolks, 2 tablespoons cornstarch, 2 tablespoons butter, and 1 teaspoon vanilla extract.

LEMON TART

LIGHT, REFRESHING, AND BEAUTIFUL, WHEN lemon tart is good it is very, very good—but when it's bad you wish you'd ordered the check instead. Despite its apparent simplicity, there is much that can go wrong with a lemon tart. It can slip over the edge of sweet into cloying; its tartness can grab at your throat; it can be gluey or eggy or, even worse, metallic tasting. Its crust can be too hard, too soft, too thick, or too sweet.

There is more than one way to fill a tart, of course. We considered briefly but dismissed the notion of an unbaked lemon filling such as a lemon pastry cream or a lemon charlotte. In each case, the filling (the former containing milk and thickened with eggs and flour, the latter containing cream and thickened with eggs and gelatin) is spooned into a baked tart shell and chilled. Not only did we find the flavor of these fillings too muted and their texture too billowy, but we realized that we wanted a proper lemon tart, one in which the filling is baked with the shell. That meant only one thing: lemon curd, and a thin, bracing layer of it at that.

Originally an old English recipe called lemon cheese and meant to be eaten like a jam, lemon curd is a stirred fruit custard made of eggs, lemon juice, sugar, and, usually, butter. Cooked over low heat and stirred continuously, the mixture thickens by means of protein coagulation. The dessert owes its bright flavor not to lemon juice but to oils released by finely grated zest, the equivalent of a lemon twist in a vodka martini. Butter further refines a lemon curd's flavor and texture. The result is a spoonable custard that can be spread on scones or used as a base for desserts. When baked, its color deepens and it "sets up," remaining supple and creamy yet firm enough to be sliced. It is intense, heady stuff, nicely modulated—if you must—by a cloud of whipped cream.

As it turned out, the lemon curd we had developed for our lemon bars (page 493) worked perfectly in this tart. Creamy and dense with a vibrant color, our yolk-only curd did not become gelatinous when baked, as did those curds made with all whole eggs, but it did set up enough to slice.

Lemon Tart

SERVES 8 TO 10

Once the lemon curd ingredients have been combined, cook the curd immediately; otherwise it will have a grainy finished texture. To prevent the curd from acquiring a metallic taste, make absolutely sure that all utensils coming into contact with it—bowls, whisk, saucepan, and strainer—are made of nonreactive stainless steel or glass. Since the tart pan has a removable bottom, it is more easily maneuvered when set on a baking sheet. If your prebaked tart shell has already cooled, place it in the oven just before you start the curd and heat it until warm, about 5 minutes. Serve the tart with Whipped Cream (page 500), which is the perfect accompaniment to the rich, intensely lemon filling.

1	recipe Sweet Tart Pastry for Prebaked Tart Shell (page 223), fully baked and still warm
7	large egg yolks, plus 2 large eggs
1	cup plus 2 tablespoons sugar (7 7/8 ounces)
2/3	cup juice plus 1/4 cup finely grated zest from 4 to 5 medium lemons
	Pinch salt
4	tablespoons (1/2 stick) unsalted butter, cut into 4 pieces
3	tablespoons heavy cream

1. Remove the baking sheet with the tart shell from the oven and place the baking sheet on a wire rack. Keep the oven temperature at 375 degrees.

2. In a medium nonreactive bowl, whisk together the yolks and whole eggs until combined, about 5 seconds. Add the sugar and whisk until just combined, about 5 seconds. Add the lemon juice, zest, and salt; whisk until combined, about 5 seconds. Transfer the mixture to a medium nonreactive saucepan, add the butter pieces, and cook over medium-low heat, stirring constantly with a wooden spoon, until the curd thickens to a thin sauce-like consistency and registers 170 degrees on an instant-read thermometer, about 5 minutes. Immediately pour the curd through a fine-mesh stainless steel strainer set over a clean nonreactive bowl. Stir in the heavy cream; pour the curd into the warm tart shell immediately.

3. Return the baking sheet with the filled tart shell to the middle rack of the oven. Bake until the filling is shiny and opaque and the center 3 inches jiggle slightly when shaken, 10 to 15 minutes. Cool on a wire rack to room temperature, about 1 hour. Remove the outer ring, slide a thin metal spatula between the bottom crust and the tart pan bottom to release, then slip the tart onto a cardboard round or serving plate. Serve the tart within several hours.

CHOCOLATE TRUFFLE TART

OF THE MYRIAD CHOCOLATE DESSERTS, A thin slice of chocolate tart is perhaps the most elegant. We wanted to develop a recipe for an intensely flavored, rich, and smooth chocolate tart, one that would be simple to prepare but that wouldn't simply be a fudgy brownie dressed up in the formal guise of a tart.

Our initial tests produced tarts that were either like fudgy brownies with a thick, rich, and dense texture or like molten chocolate cakes with a cake-like perimeter surrounding a viscous center. Both of these versions generally called for adding beaten egg yolks—usually alone, but sometimes in combination with beaten egg whites—to a sweetened chocolate and butter mixture, pouring the filling into a prebaked tart pastry, and then baking the tart until the filling was just set. While many of these tarts were appealing, none had the smooth, sophisticated texture that we were after.

We then considered a different approach. Rather than enriching our chocolate filling with egg foams, which produce a slightly aerated, cakey texture once baked, we would try reducing the filling to its essential components. Chocolate, of course, was fundamental. We briefly considered using cocoa powder, but rejected it. Cocoa powder works best in other applications, such as in combination with flour to make chocolate cakes. We knew we wanted the smooth, rich creaminess of chocolate, a mouthfeel that cocoa powder could not replicate. High-quality bittersweet chocolate was essential for this recipe. But pouring melted chocolate, no matter how good, into a tart pastry does not a chocolate tart make. So we experimented with making a ganache—a chocolate and cream mixture sometimes enriched with butter and eggs—that is often used as the filling in chocolate truffle candy. Ganache may also be used as a frosting, filling, coating, or sauce. After our first tests, we knew we were on the right path.

We divided our next tests into two categories: those that included unbeaten eggs or egg yolks and, consequently, required baking, and those that called for no eggs and did not require any time in the oven. The tarts in the former category had textures like chocolate custards. We liked these tarts but preferred the tarts in the second category. The tarts without eggs were smooth and rich with a deep chocolate flavor that had not been compromised by heat. (Chocolate flavor can disappear in the air when baking because chocolate compounds are volatile.) Ganache recipes vary in their ratios of cream to chocolate. After numerous tests, we found that 1 part cream to 1½ parts chocolate, by weight, gave us the flavor and texture that we were looking for.

The addition of 6 tablespoons butter added a silken quality to the filling. We found that the less the filling is aerated, the better. Simply bring the cream to a simmer, pour it over the finely chopped chocolate in a medium bowl, and allow the chocolate

and cream to sit for one minute before stirring slowly with a whisk to combine. At first the mixture will look granular and broken, but as you continue to stir, the mixture will become smooth and satiny. Once the cream and chocolate are mixed, add the butter and, again, stir slowly to combine.

At this point, our filling was nearly perfect. We had an intense chocolate flavor and butter-like texture. We tried adding a tablespoon of cognac and liked the result. Barely detectable, the touch of cognac heightened the chocolate flavor and added another dimension to the tart's flavor.

We added our filling to a chocolate version of our sweetened tart pastry. To make the chocolate version, we simply replaced some of the flour with cocoa powder. Because this dough has a lower gluten content (cocoa has no gluten), it is slightly softer. Tasters much preferred the silken truffle filling in the chocolate tart pastry.

Chocolate Truffle Tart
SERVES 12 TO 14

The pastry for this tart is the same as used for our Poached Pear and Almond Tart (page 232), except that ¼ cup of the flour has been replaced with ¼ cup of cocoa. After the cream is added to the chocolate, the mixture will look grainy. Stirring slowly will bring the mixture together into a smooth filling. This tart is very chocolatey and rich and would benefit from an accompaniment such as Whipped Cream (page 500), or, for a lighter touch, Berry Coulis (page 499) or fresh raspberries.

1   recipe Sweet Tart Pastry (page 232), with
    ¼ cup (¾ ounce) Dutch-processed cocoa
    substituted for an equal amount of flour

DARK CHOCOLATE TRUFFLE FILLING
12 ounces high-quality bittersweet chocolate,
    chopped
1   cup heavy cream
6   tablespoons (¾ stick) unsalted butter, at
    room temperature
1   tablespoon cognac

1. FOR THE TART PASTRY: Prepare the dough as directed, processing the cocoa with the flour,

sugar, and salt. Bake until dry and blistered, about 30 minutes, rotating the pan halfway through the baking time. Remove from the oven and carefully remove the foil and weights by gathering the edges of the foil and pulling up and out. Return the tart pan on the baking sheet to the oven and bake an additional 5 minutes. Set the baking sheet with the tart shell on a wire rack and cool to room temperature, about 30 minutes.

2. FOR THE FILLING: Meanwhile, place the chocolate in a medium bowl and set aside. Bring the cream to a simmer in a small saucepan over medium-high heat. Pour the hot cream over the chocolate and set aside for 1 minute. Using a whisk, slowly stir the chocolate and cream until smooth, being careful to avoid aerating the mixture. Slowly stir in the butter until combined. Stir in the cognac until combined.

3. Pour the filling into the cooled tart shell, using an offset spatula to spread the filling to the sides of the tart and smooth the top. Refrigerate until firm, at least 2 hours and up to 48 hours. Slice into thin wedges and serve immediately with optional accompaniments (see note).

➤ VARIATION
Caramel Chocolate Truffle Tart
Follow the recipe for the Chocolate Truffle Tart. While the tart shell is cooling, follow the recipe for Caramel Sauce (page 499), halving the recipe and stirring in 2 tablespoons butter to the finished, but still hot, sauce. Spread the warm caramel sauce evenly over the cooled tart shell. Refrigerate the crust until the sauce is set but still tacky, about 5 minutes. Pour the chocolate filling over the caramel and refrigerate as directed.

POACHED PEAR AND ALMOND TART

POACHED PEARS AND ALMONDS ARE SUCH a natural pairing that imagining them wed in a dessert is hardly difficult: slices of tender, sweet, perfumed poached pears are embedded in a nutty, rich, fragrant, custard-cake almond filling called frangipane, all contained in a crisp, buttery pastry—

HOW TO RIPEN PEARS

According to the Pear Bureau Northwest, pears are an uncommon type of fruit that do not ripen successfully on the tree. They must be harvested at maturity but before they ripen, lest their texture turn gritty and granular. This explains why virtually all pears at the grocery store are more like pet rocks than edible fruit. We tested three methods for ripening: at room temperature, in a paper bag on the counter, and in the refrigerator.

The pears went into their respective corners on a Monday, and we tasted them each day to gauge their ripeness. By the end of the week, we had a clear loser. The pears kept in the fridge were only slightly riper and softer than when they were purchased. The pears stored in a bag and those put in a basket on the counter ripened at the same speed; by Friday, they were both ready for poaching.

perfect for the holidays or other special occasions.

As a dessert made from several components, however, a pear-almond tart invites havoc. A whole day of preparation is required, and the risks are great: a soggy crust; a coarse, wet frangipane heavy-handedly flavored with almond extract; and tasteless poached pears that either retain too much crunch or are soft to the point of listlessness. Unless each element is perfect, the tart's greatness is diminished.

Unlike a pastry cream filling, which requires stovetop cooking, frangipane is baked. The question therefore was whether the tart shell required prebaking and, if so, how much. At first, we filled a completely unbaked tart shell with frangipane, but it was no good. The bottom crust of the finished tart was soggy and pasty, and it tasted of raw flour, a common downfall of this tart. On the other hand, a fully prebaked pastry became slightly overbaked after the additional time in the oven with the filling. A partially baked pastry was deep golden and had a buttery shortbread-like texture in the finished tart. It was perfect.

For a pear-almond tart, pear halves, not whole pears, are poached. Rock-hard pears never attained a tender texture no matter how long they simmered. But if the pears were too ripe, they were difficult to handle and easily cooked to mush. We tried the readily available pear varieties: Bosc, d'Anjou, Comice, and Bartlett. The favorites were the Bartlett, for its floral, honeyed notes, and the

Bosc, because it tasted like a sweet, ripe pear should taste. The other two varieties were unremarkable in flavor and the least attractive in appearance, as they experienced some discoloration during poaching.

With pear varieties selected, we went about trying to bolster their flavor by testing different poaching mediums. Our choices were a simple syrup of sugar and water or a sugar-sweetened white wine. The sugar-syrup pears were flat and dull, the wine-poached pears bright and spirited—the unanimous winner. A few spices added lush flavor: a cinnamon stick, black peppercorns, whole cloves, and, for those who like its seductiveness, a vanilla bean with its flecks of seeds.

Ripe pears poached in 10 minutes. Once the pears are tender, recipes often recommend that they be allowed to cool in their liquid. This, we found, was good advice. If the pears were plucked from the hot poaching liquid, the syrup did not penetrate to their insides, and their texture was dry. If left to cool in the liquid, the pears absorbed some syrup, took on a candied translucency, and became plump, sweet, and spicy.

Much like pastry cream, frangipane serves as a filling in numerous types of pastries. Although it seems simple because it does not require stovetop cooking, frangipane can turn out coarse, eggy, wet, and overly sweet.

Frangipane begins with fresh almonds, not almond paste or marzipan. The nuts are ground finely in a food processor and then combined with a batter of butter, sugar, eggs, and sometimes flour that has been beaten in a standing mixer. We quickly discovered that all the batter ingredients could be added directly to the food processor without resorting to a mixer. After grinding the nuts and sugar, we incorporated the eggs and finally the softened butter until the mixture was thick but pourable.

Four ounces of nuts make the right amount of filling for an 11-inch tart shell with eight poached pear halves. We made the frangipane with unblanched sliced almonds (almonds sliced with their skins on), but this gave it a dark and impure appearance and a faintly bitter aftertaste. Blanched slivered almonds worked better. We processed them with the sugar (½ cup gave the right amount of sweetness), which allowed them to be ground superfine without

turning greasy as they broke down.

Flour—just a tablespoon or two—appears in several frangipane recipes. We tried 1½ tablespoons. Astute tasters ferreted it out. Just that small amount made the frangipane not only drier and cakier but also starchier and pastier, so we took it off the list. An overabundance of butter was lethal. Eight tablespoons made a greasy frangipane. With four it was too lean and the flavor fleeting. Six tablespoons were ideal. We noted that to produce the best texture in a baked frangipane, the butter should be softened before it's added to the food processor. If too cold, it sometimes resisted incorporation and left pea-sized chunks that resulted in wet, oily pockets in the baked tart.

As for the eggs, we tested two whole eggs, one whole plus one yolk, one whole plus one white, and so on. Yolk-heavy frangipanes were gluey. The version made exclusively with whole eggs was perfectly acceptable, but the frangipane made with one whole egg plus one white was superior. It was cake-like without being dry and creamy without being wet. And it tasted of pure almond and sweet butter.

A pinch of salt and a half-teaspoon each of vanilla and almond extract were just right. Like the poached pears, the frangipane can be made in advance and refrigerated. It just needs a little softening at room temperature before use so it can be spread in the tart shell.

For assembly, the pear halves are customarily

THE WRONG TART PAN

Do not bake this tart in a 9-inch pan, as shown above. There is no room to place a pear half in the center of the tart, and the frangipane there does not brown on par with the edges and is often wet. This recipe requires an 11-inch tart pan with a removable bottom.

cut into thin crosswise slices; the slices are kept together and the pear shape is intact, but the slices are fanned slightly toward the stem end. Then they are set in the frangipane like tiles in mastic. Another option is to place uncut pear halves in the frangipane. Though quicker to whisk into the oven, a tart prepared this way was not as stunning and eating it not so pleasurable (the force needed to cut through the pear with a fork tended to dislodge the fruit from the frangipane).

We discovered that it was important to dry the pears off after removing them from their liquid and before setting them on the frangipane. To that end, after slicing the pears, we wicked away excess moisture with paper towels. Otherwise, as they baked, they released moisture that turned the layer of frangipane immediately around them sticky and wet.

Baking the tart at 350 degrees for about 45 minutes proved to be the best. At the end of baking, the tart that had begun as monochromatically straw blond had a walnut-brown crust, frangipane with a nutty tan surface, and golden pears.

❦

Poached Pear and Almond Tart

SERVES 10 TO 12

This tart has several components, but each can be prepared ahead, and the tart is baked several hours before serving. If you cannot find blanched slivered almonds, use whole blanched almonds but chop them coarse before processing to ensure that they form a fine, even texture. The pears should be ripe but firm, the flesh giving slightly when gently pressed with a finger. Purchase the pears a few days ahead and allow them to ripen at room temperature (see "How to Ripen Pears" on page 230). If they ripen before you need them, refrigerate them and use them within a day or two, or poach them and hold them in their syrup (they will keep for about 3 days). Many tasters liked the bright, crisp flavor of pears poached in Sauvignon Blanc. Chardonnay-poached pears had deeper, oakier flavors and were also well liked. See the illustrations on page 149 for tips on working with this dough.

POACHED PEARS

1	bottle (750 ml) white wine
2/3	cup (about 4 2/3 ounces) granulated sugar
2	tablespoons juice from 1 lemon plus 4 or 5 large strips zest removed with vegetable peeler
1	(3-inch) cinnamon stick
15	black peppercorns
3	whole cloves
1/8	teaspoon salt
1/2	vanilla bean, slit in half lengthwise (optional)
4	ripe but firm pears (about 2 pounds), preferably Bosc or Bartlett

SWEET TART PASTRY

1	large egg yolk
2	tablespoons heavy cream
1/2	teaspoon vanilla extract
1 1/2	cups (7 1/2 ounces) unbleached all-purpose flour, plus more for dusting the work surface

PREPARING THE PEARS FOR POACHING

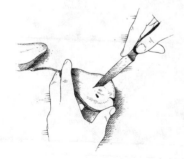  

1. Cut each pear in half lengthwise. With the tip of a paring knife, cut out the seed core from each pear half.

2. Remove the blossom end of each pear half, then remove the thin fibrous core and stem by making a V-shaped incision along both sides of the core.

3. Working quickly to avoid discoloration, peel the cored pear halves with a vegetable peeler.

³/₄ **cup (3 ounces) confectioners' sugar**

¹/₄ **teaspoon salt**

10 **tablespoons (1 ¹/₄ sticks) cold unsalted butter, cut into ¹/₂ -inch cubes**

ALMOND FILLING (FRANGIPANE)

1 **cup blanched slivered almonds**

¹/₂ **cup (3 ¹/₂ ounces) granulated sugar**

¹/₈ **teaspoon salt**

1 **large egg plus 1 large egg white**

¹/₂ **teaspoon almond extract**

¹/₂ **teaspoon vanilla extract**

6 **tablespoons (³/₄ stick) unsalted butter, cut into 6 pieces and softened to room temperature**

GLAZE

¹/₄ **cup apple jelly**

1. To POACH THE PEARS: Combine the wine, sugar, lemon juice and zest, cinnamon, peppercorns, cloves, and salt in a large, nonreactive saucepan. Scrape the seeds from the vanilla bean pod (if using) and add the seeds and pod to the saucepan. Bring the mixture to a simmer over medium heat, stirring occasionally to dissolve the sugar. Meanwhile, halve, core, and peel the pears (see the illustrations on page 232). Slide the pears into the simmering wine; increase the heat to high and return to a simmer. Reduce the heat to low and simmer, covered, until the pears are tender (a toothpick or skewer inserted into the pear should slide in and out with very little resistance) and their outer edges have turned translucent, about 10 minutes, turning the pears in the liquid halfway through the poaching time with a wooden spoon or spatula. Off the heat, cool the pears in the liquid, partially covered, until the pears have turned translucent and are cool enough to handle, about 1 hour. (The pears and liquid may be transferred to a nonreactive bowl or container, cooled to room temperature, covered, and refrigerated for up to 3 days.)

2. FOR THE TART PASTRY: Whisk together the yolk, cream, and vanilla in a small bowl. Combine the flour, sugar, and salt in a food processor with four 1-second pulses. Scatter the butter pieces over the flour mixture; process to cut the butter into the flour until the mixture resembles coarse meal, about twenty 1-second pulses. With the machine running, add the egg mixture and process until the dough comes together, about 12 seconds. Turn the dough onto a sheet of plastic wrap and press into a 6-inch disk; wrap with plastic wrap and refrigerate at least 1 hour or up to 48 hours.

3. Remove the dough from the refrigerator (if refrigerated longer than 1 hour, let stand at room temperature until malleable). Unwrap and roll out between 2 lightly floured large sheets of parchment paper or plastic wrap (or piece 4 small sheets together to form 2 large sheets) to a 15-inch round. (If the dough becomes soft and sticky, slip onto a baking sheet and refrigerate until workable, 20 to 30 minutes.) Following the illustration on page 149, transfer the dough to an 11-inch tart pan with a removable bottom by rolling the dough loosely over the rolling pin and unrolling it over the pan. Working around the circumference of the pan, ease the dough into the pan corners by gently lifting the edge of the dough with one hand while pressing into the corners with the other hand. Press the dough against the fluted sides of the pan, patching breaks or cracks if necessary. (If some sections of the edge are too thin, reinforce them by folding the excess dough back on itself.) Run the rolling pin over the top of the tart pan to remove excess dough. Set the dough-lined tart pan on a baking sheet or large plate and freeze 30 minutes. (The dough-lined tart pan can be wrapped tightly in plastic wrap and frozen up to 1 month.)

4. Meanwhile, adjust an oven rack to the middle position and heat the oven to 375 degrees. Set the dough-lined tart pan on a baking sheet; lightly spray one side of an 18-inch square of heavy-duty foil with nonstick cooking spray. Press the foil, greased side down, inside the frozen tart shell, folding the excess foil over the edge of the tart pan; fill with metal or ceramic pie weights. Bake until dry and pale gold and the edges have just begun to color, about 20 minutes, rotating halfway through the baking time. Remove from the oven and carefully remove the foil and weights by gathering the edges of the foil and pulling up and out. Set the baking sheet with the tart shell on a wire rack and cool to room temperature, about 30 minutes.

5. For the almond filling: Pulse the almonds, sugar, and salt in a food processor until finely ground, about twenty-five 2-second pulses; process until very finely ground, about 10 seconds longer. Add the egg, egg white, and both extracts; process until combined, about 10 seconds. Add the butter and process until no lumps remain, about 10 seconds. Scrape the bottom and sides of the workbowl with a rubber spatula and process to combine thoroughly, about 10 seconds longer. (The filling can be refrigerated in an airtight container up to 3 days. Before using, let stand at room temperature about 30 minutes to soften, stirring 3 or 4 times.)

6. To assemble, bake, and glaze the tart: Reduce the oven temperature to 350 degrees. Remove the pears from their poaching liquid; set the pears cut-side down on a triple thickness of paper towels and pat them dry with additional paper towels. Follow the illustrations below to spread the frangipane in the tart shell and slice and arrange the pears.

7. Bake the tart on the baking sheet until the crust is deep golden brown and the almond filling is puffed, browned, and firm to the touch, about 45 minutes, rotating the baking sheet front to back halfway through the baking time. Cool the tart on the baking sheet on a wire rack 10 minutes.

8. For the glaze: Bring the apple jelly to a boil in a small saucepan over medium heat, stirring occasionally to smooth out any lumps. When boiling and completely melted, brush the glaze on the pears. Cool the tart to room temperature, about 2 hours. (The tart can be kept at room temperature longer but should be served the day it is made.)

9. Remove the outer ring of the tart pan, slide a thin metal spatula between the bottom of the crust and the tart pan bottom to release, then slip the tart onto a cardboard round or serving platter; cut into wedges and serve.

ASSEMBLING THE TART

1. Spread the frangipane evenly into the partially baked and cooled tart shell using an offset icing spatula.

2. Cut one poached pear half crosswise into ³/₈-inch slices, leaving the pear half intact on the cutting board (do not separate the slices). Pat dry with paper towels to absorb excess moisture.

3. Discard the first 4 slices from the narrow end of the sliced pear half. Slide an icing spatula under the sliced pear and, steadying it with one hand, slide the pear off the spatula onto the center of the tart.

4. Cut and dry another pear half following step 2. Slide the spatula under the pear and gently press the pear to fan the slices toward the narrow end.

5. Slide the fanned pear half onto the frangipane, narrow end toward the center, almost touching the center pear.

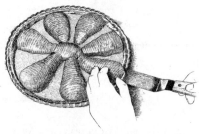

6. Repeat steps 2, 4, and 5 with the remaining pear halves, spacing them evenly and making a flower petal pattern off the center pear. If necessary, use the spatula to push the pears to space them evenly.

PASTA FROLLA

JUST LIKE FRENCH SWEET TART PASTRY (pâte sucrée), pasta frolla, the basic pastry dough of Italian baking, is quite different from American pie dough. American pie dough is typically flaky, with minimal sweetness and flavorings. It is a modest means of showcasing fillings. In contrast, pasta frolla is sweet and flavorful—good enough to eat on its own. Just as important, it is tender. In fact, the name pasta frolla literally translates as "tender dough." Where pâte sucrée is crisp and dense, pasta frolla is softer and more biscuit-like.

Many pasta frolla recipes have a small amount of butter and are heavy-handed with the sugar. The advantage of a low butter-to-sugar ratio is that the pastry is easy to manage; it rolls out beautifully and doesn't fall apart. In addition, a lean dough holds its shape better when baked, making for a more attractive final product. This is important because pasta frolla is generally used to make free-form Italian tarts called *crostate*.

However, after sampling a couple of lean, sweet doughs, we concluded that even with large amounts of sugar, they lacked flavor and tenderness. We added more and more butter until we finally settled on 7 tablespoons of butter to 1⅓ cups of flour for a single-crust batch of pasta frolla. This was the maximum amount of butter that could be worked in without compromising the manageability of the dough. With respect to the sugar, we found that ⅓ cup was just the right amount. The dough was tender and sweet, but not so sweet that it competed with the filling.

Whole eggs and/or egg yolks are almost always found in pasta frolla recipes. Whole eggs provide structure, while egg yolks provide tenderness. In a single batch of pasta frolla, one yolk did not provide enough moisture, and two yolks made the crumb too fine. A single whole egg was just right. In the double pasta frolla recipe, two whole eggs produced a crust that was airy and cake-like. Egg yolks only produced a crust with a very fine crumb. We wanted a bit of both of these qualities, so we settled on one whole egg plus one yolk for the double-crust recipe.

The last few ingredients that we needed to consider were vanilla extract, lemon zest, and baking powder. The first two are standard ingredients in pasta frolla recipes; they provide that fundamental cookie flavor. Baking powder, on the other hand, was not used in all of the recipes we uncovered in our research. We tested a version of our final pasta frolla recipe with baking powder and liked the lightness it gave to the crust. We had noticed that our free-form crostate tended to spread out when baked. The crostate made with baking powder puffed up rather than out—a definite improvement.

For all the pastry doughs we have developed over the years in the test kitchen, we have found that a food processor is the simplest and most consistent means of mixing the dough. Pasta frolla is no exception. In our standard pie dough recipe, we incorporate the fat into the flour with the processor. To avoid reducing the size of the fat particles (large fat particles create larger flakes), the mixture is transferred to a bowl and the liquid is added judiciously and stirred in with a rubber spatula. In our sweet tart pastry (pâte sucrée), the mixture is made from start to finish in the food processor. The mixture is homogenous, with few or no discrete fat particles, creating a crisp pastry.

With the pasta frolla recipe, we were aiming for somewhere between flaky pie dough and crisp pâte sucrée. To achieve this texture, we found that the liquid ingredients could be added to the butter and flour mixture in the food processor. However, once all of the liquid is incorporated, the mixture should be transferred to a large bowl and gently kneaded until it comes together.

Pasta Frolla

MAKES ENOUGH FOR I SINGLE-CRUST TART

Don't add too much water to this dough. Add a tablespoon, process the dough, test it by squeezing a handful to see if it comes together, then add more liquid if necessary. To avoid overworking the dough, finish kneading it by hand. If you process the dough in a food processor until it comes together in a ball, the baked crust will be tough and overly crisp, not flaky and biscuit-like, which is the desired texture.

1   large egg

1   teaspoon vanilla extract

1–2 tablespoons water

1⅓ cups (6⅞ ounces) unbleached all-purpose flour

⅓   cup (2⅓ ounces) sugar

¼   teaspoon salt

1¼ teaspoons baking powder

      Grated zest of 1 lemon

7   tablespoons cold unsalted butter, cut into ¼-inch pieces

1. Whisk the egg, vanilla, and 1 tablespoon of the water in a small bowl and set aside.

2. Place the flour, sugar, salt, baking powder, and lemon zest in a food processor and pulse to combine. Scatter the butter pieces over the flour mixture and process to cut the butter into the flour until the mixture resembles coarse meal, about seven 1-second pulses. With the machine running, add the egg mixture and process until all the liquid ingredients are incorporated. Squeeze a handful of the dough; if it forms a moist ball, no more water is necessary. If the mixture is crumbly and dry, add 1 more tablespoon water and process just until incorporated.

3. Remove the dough from the food processor and transfer it to a large bowl. Gently knead until cohesive, about 30 seconds. Shape the dough into a 5-inch disk. Cover with plastic wrap and refrigerate for at least 2 hours or up to 2 days.

➤ VARIATION

Pasta Frolla for a Double-Crust Tart

Follow the recipe for Pasta Frolla, whisking a large egg yolk with the whole egg, vanilla, and 2 tablespoons water in step 1. In step 2, increase the flour to 2⅓ cups (11¾ ounces), the sugar to ½ cup (3½ ounces), the salt to ½ teaspoon, the baking powder to 2 teaspoons, and the butter to 12 tablespoons (1½ sticks). Proceed as directed, kneading the dough until cohesive in step 3. Divide the dough into 2 equal pieces. Shape one piece into a 5-inch disk and the other into a 5-inch square. Cover both with plastic wrap and refrigerate for at least 2 hours or up to 2 days.

JAM CROSTATA

CROSTATA DI MARMELLATA (JAM TART) IS the quintessential Italian home dessert. This lattice-top tart, made with sweet, tender pastry and filled with fruit jam, is found throughout Italy. It is a cross between a fruit tart and a jam-filled cookie. The beauty of this dessert is its simplicity; the ingredients are usually on hand, and the recipe doesn't even require a pie or tart pan. The technique for assembling the tart is likewise quite simple. One piece of dough is rolled out to a disk, the jam is spread over the disk, a lattice of dough strips is placed on top, and the edges of the bottom dough and the lattice top are pressed together.

Having developed our pasta frolla recipe, we focused our attention on the filling and assembly procedures. Some recipes call for tart pans. While they may look attractive, they posed one major problem for us: They required too much jam to fill them. Once you press the crust into a tart pan, you need to add enough jam to come at least halfway up the sides of the crust. Use less jam and the tart just looks wrong. But imagine eating a piece of toast with ¾ inch of jam on it. It's just too sweet and intense.

A free-form crostata seemed a better alternative, and this was the route chosen in the majority of our research recipes. With the free-form method, the amount of filling isn't dictated by the size of the pan. One cup of jam translated to an ample filling about ¼ inch thick. (With a tart pan, we needed more than two cups of jam.) The pasta frolla dough was so tender and flavorful that we thought it was good enough to command a larger role in this dessert.

Although we had reduced the amount of jam filling, we still found commercial jams a bit on the sweet side. A tablespoon of lemon juice mixed into the jam balanced the sweetness and brightened the flavors of the fruit.

We experimented with several techniques for assembling the lattice-top crostata. The main issue we had to contend with was the method of incorporating the edges of the lattice with the border around the bottom piece of dough. We tried several techniques, but they all seemed a bit haphazard and sloppy. Rolling out the bottom dough, smearing it with jam, adding the lattice top, and crimping the bottom dough and lattice ends together worked, but the finished tart was unattractive. Tasters wanted a proper border, not just some puffed crust around the edge that looked like a pizza. Next, we tried folding the edge of the bottom dough over the lattice strips and fluting the dough by hand, but the crust did not hold its shape in the oven.

The best technique we found was in Nick Malgieri's *Great Italian Desserts* (Little, Brown, 1990). The tart dough is rolled out and the edges are trimmed to make a perfect circle. The jam is spread in a thin layer, and the lattice strips of dough are laid on top. A strip of dough is rolled to form a long rope, draped around the perimeter (so it covers the ends of the lattice strips), and pressed down to form a slightly raised border. This method is easy, and the finished tart is still homey but much more attractive.

One final note: When the assembled crostata was baked right away, the dough spread and lost its neat appearance. We discovered that refrigerating the assembled tart for an hour prevented the dough from spreading and losing its shape. (Refrigerating the dough chills the butter and prevents it from melting too quickly in the oven.) You could never refrigerate a tart filled with fresh fruit, which would exude its juices and create a soggy pastry. However, because the jam is relatively dry, we didn't have to worry about the dough getting soggy.

MAKING A JAM CROSTATA

 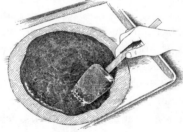 

1. Using an 11-inch pot lid or cardboard round as a guide, trim the first piece of dough to a perfect 11-inch circle with a pizza wheel or paring knife. Reserve the scraps. Slide the dough, still on the parchment, onto a baking sheet.

2. Spread the jam on the dough, leaving a 1-inch border around the edge.

3. Roll the square piece of dough between 2 sheets of lightly floured parchment paper to an 11-inch square. Peel off the parchment. With a pizza wheel or paring knife, straighten the edges of the dough (reserve the scraps), then cut the dough into ten 1-inch-wide strips.

4. Brush the strips with the egg wash and place them over the filling, 5 in each direction in a diagonal lattice. Use a spatula to help move and position the strips.

5. Combine the scraps and knead them together slightly. Roll this dough into a ³/₄-inch-thick rope about 30 inches long. Brush the rim of the pastry with the egg wash, then press the dough rope into the rim. For a decorative finish, press the tines of a fork against the dough. Brush the border with the remaining egg wash.

Jam Crostata
SERVES 8

Crostata di marmellata can be made with any smooth jam, including blackberry and cherry, although our tasters particularly liked raspberry jam. If you want to use a jam with chunks of fruit, puree it in the food processor to achieve a smooth texture.

- 1 cup raspberry jam or other smooth-textured jam
- 1 tablespoon lemon juice
- 1 recipe Pasta Frolla for a Double-Crust Tart (page 236), chilled
  Flour for dusting the work surface
- 1 large egg white, beaten with 2 tablespoons water

1. Mix the jam and lemon juice in a small bowl.

2. Remove both pieces of dough from the refrigerator (if refrigerated longer than 1 hour, let stand at room temperature until malleable). Roll the round dough disk between 2 large sheets of lightly floured parchment paper to an 11-inch circle about ¼ inch thick. Peel off the top sheet of parchment and discard. Follow the illustrations on page 237 to cut the bottom crust, spread the jam, and form the lattice top. Refrigerate the crostata on the baking sheet for 1 hour.

3. Adjust an oven rack to the middle position and heat the oven to 375 degrees. Bake until golden brown, 25 to 30 minutes. Slide the crostata (still on the parchment paper) onto a wire rack and cool to room temperature, about 3 hours. Cut into slices and serve.

FIG–WALNUT TART

FIGS, BOTH FRESH AND DRIED, ARE AN underappreciated fruit in the United States, perhaps because most people's exposure to dried figs has been through packaged fig cookies, which although good, are nothing to write home about. We developed a recipe for Fig Squares (page 495) to give ourselves an exemplary fig cookie. Next, we focused on developing a tart with a fig filling, like those popular in Europe, especially Italy. Because fresh figs are hard to come by in the United States, we developed our recipe using dried figs.

While fresh figs are moist, succulent, and not overly sweet, dried figs are leathery, tough, and chewy, with a concentrated sweetness. The first thing we needed to do was to restore their moisture and softness. We diced the figs, placed them in a small saucepan, covered them with liquid, and simmered them until they were soft and plump.

We tried rehydrating the figs in orange juice, which gave them a fresh, fruity flavor. Rehydrating the figs with brandy gave them additional richness and complexity of flavor. We also tried a dry white wine, which produced figs that tasted somewhat sour. We tried adding anise seeds (something we'd seen in several recipes) to the mixture. While some tasters thought the mild fennel flavor added a nice exotic tone, others found it overpowering, even in small doses. We settled on a mixture of brandy and water, adding orange zest at the end. The brandy added the depth we wanted, while the zest gave the mixture some bright notes.

Pleased with the flavors in our fig mixture, we nevertheless felt we needed to provide a textural balance to its sticky, jammy consistency. Enter walnuts. The fig-walnut combination is classic Italian. We found that the walnuts were best stirred into the fig mixture after it came off the stove.

We tested our tart using the three most common varieties of dried figs. We preferred Turkish and Calimyrna figs to Mission figs. Calimyrna figs are a variety of the Turkish Smyrna fig tree grown in California. Like Turkish figs, they became softer and silkier than Mission figs (also from California) when cooked.

In our experience, pastry dough generally tastes better when the crust is deeply browned rather than lightly browned. We assumed that to avoid overbaking the filling and drying it out, prebaking the tart shell before adding the filling was going to be the order of the day. We prebaked the tart shell until lightly browned, filled it with the fig and nut mixture, and placed it back in the oven for 15 minutes— just enough time for the filling to set into the crust. We were surprised that the pastry tasted dry and

Handling Nuts

SKINNING HAZELNUTS

Hazelnuts are covered with a dark brown skin that can be quite bitter. Toasting the nuts in a 350-degree oven until fragrant (about 15 minutes) improves their flavor and also causes the skins to blister and crack so they can be rubbed off. Here's how to accomplish this task.

1. Transfer the hot toasted nuts to the center of a clean kitchen towel.

2. Bring up the sides of the towel and twist it closed to seal in the nuts.

3. Rub the nuts together in the towel to scrape off as much of the brown skin as possible. It's fine if patches of skin remain.

4. Carefully open the towel on a flat surface. Gently roll the nuts away from the skins.

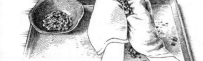

SKINNING WALNUTS

The skins from toasted walnuts can impart a bitter flavor in some dishes, especially where they are used in large quantities. To remove the skins, rub the hot toasted nuts inside a clean kitchen towel. The skins will separate easily from the nutmeats, and the skins can then be discarded.

CHOPPING ROUND NUTS NEATLY

Chopping round hazelnuts or peanuts can sometimes mean a wild chase around the cutting board as the nuts roll every which way. Here's how to contain the nuts.

1. Wet a kitchen towel, grasp both ends, and twist them in opposite directions to form a tight rope.

2. Lay the rope on a cutting board in a ring around the nuts. Leave enough room in the center of the ring to fit the knife and chop away.

CHOPPING A SMALL AMOUNT OF HAZELNUTS

The channel on a carving board can be used to trap small amounts of hazelnuts when trying to chop them. Line up a few inches' worth of nuts in the channel (keep the row shorter than your knife blade) and carefully cut through the whole row at once. Remove the cut items and repeat until you are finished.

STORING NUTS

All nuts are high in oil and will become rancid rather quickly. In the test kitchen, we store all nuts in the freezer in sealed freezer-safe, zipper-lock bags. Frozen nuts will keep for months and there's no need to defrost them before toasting or chopping.

TOASTING PINE NUTS

Because pine nuts burn so quickly, we prefer to toast these nuts on the stovetop, where we can see them, rather than in the oven. Although pine nuts can be toasted in a skillet set over medium heat, because of their flattened shape the nuts tend to rest on one side and are prone to scorching. Either shake the pan often to turn the nuts or try toasting them in a hand-cranked stovetop popcorn popper. Just heat the popper, add the nuts, and then use the crank to keep the nuts in constant motion until they are evenly toasted.

TOASTING NUTS

Toasting nuts intensifies their flavor and is a vital step in many baking recipes. For savory cooking, we often toast the nuts in a skillet on the stovetop. The nuts are easy to watch, and they will toast evenly as long as you remember to shake the pan occasionally. However, when baking, we generally toast nuts in the oven, which is already on. (Pine nuts are the one exception.)

To toast nuts, spread them in a single layer on a rimmed baking sheet and place the baking sheet in the middle of an oven heated to 325 or 350 degrees. If the recipe you are preparing calls for a higher oven temperature, toast the nuts first at 325 or 350 degrees, remove the nuts, and then finish preheating the oven. (We have found that nuts burn very quickly in hotter ovens.) To promote even toasting, it's a good idea to shake the baking sheet after several minutes. You want to toast the nuts until they are fragrant and lightly colored, a process that will take between five and 10 minutes. (With their thick skins, hazelnuts benefit from even longer toasting—generally 15 minutes.) Once the nuts are toasted, remove the baking sheet from the oven and cool the nuts to room temperature.

Sometimes we opt not to toast nuts for baked goods. For instance, if the nuts are going to be directly exposed to prolonged oven heat (on top of a batter or in cookies), we often skip the toasting step. In effect, the nuts will be toasted in the oven as the recipe bakes, and toasting them in advance may cause them to burn when they go into the oven a second time.

overcooked, even though it didn't look too brown. We then baked the tart without prebaking the crust. While the edges of the crust were lightly browned, the bottom and sides (where the filling covered the pastry) looked pale and undercooked. When we tasted it, though, the pastry was fully cooked and had a wonderful moist, biscuit-like texture.

So why did our pasta frolla taste done when it didn't look done? The dough contains baking powder, which accelerates baking by lightening the dough. As the pasta frolla bakes, it puffs in the oven, and the texture becomes almost biscuit-like. Because the dough is not dense (most sweet tart doughs are more like shortbread), it cooks quickly. Unlike other pastry doughs, we learned, pasta frolla can cook through before it fully browns. In fact, if pasta frolla browns too much, it will dry out.

Now that we were not prebaking the tart shell before filling it, we had the option of making a free-form tart. However, tasters preferred the elegant appearance of the tart made in a pan. Fitting the dough into a pan requires a couple of minutes of effort, but we think this is time well spent.

Fig-Walnut Tart

SERVES 8 TO 10

Refer to the illustrations on page 149 for tips on fitting the dough into the pan.

1	recipe Pasta Frolla (page 235), chilled
	Flour for dusting the work surface
1	pound dried Calimyrna or Turkish figs, stems removed, fruit chopped coarse
1/4	cup (1 3/4 ounces) sugar
1/2	cup brandy
1	cup water
	Grated zest from 1 medium orange
1	cup walnuts, coarsely chopped
	Confectioners' sugar for dusting on the tart

1. Remove the dough from the refrigerator (if refrigerated longer than 1 hour, let stand at room temperature until malleable). Roll the dough between 2 large sheets of lightly floured parchment paper to a 13-inch circle about 1/4 inch thick. Peel off the top sheet, loosely roll the dough around the rolling pin, then unroll it over a 10-inch tart pan with a removable bottom. Working around the circumference of the pan, ease the dough into the pan corners by gently lifting the edge of the dough with one hand while pressing into the corners with the other hand. Press the dough against the fluted sides of the pan, patching breaks or cracks if necessary. (If some sections of the edge are too thin, reinforce them by folding the excess dough back on itself.) Run the rolling pin over the top of the tart pan to remove any excess dough. The finished edge should be 1/4 inch thick. If it is not, press the dough up over the edge of the pan and pinch. Freeze the dough for 30 minutes.

2. Meanwhile, bring the figs, sugar, brandy, and water to a simmer in a medium saucepan over medium heat. Simmer, stirring occasionally, until the liquid evaporates and the figs are very soft, about 10 minutes. Stir in the orange zest and walnuts and cool to room temperature.

3. Adjust an oven rack to the middle position and heat the oven to 325 degrees.

4. Spread the cooled fig and nut mixture evenly in the tart shell. Use the back of a spoon or an offset spatula to work the filling into the edges of the tart shell. Bake until the edges of the tart are lightly browned, 25 to 30 minutes. Transfer the tart pan to a wire rack, cool for 5 minutes, then remove the outer ring of the pan. Cool the tart to room temperature, about 3 hours. (The cooled tart can be refrigerated for up to several days.) Just before serving, dust with confectioners' sugar and cut into slices.

LINZERTORTE

NAMED FOR THE AUSTRIAN CITY OF LINZ, this old-world European confection is not a torte at all but a tart with a sweet almond pastry crust and a filling of raspberry jam under a lattice top. Well executed, linzertorte is an elegant and simple addition to the dessert table, particularly excellent with coffee or tea. However, our initial tests revealed why this deceptively straightforward dessert has all but disappeared from the home kitchen. The almond crusts we sampled were either soggy from the jam or thick, tough, and dry. With loads of sugar in the crust, in the jam, and sprinkled over the top, the tart was cloyingly sweet and often heavily spiced like a gingerbread cookie. To top it off (literally), the crumbly, delicate nature of the pastry dough made weaving the traditional lattice a terrible nuisance.

We set out to make over this musty classic into a sleek and streamlined modern-day masterpiece. The dough was the obvious place to start; with such a simple filling, the almond crust would really have to shine. But how many almonds did the dough need? When the mixture contained more nuts than flour, the pastry was too crumbly and delicate. We tried reversing the ratio and the crucial almond flavor was lost. An even ratio of nuts and flour worked best. Toasting the nuts was an extra step, but the irresistible aroma of roasting almonds argued persuasively that our effort would be rewarded. Tasters agreed: Toasted almonds noticeably improved the flavor and color of the crust.

Next, we considered butter, and here our troubles began. In addition to determining the quantity of butter, we would have to choose a mixing method: Should the butter be creamed with the sugar, as one would make a cookie, or cut cold into the flour as one might make a flaky American piecrust? Crusts made by cutting cold butter into flour were more tender than their creamed butter counterparts, but they were also quite soft. The primary reason for cutting in the butter is to produce a flaky texture, but the ground nuts prevented this by interfering with the development of gluten strands. Also, the cold chunks of butter kept the dough crumbly, dry, and difficult to work with. Creaming the butter delivered a soft, malleable dough and a chewy, cookie-like crust that most tasters preferred, but it was decidedly tough and a little dry.

Puzzled, we put the issue aside for the moment and turned to the jam filling, which was making the bottom crust soggy no matter which mixing method we chose. Blind baking the crust before adding the filling seemed the obvious answer. In the course of our testing, we tried covering the crust with foil and pie weights before baking and were pleased with the results—the foil kept the crust from getting too brown, and the weights kept the dough from rising. But the use of the weights led to another discovery: The weighted crust, which had baked up thinner than the unweighted one, was also pleasantly crisp and much less tough. Sticking with the creamed butter version, we tried rolling the dough out thinner to begin with and got even better results. A finished linzertorte with the crust rolled out to less than ¼ inch was a joy to eat—crisp, tender pastry surrounding a thin layer of sweet jam. The same dessert with a thicker crust was tough and dry and sent tasters scrambling for a glass of milk. Thin was in.

Pleased at last with the texture of the crust, we began adjusting the traditional flavors to suit a more modern palate. Tasters liked a hint of cinnamon and clove but no more, so we reduced by half the quantities of spice recommended by most recipes. Grated lemon zest is a common addition to the crust, and we welcomed a bit of brightness against the backdrop of sugar, nuts, and spices. In the same vein, we experimented with adding lemon juice to the filling and found that a full tablespoon was necessary to cut the sweetness of the raspberry jam. As for the jam itself, we settled on just a cup as the right amount to cover our slimmed-down crust. Some recipes we had tested called for twice as much, and the resulting tarts were a sticky mess.

Lastly, we faced the troublesome lattice top. We loved its look but hated putting it together, as the nuts made our dough strips too delicate and crumbly to weave together in the traditional pattern. In fact, it was difficult to even pick up the strips without their falling apart. We were frustrated by the way most recipes ignored this and simply instructed us to "form the lattice." The sole exception to this was a recipe from *Maida Heatter's Book of Great Desserts* (Knopf, 1974), which suggested cutting the strips on waxed paper and then using the paper to lift the strips onto the tart. With a few changes, we were able to make this trick work for us as well. As for the weaving, we found that by rotating the pan a few times while laying out the lattice, we could make an easy woven pattern that looked impressive without having to move the strips around.

The last step was the easiest. Recipes were

unanimous in their choice of 350 degrees as the proper baking temperature for a linzertorte, and after testing a few other options, we agreed. In the oven for an hour, the crust browned slowly, and the jam had time to bubble and thicken.

Linzertorte

SERVES 8

The linzertorte may be served at room temperature the day it is baked, but it is at its best after a night in the refrigerator. Wrapped tightly in plastic wrap, the torte keeps well for up to 3 days. If at any time while forming the lattice the dough becomes too soft, refrigerate it for 15 minutes before continuing. Make sure to buy blanched almonds (without skins).

1 1/2	cups whole blanched almonds
1 1/2	cups (7 1/2 ounces) unbleached all-purpose flour, plus more for dusting the work surface
1/2	teaspoon ground cinnamon
1/8	teaspoon ground cloves
1/4	teaspoon salt
2	teaspoons grated zest and 1 tablespoon juice from 1 lemon
10	tablespoons (1 1/4 sticks) unsalted butter, softened but still cool
1/2	cup (3 1/2 ounces) granulated sugar
2	large egg yolks
1	teaspoon vanilla extract
1	cup seedless raspberry jam
	Confectioners' sugar for dusting on the tart

ASSEMBLING LINZERTORTE

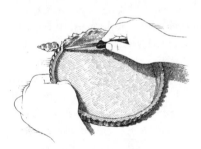
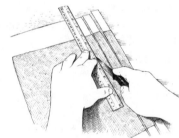

1. Use a measuring cup or ramekin to flatten the dough into an even 1/4-inch layer across the pan bottom and up the sides of the pan. Use a sharp paring knife to trim the dough to 1/2 inch below the top of the pan.

2. After rolling the remaining portion of dough into an 11-inch square, chilling it, and trimming any rough edges, cut the square into 10 strips, each 3/4 inch wide, cutting through the underlying parchment paper. Pick up a strip of dough by the parchment paper ends, then flip it over onto the tart, positioning it near the edge of the pan.

3. Remove the parchment strip and trim the ends of the dough strip by pressing down on the top edge of the pan. Reserve all of the dough scraps. Place 2 more strips parallel to the first, spacing them evenly so that one is across the center and the other is near the opposite edge of the pan.

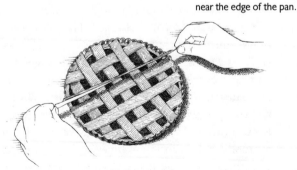

4. Rotate the pan 90 degrees. Place 3 more strips as you did the first 3. Rotate the pan 90 degrees again. Place 2 strips across the pan, spaced evenly between the first 3. Rotate the pan again and complete the lattice by placing the last 2 strips between the second set of 3.

5. Use small scraps of dough to fill in the crust around the edges between the lattice strips. The top of the crust should be just below the top of the pan.

1. Adjust an oven rack to the middle position and heat the oven to 350 degrees. Spread the almonds on a baking sheet and toast until lightly colored and fragrant, about 8 to 10 minutes. Cool to room temperature. Do not turn off the oven.

2. Process the almonds in a food processor until very finely ground, about 20 seconds, scraping down the sides of the bowl as necessary with a rubber spatula. Place the ground almonds, flour, cinnamon, cloves, salt, and lemon zest in a medium bowl and whisk to combine.

3. Place the butter and sugar in the bowl of a standing mixer and beat at medium-high speed until light and fluffy, about 3 minutes. Scrape down the sides of the mixing bowl with a rubber spatula. Add the egg yolks and vanilla and mix at medium speed until combined. Add the flour and almond mixture and mix until combined, scraping down the sides of the bowl as necessary. Form the dough into a ball, wrap in plastic, and chill until firm, about 30 minutes.

4. Divide the dough in half. Shape one half into a 6-inch square, rewrap in plastic wrap, and return to the refrigerator. Press the other half into the bottom of a 9-inch tart pan with a removable bottom. Use a measuring cup or ramekin to flatten the dough into an even ¼-inch layer across the pan bottom and up the sides of the pan. Use a sharp paring knife to trim the dough to ½ inch below the top of the pan (see illustration 1 on page 242). Chill the pan in the freezer until the dough is firm, about 15 minutes. Meanwhile, increase the oven temperature to 400 degrees.

5. Spray an 11-inch-square piece of aluminum foil with nonstick cooking spray. Prick the dough lightly with a fork across the bottom of the pan, cover with the aluminum foil, and distribute pie weights evenly in the pan.

6. Bake the crust until it is set and just slightly moist near the center, about 20 minutes. Remove the weights and foil and bake until the crust is dry and barely colored, about 5 minutes longer. Place the pan on a wire rack to cool. If the sides of the crust have risen to the top of the pan during baking, trim them down to ½ inch below the top of the pan with a paring knife. Reduce the oven temperature to 350 degrees.

7. Unwrap the remaining square of dough and roll between 2 large sheets of lightly floured parchment paper to an 11-inch square, about ⅛ inch thick. Transfer the dough and parchment onto a cookie sheet and chill until firm, about 15 minutes.

8. Meanwhile, whisk together the jam and the lemon juice in a small bowl until smooth. Spread the jam filling onto the baked crust.

9. Remove the top sheet of parchment paper from the rolled-out dough. Place the dough and the parchment paper on a cutting board. Using a ruler and a sharp knife, trim any rough edges and reserve the scraps. Following illustrations 2 through 5 on page 242, cut the dough into strips and form a lattice on the top of the tart.

10. Bake until the crust is lightly browned and the jam is bubbling, about 1 hour. Transfer the tart to a wire cooling rack and cool to room temperature, about 3 hours. When ready to serve, remove the outer ring from the tart pan and dust with confectioners' sugar.

QUICHE

THERE IS NO DISPUTE ABOUT THE CHARACTERISTICS of an ideal quiche: It must have a tender, buttery pastry case embracing a velvety smooth custard that is silken on the tongue and neither too rich nor too lean. Too often quiche filling is wet and the crust soggy.

We set out to search out the ideal quiche filling formula. In our quest, we tried every probable and improbable custard combination, from whole eggs and whole milk to whole eggs with half-and-half to whole eggs with half milk and half heavy cream to eggs with several added yolks and all heavy cream.

The leanest of these mixtures tasted so, and we rejected it as boring, with no creamy mouthfeel. The filling made with half-and-half was not as rich as one would think because half-and-half contains just 11.7 percent butterfat; it was OK but not great. The mixture containing half whole milk (which has approximately 4 percent butterfat) and half heavy cream (with 36 percent butterfat) was significantly richer; combined, the two liquids averaged 20 percent butterfat, almost twice as much as the half-and-half filling. Whole eggs, extra yolks, and all heavy cream produced a custard that was just too much of a good thing: overpoweringly rich, too creamy even for us.

The best mixture, a medium-rich custard with good mouthfeel, fine taste, and adequate firmness, combined two whole eggs with two yolks, one cup of milk and one cup of heavy cream. Baked in our favorite crust, it was just what we were looking for: a custard that was creamy but not cloyingly rich, its tender skin a luscious golden brown hue. It puffed slightly while baking and settled neatly as it cooled.

Of course, baking temperature is also an important factor regulating custard texture. High heat toughens egg proteins and shrinks the albumen, separating, or curdling, the mixture and squeezing out the water instead of keeping the egg in perfect suspension. Moderate heat works best.

We tested our different quiche formulas at temperatures ranging from 325 degrees to 400 degrees. Some cooks prefer to start baking at 400 degrees for 15 minutes, then reduce the heat to 350 degrees for the remaining time. We found 350 degrees slightly slow; by the time the custard set, the top, which remained a pallid yellow hue, had developed into a slightly rubbery, chewy skin. On the theory that warming the liquid in the custard would shorten baking time and keep the custard smoother, we tried heating the milk to 100 degrees before whisking in the eggs. Indeed, this custard set a few minutes faster, but it was otherwise unremarkable and still had a pallid color on top. We found that baking at 375 degrees was exactly right, setting the custard gently enough to maintain its creamy consistency, yet hot enough to brown the top before it dried out and became rubbery.

As a test for doneness, we advise watching the oven, not the clock, looking for a light golden brown coloring on the quiche surface, which may puff up slightly as it bakes. A knife blade inserted about 1 inch from the edge should come out clean; the center may still be slightly liquid, but internal heat will finish the baking and it will solidify when cool. If your test blade comes out clean in the center, the quiche may already be slightly overbaked and should be removed from the oven at once. Be sure to set the baked quiche on a wire rack to cool, so air circulates all around it, preventing condensation on the bottom. Allowing the quiche to cool until it is either warm or at room temperature also lets the custard settle before serving. The cooler the quiche, the more neatly it will slice.

Quiche Lorraine
SERVES 8

Quiche Lorraine is named after the region in France in which it originated, Alsace-Lorraine. The center of the quiche will be surprisingly soft when it comes out of the oven, but the filling will continue to set (and sink somewhat) as it cools. If the pie shell has been previously baked and cooled, place it in the heating oven for about five minutes to warm it, taking care that it does not burn. Because ingredients in the variations that follow are bulkier, the amount of custard mixture has been reduced to prevent overflowing the crust.

I	recipe Pie Dough for Prebaked Pie Shell (page 183)
8	ounces (about 8 slices) bacon, cut into ½-inch pieces
2	large eggs plus 2 large egg yolks
I	cup whole milk
I	cup heavy cream
½	teaspoon salt
½	teaspoon ground white pepper
	Pinch freshly grated nutmeg
4	ounces Gruyère cheese, grated (about I cup)

1. Follow the directions for partially baking the pie shell until light golden brown. Remove the pie shell from the oven but do not turn off the oven.

2. Meanwhile, fry the bacon in a skillet over medium heat until crisp, about 5 minutes. Transfer the bacon with a slotted spoon to a paper towel–lined plate. Whisk together the remaining ingredients except the cheese in a medium bowl.

3. Spread the cheese and bacon evenly over the bottom of the warm pie shell and set the shell on the oven rack. Pour the custard mixture into the pie shell (it should come to about ½ inch below the crust's rim). Bake until light golden brown and a knife blade inserted about 1 inch from the

edge comes out clean and the center feels set but soft like gelatin, 32 to 35 minutes. Transfer the quiche to a rack to cool. Serve warm or at room temperature.

➤ VARIATIONS

Crabmeat Quiche

Follow the recipe for Quiche Lorraine, reducing the quantities of milk and cream to ¾ cup each. Add 2 tablespoons dry sherry and a pinch of cayenne pepper to the custard mixture. Replace the bacon and cheese with 8 ounces (1 cup) cooked crabmeat tossed with 2 tablespoons chopped fresh chives.

Leek and Goat Cheese Quiche

Sauté the white parts of 2 medium leeks, washed thoroughly and cut into ½-inch dice (about 2 cups), in 2 tablespoons unsalted butter over medium heat until soft, 5 to 7 minutes. Follow the recipe for Quiche Lorraine, reducing the quantities of milk and cream to ¾ cup each. Omit the bacon; substitute 4 ounces mild goat cheese, broken into ½-inch pieces, for the Gruyère. Add the leeks with the goat cheese.

Ham and Asparagus Quiche

Blanch 8 asparagus spears, cut on the bias into ½-inch pieces (about 1 cup) in 1 quart salted boiling water until crisp-tender, about 2 minutes. Drain thoroughly. Follow the recipe for Quiche Lorraine, reducing the quantities of milk and cream to ¾ cup each. Replace the bacon and cheese with the asparagus and 4 ounces deli baked ham, cut into ¼-inch dice.

TOMATO AND MOZZARELLA TART

FALLING SOMEPLACE IN BETWEEN PIZZA and quiche, tomato and mozzarella tart shares the flavors of both but features problems unique unto itself. For starters, this is not fast food, as it requires some sort of pastry crust. Second, the moisture in the tomatoes almost guarantees a soggy crust. Third, tomato tarts are often tasteless. We wanted a recipe we could easily make at home with a solid bottom crust and great vine-ripened tomato flavor.

The first thing we learned is that tomato and mozzarella tarts come in all shapes and sizes: everything from overwrought custardy pies resembling quiche to stripped-down, minimalist models that are more like pizza. A test kitchen sampling of these various styles delivered dismal results—sodden bottoms and tired toppings across the board—but we agreed that one recipe stood out: a simple construction of tomatoes and cheese shingled across a plain, prebaked sheet of puff pastry. Unwilling to make puff pastry from scratch for this recipe, we grabbed some store-bought puff pastry (we found Pepperidge Farm to be the most available; two pieces of dough come in a single box) and started cooking.

The winning recipe from the taste test consisted of a flat sheet of puff pastry with a thin border to contain the topping (tomatoes easily slip off a flat sheet of anything) and a thick glaze of egg wash to seal the dough tight against the seeping tomatoes. We trimmed thin strips of dough from the edges of a single rectangular sheet of puff pastry and cemented them with some beaten egg to the top of the sheet to create a uniform 1-inch border. This single tart shell looked large enough for two to three servings. With scarcely any more effort, we found we could serve twice as many by joining the two pieces of dough that came in the box (we sealed the seam tightly with egg wash and it rolled flat) and making a long rectangular version, roughly 16 by 8 inches. Once assembled, the tart was heavily brushed with egg wash.

From the initial test results, we knew that prebaking the crust would be essential to give it a fighting chance against the moisture from the tomatoes. Following the recipe on the back of the Pepperidge Farm box, we baked our enlarged tart shell at 400 degrees until it was light, airy, and golden brown. Now we ran into our first problem. The shell was too frail to support a heavy, wet filling. Baked at 350 degrees, the shell was noticeably squatter and drier—and so better suited to a heavy filling—but it was also unpleasantly tough and chewy. We wondered if a two-step baking method might be more successful: a high temperature for initial lift and browning, then a lower temperature to dry out the shell for maximum sturdiness. Our first test—400 degrees reduced to 350 degrees once the dough had risen—proved positive, so we fiddled with temperature pairings until the crust was ideal. When baked at 425 degrees until puffed and light golden (about 15 minutes) and finished at 350 degrees until well browned (15 minutes longer), the crust was flaky yet rigid enough so that we could pick up a piece of tart at one end and hold it aloft.

Now we had half-solved the problem of the soggy crust, but there was still work to do. The egg wash coating had proven only deflective, not impermeable. Liquid from the tomatoes soaked through to the puff pastry, albeit at a slower rate than uncoated pastry. Egg wash was part of, but not the whole, solution.

Our next thought was that a layer of cheese might help. A scant ½ pound of grated mozzarella melted into a smooth, seemingly watertight layer across the tart's bottom. When the entire tart was assembled and baked, the bottom crust was vastly improved, but the tomatoes still gave off too much water, which affected the texture of the crust and the overall flavor of the tart.

Our first thought was to use tomatoes with a relatively low water content. We limited our tests to standard beefsteak (round) and Roma (plum) tomatoes because they are the most readily available. A quick side-by-side test ruled out beefsteaks as excessively high in liquid. As we had suspected, Romas were the better choice for this recipe.

As for extracting the tomatoes' juices, roasting was an obvious choice, but we ruled it out as too time- and labor-intensive. Besides, we wanted

ASSEMBLING A TOMATO TART

1. Brush some of the beaten egg along one edge of one sheet of puff pastry. Overlap with the second sheet of dough by 1 inch and press down to seal the pieces together.

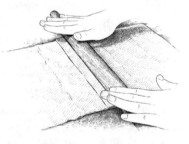

2. With a rolling pin, smooth out the seam. The dough rectangle should measure about 18 by 9 inches. Use a pizza wheel or knife to trim the edges straight.

3. With the pizza wheel or knife, cut a 1-inch strip from the long side of the dough. Cut another 1-inch strip from the same side.

4. With the pizza wheel or knife, cut a 1-inch strip from the short side of the dough. Cut another 1-inch strip from the same side.

5. Transfer the large piece of dough to a parchment-lined baking sheet and brush with more beaten egg. Gently press the long strips of dough onto the 2 long sides of the dough. Brush the long strips of dough with beaten egg. Gently press the short strips of dough onto the 2 short sides. Brush the short strips of dough with beaten egg.

6. With the pizza wheel or knife, trim any excess dough from the corners.

the brighter flavor of lightly cooked tomatoes. Salting—a step common to Mediterranean cooking and one the test kitchen has put to good use in other recipes—worked well but not perfectly. We sprinkled sliced tomatoes with salt and left them to drain on paper towels for 30 minutes. The underlying towels were soaked through, but the tomatoes were still juicy to the touch. Increasing the amount of salt and time accomplished frustratingly little. A little gentle force, however, worked magic: We sandwiched the salted slices between paper towels and pressed down with enough force to extrude any remaining juices (and the seeds) but not enough to squish the slices flat. They were as dry as could be, yet still very flavorful.

Baked quick and hot to melt the cheese and preserve the tomatoes' meaty texture (425 degrees turned out to be the best temperature), the tart looked ready for the cover of a magazine, especially when slicked with a garlic-infused olive oil and strewn with fresh basil leaves. But just a few minutes from the oven, the horrible truth revealed itself: The crust was soggy. Despite the egg wash, the melted mozzarella, and drained and pressed tomatoes, the tart continued to suffer the ills of moisture.

Discouraged but not undone, we remembered those prebaked supermarket pizza crusts and wondered if, as on those crusts, a solid layer of crisply baked Parmesan, on top of the egg wash but beneath the mozzarella, would seal the base of our tart more permanently. We sprinkled finely grated Parmesan over the tart shell for the prebake and crossed our fingers. The cheese melted to such a solid (and deliciously nutty tasting) layer that liquid rolled right off, like rain off a duck's back.

After baking a whole tart, we were stunned by the results: Slices could be lifted freely and consumed like pizza, even hours from the oven. Rich in flavor and sturdy in form, it had character to match its good looks—and it was quick, too. Ready-made dough and minimal ingredients kept preparation brief, and total cooking time was less than an hour and a half. Not only was this tart better than we expected, it was also simpler.

Tomato and Mozzarella Tart
SERVES 4 TO 6

The baked tart is best eaten warm within 2 hours of baking. If you prefer to do some advance preparation, the tart shell can be prebaked through step 1, cooled to room temperature, wrapped in plastic wrap, and kept at room temperature for up to 2 days before being topped and baked with the mozzarella and tomatoes. Use low-moisture, shrink-wrapped supermarket cheese rather than fresh mozzarella. To keep the frozen pastry from cracking, it's best to let it thaw slowly in the refrigerator overnight.

	Flour for dusting the work surface
1	(1.1-pound) box frozen puff pastry (Pepperidge Farm), thawed in the box in the refrigerator overnight
1	large egg, beaten
½	cup finely grated Parmesan cheese (about 1 ounce)
1	pound Roma tomatoes (about 3 to 4 medium), cored and cut crosswise into ¼-inch-thick slices
	Salt
2	medium garlic cloves, minced or pressed through garlic press (about 2 teaspoons)
2	tablespoons extra-virgin olive oil
	Ground black pepper
8	ounces low-moisture whole-milk mozzarella, shredded (2 cups)
2	tablespoons coarsely chopped fresh basil leaves

1. Adjust an oven rack to the lower-middle position and heat the oven to 425 degrees. Dust the work surface with flour and unfold both pieces of puff pastry onto the work surface. Follow the illustrations on page 246 to form 1 large sheet with a border, using the beaten egg as directed. Sprinkle the Parmesan evenly over the bottom of the shell; using a fork, uniformly and thoroughly poke holes in the bottom. Bake 15 minutes, then reduce the oven temperature to 350 degrees; continue to bake until golden brown and crisp, 15 to 17 minutes longer. Transfer to a wire rack; increase the oven temperature to 425 degrees.

2. While the shell bakes, place the tomato slices in a single layer on 2 layers of paper towels and sprinkle evenly with ½ teaspoon salt; let stand 30 minutes. Place 2 more layers of paper towels on top of the tomatoes and press firmly to dry the tomatoes. Combine the garlic, olive oil, and a pinch each of salt and pepper in a small bowl; set aside

3. Sprinkle the mozzarella evenly over the bottom of the warm (or cool, if made ahead) baked shell. Shingle the tomato slices widthwise on top of the cheese (about 4 slices per row); brush the tomatoes with the garlic oil. Bake until the shell is deep golden brown and the cheese is melted, 15 to 17 minutes. Cool on a wire rack 5 minutes, sprinkle with the basil, slide onto a cutting board or serving platter, cut into pieces, and serve.

➤ VARIATIONS

Tomato and Mozzarella Tart with Prosciutto

Follow the recipe for Tomato and Mozzarella Tart, laying 2 ounces thinly sliced prosciutto in a single layer on top of the mozzarella before arranging the tomato slices.

THE TALE OF THE SOGGY TART

If you neglect to salt the tomatoes and to brush the dough with egg wash, the baked tart will be soggy and limp (top). If you take both of these precautions (and add a layer of grated Parmesan), individual slices will be firm and dry and have enough structural integrity to hold their shape (bottom).

LIMP AND SOGGY

CRISP AND DRY

Tomato and Smoked Mozzarella Tart

Follow the recipe for Tomato and Mozzarella Tart, substituting 6 ounces smoked mozzarella for the whole-milk mozzarella.

PHYLLO PIE WITH SPINACH AND FETA (SPANAKOPITA)

ON PAPER, SPANAKOPITA NEVER FAILS TO make the mouth water. Recipes promise a savory blend of spinach, onions, and tangy feta cheese, spiked with lemon, garlic, and herbs and encased in crisp, buttery phyllo pastry. Unfortunately, modern-day versions of this traditional Greek dish rarely taste as good as they sound. More often than not, the basic components of spanakopita don't so much combine as collide, working at cross-purposes to produce unimpressive results. A dense, stringy layer of overcooked spinach is not enhanced by a thin, shattered crust of dried-out pastry. Scattered chunks of salty feta cheese don't do much to round out the dish. To top it off, working with store-bought phyllo dough can test the patience of a pontiff. Lots of labor and a disappointing payoff: Is spanakopita really worth it?

We wanted a spanakopita that lived up to its billing and didn't require an army of Greek grandmothers to prepare. We focused first on perfecting a spinach and feta filling with big, bold flavors. (This same filling can be used to make Phyllo Triangles with Spinach and Feta, page 251.) Spanakopita means "spinach pie," so we knew where to start—with the green stuff, and lots of it. Too many recipes skimped on the spinach, resulting in spanakopitas that are thin and greasy from all that buttery phyllo. We wanted a thick layer of filling that would stand up to the pastry crust. Many recipes call for frozen spinach, and while it may be convenient, tasters objected to its metallic, freezer-burnt flavor. Bagged curly spinach demonstrated many advantages over the bunched flat-leaf variety. It's cheaper and easier to clean, and because so much of flat-leaf spinach is stemmed and discarded, curly spinach yields much more usable product per pound.

Some recipes called for sautéing the spinach with onion and garlic, others suggested boiling or steaming the greens and then wringing out the excess water. We wanted the onion and garlic flavors, but we also knew that removing that excess moisture was crucial to avoid a soggy filling. We opted for convenience again, quickly blanching batches of spinach in rapidly boiling water and then plunging the greens into an ice bath to stop the cooking and preserve as much bright green color as possible. A potato ricer proved the perfect tool for pressing excess moisture from the spinach before adding it back to the pan with sautéed onions and garlic for a quick toss to combine. We also found that this minimal initial cooking eliminated the drab color and washed-out flavor of overcooked spinach that plagued our early efforts.

Tangy feta pairs perfectly with earthy spinach, but the marriage of flavors is ruined when big chunks of the salty cheese are found adrift in a sea of clumpy greens. Eggs are a standard ingredient in

spanakopita recipes, and rightly so. They bind the filling ingredients together, add richness and flavor, and lighten the layer of spinach that otherwise gets dense and soggy when baked in the oven. By first breaking up the feta with a fork, then whisking it with the eggs, we were able to distribute the cheese more evenly throughout the pie.

Scallions and herbs such as parsley and dill are traditional ingredients in a spanakopita but usually listed in such paltry amounts that the flavors are sunk beneath the spinach and feta. We increased the quantities of each. Lemon juice and grated nutmeg were less commonly listed, but tasters unanimously approved. We took stock: The flavors were now bright and clean, but the filling still seemed a little dry, and it lacked a certain richness. A few recipes included ricotta cheese to tame the bite of the feta, and our tasters agreed that it rounded out the flavors and gave the filling just the right creamy texture.

When spread into a 13 by 9-inch baking dish, our spinach filling stood a proud 1½ inches high, a

ASSEMBLING PHYLLO PIES

1. Butter a 13 by 9-inch glass baking dish liberally with melted butter. Place a half sheet of phyllo in the baking dish offset ³/₄ inch from the center, so that the phyllo climbs up the side of the dish but does not extend above the rim of the dish.

2. Brush lightly with melted butter. Repeat with more pieces (see recipes for the exact number) of phyllo, brushing each sheet with melted butter and alternating the direction in which each piece is offset from the center of the dish.

3. Spread half of the filling on top of the phyllo. Layer either two or four pieces of phyllo (see recipes for the exact number) centered on top of the filling. Spread the remaining filling over the top. Cover with more pieces of phyllo (see recipes for the exact number), brushing each with butter and sprinkling each with 1 tablespoon of Parmesan.

4. Place one last piece of phyllo over the layer and brush with butter (do not sprinkle with Parmesan). Using a sharp knife, lightly score into serving squares, taking care not to cut through more than the top three pieces of phyllo.

marked improvement over the sad, sunken versions we had seen earlier in our testing. A filling this thick needed more than a few paper-thin sheets of pastry to hold it all together. We found that 16 half sheets of phyllo (eight on top and eight on the bottom) made crusts that were substantial but still tender. More than that and the pastry was tough to bite through. We tried adding a middle layer of four half sheets of phyllo and found that it helped the pie keep its shape after it was sliced.

Phyllo is famous for its crisp, flaky layers, but it was this quality that gave us the most trouble once the pie hit the hot oven. In every test, the papery layers curled and separated from each other as they baked. Cutting into the pie sent shattered pieces of phyllo everywhere.

Some dessert recipes involving phyllo advise sprinkling each layer with granulated sugar, which then melts in the oven and helps the pastry stick together. We didn't want a sweet crust, but would grated cheese work the same way? A small quantity of grated Parmesan dusted across each of the top layer's sheets worked wonders, yielding a cohesive crust that was tender but offered just the right amount of chew.

Lastly, we wondered about the lengthy baking times specified by most recipes—usually an hour in the oven at 350 degrees, until the phyllo is golden and crisp. The results? Our bright flavors were washed out and flat, the spinach was well on its way to mushy and overcooked, and the phyllo was dried out and more prone to shattering. Increasing the temperature to 400 degrees and reducing the cooking time to about 35 minutes resulted in a filling and crust that were both done to perfection.

Phyllo Pie with Spinach and Feta (Spanakopita)
SERVES 6 TO 8

Frozen phyllo dough will stick together and tear unless completely thawed, either overnight in the refrigerator or for several hours at room temperature. Once unwrapped, the sheets must remain covered or they will quickly dry out. Phyllo is sold in 1-pound boxes, each of which contains about 20 sheets. This recipe will use 10 sheets, but it is important to have extra on hand as even properly thawed phyllo will sometimes stick or tear. Extra sheets can be rewrapped and kept refrigerated for 1 week or refrozen for 2 months. Leftovers are best reheated in a 350-degree oven until crisp and heated through, about 25 minutes.

	Salt
3	**pounds curly spinach, stemmed and washed**
1	**tablespoon olive oil**
1	**medium onion, chopped fine (about 1 cup)**
6	**medium garlic cloves, minced or pressed through a garlic press (about 2 tablespoons)**

MAKING PHYLLO TRIANGLES

1. With the short end near you, brush a phyllo sheet with butter. Cut the sheet lengthwise to make 2 strips about 6 inches wide. Fold each strip in half lengthwise and brush the tops.

2. Place 1 tablespoon of filling on the bottom left-hand corner. Fold up the phyllo to form a right-angle triangle.

3. Continue folding up and over, as if folding a flag, to the end of the strip.

4. Brush the triangle with butter and place seam-side down on an ungreased baking sheet. When all the triangles are on 2 baking sheets, bake as directed.

6 scallions, green and white parts, sliced thin (about ⅔ cup)

½ cup minced fresh parsley leaves

¼ cup minced fresh dill leaves

3 tablespoons juice from I large lemon
Ground black pepper

4 large eggs, lightly beaten

I teaspoon freshly grated nutmeg

12 ounces whole milk ricotta cheese

I pound feta cheese, crumbled (about 4 cups)

II tablespoons unsalted butter, melted

I pound phyllo sheets, thawed

I ounce Parmesan cheese, grated (about ½ cup)

1. Bring 4 quarts water to a boil with 2 tablespoons salt in a large, heavy-bottomed saucepan or Dutch oven. Have ready a large bowl partially filled with ice water. Add 2 large handfuls of spinach to the pan and cook until wilted, about 30 seconds. Remove the spinach with a handheld strainer and transfer to the ice-water bath until thoroughly cooled. Repeat until all of the spinach is cooked. Squeeze the excess moisture from the spinach. Roughly chop the spinach and set aside.

2. Drain the water from the pan you used to cook the spinach and wipe it thoroughly with paper towels. Heat the olive oil in the pan over medium heat until shimmering. Add the onion and cook, stirring frequently, until softened, 5 to 6 minutes. Add the garlic and cook until fragrant, about 1 minute. Add the spinach, scallions, parsley, dill, lemon juice, ¾ teaspoon salt, and ⅛ teaspoon pepper and stir until combined, about 1 minute. Transfer the filling to a large bowl and cool to room temperature.

3. Combine the eggs, nutmeg, ricotta, and feta in a mixing bowl and whisk until only small chunks of feta are visible. Add to the cooled spinach mixture and mix thoroughly.

4. Adjust an oven rack to the middle position and heat the oven to 400 degrees. Brush a 13 by 9-inch baking dish liberally with some of the melted butter. Remove 10 phyllo sheets from the package and unfold them on a cutting board. Cut the stack of sheets in half crosswise to yield 20 half sheets, then cover with plastic wrap and a damp kitchen towel. Keep the sheets covered when not using to prevent them from drying out. Following the illustrations on page 249, place 1 piece of phyllo offset ¾ inch from the center so that the phyllo climbs up the side of the dish but does not go above the rim of the dish. Brush the phyllo lightly with melted butter, starting at the edges and moving toward the center. Repeat with 7 more pieces of phyllo, brushing each with melted butter and alternating the direction in which each piece is offset from the center of the dish.

5. Spread half of the spinach mixture over the stacked phyllo in the dish, spreading it to an even thickness. Layer 4 pieces of phyllo on top of the filling, brushing each with melted butter as before. Spread the remaining spinach mixture evenly over the top. Place 1 piece of phyllo on top of the spinach and brush lightly with melted butter. Sprinkle about 1 tablespoon of Parmesan on top of the phyllo. Repeat with 6 more pieces of phyllo. Place 1 last piece over the layer and brush with butter (do not sprinkle with Parmesan). Using a sharp knife, lightly score the pie into serving squares but do not cut through more than the first 3 pieces of phyllo. Bake until the phyllo is golden and crisp, 30 to 35 minutes. Cool on a wire rack for at least 10 minutes or up to 2 hours before serving.

➤ VARIATION

Phyllo Triangles with Spinach and Feta
MAKES 40

Serve these triangles as an appetizer.

Follow steps 1 through 3 for Phyllo Pie with Spinach and Feta, reducing all the filling ingredient quantities by one half. Adjust the oven racks to the upper- and lower-middle positions and heat the oven to 375 degrees. Follow the illustrations for "Making Phyllo Triangles" on page 250, using 20 sheets of phyllo (roughly an entire package). Bake until golden, about 20 minutes, rotating the sheets halfway through the baking time.

PHYLLO PIE WITH MEAT AND RICE (KREATOPITA)

ALTHOUGH SPANAKOPITA IS THE MOST familiar of the Greek phyllo pies, we found other versions we liked just as well; kreatopita (phyllo pie with meat and rice), for example. There are more variations of this traditional Greek meat pie than there are islands in the Aegean. Though lamb is perhaps the most common choice of filling, ground beef and sometimes pork are familiar substitutes in many regional versions of this dish. Our tasters found an all-beef pie to be dry and plain, and they disliked the richness and overly strong flavors in a pie made entirely with lamb. An even mix of the two was the clear winner.

Choosing the right meat was only the beginning. The various ingredient lists we came across were baffling in their length and diversity. One version contained red wine, tomatoes, and dill. Another suggested milk and wheat germ; yet another listed cottage cheese and hard-boiled eggs. We picked and chose our way through and tried to keep it simple.

Rice, sometimes precooked and sometimes raw, was a common addition, and we liked the way it bound the filling together while counteracting the richness of the meat. While red wine imparted a sour flavor, we liked the sweetness of a little tomato paste, especially when paired with ground allspice. Milk was mentioned in a few recipes, but we preferred the clean flavor of chicken stock, which also allowed us to cook the rice in the same pot with the meat. Feta was the cheese of choice, but in this dish we balanced it with grated Parmesan, a common substitute for Kefalotiri, the unpasteurized hard Greek cheese that appears in most traditional recipes. Lastly, we stuck close to tradition and added fresh mint and lemon juice to complement the lamb.

We found we could assemble this meat pie as we did with spanakopita. The nature of the meat filling, however, required us to make a few slight adjustments. At first the finished product was extremely rich, and we reasoned that the butter coating the middle layers of phyllo wasn't helping

matters. We tried reducing the middle layer to 2 half sheets and omitting the melted butter, and the result was a cleaner, lighter-tasting dish. Secondly, the moisture from the heavier filling seemed to produce a soggy, undercooked bottom layer of phyllo. A little more oven time at a lower temperature allowed the bottom sheets to crisp up nicely.

Phyllo Pie with Meat and Rice (Kreatopita)
SERVES 6 TO 8

Try to use no more than 1½ teaspoons of melted butter to coat each sheet of phyllo as the filling is very rich. The filling can be made ahead of time and refrigerated overnight in an airtight container. See the recipe headnote on page 250 for tips on thawing and handling phyllo dough.

2	tablespoons olive oil
1	pound ground lamb
1	pound ground beef (85 percent lean)
2	medium onions, chopped fine (about 2 cups)
6	medium garlic cloves, minced or pressed through a garlic press (about 2 tablespoons)
1	tablespoon tomato paste
½	teaspoon ground allspice
1	teaspoon salt
¼	teaspoon ground black pepper
1	cup long-grain rice
2½	cups low-sodium chicken broth
½	cup minced fresh parsley leaves
⅓	cup minced fresh mint leaves
6	scallions, green and white parts, sliced thin (about ⅔ cup)
3	tablespoons juice from 1 large lemon
3	large eggs, lightly beaten
8	ounces feta cheese, crumbled (about 2 cups)
3	ounces Parmesan cheese, grated (about 1½ cups)
9	tablespoons unsalted butter, melted
1	pound phyllo sheets, thawed

1. Heat the oil in a large, heavy-bottomed saucepan or Dutch oven over medium heat until shimmering. Add the lamb and beef and cook, breaking up large chunks of the meat with a wooden spoon, until no longer pink, about 5 minutes. Remove the

meat with a slotted spoon to a platter. Pour off all but 1 tablespoon of the fat and return the pan to medium heat.

2. Add the onion to the remaining fat in the pan and cook, stirring frequently, until the onion softens, about 5 minutes. Add the garlic, tomato paste, and allspice and cook until fragrant, about 1 minute. Add the meat, salt, and pepper to the pan and cook, stirring frequently, until thoroughly combined and heated through, about 2 minutes. Stir in the rice and broth, bring to a boil, cover, and reduce the heat to low. Cook for 15 minutes, stirring every 5 minutes. Remove from the heat and let stand covered until most of the moisture is absorbed and the rice is just slightly undercooked, about 5 minutes. Add the parsley, mint, scallions, and lemon juice. Toss to combine, then transfer the filling to a medium bowl and cool to room temperature.

3. Combine the eggs, feta, and 1 cup Parmesan in a mixing bowl. Whisk the ingredients together until only small chunks of feta are visible. Add to the cooled meat mixture and mix thoroughly.

4. Adjust an oven rack to the middle position and heat the oven to 375 degrees. Brush a 13 by 9-inch baking dish with 1 tablespoon of the melted butter. Remove 9 phyllo sheets from the package and unfold them on a cutting board. Cut the stack of sheets in half crosswise to yield 18 half sheets, then cover with plastic wrap and a damp kitchen towel. Keep the sheets covered when not using to prevent them from drying out. Following the illustrations on page 249, place 1 piece of phyllo offset ¾ inch from the center so that the phyllo climbs up the side of the dish but does not go above the rim of the dish. Brush the phyllo lightly with melted butter, starting at the edges and moving toward the center. Repeat with 7 more pieces of phyllo, brushing each with melted butter and alternating the direction in which each piece is offset from the center of the dish.

5. Spread half of the meat mixture over the stacked phyllo in the dish, spreading it to an even thickness. Layer 2 pieces of phyllo on top of the filling but do not brush with melted butter. Spread the remaining meat mixture evenly over the top. Place 1 piece of phyllo on top of the meat and brush lightly with melted butter. Sprinkle about

1 tablespoon of Parmesan on top of the phyllo. Repeat with 6 more pieces of phyllo. Place 1 last piece over the layer and brush with butter (do not add Parmesan). Using a sharp knife, lightly score the pie into serving squares but do not cut through more than the first 3 pieces of phyllo. Bake until the phyllo is golden and crisp, about 50 minutes. Cool on a wire rack for at least 10 minutes or up to 2 hours before serving.

➤ VARIATION

Phyllo Triangles with Meat and Rice
MAKES 40
Serve these small triangles as an appetizer.

Follow steps 1 through 3 for Phyllo Pie with Meat and Rice, reducing the mint to 2 tablespoons and all other filling ingredients by half. Adjust the oven racks to the upper- and lower-middle positions and heat the oven to 375 degrees. Follow the illustrations for "Making Phyllo Triangles" on page 250, using 20 sheets of phyllo (roughly an entire package). Bake until golden, about 20 minutes, rotating the sheets halfway through the baking time.

PHYLLO PIE WITH CHEESE (TIROPITA)

LIGHTER THAN ITS MEAT-FILLED COUSIN and much simpler to prepare than a traditional spanakopita, this simple cheese pie is also endlessly variable. Cheese (usually feta), eggs, and phyllo are the only mandatory ingredients, and the recipes we found were often just that plain and simple. Other versions complicated matters with cream cheese, milk, and béchamel sauces, but the variation we liked best contained a mixture of feta, Parmesan, and ricotta cheeses (the latter quickly blended in a food processor to cut down on its grainy texture), onion, garlic, and herbs.

Most recipes were loaded down with eggs, as many as 10 in some cases, but the resulting pies were more like quiches or even cheesy scrambled eggs. Just three eggs were plenty to bind the ingredients together and give the filling a little lift.

A crust made from eight sheets of phyllo seemed

a little thick for this pie, which is thinner than either of the meat or spinach versions. Accordingly, we reduced the top and bottom layers to six sheets each and used just two sheets in the middle.

<hr>

Phyllo Pie with Cheese (Tiropita)

SERVES 6 TO 8

This filling is softer than the others, which can make brushing the middle and top layers a challenge. Be gentle so as not to tear the phyllo. See the recipe headnote on page 250 for tips on thawing and handling phyllo dough.

I	teaspoon olive oil
I	medium onion, chopped (about I cup)
3	medium garlic cloves, minced or pressed through a garlic press (about I tablespoon)
12	ounces ricotta cheese
3	large eggs, lightly beaten
1/2	teaspoon salt
1/8	teaspoon ground black pepper
I	pound feta cheese, crumbled (about 4 cups)
2	ounces Parmesan cheese, grated (about I cup)
1/4	cup minced fresh parsley leaves
2	tablespoons minced fresh oregano leaves
10	tablespoons (I 1/4 sticks) unsalted butter, melted
I	pound phyllo sheets, thawed

1. Heat the oil in a 10-inch nonstick skillet over medium heat. Add the onion and cook, stirring frequently, until softened, about 5 minutes. Add the garlic and cook until fragrant, about 1 minute. Remove the onion and garlic from the pan and cool.

2. Place the ricotta, eggs, salt, and pepper in the bowl of a food processor and process until smooth, about 20 seconds. Place the feta in a mixing bowl and break up the clumps with a fork. Add the ricotta mixture, 2/3 cup of the Parmesan, the parsley, and oregano and mix thoroughly.

3. Adjust an oven rack to the middle position and heat the oven to 400 degrees. Brush a 13 by 9-inch baking dish with 1 tablespoon of the melted butter. Remove 7 phyllo sheets from the package and unfold them on a cutting board. Cut the stack of sheets in half crosswise to yield 14 half sheets, then cover with plastic wrap and a damp kitchen towel. Keep the sheets covered when not using to prevent them from drying out. Following the illustrations on page 249, place 1 piece of phyllo offset 3/4 inch from the center so that the phyllo climbs up the side of the dish but does not go above the rim of the dish. Brush the phyllo lightly with melted butter, starting at the edges and moving toward the center. Repeat with 5 more pieces of phyllo, brushing each with melted butter and alternating the direction in which each piece is offset from the center of the dish.

4. Spread half of the cheese mixture over the stacked phyllo in the dish, spreading it to an even thickness. Layer 2 pieces of phyllo on top of the filling, brushing each with melted butter as before. Spread the remaining cheese mixture evenly over the top. Place 1 piece of phyllo on top of the cheese and brush lightly with melted butter. Sprinkle about 1 tablespoon of Parmesan on top of the phyllo. Repeat with 4 more pieces of phyllo. Place 1 last piece over the layer and brush with butter (do not add Parmesan). Using a sharp knife, lightly score the pie into serving squares but do not cut through more than the first 3 pieces of phyllo. Bake until the phyllo is golden and crisp, 30 to 35 minutes. Cool on a wire rack for at least 10 minutes or up to 2 hours before serving.

> VARIATION

Phyllo Triangles with Cheese

MAKES 40

Serve these small triangles as an appetizer.

Follow steps 1 and 2 for Phyllo Pie with Cheese, reducing the eggs to 1 and all other filling ingredient quantities by half. Adjust the oven racks to the upper- and lower-middle positions and heat the oven to 375 degrees. Follow the illustrations for "Making Phyllo Triangles" on page 250, using 20 sheets of phyllo (roughly an entire package). Bake until golden, about 20 minutes, rotating the sheets halfway through the baking time.

5

PASTRY

Pastry

UNLESS YOUR GRANDMOTHER WAS FRENCH (or you've attended culinary school), chances are you don't know how to make classic pastries like éclairs, croissants, and Napoleons. Have no fear. Despite their rarified reputation, making pastries isn't much more difficult than making a loaf of bread. With a little patience and a little practice, you can turn out delectable treats that seem as if they came from an authentic pâtisserie.

Cream puff pastry (pâte à choux) is a good place to start for those new to pastry making because it doesn't take long to make and the technique is fairly simple. On the stovetop, butter and flour are cooked together to form a paste. Off the heat, eggs are added and the mixture stirred. The dough should then be piped onto a sheet pan and baked. Be sure to let the pastry cool completely before filling and glazing (as for éclairs, profiteroles, and cream puffs).

The doughs used to make croissants, Danish, and puff pastry are generally composed of a few integral ingredients: flour, water or milk, sometimes yeast, and, most important, lots of butter. The butter is generally mixed with a small amount of flour, formed into a square, and folded into the dough to create multiple layers (each layer is formed by a "fold," or turn). The layers of butter and dough alternate so that when the dough is baked, the steam released from the layers of butter creates the paper-thin flaky layers characteristic of such pastry.

Pastry dough is not unlike pie dough, and it must be treated with the same attention, as it can be finicky. Although some of the doughs contain yeast for lift, butter performs double duty in that it is responsible for not only the flakiness but some of the lift and rise, as well. Therefore, keeping the butter cold and the dough relaxed (so it won't rip or tear when rolling it out, thus destroying the layers you're trying to create) is important for optimal results. If your kitchen is warm, you may find the butter in your pastry melting before you have had time to finish forming it. Simply return the dough to the refrigerator to chill. In lieu of a cool marble work surface, we have found it helpful to place a tray of ice cubes on top of the work surface to chill it down before proceeding. A pizza cutter or pastry wheel and a ruler are handy for measuring and cutting the pastry accurately. It is important that the edges of the dough line up evenly so that the layers are uniform throughout.

CREAM PUFF PASTRY

PÂTE À CHOUX, CREAM PUFF PASTRY IN English, is the most basic French pastry. It has both sweet and savory applications but is most familiar when filled with pastry cream to make éclairs or cream puffs. Fill them with ice cream and nap with chocolate sauce and they become profiteroles. Stir shredded cheese into the dough and they turn into gougères.

Pâte à choux should bake into light, airy, well-puffed pastry with a delicately crisp crust. The inside should be primarily hollow, with a soft, custardy webbing lining the interior walls. Beware the pitfalls of bad pâte à choux. The dough will spread on the baking sheet if too soft, and it may not rise properly. It may bake up lopsided, it can collapse after baking, and, finally (the most common problem), it can turn soggy as it cools.

The traditional technique of making pâte à choux is to bring water or milk, salt, and butter to a boil in a saucepan. When the mixture reaches a rolling boil, flour is stirred in to make a paste, the saucepan is returned to low heat, and the paste is cooked. During cooking, the paste is stirred constantly, stimulating the development of gluten, the protein that gives bread doughs elasticity and provides for a better, stronger rise in the oven. Then the dough is removed from the heat, and eggs are beaten in one by one. The pâte à choux is then ready to be piped onto a sheet pan and baked.

To determine how long the paste really needs to be cooked on the stovetop, we made four batches of pâte à choux and cooked each to a different degree—from not at all up to five minutes—over low heat. The uncooked batch and the one cooked for only a minute failed to attain much height when we baked them. The batches made from paste cooked for three and five minutes, however, both baked into voluminous puffs. Because none of the tasters could detect a significant difference between these two, we opted for three minutes of cooking. Since stovetops undoubtedly vary, we took the temperature of the paste and used this as an additional measure of doneness.

The traditional method of introducing the eggs is to do so gradually, stirring vigorously after each addition. If added all at once, the eggs splash about and require the patience of Job and the arm of Hercules to incorporate them into the dough. We discovered, however, that all of this grunt work was entirely unnecessary when we transferred the cooked paste to both a standing mixer and a food processor. The eggs incorporated swiftly, with nary a turn of a wooden spoon. Best of all, both machines produced pastry superior to one made by hand—the puffs rose higher and were lighter and puffier. It was the food processor, though, that became our machine of choice, because it brought the paste together with mercurial speed. (Rose Levy Beranbaum introduced this method in *The Pie and Pastry Bible*, Scribner, 1998.) We let the hot paste whirl around for a few seconds to cool it slightly, then, with the machine running, we added the eggs in a steady stream. Pâte à choux has never gone together more quickly and easily.

With the technique set, we focused next on the ingredients, beginning with the liquid. Pastry made exclusively with milk was gloriously golden but disappointingly soft; one made with only water was light and crisp but ashen and wan. Neither appealed. With equal parts milk and water, the pastry browned nicely, but its texture remained slightly soft. Three parts water to 1 part milk made a pastry that both colored and crisped agreeably.

Eggs next. Whole eggs are the norm, but both Beranbaum and Shirley Corriher, in *Cookwise* (Morrow, 1997), promote a partial replacement of whole eggs by egg whites, explaining that the whites make incredibly light, crisp pastry. To test this premise, we made pastries with whole eggs only and got puffs that, though golden from the yolks, were soft, stalwart, and bread-like. On the other end of the spectrum, an excess of whites made the puffs firm, brittle, and dry, with an unappealing pallor and texture. With the right balance of whole eggs to egg whites (in this case, 2 whole eggs to 1 egg white), the pastry was crisp and delicate, well risen, light, airy, and well colored. It was also the perfect consistency for piping—thick but soft enough to fall in great globs from a spoon.

Butter is added to pâte à choux not only for flavor but for texture; it makes the pastry tender. Three tablespoons yielded flavor-deprived pastry that had a stale, chewy texture, while 4 tablespoons delivered good results. But with 5 tablespoons, the pastry was much improved: delicately crisp, with an impeccably rich flavor.

As for flour, we stuck with all-purpose flour, whose moderate levels of gluten were just right for this pastry. The next step was placing shapely portions of dough on a baking sheet. While some recipes suggest that a pastry bag can be sidestepped and

MAKING THE PASTE

1. Occasionally stir the butter mixture until it comes to a full boil. Remove the pan from the heat.

2. Add the flour, return the pan to low heat, and cook the paste for 3 minutes, stirring constantly and using a smearing motion.

3. With the feed tube open, process the paste for 10 seconds, then add the eggs in a steady stream.

the pâte à choux simply dropped onto the baking sheet like cookie dough, we had no success with this technique; the baked puffs were uneven and unattractive. Turning to a pastry bag fitted with a plain tip, we piped the neatest, roundest mounds possible onto a greased and parchment-lined baking sheet. Some recipes suggested using the back of a teaspoon dipped in water to smooth the surface and even out the shape of the mound, and this technique proved useful.

The proper baking of pâte à choux is as key to the pastry's success as are proper cooking techniques and ingredients. If the puffs are soft and underdone but removed from the oven because they are brown, they will collapse before your very eyes. The puffs are leavened by steam pushing up from the interior so, as you might imagine, they require a blast of heat to get them going. A 400-degree oven proved too cool, as the pâte à choux sprouted to a size no larger than button mushrooms. A 425-degree oven, however, was too hot; the pastry was brown before it was done. With a little more experimentation, we hit upon the right temperature and time combination: 425 degrees for 15 minutes, then down to 375 degrees for another 8 to 10 minutes.

Recipes often warn that an overcrowded baking sheet can cause the puffs to collapse, and we found this to be true. There should be at least an inch of space between piped mounds of pâte à choux. A large baking sheet (18 by 12 inches, or a half-sheet pan) works best. Recipes also often call for sprinkling the baking sheet with water just before baking. The water, they claim, converts to steam in the oven, which prevents the exterior of the pastry from setting too quickly, affording the puffs more time to rise higher. When tested, this method proved bogus—the resulting puffs were not improved at all.

After being baked, the pastry may be crisp externally, but the inside remains moist with residual steam. If it is not released, the moisture will be absorbed into the pastry, making it soggy. This means that, immediately following baking, the puffs must be slit to release steam and returned to a turned-off, propped-open oven where they can dry out for about 45 minutes to

ensure crispness. Once dry and crisp and finally cooled, the puffs can stay at room temperature for a day or be stored in a zipper-lock plastic bag and thrown into the freezer for a month or so. Just a brief warm-up in the oven to rejuvenate them and they are ready to go. This is part of the beauty of pâte à choux.

Cream Puff Pastry (Pâte à Choux)

MAKES ENOUGH FOR 24 PROFITEROLES OR CREAM PUFFS, 16 GOUGÈRES, OR 8 ÉCLAIRS
This pastry is the basis for profiteroles, cream puffs, gougères, and éclairs. Refer to the illustrations on page 258 when making this recipe.

2	large eggs plus 1 large egg white
5	tablespoons unsalted butter, cut into 10 pieces
2	tablespoons whole milk
6	tablespoons water
1 1/2	teaspoons sugar
1/4	teaspoon salt
1/2	cup (2 1/2 ounces) unbleached all-purpose flour, sifted

1. Beat the eggs and egg white in a measuring cup or small bowl; you should have ½ cup (discard the excess). Set aside.

2. Bring the butter, milk, water, sugar, and salt to a boil in a small saucepan over medium heat, stirring once or twice. When the mixture reaches a full boil (the butter should be fully melted), immediately remove the saucepan from the heat and stir in the flour with a heatproof spatula or wooden spoon until combined and the mixture clears the sides of the pan. Return the saucepan to low heat and cook, stirring constantly, using a smearing motion, until the mixture is slightly shiny, looks like wet sand, and tiny beads of fat appear on the bottom of the saucepan, about 3 minutes (the paste should register 175 to 180 degrees on an instant-read thermometer).

3. Immediately transfer the mixture to a food processor and process with the feed tube open for 10 seconds to cool slightly. With the machine

running, gradually add the eggs in a steady stream. When all the eggs have been added, scrape down the sides of the bowl, then process for 30 seconds until a smooth, thick, sticky paste forms. (If not using immediately in one of the following recipes, transfer the paste to a medium bowl, press a sheet of plastic wrap that has been sprayed lightly with nonstick cooking spray directly on the surface, and store at room temperature for up to 2 hours.)

Profiteroles

SERVES 6

A serving of profiteroles consists of 3 baked puffs filled with ice cream and topped with sauce. This recipe makes 24 puffs, technically enough to serve 8, but inevitably a few bake up too irregularly shaped to serve to guests. Refer to the illustrations below when piping the paste.

If you're serving several guests, scooping the ice cream ahead of time makes serving quick and neat, but if you're assembling only a couple of servings or there's no room in your freezer, you can skip the prescooping step. Refer to the illustrations on page 261 when assembling the profiteroles.

I   recipe Cream Puff Pastry (page 259)
I   quart premium vanilla or coffee
    ice cream
I   recipe Bittersweet Chocolate Sauce (page 499), warmed if made ahead

1. FOR THE PASTRY: Adjust an oven rack to the middle position and heat the oven to 425 degrees. Spray a large (18 by 12-inch) baking sheet with nonstick cooking spray and line with parchment paper; set the pan aside.

2. Fold down the top 3 or 4 inches of a large pastry bag fitted with a ½-inch plain tip to form a cuff. Hold the bag open with one hand in the cuff and fill the bag with the paste. Unfold the cuff, lay the bag on the work surface, and, using your hands or a bench scraper, push the paste toward the tip of the pastry bag. Twist the top of the bag and pipe the paste into 1¼- to 1½-inch mounds on the prepared baking sheet, spacing them about 1 to 1¼ inches apart (you should be able to fit 24 mounds on the baking sheet). Use the back of a teaspoon dipped in a bowl of cold water to even out the shape and smooth the surface of the piped mounds.

3. Bake 15 minutes (do not open the oven door), then reduce the oven temperature to 375 degrees and continue to bake until golden brown and fairly firm (the puffs should not be soft and squishy), 8 to 10 minutes longer. Remove the baking sheet from the oven. With a paring knife, cut a ¾-inch slit into the side of each puff to release steam; return the puffs to the oven, turn off the oven, and prop the oven door open with the handle of a wooden spoon. Dry the puffs in the turned-off oven until the centers are just moist (not wet) and the puffs are crisp, about 45 minutes. (Use a sharp paring knife to poke a hole through the bottom or sides

PIPING CREAM PUFF PASTRY

1. Fill a pastry bag with the paste, push the paste to the bottom of the bag using your hands or a bench scraper, and twist the top of the bag to seal.

2. Pipe the paste into 1¼- to 1½-inch mounds on the prepared baking sheet.

3. Use the back of a teaspoon dipped in cold water to even out the shape and smooth the surface of the piped mounds.

to check the interior.) Transfer the puffs to a wire rack to cool. (The cooled puffs can be stored at room temperature for up to 24 hours or frozen in a zipper-lock plastic bag for up to 1 month. Before serving, crisp room-temperature puffs in a 300-degree oven 5 to 8 minutes; crisp frozen puffs 8 to 10 minutes.)

4. FOR THE ICE CREAM: Line a baking sheet with parchment paper; freeze until cold, about 20 minutes. Using a 2-inch ice cream scoop (about the same diameter as the puffs), scoop 18 portions of ice cream onto the cold baking sheet and freeze until firm, then cover with plastic wrap; keep frozen until ready to serve.

5. When ready to serve, use a paring knife to split open the puffs about ⅜ inch from the bottom; set 3 bottoms on each dessert plate. Place 1 scoop of ice cream on each bottom and gently press the tops into the ice cream. Pour the sauce over the profiteroles and serve immediately.

BAD PUFFS, GOOD PUFFS

If removed from the oven too early, cream puff pastry will collapse as it cools (left). Proper baking ensures crisp, well-risen puffs (right).

➤ VARIATIONS
Cream Puffs
MAKES 24

Cream puffs are basically profiteroles filled with pastry cream in place of ice cream and dusted with confectioners' sugar rather than drizzled with chocolate.

Follow the recipe for Profiteroles, replacing the ice cream with 1 recipe Pastry Cream (page 227). When ready to serve, use the tip of a paring knife to make a small X in the side of each puff, about halfway between the top and bottom. Fill a pastry bag fitted with a ¼-inch plain tip with the pastry cream and then pipe some pastry cream through the X in the side of each puff. (Fill each puff until the pastry cream starts to ooze out the side.) Arrange the filled puffs on a serving platter. Omit the Bittersweet Chocolate Sauce and sift ⅓ cup confectioners' sugar over the filled puffs. Serve immediately.

Gougère (Cheese Puff Ring)
MAKES ONE 12-INCH RING OR
SIXTEEN 3-INCH PUFFS

Gougères are simply pâte à choux flavored with Gruyère cheese. Traditionally, the paste is piped into a ring, but it can also be made into individual puffs. To make individual puffs, pipe the paste into 2-inch mounds, spacing them 1 to 1¼ inches apart. If Gruyère is unavailable, Swiss or Emmental cheese may be substituted. This savory application of pâte à choux is commonly served as an hors d'oeuvre or as an accompaniment to soup or salad. Gougères are best served warm, although they can be made in advance and reheated as needed.

ASSEMBLING PROFITEROLES

 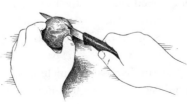 

1. Scoop the ice cream onto the prepared baking sheet, freeze until firm, and cover with plastic wrap.

2. Use a paring knife to split puffs about ³⁄₈ inch from the bottom. Set three bottoms on each dessert plate.

3. Place a scoop of ice cream on each bottom and press the tops into the ice cream. Pour the sauce over the profiteroles.

1 recipe Cream Puff Pastry (page 259),
    omitting the sugar
3 ounces Gruyère cheese, shredded
    (about ¾ cup)
    Pinch cayenne pepper

1. Prepare the pastry, adding the cheese and cayenne to the food processor after the eggs have been incorporated in step 3.

2. Adjust an oven rack to the middle position and heat the oven to 425 degrees. Spray a large (18 by 12-inch) baking sheet with nonstick cooking spray and line with parchment paper; set the pan aside.

3. Fold down the top 3 or 4 inches of a large pastry bag fitted with a ½-inch plain tip to form a cuff. Hold the bag open with one hand in the cuff and fill the bag with the paste. Unfold the cuff, lay the bag on the work surface, and, using your hands or a bench scraper, push the paste toward the tip of the pastry bag. Twist the top of the bag and pipe the paste onto the prepared baking sheet into sixteen 2-inch mounds arranged in a ring with the sides of the puffs just touching each other. Use the back of a teaspoon dipped in a bowl of cold water to even out the shape and smooth the surface of the piped mounds.

4. Bake 15 minutes (do not open the oven door), then reduce the oven temperature to 375 degrees and continue to bake until golden brown and fairly firm (the ring should not be soft and squishy), 12 to 14 minutes longer. (The puffs will have baked into each other but will still remain distinct.) Remove the baking sheet from the oven. With a paring knife, cut a ¾-inch slit into the side of each puff to release steam; return the ring to the oven, turn off the oven, and prop the oven door open with the handle of a wooden spoon. Dry the ring in the turned-off oven until the center is just moist (not wet) and the surface is crisp, about 45 minutes. Transfer the ring to a wire rack until warm. Serve warm. (The ring can be cooled completely and stored at room temperature for up to 24 hours or frozen in a zipper-lock plastic bag for up to 1 month. Before serving, crisp the room-temperature ring in a 300-degree oven 5 to 8 minutes; crisp the frozen ring 8 to 10 minutes.)

Éclairs
MAKES 8

Éclairs are simply oblong cream puffs filled with pastry cream and topped with a chocolate glaze. Be sure to use thoroughly chilled pastry cream when filling the éclairs. The pastry cream can also be made up to 2 days before serving the éclairs. Although professional bakers cut a hole in one end of each baked éclair and then pipe in the pastry cream, we find it much easier to cut off the top of the éclair and spoon the pastry cream into the bottom half. The top piece can then be dipped directly into the chocolate glaze and placed on top of the pastry cream, glazed side up, to finish the éclairs. Although vanilla is the traditional flavor for the pastry cream, mocha and chocolate make delicious alternatives.

1 recipe Cream Puff Pastry (page 259)
1 recipe Pastry Cream for Éclairs and Napoleons
    (page 227)

    CHOCOLATE GLAZE
3 tablespoons half-and-half
2 ounces semisweet or bittersweet chocolate,
    finely chopped
1 cup (4 ounces) confectioners' sugar, sifted

1. FOR THE PASTRY: Adjust the oven rack to the middle position and heat the oven to 425 degrees. Spray a large (18 by 12-inch) baking sheet with nonstick cooking spray and line with parchment paper; set aside.

2. Fold down the top 3 or 4 inches of a large pastry bag fitted with a ½-inch plain tip to form a cuff. Hold the bag open with one hand in the cuff and fill the bag with the paste. Unfold the cuff, lay the bag on the work surface, and, using your hands or a bench scraper, push the paste toward the tip of the pastry bag. Twist the top of the bag and pipe the paste into eight 5 by 1-inch strips, spaced about 1 inch apart. Use the back of a teaspoon dipped in a bowl of cold water to even out the shape and smooth the surface of the piped strips.

3. Bake 15 minutes (do not open the oven door), then reduce the oven temperature to 375 degrees and continue to bake until golden brown and fairly firm (éclairs should not be soft and squishy), 8 to

10 minutes longer. Remove the baking sheet from the oven. With a paring knife, cut a ¾-inch slit into the top of each éclair to release steam; return the éclairs to the oven, turn off the oven, and prop the oven door open with the handle of a wooden spoon. Dry the éclairs in the turned-off oven until the centers are just moist (not wet) and the éclairs are crisp, about 45 minutes. Transfer the éclairs to a wire rack to cool. (The cooled éclairs can be stored at room temperature for up to 24 hours or frozen in a zipper-lock plastic bag for up to 1 month. Before serving, crisp room-temperature éclairs in a 300-degree oven 5 to 8 minutes; crisp frozen éclairs 8 to 10 minutes.)

4. FOR THE GLAZE: Place the half-and-half and chocolate in a medium microwave-safe bowl, cover with plastic wrap, and microwave for 20 seconds at a time, until the mixture just begins to steam. Whisk together thoroughly, add the confectioners' sugar, and whisk until completely smooth.

5. To ASSEMBLE: With a paring knife, cut around the sides of each éclair to remove the top third. Dip the top of each éclair into the glaze, shaking off any excess, and transfer the tops to a wire rack to dry. Spoon 3 to 4 tablespoons of pastry cream in the bottom of each éclair. Once the glaze has set, set the tops on the éclairs and press gently to secure. Serve within several hours.

➤ VARIATIONS

Double Chocolate Éclairs
Follow the recipe for Éclairs. When preparing the Pastry Cream, add 2 ounces finely chopped bitter-sweet chocolate along with the butter and vanilla and reduce the vanilla to ½ teaspoon.

Mocha Éclairs
Follow the recipe for Éclairs. When preparing the Pastry Cream, whisk 1½ teaspoons instant espresso powder into the heated half-and-half mixture and reduce the vanilla to ½ teaspoon.

CROISSANTS

IN FRANCE, CROISSANTS ARE A TRADITIONAL breakfast pastry, but when filled with chocolate or the almond filling called frangipane, they become a decadent afternoon snack. What makes great croissants so seductive? This yeast-raised pastry contains the best of both worlds: Part pastry, part bread, it has a buttery crust on the outside and tender, pillow-soft layers on the inside—perfect for dipping into a cup of café au lait or hot chocolate. Sadly, the gargantuan, bready, mass-produced versions found in supermarkets and mall cafés are the norm in the United States. We were after authentic French bakery croissants that could be made in the home kitchen.

The ingredient list for croissant dough is short: flour, milk or water, yeast, sugar, butter, and salt. We began our quest for the best croissant recipe by examining the flour. The high amount of gluten in bread flour made the dough too elastic and difficult to roll out and resulted in an overly chewy croissant. Croissants made with cake flour lacked the height and texture we wanted and were flimsy. In addition, cake flour, which contains less gluten than either all-purpose or bread flour, didn't stand up well to the kneading required for croissant dough. We found that all-purpose flour split the difference and made the best croissant. Three cups of flour was enough to make 12 croissants.

We compared croissants made with milk and with water and found that we preferred the version made with milk. The milk contributed a small amount of fat and sweetness that gave the croissants a slightly more tender texture and a richer flavor. As for sugar, ¼ cup was just the right amount, and 1¼ teaspoons of salt balanced the flavors nicely. Having eaten too many croissants with a strong yeasty flavor, we took special care in determining its amount in our recipe. One tablespoon of yeast gave the croissants the right amount of lift.

Next, we looked at the star ingredient of croissants: butter. Traditionally, a small amount of butter goes into the croissant dough, which makes it relatively lean. A much larger amount of butter is then mixed with a little flour and formed into a square. This rich butter square is then folded into the lean dough. The alternating rich and lean layers are what make croissants so flaky and decadent. For our butter square, we tried butter amounts ranging from 4 ounces to 1 pound of butter. We had assumed that the more butter, the better. Not surprisingly, the croissants made with less butter were dry and bready. However, a pound was far too much, making the croissants greasy and heavy. We found 12 ounces (three sticks) of butter to be just right for our butter square.

The next issue to address was forming the croissant dough. The croissant's flakiness depends on successfully creating layers of butter and dough. The dough is wrapped around the flattened butter square and rolled out to a thin square. Then the square of dough is folded into thirds, like a letter about to go into an envelope. This folding procedure is called a "turn," and traditionally, up to six turns are given (chilling the dough after each one) to create multiple layers and achieve the ideal flaky texture. We tried as few as three turns and as many as six. Three turns made for a heavy, bready croissant. Six was too many and resulted in thin, brittle layers of dough that were all crust. Four turns did the trick, providing the perfect amount of flakiness and tenderness.

We were pleased to be able to reduce the number of turns, but because we needed to chill the dough after each turn, our process was still a very lengthy affair. Croissant recipes recommend thoroughly chilling the dough between turns in order to relax the gluten and make the dough more pliable so it can be easily rolled out. Chilling the dough for at least two hours between the turns as well as after the final turn is optimal. Could we find a way to streamline the process? Yes. We found that we could give the dough two turns before chilling it. By chilling the dough just once in between the two double turns (and once after we were done), we made the process much more manageable.

Our dough was ready and now we needed to find the best way to shape the croissants. The dough was cut into triangles of varying sizes, rolled, and baked. To our chagrin, the croissants ended up resembling fat triangles, rather than the elegantly curved, crescent-shaped pastries we were looking for. Stretching the triangles of dough

before and during shaping helped a little, but it was still difficult to coax the ends into the desired shape. The solution was to make a small cut in the shortest side of the triangle, which made stretching the ends into a crescent much easier.

Next, we experimented with different proofing times and temperatures. We tried giving the croissants a slow, cool rise in the refrigerator, a method that worked well with our Brioche (page 107). We left the shaped croissants in the refrigerator overnight and baked them the next day. The results were less than satisfactory; the croissants had developed the characteristic tang of breads made with a starter or sponge—OK for bread, but not for a delicate croissant. We found they had the best flavor when they were allowed to rise at room temperature for two hours.

The last thing to test was the baking temperature. Because of the amount of butter (a browning agent), we found that 400 degrees was best, giving the croissants a crisp, browned exterior and a tender interior. Any higher and the croissants browned on the outside before the interior was baked through; any lower and the croissants did not achieve the proper lift. High-fat doughs like croissants rely on fairly high temperatures for lift as the moisture contained within the fat evaporates rapidly, creating steam and lifting the dough upward.

Croissants
MAKES 12

Make sure the dough is thoroughly chilled before it is rolled out. If the butter becomes too warm, it will melt, making the dough difficult to roll and shape. If the dough becomes too warm and sticky at any time during the rolling and folding process, wrap the dough in plastic and chill until the dough becomes workable. This dough is best made in a cool kitchen; if your kitchen is warm, place a large tray of ice on your work surface to chill it down before rolling the dough.

DOUGH
3	cups (15 ounces) unbleached all-purpose flour, plus extra for rolling
1	tablespoon instant yeast
¼	cup (1 ¾ ounces) sugar

1¼	teaspoons salt
1¼	cups whole milk, cold
2	tablespoons unsalted butter

BUTTER SQUARE

| 24 | tablespoons (3 sticks) unsalted butter, cut into 1-tablespoon pieces and kept cold |
| 2 | tablespoons unbleached all-purpose flour |

EGG WASH

| 1 | large egg, lightly beaten |

1. FOR THE DOUGH: Whisk 2¾ cups of the flour together with the yeast, sugar, and salt in a medium bowl. Place the milk in the bowl of a standing mixer fitted with the dough hook. Add the flour mixture and knead at low speed until a ball of dough forms, about 5 minutes. Cut the butter into small pieces and add them to the dough. Continue to knead until the butter becomes fully incorporated and the dough becomes smooth, begins to form a ball, and clears the sides of the bowl, an additional 5 to 6 minutes. (The dough should be sticky, but if more dough is sticking to the sides of the bowl than to itself, add the remaining ¼ cup flour, 1 tablespoon at a time, as necessary.) Wrap the dough in plastic and refrigerate it for 1 hour.

2. FOR THE BUTTER SQUARE: Follow the illustrations for forming the butter square (at right), forming the mixture into an even 7-inch square. Refrigerate the butter square until ready to use, at least 30 minutes.

3. Lightly dust a work surface with flour. Following the illustrations for making the turns on page 266, roll the dough into an 11-inch square. Place the chilled butter square diagonally onto the dough. Fold the corners of the dough up over the butter square so that they meet in the middle and pinch the ends of the dough together to seal them.

4. Using a rolling pin, gently tap the dough, starting from the center of the dough and going outward, until the square becomes larger and the butter begins to soften. At this point, start gently rolling the dough into a 14-inch square, checking often to make sure the dough is not sticking and dusting with additional flour as necessary. Fold the square into thirds to form a long rectangle. This method of folding is called a "turn" and resembles folding a business letter. Starting from the narrow ends, fold the rectangle into thirds again to form a square. You have now given the dough two turns. Wrap the dough in plastic wrap and refrigerate for 2 hours.

5. Repeat step 4, giving the dough two additional turns (for a total of four turns) and chilling again for at least 2 hours.

6. TO SHAPE THE CROISSANTS: Line 2 baking sheets with parchment paper. Place the chilled dough on a floured surface and gently roll the dough into a 20-inch square. Following the illustrations for shaping the dough on page 267, cut the dough into 2 rectangles, then cut each rectangle into thirds. Cut each rectangle on the diagonal to yield a total of 12 triangles. One at a time, lift a triangle off the work surface, holding the base (the triangle's short side) in one hand and the tip in the other and gently

FORMING THE BUTTER SQUARE

1. Using a bench scraper, toss together the butter pieces and flour on a clean work surface. Smear the butter and flour back and forth against the work surface until they have combined into a smooth, homogenous mixture.

2. Wrap the butter mixture in plastic wrap and use the edges of the plastic to form it into an even 7-inch square for croissants or a 5-inch square for Danish. Refrigerate until firm.

stretch. With the base closest to you, cut a 1-inch slit into the center of the base. (The small slit will allow the croissant to roll evenly.) Fold the two sides of the slit outward and with both hands, roll the triangle, gently stretching the dough as you roll, leaving the last ¼ inch of the tip unrolled. Gently transfer the croissant to a prepared baking sheet (unrolled tip facing downward). Bring the ends of the croissant toward each other to form a crescent shape. Repeat with the remaining triangles.

7. Cover the croissants loosely with plastic wrap. Let them rise at room temperature until puffy (they will not double in size), 45 to 60 minutes.

8. TO BRUSH WITH EGG WASH AND BAKE: Meanwhile, adjust the oven racks to the upper- and lower-middle positions and heat the oven to 400 degrees. Brush the croissants with the beaten egg. Bake until the croissants are golden brown, 18 to 22 minutes, rotating the baking sheets from front to back and top to bottom halfway through the baking time. Cool the croissants on a wire rack until warm, about 15 minutes. Serve warm or at room temperature. (Although they are best eaten fresh out of the oven, baked croissants will keep at

MAKING TURNS

The second step of the croissant-making process is called making turns, which means adding the butter square to the dough to create 2 distinct layers: one lean and one fat. These 2 layers are then "turned" or folded upon themselves to create more alternating layers of lean and fat, which is what makes the tender and flaky layers in croissants. The same technique is used to make Danish.

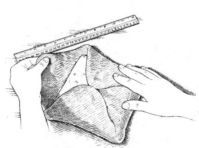

1. Place the chilled dough on a floured surface and roll into an 11-inch square for croissants or a 9-inch square for Danish. Place the butter square diagonally on top of the dough and remove the plastic wrap.

2. Fold the corners of the dough over the butter so that they meet in the middle of the butter square. Pinch the ends of the dough together to seal.

3. Using a rolling pin, tap the dough from the center outward until the butter begins to soften and become malleable. Gently roll the dough into a 14-inch square for croissants or an 11-inch square for Danish, dusting the work surface as necessary with flour to prevent sticking.

4. Fold one outside edge of the dough in toward the center and bring the opposite outside edge in over the top (like a business letter).

5. Repeat the process, but folding over each end to make a square. This is 2 turns. Wrap the dough in plastic wrap and refrigerate for 2 hours before making the final 2 turns (roll the dough to a 14-inch square for croissants or an 11-inch square for Danish and fold in the same fashion as before). When you have finished, you will have made a total of 4 turns.

room temperature for 2 days or well wrapped, in plastic, in the freezer for up to 2 weeks. To reheat frozen croissants, place them in a 300-degree oven for 5 to 10 minutes.)

Chocolate Croissants

MAKES 12

Chocolate croissants (or pain au chocolat) *are best made with high-quality chocolate. Their rectangular shape is easier to execute than the classic crescent shape used for regular croissants.*

1	recipe Croissants (page 264), prepared through step 5
8	ounces bittersweet or semisweet chocolate, chopped fine
1	large egg, lightly beaten

1. Line 2 baking sheets with parchment paper. Place the chilled dough on a floured work surface and gently roll the dough into a 20-inch square. Use a pizza cutter and ruler to cut the dough into 4 equal 10-inch squares. Cut each square into thirds to make a total of 12 rectangles, each approximately 10 by 3¼ inches. Place ½ ounce (about 1 tablespoon) chocolate in the middle of each rectangle. Following the illustration on page 268, fold each rectangle into thirds and place it, seam-side down, on a baking sheet.

2. Cover the croissants loosely with plastic wrap and let them rise at room temperature until puffy (they will not double in size), 45 to 60 minutes.

3. Meanwhile, adjust the oven racks to the upper- and lower-middle positions and heat the oven to 400 degrees. Brush the croissants with the beaten egg. Bake until the croissants are golden brown,

SHAPING CROISSANTS

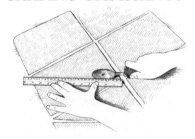 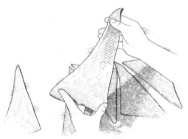 

1. After rolling the dough into a 20-inch square, use a pizza cutter and ruler to cut the dough into two equal rectangles. Cut each rectangle into thirds widthwise and then into triangles, to yield a total of 12 triangles.

2. Working one at a time, lift a triangle off the work surface, holding the base (the triangle's short side) in one hand and the tip in the other. Gently stretch into an isosceles triangle with two sides equal in length.

3. With the base closest to you, cut a 1-inch slit into the center of the base (the short side) of each triangle.

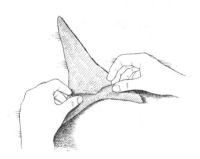  

4. Fold the two sides of the slit outward.

5. With both hands, roll the triangle from the base, gently stretching the dough as you roll, leaving the last ¼ inch of the tip unrolled.

6. Transfer the croissant to a parchment paper–lined baking sheet, unrolled tip facing downward. Bring the ends of the croissant toward each other to form a crescent shape.

18 to 22 minutes, rotating the baking sheets from front to back and top to bottom halfway through the baking time. Cool the croissants on a wire rack until warm, about 20 minutes. Serve warm or at room temperature.

Almond Croissants

MAKES 12

This almond filling, commonly called frangipane, is a classic French filling also used in other pastries, such as Poached Pear and Almond Tart (page 230). The filling can be made ahead of time and kept refrigerated for up to 3 days.

FRANGIPANE

³/₄	cup blanched sliced almonds, plus ¹/₄ cup for garnish
¹/₃	cup (2¹/₃ ounces) sugar
¹/₈	teaspoon salt
1	large egg
¹/₄	teaspoon almond extract
¹/₄	teaspoon vanilla extract
3	tablespoons unsalted butter, cut into 3 pieces and softened

1	recipe Croissants (page 264), prepared through step 5
1	large egg, lightly beaten

SHAPING CHOCOLATE AND ALMOND CROISSANTS

Place 1 tablespoon of chocolate or 2 teaspoons of frangipane in the center of each rectangle. Fold the two edges, slightly overlapping, over the filling to form a rectangle. Transfer to the parchment paper–lined baking sheet, seam-side down.

1. FOR THE FRANGIPANE: Place the ³/₄ cup almonds, the sugar, and salt in a food processor. Process until the almonds are finely ground, about twenty-five 2-second pulses; process until very finely ground, about 10 seconds longer. Add the egg, almond extract, and vanilla extract and process until combined, about 10 seconds. Add the butter and process until no lumps remain, about 10 seconds. Scrape the bottom and sides of the workbowl with a rubber spatula and process to combine thoroughly, about 10 seconds longer.

2. TO SHAPE AND BAKE: Line 2 baking sheets with parchment paper. Place the chilled dough on a floured work surface and gently roll the dough into a 20-inch square. Use a pizza cutter and ruler to cut the dough into 4 equal 10-inch squares. Cut each square into thirds to make a total of 12 rectangles, each approximately 10 by 3¼ inches. Place about 2 teaspoons of the filling in the middle of each rectangle. Following the illustration at left, fold each rectangle into thirds and place it, seam-side down, on a baking sheet.

3. Cover the croissants loosely with plastic wrap and let them rise at room temperature until puffy (they will not double in size), 45 to 60 minutes.

4. Meanwhile, adjust the oven racks to the upper- and lower-middle positions and heat the oven to 400 degrees. Brush the croissants with the beaten egg and sprinkle with the remaining ¼ cup sliced almonds. Bake until the croissants are golden brown, 18 to 22 minutes, rotating the baking sheets from front to back and top to bottom halfway through the baking time. Cool the croissants on a wire rack until warm, about 20 minutes. Serve warm or at room temperature.

DANISH

THE COMBINATION OF A FLAKY, TENDER pastry and a sweet, decadent filling makes Danish the most elegant of breakfast pastries. Unfortunately, bad versions can be found everywhere, from grocery stores to coffeehouse franchises to fast-food restaurants. Most of these mass-produced pastries are leaden, bready hockey pucks smeared with a thick coating of sweet icing—a far cry from the real thing. We wanted to make Danish that were buttery rich and tender, with a flavorful, not-too-sweet filling, and drizzled with just enough icing to satisfy our sweet tooth.

Danish are made using a rich yeasted dough, similar to that of croissants. The only difference lies in the addition of eggs, which contribute to a richer and slightly more cakelike texture. Like croissant dough, Danish dough is wrapped around a square of butter, rolled into a thin sheet, and given turns or folds, which create layers. Once filled (with jam, fruit, or sweetened cream cheese), the dough can then be formed into a variety of shapes: large braids and simple rectangles, to name just two. After the Danish are baked, they are finished with a drizzle of icing.

We used our own croissant recipe as our starting point. We made half batches of the croissant dough (enough to make 16 individual Danish or one large braid) to which we added various amounts of eggs, as well as combinations of egg yolks and whites. We found that adding just one whole egg made the pastry with the most tender texture. Any more and the flavor of the eggs became overwhelming. Because the egg added extra moisture to the dough, the amount of milk needed to be reduced. The egg also made the dough richer, eliminating the need for the small amount of butter mixed into the croissant dough. Because Danish should be sweeter than croissants, we increased the amount of sugar slightly.

What about turning the dough? Just as with the croissants, four turns (two turns of two folds each) did the trick to give the Danish a perfect flaky texture. Once the Danish were shaped, filled, and proofed, we needed to find the ideal baking temperature. We tried temperatures ranging from 325 to 425 degrees. Once again, what was best for the croissants was best for the Danish. Four hundred degrees was perfect, baking the Danish to a golden brown on the outside without overcooking the fillings.

Even with the filling, the Danish were a bit dry and lacked the sweet flavor that we were striving for. We added the traditional drizzle of icing made with milk and confectioners' sugar, but that wasn't enough. We didn't want to obliterate the pastry with too much of the icing, so we tried brushing them with a light glaze made with confectioners' sugar, milk, and a little lemon juice. The flavor was great, but there was one problem: The glaze left the Danish with a damp outer crust. What could we do to eliminate the unappetizing sogginess? We tried letting the Danish dry, but even after several hours, they were still soggy. We then tried making the glaze thicker, but that only made the pastries overwhelmingly sweet and sticky. The answer turned out to be simple: The pastries needed to be glazed while they were still hot. The hot pastry soaked up the glaze like a sponge, which flavored the Danish without making them wet. The glaze also gave the Danish a beautiful sheen.

SHAPING A DANISH BRAID

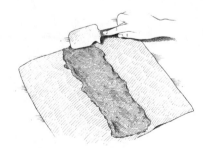

1. Spread the filling or jam onto the center third of the dough.

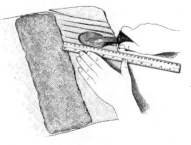

2. Using a pizza cutter or paring knife, cut the outer thirds into $3/4$-inch strips (so that the cuts are at an angle to the filling).

3. Alternating sides, fold the strips over the filling, crisscrossing the strips over the center and pressing the ends to seal, until the entire Danish is braided.

Danish Dough

MAKES ENOUGH FOR I LARGE BRAID
OR I6 INDIVIDUAL DANISH

If the dough becomes too warm and sticky at any time during the rolling and folding process, wrap the dough in plastic and chill until it becomes workable.

DOUGH

1 ½	cups (7 ½ ounces) all-purpose flour, plus extra for rolling
1 ½	teaspoons instant yeast
¼	cup (1 ¾ ounces) sugar
¾	teaspoon salt
⅓	cup whole milk
1	large egg, lightly beaten

BUTTER SQUARE

12	tablespoons (1 ½ sticks) unsalted butter, cut into 1-tablespoon pieces and kept cold
1	tablespoon all-purpose flour

1. FOR THE DOUGH: Whisk 1¼ cups of the flour together with the yeast, sugar, and salt in a medium bowl. Place the milk and egg in the bowl of a standing mixer fitted with the dough hook. Add the flour mixture and knead at low speed until a smooth ball of dough forms, 7 to 8 minutes. (The dough should be sticky, but if more dough is sticking to the sides of the bowl than to itself, add the remaining ¼ cup flour, 1 tablespoon at a time, as necessary.) Wrap the dough in plastic and refrigerate it for 1 hour.

2. FOR THE BUTTER SQUARE: Follow the illustrations for forming the butter square on page 265, forming the mixture into an even 5-inch square. Refrigerate the butter square until ready to use, at least 30 minutes.

3. Lightly dust a work surface with flour. Following the illustrations for making the turns on page 266, roll the dough into a 9-inch square. Place the chilled butter square diagonally onto the dough. Fold the corners of the dough up over the butter square so that they meet in the middle and pinch the ends of the dough together to seal.

4. Using a rolling pin, gently tap the dough, starting from the center of the dough and going outward, until the square becomes larger and the butter begins to soften. At this point, start gently rolling the dough into an 11-inch square, checking often to make sure the dough is not sticking and dusting with additional flour as necessary. Fold the square into thirds to form a long rectangle. This method of folding is called a "turn" and resembles folding a business letter. Starting at the narrow ends, fold the rectangle in thirds again to form a square. You have now given the dough 2 turns. Wrap the dough in plastic and refrigerate for 2 hours.

5. Repeat step 4, giving the dough 2 additional turns (for a total of 4 turns) and chilling again for at least 4 hours. Fill and shape the dough using one of the recipes on page 271.

SHAPING INDIVIDUAL DANISH

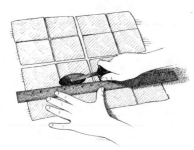

1. Using a pizza cutter, cut the dough into 4-inch squares.

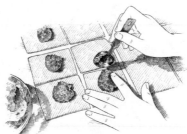

2. Spoon 1 tablespoon of filling or jam into the center of each square.

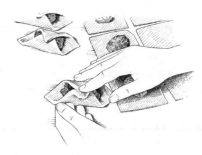

3. Fold two opposite corners of the dough over the filling (to form a rectangle with two pointed ends), gently pressing the corners to seal.

Danish Braid

MAKES ONE 14 BY 5-INCH BRAID, SERVING 6
This long braided shape should be lightly filled, so you need only half of either filling recipe.

1	recipe Danish Dough (page 270)
½	recipe Apricot Filling or Cream Cheese Filling (recipes follow) or ½ cup fruit jam
1	recipe Danish Glaze (page 272)
1	recipe Danish Icing (page 272)

1. Adjust an oven rack to the middle position and heat the oven to 400 degrees.

2. On a large sheet of parchment paper, roll the chilled dough into a 14-inch square. Follow the illustrations on page 269 to spread the filling or jam onto the center third of the dough and to form the braid. Transfer the braid, still on the parchment, to a large baking sheet. Cover the braid loosely with plastic wrap and let rise at room temperature until puffy (it will not double), about 30 minutes.

3. Bake until the braid is golden brown, 22 to 26 minutes, turning halfway through the baking time. Place the braid on a cooling rack and brush with the glaze while still hot. Cool to room temperature, about 1 hour. Using a soupspoon, drizzle the braid with the icing. Slice crosswise and serve.

Individual Danish

MAKES 16

These Danish are traditionally called spandauer and are shaped somewhat like bow ties.

1	recipe Danish Dough (page 270)
1	recipe Apricot Filling or Cream Cheese Filling (recipes follow) or 1 cup fruit jam
1	recipe Danish Glaze (page 272)
1	recipe Danish Icing (page 272)

1. Adjust the oven racks to the lower- and upper-middle positions and heat the oven to 400 degrees. Line 2 baking sheets with parchment paper and set aside.

2. On a floured work surface, roll the dough into a 16-inch square, checking frequently to make sure that the dough is not sticking to the surface. Follow the illustrations on page 270 to cut and shape the Danish. Place the Danish on the baking sheets, cover loosely with plastic wrap, and let rise at room temperature until puffy (they will not double), about 30 minutes.

3. Bake until the Danish are golden brown, 15 to 20 minutes, rotating the baking sheets from front to back and top to bottom halfway through the baking time. Place the Danish on a wire rack and brush with the glaze while still hot. Cool to room temperature, about 1 hour. Using a soupspoon, drizzle the Danish with the icing.

Apricot Filling

MAKES ABOUT 1 CUP, ENOUGH FOR
2 BRAIDS OR 16 INDIVIDUAL DANISH

This filling can be refrigerated for up to 1 week.

1	cup (about 6 ounces) dried apricots, roughly chopped
½	cup orange juice
⅓	cup (2⅓ ounces) sugar
	Pinch salt

1. Combine the apricots and orange juice in a small microwave-safe bowl; cover tightly with plastic wrap, and microwave on high until simmering, about 1 minute. Let stand, covered, until the apricots have soaked up most of the juice, about 10 minutes.

2. Place the apricots, any remaining orange juice, sugar, and salt in a food processor and process until a puree forms, about 20 seconds. Scrape the apricot puree into a small bowl, cover with plastic wrap, and set aside until ready to use.

Cream Cheese Filling

MAKES ABOUT 1 CUP, ENOUGH FOR
2 BRAIDS OR 16 INDIVIDUAL DANISH

Don't use reduced-fat or fat-free cream cheese for this recipe.

1	(8-ounce) package cream cheese, cut into 1-inch pieces and softened at room temperature

$^1/_2$　teaspoon grated zest from 1 lemon

$^1/_4$　cup (1 $^3/_4$ ounces) sugar

Using a spoon, mix all the ingredients together thoroughly in a medium bowl. Cover with plastic wrap and chill until ready to use.

Danish Glaze

MAKES ABOUT $^1/_3$ CUP

Make this glaze while the Danish is in the oven and apply it as soon as the Danish is baked.

1 $^1/_2$　cups (6 ounces) confectioners' sugar, sifted

1　teaspoon juice from 1 lemon

5　teaspoons milk

Whisk the ingredients together in a small bowl, cover with plastic wrap, and set aside until ready to use.

Danish Icing

MAKES ABOUT $^1/_4$ CUP

Drizzle this white icing over the Danish when it has fully cooled.

1　cup (4 ounces) confectioners' sugar, sifted

1　tablespoon milk

Whisk the ingredients together in a small bowl, cover with plastic wrap, and set aside until ready to use.

PUFF PASTRY

PÂTE FEUILLETÉE, OR PUFF PASTRY, IS A basic dough used to make a variety of pastries, such as cheese straws, palmiers, turnovers, and Napoleons. Traditionally, it is made like croissant dough: The dough is wrapped around a square of butter, rolled, and folded (or turned) up to six times, chilling the dough for at least one hour before, between, and after the turns. Paper-thin sheets of dough and butter are created by the turns, and when baked, the butter steams and separates the many layers of dough, creating puff pastry's characteristic flaky texture. This time-intensive traditional method takes the better part of a day. We wondered if it was possible to find a quick way of making puff pastry without sacrificing any of the flaky texture.

We began our tests by pitting a traditional puff recipe against a "quick" puff. The quick puff was made in a fashion similar to pie dough: Small chunks of butter were cut into the dough, water was added to bring it all together, and the dough was rolled out and given four turns, resting in the refrigerator for an hour between turns. The "quick" puff was hardly that. Making it took almost four hours, from start to finish. The traditional puff, which was turned six times and refrigerated in between, took nearly six hours. We liked the faster method, but the quick puff lacked the super-flaky layers of the traditional. More layers of dough and butter were necessary to boost the pastry's flakiness. But adding turns would also make it a longer process, something we wanted to avoid. We needed to find another method.

The ingredients in puff pastry are identical to pie dough, which got us to thinking about the fraisage method, a method often used to bring together pie dough ingredients. The butter and dry ingredients are placed on a counter, sprinkled with water, and smeared by hand, forcing the butter and dough into thin sheets. Not only would this create more thin layers, but it was also a time saver. By fraisaging the dough, the need for any additional turns was eliminated. (Not to mention that we could also skip forming the butter square.) However, this was still a four-hour project. Could we streamline the process even further?

One of the test cooks suggested that we abandon turning the dough in the traditional method (folding it into thirds, like a letter going into an envelope). Instead, she suggested folding the dough into thirds and then rolling it up, starting at the open end. This created the layers we were looking for easily and quickly. Folding and rolling the dough twice took a fraction of the time of the six-hour, six-turn method and produced identical results. With just an hour's chilling time before and after the turns, we trimmed the process from a tedious six hours to a mere two.

With puff pastry in the refrigerator (or freezer), you can make a variety of recipes. Cheese straws, almond straws, and palmiers are basically just puff pastry brushed with beaten egg (which acts as glue) and dusted with cheese, sugared almonds, or cinnamon sugar. Apple turnovers require the preparation of a filling and a somewhat more elaborate shaping method (see page 275 for details), and Napoleons are layers of baked puff pastry spread with pastry cream and topped off with a chocolate and vanilla glaze (see page 276 for details).

Quick Puff Pastry

MAKES ENOUGH FOR 18 STRAWS,
28 PALMIERS, OR 12 TURNOVERS

If well wrapped, puff pastry will keep in the refrigerator for 2 days or in the freezer for 1 month.

3	cups (15 ounces) unbleached all-purpose flour
1 1/2	tablespoons sugar
1 1/2	teaspoons salt
1 1/2	cups (3 sticks) cold unsalted butter, cut into 1/4-inch cubes
9	tablespoons ice water
2	teaspoons juice from 1 lemon

1. Place the flour, sugar, and salt in a food processor and pulse to combine. Add a quarter of the butter cubes and process until the butter is in

SHAPING PUFF PASTRY STRAWS

One at a time, twist each strip into a corkscrew shape. Place the strips on a parchment-lined baking sheet about 1/2 inch apart.

dime-size pieces, four 1-second pulses. Add the remaining butter and process to coat the cubes with flour, two 1-second pulses. Transfer the mixture to a medium bowl.

2. Combine the ice water and lemon juice in a small bowl. Add half the liquid to the flour and butter mixture and toss until just combined. Keep adding the liquid, 1 tablespoon at a time, until the dough will clump together in your hand. Turn the dough out onto a work surface. The dough will be quite dry and shaggy at this point. Follow the illustration on page 150 to fraisage the dough; wrap the dough in plastic and refrigerate for 1 hour.

3. Unwrap the dough and follow the illustrations on page 150 for turning the dough twice. (If the dough becomes soft and sticky after the first set of turns, wrap it in plastic and refrigerate 30 minutes until workable, then repeat rolling and pressing.) When the second rolling and folding is complete, wrap the dough in plastic and chill for at least 1 hour.

Cheese Straws

MAKES 18

If you've never baked with puff pastry before, cheese straws are a great place to start. They are simply strips of puff pastry dusted with grated cheese, twisted, and baked. They can be made with any hard cheese; feel free to substitute Asiago or Pecorino Romano for the Parmesan. For an herb variation, add 1 tablespoon finely chopped fresh chives or parsley to the grated cheese. Serve them as an hors d'oeuvre, an appetizer, or with salads or soups. The cheese straws will keep at room temperature in an airtight container for up to 3 days.

1	recipe Quick Puff Pastry (at left), chilled
1	large egg, lightly beaten
1	cup (2 ounces) finely grated Parmesan cheese (see note)

1. Adjust the oven racks to the upper- and lower-middle positions. Heat the oven to 400 degrees. Line 2 baking sheets with parchment paper.

2. Lightly flour a large sheet of parchment. Place the dough on the floured parchment and roll it into a 16 by 14-inch rectangle about 1/4 inch thick. Brush

with the beaten egg and sprinkle with the Parmesan, patting it onto the dough with your hand. Using a pizza cutter, cut the dough into eighteen ¾-inch strips. Following the illustration on page 273, twist the strips into a corkscrew shape and place them on a prepared baking sheet about ½ inch apart (you should be able to fit 9 strips onto each baking sheet).

3. Bake until the cheese straws are golden brown, 22 to 26 minutes, rotating the baking sheets from front to back and top to bottom halfway through the baking time. Cool on a wire rack until they reach room temperature, about 20 minutes. Serve.

Sugared Almond Straws

MAKES 18

These straws are made the same way as cheese straws, except the cheese is replaced with sugar and sliced almonds. Also, both sides of the dough are coated with the mixture.

- I   cup (7 ounces) sugar
- I   cup sliced almonds
- I   recipe Quick Puff Pastry (page 273), chilled
- I   large egg, lightly beaten

1. Adjust the oven racks to the upper- and lower-middle positions. Heat the oven to 400 degrees. Line 2 baking sheets with parchment paper. In a small bowl, mix together the sugar and sliced almonds; set aside.

2. Lightly flour a large sheet of parchment paper. Place the dough onto the floured parchment and roll it into a 16 by 14-inch rectangle about ¼ inch thick. Brush with half of the beaten egg and sprinkle with half of the sugar mixture. Using a rolling pin, gently press the sugar mixture into the dough. Carefully turn the dough over, brush with the remaining egg, sprinkle with the remaining sugar mixture, and press the sugar and almonds into the dough with the rolling pin. Using a pizza cutter, cut the dough into eighteen ¾-inch strips. Following the illustration on page 273, twist the strips to form a corkscrew shape and place them on a prepared baking sheet about ½ inch apart (you should be able to fit 9 strips onto each baking sheet).

3. Bake until the straws are golden brown, 22 to 26 minutes, rotating the baking sheets from front to back and top to bottom halfway through the baking time. Cool on a wire rack until they reach room temperature, about 20 minutes. Serve the day they are made.

Palmiers

MAKES ABOUT 28

Palmiers are crispy palm leaf–shaped cookies made with puff pastry dough and usually served with tea or coffee. The dough is rolled into a thin sheet, dusted with sugar and cinnamon, folded, sliced, and baked. In the oven, the sugar turns into crunchy caramel, and the folds create an attractive palm leaf pattern. Rolled uncut palmier dough can be wrapped well and stored in the freezer for up to 2 weeks (the frozen dough can be cut and baked directly from the freezer). Once baked,

SHAPING PALMIERS

1. With the long side of the 16 by 14-inch rectangle closest to you, fold 3½ inches of the outer edges in toward the center, maintaining a 2-inch strip separating the two sides.

2. Fold the outer edges in again so that both sides of the rectangle are folded in (on top of themselves), still maintaining a 2-inch strip in the middle.

3. Fold the dough in half, forming a rectangular log measuring about 14 by 4 inches. Wrap in plastic wrap and refrigerate until firm.

4. Slice the chilled roll into ½-inch-thick slices and position the pieces 1 inch apart on a baking sheet lined with parchment.

the palmiers can be kept at room temperature in an airtight container for up to 3 days.

- ½   cup (3½ ounces) sugar
- 1½   teaspoons ground cinnamon
- 1   recipe Quick Puff Pastry (page 273), chilled
- 1   large egg, lightly beaten

1. In a small bowl, mix together the sugar and cinnamon. Lightly flour a large piece of parchment paper. Place the dough onto the floured parchment and roll it into a 16 by 14-inch rectangle about ¼ inch thick. Brush with the beaten egg and sprinkle with the cinnamon sugar, gently smoothing the sugar and patting it onto the dough with your hand. Following the illustrations on page 274, form the dough into a log. Wrap the dough in plastic and refrigerate it until firm, about 1 hour.

2. Adjust the oven racks to the upper- and lower-middle positions. Heat the oven to 400 degrees. Line 2 baking sheets with parchment paper and set aside.

3. Remove the dough roll from the refrigerator and remove the plastic wrap. Cut the dough into ½-inch-thick pieces and arrange the pieces on the prepared baking sheets, spacing them about 1 inch apart. Bake until the palmiers are golden brown, 20 to 24 minutes, rotating the baking sheets from front to back and top to bottom halfway through the baking time. Cool on a wire rack until they reach room temperature, about 20 minutes. Serve.

APPLE TURNOVERS

WHEN YOU EAT AN APPLE TURNOVER—AND we mean a real turnover, not those mass-produced imitations—the flaky dough should shatter all over your plate and yourself, requiring a stand-up and shakedown to get your clothes presentable again. Eating bad apple turnovers, on the other hand, may be neater, but the experience couldn't be more disheartening—the filling is bland and mushy and the dough soggy.

Our puff pastry dough is perfect for turnovers so we concentrated on the filling. Most recipes dice or chop the apples and they are too chunky, often breaking through the dough during the shaping process. At the other extreme, some recipes rely on a cooked filling. Although a cooked filling won't puncture the dough, it doesn't have the freshness we wanted. The turnovers are baked, so why cook the filling in advance? We found the solution was to grate the apples on the large holes of a box grater. Unlike the other fillings, the turnovers with the shredded apples exuded fresh apple flavor, providing just the right contrast with the rich pastry.

We felt that a plain apple filling did not do the pastry justice. After trying various options, we found that turnovers made with lemon juice, sugar, and just a pinch of salt were the biggest crowd pleasers. We added cinnamon by dusting the surface of the turnovers with cinnamon sugar just before they went into the oven.

SHAPING TURNOVERS

1. On a large sheet of parchment paper lightly dusted with flour, roll the dough to a 20-inch by 15-inch rectangle that is slightly under ⅛ inch thick. Using a ruler and a pizza cutter, trim the edges to make them neat and even.

2. Make incisions at 5-inch intervals on all four sides of the rectangle. Line the ruler up with the incisions and cut the dough into twelve 5-inch squares.

3. Grate the peeled apples on the large holes of a box grater, discarding the core and seeds.

4. With a fork dipped in flour, press to seal and crimp the edges.

With the dough and filling good to go, we focused on the proper oven temperature. We tested several options and found that turnovers baked at 375 degrees were the flakiest, with the best rise. After 20 minutes in the oven and a 15-minute cool-down on a wire rack, these turnovers are ready to be eaten. Just make sure you're not wearing black—it won't sufficiently camouflage the flakes bound to dust your clothes on impact.

Flaky Apple Turnovers

MAKES 12

If at any point during rolling the dough becomes sticky and difficult to work with, transfer it to a baking sheet or cutting board, wrap it in plastic, and chill until it becomes workable. Refer to the illustrations on page 275 when forming the turnovers.

1	recipe Quick Puff Pastry (page 273), chilled

APPLE FILLING

4	large Granny Smith apples (about 2 pounds)
1 1/2	cups (10 1/2 ounces) sugar
3	teaspoons juice from 1 lemon
1/2	teaspoon salt

CINNAMON SUGAR

1/2	cup (3 1/2 ounces) sugar
2	teaspoons ground cinnamon

1. Roll the dough into a 20 by 15-inch rectangle, about 1/8 inch thick. Line 2 baking sheets with parchment paper, trim and cut the dough into twelve 5-inch squares, and place 6 on each sheet. Refrigerate the dough squares while making the filling.

2. FOR THE FILLING: Peel the apples and grate them on the large holes of a box grater. Combine the grated apples, sugar, lemon juice, and salt in a medium bowl. Remove one sheet of dough squares from the refrigerator. Working with one square at a time, place a dough square on a work surface. Place 2 tablespoons of the grated apple filling (squeezed of excess liquid) in the center of the dough. Moisten two adjoining edges of the dough square with a finger dipped in the apple liquid, then fold the top portion of dough over the bottom, making sure to overlap the bottom portion by 1/8 inch. Crimp the edges of the turnover with a fork. Using a wide metal spatula, transfer the turnover to the prepared baking sheet. Repeat with the remaining dough squares. Return the sheet of turnovers to the refrigerator and repeat with the second sheet of dough squares. Refrigerate the filled turnovers 30 minutes or cover with plastic wrap and refrigerate up to 24 hours.

3. FOR THE CINNAMON SUGAR: While the turnovers are chilling, adjust the oven racks to the upper- and lower-middle positions and heat the oven to 375 degrees. Combine the sugar and cinnamon in a small bowl.

4. Brush or mist the turnovers lightly with water and sprinkle them evenly with the cinnamon sugar. Bake until golden brown, 30 to 35 minutes, rotating the baking sheets front to back and top to bottom halfway through the baking time. Using a wide metal spatula, transfer the turnovers to a wire rack to cool. Serve warm or at room temperature.

NAPOLEONS

NAPOLEONS (ALSO KNOWN AS MILLE-FEUILLES) are made of layers of flaky puff pastry filled with rich pastry cream, cut into small rectangles, and topped with chocolate and vanilla icings. Although frequently found in bakeries, homemade Napoleons are rare. We set out to change that.

The Napoleon may look complicated, but its two main components (puff pastry and pastry cream) are actually quite basic. We started with a smaller yield of both our Pastry Cream (page 150) and our Quick Puff Pastry (page 273).

There is one major difference with the way the puff pastry is treated for Napoleons as opposed to other pastries. In order to keep the pastry from rising too much, it is weighed down while baking, usually by a second baking sheet placed on top of the pastry. (The goal is to achieve thin, crisp sheets of pastry.) We tried this but found that the second baking sheet shielded the puff from the oven's heat and prevented it from browning adequately. The perfect tool for this job turned out to be a sheet of aluminum foil lined with pie weights, which were just heavy enough to keep the puff from rising, while allowing it to brown.

Traditional Napoleon recipes use fondant for their icing, but we found that making fondant (which requires making a sugar syrup and using a candy thermometer) was too fussy for an already involved recipe. We made our icing as simple as possible: a combination of confectioners' sugar and half-and-half (and the addition of melted chocolate for the chocolate version). The pastry is covered with chocolate icing and the vanilla icing is drizzled over the chocolate.

Now it was time to assemble our Napoleons. Some cookbooks suggested cutting all the pastry into small rectangles, then filling and assembling the Napoleons one at a time, but we found this to be unnecessarily time-consuming. We found it best to fill and assemble one large pastry and then cut it into individual portions. We began by cutting the layers into four strips. We spread three strips with pastry cream, placing one on top of another. We frosted the remaining strip with the icings and carefully placed it on top of the filled pastry. Chilling the assembled pastry helped the pastry cream firm up further and prevented it from oozing out when we cut through the layers to make individual pieces. We chilled the assembled pastry for two hours, then used a sharp serrated knife and a gentle sawing motion to cut individual portions.

Napoleons

MAKES 8

We have reduced the yield on our puff pastry to accommodate this recipe. Assemble the Napoleons at least 2 hours before you plan to serve them to making cutting them neatly easier. Although Napoleons will hold for up to 2 days, the pastry will not be as crisp.

QUICK PUFF PASTRY

1 1/4   cups (6 1/4 ounces) unbleached all-purpose flour

1   tablespoon sugar

1/2   teaspoon salt

3/4   cup (1 1/2 sticks) cold unsalted butter, cut into 1/4-inch cubes

3   tablespoons ice water

1   teaspoon juice from 1 lemon

1   recipe Pastry Cream for Éclairs and Napoleons (page 227)

CHOCOLATE GLAZE

2   tablespoons half-and-half

1   ounce bittersweet or semisweet chocolate, chopped fine

3/4   cup (3 ounces) confectioners' sugar, sifted

VANILLA GLAZE

1 1/2   teaspoons half-and-half

1/4   cup (1 ounce) confectioners' sugar, sifted

1/8   teaspoon vanilla extract

1. FOR THE PUFF PASTRY: Place the flour, sugar, and salt in a food processor and pulse to combine. Add a quarter of the butter cubes and cut the butter into the flour until the butter is in dime-size pieces, four 1-second pulses. Add the remaining butter and process to coat the cubes with flour, two 1-second pulses. Transfer the mixture to a medium bowl.

2. Combine the ice water and lemon juice in a small bowl. Add half the liquid to the flour and butter mixture and toss until just combined. Keep adding the liquid, 1 teaspoon at a time, until the dough will clump together in your hand. Turn the dough out onto the work surface. The dough will be quite dry and shaggy at this point. Follow the illustration on page 150 to fraisage the dough; wrap the dough in plastic and refrigerate for 1 hour.

3. Unwrap the dough and follow the illustrations on page 150 for turning the dough. To accommodate the smaller yield of pastry, roll the Napoleon dough to a 12 by 9-inch rectangle instead of a 15 by 10-inch rectangle. The folded dough should measure a 5 by 4-inch rectangle, instead of a 6 by 5-inch rectangle. (If the dough becomes soft and sticky after the first set of turns, wrap it in plastic and refrigerate 30 minutes until workable, then repeat rolling and pressing.) When the second rolling and folding is complete, wrap the dough in plastic and chill for at least 1 hour. (At this point, the dough

will keep in the refrigerator for up to 2 days.)

4. Adjust an oven rack to the middle position and heat the oven to 400 degrees. On a large piece of parchment paper, roll the dough to a 16 by 11-inch rectangle about ⅛ inch thick, trimming the edges if necessary to make them even. Transfer the dough, still on the parchment, to a large baking sheet. Using a fork, prick holes into the pastry at 2-inch intervals. Place a large sheet of aluminum foil over the puff pastry. Crimp the edges of the foil (to prevent the pie weights from sliding off) and distribute the pie weights evenly over the top. If the pastry has become warm at this point, refrigerate it until firm, about 30 minutes.

5. Bake the pastry for 20 minutes, turning the baking sheet halfway through the baking time. Remove the foil and pie weights and continue baking until the pastry is golden brown, 3 to 5 minutes. Remove the pastry from the oven. Grasp the sides of the foil to lift it (and the weights) off the pastry and place the pan on a cooling rack until the pastry is at room temperature, about 1 hour.

6. For the chocolate glaze: While the pastry cools, place the half-and-half and chocolate in a small microwave-safe bowl. Cover with plastic wrap and microwave until the half-and-half is hot and the chocolate begins to melt, 20 to 30 seconds. Add the confectioners' sugar and whisk together until smooth. Cover the bowl with plastic wrap and set aside.

7. For the vanilla glaze: In a small bowl, whisk together the half-and-half, confectioners' sugar, and vanilla until smooth. Cover the bowl with plastic wrap and set aside.

8. Cut the puff pastry lengthwise into 4 pieces measuring approximately 16 by 2½ inches, trimming the edges to make straight sides if necessary. Spread a third of the pastry cream onto one of the unfrosted pieces of puff pastry and place this piece on a parchment-lined baking sheet. Place another piece of puff pastry on top of the pastry cream, and repeat twice more, so you have three layers of puff pastry and pastry cream.

9. Spread the chocolate glaze onto the remaining piece with a small offset spatula. Dip a soupspoon into the vanilla glaze. Move the spoon back and forth over the pastry, working from one end to the other, letting the glaze drop onto the chocolate-covered surface. When you are done, the entire length of the pastry should be marked by thin lines of the vanilla glaze. Cover the top layer of the pastry cream–filled pastry with the glazed piece of puff pastry. Place the assembled Napoleon in the refrigerator until chilled and the pastry cream is totally set, at least 2 hours and up to overnight.

10. Using a sharp serrated knife, carefully cut the Napoleon crosswise into 2-inch pieces and serve. (Napoleons are best served within 1 day of assembly.)

ASSEMBLING NAPOLEONS

1. Cut the baked puff pastry lengthwise into 4 pieces measuring approximately 16 by 2½ inches, trimming the edges to make straight sides if necessary.

2. Spread one-third of the pastry cream onto one of the unfrosted pieces of puff pastry and place this pastry on a parchment-lined baking sheet. Repeat with 2 more pieces of pastry, stacking them one on top of another, so you have three layers of pastry cream.

3. Spread the chocolate glaze onto the remaining piece of pastry with a small offset spatula. Dip a soupspoon into the vanilla glaze. Move the spoon back and forth across the pastry, working from one end to the other. When you are done, the entire length of the pastry should be marked by thin lines of the vanilla glaze.

4. Cover the top layer of the pastry cream–filled pastry with the glazed piece of puff pastry. Place the assembled Napoleon in the refrigerator until chilled and the pastry cream is totally set, at least 2 hours and up to overnight. Using a sharp serrated knife, carefully cut the Napoleon crosswise into 2-inch pieces.

CORN AND APRICOT MUFFINS WITH ORANGE ESSENCE **PAGE 49**

CREAM BISCUITS **PAGE 56**

BANANA BREAD **PAGE 24**

RUSTIC ITALIAN BREAD **PAGE 98**

CRESCENT ROLLS **PAGE 112**

RICOTTA CALZONES WITH SAUSAGE AND BROCCOLI RABE   **PAGE 169**

DEEP-DISH PIZZA WITH FRESH TOMATO TOPPING, MOZZARELLA, AND BASIL **PAGE 166**

DEVIL'S FOOD CAKE WITH RICH VANILLA BUTTERCREAM FROSTING   **PAGE 364**

NEW YORK CHEESECAKE WITH FRESH STRAWBERRY TOPPING **PAGE 391**

YELLOW CUPCAKES WITH SIMPLE CHOCOLATE FROSTING   **PAGE 345**

FLOURLESS CHOCOLATE CAKE   **PAGE 381**

CARROT CAKE WITH CREAM CHEESE FROSTING **PAGE 337**

CHOCOLATE SHEET CAKE WITH CREAMY MILK CHOCOLATE FROSTING **PAGE 342**

SOUR CREAM COFFEECAKE **PAGE 340**

FRESH NECTARINE UPSIDE-DOWN CAKE **PAGE 332**

LEMON CHEESECAKE **PAGE 393**

6

CRISPS, COBBLERS, AND OTHER FRUIT DESSERTS

Crisps, Cobblers, and Other Fruit Desserts

WE LOVE A SIMPLE BOWL OF FRESH SUMMER berries or a crisp autumn apple, but who says nature can't be improved upon a little? Baking fruit intensifies its natural sweetness and softens its texture. Likewise, macerating fruit (mixing and sometimes mashing fruit with sugar or other sweeteners) enriches the fruit's natural juices (as in strawberry shortcake, for example). Whether cooked or not, these fruit desserts are complemented by a crust formed with bread, cake crumbs, flour and butter, oats, and the like.

There is an astonishing array of old-fashioned American desserts that fall under this category. In the days when home cooks were frugal, these desserts were an easy way to use up stale leftovers while providing a bit of variety in terms of texture and flavor. Most of these simple desserts have funny names that are hard to keep straight. While regional differences exist, most American cookbooks agree on the following formulations:

A crisp is fruit topped with a "rubbed" mixture of butter, sugar, and flour, then baked. The topping often includes nuts or oats.

A pandowdy is fruit covered with pastry dough and baked. The dough is cut, scored, and pressed into the fruit.

A cobbler is fruit topped with a crust, which can be made from cookie dough, pie pastry, or biscuit topping, and baked.

Shortcakes are often grouped with crisps, cobblers, and such, although this dessert is made with fruit that has not been baked. Rather, the fruit is macerated and then layered between split biscuits with whipped cream.

The following pages contain recipes for our favorite baked fruit desserts. Please refer to "Preparing Fruit" on pages 308 and 309 for tips on peeling, pitting, and cutting all the types of fruit used in this chapter.

CRISP

THERE IS SELDOM ANYTHING CRISP ABOUT most crisps. This simple baked dessert, made from sweetened fruit topped with a combination of sugar, butter, and flour, almost invariably comes out of the oven with a soggy top crust. A few recipes go so far as to refer to this classic dish as a crunch, a term that does little to suggest the flat, dull, overly sweetened crust that serves as a streusel topping for the fruit.

We tried covering fruit with sweetened and buttered oats (for a British take on a crisp, called a crumble), as well as plain toppings without oats or nuts, and were unimpressed. None of these toppings merited the name "crisp." We found that two ingredients are essential to a successful crisp—spices (we recommend cinnamon and nutmeg) and nuts (particularly whole almonds or pecans). The spices add flavor to the topping, while the nuts give it some texture and much-needed crunch. We also found that the food processor does the best job of making the topping, although you can also use your fingers or a fork.

Firm fruits, such as apples, pears, nectarines, peaches, and plums, work best in crisps. Berries are quite watery and will make the topping soggy if used alone. However, they will work in combination with firmer fruits. If you like, replace up to one cup of the fruit in the fillings with an equal amount of berries. We think that raspberries are especially good with apples, while blueberries work nicely with peaches.

Our tests revealed that when using apples, a combination of Granny Smith and McIntosh apples works best. The McIntosh apples have good flavor and cook down to form a thick sauce. The Granny Smiths cut some of the sweetness and hold their shape.

We found it unnecessary to thicken the fruit in all but two cases. Plums are a bit watery and benefit from the addition of a little quick-cooking tapioca. Peaches will thicken up on their own but need some help when blueberries are added to the mix. Juices thrown off by any of the other fruits will evaporate or thicken nicely without causing the topping to become soft.

As for flavoring the fruit, we found ¼ cup sugar to be adequate, especially since the toppings are fairly sweet. We also like to add some lemon juice and zest. One-half teaspoon of grated ginger makes a nice addition to any of the fillings.

Apple Crisp

SERVES 4 TO 6

Although almost any unsalted nut may be used in the topping, our preference is for almonds or pecans. A dollop of whipped cream or vanilla ice cream is always welcome, especially if serving the crisp warm. To double the recipe, place the ingredients in a 13 by 9-inch baking dish and bake for 55 minutes at 375 degrees without increasing the oven temperature.

TOPPING

6	tablespoons (1 7/8 ounces) unbleached all-purpose flour
1/4	cup packed (1 3/4 ounces) light brown sugar
1/4	cup (1 3/4 ounces) granulated sugar
1/4	teaspoon ground cinnamon
1/4	teaspoon ground nutmeg
1/4	teaspoon salt
5	tablespoons cold unsalted butter, cut into 1/2-inch pieces
3/4	cup coarsely chopped nuts, such as almonds, pecans, or walnuts

FILLING

3	medium Granny Smith apples (about 1 1/4 pounds)
3	medium McIntosh apples (about 1 1/4 pounds)
1/2	teaspoon grated zest and 1 1/2 tablespoons juice from 1 lemon
1/4	cup (1 3/4 ounces) granulated sugar

1. FOR THE TOPPING: Place the flour, sugars, spices, and salt in a food processor and process briefly to combine. Add the butter and pulse 10 times, about 4 seconds for each pulse. The mixture will first look like dry sand, with large lumps of butter, then like coarse cornmeal. Add the nuts, then process again, four or five 1-second pulses. The topping should look like slightly clumpy wet sand. Be sure not to overmix or the mixture will become too wet and homogeneous. Refrigerate the topping while preparing the fruit, at least 15 minutes.

2. Adjust an oven rack to the lower-middle position and heat the oven to 375 degrees.

3. FOR THE FILLING: Peel, quarter, core, and cut the apples into 1-inch chunks. (You should have 6 cups.) Toss the apples, zest, juice, and sugar in a medium bowl. Scrape the fruit mixture with a rubber spatula into an 8-inch square baking pan or 9-inch deep-dish pie plate.

4. TO ASSEMBLE AND BAKE THE CRISP: Distribute the chilled topping evenly over the fruit. Bake for 40 minutes. Increase the oven temperature to 400 degrees and continue baking until the fruit is bubbling and the topping turns deep golden brown, about 5 minutes more. Serve warm. (The crisp can be set aside at room temperature for a few hours and then reheated in a warm oven just before serving.)

VARIATIONS

Pear Crisp

Follow the recipe for Apple Crisp, replacing the apples with 6 medium pears (2½ to 3 pounds).

Peach Crisp

Nectarines can be used in place of peaches if desired. For peach-blueberry crisp, reduce the cut peaches to 5 cups (about 2½ pounds) and add 1 cup fresh blueberries and 1 tablespoon quick-cooking tapioca to the fruit mixture.

Follow the recipe for Apple Crisp, replacing the apples with 6 peaches (about 3 pounds), peeled, pitted, and cut into ⅓-inch wedges.

Plum Crisp

Follow the recipe for Apple Crisp, replacing the apples with 8 plums (2½ to 3 pounds), pitted and cut into ⅓-inch wedges, and adding 1 tablespoon quick-cooking tapioca to the fruit mixture.

APPLE PANDOWDY

PANDOWDY IS A SORT OF DEEP-DISH PIE, originally made with sweetened apples covered with a very thick piece of pastry and baked. Some time before serving, the pastry is scored and pushed into the fruit so it absorbs their juices. Like its fruit dessert cousins, which may be described according to how they look when served or even how they sound when eaten, pandowdy got its name for being just that—dowdy, or on the homely side.

When we began our recipe development by making five pandowdies from various sources, we realized that making this dessert was not without its pitfalls. Though "soggy" is not too far off in describing the texture of the submerged pastry in a good pandowdy, we considered doughs that qualified as "waterlogged," "saturated," or "total mush" to be failures. We wanted to produce a crust that preserved some of its baked structure, one that was at once soggy and crisp. Likewise, some of our first attempts at apple fillings fell short of acceptable, ranging from "overspiced" to "tasteless." We knew our charge would be to develop something in between.

We started with the apples, not only concentrating on their flavor and texture but also knowing that the variety we used would determine the amount of juices released during baking. As with other apple desserts (including apple pie), we found that a combination of Granny Smith and McIntosh apples delivered the best results. An all-Granny Smith pandowdy left a lot to be desired. In the short time that the dowdy is in the oven, the apples held their shape, retained most of their firm texture, and shed only a minimal amount of juices. While we liked their tart assertive flavor, we could not "dowdy" the pastry—there were no juices for it to soak up—and crunchy apples were not the tasters' ideal. The all-McIntosh version came out of the oven on the other end of the spectrum. The apples

were broken down and listless, like applesauce, and there was too much juice. The pastry crust, which had already been steamed in the oven, soaked the juices right up and turned into a waterlogged mess. A 50-50 ratio of the two apple varieties produced a perfect balance of delicate apple juices and yielding yet sturdy apple chunks.

Seasoning the filling came next. A traditional dowdy is not a fancy dish. We decided to keep it simple and limit the flavorings to brown sugar for a caramel-like sweetness, vanilla extract for roundness, and lemon zest for brightness. Although the combination of these ingredients with two types of apples was pleasing, tasters were looking for a hint of cinnamon. In the end, a sprinkling of cinnamon sugar on the pastry's surface added cinnamon flavor without compromising the freshness of the apples.

It was time to focus on the pastry. We found that our standard pie pastry (see page 181), made with both butter and shortening, yielded good results. The most pressing problem was the overrun of dough around the 8-inch dish in which we were baking the dowdy. When we tucked the excess pastry around the sides of the pan (as recommended in a few recipes), the pastry dropped below the apple layer and "boiled" into a mass of unappealing mush. To avoid such oversaturated dough, especially on the sides and in the corners, we found that it was best to trim the dough to

MAKING A PANDOWDY

1. As soon as it emerges from the oven, score the pastry with a sharp knife by running the knife lengthwise and crosswise to form 2-inch squares.

2. Use the edge of a spoon or metal spatula to press the edges of the crust squares down into the fruit. Don't completely submerge the pieces or they will become exceedingly soggy.

size, eliminating any chance of boiling the dough. Cutting air vents into the surface of the raw dough before baking also helped to prevent excessive steaming and subsequent rubberizing of the pastry. With the edges untucked and the vents opened, the pastry came out of the oven crisp, tender, and flaky, perfect for dunking in the fruit and soaking up its juices.

A few recipes suggested submerging the crust during baking. We quickly rejected this notion, as it made the crust unbearably soggy. Scoring the crust when it emerged from the oven and then pressing the crust down into the juices was a far better option.

Apple Pandowdy
SERVES 4 TO 6

Serve the pandowdy warm in deep bowls with scoops of vanilla ice cream.

CRUST

1	cup (5 ounces) unbleached all-purpose flour, plus more for dusting the work surface
1/2	teaspoon salt
2	tablespoons granulated sugar
2	tablespoons vegetable shortening, chilled
6	tablespoons (3/4 stick) cold unsalted butter, cut into 1/4-inch pieces
3–4	tablespoons ice water
1/2	teaspoon ground cinnamon
1	tablespoon milk

FILLING

2	large Granny Smith apples (about 1 pound), peeled, cored, and cut into 1/4-inch slices
2	large McIntosh apples (about 1 pound), peeled, cored, and cut into 1/4-inch slices
1/3	cup packed (2 1/3 ounces) light brown sugar
1	teaspoon grated zest from 1 lemon
1/2	teaspoon vanilla extract

1. FOR THE CRUST: Place the flour, salt, and 1 tablespoon of the granulated sugar in a food processor and pulse until combined. Add the shortening and process until the mixture has the texture of coarse sand, about 10 seconds. Scatter the butter pieces over the flour mixture; cut the butter into the flour until the mixture is pale yellow and resembles coarse crumbs, with butter bits no larger than small peas, about ten 1-second pulses. Turn the mixture into a medium bowl.

2. Sprinkle 3 tablespoons ice water over the mixture. With the blade of a rubber spatula, use a folding motion to mix. Press down on the dough with the broad side of the spatula until the dough sticks together, adding up to 1 tablespoon more ice water if the dough will not come together. Place the dough on a sheet of plastic wrap and press into either a square or a circle, depending on whether you are using a square or round pan. Wrap the dough in the plastic and refrigerate at least 1 hour, or up to 2 days, before rolling out.

3. FOR THE FILLING: Adjust the oven rack to the middle position and heat the oven to 425 degrees. Toss the apple slices, brown sugar, lemon zest, and vanilla together in a large bowl until the apples are evenly coated with the sugar. Place the apples in an 8-inch square or 9-inch round glass baking pan.

4. TO ASSEMBLE AND BAKE THE PANDOWDY: Mix together the remaining 1 tablespoon of granulated sugar and the cinnamon in a small bowl and set aside. If the dough has been refrigerated longer than 1 hour, let it stand at room temperature until malleable. Roll the dough on a lightly floured work surface or between two large sheets of plastic wrap to a 10-inch square or circle. Trim the dough to the exact size of the baking dish. Place the dough on top of the apples. Brush the dough with the milk and sprinkle with the cinnamon sugar mixture. Cut four 1-inch vents into the dough. Bake until golden brown, 35 to 40 minutes.

5. Following the illustrations on page 299, score the pastry with a knife as soon as it emerges from the oven. Use the edge of a spoon or spatula to press the edges of the crust squares down into the fruit without completely submerging them. Because the crust will soften quickly, serve pandowdy warm.

➤ VARIATION
Pear Pandowdy
It's important to use perfectly ripe pears in this recipe. Firm pears don't exude enough juice, and overly ripe

pears will break down into mush when baked.

Follow the recipe for Apple Pandowdy, replacing the apples with 4 large ripe pears (2 pounds) and replacing the lemon zest with 1 teaspoon grated fresh ginger.

GERMAN APPLE PANCAKE

FOUND UNDER A VARIETY OF ALIASES, including Dutch pancake, Dutch baby, and puff pancake (to name just a few), a German apple pancake is a crisp, puffy baked pancake packed with apples. A few renowned pancake houses around the country have daily lines of hungry breakfast-goers snaking out the door waiting for this simple yet deeply satisfying breakfast treat. But, as we found out, apple pancakes worth waiting for are few and far between. The average pancake falls far short of what we consider ideal: a crisp, brittle top, a rich but neutral-flavored pancake, and well-caramelized apples.

German apple pancake batter is a simple affair, closer in composition and consistency to thin crêpe batter than to thicker conventional pancake batter. It should be a very loose mixture of eggs, milk or cream, flour, and a pinch of salt. The secret to the batter is balancing the amount of eggs with the milk or cream. Many of the batters we tested yielded pancakes that were far too eggy. For a 10-inch pancake, tasters agreed that two eggs was just enough for structure and flavor. Three eggs made a dense, gummy pancake predominantly flavored with egg.

As for the dairy component, we tried milk, cream, and half-and-half. Milk alone made a loose, relatively flavorless pancake dominated by the eggs. All cream produced an over-the-top rich pancake that almost resembled a custard in texture. Half-and-half proved a great compromise between milk and cream. It gave the pancake body and depth without being too rich.

To round out the pancake's flavors, we added vanilla extract and a small amount of granulated sugar. The apples provide the sweetening for this pancake, but sugar in the batter wedded the flavors.

Unlike stovetop pancakes that are packed with chemical leaveners and buttermilk, oven-baked pancakes rely on heat and eggs for an explosive rise. While a very high heat—500 degrees—guaranteed a dramatic rise and golden crust, it failed to fully cook the pancake's interior. Leaving the pancake in the oven for more time at this high temperature caused the crust to burn, so to remedy the problem we tried starting the pancake at a high temperature and quickly reducing the heat to finish cooking. We discovered that if the oven temperature is brought too low, the pancake needs to bake too long and the exterior dries out by the time the interior is set. After several tests, we found it best to heat the oven to 500 degrees and then lower the temperature to 425 degrees when the pancake goes into the oven.

Much to our surprise, cooking the apples proved to be a bigger issue than assembling the batter. We wanted well-caramelized apples for the best flavor, but we also wanted the apples to retain a bit of bite for contrast with the soft and creamy pancake. We knew firm Granny Smith apples would be the best choice because they stand up well to cooking. These tart apples would also keep the dish from becoming too sweet.

We started with the simplest method—cooking the apples in some butter until they turned golden brown and their natural sugars caramelized. Our first few attempts at cooking the apples were frustrating. Over medium heat, the apples verged on chunky applesauce before they caramelized; over high heat, they scorched before the apples' sugars browned.

One of the test cooks then suggested an eccentric method—sautéing the apples in caramel, a common technique in Vietnamese cooking. In this manner, the caramel flavor is already developed, and the apples are cooked until the desired texture is reached. The technique worked beautifully, but making caramel prior to cooking the apples was time-consuming and a bit daunting for early-morning cooking.

Hoping to avoid making caramel, we tried adding sugar to the apples as they cooked over high heat in the hope that the sugar would caramelize as the apples cooked. It was close, but not quite there. The apples were slightly overcooked by the time the sugars had caramelized. When we switched to light brown sugar, the technique worked beautifully; the apple slices were uniformly golden and retained some body. This technique works well, but we found that it is crucial to cut the apples into even slices; otherwise, they cook unevenly and the smaller slices burn.

Straight from the oven, German apple pancake is quite dramatic and will certainly impress your breakfast companions. Get to the table fast, though—the pancake sinks within a couple of minutes. A dusting of confectioners' sugar and warm maple syrup are the classic accompaniments.

~≈~

German Apple Pancake

SERVES 4

Tradition dictates that this supersized pancake should be cooked in a cast-iron skillet, but we found that an oven-safe, nonstick skillet worked significantly better. If you want to use cast iron, reduce the heat to medium-high after 5 minutes when cooking the apples; otherwise, they may burn in the oven because the cast iron retains so much heat. And be careful removing the pancake from a cast-iron skillet; it may stick unless your pan is very well seasoned.

2	large eggs
³/₄	cup half-and-half
l	teaspoon vanilla extract
¹/₂	teaspoon salt
l	tablespoon granulated sugar
¹/₂	cup (2¹/₂ ounces) unbleached all-purpose flour
l	tablespoon unsalted butter
3	medium Granny Smith apples (about 1¹/₄ pounds), peeled, cored, and cut into ¹/₄-inch slices
¹/₄	cup packed (1³/₄ ounces) light brown sugar
2	tablespoons confectioners' sugar
	Maple syrup, warmed

1. Adjust an oven rack to the middle position and heat the oven to 500 degrees. Combine the eggs, half-and-half, vanilla, salt, and granulated sugar in a food processor or a blender and process until well combined, about 15 seconds. Add the flour and process until thoroughly mixed and free of lumps, about 30 seconds; set the batter aside.

2. Add the butter to a 10-inch ovenproof nonstick skillet and heat over medium-high heat until the butter foams. Add the apples and sprinkle the brown sugar evenly over them. Cook, stirring occasionally, until the apples begin to turn light brown, about 5 minutes. Continue to cook over medium-high heat, stirring constantly, until the apples are golden brown, 4 to 5 minutes.

3. Remove the pan from the heat. Following illustration 1 below, quickly pour the batter around the edge of the pan over the apples; place the pan in the oven. Reduce the heat to 425 degrees and cook until browned and puffed, 16 to 17 minutes. With a heatproof spatula, loosen the edges of the pancake (see illustration 2). Invert the pancake onto a serving platter (see illustration 3), dust it with the confectioners' sugar, and serve immediately, accompanied by the warmed maple syrup.

PREPARING GERMAN APPLE PANCAKE

1. Pour the batter around the edge of the pan, then over the apples.

2. Loosen the edges of the pancake with a heatproof spatula.

3. Invert the pancake onto a large plate or serving platter.

➤ VARIATION
German Apple Pancake with Caramel Sauce

For a rustic dessert or a truly hedonistic breakfast experience, make a batch of Caramel Sauce (page 499). You will have extra caramel sauce, but it keeps well in the refrigerator for up to 2 weeks.

Follow the recipe for German Apple Pancake, replacing the maple syrup with Caramel Sauce (page 499).

QUICK APPLE STRUDEL

CLASSIC STRUDEL INVOLVES HOURS OF hands-on preparation, rolling and pulling the dough until it is so thin you can read a newspaper through it. Chucking the notion of homemade strudel dough, we started with a simpler option— store-bought phyllo dough—and set out to dramatically simplify this classic dessert while keeping the rich apple filling and as much of the crisp, flaky texture as possible.

A classic apple strudel contains apples, bread crumbs, sugar, cinnamon, raisins, and sometimes walnuts. Although this combination sounds appealing, the strudel recipes we tested initially were in a sad state: dry, bready fillings overpowered by the flavor of the spices and leathery, bland crusts that separated from the filling as soon as a fork came near.

We wanted the filling and pastry in our strudel to come together as a unified whole. The crust must be crisp and flaky yet still hold its shape. The filling should be moist but not wet, and the flavor of apple should shine through.

BEST PHYLLO DOUGH

We tried an expensive organic brand of phyllo, but Athens phyllo dough, which is widely available in supermarkets nationwide, yielded the crispiest crust.

Our first strudels threatened to shatter to bits if we so much as looked at them askance. Butter is usually brushed between the layers of phyllo dough to help keep them crisp and flaky, so we thought that by eliminating the butter we might get a more cohesive crust. But the phyllo crust without butter was still crisp, only now it was also dry and unappealing. We tried adding a bit of milk to the butter, in the hope that the added moisture might help, but that strudel was simply soggy. Then a test cook recalled a method she used while working as a pastry chef. For crisp, cohesive Napoleon layers that retained a bit of chew, she sprinkled sugar on each layer of phyllo with the butter. The melted sugar acted as glue between the layers and added flavor to an otherwise bland dough. The results weren't perfect, but we knew we were on the right track.

Working with phyllo requires constant attention. Left alone, the layers dry out and crack almost instantly. We were careful to keep damp towels over the unused phyllo while layering the sheets, but then we were sending our strudel into a hot oven for upward of 40 minutes, totally unprotected. With sugar between the layers, the strudel held its shape better, but as it cooled on the rack, the outer layers curled and flaked like a bad sunburn. We thought the long time in the oven might be drying out the phyllo, so we tried baking the strudel at very high heat—475 degrees—for just 15 minutes. This crust was perfect: toothsome yet slightly

WHY STRUDEL SHATTERS

We found that the phyllo on most strudels, including this one, curled and shattered as it cooled. Sprinkling sugar between the layers of phyllo "glues" them together in the oven and prevents this problem.

yielding, with a deeply caramelized exterior. And it could be cut into clean, solid slices. There was only one problem: The apples were still raw.

Up until this point, we had been using sliced Granny Smiths, figuring that a firm, tart apple would be best. The quick blast of heat was perfect for the phyllo, but the apples never had a chance to cook and soften. We tried slicing the apples thinner, about ⅛ inch. Still too firm. In the past, the test kitchen has found that a combination of apples works well in pies, so we applied the combination to strudel. Our half-McIntosh, half-Golden Delicious strudel was a success, the former adding body and apple flavor, the latter a toothsome texture.

Lemon juice replaced some of the tartness that had departed with the Granny Smiths. A scant ¼ teaspoon of cinnamon made the filling sweet and

well rounded. After testing various combinations of brown and granulated sugars, we discovered that less was more—just ¼ cup of granulated sugar added a clean sweetness that tasters liked.

Almost every recipe we'd seen called for raisins of some kind, and tasters preferred milder golden raisins to dark ones. Added straight to the apples, the raisins were a bit dry and chewy, but we found that simmering the raisins in liquid plumped them up in no time. For the liquid, we tried Calvados (apple brandy), which added a great layer of sweet apple flavor that everyone liked. Knowing that not many houses stock Calvados and that some cooks might not want to use alcohol, we looked for an alternative. Readily available apple cider proved to be the best substitute for Calvados.

Tasters were split on whether they liked chopped

ASSEMBLING STRUDEL

1. Place large sheet of parchment or waxed paper on a large work surface, long side toward you. Place 1 sheet of phyllo on the parchment paper, brush liberally with melted butter, and sprinkle with 1 teaspoon sugar. Repeat with the remaining 4 sheets of phyllo.

2. Place the apple filling in a 3-inch strip about 2½ inches from the bottom of the phyllo, leaving about 2 inches on either short side.

3. Fold the short ends of the phyllo over the apples.

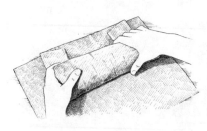

4. Fold the end closest to you over the apples and continue rolling loosely, using the parchment paper as a guide. Don't roll too tight, as this can cause tearing during baking.

5. Place the finished strudel, seam-side down, on an ungreased baking sheet. Brush the strudel with the remaining butter and sprinkle with the remaining 1 teaspoon sugar.

6. Cut four 1-inch vents into the top of the strudel for steam to escape.

nuts in the filling. We decided to make the nuts optional. We knew the bread crumbs, a classic component of strudel, were there to absorb the juices from the apples and prevent a damp crust, but we weren't completely convinced they were necessary. We were wrong. Strudel made without bread crumbs was soggy and loose. But the ½ to ¾ cup of bread crumbs most recipes called for resulted in a strudel that stuck to the roof of the mouth. We settled on ¼ cup of fresh bread crumbs, which gave us a strudel that was moist without being too wet. The flavor, however, was still bready. We browned the crumbs in butter, and tasters loved the results. The filling was now buttery and rich, moist but solid.

Quick Apple Strudel

SERVES 6 TO 8

The best ways to defrost phyllo dough are in the refrigerator overnight or at room temperature for 3 to 4 hours; it doesn't defrost well in the microwave. Make sure that the phyllo sheets you use for the strudel are not badly torn. If they have small cuts or tears in the same location (sometimes an entire package sustains cuts in the same spot), flip alternating layers when forming the strudel so that the cuts will not line up and create a weak spot that can cause the strudel to burst during baking. Serve the strudel warm with Whipped Cream (page 500).

½	cup golden raisins
2	tablespoons Calvados or apple cider
6	tablespoons (¾ stick) unsalted butter
¼	cup fresh white bread crumbs
2	small Golden Delicious apples (about 10 ounces)
2	medium McIntosh apples (about 13 ounces)
¼	cup (1¾ ounces) plus 2 tablespoons granulated sugar
⅓	cup finely chopped walnuts (optional), toasted in small dry skillet over medium heat until lightly browned and fragrant, about 4 minutes
¼	teaspoon ground cinnamon
⅛	teaspoon salt
1	teaspoon juice from 1 lemon
5	sheets defrosted phyllo (see note)
1½	teaspoons confectioners' sugar

1. Adjust an oven rack to the lower-middle position and heat the oven to 475 degrees. Heat the raisins and Calvados in a small saucepan over medium heat (or in the microwave, covered with plastic wrap) until simmering. Cover, remove from the heat, and let stand until needed.

2. Melt 1 tablespoon of the butter in a small skillet over medium heat; when the foaming subsides, stir in the bread crumbs and cook, stirring frequently, until golden brown, about 2 minutes. Transfer the bread crumbs to a small bowl and set aside.

3. Peel, quarter, and core the apples; cut each quarter lengthwise into slices ⅛-inch thick. Drain off and discard any remaining liquid from the raisins. Toss the apples, raisins, bread crumbs, ¼ cup of the sugar, the walnuts (if using), cinnamon, salt, and lemon juice in a large bowl to combine.

4. Melt the remaining 5 tablespoons of butter. Place a large sheet of parchment paper horizontally on a work surface. Following the illustrations on page 304, fill and roll the strudel. Place the strudel, seam-side down, on an ungreased baking sheet; brush with the remaining butter and sprinkle with the remaining sugar. Cut four 1-inch crosswise vents into the top of the strudel and bake until golden brown, 15 minutes. Cool on the baking sheet on a wire rack until warm, about 40 minutes.

5. Sieve the confectioners' sugar over the strudel. Using 2 large metal spatulas, transfer the strudel to a platter or cutting board, cut into slices with a serrated knife, and serve with whipped cream, if desired.

BLUEBERRY COBBLER

NO MORE THAN A FLEET OF TENDER BISCUITS on a sea of sweet fruit, good cobblers hold their own against fancy fruit desserts. But unlike fancy fruit desserts, cobblers come together in a couple of quick steps and can be dished up hot, with a scoop of vanilla ice cream.

As simple (and appealing) as this sounds, why do so many of us end up with a filling that is sickeningly sweet and overspiced? Why is the filling so often runny, or, on the flip side, so thick and gloppy? Why are the biscuits, the most common choice of topping for cobblers, too dense, dry, and heavy?

We decided to begin by developing a recipe for the most popular cobbler of all—blueberry. Our goal was to create a filling in which the berries were allowed to cook until lightly thickened. We wanted their natural sweetness to come through without being overshadowed by the sugar and spice. The biscuit should stand tall with structure, be crisp on the outside and light and buttery on the inside, and complement the filling. Most important, it had to be easy.

The basic ingredients found in most cobbler fillings are fruit, sugar, thickener (flour, arrowroot, cornstarch, potato starch, or tapioca), and flavorings (lemon zest, spices, etc.). The fruit and sugar are easy: Take fresh blueberries and add enough sugar so that the fruit neither remains puckery nor turns saccharine. For 6 cups of berries, we found ½ cup sugar to be ideal—and far less than the conventional amount of sugar, which in some recipes exceeds 2 cups.

Some recipes swear by one thickener and warn that other choices will ruin the filling. We found this to be partly true. Tasters were all in agreement that flour—the most common choice in recipes—gave the fruit filling an unappealing starchy texture. Most tasters agreed that tapioca thickened the berry juices nicely, but the soft beads of starch left in the fruit's juices knocked out this contender.

INGREDIENTS: Blueberries

When local berries are not in season, can you still make blueberry cobbler? Should you rely on fresh berries from South America or frozen berries? If you choose the latter, should you pick cultivated or wild?

Last winter, the test kitchen tried fresh berries from Chile as well as four frozen brands. Easily beating the fresh imported berries as well as the other frozen contenders were Wyman's frozen wild berries. (Compared with cultivated berries, wild berries are smaller, more intense in color, firmer in texture, and more sweet and tangy in flavor.) The fresh imported berries finished in a respectable second place. While frozen cultivated berries trailed in the tasting, all but one brand received decent scores.

Flavor aside, the cost of frozen berries is $8 per cobbler versus $25 for the fresh South American berries. You could make three cobblers using the frozen berries for that price, and the money would also buy better quality.

Why did frozen wild berries beat fresh berries? The imported berries are picked before they have a chance to fully ripen to help them survive the long trip north. As a result, they are often tart and not so flavorful. Frozen berries have been picked at their peak—when perfectly ripe—and are then individually quick frozen (IQF) at -20 degrees. The quick freezing preserves their sweetness, letting us enjoy them year-round—and at a price just about anyone can afford.

1ST PLACE
WYMAN'S FROZEN WILD BLUEBERRIES
These small blueberries were intense in color and flavor, with a pleasing balance of sweetness and tanginess and a clean, fresh berry finish.

2ND PLACE
FRESH BLUEBERRIES (SOUTH AMERICAN)
Imported fresh berries lacked that "picked at peak ripeness" flavor you get with local fresh berries, but they were still sweet/tart and juicy.

3RD PLACE
CASCADIAN FARMS 100% ORGANIC FROZEN BLUEBERRIES
This mix of berries includes "wild" blueberries. Berries had a tart punch characteristic of wild berries and a pleasant "jammy" sweetness.

4TH PLACE
365 GRADE A FANCY FROZEN BLUEBERRIES
These cultivated berries were very sweet, with just a hint of tartness. Compared with other brands, they lacked complexity.

5TH PLACE
SHAW'S INDIVIDUALLY QUICK FROZEN WHOLE
This supermarket brand was the most disappointing. The berries were watery, bland, and flat tasting, with a mushy consistency.

Arrowroot worked beautifully, but this starch can sometimes be difficult to find. Cornstarch and potato starch, the winners, proved to be interchangeable. They both thickened the juices without altering the blueberry flavor or leaving any visible traces of starch behind.

Lemon juice as well as grated lemon zest brightened the fruit flavor, and as for spices, everyone preferred cinnamon. Other flavors simply got in the way.

For the topping, our guiding principle was ease of preparation. A biscuit topping is the way to go, and we had our choice of two types: dropped and rolled. Most rolled biscuit recipes call for cold butter cut into dry ingredients with a pastry blender, two knives, or sometimes a food processor, after which the dough is rolled and cut. The dropped biscuits looked more promising (translation: easier)—mix the dry ingredients, mix the wet ingredients, mix the two together, and drop (over fruit). Sounded good to us!

To be sure that our tasters agreed, we made two cobblers, one with rolled and one with dropped biscuits. The dropped biscuits, light and rustic in appearance, received the positive comments we were looking for but needed some work. To start, we had to fine-tune the ingredients, which included flour, sugar, leavener, dairy, eggs, shortening, and flavorings. We immediately eliminated eggs from the list because they made the biscuits a tad heavy. As for dairy, heavy cream was too rich, whereas milk and half-and-half lacked depth of flavor. We finally tested buttermilk, which delivered a much-needed flavor boost as well as a lighter, fluffier texture. As for the choice of fat, butter was in and Crisco was out—butter tasted much better.

We soon discovered that the big problem with drop biscuits is getting them to cook through. (The batter is wetter than rolled biscuit dough and therefore has a propensity for remaining doughy.) No matter how long we left the biscuits on the berry topping in a 400-degree oven, they never baked through, turning browner and browner on top while remaining doughy on the bottom. We realized that what the biscuits needed might be a blast of heat from below—that is, from the berries.

We tried baking the berries alone in a moderate 375-degree oven for 25 minutes and then dropping and baking the biscuit dough on top. Bingo! The heat from the bubbling berries helped to cook the biscuits from underneath, while the dry heat of the oven cooked them from above.

There was one final detail to perfect. We wanted the biscuits to be more crisp on the outside and to have a deeper hue. This was easily achieved by bumping the oven to 425 degrees when we added the biscuits. A sprinkling of cinnamon sugar on the dropped biscuit dough added just a bit more crunch.

Blueberry Cobbler
SERVES 6 TO 8

While the blueberries are baking, prepare the ingredients for the biscuit topping, but do not stir the wet ingredients into the dry ingredients until just before the berries come out of the oven. A standard or deep-dish 9-inch pie pan works well; an 8-inch square baking dish can also be used. Vanilla ice cream or lightly sweetened whipped cream is the perfect accompaniment. To reheat leftovers, put the cobbler in a 350-degree oven for 10 to 15 minutes, until heated through.

FILLING

½	cup (3½ ounces) sugar
1	tablespoon cornstarch
	Pinch ground cinnamon
	Pinch salt
6	cups (30 ounces) fresh blueberries, picked over
1½	teaspoons grated zest plus 1 tablespoon juice from 1 lemon

BISCUIT TOPPING

1	cup (5 ounces) unbleached all-purpose flour
2	tablespoons stone-ground cornmeal
¼	cup (1¾ ounces) sugar, plus 2 teaspoons for sprinkling
2	teaspoons baking powder
¼	teaspoon baking soda
¼	teaspoon salt
4	tablespoons (½ stick) unsalted butter, melted
⅓	cup buttermilk
½	teaspoon vanilla extract
⅛	teaspoon ground cinnamon

Preparing Fruit

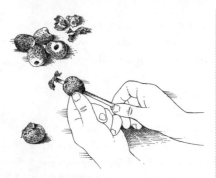

HULLING STRAWBERRIES

Early-season strawberries can have tough, white cores that are best removed. If you don't own a strawberry huller (and almost no one does), you can improvise with a plastic drinking straw. Push the straw through the bottom of the berry and up through the leafy stem end. The straw will remove the core as well as the leafy top.

JUICING LEMONS

Everyone seems to have a trick for juicing lemons. We find that this one extracts the most juice possible from lemons as well as limes.

1. Roll the lemon on a hard surface, pressing down firmly with the palm of your hand to break the membranes inside the fruit.

2. Cut the lemon in half. Use a wooden reamer (preferably one with sharp ridges and a pointed tip) to extract the juice into a bowl. To catch the seeds and pulp, place a mesh strainer over the bowl.

PEELING PEACHES

A vegetable peeler will mash the fruit on most peaches, especially ripe ones. Instead, we prefer to dip the peaches into a pot of simmering water to loosen their skins.

1. With a paring knife, score a small x at the base of each peach.

2. Lower the peaches into a pan of boiling water with a slotted spoon. Turn the peaches occasionally and simmer until their skins loosen, 30 seconds to 1 minute, depending on the ripeness of the peaches.

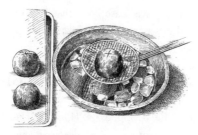

3. Transfer the peaches to a bowl of ice water. Let stand to stop the cooking process, about 1 minute and cool.

4. Starting from the scored x, peel each peach. Use a paring knife to lift the skin from the flesh and pull the skin off in strips.

PEELING RHUBARB

Rhubarb stalks, especially thick ones, can be covered with a stringy outside layer that should be removed before cooking. Make sure to cut away and discard any leaves, which are inedible.

1. Trim both ends of the stalk and then partially slice a thin disk from the bottom of the stalk, being careful not to cut all the way through. Gently pull the partially attached disk away from the stalk, pull back the outer peel, and discard.

2. Make a second cut partway through the bottom of the stalk in the reverse direction. Pull back the peel on the other side of the stalk and discard. The rhubarb is now ready to be sliced or chopped as needed.

PEELING KIWI

A vegetable peeler can crush soft kiwi flesh if you attempt to remove the hairy skin with this tool. We like this method, which won't bruise the fruit.

1. Trim the ends of the fruit and insert a small spoon between the skin and the flesh, with the bowl of the spoon facing the flesh. Push the spoon down and carefully move it around the fruit, separating the flesh from the skin.

2. Gently remove the spoon and pull the loosened skin away from the flesh.

CORING PEARS

Pears are best halved, from stem to blossom end, and then cored. We like to use a melon baller for this task.

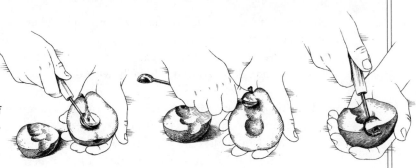

1. Use a melon baller to cut around the central core with a circular motion.

2. Draw the melon baller from the central core to the top of the pear, removing the interior portion of the stem as you go.

3. Use the melon baller to remove the blossom end as well.

PREPARING PINEAPPLE

A pineapple can seem daunting to peel and core. We find that the following method is reliable and easy.

1. Start by trimming the ends of the pineapple so it will sit flat on a work surface. Cut the pineapple through the ends into four quarters.

2. Place each quarter, cut-side up, on a work surface and slide a knife between the skin and the flesh to remove the skin.

3. Stand each peeled quarter on end and slice off the portion of the tough, light-colored core attached to the inside of the piece. The peeled and cored pineapple can be sliced as desired.

PITTING CHERRIES

Pitting sour cherries for pie is a tedious but essential task if you want to use fresh fruit. If you don't own a cherry pitter, you can use one of these 3 methods for removing the pits. Always work over a bowl to catch the flavorful juices.

A. Push the cherry firmly down against the pointed, jagged end of a small pastry bag tip. Take care not to cut your fingers on the points as they pierce the fruit.

B. Pierce the skin at the stem end with a clean pair of needle-nose pliers. Spread the pliers just enough to grasp the pit, then pull it straight out.

C. Push a drinking straw through the bottom of the cherry, forcing the pit up and out through the stem end.

PEELING MANGOES

Because of their odd shape and slippery texture, mangoes are notoriously difficult to peel. Here's how we handle this task. This method ensures long, attractive strips of fruit.

1. Remove a thin slice from one end of the mango so that it sits flat on a work surface.

2. Hold the mango cut-side down and remove the skin with a sharp paring knife in thin strips, working from top to bottom.

3. Cut down along the side of the flat pit to remove the flesh from one side of the mango. Do the same on the other side of the pit.

4. Trim around the pit to remove any remaining flesh. The mango flesh can now be chopped or sliced as desired.

1. Adjust an oven rack to the lower-middle position and heat the oven to 375 degrees.

2. FOR THE FILLING: Stir the sugar, cornstarch, cinnamon, and salt together in a large bowl. Add the berries and mix gently with a rubber spatula until evenly coated; add the lemon zest and juice and mix to combine. Transfer the berry mixture to a 9-inch glass pie plate, place the pie plate on a rimmed baking sheet, and bake until the filling is hot and bubbling around the edges, about 25 minutes.

3. FOR THE BISCUIT TOPPING: Meanwhile, whisk the flour, cornmeal, ¼ cup of the sugar, the baking powder, baking soda, and salt in a large bowl to combine. Whisk the melted butter, buttermilk, and vanilla together in a small bowl. Mix the remaining 2 teaspoons sugar with the cinnamon in a second small bowl and set aside. One minute before the berries come out of the oven, add the wet ingredients to the dry ingredients; stir with a rubber spatula until just combined and no dry pockets remain.

4. TO ASSEMBLE AND BAKE THE COBBLER: Remove the berries from the oven; increase the oven temperature to 425 degrees. Pinch off 8 equal pieces of biscuit dough and place them on the hot berry filling, spacing them at least ½ inch apart (they should not touch). Sprinkle each mound of dough with cinnamon sugar. Bake until the filling is bubbling and the biscuits are golden brown on top and cooked through, 15 to 18 minutes. Cool the cobbler on a wire rack 20 minutes and serve.

➤ VARIATIONS

Blueberry Cobbler with Gingered Biscuits

Follow the recipe for Blueberry Cobbler, adding 3 tablespoons minced crystallized ginger to the flour mixture and substituting an equal amount of ground ginger for the cinnamon in the sugar for sprinkling on the biscuits.

All-Season Blueberry Cobbler (with Frozen Blueberries)

Thawed berries shed a lot of flavorful liquid that must be reduced to a syrup on the stovetop before baking.

Thaw 36 ounces (about 6 cups) frozen blueberries (preferably wild) in a colander set over a bowl to catch the juices. Transfer the juices (you should have about 1 cup) to a small saucepan; simmer over medium heat until syrupy and thick enough to coat the back of a spoon, about 10 minutes. Follow the recipe for Blueberry Cobbler, mixing the syrup with the berries and other filling ingredients, increasing the baking time for the berry mixture to 30 minutes, and increasing the biscuit baking time to 20 to 22 minutes.

SOUR CHERRY COBBLER

HAVING TACKLED THE MYSTERIES BEHIND great Blueberry Cobbler (page 307), the test kitchen was ready for something a little more challenging. We recalled picking up sour cherries the summer before at the farmers market for a compote we were developing. This got us thinking. Sour cherries have sufficient acidity to cook up well and become truly expressive with a touch of sugar and some heat. (Sweet eating cherries, like Bings, lose their flavor when cooked.) We suspected sour cherries would feel at home in a cobbler—if we could find good ones. Another requirement we had for this cobbler was size. We wanted a large enough cobbler to feed about 12—a dessert perfect for an outdoor barbecue on the Fourth of July or as part of a buffet during the winter holidays.

Until we saw them at the farmers market, the only sour, or baking, cherries we had known of were the canned variety. Though sour cherries are grown in relatively large quantities in Michigan, here in the Northeast our grocery shelves are bereft of sour cherry products, save the crayon-red canned gravy with lumps called "pie filling." So we were grateful to find two different kinds of jarred sour cherries at our local Trader Joe's during the off-season (all 11 months of it). In addition, the Cherry Marketing Institute of Michigan provided us with variously processed sour cherries—frozen, canned, and dried. Since it would be months before we could try making cobbler with fresh cherries, we began our tests with processed ones.

Early tests in which we prepared quick fruit fillings elicited unenthusiastic comments from tasters.

While frozen Michigan sour cherries maintained their color well, their flavor was left largely to the imagination. Both canned and jarred sour cherries from Michigan were flaccid and developed an anemic pallor when cooked. Only Trader Joe's jarred Morello cherries drew a crowd. Deep ruby red, plump, meaty, and tart, they delivered bracing flavor and a great texture right out of the jar.

This experience prompted us to do a little research. Sour cherries, we learned, are classified in two groups, amarelles and griottes. The former have lighter flesh that's tan on the inside and clear juices; the latter are dark, even black, with deep red juice. The best known examples of each group are Montmorency (an amarelle) and Morello (a griotte). Most tart cherries grown in the United States are Montmorency. Those from Eastern Europe are Morello. With a couple of us remembering the stellar cherries we had tasted in baked goods in Germany, we decided to base our recipe on jarred Morellos.

A cobbler should be juicy but not swimming in juice, and it should taste like the fruit whose name it bears. Jarred and canned cherries come awash in juices, which we used to produce the sauce. Since jarred and canned cherries have already been processed, they are already cooked, so the less heat they're exposed to thereafter, the better. Straining off the juice, we dumped the drained contents of four 24-ounce jars of Morellos into a 13 by 9-inch baking dish, then thickened and sweetened 3 cups of the juice. The resulting flavor was a bit flat. We replaced 1 cup of the cherry juice with red wine and added a cinnamon stick, a pinch of salt, and a whiff of almond extract. Much better. Red wine and sour cherries have a natural affinity; the cinnamon stick added a fragrant woody depth; and, as with all fruits, salt performed its usual minor miracle. The almond extract brought the entire flavor experience up a couple of notches. For thickener, we resolved to go with cornstarch. It could be mixed in with the sugar and brought directly to a simmer with the reserved cherry juices, then poured over the waiting cherries and baked. Lightly thickened fruit is best; a cobbler shouldn't be thick enough to spread on toast.

For the topping, we wanted our biscuits to be light and feathery but able to withstand the juices of our cherry filling. We started with a biscuit similar to our blueberry cobbler topping but needed to make adjustments to allow for not only a different filling but a larger amount, as well. Following the method employed in our blueberry cobbler—dropping the biscuit topping on hot, partially baked fruit and increasing the oven temperature—did not quite do the trick. Having the undersides of the topping touching the fruit resulted in biscuits with pale bellies, so we undertook to bake the biscuits for 15 minutes on a baking sheet while the filling was coming together on the stove. We then wedded them to the fruit for only 10 minutes in the oven. By then the fruit (already hot from the cooked sauce) was bubbling around the biscuits, which were deeply browned on top and baked through underneath. Heaven in about a half hour.

Jarred Morellos made a fine cobbler, but we wanted more and, finally, summer came. We used both Morellos and Montmorency cherries. Both varieties of fresh cherries yielded cobblers with plump, gorgeous, deeply flavorful fruit. The Montmorency cherries were candy-apple red and had a flavor resonant with almond accents; the fresh Morellos were transcendent, with a smooth richness and complex flavor notes. If you can get your hands on fresh sour cherries during their brief season in July, buy them—quickly—and start baking.

Sour Cherry Cobbler
SERVES 12

Use the smaller amount of sugar in the filling if you prefer your fruit desserts on the tart side and the larger amount if you like them sweet.

BISCUIT TOPPING

2	cups (10 ounces) unbleached all-purpose flour
6	tablespoons (2½ ounces) sugar, plus 2 tablespoons for sprinkling
½	teaspoon baking powder
½	teaspoon baking soda
½	teaspoon salt
6	tablespoons (¾ stick) cold unsalted butter, cut into ½-inch cubes
1	cup buttermilk

FILLING

4	(24-ounce) jars Morello cherries, drained (about 8 cups drained cherries), 2 cups juice reserved
³/₄–1	cup (5¼ to 7 ounces) sugar
3	tablespoons plus 1 teaspoon cornstarch
	Pinch salt
1	cup dry red wine
1	(3-inch) cinnamon stick
¼	teaspoon almond extract

1. FOR THE BISCUIT TOPPING: Adjust an oven rack to the middle position and heat the oven to 425 degrees. Line a baking sheet with parchment paper.

2. In a food processor, pulse the flour, 6 tablespoons of the sugar, the baking powder, baking soda, and salt to combine. Scatter the butter pieces over the flour and process until the mixture resembles coarse meal, about fifteen 1-second pulses. Transfer to a medium bowl; add the buttermilk and toss with a rubber spatula to combine. Using a 1½- to 1¾-inch spring-loaded ice cream scoop, scoop 12 biscuits onto the baking sheet, spacing them 1½ to 2 inches apart. Sprinkle the biscuits evenly with the remaining 2 tablespoons sugar and bake until lightly browned on the tops and bottoms, about 15 minutes. (Do not turn off the oven.)

3. FOR THE FILLING: Meanwhile, spread the drained cherries in an even layer in a 13 by 9-inch glass baking dish. Stir the sugar, cornstarch, and salt together in a medium nonreactive saucepan. Whisk in the reserved cherry juice and wine and add the cinnamon stick; set the saucepan over medium-high heat and cook, whisking frequently, until the mixture simmers and thickens, about 5 minutes. Discard the cinnamon stick, stir in the almond extract, and pour the hot liquid over the cherries in the baking dish.

4. TO ASSEMBLE AND BAKE THE COBBLER: Arrange the hot biscuits in 3 rows of 4 over the warm filling. Bake the cobbler until the filling is bubbling and the biscuits are deep golden brown, about 10 minutes. Cool on a wire rack 10 minutes; serve warm.

➤ VARIATION

Fresh Sour Cherry Cobbler

Morello or Montmorency cherries can be used in this cobbler. Do not use sweet Bing cherries. If the cherries do not release enough juice after macerating for 30 minutes, use cranberry juice to make up the difference. A cherry pitter is almost essential for this recipe, although you can try one of the improvised methods on page 309; they will get the job done but at a slow pace, especially with so many cherries to pit.

FILLING

1¼	cups (8¾ ounces) sugar
3	tablespoons plus 1 teaspoon cornstarch
	Pinch salt
4	pounds fresh sour cherries, pitted (about 8 cups), juices reserved
1	cup dry red wine
	Cranberry juice (if needed)
1	(3-inch) cinnamon stick
¼	teaspoon almond extract
1	recipe Biscuit Topping (page 311)

1. FOR THE FILLING: Stir together the sugar, cornstarch, and salt in a large bowl; add the cherries and toss well to combine. Pour the wine over the cherries; let stand 30 minutes. Drain the cherries in a colander set over a medium bowl. Combine the drained and reserved juices (from pitting the cherries); you should have 3 cups. If not, add enough cranberry juice to equal 3 cups.

2. FOR THE BISCUIT TOPPING: While the cherries macerate, prepare and bake the biscuit topping.

3. TO ASSEMBLE AND BAKE THE COBBLER: Spread the drained cherries in an even layer in a 13 by 9-inch glass baking dish. Bring the juices and cinnamon stick to a simmer in a medium nonreactive saucepan over medium-high heat, whisking frequently, until the mixture thickens, about 5 minutes. Discard the cinnamon stick, stir in the almond extract, and pour the hot juices over the cherries in the baking dish.

4. Arrange the hot biscuits in 3 rows of 4 over the warm filling. Bake the cobbler until the filling is bubbling and the biscuits are deep golden brown, about 10 minutes. Cool on a wire rack 10 minutes; serve warm.

SUMMER BERRY GRATIN

QUICKER THAN A CRISP AND DRESSIER than a shortcake, a gratin is a layer of fresh fruit piled into a shallow baking dish, gussied up with crumbs, and run under a broiler. The topping browns, and the fruit is warmed just enough to juice a bit.

We wanted to travel the simplest route to this summer dessert. Even though gratins can be made with all types of summer fruits, we confined our subject matter to berries (easy; no slicing), the topping to crumbs (easy; no mixing), and the ingredients to a minimum (five, to be precise).

We discovered straight off that a dish of this simplicity requires much attention. The berries, in whatever combination, had to be perfect: ripe, dry, unbruised, and clean. Woody and unyielding berries delivered indifferent results. No flavors coalesced, no juices were exchanged, nothing happened. Overripe or moldy berries, on the other hand, which found their way in among the others, disgraced the flavor of the gratin instantly. What's more, to cook correctly and to look and taste good, the berries needed to be of relatively similar size.

Strawberries, raspberries, and blueberries were superb when used alone; they were also compatible in combination. Smallish strawberries, halved lengthwise, complemented the other berry shapes. Blackberries tasted best when paired with raspberries or blueberries. (For anyone lucky enough to have access to fresh currants, they would doubtless be wonderful with any of the other berries.) Four cups of berries, whatever the selection, fit nicely into a 9-inch glass or porcelain pie plate.

Then there were the crumbs. Cake and muffin crumbs—even stale ones—collapsed into the filling and disappeared. French chef Jacques Pépin uses dry croissant crumbs in his raspberry gratin. Translate croissant into American English and you come up with, well, white bread. So we tried both dried and fresh bread crumbs and dried and fresh croutons.

The dried bread crumbs were granular and texturally at odds with the soft flesh of the berries. Croutons, too, were somewhat standoffish. Weary of this unproductive fussing, we took three pieces of soft white bread and tossed them into the food processor with a couple tablespoons of sugar and a little chunk of soft butter. The resulting fluffy crumbs embraced the berries like a fresh snowfall. Once broiled, the surface of the crumbs became lightly crunchy and the undercoat soft enough to absorb the berries' juices. We modified this combination only slightly by switching from white sugar to light brown and by adding a pinch of ground cinnamon—both for a small flavor bonus.

The berries themselves needed just a bit of sweetness to brighten them and coax forth their juices. A modest tablespoon of granulated sugar brought out the best in them. Many of the tasters also liked a tablespoon of kirsch (a clear cherry brandy) or another eau de vie tossed with the berries and sugar. Taken together on a spoon, the flavors of the gratin were soft but deeply pleasing. The clear berry tastes shone forth against the light, buttery crumbs, and the berries and crust formed a nice textural counterpoint.

Broiling the gratin, as we had been doing, required more vigilance than we deemed desirable, and often the crust browned unevenly. We thought perhaps a moderately high oven heat lasting a bit longer might melt the berries slightly and brown the crust more evenly while also needing less monitoring. This proved to be true: a 400-degree oven and 15 or 20 minutes gave us a chance to put the coffee on and whip a bit of cream or soften vanilla ice cream before the dome of the crust grew deep golden and the berries warm and fragrant.

Summer Berry Gratin

SERVES 4 TO 6

Though a mixture of berries offers a wonderful combination of color, flavor, and texture, it's also fine to use just one or two types of berries. A half pint of fresh berries equals about 1 cup of fruit. Later in the season, ripe, peeled peach or nectarine slices can be used in combination with blueberries or raspberries. We recommend using only fresh fruit, but if you must use frozen, raspberries are the best option. Do not thaw them before baking. Avoid using a metal pie pan, which may react with the acidity of the fruit and impart a metallic flavor. Serve the fruit gratin with lightly sweetened whipped cream or vanilla ice cream.

FRUIT MIXTURE

4 1/2   cups (about 22 ounces) mixed raspberries, blueberries, blackberries, and strawberries (hulled and left whole if small, halved lengthwise if medium, quartered lengthwise if large)

1   tablespoon granulated sugar

1   tablespoon kirsch or other eau de vie (optional)
    Pinch salt

TOPPING

3   slices sandwich bread, each slice torn into quarters

2   tablespoons unsalted butter, softened

1/4   cup packed (1 3/4 ounces) light or dark brown sugar
    Pinch ground cinnamon

1. FOR THE FRUIT MIXTURE: Adjust an oven rack to the lower-middle position and heat the oven to 400 degrees. Toss the fruit gently with the sugar, kirsch (if using), and salt in a medium nonreactive bowl and transfer to a 9-inch glass or ceramic pie plate.

2. FOR THE TOPPING: Pulse the bread, butter, sugar, and cinnamon in a food processor until the mixture resembles coarse crumbs, about ten 1-second pulses. Sprinkle the crumbs evenly over the fruit and bake until the crumbs are deep golden brown and the fruit is hot, 15 to 20 minutes. Cool on a wire rack 5 minutes and serve.

MASHING STRAWBERRIES FOR SHORTCAKE

For best flavor and appearance, crush one third of the berries for the filling with a potato masher. This thick puree will anchor the remaining whole or sliced berries so that they don't slip off the split biscuit.

STRAWBERRY SHORTCAKE

SHORTCAKES MAY SEEM SIMILAR TO CRISPS and cobblers, but there is one important difference—the fruit is not cooked. For a true shortcake, sweetened fruit, usually strawberries, is spread between a split biscuit. A dollop or two of whipped cream is also added. The contrast of the cool fruit, warm and crisp biscuit halves, and chilled whipped cream places this dessert in a category by itself.

Because the fruit is not cooked, frozen fruit is not an option. The fruit must be ripe as well. Half-ripe berries will bake up fine in a pandowdy but will make a second-rate shortcake. Also, because the fruit is not baked, only softer fruits are appropriate. A pear or apple shortcake does not make sense. Strawberries are soft enough and have enough flavor to be used uncooked.

We don't like quartered or sliced strawberries in shortcakes—they often slide off the split biscuit—but we don't like the look of a crushed fruit shortcake either. So we found a happy compromise by slicing most of the strawberries and then crushing the remaining portion of the berry mixture to unify the sliced fruit. The thick puree anchors the remaining whole or sliced fruit so that it won't slip off the split biscuit.

Our testing for this recipe revolved mostly around the biscuit. Strawberry shortcake requires something different from the biscuit topping used in our blueberry or cherry cobbler recipe. There, the fruit is so juicy and sweet that a light, tender biscuit works best. Shortcake, on the other hand, must be substantial enough to withstand splitting and layering with juicy fruit and whipped cream. It should be more dense and cakey. We assumed that a richer biscuit—that is, one made with eggs—would work best.

To make sure, we tried four very different sweetened biscuits: a baking powder version with fat cut into flour, baking powder, salt, and sugar and then moistened with milk; buttermilk biscuits, with buttermilk in place of milk and baking soda substituted for part of the baking powder; cream biscuits, with heavy cream standing in for the milk and some of the fat; and egg-enriched cream biscuits, with an egg and half-and-half replacing the milk. After sampling each, we felt that the egg-enriched biscuits had the advantage. The baking powder and buttermilk biscuits weren't rich enough. The cream biscuits were good looking but gummy inside. The egg and half-and-half biscuits were finer-textured and more cake-like.

With our general direction settled, we began to test individual ingredients. Because biscuits should be tender, we assumed that low-protein cake flour would deliver the best results. Defying our predictions, the cake flour biscuit came in last, with a meltingly tender yet powdery and dry texture that was too much like shortbread. There was not enough gluten in this flour to support all the fat. Shortcakes made with all-purpose flour were tender, moist, and cakey. They were our clear favorites, besting a combination of cake and all-purpose flours as well as the plain cake flour.

We then experimented with liquids, figuring that the egg might be crucial but maybe not the half-and-half, which had won in our initial test. Buttermilk made the biscuits too savory, while heavy cream made them squat and dense. Milk was fine, but the richer flavor of half-and-half makes it our first choice.

The food processor is foolproof and is our preferred method for mixing biscuits. For cooks without a food processor, we suggest freezing the butter and then using a box grater to shave the butter into bits before cutting it into the flour.

When testing dough shaping, we made an interesting discovery. Although hand-formed biscuits look attractive and rustic, we found they were fairly easy to overwork, since warm hands can cause the dough's surface butter to melt. Using a biscuit cutter requires less handling, and dough rounds cut this way develop a natural crack around the circumference during baking, making them easy to split by hand. We also realized we didn't need a rolling pin. Patting the dough to a thickness of ¾ inch on a floured work surface was fast and simple.

Strawberry Shortcake
SERVES 6

Start the recipe by preparing the fruit, then set the fruit aside while preparing the biscuits to allow the juices to become syrupy. After cutting 6 perfect rounds of dough, we found that the scraps could be pulled together, kneaded, and cut to get 1 or 2 more rounds. These shortcakes will be a little tougher and less attractive than those from the first cutting.

FRUIT
8	cups strawberries (about 2½ pounds), hulled
6	tablespoons (2½ ounces) sugar

SHORTCAKES
2	cups (10 ounces) unbleached all-purpose flour, plus more for dusting the work surface and biscuit cutter
5	tablespoons (about 2¼ ounces) sugar
I	tablespoon baking powder
½	teaspoon salt
8	tablespoons (I stick) cold unsalted butter, cut into ½-inch cubes
I	large egg, lightly beaten
½	cup plus I tablespoon half-and-half or whole milk
I	large egg white, lightly beaten
2	cups Whipped Cream (page 500)

1. FOR THE FRUIT: Place 3 cups of the hulled strawberries in a large bowl and crush with a potato masher (see the illustration on page 314). Slice the remaining 5 cups berries and stir into the crushed berries along with the sugar. Set the fruit aside to macerate for at least 30 minutes and up to 2 hours.

SPLITTING SHORTCAKES

When the shortcakes have cooled, look for a natural crack around the circumference. Gently insert your fingers into the crack and split the shortcake in half.

2. FOR THE SHORTCAKES: Adjust an oven rack to the lower-middle position and heat the oven to 425 degrees. In a food processor, pulse the flour, 3 tablespoons of the sugar, the baking powder, and salt to combine. Scatter the butter pieces over and process until the mixture resembles coarse meal, about fifteen 1-second pulses. Transfer to a medium bowl.

3. Mix the beaten egg with the half-and-half in a measuring cup. Pour the egg mixture into the bowl with the flour mixture. Combine with a rubber spatula until large clumps form. Turn the mixture onto a floured work surface and lightly knead until it comes together.

4. Use your fingertips to pat the dough into a 9 by 6-inch rectangle about ¾ inch thick, being careful not to overwork the dough. Flour a 2¾-inch biscuit cutter and cut out 6 dough rounds. Place the rounds 1 inch apart on a small baking sheet, brush the tops with the beaten egg white, and sprinkle with the remaining 2 tablespoons sugar. (Dough rounds can be covered and refrigerated for up to 2 hours before baking.)

5. Bake until the shortcakes are golden brown, 12 to 14 minutes. Place the baking sheet on a wire rack and cool the cakes until warm, about 10 minutes.

6. TO ASSEMBLE: When the shortcakes have cooled slightly, split them in half (see the illustration on page 315). Place each cake bottom on an individual serving plate. Spoon a portion of the fruit and then a dollop of the whipped cream over each cake bottom. Cap with the cake top and serve immediately.

PAVLOVA

DELICATE MERINGUE SHELLS FILLED WITH fresh fruit and topped with whipped cream, pavlova makes a light and flavorful ending to a meal. Created down under as the culinary expression of the ethereal dancing of legendary Russian prima ballerina Anna Pavlova, the dish has become a national treasure for both Australians and New Zealanders. Properly made, the dessert is an airy study in textural contrasts. The thin, crisp meringue should give way to just a hint of a chew

before dissolving on the tongue along with the rich whipped cream. The fruit should be fresh, flavorful, and abundant. Although simple to prepare, pavlovas fall short when the meringues are cloyingly sweet and sticky, the fruit unripe, and the whipped cream granular and saccharine.

Broadly defined, meringue refers to a voluminous mixture of beaten egg whites and sugar that can be used in any number of applications. In our research on meringue cookies (see page 479), we thoroughly tested different methods for beating egg whites and sugar as well as testing differences between granulated and confectioners' sugar. Our final recipe calls for 4 egg whites at room temperature, ¼ teaspoon cream of tartar, 1 cup granulated sugar, and ¾ teaspoon vanilla. The whites are beaten in the bowl of an electric mixer with the cream of tartar until they are white, thick, voluminous, and the consistency of shaving cream. Half of the sugar is beaten into the mixture. The bowl of whites is removed from the mixer and the remaining sugar is folded in until incorporated. The meringues are then immediately shaped and baked in a low oven until dry and crisp on the outside. The oven is then turned off, and the meringues are left in the oven for several hours to cool.

We went into the test kitchen armed with the extensive results of our meringue research as the basis for our pavlova testing. For our first test we followed traditional presentation and made one large pavlova, about 9 inches in diameter. The entire dessert is presented on a platter and sliced into wedges at the table. We quickly considered other ways of shaping and serving the dessert. It was impossible to transfer a clean slice of the pavlova without spilling the meringue, whipped cream, and fruit all over the table. Leftovers were impossible to store (the filled meringue quickly became soggy), and while the dessert did look light and ethereal, it also looked sloppy. We wanted a version of the dessert that would be easier to serve and look more sophisticated.

Restaurants often serve individual pavlovas, and we soon found out why. The meringue shells look very attractive—delicate and not at all messy. Making individual meringues also allowed us the option of filling and serving just the amount we needed—extras could be stored for another day. And best of all, serving the dessert was simple and did not involve complicated transfers from platter to plate. We tried different techniques for making the shells, using ice cream scoops and large soupspoons, among other utensils, and found that using a ¼ cup dry measure to scoop up the meringue and a soupspoon to scrape it out produced a dozen evenly proportioned mounds of meringue on two parchment-lined baking sheets. By gently pressing the back of the soupspoon into the center of the mounds, we created hollows in the cloud-like mounds for the whipped cream and fruit to fill.

We found that baking the shells like our meringue cookies, at 200 degrees for about an hour and a half until the shells were slightly firm to the touch and dry, kept the meringues white. At a higher temperature, the meringues baked too quickly and began to turn a light caramel color. Like the meringue cookies, the pavlova shells remain in the oven, with the heat off, until they are cool. Once they're cooled, we found that the meringue shells could be stored in an airtight container for several weeks.

We tested the pavlovas with our sweetened Whipped Cream (page 500) and found that the sweetness of the meringue made adding sugar to the cream not only unnecessary but undesirable. In the test kitchen, tasters preferred the contrast of the crisp, sweet meringue to the rich, soft, unsweetened whipped cream. Adding a tablespoon of sugar to the fruit, however, was necessary to extract some of the juices from the fruit and create a flavorful syrup that soaked into the meringue and whipped cream.

To assemble the pavlovas, simply place a dried, cooled meringue shell on each dessert plate. Fill the recess in each shell with ½ cup whipped cream and then top it with ½ cup fruit. Although traditional pavlovas use kiwi and strawberries, almost any fruit combination will work well. In the test kitchen, we liked a tropical fruit mixture of mangoes, kiwis, and pineapple. Summer fruit like mixed berries, peaches, and nectarines also are good options. Once assembled, this dessert should be served immediately.

Individual Pavlovas with Tropical Fruit
SERVES 12

Avoid making pavlovas on humid days when preventing the meringue from becoming sticky and soft will be nearly impossible. The meringue shells keep, covered, in an airtight container for up to 2 weeks, allowing you to serve just as many as you need the day you make them; adjust the amounts of fruit and whipped cream accordingly. See the illustrations on pages 308 and 309 for tips on preparing mangoes, kiwi, and pineapple.

MERINGUES

4	large egg whites (about 1 cup plus 2 tablespoons), at room temperature
¼	teaspoon cream of tartar
1	cup (7 ounces) sugar
¾	teaspoon vanilla extract

TROPICAL FRUIT

2	large ripe mangoes (about 2 pounds), peeled and cut into ¼-inch cubes
4	kiwis, peeled, halved lengthwise, and cut into half-moon slices about ⅜ inch thick
½	large pineapple, cut into ½-inch cubes (about 3 cups)
1	tablespoon sugar

WHIPPED CREAM

3	cups (1 ½ pints) chilled heavy cream

1. FOR THE MERINGUES: Adjust the oven racks to the upper- and lower-middle positions and heat the oven to 200 degrees. Line 2 large baking sheets with parchment paper.

2. In the bowl of an electric mixer, beat the egg whites at medium-low speed until they are opaque and frothy, about 30 seconds. Add the cream of tartar, increase the speed to medium-high, and, watching carefully, beat the egg whites until they are white, thick, voluminous, and the consistency of shaving cream, about 90 seconds. Slowly sprinkle in ½ cup of the sugar and then the vanilla and continue to beat until incorporated, about 60 seconds. Remove the bowl from the mixer and sprinkle in the remaining ½ cup sugar and fold in

just until incorporated. Using a ¼-cup dry measuring cup and a soupspoon, place 6 heaping ¼-cup dollops of meringue about 1 inch apart on each sheet. Gently press the back of the soupspoon into the center of the mounds to create hollows (see the illustration below). Bake for 1½ hours or until the meringues have smooth, dry, and firm exteriors. Turn the oven off and allow the meringues to cool in the oven for several hours. Once cool, store the meringues in an airtight container, where they will keep for a couple of weeks, until ready to use.

3. FOR THE FRUIT: Place the prepared fruit in a medium bowl and sprinkle with the sugar. Using a rubber spatula, stir gently to combine. Cover with plastic wrap and set aside at room temperature until the fruit begins to exude its juices, about 30 minutes.

4. FOR THE WHIPPED CREAM: Just before serving, beat the cream in a chilled bowl of an electric mixer on low speed until small bubbles form, about 30 seconds. Increase the speed to medium; continue beating until the beaters leave a trail, about 30 seconds more. Increase the speed to high; continue beating until the cream is smooth, thick, and nearly doubled

in volume, about 20 seconds for soft peaks. If necessary, finish beating by hand to adjust consistency.

5. TO ASSEMBLE THE PAVLOVAS: Place a meringue shell on a dessert plate. Top with ½ cup whipped cream. Spoon ½ cup fruit over the whipped cream, allowing some fruit to fall onto the plate. Repeat with the remaining meringue shells, whipped cream, and fruit. Serve immediately.

➤ VARIATIONS
Individual Pavlovas with Mixed Berries
Combine 2 cups each raspberries, blackberries, and blueberries (about 30 ounces total) in a large colander and gently rinse (taking care not to bruise them); spread the berries on a paper towel–lined rimmed baking sheet and gently pat dry with additional paper towels. Transfer the fruit to a medium bowl. Sprinkle 1 tablespoon sugar over the fruit and, using a rubber spatula, stir gently to combine. Cover with plastic wrap and set aside at room temperature until the berries begin to exude their juices, about 30 minutes. Follow the recipe for Individual Pavlovas with Tropical Fruit, using the macerated berries in place of the tropical fruit.

Individual Pavlovas with Strawberries, Blueberries, and Peaches
Combine 2 cups (about 10 ounces) strawberries, hulled and halved, and 2 cups (about 10 ounces) blueberries in a large colander and gently rinse (taking care not to bruise them); spread the berries on a paper towel–lined rimmed baking sheet and gently pat dry with additional paper towels. Transfer the fruit to a medium bowl and add 3 medium peaches, peeled and sliced into ¼-inch slices (about 2 cups). Sprinkle 1 tablespoon sugar over the fruit and, using a rubber spatula, stir gently to combine. Cover with plastic wrap and set aside at room temperature until the fruits begin to exude their juices, about 30 minutes. Follow the recipe for Individual Pavlovas with Tropical Fruit, using the macerated fruit in place of the tropical fruit.

SHAPING PAVLOVAS

Use a ¼-cup measuring cup and a soupspoon to place six ¼-cup dollops of meringue evenly spaced on a parchment-paper lined sheet tray. Use the soupspoon to hollow out a bowl-like indentation in the center of each meringue (taking care not to reach the parchment). Each meringue should be 3½ to 4 inches in diameter.

7
CAKES

Cakes

WE MAKE CAKES TO CELEBRATE BIRTHDAYS, weddings, anniversaries, and almost any other holiday you can think of. Cakes can be as simple as a sheet cake sprinkled with confectioners' sugar or as special as a multitiered affair with filling, frosting, and nuts.

Cake making requires precision and careful attention to detail. A slight mismeasurement of ingredients or the failure to follow a specific mixing instruction can have drastic consequences in terms of flavor and texture. Over the years, we have developed a list of general tips designed to head off the mistakes home cooks are most likely to make.

OVEN TEMPERATURE is always important, especially when baking a cake, so periodically check your oven temperature with an oven thermometer. If your oven is too hot, the sides of the cake will set before the middle does, and the cake will hump or crack. If your oven is too cold, the air will escape from the batter before the batter begins to set, and the cake will have a coarse texture and may even fall.

CAKE PANS You should own two sets—two pans that measure 8 inches across and two that measure 9 across. Some recipes call for 8-inch cake pans, others for 9-inch pans. Use the correct size. If the pans are too large, they overheat the rim of the cake, causing the same sorts of problems as an overheated oven. If the pans are too small, batter may rise right out of them. Choose sturdy aluminum pans with absolutely vertical sides. Do not use disposable foil pans, which often produce misshapen cakes. (For more information about what to look for when buying cake pans, see page 11.)

Generously grease the pans with vegetable shortening (such as Crisco) or butter and coat them well with flour. The flour holds the fat in place and keeps the batter from seeping through to the pan bottom. As an extra precaution you may want to grease the pan, line the bottom with a piece of parchment or waxed paper, grease the paper, and then flour the pan and paper.

INGREDIENT PREPARATION Have all ingredients, especially butter, eggs, and milk, at room temperature. Chilled ingredients do not emulsify well, which leads to a dense cake, and cold butter won't incorporate into a batter. Very warm ingredients may cause air cells in creamed butter to dissolve. Unless specified otherwise in a recipe, all ingredients should register between 65 and 70 degrees on an instant-read thermometer. Sticks of softened butter should give when pressed but still hold their shape with no signs of melting (see illustrations on page 140).

To bring eggs to room temperature quickly, submerge uncracked eggs in a bowl of warm water for five to 10 minutes. Since separating eggs is somewhat easier when they are cold, you may want to separate the eggs first and then let them warm up while you assemble and measure the remaining ingredients. You may also place a bowl or measuring cup filled with yolks or whites in a bowl of warm water if necessary.

Unless otherwise noted, measure flour carefully by the dip-and-sweep method (see page 38 for details). Dip the measuring cup into the container of flour, scoop out a heaping cupful, and then level the top with the straight edge of a butter knife or icing spatula. Do not shake, tap, or pack the cup. If the cup is not completely filled on the first try, dump the flour back into the container and dip again. A kitchen scale is the most accurate way to measure ingredients like flours, sugars, cornmeal, and cocoa. (See page 15 for information about kitchen scales.)

MIXING We developed the recipes in this chapter using a standing mixer, and the mixing times in the recipes reflect that. But you don't need a standing mixer to make the cakes in this chapter. Although we like the convenience of standing mixers—they keep our hands free to measure an ingredient, crack eggs into a bowl, or just wipe the counter—a good handheld mixer does the job just as well (in just a little more time). It is more important to rely on the visual cues we give, like "beat until light and fluffy." To read more about mixers, both standing and handheld, see pages 13 and 14.

BAKING Give pans enough space in the oven. Cakes placed too close together will rise toward each other and end up lopsided. Cakes placed too close to the oven walls won't rise as high on the side nearest the wall. Keep pans at least 3 inches from each other and the oven walls and on the middle rack of the oven. If your oven is small, stagger the pans on racks set at the upper-middle and lower-middle positions to allow for proper air circulation.

TESTING FOR DONENESS How do you tell when a cake is done? It depends upon the cake. For cakes like angel food, chiffon, layer cakes, and the like, use your finger and a toothpick or thin skewer to judge when they are done. Cakes should be baked until firm in the center when lightly pressed and a toothpick or skewer inserted in the center comes out clean or with just a crumb or two adhering. If the tester comes out perfectly clean, the cake is probably overcooked and dry.

For cakes whose texture does not depend on crumb, like cheesecakes and pudding cakes, the rules vary. Cheesecakes are done when an instant-read thermometer inserted in the center registers 150 degrees. For pudding cakes, look for visual cues provided in the individual recipes, as they vary. It is important not to overbake these moist cakes, because their texture can become unpalatably dry.

ANGEL FOOD CAKE

AT ITS BEST, AN ANGEL FOOD CAKE SHOULD be tall and perfectly shaped, have a snowy-white, tender crumb, and be encased in a thin, delicate, golden crust. Although most angel food cakes contain no more than six ingredients, there are literally hundreds of variations on this basic theme. The type of flour used, the baking temperature, the type of sugar, and even the use of baking powder—a serious transgression, according to most experts—are all in dispute. What is not in dispute is that angel food cake requires a delicate balance of ingredients and proper cooking techniques. If leavened with just beaten egg whites (as is the custom), this cake can be fickle.

An angel food cake is distinguished by its lack of egg yolks, chemical leaveners, and fat. Other cakes also use beaten egg whites for leaveners, but there are differences. Chiffon cake (page 325) contains

egg yolks, which makes for a slightly heavier, moister cake. Sponge cake (page 357) also includes whole or separated eggs; it, too, is denser and more yellow than angel food cake.

The six ingredients found in every angel food cake are egg whites, sugar, flour, cream of tartar, salt, and flavorings. Most recipes start by beating the egg whites. Mixer speed is critical for well-beaten whites. We found that starting at high speed will produce quick but inconsistent results. To create the most stable foam, beat the whites at low speed to break them up into a froth. Add the cream of tartar and salt, increase the speed to medium, and beat until the whites form very soft, billowy mounds. When large bubbles stop appearing around the edges, and with the mixer still on medium, add the sugar, a tablespoon at a time, until all the sugar has been incorporated and the whites are shiny and form soft peaks when the beater is lifted. The mass should still flow slightly when the bowl is tilted. Do not beat until the peaks are stiff; we found that this makes it difficult to fold in the flour, deflating the whites and therefore reducing volume.

Because there is no fat in angel food cake, sugar is critical to its taste and texture. We tested confectioners' sugar and found that the cornstarch in it makes the cake too dense. Superfine sugar is simply too fine, making a soft cake with little substance. We found that granulated sugar is best in this recipe.

Flour sets the cake batter, but because it also adds weight, the flour should be as light and airy as possible. We found that cake flour, which is finer than all-purpose flour, is easier to incorporate into the beaten whites without deflating them. The lower protein content of cake flour results in a more delicate, tender crumb, which we preferred. No matter what kind of flour is used, we found sifting to be essential; it makes the flour lighter in texture and easier to incorporate into the whites. Sift the flour twice—once before measuring and once before adding it to the beaten whites—for maximum lightness.

Egg whites, sugar, flour, and cream of tartar will produce a good-looking angel food cake that is sweet but bland. Salt is added for flavor and also helps stabilize the beaten whites. Other common additions are vanilla and almond extracts (we like to use both), which add flavor without changing the basic chemistry of the batter. You can add grated citrus zest or a little citrus juice; we prefer the latter because zest can mar the perfectly soft, white texture of the cake. We found that high-fat flavorings, such as grated chocolate and nuts, greatly affect the cake's texture, and we prefer to stick with simpler flavorings.

We tried using some baking powder for added leavening and stability but found that the resulting cake was not as white and had a coarser crumb. Adding baking powder also felt like cheating. If you separate and beat the egg whites properly, there should be no need to add baking powder.

Our most intriguing experiment involved oven temperatures. We baked the same recipe in the same pan at 300, 325, 350, and 375 degrees, baking each cake until it tested done with a skewer and the top bounced back when pressed lightly. Surprisingly, all the cakes cooked evenly, but those baked at 350 and 375 degrees had a thicker, darker crust, while the cakes baked at 300 and 325 degrees had a more desirable, delicate, evenly pale golden crust. After many taste tests, we decided that 325 degrees was the ideal temperature.

The best tool we found to remove an angel food cake from the pan is a thin, flexible, nonserrated knife that is at least five inches long. Tilt the pan at a right angle to the counter to make it easy to work the knife around the sides. Insert the knife between the crust and the pan, pressing hard against the side of the pan, and work your way all around the cake. To cut around the central core of the pan, use a long, thin skewer. Invert the pan so that the cake slides out, then peel off the parchment or waxed paper. If using a pan with a removable bottom, slide the knife blade between the cake and the sides of the pan to release it. Present the cake sitting on its wide, crustier top, with the delicate and more easily sliced bottom crust facing up.

To cut the cake, use a long, serrated knife, and pull it back and forth with a gentle sawing motion. When we tried using the specially made tool for cutting angel food cake—a row of prongs attached to a bar—it mashed and squashed this tender cake.

Angel Food Cake

SERVES 10 TO 12

Sift both the cake flour and the granulated sugar before measuring to eliminate any lumps and ensure the lightest possible texture.

1	cup (3 ounces) sifted plain cake flour
1½	cups (10½ ounces) sifted sugar
12	large egg whites (1¾ cups plus 2 tablespoons), at room temperature
1	teaspoon cream of tartar
¼	teaspoon salt
1½	teaspoons vanilla extract
1½	teaspoons juice from 1 lemon
½	teaspoon almond extract

1. Adjust an oven rack to the lower-middle position and heat the oven to 325 degrees. Have ready an ungreased large tube pan (9-inch diameter, 16-cup capacity), preferably with a removable bottom. If the pan bottom is not removable, line it with parchment paper or waxed paper.

2. Whisk the flour and ¾ cup of the sugar in a small bowl. Place the remaining ¾ cup sugar in another small bowl next to the mixer.

3. Beat the egg whites in the bowl of a standing mixer at low speed until just broken up and beginning to froth. Add the cream of tartar and salt and beat at medium speed until the whites form very soft, billowy mounds. With the mixer still at medium speed, beat in the remaining ¾ cup sugar, 1 tablespoon at a time, until all the sugar is added and the whites are shiny and form soft peaks. Add the vanilla, lemon juice, and almond extract and beat until just blended.

4. Place the flour-sugar mixture in a sifter set over waxed paper. Sift the flour-sugar mixture over the whites, about 3 tablespoons at a time, and gently fold in, using a large rubber spatula. Sift any flour-sugar mixture that falls onto the paper back into the bowl with the whites.

5. Gently scrape the batter into the pan, smooth the top with a spatula, and give the pan a couple of raps on the counter to release any large air bubbles.

323

6. Bake until the cake is golden brown and the top springs back when pressed firmly, 50 to 60 minutes.

7. If the cake pan has prongs around the rim for elevating the cake, invert the pan onto them. If the pan does not have prongs, invert the pan onto the neck of a bottle or funnel. Let the cake cool completely, 2 to 3 hours.

8. To unmold, run a knife around the edges of the pan, being careful not to separate the golden crust from the cake. Slide the cake out of the pan and cut the same way around the removable bottom to release or peel off the parchment or waxed paper, if using. Place the cake, bottom-side up, on a platter. Cut slices by sawing gently with a large, serrated knife. Serve the cake the day it is made.

CHIFFON CAKE

A MILE HIGH AND LIGHT AS A FEATHER, chiffon cake is also tender and moist; qualities that angel food and sponge cakes typically lack.

Chiffon cake was revolutionary in its day. Made with vegetable oil, which was a brand-new idea in 1950, this cake required none of the tedious creaming and incremental adding of ingredients demanded by a butter cake. One simply mixed flour, sugar, baking powder, egg yolks, water, and oil as if making a pancake batter and then folded in stiffly beaten egg whites. The whipping of the whites—"They should be much stiffer than for angel food or meringue," warned Betty Crocker— was the only tricky feat required, and even this was no longer an arduous task. More than a few households could boast a snappy new electric mixer.

Chiffon cake had been invented in 1927 by the aptly named Harry Baker, a Los Angeles insurance salesman turned caterer. When the cake became a featured attraction at the Brown Derby, then the restaurant of the stars, Baker converted a spare room into his top-secret bakery, fitted it with 12 tin hot-plate ovens, and personally baked 42 cakes a day.

Baker kept his recipe a secret for 20 years, before selling it to General Mills. There ensued considerable testing, but with only a couple of minor changes to the technique and a new name—"chiffon cake"—the cake appeared before the American public in a 1948 pamphlet called "Betty Crocker Chiffon," containing 14 recipes and variations in addition to umpteen icings, fillings, serving ideas, and helpful hints. It was an instant hit and became one of the most popular cakes of the time.

Although we have been delighted by the uniquely light yet full richness and deep flavor of this American invention, we also know that chiffon cakes can be dry or cottony. Ideally, chiffon cake should be moist and tender with a rich flavor. To perfect this 20th-century classic, we decided to go back to Betty Crocker's version.

With the exception of the chocolate variation, all of Betty Crocker's original chiffon cakes call for 2¼ cups sifted cake flour (which translates to about 1⅔ cups as measured by the dip-and-sweep method), 1½ cups sugar, 1 tablespoon baking powder, 1 teaspoon salt, ½ cup oil, 5 egg yolks, ¾ cup water or other liquid, 1 cup egg whites, and ½ teaspoon cream of tartar.

We made a plain, an orange, and a walnut chiffon cake according to the original formula and found that we had three complaints. The cakes were a bit dry—cottony and fluffy rather than moist and foamy, the way we thought chiffon

QUICK DRY FOR BAKING UTENSILS

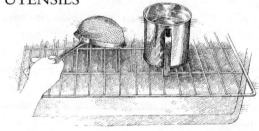

Most home bakers have just one piece of any given type of equipment, such as a strainer or sifter. Of course, these tools must be completely dry before you use them, but waiting for a strainer or sifter to dry fully can be frustrating, and it can't always be accomplished by hand-drying with a dish towel. Because the oven is on anyway, put the utensil in it to dry out. Set a timer for about 2 minutes to remind yourself that the utensil is in the oven. Be sure that the utensil doesn't have any plastic parts that can melt. Because the utensil will be quite hot, use an oven mitt to protect your hand when removing it from the oven.

cakes should be—and they seemed to lack flavor, punch, pizzazz. In addition, the cakes rose a bit too high for the pan, a consequence of the downsizing of tube pans, from 18 to 16 cups, that took place around 1970.

Since fat increases perceived moistness and also transmits flavor, we thought that adding more oil might help, but it did not. An orange chiffon cake made with an additional quarter cup of oil (up from ½ cup) turned out not only dry and flavorless but also greasy and heavy, an outcome that was as unexpected as it was disappointing.

We increased the number of eggs, and the cakes, even though they were lighter and richer than Betty Crocker's original, still tasted dry. We instinctively felt that adding more liquid would be a poor idea, but at this point we felt we had no choice but to try. Unfortunately, increasing the water from ¾ cup to 1 cup made the texture gummy and heavy—and the cake still managed to taste dry!

There was now only one ingredient left to play with, the flour. Since the problem was dryness, the flour obviously had to be decreased, but we knew from our experience with other sponge-type cakes that decreasing the flour could have very messy consequences. We might end up with a rubbery sponge or, worse, with a demonic soufflé that heaved blobs of batter onto the floor of the oven.

Whenever a sponge-type cake decides to collapse or explode, the culprit is the same: a lack of structure. Since eggs as well as flour provide structure, we reasoned that we could compensate for a decrease in flour by adding an extra egg yolk. We made an orange chiffon cake using the Betty Crocker formula but decreasing the flour by one-third cup and increasing the yolks from five to six. The effect was magical. Instead of being fluffy, cottony, and crumbly, the cake was wonderfully moist and so tender that slices flopped over at the middle if cut too thin. And the moistness transmitted all of the taste that had been lacking in our first experiments.

The cake, however, was not quite perfect. Evidently the structure was borderline, and so the cake rose very high, spilling over onto the lip of the pan. This made it difficult to cut the cake free from the pan without tearing the top crust.

Furthermore, because its top was humped, the cake did not sit flat when turned upside down onto a serving plate. We figured that removing an egg white would help to shrink the cake, but we feared that it might also undercut the structure to the point where the cake wouldn't rise at all. Nonetheless, we gave the idea a try. The resulting cake was lovely coming out of the oven, risen just to the top of the pan and perfectly flat—but its perfection was illusory. We hung the cake upside down to cool and started to clean up the kitchen when we heard a soft plop: the cake had fallen out of the pan.

Once we had taken a few nibbles of the mess, our fears were confirmed. The cake was pasty and overly moist. There was simply not enough structure to hold it together. We then remembered a chiffon cake recipe in Carole Walter's *Great Cakes* (Ballantine, 1991). Rather than whipping all of the egg whites, Walter mixed some of them, unbeaten, into the dry ingredients along with the yolks, water, and oil. Thus she incorporated less air into the batter, which should, we reasoned, make for a smaller cake. We tried Walter's technique using seven eggs, two of them added whole to the batter and five of them separated with the whites beaten. Eureka! At last we had the perfect chiffon cake: moist, tender, flavorful, and just the right size for the pan.

Chiffon Cake
SERVES 12

In the original recipes for chiffon cake published by General Mills, the directions for beating the egg whites read, "WHIP until whites form very stiff peaks. They should be much stiffer than for angel food or meringue. DO NOT UNDERBEAT." These instructions, with their anxiety-inducing capitalized words, are well taken. If the whites are not very stiff, the cake will not rise properly, and the bottom will be heavy, dense, wet, and custard-like. Better to overbeat than underbeat. After all, if you overbeat the egg whites and they end up dry and "blocky," you can simply smudge and smear the recalcitrant clumps with the flat side of the spatula to break them up. Although we prefer chiffon cake glazed, the cake can also be served as is or dusted with confectioners' sugar.

CAKE

1 1/2	cups (10 1/2 ounces) sugar
1 1/3	cups (5 1/3 ounces) plain cake flour
2	teaspoons baking powder
1/2	teaspoon salt
7	large eggs, 2 whole, 5 separated, at room temperature
3/4	cup water
1/2	cup vegetable oil
1	tablespoon vanilla extract
1/2	teaspoon almond extract
1/2	teaspoon cream of tartar

GLAZE

4	tablespoons (1/2 stick) unsalted butter, melted
4–5	tablespoons orange juice, lemon juice, milk, or coffee (for date-spice or mocha-nut variations)
2	cups (8 ounces) sifted confectioners' sugar

1. FOR THE CAKE: Adjust the rack to the lower-middle position and heat the oven to 325 degrees. Whisk the sugar, flour, baking powder, and salt together in a large bowl. Whisk in the 2 whole eggs, 5 egg yolks (reserve whites), water, oil, and extracts until the batter is just smooth.

2. Pour the reserved egg whites into the bowl of a standing mixer; beat at low speed until foamy, about 1 minute. Add the cream of tartar, gradually increase the speed to medium-high, then beat the whites until very thick and stiff, just short of dry (as little as 7 minutes in a standing mixer and as long as 10 minutes with a handheld mixer). With a large rubber spatula, fold the whites into the batter, smearing in any blobs of white that resist blending with the flat side of the spatula.

3. Pour the batter into an ungreased large tube pan (9-inch diameter, 16-cup capacity). Rap the pan against the countertop 5 times to rupture any large air pockets. If using a pan with a removable bottom, grasp both sides with your hands while firmly pressing down on the tube with your thumbs to keep the batter from seeping from the pan during the rapping process. Wipe off any batter that may have dripped or splashed onto the inside walls of the pan with a paper towel.

4. Bake the cake until a toothpick or thin skewer inserted in the center comes out clean, 55 to 65 minutes. Immediately turn the cake upside down to cool. If the pan does not have prongs around the rim for elevating the cake, invert the pan onto the neck of a bottle or funnel. Let the cake cool completely, 2 to 3 hours.

5. To unmold, turn the pan upright. Run a thin knife around the pan's circumference between the cake and the pan wall, always pressing against the pan. Use a skewer to loosen the cake from the tube. For a one-piece pan, bang it on a counter several times, then invert it over a serving plate. For a two-piece pan, grasp the tube and lift the cake out of the pan. If glazing the cake, use a fork or paring knife to gently scrape all the crust off the cake. Loosen the cake from the pan bottom with a spatula or knife, then invert the cake onto a serving plate. (The cake can be wrapped in plastic and stored at room temperature up to 2 days or refrigerated up to 4 days.)

6. FOR THE GLAZE: Beat the butter, 4 tablespoons of the liquid, and the sugar in a medium bowl until smooth. Let the glaze stand 1 minute, then try spreading a little on the cake. If the cake starts to tear, thin the glaze with up to 1 tablespoon more liquid. A little at a time, spread the glaze over the cake top, letting any excess dribble down the sides. Let the cake stand until the glaze dries, about 30 minutes. If you like, spread the dribbles (before they have a chance to harden) to make a thin, smooth coat. Serve.

➤ VARIATIONS

Banana-Nut Chiffon Cake

Follow the recipe for Chiffon Cake, decreasing the baking powder to 1 1/4 teaspoons and adding 1/4 teaspoon baking soda. Decrease the water to 2/3 cup and vanilla to 1 teaspoon; omit the almond extract. Fold in 1 cup very smoothly mashed bananas (about 2 medium) and 1/2 cup finely ground toasted walnuts or pecans to the batter before folding in the whites. Increase the baking time to 60 to 70 minutes.

Chocolate Marble Chiffon Cake

Combine 1/4 cup (3/4 ounce) unsweetened cocoa powder and 2 tablespoons packed dark brown sugar in a small bowl. Stir in 3 tablespoons boiling water, mixing until smooth. Follow the recipe for Chiffon Cake, equally dividing the batter into 2 separate bowls. Mix a scant 1/2 cup of batter from 1 bowl into the cocoa mixture, then partially fold this mixture back into the same bowl so you have 1 bowl of chocolate batter. Sieve or sift 3 tablespoons cake flour over the chocolate batter and continue to fold until just mixed. Pour half of the white and then half of the chocolate batter into the pan; repeat. Do not rap the pan against the countertop. Bake as directed.

Date-Spice Chiffon Cake

Follow the recipe for Chiffon Cake, substituting 1½ cups packed (10½ ounces) dark brown sugar for the granulated sugar and adding ¾ cup chopped dates, 2 teaspoons ground cinnamon, ½ teaspoon freshly grated nutmeg, and ¼ teaspoon ground cloves to the dry ingredients. Process the dry ingredients in a food processor until the dates are reduced to ⅛-inch bits and any lumps of brown sugar are pulverized. Transfer the dry ingredients to a bowl and whisk in the eggs, yolks, water, oil, and vanilla as directed. Omit the almond extract.

Lemon or Lemon-Coconut Chiffon Cake

Follow the recipe for Chiffon Cake, substituting ½ teaspoon baking soda for the baking powder, decreasing the water to ⅔ cup and vanilla to 1 teaspoon, and omitting the almond extract. Along with the vanilla, add the grated zest of 2 large lemons (about 3 tablespoons) plus 2 tablespoons strained lemon juice. (For Lemon-Coconut Chiffon Cake, proceed as above, adding ⅔ to 1 cup lightly packed sweetened flaked coconut, chopped a bit with a chef's knife, to the batter before folding in the whites.)

Mocha-Nut Chiffon Cake

Follow the recipe for Chiffon Cake, substituting ¾ cup brewed espresso-strength coffee for the water and omitting the almond extract. Add ½ cup finely chopped toasted walnuts and 1 ounce grated unsweetened baking chocolate to the batter before folding in the whites.

CHIFFON CAKE 101

1. Before the batter goes into the oven, grasp the pan on both sides while firmly pressing down on the tube with your thumbs. Rap the pan against the counter five times to rupture any air pockets.

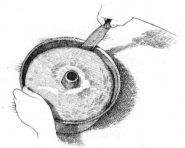

2. After the cake has cooled, with the pan upright on the counter, insert a thin knife between the cake and the wall of the pan. Pressing against the pan, run the knife around the circumference of the cake.

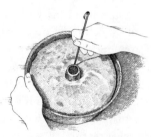

3. To loosen the cake from the tube, scrape around the tube with a wire cake tester.

4. If glazing the cake, use a fork or a paring knife to gently scrape all the crust off the cake.

5. Carefully invert the cake onto a plate.

6. If you like, spread the dribbles, before they have a chance to harden, to make a thin smooth coat.

Orange or Cranberry-Orange Chiffon Cake

Follow the recipe for Chiffon Cake, substituting 2 tablespoons grated orange zest and ¾ cup strained orange juice for the water, decreasing the vanilla to 1 teaspoon, and omitting the almond extract. (For Cranberry-Orange Chiffon Cake, proceed as above, adding 1 cup cranberries, chopped to ⅛-inch flecks in a food processor, and ½ cup finely chopped toasted walnuts to the batter before folding in the whites.)

POUND CAKE

UNLIKE THEIR MODERN DESCENDANTS, classic pound cakes contain no chemical leaveners. Instead, they depend for lightness on the innate puffing power of eggs and on the air incorporated into the batter through beating. This gives these cakes (which take their name from what is believed to be their original ingredients: a pound each of flour, sugar, butter, and eggs) a wonderful flavor but can cause problems with texture. After testing 31 old-style pound cake recipes, however, we have found one that is perfect in every regard, and because the cake is made without a speck of baking powder, it tastes of pure butter and eggs.

We embarked on this orgy of baking knowing that the main difficulty with pound cakes of the classic type is textural. Cakes might be said to have five "texture points": moist/dry, soft/hard, dense/porous, light/heavy, rich/plain. To contemporary tastes, cakes must be relatively moist and soft; the three remaining texture points are negotiable.

The problem with pound cake is that we ask it to be moist and soft on the one hand but also dense, light, and rich on the other. This is an extremely difficult texture to achieve unless one resorts to baking powder, with its potent chemical magic. Air-leavened cakes that are light and soft also tend to be porous and plain, as in sponge or angel cakes; moist and dense cakes inevitably also turn out heavy, as in the various syrup-soaked Bundt cakes that are so popular. From pound cake we ask all things.

In our early experiments, our interest was in comparing the merits of the two major mixing methods for pound cake. Accordingly, we prepared all of the cakes with exactly one-half pound each of flour, sugar, butter, and eggs. When we got what looked to be a promising result, we also tried adding varying amounts of liquid in the hope of achieving perfection.

The first mixing method we tried is probably the most common, and it produced good cakes but not great ones. It entails creaming the butter, sugar, and egg yolks until fluffy, adding the flour, and then folding in the stiffly beaten egg whites. The cakes made this way were a little tough, dry, and heavy, and they did not taste quite rich enough. We next tried adding some of the sugar to the egg whites during beating to give the whites more strength and puffing power. This did make the cakes lighter and more tender, but we still found them dry and insufficiently rich. Adding a quarter cup of liquid, as older cookbooks recommend, made the cakes moister but also turned them rubbery.

The simplest, most straightforward method of making pound cake involves beating the butter and sugar to a fluffy cream, adding the eggs (whole) one at a time, creaming the batter some more, and then mixing in the flour. No matter how we tried to work this method—adding and withholding liquid, beating the batter after putting in the flour (as some old cookbooks recommend)—we got simply awful results. The cakes were rubber doorstops.

Having thus far failed to make a perfect pound cake with either mixing method, we turned our attention to the ingredients themselves. In our readings of old cookbooks, we had long noted that pound cake, in the period of its greatest popularity, was rarely made with precisely 1 pound each of flour, sugar, butter, and eggs; nor were these necessarily the only ingredients used. For example, Eliza Leslie, the Julia Child of the 1830s and 1840s, specifies a "small pound of flour" (around 14 ounces), "a large pound of sugar" (perhaps 18 ounces), and somewhat better than one-half cup of liquid (eggs plus brandy, sherry, or rose water). Leslie's fiddling with the flour and sugar are atypical, but her use of one-half cup liquid is virtually invariable in pound cake recipes written before 1850. Meanwhile, other authors play around with the eggs. In *The Virginia House-Wife* (1824), Mary Randolph specifies a dozen eggs; in her time, 10 eggs were generally considered to weigh 1 pound. Susannah Carter, an English author whose cookery book was published in America in 1772, calls for six whole eggs and six yolks. Carter's idea to use extra yolks eventually proved a cornerstone in our own recipe.

Before tinkering with the sacrosanct pound formula, we decided to consult some modern cookbooks. We could hardly believe what we found in Flo Braker's *The Simple Art of Perfect Baking* (Morrow, 1985). Her classic pound cake is mixed in a way very similar to the second method we had tried, the one that we had found disastrous! We made her pound cake exactly as directed, and it turned out, indeed, to be the very best one we had baked so far. What made the difference?

First of all, Braker refined the mixing method. Instead of adding whole eggs one at a time to the creamed butter and sugar, she directs that the eggs first be lightly beaten in a bowl and then added by the tablespoon to the butter mixture. The butter and sugar mixture is evidently incapable of absorbing whole eggs; the mixture "curdles" and all the air is let out, resulting in tough, shrunken, wet pound cakes. But dribbling in the egg a little at a time preserves the emulsion—Braker astutely compares the process

to making mayonnaise—and allows all the air to be retained, making for a light, soft, tender cake. In baking, everything is in the details.

We also noted that Braker slightly modified the one-pound-each proportions. Her recipe, a "half-pound" cake like the ones we had been working with, calls for roughly 7 ounces of flour, 9 ounces of sugar, and 5 eggs (10 ounces weighed with the shells, the usual method of computation, or 8¾ ounces weighed without). She calls for 8 ounces of butter, the standard amount, and no added liquid other than almond and vanilla extracts. What a brilliant formula this is. Decreasing the flour makes the cake moister; increasing the sugar makes it more tender and, of course, sweeter; and adding an extra egg adds both moistness and lightness while at the same time compensating for the loss of structure caused by removing a little of the flour.

For many people, Braker's Viceroy Pound Cake will prove to be the only pound cake recipe they will ever need. It is a truly wonderful cake. We were hoping, however, to make a slightly denser cake. Adding liquid to Braker's pound cake made it rubbery; increasing the butter by a mere two tablespoons made it heavy. We tried any number of other small modifications, all to no avail, until finally we remembered Carter's recipe, with those extra egg yolks. Because they contain lecithin, yolks are good emulsifiers and thus help the batter retain air, making the cake light. Their fattiness contributes richness, tenderness, and moistness, while tamping the batter down a bit and thus militating against too fluffy an effect. Finally, the deep yellow of egg yolks gives the cake a beautiful golden color. Herewith is our own version of the perfect classic pound cake, inspired by gifted bakers living two centuries apart.

STORING PARCHMENT PAPER

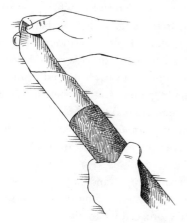

Parchment paper is a must for many baking projects. To save money, we like to buy it in bulk in sheets (rather than in rolls), but storing a large quantity can be a challenge. To keep parchment safe and out of the way, we roll a quantity of parchment paper sheets into a tight cylinder and slide it inside an empty gift-wrap tube that can be stored easily. The sheets can be pulled out easily, one at a time.

Classic Pound Cake
SERVES 8 TO 10

You may double the recipe and bake the cake in a large nonstick Bundt pan (14-cup capacity); the baking time remains the same. The recipe also makes 4 miniature pound cakes; use four 2-cup pans and reduce the baking time to 40 minutes. Though best when freshly baked, the cake will keep reasonably well for up to 5 days.

16	tablespoons (2 sticks) unsalted butter, softened but still cool
1⅓	cups (9⅓ ounces) sugar
3	large eggs plus 3 large egg yolks, at room temperature
1½	teaspoons vanilla extract
1½	teaspoons water
½	teaspoon salt
1½	cups (6 ounces) plain cake flour

1. Adjust an oven rack to the middle position and heat the oven to 325 degrees. Grease a 9 by 5-inch loaf pan (7½-cup capacity). Following the illustrations on page 141, fit a sheet of foil or parchment paper lengthwise in the bottom of the greased pan, pushing it into the corners and up the sides. Fit a second sheet crosswise in the pan in the same manner.

2. Beat the butter in the bowl of a standing mixer at medium-high speed until smooth and shiny, about 15 seconds. With the machine still on, sprinkle the sugar in slowly, taking about 30 seconds. Beat the mixture until light, fluffy, and almost white, 4 to 5 minutes, stopping the mixer once or twice to scrape down the sides of the bowl with a rubber spatula.

3. Stir together the eggs, yolks, vanilla, and water in a 2-cup liquid measuring cup. With the mixer running at medium-high speed, add the egg mixture to the butter and sugar in a very slow, thin stream. Finally, beat in the salt.

4. Place ½ cup of the flour in a sieve and sift it over the batter. Fold gently with a rubber spatula, scraping up from the bottom of the bowl, until the flour is incorporated. Repeat twice more, adding flour in ½-cup increments.

5. Scrape the batter into the prepared pan, smoothing the top with a spatula or wooden spoon. Bake until a toothpick or thin skewer inserted into the crack running along the top comes out clean, 70 to 80 minutes. Let the cake rest in the pan for 5 minutes, then invert onto a wire rack. Place a second wire rack on the cake bottom, then turn the cake top-side up. Cool to room temperature, remove and discard the foil, and serve. If not serving immediately, wrap the cake in plastic, then in foil. Store the cake at room temperature.

➤ VARIATIONS

Ginger Pound Cake

Follow the recipe for Classic Pound Cake, adding 3 tablespoons very finely minced crystallized ginger, 1½ teaspoons ground ginger, and ½ teaspoon mace along with the salt.

Citrus Pound Cake

Follow the recipe for Classic Pound Cake, adding any of the following along with the salt: the grated zest of 2 lemons, the grated zest of 1 orange, or the grated zest of 1 lemon and 1 orange. You can replace the water and vanilla extract with 1 tablespoon orange or lemon blossom water.

FRUIT UPSIDE-DOWN CAKE

THE IDEAL FRUIT UPSIDE-DOWN CAKE HAS a glistening, caramelized, deep amber topping encasing plump fruit on top of a flavorful, tender butter cake. The proportions and textures must marry well, providing the perfect balance of topping, fruit, and cake in each bite. Unfortunately, when we tested the standard recipes, we were left with pale blond, anemic-looking desserts consisting of fruit and topping that just sat on the cake component, not blending with it at all.

We set out to determine what proportions of brown sugar topping, fruit, and batter and what techniques worked most harmoniously. We also wanted to see if a master recipe could be developed that would support a variety of fresh fruits, including pineapple, plums, and peaches, in place of the more common canned pineapple.

Most recipes for this cake, including the original and the current recipe from Dole's test kitchen (where the recipe was first developed in 1925), combine brown sugar and butter for the topping by melting the butter, adding the brown sugar, and immediately proceeding to the fruit. This is why these cakes turn out very blond and light in taste. We knew we wanted a darker, richer, caramelized topping, so we opted to try the technique used in recipes that follow the method of tarte Tatin, in which the sugar and butter combination is lightly caramelized on top of the stove before the fruit is added.

We tested butter with granulated sugar, with light brown sugar, and with a combination of granulated and brown. The traditional brown sugar won out, since it added complexity to the final taste. As far as proportions were concerned, we settled on ¼ cup of butter to ¾ cup of brown sugar. The proportions were right, and by simmering and stirring for a few minutes to really combine the butter and sugar and produce a slightly reduced caramel, we hit the mark.

Coincidentally, this important step of caramelizing and thickening the topping affected unmolding as well. If the butter and sugar for the topping were simply stirred together, the cake, after being turned out of the pan, had a greasy top, with fruit that tended to alternately stick to the pan or fall off the sides of the cake. By cooking the topping first, we discovered that the unmolded cakes consistently yielded beautiful-looking tops with fruit that stayed put and never stuck.

We assumed initially that using fresh pineapple would be a problem and that we might end up preferring the ease of canned fruit. To our surprise, the fresh pineapple worked wonderfully with little preparation.

Fresh peaches, nectarines, and plums were also excellent and easy to prepare. We simply pitted and sliced them into thin half-inch wedges—no peeling was necessary. Mangoes required a bit more work because they had to be peeled as well as pitted and sliced but were wonderfully delicious. For all fruits, the slices were placed in concentric circles, filling

up the pan in the same way as the pineapple slices.

Having arrived at the proper topping and the right approach to each fruit, we turned to the question of the cake batter. Our aim was to make a cake that tasted good in its own right and that would physically support the fruit and caramelized topping, yet not detract from it. The proportions of cake to topping also had to be just right, and the cake had to merge with the topping and fruit to present a unified whole.

We thought a classic butter-type cake would work best, but we also had a notion that a light, low-fat sponge cake might balance well with the rich topping. We theorized that the syrupy caramel and fruit juices would be soaked up by the intentionally dryish sponge. We were pretty sure that a rich pound cake would be too heavy, but we decided to try both of these extremes first to establish whether or not they were even in the running.

We began with the sponge, and the results were poor. Its excessive dryness in juxtaposition to the unctuous topping did not make a happy pairing. The pound cake similarly placed poorly in taste tests; its heaviness prevented it from melding with the topping, and its extra butteriness competed with the caramel. We knew the ideal lay somewhere in between, so the next tests would be with butter cakes.

We began by using all-purpose flour, whole eggs, and milk. The cake texture was a bit coarse, so we tried using cake flour and separating the eggs, in both separate and combined tests. We found that the differences between flours in this cake were negligible but that the separated eggs

Fruit for Upside-Down Cake

Our favorite fruits for upside-down cakes are peaches, nectarines, plums, mangoes, and, of course, pineapple. Below are instructions to prepare enough of each fruit for one upside-down cake. See the illustrations on page 309 for tips on peeling mangoes and pineapples.

FRUIT	QUANTITY	PREPARATION
Peaches or Nectarines	4 medium	Halve fruits pole to pole; remove stones. Cut each half into slices ½ inch thick.
Plums	5 medium	Halve fruits pole to pole; remove stones (cutting halves in half again, if needed). Cut into slices ½ inch thick.
Mangoes	2 medium	Peel fruits and remove pits. Cut into slices ¼ inch thick.
Pineapple	1 small	Stem, quarter, peel, and core. Cut each quarter into pieces ⅜ inch thick.

improved the texture dramatically. When the whites were whipped separately and then folded in, the resulting cake was extremely tender, with a crumb so fine that it was almost too velvety. The combination of all-purpose flour and separated eggs was a winner. To give the cake a slightly coarser crumb and help balance the rich topping, we added 3 tablespoons of cornmeal.

The milk helped to produce a smooth, moist cake and batter, but we wanted to try buttermilk because it often works so well in butter cake recipes. We thought the sharp flavor might also complement the sweetness of the topping. We reduced the amount of baking powder and added baking soda to offset the acidic nature of the buttermilk. The cakes baked well and looked fine, but a more open crumb, a result of the baking soda, was not right for this cake.

As far as flavorings were concerned, we had always thought vanilla should be included, and it did provide the butter cake with a rounder, fuller flavor. We experimented with cinnamon and ginger, which were interesting, and lemon zest added a nice tangy flavor, but all of these additions veered away from what we thought a very basic pineapple upside-down cake should taste like. Vanilla was necessary, but no other flavoring was required.

While we had discovered early on the value of the caramelized topping to easier unmolding, we also came to understand that the length of the cooling period is crucial. In short, the best procedure is to remove the cake from the oven when done, let it sit for two minutes on a rack, then flip it over onto a plate. This minimal cooling time allows the caramelized top to solidify enough to keep it from flowing off the cake after unmolding yet does not allow the caramelized sugar to set, which would lead to unmolding problems. If any fruit does stick, it is easy enough to remove the pieces and place them properly on the cake top.

Fresh Fruit Upside-Down Cake
SERVES 8 TO 10

Using a 3-inch deep, 9-inch round pan to bake the cake gives it straight sides. If you prefer slightly flared sides on your cake, bake it in a 10-inch cast-iron skillet, which streamlines the process in three ways. First, the skillet need not be buttered; second, the caramel topping can be prepared in it directly; and third, the total baking time is cut to 50 minutes, which is 10 to 15 minutes faster than with the cake pan.

TOPPING
4 tablespoons (1/2 stick) unsalted butter
3/4 cup packed (5 1/4 ounces) light brown sugar
1 recipe Fruit for Upside-Down Cake (see chart, page 331)

CAKE
1 1/2 cups (7 1/2 ounces) unbleached all-purpose flour
3 tablespoons cornmeal
1 1/2 teaspoons baking powder
1/2 teaspoon salt
8 tablespoons (1 stick) unsalted butter, softened but still cool
1 cup (7 ounces) plus 2 tablespoons granulated sugar
4 large eggs, separated, at room temperature
1 1/2 teaspoons vanilla extract
2/3 cup milk

1. FOR THE TOPPING: Grease the bottom and sides of a 3-inch deep, 9-inch round cake pan. Melt the butter in a medium saucepan over medium heat; add the brown sugar and cook, stirring occasionally, until the mixture is foamy and pale, 3 to 4 minutes. Pour the mixture into the prepared cake pan; swirl the pan to distribute evenly. Arrange the fruit slices in concentric circles over the topping; set aside.

2. FOR THE CAKE: Adjust an oven rack to the lower-middle position and heat the oven to 350 degrees. Whisk the flour, cornmeal, baking powder, and salt together in a medium bowl; set aside. Cream the butter in the bowl of a standing mixer at medium speed. Gradually add 1 cup of the sugar; continue beating until light and fluffy, about 2 minutes. Beat in the yolks and vanilla (scraping the sides of the bowl with a rubber spatula if necessary); reduce the speed to low and add the dry ingredients and the milk alternately in 3 or 4 batches, beginning and ending with the dry ingredients, until the batter is just smooth.

3. Beat the egg whites in the large bowl of a standing mixer at low speed until frothy. Increase the speed to medium-high; beat to soft peaks. Gradually add the remaining 2 tablespoons sugar; continue to beat to stiff peaks. Fold a quarter of the beaten whites into the batter with a large rubber spatula to lighten. Fold in the remaining whites until no white streaks remain. Gently pour the batter into the pan and spread evenly on top of the fruit, being careful not to dislodge the fruit. Bake until the top of the cake is golden and a toothpick or thin skewer inserted into the center (but not into the fruit, which remains gooey) comes out clean, 60 to 65 minutes.

4. Rest the cake on a wire rack for 2 minutes. Slide a paring knife around the edge of the cake to loosen it from the pan. Place a serving platter over the pan and hold tightly. Invert the cake onto the platter. Carefully remove the cake pan. If any fruit sticks to the pan bottom, remove and position it on top of the cake.

APPLE CAKE

EASIER TO BAKE THAN A HOMEMADE APPLE pie but more refined than a quick-cooking apple crisp, an apple cake serves up sweet-tart apples married to a gracious, buttery cake. It can be baked in many forms—loaf pan, cake pan, glass baking dish, even cast-iron skillet. Another part of the apple cake's changing wardrobe is the placement of the apples. They can be found inside, on top of, or underneath the cake. In fact, the only constant in the apple cake recipes we explored was the apples themselves.

We began our tests by gathering a small mountain of apple cake recipes and baked off five that were representative of the group. Most were disappointing. One cake tasted like an overly spiced apple muffin, with flavorless apple chunks suspended in a grainy, gingerbread-colored interior. A loaf cake made by layering McIntosh apples in the batter came out heavy and eggy, with wet pockets of cake and steamed, supersoft apples. We tried an apple upside-down cake consisting of partially cooked apples arranged in a round cake pan with the cake batter poured on top. This one turned out like a third-grade craft project, shellacked, inedible, and ready to hang on the wall. The fourth recipe sounded easy—toss sliced apples in a baking dish and pour batter on top—but it resulted in a loose apple crisp–like dessert. The fifth cake showed some promise. Baked in a springform pan, it consisted of a stiff layer of batter topped with raw chopped apples. Although tasters found the cake too tightly bound and the apples too heavily spiced, we took a shine to its stand-up presentation. The cake was clean-edged and pretty, with a ring of apples jutting up above its crown.

From these initial tests, we gathered our wish list: We wanted the apples to retain their sweet character and to refrain from exuding so much juice as to affect the cake. The cake should contribute a subtle backdrop of flavor, not a barrage of overwhelming spices, and its texture should be sturdy enough to support the apples without being firm and dense, the way a quick bread is.

To find a cake suitable to serve as the foundation for the apples, we turned to our recipe for yellow cake (see page 347). While it was buttery, tender, and rich, this cake was also too delicate to stand up to the weight and released juices of the sliced apples, which we had shingled across the top.

To give the cake base more muscle, we increased the ratio of flour to liquids and added a bit more baking powder for greater lift. We then topped the cake with raw sliced apples coated in sugar. Although improved, this cake was too spongy. It was also a touch sodden from the exuded apple liquid, and it dipped slightly in the center from the apples' weight and juices.

We found a partial solution in the choice of apples: Granny Smith. While Grannies have a very tart flavor, they hold their shape nicely during baking and don't give off much juice. Even better choices, if you can find them, are Pink Lady, Cameo, and Gala. Even with the Grannies, however, the cake was still unable to fully support the fruit. After a host of additional tests, including broiling the apple slices ahead of time, fiddling with ingredient ratios, and baking the cake at different temperatures and on different rack levels in the oven, the center still sank. How could we produce a stand-up cake with a thick top layer of richly flavored apples?

The solution dawned on us when we noticed a Bundt pan sitting inconspicuously on a corner shelf. With this pan, we wouldn't have a sinking problem—there would be no center to sink. What's more, the hollow center of the pan might knock down the baking time (which until this point had been 1½ hours). And if we placed the apples in the bottom of the pan and then inverted it after baking, the fruit could still be perched on top. We happily dusted off the Bundt pan and increased our working recipe by half to fill its larger size.

To prevent sticking, we greased the pan with 2 tablespoons of softened butter, then tossed raw, cubed apples in brown sugar and laid them in the pan. (Cubes fit better than slices in a Bundt's fluted shape.) We topped the apples with batter and popped the pan into the oven. Forty-five minutes later, we pulled out the cake and inverted it onto a cake stand. Although perfectly baked, the cake was no showstopper, with some apples hugging the cake and others glued to the pan.

To solve this problem, we tried sprinkling 6 tablespoons of sugar over the bottom of the pan before adding the brown sugar–tossed apples, hoping that the sugar would melt and trap the apples' juices before they hit and then stuck to the pan. This apple cake fell out of the pan without any coaxing, and the chopped apples clung to the swells

of the cake—not the valleys of the pan.

But this cake wasn't without fault. It was pale and gummy at its apex. When we tested dark brown sugar in the pan instead of granulated, the apples looked bruised, a result we attributed to uneven melting of the brown sugar. But the cake wasn't gummy anymore, as the brown sugar had created a semicrisp shell around the apples. Next, we gave a combination of granulated and brown sugars a try. We sprinkled 6 tablespoons of granulated sugar in the pan. Then, as evenly as possible, we added 2 tablespoons of light brown sugar on top. We added the sugared apples and, finally, the batter. When unmolded, the cake practically glowed with a haloed ring of lovely, flaxen gold apples. This apple cake was the one—tall, bountiful, and with great apple flavor.

Apple Cake
SERVES 10 TO 12

Cake flour does this cake the most justice, but if there's none available, use a lower-protein, unbleached all-purpose flour instead. Pillsbury and Gold Medal are good options. The cake must be unmolded right after baking. If bits of apple or caramelized sugar stick to the pan, use a toothpick to remove them and return them to their rightful spots on the cake while still warm. Try Pink Lady, Cameo, or Gala apples rather than Granny Smiths if you can find them. This cake is best served the day it is made, with a dusting of confectioners' sugar, if you like.

DISTRIBUTING APPLE CAKE BATTER

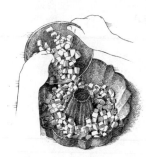

1. Distribute the cubed apples evenly on the bottom of the buttered and sugared pan.

2. Dip a rubber spatula into the mixing bowl, scooping out a large dollop of batter. Drop the batter off the end of the spatula in quadrants.

3. Smooth the batter with an offset spatula or the back of a soupspoon.

CAKE

16	tablespoons (2 sticks) unsalted butter, cut into 16 pieces, softened but still cool, plus 2 tablespoons for greasing the pan
1 1/4	cups (8 3/4 ounces) granulated sugar, plus 6 tablespoons for dusting the pan
2	tablespoons light brown sugar for the pan
3	large eggs plus 2 large egg yolks
1/2	cup heavy cream
2	teaspoons vanilla extract
2 1/4	cups (9 ounces) plain cake flour
1	tablespoon baking powder
3/4	teaspoon salt

APPLES

2	large Granny Smith apples (about 1 pound), peeled, cored, and cut into 1/2-inch cubes
2	tablespoons light brown sugar

1. FOR THE CAKE: Adjust an oven rack to the lower-middle position and heat the oven to 350 degrees. Grease a standard nonstick 12-cup Bundt pan with the 2 tablespoons softened butter; dust the sides with 2 tablespoons of the granulated sugar, then evenly distribute the remaining 4 tablespoons granulated sugar in the bottom of the pan. Evenly sprinkle the brown sugar on top of the granulated sugar, breaking up any large lumps with your fingers.

2. Whisk the eggs and yolks in a 2-cup liquid measuring cup to combine. Add the cream and vanilla and beat until thoroughly combined.

3. In the bowl of a standing mixer set at the lowest speed, combine the flour, the 1 1/4 cups sugar, baking powder, and salt, about 30 seconds. With the mixer still running on the lowest speed, add the butter 1 piece at a time in 1-second intervals and beat until the mixture resembles coarse meal, with butter bits no larger than small peas, 1 to 1 1/2 minutes.

4. With the mixer still running, add 1/2 cup of the egg mixture; mix at the lowest speed until incorporated, 5 to 10 seconds. Increase the speed to medium-high and beat until light and fluffy, about 1 minute. With the mixer still running, add the remaining liquid in a steady stream (this should take about 30 seconds). Stop the mixer and scrape down the bowl with a rubber spatula, then beat at medium-high speed to combine, about 30 seconds.

5. FOR THE APPLES: Toss the cubed apples with the light brown sugar and distribute in an even layer over the sugar in the pan. Add the batter in 4 portions and gently level with an offset spatula or the back of a soupspoon.

6. Bake until the cake begins to pull away from the sides of the pan, springs back when pressed with a finger, and a toothpick or skewer inserted into the center of the cake comes out clean, 35 to 45 minutes. Meanwhile, place a 12-inch square of foil on a wire rack. Immediately invert the cake onto the foil-covered rack. Cool at least 1 hour, then slide onto a serving plate; cut into slices and serve.

CARROT CAKE

A RELIC OF THE HEALTH FOOD CRAZE, CARROT cake was once heralded for its use of vegetable oil in place of butter and carrots as a natural sweetener. But healthy or not (and we doubt that it ever was), we have eaten far more bad carrot cake than good. Sure, the carrots add some sweetness, but they also add a lot of moisture, which is why carrot cake is invariably soggy. And oil? It makes this cake dense and, well, oily. Save for the mercifully thick coating of cream cheese frosting, most carrot cakes seem nothing but a good spice cake gone bad.

We wanted to create a truly great carrot cake. It should be a moist (not soggy) cake that was rich (not greasy). The crumb should be relatively tight and tender, while the spices should be nicely balanced. And what about the cake's namesake? We wanted our cake to contain enough carrots to confirm at first glance that it was indeed carrot cake. We also wanted it to be simple—from ingredient list to mixing method.

Our initial research turned up numerous recipes, and we chose several that seemed promising. Although very different in shape and ingredients, they were, with the exception of one, very bad (see "Some Failed Carrot Cakes," page 336). But the test wasn't a complete wash, as we learned two very important things.

First, shape matters. Layer cakes could hardly be considered part of our "simple" plan. Loaf cakes were easy but looked more like quick bread than cake. A Bundt cake was easy as well as attractive but difficult to ice with the thick coating of cream cheese frosting that our ultimate cake must have. For our purposes, there was nothing easier than a sheet cake baked in a standard 13 by 9-inch pan.

Second, there are carrot cakes out there made with just about anything and everything. Canned crushed pineapple, toasted coconut, wheat germ, raisins, and nuts all made appearances in the cakes. The first three were unanimously voted out, but the raisins and nuts were liked well enough to make them an option.

All-purpose flour worked better than cake flour (the latter proved too delicate for this sturdy American classic), and we used 2½ cups as the base for our tests. We quickly found that this cake would need healthy amounts of baking soda and baking powder, 1 teaspoon and 1¼ teaspoons, respectively (nearly twice the amount found in many recipes), to give it sufficient lift and a beautiful brown color. Four eggs gave the cake a slight spring and a tender crumb. As for sugar, this cake clearly benefited from both granulated and light brown sugar, the former giving the cake clean sweetness, the latter bringing out the warmth of the spices. While many recipes use handfuls of every baking spice in the pantry, we found that a conservative touch with cinnamon, along with a little help from nutmeg and cloves, won the approval of tasters.

Now that we had a reasonably simple working recipe, we introduced carrots to the mix. We rejected any idea of first boiling, steaming, or pureeing the carrots, as was called for in some recipes. It was just too much work. Grating the carrots was clearly the way to go, but it took a few failed efforts before we realized that just the right amount of carrots was paramount, because their high moisture content could determine whether a cake was moist or soggy. After baking cakes with as few grated carrots as 1 cup (no carrot presence) and as many as 5 cups (soaking-wet cake), we found that 3 cups was the perfect amount to give the cake a pleasantly moist texture. To hasten the grating of the carrots (as well as to spare ourselves a few grazed knuckles), we put away our box grater in favor of the food processor.

About 99 percent of carrot cake recipes use oil instead of softened butter in the batter, and while the idea of not having to wait for butter to soften fit into our simple approach, the thought of using oil gave us pause; after all, butter adds flavor and oil does not. As a compromise, we tested melted butter versus oil. We were shocked to find that all the tasters preferred the cleaner taste of the cake made with oil. Any more than 1½ cups of oil and the cake was too dense and greasy; any less and tasters found the cake too lean.

Just as we would with a butter-based cake, we beat the oil with the sugar and then beat the eggs in with an electric mixer before adding the dry ingredients and the carrots. The cake was good, but we still weren't happy with two aspects. First, the bottom of the cake was too dense. Second, we weren't thrilled with the idea of pulling out both a food processor and an electric mixer to bake a "simple" cake. Deciding to work with the easier problem

SOME FAILED CARROT CAKES

We uncovered a number of problems in our initial round of testing. Pureed carrots gave one cake (left) an odd texture. The curved Bundt shape (center) was hard to ice, and the cake was bland. One layer cake (right) was so delicate that we had to slice it cold.

TOO SOGGY

TOO BLAND

TOO DELICATE

first, we examined our mixing method. Since we were using the food processor to grate the carrots, we wondered if we could use it to mix the cake. We processed the eggs and oil together with the sugar, then added the dry ingredients and finally the carrots. This cake was tough from the beating of the flour. Next time around, we again processed the eggs, oil, and sugar but then transferred the mixture to another bowl, into which we could stir the carrots and dry ingredients. This was much better, but still there was that annoyingly dense bottom.

On a whim, we wondered if gradually adding the oil to the sugar and eggs while the machine was running (much like making a mayonnaise) would have any impact on the cake. You bet it did. By first creating this stable emulsion of eggs and oil, we were breaking up the oil into tiny particles that were less likely to sink to the bottom, instead dispersing themselves evenly throughout the cake. No more soggy bottom, no more heavy texture. This cake was light, tender, and pleasantly moist.

Our cake was now good enough to eat on its own, but there was no way we were going to pass up the frosting. Made with cream cheese, butter, and confectioners' sugar, cream cheese frosting is one of those things that, even when it's bad, it's still good. So we made (and happily ate) several frostings made with various amounts of each ingredient. We added vanilla for depth of flavor, but it wasn't until we added a little sour cream that the frosting really shone on top of the cake—at last, we had a carrot cake worth eating.

Carrot Cake with Cream Cheese Frosting
SERVES 10 TO 12

If you like nuts in your cake, stir 1½ cups toasted chopped pecans or walnuts into the batter along with the carrots. Raisins are also a good addition; 1 cup can be added along with the carrots. If you add both nuts and raisins, the cake will need an additional 10 to 12 minutes in the oven.

CARROT CAKE
2½	cups (12½ ounces) unbleached all-purpose flour
1¼	teaspoons baking powder
1	teaspoon baking soda
1¼	teaspoons ground cinnamon
½	teaspoon freshly grated nutmeg
⅛	teaspoon ground cloves
½	teaspoon salt
1	pound (6 to 7 medium) carrots, peeled
1½	cups (10½ ounces) granulated sugar
½	cup packed (3½ ounces) light brown sugar
4	large eggs
1½	cups safflower, canola, or vegetable oil

CREAM CHEESE FROSTING
8	ounces cream cheese, softened but still cool
5	tablespoons unsalted butter, softened but still cool
1	tablespoon sour cream
½	teaspoon vanilla extract
1¼	cups (5 ounces) confectioners' sugar

1. FOR THE CAKE: Adjust an oven rack to the middle position; heat the oven to 350 degrees. Spray a 13 by 9-inch baking pan with nonstick cooking spray. Line the bottom of the pan with parchment paper and spray the parchment.

2. Whisk together the flour, baking powder, baking soda, spices, and salt in a medium bowl; set aside.

3. In a food processor fitted with the large shredding disk, shred the carrots (you should have about 3 cups); add the carrots to the bowl with the dry ingredients and set aside. Wipe out the food processor and fit with the metal blade. Process both sugars with the eggs until frothy and thoroughly combined, about 20 seconds. With the machine running, add the oil through the feed tube in a steady stream. Process until the mixture is light in color and well emulsified, about 20 seconds longer. Scrape the mixture into a large bowl. Stir in the carrots and dry ingredients until incorporated and no streaks of flour remain. Pour into the prepared pan and bake until a toothpick or skewer inserted into the center of the cake comes out clean, 35 to 40 minutes, rotating the pan from front to back halfway through the baking time. Cool the cake to room temperature in the pan on a wire rack, about 2 hours.

4. FOR THE FROSTING: When the cake is cool, process the cream cheese, butter, sour cream, and

vanilla in a clean food processor until combined, about 5 seconds, scraping down the workbowl with a rubber spatula as needed. Add the confectioners' sugar and process until smooth, about 10 seconds.

5. Run a paring knife around the edge of the cake to loosen it from the pan. Invert the cake onto a wire rack, peel off the parchment, then invert it again onto a serving platter. Using an offset spatula, spread the frosting evenly over the surface of the cake. Cut into squares and serve.

➤ VARIATIONS

Spiced Carrot Cake with Vanilla Bean–Cream Cheese Frosting

The Indian tea called chai inspired this variation.

Follow the recipe for Carrot Cake with Cream Cheese Frosting, substituting an equal amount of ground black pepper for the nutmeg, increasing the cloves to ¼ teaspoon, and adding 1 tablespoon ground cardamom along with the spices. For the frosting, halve and scrape the seeds from 2 vanilla beans, using a paring knife, and add the seeds to the food processor along with the vanilla extract.

Ginger-Orange Carrot Cake with Orange–Cream Cheese Frosting

Follow the recipe for Carrot Cake with Cream Cheese Frosting, reducing the cinnamon to ½ teaspoon, adding 1½ teaspoons ground ginger along with the spices, processing 1 tablespoon grated orange zest along with the sugar and eggs, and adding ½ cup finely chopped crystallized ginger along with the carrots. For the frosting, substitute an equal amount of orange juice for the sour cream and 1 tablespoon grated orange zest for the vanilla.

CRUMB COFFEECAKE

GREAT WITH A STRONG CUP OF COFFEE or a tall glass of cold milk, crumb coffeecake is a classic. Made well, it's a far cry from the cellophane-wrapped supermarket versions so often seen today: heavy, leaden cake, achingly sweet crumb topping—and too much of it. We wanted to develop a simple old-fashioned crumb cake with good buttery flavor and just enough crumb topping for balance.

Crumb coffeecake is nothing more than a single layer of buttery yellow cake topped with crumbs made from sugar, flour, and butter. We had seen recipes that used the same flour-sugar mixture for the topping and as the basis of the batter. We were intrigued. Although these recipes might seem odd, they do make some sense. Cake batters and crumb toppings are composed of the same basic ingredients; namely, flour, sugar, and butter. The main difference between the two is that cake batters contain liquid, which binds the protein and starch in flour into a springy, cohesive mass, while crumb toppings are made without liquid and thus remain loose. A recipe that derives both cake and crumbs from the same basic mixture seemed like a great way to simplify the preparation process.

We baked up cakes from several sources but were disappointed. First of all, there were not nearly enough crumbs, although this problem was easily remedied. The bigger issue was the lack of contrast between the batter and the topping. Either the cake was too brown or the crumbs were insipid—they needed the molasses flavor of brown sugar. We devised a two-tone cake (a yellow cake topped with dark brown crumbs) by making the initial crumb mixture with granulated sugar and then adding brown sugar to the topping crumbs only.

Other problems proved trickier to solve. None of the recipes that we tested were quite buttery enough, but when we tried adding more butter to the batter, the cake became too weak to support the crumbs and collapsed in the center. Increasing the flour shored up the cake but also made it dry and puffy.

We knew that adding a bit more buttermilk (our liquid of choice) would strengthen the structure by promoting the gelatinization of the starch in the flour, but we resisted this option because we thought the resulting batter would be too liquid to hold fruit (an ingredient in some variations) in suspension. When we finally bit the bullet and put a little more buttermilk in, we were pleasantly surprised. The batter was less stiff and easier to beat, and we found that a thorough beating aerated and emulsified the ingredients, making the batter wonderfully thick and fluffy. Even with a goodly quantity of butter added, the cake with more buttermilk rose perfectly, and the fruit stayed firmly suspended.

Old-Fashioned Crumb Coffeecake

SERVES 8 TO 10

This cake is best eaten on the day it is baked, though it may be made a day ahead. The batter is quite heavy, so you may prefer to beat it with an electric mixer at medium-high speed for a minute or so rather than whisk it by hand.

1	tablespoon dry bread crumbs
2	cups (10 ounces) unbleached all-purpose flour
1	cup plus 2 tablespoons (7⁷⁄₈ ounces) granulated sugar
1	teaspoon salt
10	tablespoons (1¼ sticks) unsalted butter, softened but still cool
1	teaspoon baking powder
½	teaspoon baking soda
¾	cup buttermilk or low-fat (not nonfat) plain yogurt, at room temperature
1	large egg, at room temperature
1	teaspoon vanilla extract
¾	cup walnuts or pecans, chopped fine
½	cup packed (3½ ounces) dark brown sugar
1	teaspoon ground cinnamon

1. Adjust an oven rack to the middle position and heat the oven to 350 degrees. Generously grease the bottom and lightly grease the sides of a 10-inch springform pan. Sprinkle the bottom of the pan with the bread crumbs, then shake lightly to coat. Tap out excess crumbs.

2. Whisk the flour, sugar, and salt in a large mixing bowl until blended. Add the butter and cut in with the whisk until the mixture resembles coarse crumbs. Remove 1 cup of the flour mixture to a separate bowl and set aside.

3. Whisk the baking powder and baking soda into the flour mixture remaining in the mixing bowl. Add the buttermilk, egg, and vanilla; whisk vigorously until the batter is thick, smooth, fluffy, and frosting-like, 1½ to 2 minutes. Using a rubber spatula, scrape the batter into the prepared pan and smooth the top.

4. Add the nuts, brown sugar, and cinnamon to the reserved crumbs of flour, sugar, and butter; toss with a fork or your hands until blended. Sprinkle the crumbs over the batter, pressing lightly so that they adhere. Bake the cake until the center is firm and a cake tester comes out clean, 50 to 55 minutes. Transfer the cake to a wire rack; remove the sides of the pan. Let the cake cool completely, about 2 hours, before serving. When completely cooled, the cake can be slid off the pan bottom onto a serving plate.

➤ VARIATIONS

Apple-Cinnamon Coffeecake

Peel and core 2 medium-large Granny Smith apples and cut them into ¼-inch dice. Heat 1 tablespoon butter in a 10-inch skillet (preferably nonstick) over high heat until golden. Add the apples, cover, and cook over high heat, stirring frequently, until they are dry and very tender, 2 to 3 minutes. Remove from the heat, sprinkle the apples with 2 tablespoons sugar, and lightly toss until glazed. Cool to room temperature. Follow the recipe for Old-Fashioned Crumb Coffeecake, adding 1 teaspoon cinnamon with the baking powder and baking soda and folding the apples into the finished batter.

Raspberry-Almond Coffeecake

Follow the recipe for Old-Fashioned Crumb Coffeecake, adding 1 teaspoon almond extract along with the vanilla. Turn the batter into the pan. Beat ½ cup seedless raspberry jam until smooth and fluid, then carefully spread it over the batter with the back of a teaspoon. For the crumb topping, substitute ¾ cup ground almonds for walnuts and ½ cup granulated sugar for the dark brown sugar; omit the cinnamon. Add 1 large egg yolk and 1 teaspoon almond extract to the topping and mix with a fork. Thoroughly knead the mixture with your fingers until the color is uniform.

SOUR CREAM COFFEECAKE

A STATUESQUE SOUR CREAM COFFEECAKE with delicate streusel swirls and mounds of streusel topping is the king of coffeecakes. Not only does it taste fabulously rich and hearty, but it is easy to make, looks impressive on a cake stand, is apropos morning through night, and has the potential to last well beyond its first day out of the oven.

But in the recipes we tried, the coffeecakes were either too stout or too sweet, too spicy or too bland, and sometimes even too tough. The streusel inside of the cake was most often wet and pasty, and the streusel topping sometimes melted into the cake, while other times it stayed sandy and granular.

In our efforts to revamp sour cream coffeecake, we decided to first isolate what was important to us. We all agreed that a tube pan lent the most handsome presentation to the cake shape and that we liked streusel so much that we wanted two layers of it—plus the crowning topping.

Because this cake is a behemoth, with hefty amounts of sour cream, butter, eggs, and streusel, a strong flour like all-purpose is required. For the traditional buttery yellow cake color, we decided on four eggs, enough to give structure to the cake and provide for a tight crumb. We also added a generous amount of baking powder to help lighten the cake's load and baking soda to react with the acidity of the sour cream. As far as fat goes, the more the better, since this is what gives the strong cake its sensitive side and its ability to stay moist for days. One-and-a-half sticks of butter and 1½ cups of sour cream seemed to do the trick. To keep the cake from being too heavy, we chose to use only granulated sugar in the cake base.

Crispy, crunchy, yet melt-in-your-mouth streusel requires a careful balance among sugar, flour, and butter; nuts and spices also warrant careful scrutiny. Our first discovery was to treat the top streusel and the interior streusel separately. We enjoyed the contrast of tender cake to crunchy topping and so decided to use nuts only in the topping. One cup was just the right amount. We also found that the interior layers of streusel became pasty when we included butter in the mix, so butter, like nuts, would be reserved for the topping. We did like the appearance and flavor from the combined use of granulated and dark brown sugar for both the topping and the inner layers of streusel. In both cases we also found flour necessary to keep the sugar in the streusel from melting or congealing in cement-like shards. Cinnamon—and a hefty dose of it at

2 tablespoons—was the only spice needed to lend warmth to the streusel's flavor.

One hour in the oven at 350 degrees proved to be the best and easiest option for baking; at higher temperatures the streusel became too dark, requiring an aluminum foil shield to protect it from the heat. Because the recipe is quite saturated with fat, we found it best to let the cake cool in the pan for at least one hour to become crack-proof before unmolding. We were pleased to find that if stored well, this cake actually improves with age.

Sour Cream Coffeecake
SERVES 16

To prevent leakage and for best results, we strongly recommend using a tube pan made of one piece of metal (rather than a two-piece angel food cake pan, which has a removable bottom). In a pinch, you can wrap the bottom of an angel food cake pan with foil before baking, although this improvisation will not work with the variation, Lemon-Blueberry Sour Cream Coffeecake, which contains more moisture (from the berries) than the other cakes. Note, too, that with an angel food cake pan wrapped in foil, the cake may take longer to bake and will not brown as well as a cake made in a one-piece pan.

STREUSEL

³/₄	cup (3³/₄ ounces) unbleached all-purpose flour
³/₄	cup (5¹/₄ ounces) granulated sugar
¹/₂	cup packed (3¹/₂ ounces) dark brown sugar
2	tablespoons ground cinnamon
2	tablespoons cold unsalted butter
I	cup pecans, chopped

CAKE

4	large eggs
I¹/₂	cups sour cream
I	tablespoon vanilla extract
2¹/₄	cups (11¹/₄ ounces) unbleached all-purpose flour
I¹/₄	cups (8³/₄ ounces) granulated sugar
I	tablespoon baking powder
³/₄	teaspoon baking soda
³/₄	teaspoon salt
12	tablespoons (1¹/₂ sticks) unsalted butter, softened but still cool, and cut into 1-inch cubes

1. FOR THE STREUSEL: Place the flour, granulated sugar, ¼ cup of the dark brown sugar, and the cinnamon in a food processor and process to combine. Transfer 1¼ cups of this mixture to a small bowl and stir in the remaining ¼ cup brown sugar; set aside (this will be the streusel for the inside of the cake). Add the butter and pecans to the remaining dry ingredients in the food processor bowl. Process the mixture until the nuts and butter have been broken down into small pebbly pieces, about ten 1-second pulses. Set aside. (The streusel with the butter and nuts will be for the top of the cake.)

2. FOR THE CAKE: Adjust the oven rack to the lowest position and heat the oven to 350 degrees. Grease a tube pan (10-inch diameter, 10-cup capacity). Combine the eggs, 1 cup of the sour cream, and vanilla in a medium bowl.

3. In the bowl of a standing mixer, combine the flour, sugar, baking powder, baking soda, and salt at low speed, about 30 seconds. Add the butter and the remaining ½ cup sour cream and mix at low speed until the dry ingredients are moistened. Increase to medium speed and beat 30 seconds. Scrape down the sides of the bowl with a rubber spatula. Decrease the mixer speed to medium-low and slowly incorporate the egg mixture in 3 additions, beating for 20 seconds after each addition and scraping the sides of the bowl as necessary. Increase the speed to medium-high and beat for 1 minute (the batter should increase in volume and become aerated and pale in color).

4. Add 2 cups of the batter to the prepared pan. With an offset metal spatula or rubber spatula, smooth the surface of the batter. Sprinkle with ¾ cup of the streusel filling (without butter or nuts). Drop 2 cups of the batter over the streusel, spread evenly, and then add the remaining streusel filling. Top with the remaining batter and then the streusel topping (with the butter and nuts).

5. Bake until the cake feels firm to the touch and a toothpick or thin skewer inserted into the center comes out clean (although there may be bits of sugar from the streusel clinging to the tester), 50 to 60 minutes. Cool the cake in the pan for 30 minutes. Place a rimmed baking sheet over the top of the cake and invert the cake onto the pan (the cake should now be upside down, with the streusel on the bottom). Remove the tube pan, place a wire rack on the cake, and reinvert so the streusel is facing up. Cool for 2 hours and serve or cool completely and wrap the cake in aluminum foil.

➤ VARIATIONS

Chocolate Chip Sour Cream Coffeecake
Follow the recipe for Sour Cream Coffeecake, sprinkling ½ cup chocolate chips on top of the cake batter before adding the first and second streusel layers, for a total of 1 cup chips. Finish the assembly and bake as instructed.

Lemon–Blueberry Sour Cream Coffeecake
Toss 1 cup frozen blueberries with 1 teaspoon grated lemon zest in a small bowl. Follow the recipe for Sour Cream Coffeecake, sprinkling ½ cup blueberries on top of the cake batter before adding the first and second streusel layers for a total of 1 cup blueberries. Finish the assembly and bake as instructed.

LAYERING COFFEECAKE BATTER AND STREUSEL

1. Using a rubber spatula, spread 2 cups of batter in the bottom of the prepared pan, smoothing surface.

2. Sprinkle evenly with ¾ cup streusel filling without butter or nuts.

3. Repeat steps 1 and 2 with 2 cups batter and the remaining streusel without butter or nuts.

4. Spread the remaining batter over, then sprinkle with streusel topping with butter and nuts.

Almond–Apricot Sour Cream Coffeecake
Follow the recipe for Sour Cream Coffeecake, substituting blanched slivered almonds for the pecans and adding ½ teaspoon almond extract with the vanilla extract. Spoon ½ cup apricot preserves into a zipper-lock bag. Cut off a corner tip. Squeeze 6 dollops of apricot preserves on top of the cake batter before adding the first and second streusel layers, for a total of 12 dollops. Finish the assembly and bake as instructed.

CHOCOLATE SHEET CAKE

A SHEET CAKE IS LIKE A TWO-LAYER CAKE with training wheels—it's hard to fall off. Unlike regular cakes, which often require trimming and decorating skills to make sure the cake doesn't turn out lopsided, domed, or altogether amateurish, sheet cakes are single-story and easy to frost. These are the sorts of cakes made for church suppers, old home days, bake sales, and Fourth of July picnics, decorated with red, white, and blue frosting.

But sheet cakes are still cakes. They can still turn out dry, sticky, or flavorless and, on occasion, can even sink in the middle. So we set out to find the simplest, most dependable recipe for a chocolate sheet cake, one that was moist yet also light and chocolatey.

First off, a sheet cake is nothing more than cake batter baked in one layer, usually in a square or rectangular pan. We started with a test batch of five different recipes that required a variety of mixing techniques, everything from creaming butter to beating yolks, whipping whites, and gently folding everything together at the end. The best of the lot was the most complicated to make. But we were taken with another recipe that simply whisked together the ingredients without beating, creaming, or whipping. Although the recipe needed work, its approach was clearly a good match for the simple, all-purpose nature of a sheet cake.

The recipe called for 2 sticks of butter, 4 eggs, 1½ cups flour, 2 cups sugar, ½ cup cocoa, 1 teaspoon vanilla, and ⅛ teaspoon salt. Our first change was to add buttermilk, baking powder, and baking soda to lighten the batter, as the cake had been dense and chewy in its original form. To increase the chocolate flavor, we reduced the sugar and flour, increased the cocoa, and decreased the butter. To further deepen the chocolate taste, we decided to use semisweet chocolate in addition to the cocoa. With this revised recipe and our simple mixing method, we actually had a cake that was superior to those whose recipes called for creaming butter or whipping eggs.

The only significant problem came when we tested natural versus Dutch-processed cocoa and discovered that the cake fell a bit in the center when we used the former. A few tests later, we eliminated the baking powder entirely, relying instead on baking soda alone, and the problem was fixed. (Natural cocoa is more acidic than Dutch-processed, and when it was combined with baking powder, which also contains acid, it produced an excess of carbon dioxide gas. This in turn caused the cake to rise very fast and then fall like a deflated balloon.)

Also of note is the low oven temperature—325 degrees—which, combined with a relatively long baking time of 40 minutes, produced a perfectly baked cake with a lovely flat top. Using a microwave oven rather than a double boiler to melt the chocolate and butter also saved time and hassle.

This cake can be frosted with almost anything—buttercream, Italian meringue, sour cream frosting, or whipped cream frosting—but we developed a classic American milk chocolate frosting that pairs well with the darker flavor of the cake. Unlike a two-layer cake, this cake is a snap to frost.

Chocolate Sheet Cake
SERVES 10 TO 12

Melting the chocolate and butter in the microwave is quick and neat, but it can also be done in a heatproof bowl set over a saucepan containing 2 inches of simmering water. We prefer Dutch-processed cocoa (see page 10) for the deeper chocolate flavor it gives this cake. If you prefer the cake unfrosted, lightly sweetened Whipped Cream (page 500) makes a nice accompaniment.

³⁄₄ **cup (2¼ ounces) cocoa, preferably Dutch-processed**
1¼ **cups (6¼ ounces) unbleached all-purpose flour**

$1/2$	teaspoon baking soda
$1/4$	teaspoon salt
8	ounces semisweet chocolate, chopped
12	tablespoons ($1\,1/2$ sticks) unsalted butter
4	large eggs
$1\,1/2$	cups ($10\,1/2$ ounces) sugar
1	teaspoon vanilla extract
1	cup buttermilk

**Creamy Milk Chocolate Frosting
(recipe follows)**

1. Adjust an oven rack to the middle position and heat the oven to 325 degrees. Grease the bottom and sides of a 13 by 9-inch baking pan.

2. Sift together the cocoa, flour, baking soda, and salt in a medium bowl; set aside. Heat the chocolate and butter in a microwave-safe bowl covered with plastic wrap for 2 minutes at 50 percent power; stir until smooth. (If not fully melted, heat 1 minute longer at 50 percent power.) Whisk together the eggs, sugar, and vanilla in a medium bowl. Whisk in the buttermilk until smooth.

3. Whisk the chocolate mixture into the egg mixture until combined. Whisk in the dry ingredients until the batter is smooth and glossy. Pour the batter into the prepared pan; bake until firm in the center when lightly pressed and a toothpick inserted in the center comes out clean, about 40 minutes. Cool on a wire rack until room temperature, at least 1 hour; ice with frosting, if desired, and serve.

Creamy Milk Chocolate Frosting

MAKES ABOUT 2 CUPS,
ENOUGH TO ICE ONE 13 BY 9-INCH CAKE

This frosting needs about an hour to cool before it can be used, so begin making it when the cake comes out of the oven.

$1/2$	cup heavy cream
	Pinch salt
1	tablespoon light or dark corn syrup
10	ounces milk chocolate, chopped
$1/2$	cup (2 ounces) confectioners' sugar
8	tablespoons (1 stick) cold unsalted butter, cut into 8 pieces

1. Heat the cream, salt, and corn syrup in a microwave-safe measuring cup on high until simmering, about 1 minute, or bring to a simmer in a small saucepan over medium heat.

2. Place the chocolate in a food processor. With the machine running, gradually add the hot cream mixture through the feed tube; process 1 minute after the cream has been added. Stop the machine; add the confectioners' sugar and process to combine, about 30 seconds. With the machine running, add the butter through the feed tube 1 piece at a time; process until incorporated and smooth, about 20 seconds longer.

3. Transfer the frosting to a medium bowl and cool to room temperature, stirring frequently, until thick and spreadable, about 1 hour.

CUPCAKES

CUPCAKES ARE MANAGEABLE. THEY ARE EASY to transport, easy to serve (no plate and fork required) and, when made well, delicious. The cupcakes we remember from childhood birthday parties were rich, dense, and moist little yellow cakes lavishly topped with mounds of fluffy, lush, sweet chocolate. Unfortunately, times have changed. It's too easy for busy parents to pick up a box of cupcakes from the supermarket bakery. Often, these cupcakes are dry and crumbly, topped with greasy frosting or, even worse, cloyingly sweet, rubbery, and leaden. We wanted to make a better cupcake, one so delicious that children would savor the cake itself instead of just licking off the icing. We also wanted a cupcake good enough to satisfy grown-ups, too.

We tried almost every cupcake recipe we could find and discovered no clear winners. The major ingredients (flour, sugar, eggs, butter, and some sort of dairy product) were consistent enough among the recipes we tested, but their proportions and the exact type were up for grabs. We started with an investigation of which kind of flour to use and whether or not to sift it. We tested cake flour, pastry flour, and all-purpose flour. Cake flour and pastry flour were rejected by the panel of tasters almost immediately. Both produced too fine a texture; besides, pastry flour is difficult to find. All-purpose flour was the flour of choice. Most recipes we tested called for sifting because it aerates the flour, making it lighter. We sifted once. We sifted twice. We even sifted three times. When we made cupcakes using sifted flour, tasters found them extremely airy, a desirable quality in certain cakes but not in a cupcake. In fact, one taster who initially described the sifted-flour cupcakes as "too fluffy" later admitted, reluctantly, that they reminded her of Twinkies.

Once we had nailed down the type and texture of the flour, we tackled the eggs. Quantities ranged from three yolks to three whole eggs to varying combinations of yolks and whole eggs. The version we liked best included one whole egg and two yolks; these cupcakes had the golden beauty of the cupcakes with three whole eggs, but without the two whites they were richer.

We moved on to the dairy, trying whole milk, buttermilk, yogurt (low-fat and full fat), heavy cream, and sour cream. Although we all ended up preferring the slightly tangy richness of the sour cream, none of the options, except for the yogurt, were considered flops. When it came to butter, ½ cup of unsalted butter at room temperature was the right choice. We did try melting the butter, but it produced a slightly heavier cake that tasters found to be less appealing. We next tried varying amounts of sugar and found that 1 cup was best. More sugar reminded us of the cloyingly sweet cupcakes we've had the misfortune to sample, but less sugar produced something akin to a muffin.

It was time to test mixing methods more methodically. We tested two quite different options. First we used the classic creaming method, which starts by creaming the butter and sugar together, adding eggs, and then alternately adding dry and wet ingredients. Next we tried the two-stage method (recommended when you want a finer, more velvety texture), whereby butter is cut into the flour and other dry ingredients, after which the eggs and liquid are added. The results? Both techniques worked fine, and the cupcakes were barely distinguishable from each other.

At this point, we had made about 25 batches of cupcakes. On a whim, we simply threw everything—dry ingredients, butter, and wet ingredients—into a bowl in no particular order and turned on the mixer. Some members of the test kitchen staff were skeptical (to say the least), but in a blind tasting, everyone preferred this kitchen-sink method over the two more conventional mixing methods. The obvious question was, Why? One possible answer is that egg yolks contain emulsifiers that hold the fat and liquid together even when mixed in such a haphazard fashion. We continued testing this method by mixing the batter by hand (instead of with an electric mixer) and by using it to bake muffin tops and a cake. All three tests were winners. This cupcake batter was simple and invincible.

After much anticipation from tasters, it was time to perfect a chocolate frosting. The classic choice is buttercream, which entails whisking eggs and sugar over simmering water until the temperature reaches 160 degrees, whipping this mixture for 5 minutes until it is light and airy, and finally beating in softened butter a few tablespoons at a time. This seemed like an awful lot of work for something as simple as cupcakes, so we opted for an easy frosting, in which hot heavy cream is whisked together with chopped chocolate. Adding vanilla extract and cocoa to pump up the flavor seemed like a good idea, but they turned out to be extraneous. Experiments with amounts and types of chocolate resulted in a combination of 8 ounces semisweet chocolate and 1 cup heavy cream. Most tasters

BAKING OUTSIDE THE TIN

If you don't own a muffin tin, we found that foil liners are sturdy enough to hold our cupcake batter. Simply arrange the liners on a rimmed baking sheet and then fill them with batter. Note that cupcakes baked in a muffin tin brown on both the bottom and sides. If cupcakes are baked without a muffin tin, only the bottoms (and not the sides) will brown.

wanted a massive amount of frosting, but they also wanted it to be light. The solution was to whip the frosting after it had cooled, which produced a fluffy, rich chocolate frosting.

Now the next time your kids ask you to make cupcakes, it will be a lot easier to say yes. You can throw the batter together and produce a cupcake that even adults will want to eat.

Yellow Cupcakes with Simple Chocolate Frosting

MAKES 12

Make the frosting first. While it cools, prepare and bake the cupcakes; when the cupcakes are cooled, the frosting will be ready to be whipped and used. If you prefer, you may opt not to whip the frosting. It will be denser and have slightly less volume (see the photos on page 346 for more information). Bittersweet, milk, or white chocolate can be substituted for the semisweet chocolate. The recipe can be doubled.

These cupcakes are best eaten the day they are made, but unfrosted extras will keep in an airtight container at room temperature for up to 3 days. To double the recipe, use 3 whole eggs and 2 yolks and double the remaining ingredients.

SIMPLE CHOCOLATE FROSTING
- 1 **cup heavy cream**
- 8 **ounces semisweet chocolate, chopped**

CUPCAKES
- 1½ **cups (7½ ounces) unbleached all-purpose flour**
- 1 **cup (7 ounces) sugar**
- 1½ **teaspoons baking powder**
- ½ **teaspoon salt**
- 8 **tablespoons (1 stick) unsalted butter, softened**
- ½ **cup sour cream**
- 1 **large egg plus 2 large egg yolks, at room temperature**
- 1½ **teaspoons vanilla extract**

1. FOR THE FROSTING: Bring the cream to a simmer in a small saucepan or in a microwave. Place the chocolate in a medium bowl and pour the hot cream over it. Cover the bowl with foil and let

stand 5 minutes. Whisk the mixture until smooth, then cover with plastic wrap and refrigerate until cool and slightly firm, 45 minutes to 1 hour.

2. Transfer the frosting to the bowl of a standing mixer. Whip the mixture at medium speed until it is fluffy and mousse-like and forms medium-stiff peaks, about 2 minutes. Set aside.

3. FOR THE CAKE: Meanwhile, adjust an oven rack to the middle position; heat the oven to 350 degrees. Line a standard muffin tin with paper or foil liners.

4. Whisk together the flour, sugar, baking powder, and salt in the bowl of a standing mixer. Add the butter, sour cream, egg, yolks, and vanilla and beat the wet ingredients into the dry at medium speed until smooth and satiny, about 30 seconds. Scrape down the sides of the bowl with a rubber spatula and stir by hand until smooth and no flour pockets remain.

5. Divide the batter evenly among the cups of the prepared tin using a 2-ounce ice cream scoop or a spoon. Bake until the cupcake tops are pale gold and a toothpick or skewer inserted into the center comes out clean, 20 to 24 minutes. Use a skewer or paring knife to lift the cupcakes from the tin and transfer to a wire rack; cool the cupcakes to room temperature, about 45 minutes.

6. Spread 2 to 3 generous tablespoons of the frosting on top of each cooled cupcake; serve.

YELLOW LAYER CAKE

YELLOW LAYER CAKE IS AS FAMILIAR TO Americans as apple pie. Its buttery vanilla flavor makes it almost good enough to eat on its own, although iced with a creamy frosting is how we like it best. Its popularity drove companies like Betty Crocker and Pillsbury (and many others) to create boxed mix versions of the cake, as well as plastic cans of ready-made frostings, that today take up most of the baking aisle at the supermarket.

As easy as the boxed mixes are to put together, nothing can beat the flavor of a home-baked cake. And it is not difficult or time consuming. Yellow cake has always been a broad category, but most of the recipes for making it are very similar. For example, in *The Boston Cook Book*, published in 1884, Mary Lincoln, one of Fannie Farmer's colleagues at the Boston Cooking School, outlined several recipes for yellow cake. But she singled out one as "the foundation for countless varieties of cake, which are often given in cook books under different names." Mrs. Lincoln's master cake formula turns out to be similar to what we today call a 1-2-3-4 cake, made with 1 cup of butter, 2 cups of sugar, 3 cups of (sifted) cake flour, and 4 eggs, plus milk and small amounts of baking powder, vanilla, and salt.

As it turns out, things have not changed much since more than a century ago. When analyzed, most of the yellow cake recipes in today's cookbooks are 1-2-3-4 cakes or something very similar.

So when we set out in search of the perfect yellow cake, the first thing we did was bake a 1-2-3-4 cake. It wasn't a bad cake; it just wasn't very interesting. Instead of melting in the mouth, the cake seemed crumbly, sugary, and a little hard. The crust was tacky and separated from the underlying cake. Above all, the cake lacked flavor. It did not taste of butter and eggs, as all plain cakes ought to, but instead seemed merely sweet.

Before tinkering with the ingredients, we decided to try a different mixing method. We had mixed our 1-2-3-4 cake in the classic way, first beating the butter and sugar until light and fluffy, then adding the eggs one at a time, and finally adding the dry ingredients and milk alternately. Now we wanted to try mixing the batter by the so-called two-stage method, developed by General Mills and Pillsbury in the 1940s and later popularized by Rose Levy Beranbaum in *The Cake Bible* (William Morrow, 1988).

In the two-stage method, the flour, sugar, baking powder, and salt are combined; the butter and about two-thirds of the milk and eggs are added; and the batter is beaten until thick and fluffy, about a minute. Then, in the second stage, the rest of the milk and eggs are poured in and the batter is beaten about half a minute more. The two-stage method is simpler, quicker, and more nearly foolproof than the conventional creaming method.

The results exceeded our expectations. The two-stage method is often touted for the tender texture it promotes in cakes, and our two-stage 1-2-3-4 cake was indeed tender. But, more important, its consistency was improved. Whereas the conventionally mixed 1-2-3-4 cake had been crumbly, this cake was fine-grained and melting, and, interestingly enough, it did not seem overly

CHANGING FROSTING TEXTURE

The unwhipped frosting is dense and shiny. The whipped frosting is fluffier, a bit lighter in color, and not as shiny. Although most tasters preferred the fluffier texture of the whipped frosting, several tasters liked the shinier unwhipped frosting. Either may be used to frost our cupcakes. Don't let the frosting chill for more than an hour before whipping or it can separate. Excessive whipping may cause the frosting to curdle.

UNWHIPPED FROSTING   **WHIPPED FROSTING**   **CURDLED FROSTING**

sweet. Even the crust was improved. It was still a bit coarse but only slightly sticky. This was a cake with a texture that we truly liked.

The problem was the taste; the cake still didn't have any. In fact, oddly enough, it seemed to have less taste than the conventionally mixed version. Certainly it had less color. The 1-2-3-4 cake, it seemed, conformed to a typical cake pattern; as the texture lightened, the taste and color faded.

After trying to remedy the taste deficit by playing around with the ingredients in many ways—primarily adjusting the amounts and proportions of the sugar and eggs—we finally recalled a recipe called Bride's Cake in *Mrs. Rorer's New Cook Book*, published exactly a century ago. This is basically an egg-white pound cake—made of a pound each of flour, sugar, butter, and egg whites—with a cup of milk and a chemical leavener added. What would happen, we wondered, if we made Mrs. Rorer's cake with whole eggs instead of egg whites? It seemed worth a try.

We cut all of Mrs. Rorer's ingredients by half; that is, we made a half-pound cake, so that the batter would fit into two standard 9-inch round layer pans. When mixing the batter, we followed the two-stage method.

The resulting cake was richer, more flavorful, and generally more interesting than any of the 1-2-3-4 cakes we had baked, but it was not perfect. The layers were low, and the cake was just a tad dense and rough on the tongue (though not rubbery). We had several options. We could try to open up the crumb by adding more milk and baking powder; we could try to lighten the cake up with an extra egg or a couple of extra yolks; or we could try to increase the volume and tenderize the texture by adding a few more ounces of sugar. We tried all three strategies. The last one—the extra sugar—did the trick. This cake was fine-grained, soft, and melting, and it tasted of butter and eggs. It had elegance and finesse and yet was still sturdy enough to withstand the frosting process.

Both the 1-2-3-4 cake and our improved yellow cake based on Mrs. Rorer's recipe are made with a half pound each of butter and eggs. But while the 1-2-3-4 cake contains 3 cups of sifted cake flour and 1 cup of milk, our improved

yellow cake contains just 1¾ cups of sifted cake flour and only ½ cup of milk. So, while the 1-2-3-4 cake contains, by weight, 3 ounces more flour and milk than butter and eggs, our yellow cake contains 3 ounces less flour and milk than butter and eggs. This difference in basic proportions, as it turns out, makes a tremendous difference in texture and taste.

Yellow Layer Cake
SERVES 8 TO 10

Adding the butter pieces to the mixing bowl one at a time prevents the dry ingredients from flying up and out of the bowl. This yellow cake works with any of the frostings that follow.

1¾	cups (7 ounces) plain cake flour, sifted, plus more for dusting the pans
4	large eggs, at room temperature
½	cup whole milk, at room temperature
2	teaspoons vanilla extract
1½	cups (10½ ounces) sugar
2	teaspoons baking powder
¾	teaspoon salt
16	tablespoons (2 sticks) unsalted butter, softened but still cool, cut into 16 pieces
1	recipe Rich Vanilla Buttercream Frosting, Rich Coffee Buttercream Frosting, or Rich Chocolate Cream Frosting (pages 350 and 351)

1. Adjust an oven rack to the lower-middle position and heat the oven to 350 degrees. Generously grease two 9-inch round cake pans and cover the pan bottoms with rounds of parchment paper or waxed paper. Grease the parchment rounds and dust the cake pans with flour, tapping out the excess.

2. Beat the eggs, milk, and vanilla with a fork in a small bowl; measure out 1 cup of this mixture and set aside. Combine the flour, sugar, baking powder, and salt in the bowl of a standing mixer. Beat the mixture at the lowest speed to blend, about 30 seconds. With the mixer still running at the lowest speed, add the butter 1 piece at a time; mix until the butter and flour begin to clump together

Simple Ideas for Cake Decorating

WRITING ON A CAKE

When writing a message on top of a frosted cake, it's easiest to use chocolate on a light-colored frosting.

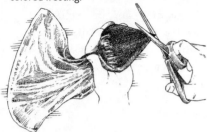

1. Put chopped semisweet or bittersweet chocolate in a zipper-lock plastic bag and immerse the bag in hot water until the chocolate melts. Dry the bag, then snip off a small piece from one corner.

2. Holding the bag in one hand, gently squeeze the chocolate from the hole as you write.

DECORATING WITH A TWO-TONE PATTERN

Confectioners' sugar and cocoa powder can be used together to give a frosted cake a professional look. Since confectioners' sugar will dissolve, apply this decoration right before serving. Start by freezing the cake 15 minutes to firm up the frosting.

1. Gather 6 jar lids of varying sizes. Place the lids face down on the surface of the cake in a random arrangement, letting some hang over the edge. Dust the cake with cocoa or confectioners' sugar.

2. Remove the lids by grasping them by the lip and lifting them straight up. Rearrange the lids randomly again, then dust with a contrasting color, using confectioners' sugar, cocoa, or very finely ground nuts. Remove the lids carefully and serve the cake.

REMOVING STENCILS

Store-bought stencils are an easy way to decorate with confectioners' sugar or cocoa powder. Removing the stencil without marring the design can be tricky. Here's how we do it.

1. Create 2 handles for the stencil by folding 2 short lengths of masking tape back onto themselves, pinching the middle sections together. Stick the ends of the tape to the top and bottom of the stencil, placing a handle on either side.

2. Place the stencil on top of the cake and dust with confectioners' sugar or cocoa powder. When you are done, use the tape handles to grasp and lift the stencil straight up and off the cake.

DUSTING WITH CONFECTIONERS' SUGAR

Simple single-layer cakes, such as a flourless chocolate cake, are rarely frosted, but they can be dressed up with some confectioners' sugar. This trick adds a bit of flair to an otherwise plain sugar dusting.

1. Lay strips of paper about ¾ inch wide across the top of the cake, then sieve the confectioners' sugar over the cake.

2. Carefully lift away the paper strips to reveal an attractive striped pattern.

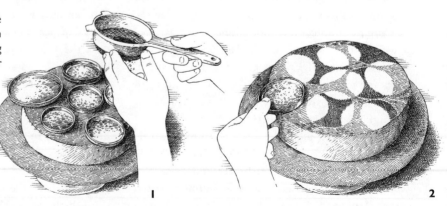

1   2

DECORATING WITH COLORED SUGAR

Colored sugar or sprinkles can add a special touch to freshly frosted cakes or cupcakes. To apply the colored sugar in neat shapes, use a cookie cutter outline as a guide. Once you've covered the area outlined by the cookie cutter with colored sugar, carefully remove the cutter to reveal a fanciful decoration.

GIVING FROSTING A SILKY LOOK

Professionally frosted cakes seem to have a molten, silky look. To get that same appearance at home, frost as usual and then use a hair dryer to "blow-dry" the surface of the cake. The slight melting of the frosting gives it that smooth, lustrous appearance.

DECORATING WITH CHOCOLATE

If the block of chocolate is too hard, it can be difficult to pull off thick shavings. Even if you do cut off nice shavings, warmth from your fingers can cause the pieces to melt as you try to place them on the cake. Here's how to avoid both problems.

1. Warm a block of bittersweet or semisweet chocolate by sweeping a hair dryer over it, taking care not to melt the chocolate. Holding a paring knife at a 45-degree angle against the chocolate, scrape toward you, anchoring the block with your other hand.

2. Pick up the shavings with a toothpick and place them as desired on the frosted cake.

DECORATING WITH ALMONDS

The shape and color of sliced almonds lend them to simple, elegant designs. Use these tips separately or in combination.

 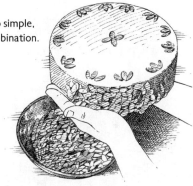

A. Arrange sliced almonds in a fleur-de-lis design around the perimeter of the frosted cake. Use four slices to make a flower design in the center of the cake.

B. Hold the cake with one hand by the cardboard round on its underside. Use the other hand to press nuts into the frosting, letting the excess fall back into the bowl of nuts. You will need about 1 cup of nuts to coat the sides of a 9-inch cake. Sliced almonds (pictured here) or chopped pecans or walnuts work well.

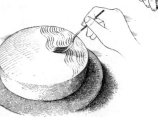 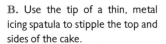 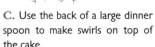

PUTTING A PATTERN IN FROSTING

A frosted cake can be easily styled in three ways. All of these designs are best accomplished when the frosting has just been applied and is still soft.

A. Use the tines of a dinner fork to make wave designs in the frosting. Wipe the fork clean intermittently. You can make this pattern on the top of the cake or on the top and sides.

B. Use the tip of a thin, metal icing spatula to stipple the top and sides of the cake.

C. Use the back of a large dinner spoon to make swirls on top of the cake.

and look sandy and pebbly, with pieces about the size of peas, 30 to 40 seconds after all the butter is added. Add the reserved 1 cup of egg mixture and mix at the lowest speed until incorporated, 5 to 10 seconds. Increase the speed to medium-high and beat until light and fluffy, about 1 minute. Add the remaining egg mixture (about ½ cup) in a slow steady stream, taking about 30 seconds. Stop the mixer and scrape the sides and bottom of the bowl with a rubber spatula. Beat at medium-high speed until thoroughly combined and the batter looks slightly curdled, about 15 seconds.

3. Divide the batter equally between the prepared cake pans; spread to the sides of the pans and smooth with a rubber spatula. Bake until the cake tops are light gold and a toothpick or thin skewer inserted in the centers comes out clean, 20 to 25 minutes. (Cakes may mound slightly but will level when

cooled.) Cool on a wire rack for 10 minutes. Run a knife around the pan perimeters to loosen. Invert one cake onto a large plate, peel off the parchment, and reinvert onto another wire rack. Repeat with the other cake. Cool completely before icing.

4. Assemble and frost the cake according to the illustrations on page 144. Cut the cake into slices and serve.

Rich Vanilla Buttercream Frosting

MAKES ABOUT 4 CUPS, ENOUGH TO ICE ONE 8- OR 9-INCH TWO-LAYER CAKE OR ONE 8-INCH THREE-LAYER CAKE

The whole eggs, whipped until airy, give this buttercream a light, satiny smooth texture that melts on the tongue.

- 4 large eggs
- I cup (7 ounces) sugar
- 2 teaspoons vanilla extract
- Pinch salt
- I pound (4 sticks) unsalted butter, softened but still cool, each stick cut into quarters

1. Combine the eggs, sugar, vanilla, and salt in the bowl of a standing mixer; place the bowl over a pan of simmering water. (Do not let the bottom of the bowl touch the water.) Whisking gently but constantly, heat the mixture until it is thin and foamy and registers 160 degrees on an instant-read thermometer.

2. Beat the egg mixture at medium-high speed until light, airy, and cooled to room temperature, about 5 minutes. Reduce the speed to medium and add the butter, one piece at a time. (After adding half the butter, the buttercream may look curdled; it will smooth out with additional butter.) Once all the butter is added, increase the speed to high and beat 1 minute until light, fluffy, and thoroughly combined. (The buttercream can be covered and refrigerated up to 5 days.)

> VARIATION

Rich Coffee Buttercream Frosting
Dissolve 3 tablespoons instant espresso in 3 tablespoons warm water. Follow the recipe for Rich

CUTTING ROUNDS OF PARCHMENT TO LINE CAKE PANS

1. Trace the bottom of your cake pan roughly in the center of a sheet of parchment paper (use a double sheet if using two pans).

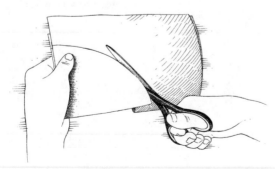

2. Fold the traced circle in half and then in half again, then cut just inside the outline of the quarter circle formed in this way. The resulting rounds of parchment will exactly fit your pan.

Vanilla Buttercream Frosting, omitting the vanilla and beating the dissolved coffee into the buttercream after the butter has been added.

Rich Chocolate Cream Frosting

MAKES ABOUT 3 CUPS, ENOUGH TO ICE ONE 8- OR 9-INCH TWO-LAYER CAKE

This soft, rich frosting is the perfect companion to a tender yellow layer cake.

16	ounces bittersweet or semisweet chocolate, chopped fine
1½	cups heavy cream
⅓	cup light corn syrup
1	teaspoon vanilla extract

Place the chocolate in a heatproof bowl. Bring the heavy cream to a simmer in a small saucepan over medium-high heat; pour over the chocolate. Add the corn syrup and let stand 3 minutes. Whisk gently until smooth; stir in the vanilla. Refrigerate 1 to 1½ hours, stirring every 15 minutes, until the mixture reaches a spreadable consistency. This frosting does not keep well, so it should be served within a day.

WHITE LAYER CAKE

WHITE LAYER CAKE HAS BEEN A CLASSIC birthday cake for more than a hundred years. Today, white layer cakes are often served at weddings, baby showers, and anniversary parties. The cake's snowy white interior is stunning against the pale frostings with which it is so often paired.

White cake is simply a basic butter cake made with egg whites instead of whole eggs. The whites produce the characteristic color, and they also make the cake soft and fine-grained, a bit like pound cake but much lighter and more delicate. Unfortunately, the white cakes we have baked over the years, although good enough, always fell short of our high expectations. They came out a little dry and chewy—one might say cottony—and we noticed that they were riddled with tunnels and small holes. What was going wrong?

Early on, we suspected the mixing method might be to blame. We had always mixed white cakes according to standard cookbook procedure; that is, we had creamed the butter and sugar, added the flour and milk alternately, and finally folded in stiffly beaten egg whites. Because this mixing method brings the flour into direct contact with liquid, it encourages the flour to form the elastic protein gluten. When beaten, gluten forms a stretchy net of rope-like fibers that not only make the cake tough but also press the air cells together into holes and tunnels. Cookbook recipes generally recommend deft, gentle handling of the batter to minimize gluten development, but it seemed that no matter how little we beat or how delicately we folded, the cakes did not improve.

In trying to avoid an "overglutenized" cake batter, we ordinarily use the so-called two-stage mixing method. This method entails creaming the flour, butter, and sugar together (rather than just the butter and sugar) before adding the eggs and other liquid ingredients. Because the flour is mixed with butter at the start, it is partially waterproofed and thus less prone to develop gluten. In the case of white cake, however, we could not bring ourselves to try this method because it uses unbeaten eggs, and every traditional recipe for white cake calls for stiffly beaten egg whites folded into the batter at the end. Surely the cake's special texture depended on beating the whites first, we thought. So we stuck with the creaming method and tried to improve the results by fiddling with the proportions. Into the garbage went a dozen cakes.

Luckily, we happened upon a recipe called Old-Fashioned White Cake in the 1943 edition of the *Joy of Cooking* (Scribner). The recipe called for working the butter into the flour with one's fingertips, as when making piecrust, and then whisking in beaten egg whites. We were intrigued—here was a two-stage white cake, but with the beaten egg whites we thought were necessary. Upon testing, the cake indeed proved to be more tender than the others we had made, and it also had a finer crumb. After a few more experiments, we eventually arrived at a white cake that we thought very good but, alas, still not quite perfect. There were still those holes.

We were stumped and might have stayed stumped if we had not been paying particularly close attention one day while we were folding egg whites into a soufflé batter. As the rubber spatula drew the egg whites up from the bottom of the bowl and over the top of the batter, we noticed how coarse and bubbly the whites were, even though they were not overbeaten and had seemed perfectly smooth and thick when taken from the mixer just moments before. Could it be that beaten egg whites, instead of promoting an ethereal texture in white cakes, actually formed large air pockets and caused those unsightly holes?

We tried the "old-fashioned" recipe again, only this time we simply mixed the egg whites with the milk before beating them into the flour and butter mixture. The results were fantastic. The cake was not only fine-grained and without holes but, to our surprise, also larger and lighter than the ones we'd prepared with beaten whites. And the method couldn't be simpler, quicker, or more nearly failure-proof. The two-stage method had proved, after all, to be the way to go.

Of course, we were curious to know the reason for this surprising outcome, so we did some boning up on egg whites. Apparently, beating has something of the same effect on egg whites that cooking does. Both beating and heating cause some of the individual protein strands to uncoil, whereupon they bump into each other and start linking up into an increasingly tight, dense web. It is this linking process that causes cooked whites to coagulate and beaten whites to stiffen. The problem, then, with putting beaten egg whites into a batter is that the whites have, in this respect, already been partially cooked. Because of this, the whites do not mix well with the rest of the batter and tend instead to create large air pockets when the cake bakes. Unbeaten egg whites, on the other hand, mix easily with the rest of the ingredients. When, during baking, they set and stiffen, they provide the structure necessary to hold the fine air bubbles beaten into the batter by creaming. The result is a wonderfully velvety cake, perfect for any special occasion.

Classic White Layer Cake with Butter Frosting and Raspberry-Almond Filling
SERVES 12

If you have forgotten to bring the milk and egg white mixture to room temperature, set the bottom of the measuring cup containing it in a pan of hot water and stir until the mixture feels cool rather than cold, around 65 degrees. The cake layers can be wrapped in plastic wrap and stored for 1 day; the frosting can be covered with plastic wrap and set aside at room temperature for several hours. Once assembled, the cake should be covered with an inverted bowl or cake cover and refrigerated. Under its coat of frosting, it will remain fresh for up to 3 days. Bring it to room temperature before serving. There is enough frosting to pipe a border around the base and top of the cake. If you want to decorate the cake more elaborately, you should make 1½ times the frosting recipe.

CLASSIC WHITE CAKE

2¼	cups (9 ounces) plain cake flour, plus more for dusting the pans
1	cup milk, at room temperature
6	large egg whites, at room temperature
2	teaspoons almond extract
1	teaspoon vanilla extract
1¾	cups (12¼ ounces) granulated sugar
4	teaspoons baking powder
1	teaspoon salt
12	tablespoons (1½ sticks) unsalted butter, softened but still cool

BUTTER FROSTING

16	tablespoons (2 sticks) unsalted butter, softened but still cool
4	cups (1 pound) confectioners' sugar
1	tablespoon vanilla extract
1	tablespoon milk
	Pinch salt

RASPBERRY-ALMOND FILLING

½	cup blanched slivered almonds, toasted and chopped coarse
⅓	cup seedless raspberry jam

1. FOR THE CAKE: Adjust an oven rack to the middle position and heat the oven to 350 degrees. Generously grease two 9-inch round cake pans and cover the pan bottoms with rounds of parchment paper or waxed paper. Grease the parchment rounds and dust the cake pans with flour, tapping out the excess.

2. Pour the milk, egg whites, and extracts into a 2-cup liquid measuring cup and mix with a fork until blended.

3. Mix the flour, granulated sugar, baking powder, and salt in the bowl of a standing mixer set at low speed. Add the butter; continue beating at low speed until the mixture resembles moist crumbs, with no powdery streaks remaining.

4. Add all but ½ cup of the milk mixture to the crumbs and beat at medium speed (or high speed if using a handheld mixer) for 1½ minutes. Add the remaining ½ cup of the milk mixture and beat 30 seconds more. Stop the mixer and scrape the sides of the bowl with a rubber spatula. Return the mixer to medium (or high) speed and beat 20 seconds longer.

5. Divide the batter evenly between the two prepared cake pans; using a rubber spatula, spread the batter to the pan walls and smooth the tops. Arrange the pans at least 3 inches from the oven walls and 3 inches apart. (If your oven is small, place the pans on separate racks in staggered fashion to allow for air circulation.) Bake until a toothpick or thin skewer inserted in the center of the cakes comes out clean, 23 to 25 minutes.

6. Let the cakes rest in the pans for 3 minutes. Loosen from the sides of the pans with a knife, if necessary, and invert onto wire racks. Reinvert onto additional wire racks. Let cool completely, about 1½ hours.

7. FOR THE FROSTING: Beat the butter, confectioners' sugar, vanilla, milk, and salt in the bowl of a standing mixer at low speed until the sugar is moistened. Increase the speed to medium-high; beat, stopping twice to scrape down the bowl, until creamy and fluffy, about 1½ minutes. Avoid overbeating or the frosting will be too soft to pipe.

8. FOR THE FILLING: Before assembling the cake, set aside ¾ cup of the frosting for decoration. Spread a small dab of frosting in the center of the cake plate to anchor the cake and set down one cake layer. Combine ½ cup of the remaining frosting with the almonds in a small bowl and spread over the first layer. Carefully spread the jam on top, then cover with the second cake layer. Spread the frosting over the top and sides of the cake (see the illustrations on page 144). Pipe the reserved frosting around the perimeter of the cake at the base and the top. Cut the cake into slices and serve.

COCONUT LAYER CAKE

COCONUT CAKE SHOULD BE PERFUMED inside and out with the cool, subtle, mysterious essence of coconut. Its layers of snowy white cake should be moist and tender, with a delicate, yielding crumb, and the icing should be a silky, gently sweetened coat covered with a deep drift of downy coconut. So it's irksome and disappointing that coconut cakes are often frauds, no more than plain white cakes with plain white icing slapped with shredded coconut. We decided to pursue a coconut cake that lived up to our dreams.

Presented with a roundup of cakes baked according to different recipes, likes and dislikes among the members of the tasting panel surfaced. Cakes baked in a 13 by 9-inch baking pan defied the archetypal sky-high layer-cake form. Coarse, crumbly textured cakes did not fill the bill, nor did cakes tinted yellow from yolks or whole eggs. Light, spongy, cottony cakes were too dry for a coconut cake. Doctored with coconut milk and a bit of coconut extract and tweaked ever so slightly, a basic white cake earned the most praise for its buttery flavor and its tender, fine crumb.

The cake doctored with coconut milk and extract was good, but it wasn't perfect. We found that, from batch to batch, coconut milk could produce mystifyingly different results—sometimes a flat cake, sometimes a mounded cake, sometimes a heavy, greasy cake. We discovered that the source of the problem was the variation in fat content—as much as 33 percent—among brands of coconut milk. Cream of coconut, a sweetened coconut product that contains a few inscrutable emulsifiers, seemed to be a more consistent product, perhaps because there are fewer brands (Coco Lopez being the best known). So we cut back on some of the sugar that went into the batter and used cream of coconut instead of coconut milk. These cakes baked up beautifully, their exteriors an appealing burnished brown color that the coconut milk versions lacked, and they tasted more strongly of coconut as well.

Unfortunately, these cakes also baked up with a giant mound at their centers, which made them look more like desert turtles than dessert. Because the batter was a very thick one that could use gentler heat (which would facilitate a more even rise in the oven), we were able to lower the mounds by reducing the oven temperature to 325 degrees. The resulting cakes were significantly improved. Then, to level things out even more, we manipulated the quantity of eggs. During these trials, we discovered that one yolk in addition to six egg whites gave the cakes a richer, fuller flavor without tainting their saintly color. This did nothing to alleviate the remaining slight mounding problem, however, so we tried scaling back on the cream of coconut and diluting the batter with a bit of water. This thinner batter baked into nice, even cakes.

It was time to work on the icing. Most tasters acknowledged that seven-minute meringue icing is what they'd expect on a coconut cake, but we found this icing to be painfully sweet and devoid of appealing texture. So we assembled one coconut cake with a butter and confectioners' sugar icing and one with an egg white buttercream that was an offshoot of the whole-egg buttercream we like to use with our yellow layer cake and devil's food cake. Both icings garnered applause, but the egg white buttercream was the favorite. Not only was it incredibly lithe, but it was also less sweet, significantly more silky and smooth, and much more fluffy and light than its competitor. In some ways, it was reminiscent of the traditional seven-minute icing, just not as sweet or as sticky, and with a creamier consistency.

This buttercream begins with a meringue, and softened butter is eventually beaten in. We tried two approaches to building the meringue. In the first, the whites and sugar are simply beaten to soft peaks in a standing mixer. In the second, the whites

---

INGREDIENTS: Coconut Extract

Pure extracts are essential oils extracted from natural flavoring agents such as fruit rinds, nuts, and herbs and then dissolved in alcohol. Imitation extracts are fabricated from chemical compounds that mimic natural flavors; these compounds are then also dissolved in alcohol. As with most things natural and synthetic, natural extracts cost more. When it came to coconut extract, we wanted to know whether "pure" was worth the price. So we made our buttercream frosting using three extracts—McCormick Imitation Coconut Extract, Spices Etc. Natural Coconut Flavoring, and LorAnn Gourmet Coconut Flavor—and put them to the test.

LorAnn Gourmet Coconut Flavor was uniformly rejected, bringing new meaning to the word artificial. One taster commented, "I feel like I'm eating suntan lotion." McCormick Imitation Coconut Extract came in second. Tasters didn't note any off flavors and considered this extract "subtle" and "good." Spices Etc. Natural Coconut Flavoring, made from the pulp of coconuts, was the most "deeply coconutty" and highly praised of the group. Ringing in at $3.25 for a 1-ounce bottle compared with $2.42 for the McCormick, the natural is worth the extra 80 cents.

---

and sugar are whisked together over a hot water bath until the sugar dissolves and the mixture is warm to the touch. The former straightforward meringue fell quickly as the butter was added, and the resulting buttercream was incredibly heavy and stiff, almost no better than the butter and confectioners' sugar icing. The meringue that went over heat was much more stable. Although it did fall when butter was added, the completed icing was soft, supple, and dreamy. (Note that the mixture does not become hot enough to eliminate the unlikely presence of salmonella bacteria in the eggs.)

The textural coup de grâce of a coconut cake is its woolly coconut coat. Indeed, pure white shredded coconut straight from the bag makes for a maidenly cake. Toasted coconut, however, has both chew and crunch as well as a much more intense flavor. And when toasted not to the point of even brownness but just until it resembles a toss of white and bronze confetti, it dresses this cake to be belle of the ball.

Coconut Layer Cake

SERVES 8 TO 10

Cream of coconut is often found in the soda and drink-mix aisle in the grocery store. One 15-ounce can is enough for both the cake and the buttercream; make sure to stir it well before using because it separates upon standing.

CAKE

2¼	cups (9 ounces) plain cake flour, sifted, plus more for dusting the pans
1	large egg plus 5 large egg whites
¾	cup cream of coconut
¼	cup water
1	teaspoon coconut extract
1	teaspoon vanilla extract
1	cup (7 ounces) sugar
1	tablespoon baking powder
¾	teaspoon salt
12	tablespoons (1½ sticks) unsalted butter, softened but still cool, cut into 12 pieces
2	cups packed sweetened shredded coconut

COCONUT BUTTERCREAM

4	large egg whites
1	cup (7 ounces) sugar
	Pinch salt
1	pound (4 sticks) unsalted butter, softened but still cool, each stick cut into 6 pieces
¼	cup cream of coconut
1	teaspoon coconut extract
1	teaspoon vanilla extract

1. FOR THE CAKE: Adjust an oven rack to the lower-middle position and heat the oven to 325 degrees. Grease two 9-inch round cake pans and dust with flour, tapping out the excess.

2. Beat the whole egg and egg whites in a large liquid measuring cup with a fork to combine. Add the cream of coconut, water, and coconut and vanilla extracts and beat with a fork until thoroughly combined.

3. Mix the flour, sugar, baking powder, and salt in the bowl of a standing mixer at the lowest speed to combine, about 30 seconds. With the mixer still running at the lowest speed, add the butter 1 piece at a time, then beat until the mixture resembles coarse meal, with butter bits no larger than small peas, 2 to 2½ minutes.

4. With the mixer still running, add 1 cup of the egg mixture to the flour and butter mixture. Increase the speed to medium-high and beat until light and fluffy, about 45 seconds. With the mixer still running, add the remaining 1 cup liquid in a steady stream (this should take about 15 seconds). Stop the mixer and scrape down the bowl with a rubber spatula, then beat at medium-high speed to combine, about 15 seconds. (Batter will be thick.)

5. Divide the batter between the cake pans and level with a rubber spatula. Bake until the cakes are deep golden brown, have pulled away from the sides of the pans, and a toothpick or thin skewer inserted into the center of the cakes comes out clean, about 30 minutes (rotate the pans from front to back after about 20 minutes). Do not turn off the oven.

6. Cool the cakes in the pans on wire racks for about 10 minutes, then loosen the cakes from the sides of the pans with a paring knife, invert the cakes onto the racks, and reinvert them so the top sides face up; cool to room temperature.

7. TO TOAST THE COCONUT: While the cakes are cooling, spread the shredded coconut on a rimmed baking sheet; toast in the oven until the shreds are a mix of golden brown and white, 15 to 20 minutes, stirring 2 or 3 times. Cool to room temperature.

8. FOR THE BUTTERCREAM: Combine the egg whites, sugar, and salt in a mixing bowl; set the bowl over a saucepan containing 1½ inches of barely simmering water. Whisk constantly until this mixture is opaque and warm to the touch and registers 120 degrees on an instant-read thermometer, about 2 minutes. (Note that this temperature is not hot enough to eliminate the unlikely presence of salmonella bacteria in the eggs.) Remove from the heat.

9. Using a standing mixer, beat the whites at high speed until they are barely warm (about 80 degrees), glossy, and sticky, about 7 minutes. Reduce the speed to medium-high and beat in the butter 1 piece at a time. Beat in the cream of coconut and the coconut and vanilla extracts. Stop the mixer and scrape the bottom and sides of the bowl with a rubber spatula. Continue to beat at medium-high speed until well combined, about 1 minute.

10. To ASSEMBLE THE CAKE: Following the illustrations on page 368, cut the cakes in half horizontally so that each cake forms 2 layers. Assemble and frost the cake according to the illustrations on page 144. Sprinkle the top of the cake with the toasted coconut, then press the coconut into the sides of the cake with your hand, letting the excess fall back onto a baking sheet or piece of parchment paper. Cut the cake into slices and serve.

SPONGE CAKE

IDEALLY, SPONGE CAKE IS LIGHTER THAN the standard butter-based layer cake, with a springy but delicate texture that stands up nicely to fillings and/or glazes. We like to use it in our Boston Cream Pie (filled with custard and iced with a sweet chocolate glaze) as well as a simple layer cake like Blackberry Jam Cake. It should not be dry or tough, the curse of many classic sponge cakes, nor should it be difficult to make. We were seeking a basic building-block cake recipe, just as dependable and useful as a classic American layer cake.

There are several kinds of sponge or "foam" cakes, so named because they depend on eggs (whole or separated) beaten to a foam to provide lift and structure. They all use egg foam for structure, but they differ in two ways: whether fat (butter or milk) is added and whether the foam is made from whole eggs, egg whites, or a combination.

We started by making a classic American sponge cake, which adds no fat in the form of butter or milk and calls for eight beaten egg whites folded into four beaten egg yolks. The cake certainly was light, but it lacked flavor, and the texture was dry and a bit chewy. To solve these problems, we turned to a recipe for a hot-milk sponge cake, in which a small amount of melted butter and hot milk is added to the whole-egg foam. This cake turned out much better on all counts. The added fat not only provided flavor but also tenderized the crumb. This particular recipe also used fewer eggs than our original sponge cake recipe.

We were now working with a recipe that used ¾ cup cake flour, 1 teaspoon baking powder, ¾ cup sugar, and five eggs. We started by separating out all

five whites and found that the cake was too light, its insufficient structure resulting in a slightly sunken center. We then separated out and beat just three of the whites, and the resulting cake was excellent. When all-purpose flour was substituted for cake flour, the cake had more body and was a bit tougher than the version with cake flour. We then tried different proportions of the two flours, finally settling on a 2-1 ratio of cake flour to all-purpose. We also tested to find the proper ratio of eggs to flour and found that five eggs to ¾ cup flour (we also tested ½ cup and 1 cup) was best. Five eggs also turned out to be appropriate: Six eggs produced an "eggy" cake, while four eggs resulted in a lower rise and a cake with a bit less flavor.

We had thought that the baking powder might be optional, but it turned out to be essential to a properly risen cake. Although angel food and classic sponge cakes, which use no added fat, do not require chemical leaveners, our sponge cake, with its fat from milk and melted butter, would require baking powder.

Two tablespoons of melted butter was just the right amount; three tablespoons made the cake a bit oily and the butter flavor too prominent. As for the milk, three tablespoons was best; larger quantities resulted in a wet, mushy texture.

With our basic recipe in hand, we played with the order of the steps. Beating the whole-egg foam first, and then the whites, allowed the relatively fragile foam to deteriorate, producing less rise. We found that beating the whites first was vastly better. After much experimentation, we also found it best to fold together, all at the same time, the beaten whole eggs, the beaten whites, and the flour, and then, once the mixture was about half mixed, to add the warm butter and milk. This eliminated the possibility that the liquid would damage the egg foam and also made the temperature of the butter and milk mixture less important.

Determining when a sponge cake is properly baked is a little more difficult than it is with a regular American layer cake. A sponge cake should provide some resistance and not feel as if one has just touched the top of a soufflé. Another good test is color. The top of the cake should be a nice light brown, not pale gold or a dark, rich brown.

We also tested the best way to handle the cake once out of the oven. When left to cool in a baking pan, the cake shrinks away from the sides and the edges become uneven. The best method is to immediately place the hot cake pan on a towel, cover it with a plate, and then use the towel to invert the cake. Finally, reinvert the cake and slip it back onto the wire rack.

Foolproof Sponge Cake

MAKES TWO 8- OR 9-INCH CAKE LAYERS

The egg whites should be beaten to soft, glossy, billowy peaks. If beaten until too stiff, they will be very difficult to fold into the whole-egg mixture.

- 1/2 cup (2 ounces) plain cake flour
- 1/4 cup (1 1/4 ounces) unbleached all-purpose flour
- 1 teaspoon baking powder
- 1/4 teaspoon salt
- 3 tablespoons milk
- 2 tablespoons unsalted butter
- 1/2 teaspoon vanilla extract
- 5 large eggs, at room temperature
- 3/4 cup (5 1/4 ounces) sugar

1. Adjust an oven rack to the lower-middle position and heat the oven to 350 degrees. Grease two 8- or 9-inch cake pans and cover the pan bottoms with rounds of parchment paper or waxed paper. Whisk the flours, baking powder, and salt in a medium bowl (or sift onto waxed paper). Heat the milk and butter in a small saucepan over low heat until the butter melts. Remove from the heat and add the vanilla; cover and keep warm.

2. Separate 3 of the eggs, placing the whites in the bowl of a standing mixer, reserving the 3 yolks plus the remaining 2 whole eggs in another mixing bowl. Beat the 3 whites at low speed until foamy. Increase the mixer speed to medium and gradually add 6 tablespoons of the sugar; continue to beat the whites to soft, moist peaks. (Do not overbeat.) Transfer the egg whites to a large bowl and add the whole-egg mixture to the mixer bowl.

3. Beat the whole-egg mixture with the remaining 6 tablespoons sugar. Beat at medium-high speed until the eggs are very thick and a pale yellow color, about 5 minutes. Add the beaten eggs to the whites.

4. Sprinkle the flour mixture over the beaten eggs and whites; fold very gently 12 times with a large rubber spatula. Make a well in one side of the batter and pour the milk mixture into the bowl. Continue folding until the batter shows no trace of flour and the whites and whole eggs are evenly mixed, about 8 additional strokes.

5. Immediately pour the batter into the prepared cake pans; bake until the cake tops are light brown and feel firm and spring back when touched, about 16 minutes for 9-inch cake pans and 20 minutes for 8-inch cake pans.

6. Immediately run a knife around the pan perimeters to loosen the cakes. Place one pan on a towel and cover the pan with a large plate. Using the towel to protect your hands and catch the cake, invert the pan and remove the pan from the cake. Peel off the parchment. Reinvert the cake from the plate onto the rack. Repeat with the remaining cake. Cool the cake layers to room temperature before proceeding with Boston Cream Pie (recipe follows) or Blackberry Jam Cake (recipe follows).

Boston Cream Pie

SERVES 8 TO 10

Why is this cake called Boston cream pie? It seems that the cake does indeed have its roots in Boston, where it developed in the middle of the 19th century. Modern baking experts believe that since pies predated cakes in the American kitchen, pie pans were simply more common kitchen equipment than cake pans. Hence the name pie was originally given to this layer cake. Prepare the pastry cream first, then the cake, and last, the glaze.

GLAZE
- 1 cup heavy cream
- 1/4 cup light corn syrup
- 8 ounces semisweet chocolate, chopped into small pieces
- 1/2 teaspoon vanilla extract

- 1 recipe Pastry Cream (page 227), chilled
- 1 recipe Foolproof Sponge Cake (at left), baked and cooled

1. FOR THE GLAZE: Bring the cream and corn syrup to a full simmer over medium heat in a medium saucepan. Remove from the heat and add the chocolate; cover and let stand for 8 minutes. (If the chocolate has not completely melted, return the saucepan to low heat; stir constantly until melted.) Add the vanilla; stir very gently until the mixture is smooth. Cool until tepid so that a spoonful drizzled back into the pan mounds slightly. (The glaze can be refrigerated to speed up the cooling process, stirring every few minutes to ensure even cooling.)

2. TO ASSEMBLE: While the glaze is cooling, place one cake layer on a cardboard round on a wire rack set over waxed paper. Carefully spoon the pastry cream onto the cake and spread it evenly up to the edges. Place the second cake layer on top, making sure the layers line up properly.

3. Pour the glaze onto the middle of the top layer and let it flow down the cake sides. Use a metal spatula, if necessary, to completely coat the cake. Use a small needle to puncture any air bubbles. Let the cake sit until the glaze fully sets, about 1 hour. Serve the same day, preferably within a couple of hours.

Blackberry Jam Cake

SERVES 8

Although blackberry jam is traditional, you can fill this cake with any favorite jam as long as it doesn't contain large chunks of fruit, which would be difficult to spread on the cake.

I   recipe Foolproof Sponge Cake (page 357)
I   (8-ounce) jar blackberry jam
      Confectioners' sugar for dusting

Place one cake layer on a cardboard round on a sheet of waxed paper. Evenly spread the jam over the cake. Place the second cake layer on the jam, making sure the layers line up properly. Sieve confectioners' sugar over the cake and serve.

CHOCOLATE LAYER CAKE

COOKBOOKS ARE FILLED WITH A VARIETY of chocolate layer cakes, which tend to hew closely to the yellow cake formula (including the addition of milk or some sort of dairy) but with chocolate added to the mix.

From past experience, we have found that recipes for chocolate layer cake can be maddening. One promises an especially fudgy and rich cake, the next guarantees a light and tender one. The secret to the recipe, we are told, is Dutch-processed cocoa, or dark brown sugar, or sour cream, or buttermilk, or some special mixing method—and so on and so forth. If you've made as many chocolate cakes as we have over the years, you can fill in the blanks yourself.

Finally, you make the cake, and you think, well, it is a little fudgy, or tender, or a little like devil's food, or whatever. But isn't it also very much like the chocolate cake you made just the other week, from a recipe that called for very different ingredients and promised a very different result?

We set out to make sense of this muddle. After baking and comparing dozens of different chocolate cakes, we have devised three truly distinctive chocolate layer cakes. In the process, we discovered a couple of general principles that apply to whatever type of chocolate layer cake you are making. Perhaps more important, we also learned a great deal about how various ingredients function and what results they produce, so that each of these recipes delivers exactly the type of chocolate cake it promises.

Bakers can (and do) argue endlessly over whether cocoa-based chocolate cakes are best made with standard American cocoa, such as Hershey's, or with a European-style cocoa, such as Droste, that has been alkalized, or "Dutched," to neutralize some of the natural acid. (See page 10 for more information on cocoa powder.)

To settle this question, we prepared several recipes using both types of cocoa and found that there was not an enormous difference. Cakes made with Hershey's were a little blacker and had a slight bitter edge; in the Droste cakes, the chocolate flavor was perhaps a bit mellower but also fainter. But these distinctions were minor, and the bottom line was that we liked both cocoas just fine. Since natural (nonalkalized) and Dutch-processed react differently with leaveners, we choose to base our recipes on widely available natural cocoa.

A second cocoa experiment, however, proved much more conclusive. In cakes made with cocoa and water, the chocolate flavor was much stronger and the color twice as dark when the cocoa was first dissolved in boiling water rather than simply being mixed into the batter dry. We therefore recommend following this procedure in any cocoa-based chocolate cake in which water is the liquid.

Next, we sought to discover the effects of substituting unsweetened baking chocolate or semisweet chocolate for cocoa. Following standard substitution tables, we prepared our master recipe using 3 ounces of unsweetened chocolate in place of the cocoa and subtracted 3 tablespoons of butter to compensate for the fat in the chocolate. We also made the master recipe with 5 ounces of semisweet chocolate in lieu of cocoa, cutting the butter by 2 tablespoons and the sugar by 6 tablespoons.

In the first set of experiments, we simply melted the chocolate over boiling water. Both the unsweetened and the semisweet chocolates produced terrible cakes: pale, dry, hard, and lacking in flavor. We remembered, however, that Rose Levy Beranbaum, author of *The Cake Bible* (William Morrow, 1988), counsels actually cooking the chocolate over boiling water for several minutes to rupture the cocoa particles and release the flavor. A second round of experiments substantiated the wisdom of this advice: Both unsweetened and semisweet chocolate responded dramatically, producing cakes with a much richer, darker flavor. Even when made with cooked chocolate, however, the cakes were neither as moist nor as flavorful as when made with cocoa. We will therefore venture a rule: In butter cakes, at least (if not necessarily in chocolate cakes of other types), cocoa is always better than chocolate.

Our second—and most extensive—set of experiments concerned the effect of dairy liquids on the cake. We checked out everything from sweet milk to buttermilk to yogurt to sour cream.

Sour cream and buttermilk have a seductively mouthwatering effect in chocolate cake recipes, but we have long had reservations about using milk products when baking with chocolate. Hot chocolate prepared with water (with a spoonful of cream added for richness, if you wish) has a far more intense flavor than hot chocolate made with milk. If milk is a flavor-blocker in hot chocolate, we reasoned, why wouldn't dairy products have a similar effect in chocolate cakes? Our experiments prove that they do, but the whole business turned out to be surprisingly complicated.

When we replaced the water with milk, we got a cake that we liked a great deal. As we had predicted, the chocolate flavor was somewhat muted, but to some tastes, this was for the better. The cake was a little less tender and more crumbly than the one made with water, but on the plus side, it also felt pleasantly substantial in the mouth. Milk produced the kind of chocolate cake that we remember from childhood, so we call this milk-based variation Old-Fashioned Chocolate Layer Cake.

Further experiments revealed that neither dissolving the cocoa in hot milk nor cooking the cocoa and milk together made for an appreciably stronger flavor than simply adding the cocoa to the batter dry. Evidently, dissolving the cocoa in boiling liquid improves its flavor only if the liquid in question is water.

Buttermilk and yogurt proved to be far more problematic ingredients. In our myriad tests, both had a paradoxical effect on texture, on the one hand velvetizing the crumb and adding a nice moistness, but on the other compacting the cakes and making them seem a little hard and chewy and also a bit pasty. Taste, though, was the real issue. While milk had a gentling effect on the flavor of chocolate, buttermilk and yogurt nearly killed it.

By testing various cookbook recipes, we eventually learned how to use buttermilk in such a way as to maximize its tenderizing qualities without obliterating all chocolate taste. One solution is to make your cake with a great deal of sugar; sugar speeds melting, and rapid melting intensifies flavor. We discovered that extra fat also mitigates the chocolate-blocking effects of buttermilk, though fat seems at the same time to undercut buttermilk's tenderizing properties, resulting in a fudgy texture.

Of course, if you actually prefer a chocolate cake with a mild flavor, buttermilk can be very helpful, for the velvetiness it imparts reinforces the flavor impression you are trying to create. The trick, we think, is to use the buttermilk in sparing quantities. Our German Chocolate Layer Cake is a reconfiguration of a cake popularly made with German sweet chocolate and a cup or more of buttermilk. We are not particularly fond of the cake made according to the standard recipe, but when the buttermilk is reduced, the cake turns out quite nice.

To use sour cream in a chocolate layer cake recipe, we found it necessary to decrease the butter to compensate for the milk fat in sour cream. Like buttermilk, sour cream made for a more velvety crumb, but there was a marked difference in degree—the sour cream cake was so feathery and soft as to seem almost pudding-like.

The effects of sour cream on flavor were complicated. It did make for a less pungent chocolate taste, but at the same time it imparted a pleasing, lingering mellowness. Strangely enough, it seemed to sweeten the cake rather than making it more tart, as buttermilk had. Sour cream and buttermilk, of course, are two very different things, so perhaps we shouldn't have been so surprised by the results. For our Sour Cream Fudge Layer Cake, we use the unique properties of sour cream to produce a cake with a dense yet melting texture and a rich taste.

Old-Fashioned Chocolate Layer Cake

SERVES 12

This chocolate cake resembles a traditional yellow cake with a great deal of chocolate added. The milk mutes the chocolate flavor slightly while giving the cake a sturdy, pleasantly crumbly texture. Cream enriches the frosting, making it compatible with this less assertive chocolate cake.

1¼	cups (6¼ ounces) unbleached all-purpose flour, plus more for dusting the pans
12	tablespoons (1½ sticks) unsalted butter, softened but still cool
1¼	cups (8¾ ounces) sugar
2	large eggs, at room temperature
½	teaspoon baking soda
½	teaspoon salt
½	cup (1½ ounces) nonalkalized cocoa, such as Hershey's, sifted
2	teaspoons instant espresso or coffee powder
1	cup plus 2 tablespoons milk
2	teaspoons vanilla extract
1	recipe Rich Chocolate Cream Frosting (page 351)

1. FOR THE CAKE: Adjust an oven rack to the middle position and heat the oven to 350 degrees. Generously grease two 8-inch round cake pans and cover the pan bottoms with rounds of parchment paper or waxed paper. Grease the parchment rounds and dust the pans with flour, tapping out the excess.

2. Beat the butter in the bowl of a standing mixer at medium-high speed until smooth and shiny, about 30 seconds. Gradually sprinkle in the sugar; beat until the mixture is fluffy and almost white, 3 to 5 minutes. Add the eggs 1 at a time, beating 1 full minute after each addition.

3. Whisk the flour, baking soda, salt, cocoa, and instant espresso powder in a medium bowl. Combine the milk and vanilla in a liquid measuring cup. With the mixer at the lowest speed, add about a third of the dry ingredients to the batter, followed immediately by about a third of the milk mixture; mix until the ingredients are almost incorporated into the batter. Repeat the process twice more. When the batter appears blended, stop the mixer and scrape the sides of the bowl with a rubber spatula. Return the mixer to low speed; beat until the batter looks satiny, about 15 seconds longer.

4. Divide the batter evenly between the prepared pans. With a rubber spatula, spread the batter to the pan sides and smooth the tops. Bake the cakes until they feel firm in the center when lightly pressed and a toothpick or thin skewer comes out clean or with just a crumb or two adhering, 23 to 30 minutes. Transfer the pans to wire racks; cool for 10 minutes. Run a knife around the perimeter of each pan, invert the cakes onto the racks, and peel off the paper liners. Reinvert the cakes onto additional racks; cool completely before frosting.

5. Assemble and frost the cake according to the illustrations on page 144. Cut the cake into slices and serve. (Cover leftover cake with plastic and refrigerate; bring to room temperature before serving.)

German Chocolate Layer Cake with Coconut-Pecan Filling

SERVES 12

Buttermilk gives this cake a pleasantly mild chocolate flavor with a very light, soft texture. The pecan and coconut filling provides textural contrast. Be sure to divide the batter evenly between the pans, as the cakes will rise high.

GERMAN CHOCOLATE CAKE

1 1/4	cups (6 1/4 ounces) unbleached all-purpose flour, plus more for dusting the pans
1/4	cup (3/4 ounce) nonalkalized cocoa, such as Hershey's
2	teaspoons instant espresso or coffee powder
1/3	cup boiling water
1/3	cup buttermilk or plain yogurt
2	teaspoons vanilla extract
12	tablespoons (1 1/2 sticks) unsalted butter, softened but still cool
1 1/4	cups (8 3/4 ounces) sugar
3	large eggs, at room temperature
1/2	teaspoon baking soda
1/2	teaspoon salt

COCONUT-PECAN FILLING

4	large egg yolks
1	cup (7 ounces) sugar
1/4	teaspoon salt
8	tablespoons (1 stick) unsalted butter, softened but still cool
1	cup heavy cream
1	teaspoon vanilla extract
1 1/2	cups chopped pecans, toasted
2	cups lightly packed sweetened flaked coconut

1. FOR THE CAKE: Adjust an oven rack to the middle position and heat the oven to 350 degrees. Generously grease two 8-inch round cake pans and cover the pan bottoms with rounds of parchment paper or waxed paper. Grease the parchment rounds and dust the pans with flour, tapping out the excess.

2. Mix the cocoa and instant espresso powder in a small bowl; add the boiling water and mix until smooth. Cool to room temperature, then stir in the buttermilk and vanilla.

3. Beat the butter in the bowl of a standing mixer at medium-high speed until smooth and shiny, about 30 seconds. Gradually sprinkle in the sugar; beat until the mixture is fluffy and almost white, 3 to 5 minutes. Add the eggs 1 at a time, beating 1 full minute after each addition.

4. Whisk the flour, baking soda, and salt in a medium bowl. With the mixer at the lowest speed, add about a third of the dry ingredients to the batter, followed immediately by about a third of the cocoa mixture; mix until the ingredients are almost incorporated into the batter. Repeat the process twice more. When the batter appears blended, stop the mixer and scrape the sides of the bowl with a rubber spatula. Return the mixer to low speed; beat until the batter looks satiny, about 15 seconds longer.

5. Divide the batter evenly between the pans. With a rubber spatula, spread the batter to the pan sides and smooth the tops. Bake the cakes until they feel firm in the center when lightly pressed and a toothpick or thin skewer comes out clean or with just a crumb or two adhering, 23 to 30 minutes. Transfer the pans to wire racks; cool for 10 minutes. Run a knife around the perimeter of each pan, invert the cakes onto the racks, and peel off the paper liners. Reinvert the cakes onto additional racks; cool completely before frosting.

6. FOR THE FILLING: Mix the egg yolks, sugar, and salt in a medium bowl; beat in the butter, then gradually beat the cream and vanilla into the mixture. Pour into a medium, nonreactive saucepan and cook over low heat, stirring constantly, until the mixture is puffy and just begins to thicken and the temperature reaches 180 degrees on an instant-read thermometer, 15 to 20 minutes. Pour the mixture into a medium bowl and cool to room temperature. Stir in the pecans and coconut.

7. TO ASSEMBLE: Following the illustrations on page 368, use a long serrated knife to cut the cakes in half horizontally so that each cake forms 2 layers. Place 1 of the cake bottoms on a serving plate. Spread about 1 cup filling over the cake half. Place another halved cake round over the filling. Repeat this stacking and spreading process with the remaining filling and cake, ending with a final layer of filling. Cut the cake into slices and serve.

Sour Cream Fudge Layer Cake

SERVES 12

Sour cream gives this cake its smooth, rich chocolate taste with a dense yet melting texture, almost like fudge. An equally intense chocolate icing stands up to the rich cake.

SOUR CREAM FUDGE CAKE

1 1/4	cups (6 1/4 ounces) unbleached all-purpose flour, plus more for dusting the pans
1	cup (3 ounces) nonalkalized cocoa, such as Hershey's
2	teaspoons instant espresso or coffee powder
1	cup boiling water
1/2	cup sour cream
2	teaspoons vanilla extract
16	tablespoons (2 sticks) unsalted butter, softened but still cool
1 3/4	cups (12 1/4 ounces) sugar
2	large eggs, at room temperature
3/4	teaspoon baking soda
1/2	teaspoon salt

CHOCOLATE BUTTER ICING

9	ounces bittersweet or semisweet chocolate, chopped
8	tablespoons (1 stick) unsalted butter
1/3	cup light corn syrup

1. FOR THE CAKE: Adjust an oven rack to the middle position and heat the oven to 350 degrees. Generously grease two 9-inch round cake pans and cover the pan bottoms with rounds of parchment paper or waxed paper. Grease the parchment rounds and dust the pans with flour, tapping out the excess.

2. Mix the cocoa and instant espresso powder in a small bowl; add the boiling water and mix until smooth. Cool to room temperature, then stir in the sour cream and vanilla.

3. Beat the butter in the bowl of a standing mixer at medium-high speed until smooth and shiny, about 30 seconds. Gradually sprinkle in the sugar; beat until the mixture is fluffy and almost white, 3 to 5 minutes. Add the eggs 1 at a time, beating 1 full minute after each addition.

4. Whisk the flour, baking soda, and salt in a medium bowl. With the mixer at the lowest speed, add about a third of the dry ingredients to the batter, followed immediately by about a third of the cocoa mixture; mix until the ingredients are almost incorporated into the batter. Repeat the process twice more. When the batter appears blended, stop the mixer and scrape the sides of the bowl with a rubber spatula. Return the mixer to low speed; beat until the batter looks satiny, about 15 seconds longer.

5. Divide the batter evenly between the pans. With a rubber spatula, spread the batter to the pan sides and smooth the tops. Bake the cakes until they feel firm in the center when lightly pressed and a toothpick or thin skewer comes out clean or with just a crumb or two adhering, 23 to 30 minutes. Transfer the pans to wire racks; cool for 10 minutes. Run a knife around the perimeter of each pan, invert the cakes onto the racks, and peel off the paper liners. Reinvert the cakes onto additional racks; cool completely before frosting.

6. FOR THE ICING: Melt the chocolate and butter in a medium bowl set over a pan of almost-simmering water. Stir in the corn syrup. Set the bowl of chocolate mixture over a larger bowl of ice water, stirring occasionally, until the icing is just thick enough to spread.

7. Assemble and frost the cake according to the illustrations on page 144. Cut the cake into slices and serve.

DEVIL'S FOOD CAKE

THE CRAZE FOR FANCY CAKE NAMES DATES back to the latter part of the 19th century. But only one of these cakes has truly survived from that period to ours—the devil's food cake. Its success is a testament both to its utter simplicity and its appealing moistness.

The obvious question is, "Just what is this cake?" The short answer is that the name refers to the color of the cake, not the texture, taste, shape, or fancy decorations. One group of food historians would argue that devil's food is a black cake; others would point to a reddish hue (cocoa naturally contains red pigments) as the distinguishing characteristic.

The problem with defining the devil's food cake, beyond the obvious issue of color, is that over time the recipe has been changed and embellished to the point where different recipes have little in common. To get a better handle on the situation, we pulled together two dozen or so recipes from cookbooks and the Internet, and our test kitchen baked the most promising five. The blind tasting that followed helped us put together a good working definition of our ideal devil's food cake. Although some of the recipes were similar to a regular chocolate cake (crumbly, a bit dry, and mild in flavor), we found the essence of devil's food to be a very moist, velvety texture combined with an intense chocolate experience. In addition, the better cakes were very dark, almost black. Here was a chocolate cake that was rich in both color and texture.

The next question was how to construct the ideal recipe. Despite their several differences, we first noted that all the recipes used the basic layer cake method. Butter and sugar were creamed, and then eggs were beaten in, followed by flour, cocoa, milk or water, and other ingredients. The next things we noticed were that the majority of recipes for this cake called for both cocoa and baking soda (not baking powder) and that many also suggested the addition of melted chocolate. Almost all of them used boiling water as the liquid of choice, although recipes from the early 1900s preferred milk, sour milk, or buttermilk. So the four key ingredients—those that really stood out in our research—were chocolate, cocoa, baking soda, and water.

The first issue was whether both chocolate and cocoa were necessary for the best flavor. The one cake out of five that used only cocoa was the driest and least flavorful. Clearly, a bit of chocolate was a must, and we finally settled on 4 ounces after testing smaller and larger amounts. As expected, the cake that used milk instead of water had less flavor, since milk tends to dull the flavor of chocolate (think of milk chocolate versus dark chocolate).

Baking soda was the leavener of choice in virtually every recipe we found, but we tested this anyway. To our great surprise, baking powder produced a totally different cake. It was much lighter

in color, and, more to the point, it was fudgy, almost like a brownie. It shared none of the delicate, velvety texture that we had come to expect of a classic devil's food cake. We also tested the proper amount of baking soda and settled on 1 teaspoon. More caused the cake to fall in the center, and any less didn't provide enough lift.

We continued our testing to refine the recipe and found that a mixture of cake flour and all-purpose was best. The all-purpose flour provided structure, while the addition of the cake flour made the cake a bit more delicate. On a lark, we made one cake by whipping the egg whites separately from the yolks, but the result was a much too flimsy cake that could not support the large amount of water called for in most recipes and sank. We played with the number of eggs, trying two, three, and then four. The middle road proved best—three eggs was just right. Granulated sugar was tested against brown sugar, and the latter won, improving the flavor. Many devil's food recipes do indeed call for brown sugar, whereas those for regular chocolate cakes tend to use granulated.

Although we had tested milk and buttermilk against water—the water produced a more intense chocolate experience—we tried adding sour cream to the recipe and were impressed. It deepened the flavor, added substance to the texture, and provided a richer taste experience, the chocolate flavor lingering in the mouth and coating the tongue.

Finally, we wondered if boiling water was really necessary. To find out, we made a cake with room-temperature water and found that it made virtually no difference. But when we tested dissolving the cocoa in the boiling water (as opposed to simply mixing it in with the flour), we found that this significantly enhanced the cocoa's flavor.

We had finally discovered the essence of a great devil's food cake. Unlike chocolate cake, which is usually made with milk and has a higher proportion of fat (butter), devil's food provides a velvety, more intense chocolate experience. And it is a particularly dark cake when made with Dutch-processed cocoa; natural (nonalkalized) cocoa will give it a redder hue. It is, ultimately, a singular cake in its devotion to a pure chocolate experience, subordinating everything to this simple but tasty proposition.

Devil's Food Cake

SERVES 8 TO 10

Regular, or natural, cocoa like Hershey's regular can be used, but you'll get best results with Dutch-processed cocoa.

4	ounces unsweetened chocolate, chopped
1/4	cup (3/4 ounce) Dutch-processed cocoa
1 1/4	cups boiling water
3/4	cup (3 3/4 ounces) unbleached all-purpose flour
3/4	cup (3 ounces) plain cake flour
1	teaspoon baking soda
1/4	teaspoon salt
16	tablespoons (2 sticks) unsalted butter, softened but still cool
1 1/2	cups packed (10 1/2 ounces) dark brown sugar
3	large eggs, at room temperature
1/2	cup sour cream
1	teaspoon vanilla extract
1	recipe Rich Vanilla Buttercream Frosting or Rich Coffee Buttercream Frosting (page 350)

1. Adjust the oven racks to the upper- and lower-middle positions; heat the oven to 350 degrees. Meanwhile, grease three 8-inch cake pans and line the bottom of each pan with a round of parchment paper or waxed paper. Combine the chocolate and cocoa in a medium bowl; pour the boiling water over and whisk until smooth. Sift together the flours, baking soda, and salt onto a large sheet of parchment or waxed paper; set aside.

2. Beat the butter in the bowl of a standing mixer at medium-high speed until creamy, about 1 minute. Add the brown sugar and beat at high speed until light and fluffy, about 3 minutes. Stop the mixer and scrape down the bowl with a rubber spatula. With the mixer at medium-high speed, add the eggs 1 at a time, beating 30 seconds after each addition. Reduce the speed to medium; add the sour cream and vanilla and beat until combined, about 10 seconds. Stop the mixer and scrape down the bowl. With the mixer at low speed, add about a third of the flour mixture, followed by about half of the chocolate mixture. Repeat, ending with the flour mixture; beat until just combined, about 15 seconds. Do not overbeat. Remove the bowl from the mixer; scrape the bottom and sides of the bowl with a rubber spatula and stir gently to thoroughly combine.

3. Divide the batter evenly among the cake pans and smooth the batter to the edges of each pan with a rubber spatula. Place 2 pans on the lower-middle rack and 1 on the upper-middle rack. Bake the cakes until a toothpick or skewer inserted in the center comes out clean, 20 to 23 minutes. Cool the cakes on wire racks 15 to 20 minutes. Run a knife around each pan perimeter to loosen. Invert each cake onto a large plate; peel off the parchment and reinvert onto a rack. Cool completely.

4. Assemble and frost the cake according to the illustrations on page 144. Cut the cake into slices and serve.

GÉNOISE LAYER CAKE

GÉNOISE IS A SOPHISTICATED CAKE, AND when the cake is cut into multiple layers, filled, and frosted, it's a looker too. Peek into the cases of fine French pastry shops and this is the cake you're most likely to see. Less rich than the more buttery American layer cake, the lean, light crumb of génoise is often brushed with a flavorful soaking syrup and coated in extra-rich buttercream frosting. Génoise is an occasion cake that has a reputation for being fickle. Poorly done génoise is squat, dry, and flavorless. We went into the test kitchen intent on developing a foolproof recipe.

The standard génoise method calls for warming a mixture of whole eggs and sugar over a water bath and beating the mixture until it is voluminous and billowy. Then, a small amount of the beaten egg mixture is transferred to a bowl with melted butter and stirred gently until combined. After flour is folded into the egg mixture, the lightened butter mixture is returned to the batter and folded in gently until combined. In the test kitchen, we liked this method. Another technique, pouring the melted butter directly into the batter, causes the egg mixture to deflate somewhat. Also, it is difficult to incorporate the butter fully. Diffusing the butter in a small amount of egg foam lightens it and allows it to combine thoroughly into the batter with minimum effect on the batter's volume.

For many home cooks, one of the most mysterious steps to making a génoise is identifying when the egg mixture is properly beaten. Recipes generally call for beating the egg mixture until it has tripled in volume. Gauging volume can be imprecise, so we looked for other ways of judging when the egg mixture was done. Some recipes call for beating the egg mixture until it has reached the heavy ribbon stage, when it falls from a whisk held several inches above the bowl into the remaining mixture in thick, billowy, serpentine strands that rest on the surface for several seconds. These guidelines were more helpful. After numerous tests and careful attention to the change in appearance and texture of the egg and sugar mixture, we found that the egg mixture is generally ready after six to eight minutes of beating in a electric mixer at medium-high speed. After just two minutes of beating, the mixture is wet looking, shiny, and pale yellow with fragile, tiny bubbles. By four minutes, the mixture is cream colored and voluminous, and the bubbles are numerous but still somewhat uneven in size. Between six and eight minutes, the egg mixture is pale, is slightly shiny but not wet looking, and forms a thick, billowy, stable ribbon. We found that the cakes baked from a more stable egg foam were lighter and more airy in texture.

In an attempt to lighten an already light and airy cake, many recipes add cake flour or cornstarch, alone or in combination with all-purpose flour, to the cake batter. We tested a number of combinations and proportions and found that cakes made with cornstarch or cake flour were so light as to be weak and flimsy. Soaked with flavored sugar syrup and coated with rich buttercream, the cakes were unpalatable and unsubstantial. In the test kitchen, tasters preferred the texture of the cakes made with all-purpose flour alone.

We tried baking our génoise in two standard round cake pans and were disappointed with the resulting cakes. Although the interior texture of the cake was fine, the exterior crust was slightly thicker than we wanted, and the tops of the two cakes domed slightly. In order to get the soaking syrup

to penetrate the interior crumb and to achieve a smooth surface on the finished, frosted cake, we had to remove the top crusts with a serrated knife. Although the technique worked, we didn't like cutting away and discarding what turned out to be a significant amount of cake. We then tried baking the cake in a springform pan and were thrilled with the results. The crust was thin and even. Because the pan is deep (2½ inches), we were able to bake the entire batter in one pan and, consequently, didn't have to cut away substantial portions of the cake to make uniform layers. We simply sliced the cake into three even layers and inverted them as we brushed them with soaking syrup and covered them with filling. What had been the smooth, flat bottom layer with crisp edges became the top layer, giving the finished, frosted cake an even top.

We also found that the cake bakes best in a springform pan that is simply lined with a circle of parchment. If the pan is buttered and floured, the preparation we typically recommend for our cake pans, the batter sticks to the flour on the sides of the pan and then begins to fall away as the cake nears the end of its baking time. Although this is generally seen as an indication that the cake is nearly ready to be removed from the oven, it has an unfortunate consequence with the génoise cake. If the pan is left unbuttered and unfloured, the egg

ADDING FLOUR TO A STANDING MIXER

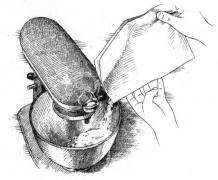

For one less dirty bowl to wash when making cakes, we recommend adding dry ingredients to the bowl of an electric mixer with a parchment "funnel." Measure flour, spices, leaveners, and other dry ingredients directly onto a piece of parchment paper, then fold the parchment in half and pour the dry ingredients into the mixing bowl.

foam in the génoise batter rises and sticks to the sides of the pan. A springy center and deep golden color (with the vanilla génoise) are good indications of when the cake is done. We found that if the cake pan is removed from the oven and the cake allowed to cool completely in the pan, the top of the génoise stays flat and even. To release the cake from the pan, we simply ran the blade of a thin metal spatula around the interior circumference of the pan, then removed the sides of the pan. The result was a perfectly round cake with a uniform height and thin crust.

Unlike American butter cakes, which contain enough butter and sugar to keep them rich and tender, génoise cakes require a soaking syrup to add moisture and flavor. Simply bring a mixture of sugar and water to a rolling boil in a small saucepan over medium-high heat, remove it from the heat, allow it to cool, and add the liqueur of your choice. Jam is also traditional; it adds not only moisture and flavor to the cake but a burst of color as well.

Génoise is traditionally frosted with buttercream. We have made many versions of buttercream in the test kitchen and decided to pair our génoise with the egg-white buttercream we used to frost our Coconut Layer Cake (page 355). This egg-white buttercream is particularly light and lithe and is a complement to the syrup-soaked cake.

In the test kitchen, tasters preferred thin layers of cake alternating with paper-thin layers of buttercream and jam, rather than one thick layer of filling between two cake layers, so we began by using a serrated knife to slice the cake into three equal layers. We then placed a small amount of buttercream in the center of a cardboard round cut slightly larger in diameter than the cake and inverted the top layer of the cake onto the cardboard round so that it became the bottom layer of our assembled cake. (The buttercream helps anchor the cake, so it will not slip and slide as you assemble it.) With a pastry brush, we brushed this layer with soaking syrup. (You can also use a spoon if a pastry brush is not handy.) Then, using an offset metal spatula, we spread thin layers of jam and buttercream on this cake layer. Next, we brushed both sides of the middle cake layer with soaking syrup and placed it on top of the first filled layer. Again,

we spread thin layers of jam and buttercream on the second layer. We then finished by inverting the bottom layer of cake, with its even crust, on top of the assembled cake layers to give the finished cake a smooth, flat surface.

Now we were ready to frost the cake. We found that frosting the cake with what pastry chefs call a crumb coat helped make the surface of the cake smooth, with no cake crumbs peeking through the frosting. We frosted the entire cake in a thin, even layer of frosting and then chilled it in the refrigerator until the buttercream was firm. We then finished the cake by spreading the remaining buttercream in a thicker layer over the top and sides of the cake.

Génoise

MAKES ONE 9-INCH CAKE

When transferring the batter from the bowl to the prepared pan, hold the bowl as close to the bottom of the pan as possible and use a rubber spatula to gently push the batter into the pan. To avoid deflating the voluminous batter, do not dump or pour the batter from a height of several inches or more above the pan.

4	tablespoons (½ stick) unsalted butter
1	cup (5 ounces) unbleached all-purpose flour
½	teaspoon salt
6	large eggs
1	cup (7 ounces) sugar
1	teaspoon vanilla extract

1. Adjust an oven rack to the middle position and heat the oven to 350 degrees. Line the bottom of a 9-inch springform pan with a circle of parchment paper.

2. Melt the butter in a small saucepan over low heat. Remove from the heat and set aside. Sift the flour and salt together onto a large piece of parchment paper; set aside.

3. Whisk together the eggs and sugar in the bowl of a standing mixer until combined. Place the bowl over a pan of barely simmering water, making sure that the water does not touch the bottom of the bowl, and heat the egg mixture, whisking constantly, until warm to the touch, about 110 degrees on an instant-read thermometer. Remove from the

heat and beat at medium-high speed until the eggs are pale, cream-colored, voluminous, and form a thick ribbon of tiny billowy bubbles that falls from the whisk and rests on top of the batter for several seconds when the whisk is held about 4 inches above the egg mixture (this should take 6 to 8 minutes). Beat in the vanilla. Turn off the mixer, transfer 1 cup of the egg mixture to a medium bowl, and stir in the melted butter until combined; set aside. Grab the two ends of the sheet of parchment paper holding the flour mixture and, with the mixer running at the lowest speed, slowly sprinkle the flour mixture into the batter until just barely incorporated, following the illustration on page 365. Add the melted butter mixture back to the batter in the standing mixer bowl and, with the mixer still running at the lowest speed, fold gently to incorporate, being careful not to deflate the batter.

4. Immediately push the batter from the bowl into the prepared springform pan with a rubber spatula, holding the bowl close to the bottom of the pan. Smooth the top with an offset spatula. Bake until the cake is deep golden brown and springs back lightly when pressed with a finger, about 35 minutes. Transfer the pan to a wire rack and cool completely. When the cake is cool, run the blade of a thin metal spatula around the inside circumference of the springform pan to loosen the cake from the sides of the pan and remove. Invert the cake onto a plate or baking sheet, remove the pan bottom and parchment paper, and reinvert the cake onto the rack. Proceed with the Génoise Layer Cake with Almond Buttercream and Raspberry Filling or the Génoise Layer Cake with Mocha Buttercream.

➤ VARIATION

Chocolate Génoise

This chocolate génoise is used in our Sacher Torte (page 376) and Black Forest Cake (page 378).

Follow the recipe for Génoise, replacing ¼ cup of the flour with ¼ cup Dutch-processed cocoa. Proceed as directed, baking the cake until it springs back lightly when pressed with a finger, about 35 minutes.

Génoise Layer Cake with Almond Buttercream and Raspberry Filling

SERVES 10 TO 12

Unlike butter cakes, génoise benefits from refrigeration. For the best flavor, assemble the cake a day in advance and refrigerate it for at least 12 hours to allow the flavors to meld and the cake to absorb the moisture of the soaking syrup.

AMARETTO SOAKING SYRUP

¼	cup (1 ¾ ounces) sugar
⅓	cup water, plus additional water if necessary
¼	cup amaretto or other almond-flavored liqueur

ALMOND BUTTERCREAM

4	large egg whites
1	cup (7 ounces) sugar
	Pinch salt
1	pound (4 sticks) unsalted butter, softened but still cool, each stick cut into 6 pieces
¼	cup amaretto

FILLING AND DECORATION

1	cup seedless raspberry jam
1 ½	cups sliced almonds
1	recipe Génoise (page 366), cooled and split into 3 layers following the instructions on page 368

1. FOR THE SOAKING SYRUP: Bring the sugar and water to a rolling boil in a small saucepan over high heat. Remove the pan from the heat, cover, and cool completely. Transfer the syrup to a liquid measuring cup, add the amaretto, and add additional water if necessary to bring the liquid to ⅔ cup. Set aside. (The syrup can be refrigerated in an airtight container for up to 1 month.)

2. FOR THE BUTTERCREAM: Combine the whites, sugar, and salt in the clean bowl of a standing mixer; set the bowl over a saucepan of barely simmering water, making sure that the water does not touch the bottom of the bowl. Whisk constantly until the mixture is opaque and warm to the touch and registers about 120 degrees on an instant-read thermometer, about 2 minutes. (Note that this temperature is

not hot enough to eliminate the unlikely presence of salmonella bacteria in the eggs.)

3. Beat the whites at medium-high speed until barely warm (about 80 degrees) and the whites are glossy and sticky, about 7 minutes. Reduce the speed to medium and beat in the butter 1 piece at a time. Beat in the amaretto. Stop the mixer and scrape down the bottom and sides of the bowl. Continue to beat at medium speed until well combined, about 1 minute. Cover the bowl with plastic wrap and set aside at room temperature for up to 6 hours. (The buttercream may be refrigerated in an airtight container for 1 week or frozen for up to 1 month. Bring to room temperature and whisk well before using.)

4. FOR THE FILLING AND DECORATION: Adjust an oven rack to the middle position and heat the oven to 350 degrees. Stir the jam in a small bowl until smooth; set aside. Spread the sliced almonds on a rimmed baking sheet and cook until golden brown, redistributing the almonds several times throughout the baking time to avoid uneven browning, about 12 minutes. Transfer the almonds to a plate to cool completely.

5. TO ASSEMBLE THE CAKE: Put a dab of buttercream frosting on a cardboard round cut just larger than the diameter of the cake. Invert and center the top cake layer on the round. Using a pastry brush, brush some of the soaking syrup over the cake layer. Place ½ cup raspberry jam on the center of the cake layer and spread a thin layer of jam over the cake. Place a large dollop of buttercream on top of the jam and spread the buttercream in a thin even layer over the cake. Brush both sides of the middle layer with more soaking syrup and place the middle layer on top of the first, filled layer. Spread the remaining jam and another dollop of buttercream over the middle layer. Finally, brush the final layer of cake with the remaining soaking syrup and invert this layer over the filled layers. Frost the cake according to the illustrations on page 144. Refrigerate until ready to serve.

6. TO SERVE: Finish the cake by pressing sliced almonds into the sides of the cake (see the illustration on page 349). Cut into slices and serve.

➤ VARIATION

Génoise Layer Cake with Mocha Buttercream

Follow the instructions for Génoise Layer Cake with Almond Buttercream and Raspberry Filling, omitting the jam, substituting Kahlúa for the amaretto in the soaking syrup, adding only 3 sticks butter to the buttercream instead of 4, whisking in 8 ounces melted bittersweet chocolate, and adding 1 tablespoon instant espresso powder dissolved in 1 tablespoon water to the finished buttercream in place of the amaretto.

LEVELING AND SPLITTING A CAKE

1. If the cake has mounded in the center, it should be leveled before being split. Gently press an out-stretched hand on its surface and, holding a serrated knife parallel to the work surface, use a steady sawing motion to begin cutting at the same level as the cake's lowest point, slicing off the mound.

2. To cut into even layers, measure the height of the cake with a ruler and cut a small incision into the side with a paring knife to mark the desired thickness of your layers. Repeat every 3 to 4 inches around the circumference of the cake.

3. With a long serrated knife held parallel to the work surface, score the cake: With an outstretched palm gently pressed on the surface, slowly spin the cake away from you while pulling the knife toward you. The goal is to connect the incisions and score the cake, not to slice it.

4. Following the markings on the cake, cut deeper and deeper in the same manner. Gradually move the knife closer to the cake's center with each rotation. When the knife progresses past the cake's center, the cut is complete. Carefully slide the knife out and separate the layers.

RASPBERRY JELLY ROLL

IMPRESSIVE LOOKING WITH ITS INWARD spiral of fruit preserves, the classic jelly roll cake is a sure-fire crowd pleaser that has a reputation for being more complicated than its simple, elegant appearance would suggest. A basic sponge cake slathered with jam, rolled into a spiral, and dusted with powdered sugar, the cake becomes complicated when it resists assuming its characteristic shape, cracks, or becomes soggy and squat. We entered the test kitchen eager to make the simple jelly roll cake reliably uncomplicated to make.

Sponge cakes are the cake of choice for jelly rolls. Unlike butter cakes, sponge cakes depend upon eggs, whole or separated, beaten to a foam to provide lift and structure. Because of their airy, light crumb, sponge cakes are flexible and take well to rolling. While in the past we have made jelly rolls with a variety of sponge cakes, we decided to develop a jelly roll based on a génoise, a classic French cake leavened by beaten whole eggs that takes well to a variety of applications and bakes well in a number of different baking pans. (For detailed instructions on making a génoise, see page 364.) To make the characteristic jelly roll shape, the cake batter must be baked in an 18 by 12-inch rimmed baking sheet, otherwise known as a jelly roll pan. We found that an offset spatula makes pushing the cake batter against the sides of the pan and into the corners a breeze. Determining when the cake is properly cooked is a little more difficult than it is with a regular American layer cake. A génoise, like all sponge cakes, should provide some resistance and not feel as if one just touched the top of a soufflé. Another good test is color. The top of the cake should be a nice light brown color, not pale golden or a dark, rich brown.

We knew when we began testing that the trick would be forming the jelly roll's classic spiral shape. We tried two different methods of coaxing the cake out of the baking pan and rolling it into a cylinder. First, we tried inverting the just-baked cake onto parchment paper and then rolling the cake and paper together into the jelly roll shape. We found that the parchment paper was difficult to roll smoothly and occasionally stuck to the cake, making reshaping the cake once the jam

was added difficult. We then tried inverting the just-baked cake onto a clean kitchen towel dusted liberally with confectioners' sugar and then rolling the cake and towel together into a jelly roll shape to cool. We much preferred this method. The soft, pliable towel—which should be at least 2 inches longer and wider than the cake—rolled easily, and the confectioners' sugar prevented the towel from sticking to the cake. After we rolled it into a spiral—towel and all—we cooled the cake about ten minutes, unrolled it carefully, spread the jam on the cake in a thin, even layer with an offset spatula, sprinkled the cake with fresh raspberries, and rerolled the cake, this time gently pulling the towel away from the cake.

We also uncovered several other steps toward rolling the cake easily and reliably. We found that the cake rolls best when it has just barely finished baking. If the cake is overbaked, it forms a firm crust that causes the cake to crack when rolled. Also, if the cake is left to cool completely before it is rolled up, the crumb becomes less flexible and resists bending into the required shape. We found that trimming the crisp edges of the cake also helped the cake roll easily.

To serve the cake, trim the edges of the roll and dust the cake with powdered sugar. Using a serrated knife, cut the cake into slices and serve with fresh raspberries as a garnish. Like all cakes made from a génoise batter, this cake stores well. Cover the cake with plastic wrap and refrigerate for up to four days.

Raspberry Jelly Roll

SERVES 8 TO 10

Although this recipe calls for a standing mixer, the cake may be made with a handheld mixer. Beat the eggs and sugar for an additional 6 to 8 minutes and incorporate the flour mixture and the lightened butter mixture with a rubber spatula. When transferring the batter from the bowl to the prepared pan, hold the bowl as close to the bottom of the pan as possible and use a rubber spatula to gently push the batter into the pan. To avoid deflating the voluminous batter, do not dump or pour the batter from a height of several inches or more above the pan. Use an offset spatula to gently push the batter against the sides and into the corners of the baking pan.

GÉNOISE

I	cup (5 ounces) unbleached all-purpose flour, plus extra for dusting the pan
4	tablespoons (½ stick) unsalted butter
½	teaspoon salt
6	large eggs
I	cup (7 ounces) granulated sugar
I	teaspoon vanilla extract
¼	cup (I ounce) confectioners' sugar

FILLING AND GARNISH

¾	cup raspberry jam
2	cups (9 ounces) fresh raspberries
¼	cup (I ounce) confectioners' sugar

1. For the génoise: Adjust an oven rack to the middle position and heat the oven to 350 degrees. Grease the bottom and sides of an 18 by 12-inch rimmed baking sheet, cover the pan bottom with parchment paper or waxed paper, grease the paper, and dust with flour, tapping out the excess.

2. Melt the butter in a small saucepan over low heat. Remove from the heat and set aside. Sift the flour and salt together onto a large piece of parchment paper. Set aside.

3. Whisk together the eggs and sugar in the bowl of a standing mixer until combined. Place the bowl over a pan of barely simmering water and heat the egg mixture, whisking constantly, until warm to the touch, about 110 degrees on an instant-read thermometer. Remove from the heat and beat at medium-high speed until the eggs are

pale, cream-colored, voluminous, and form a thick ribbon of tiny billowy bubbles that falls from the whisk and rests on top of the batter for several seconds when the whisk is held about 4 inches above the egg mixture (this should take 6 to 8 minutes). Beat in the vanilla. Turn off the mixer and transfer 1 cup of the egg mixture to a medium bowl and stir in the reserved melted butter until combined; set aside. Grab the two ends of the sheet of parchment paper holding the flour mixture and, with the mixer at the lowest speed, slowly sprinkle the flour mixture into the batter until just barely incorporated, following the illustration on page 365. Add the melted butter mixture back to the batter in the standing mixer bowl and, with the mixer at the lowest speed, fold gently to incorporate, being careful not to deflate the batter.

4. Holding the bowl close to the bottom of the prepared pan, immediately pour the batter into the prepared pan, using an offset spatula to push the batter against the sides and into the corners of the pan and smooth the top. Bake until the cake is deep golden brown, springs back lightly when pressed with a finger, and is beginning to pull away from the sides of the pan, about 25 minutes.

5. Meanwhile, sift the confectioners' sugar evenly over a kitchen towel measuring at least 20 by 14 inches. When the cake is done, run the blade of a metal spatula around the edge of the pan and immediately invert the cake onto the towel. Remove the parchment paper the cake was baked on. With a serrated knife, trim a scant ⅛-inch strip of crust from

ASSEMBLING A JELLY ROLL CAKE

1. Starting from a short side, roll the cake—towel and all—into a jelly roll shape. Cool for 10 minutes.

2. Unroll the cooled cake. Using an offset spatula, spread the jam over the surface of the cake, leaving a 1-inch border around the edges. Sprinkle half the raspberries evenly over the cake.

3. Reroll the cake gently but snugly around the filling, carefully peeling off the towel as you roll. Dust the top of the cake with confectioners' sugar.

4. Trim thin slices from both ends and then cut the cake into individual slices, using an electric or serrated knife, and garnish with raspberries.

all four sides of the cake. Fold one end of the sugared kitchen towel over a short end of the cake and, beginning at the short end, roll the towel and cake together into a spiral. Set the cake aside on a rack, seam-side down, until cool, about 10 minutes.

6. FOR THE FILLING: Meanwhile, stir the jam with a rubber spatula in a medium bowl until smooth and spreadable. Set aside.

7. TO ASSEMBLE THE CAKE: When the cake is almost cool, unroll the cake and, using an offset spatula, evenly spread a thin layer of jam over the cake, leaving a 1-inch border around the edges. Sprinkle half the raspberries evenly over the cake. Reroll the cake gently but snugly around the filling, carefully peeling off the kitchen towel as you roll. Trim both ends of the jelly roll cake on the diagonal. Sprinkle the cake with the confectioners' sugar. Using an electric or serrated knife, cut the cake into evenly proportioned slices, garnish with the remaining raspberries, and serve.

BAKED ALASKA

A TOWERING MOUND OF SPIKY GOLDEN meringue hiding a dome of cake and ice cream, baked Alaska is not only a visually spectacular dessert but also an example of the marvels of heat transfer. A frozen dome of génoise cake and ice cream is inverted onto an ovenproof platter, covered in peaks and valleys of meringue, and then placed in a hot oven until the meringue turns golden brown. Miraculously, it seems, the ice cream remains frozen while the meringue cooks. A study in contrasting textures and temperatures— the soft, warm meringue against the firm, frozen ice cream—the dessert demonstrates the insulating properties of air. Trapped among the meringue's protein bonds are tiny air bubbles that prevent the hot air in the oven from reaching the ice cream before the meringue achieves the proper color. In the test kitchen we set out to find the right cake and perfect meringue for this classic dessert.

Traditionally, baked Alaska is made with a sponge cake that, once baked and cooled, has the flexibility to conform to a mold. After reviewing a number of different cakes collected within these pages, our génoise cake proved the natural choice (see page 364 for more information on this cake). We experimented with several different ways of baking the cake and shaping the mold. After baking the cake batter in a springform pan, two cake pans, a loaf pan, and a rimmed baking sheet, we opted for the final choice. Although recipes call for a range of shapes, our tasters liked the dome, or mound, shape that is traditional for the dessert, and a 1½-quart bowl serves well as a mold.

We developed different templates to cut the cake into the correct shape to line the bowl. Transferring detailed measurements of the bowl's diameter and depth onto a piece of parchment paper and then using that as a guide helped us slice the cake into the precise shapes to line the bottom, sides, and top of the mold. But it was all very complicated. Looking for a simpler method, we instead used a serrated knife to slice the cooled cake crosswise into 10 strips and then essentially cut-and-pasted the strips along the sides and bottom of the plastic wrap–lined bowl. After filling it with ice cream, we covered the top of the mold with the remaining cake strips. This simple method required no complicated template; we just packed the strips close together to properly insulate the ice cream from the oven's high heat. The thick coating of meringue hid the chinks in the cake from view. The cake needs to cover the entire interior of the bowl, so we cut smaller pieces as needed and trimmed strips of cake flush with the top edge of the bowl. When the cake was in place, we used a pastry brush to brush it with flavored soaking syrup.

Filling the cake mold with ice cream was initially tricky. We started by softening the ice cream at room temperature, transferring it to a bowl, and stirring it with a rubber spatula to make it spreadable. Too often, however, the ice cream did more than soften. Some of the ice cream melted completely, and once refrozen, it had an icy, granular texture because the ice crystals in the melted ice cream were too large when they froze again. We solved this problem by cutting the ice cream from its container while quite cold and then breaking it into small, evenly sized pieces in a large bowl using a wooden spoon. This way, all of the ice cream became soft and pliable at the same time. It was quick work to pack the soft ice cream into the cake-lined mold. Once we topped it with the remaining syrup-soaked cake, we wrapped the molded cake tightly in plastic and froze it until firm.

Baked Alaska calls for a sturdy meringue, one that will be able to withstand the withering heat of the oven. We knew that the simple French meringue that we developed for our cookies would not work well in this application since it was so delicate. Baked Alaska requires the most stable meringue, an egg white and sugar combination called Italian meringue. This form of meringue is made by beating egg whites and adding hot sugar syrup to them as they are being beaten. We found that using room temperature egg whites was important because it enabled the whites to reach the correct temperature when the hot syrup was added (for bringing eggs to room temperature quickly, see page 321). Also, we found that adding the sugar syrup at the soft-ball stage, around 238 degrees, to the whites when they had just reached the soft peak stage ensured the best texture. Because this step must be timed right, we found that beating the eggs on a work surface next to the stovetop made coordinating the whites and the syrup easier. Once the syrup is added, we beat the mixture until cool and then added vanilla extract.

Just before serving the baked Alaska, we inverted the génoise–ice cream dome onto an ovenproof plate and removed the plastic wrap and bowl. We found that a 9-inch Pyrex pie plate works perfectly with a 7½-inch diameter, 1½-quart bowl. We covered the cake with the meringue, placed the plate on a sheet pan, and baked it in a 425-degree oven until the meringue turned golden brown, about 5 minutes. (A properly heated oven is crucial; at cooler oven temperatures, the ice cream will melt before the meringue browns.) Dramatic and delicious, our baked Alaska was ready to be cut and served on individual plates.

Baked Alaska

SERVES 6 TO 8

For the soaking syrup, choose a liqueur that best complements your choice of ice cream. Rum, Kahlúa, amaretto, and Grand Marnier all work well with vanilla, chocolate, coffee, chocolate chip, or caramel-flavored dulce de leche ice cream. The cake can be prepared and assembled, excluding the meringue, up to 1 week in advance and stored, well wrapped, in the freezer. The meringue, however, must be applied and baked just before serving. Follow the illustrations on page 373 for tips on assembling this cake.

CAKE, SYRUP, AND ICE CREAM
1	recipe Génoise for Raspberry Jelly Roll (page 369), prepared through step 4 and omitting confectioners' sugar
2	tablespoons sugar
⅓	cup water
¼	cup liqueur of your choice
2	pints ice cream of your choice

MERINGUE
½	cup water
1	cup (7 ounces) sugar
4	large egg whites, at room temperature
	Pinch salt
¼	teaspoon cream of tartar
½	teaspoon vanilla extract

1. FOR THE CAKE, SYRUP, AND ICE CREAM: When the cake is cool, run the blade of a metal spatula around the edge of the pan, place a large sheet of parchment paper over the cake followed by a wire rack, invert the cake onto the rack, and remove the parchment paper the cake was baked on. Place an inverted jelly roll pan on the cake and reinvert the cake so that it is right side up on the inverted jelly roll pan; remove the second sheet of parchment paper. Use a serrated knife to slice the cake widthwise into ten 1¾-inch slices.

2. Place the sugar and water in a small saucepan, cover, and bring to a boil. Remove the pan from the heat, cool, and add the liqueur. Set aside.

3. Line a 1½-quart bowl with plastic wrap, letting the ends of the plastic wrap overhang the

bowl by 6 inches. Line the sides and bottom of the bowl with cake by placing the strips snugly next to each other and cutting them flush with the edge of the bowl. Using a pastry brush, brush the soaking syrup over the cake in the bowl and the remaining strips of cake.

4. Cut the ice cream from its container and transfer it to a large bowl (or 2 medium bowls if using 2 flavors of ice cream). Using a wooden spoon, break the ice cream into small pieces. Let the ice cream sit at room temperature until it is pliable but not melted, 2 to 7 minutes. Transfer the ice cream to the cake-lined bowl and use a rubber spatula to press the ice cream along the sides and bottom of the mold. (If using 2 flavors, place the mold in the freezer until the ice cream is firm before adding the second flavor.) Cover the ice cream with the remaining strips of cake. Fold the edges of the plastic wrap over the cake and ice cream and freeze until firm, at least 2 hours.

5. FOR THE MERINGUE: Combine the water and sugar in a small saucepan. Cover and bring to a boil over medium-high heat. Boil, swirling the pan once or twice, until the sugar has dissolved, 1 to 2 minutes. If necessary, wash down any sugar crystals on the side of the pan with a damp pastry brush. Cook, uncovered, until the temperature registers 238 degrees on a candy thermometer, about 10 minutes.

6. While the syrup is cooking, place the egg whites in the bowl of a standing mixer fitted with the whisk. Beat the whites at medium-low speed until frothy, about 1 minute. Add the salt and cream of tartar and beat, gradually increasing the speed to medium-high, until the whites hold soft peaks, about 1 minute.

7. Adjust an oven rack to the middle position and heat the oven to 425 degrees.

8. With the mixer at medium speed, slowly pour the hot syrup into the egg whites, avoiding the whisk. Increase the speed to medium-high and continue to beat until the meringue cools to room temperature and becomes very thick and shiny, 5 to 10 minutes. Whisk in the vanilla; cover and refrigerate up to 2 hours.

9. Remove the chilled cake from the freezer and unfold the plastic wrap. Invert onto an ovenproof pie plate or platter and remove the bowl and plastic wrap. Using an offset spatula, spread the meringue all over the top and sides of the dome, sealing the meringue onto the plate. Make spikes of meringue by pulling the spatula off the meringue in short, quick strokes. Place on a baking sheet and bake until the meringue is golden brown, about 5 minutes. Remove from the oven, cut into wedges, and serve immediately.

ASSEMBLING BAKED ALASKA

  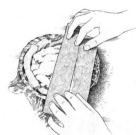 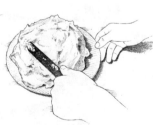

1. With a serrated knife and a ruler, cut the cake widthwise into ten 1³/₄-inch-wide strips.

2. Line the sides and bottom of the prepared bowl with cake by placing the strips snugly next to each other and cutting them flush with the edge of the bowl.

3. After filling the bowl with the softened ice cream, cover the ice cream with remaining strips of cake. (There may be a strip or two of cake remaining.) Trim the edges flush with the sides of the bowl and wrap tightly with plastic wrap.

4. After chilling and unmolding, use an offset spatula to spread the meringue all over the top and sides of the dome, completely covering the cake. Make spikes of meringue by pulling the spatula off the meringue in short, quick strokes.

FRESH FRUIT TRIFLE

A CELEBRATORY DESSERT WITH A LONG HISTORY in both England and America, the trifle is what its name implies: a little bit of this and a little bit of that. Alternating layers of liqueur-soaked sponge cake, custard, and fruit or jam are topped with billowy clouds of whipped cream, all visible through the sides of the clear glass, straight-sided bowl in which it is traditionally served. The trifle has unfairly fallen out of fashion, perhaps because it is too often thought of as a heavy, soggy, and bland dessert served at stiflingly formal family gatherings with distant relatives. We wanted to rejuvenate this tired classic and make it the delicate and creamy dessert it is meant to be.

Trifle is traditionally made with sponge cake, a broad category of cake that generally relies on beaten eggs, whole or separated, to provide lift and structure. Sponge cakes have a lower proportion of fat than traditional American butter cakes and are consequently lighter in texture and flavor. Sponge cakes work well in trifles because they readily absorb the flavors of the liqueur, fruit, and custard and keep the texture of the assembled dessert buoyant rather than heavy. We tested cake recipes and decided to use our favorite génoise recipe. Leavened by beaten whole eggs, the génoise has a lean, airy crumb and a delicate texture that absorbs flavors well and complements, but does not compete with, the rich texture of the custard. Baking the génoise cake in a rimmed baking sheet allowed us to soak the cake evenly in liqueur and then cut

ASSEMBLING THE TRIFLE

1. Using a serrated knife, cut the cake into 6 lengthwise and 8 crosswise strips to yield 48 approximately 2-inch squares.

2. Arrange 16 cake squares, fallen-domino style, around the bottom of a 14- to 16-cup glass trifle dish, placing 12 or 13 squares in a ring against the wall of the dish and the remaining squares in the center.

3. Arrange about ²/₃ cup each raspberries, strawberries, and blueberries and one half sliced kiwi over the cake squares.

4. Spread a third of the pastry cream, about 1 cup, over the layer, coming to within ¹/₂ inch of the edge. Repeat layering cake, fruit, and pastry cream to make a total of 3 layers, reserving ¹/₄ cup raspberries, ¹/₄ cup strawberries, ¹/₄ cup blueberries, and half a kiwi for garnish. Pipe or spoon the whipped cream over the top before garnishing with the reserved fruit.

the cake into uniform 2-inch squares, which we found were the ideal size to fan into layers in the trifle. Tasters gave high marks to cake soaked in Grand Marnier, although other wines and liqueurs such as amaretto or cognac may also be used.

Trifle recipes vary in the type of custard called for. Some use thick, eggy custard, while others call for smoother, creamier custard. We made several different versions in the test kitchen and preferred a type of custard called pastry cream. Cooked in a saucepan on the stovetop like a homemade pudding, pastry cream combines milk or cream with eggs, sugar, and starch—usually either cornstarch or flour. (For a detailed discussion of pastry cream, see page 226.)

Following recipes we found in our research, we made versions of trifle with jam, fresh fruit, and a combination of the two. Tasters preferred the trifle with fruit alone. The fruit was more flavorful and provided better textural contrast to the cake and custard than the jam. Also, artfully arranged along the outside perimeter of the bowl, the fresh fruit elevated the presentation to a new level and made it as visually stunning as it was delicious.

Making trifle requires advance preparation. The custard and cake may both be made in advance. The cake may be stored, wrapped in an airtight container, up to three days in the refrigerator or up to one month in the freezer. The custard may be stored, covered in an airtight container, up to two days in the refrigerator before assembling the trifle. Soak the cake with the Grand Marnier just before assembling it.

Fresh Fruit Trifle

SERVES 8 TO 10

The trifle should be made at least 6 hours before serving so that the flavors of the fruit, custard, and liqueur can meld. Once assembled, refrigerate the trifle, covered well with plastic wrap, for up to 36 hours. Top the trifle with freshly made whipped cream and additional fresh fruit just before serving. If you don't own a trifle bowl, a large glass bowl, roughly 2 to 3 quarts, can work as well.

1	recipe Génoise for Raspberry Jelly Roll (page 369), prepared through step 4 and omitting confectioners' sugar
1/2	cup Grand Marnier

2¼	cups (about 10 ounces) raspberries
2¼	cups (about 12 ounces) strawberries, hulled and quartered
2¼	cups (about 10 ounces) blueberries
2	kiwi, peeled, halved vertically and sliced into ¼-inch half moons
1	recipe Pastry Cream (page 227), covered and chilled

WHIPPED CREAM

1½	cups heavy cream, chilled
1½	tablespoons sugar
1½	teaspoons vanilla extract

1. Immediately after baking the cake, free the cake edges from the pan sides with a knife and smooth a sheet of parchment paper over the cake top. Place a second baking sheet on top of the cake. Invert the cake, then lift off the baking pan. Let the cake cool completely, then gently peel the parchment paper off the cake bottom, removing the bottom crust. Reinvert the cake, top-side up, then peel off the second sheet of parchment paper, removing the top crust. Brush the cake evenly with the Grand Marnier; let stand about 10 minutes. Following the illustrations on page 374, use a serrated knife to cut the cake into 6 lengthwise and 8 crosswise strips to yield 48 approximately 2-inch squares. Set aside.

2. Arrange 16 cake squares, fallen-domino style, around the bottom of a 14- to 16-cup footed glass trifle dish (or equivalent glass bowl), placing 12 to 13 squares in a ring against the dish wall and the remaining squares in the center. Arrange about ⅔ cup each raspberries, strawberries, and blueberries, and a quarter of the kiwi slices over the cake squares. Spread a third of the pastry cream, about 1 cup, over the layer, coming to within ½ inch of the edge. Repeat layering cake, fruit, and pastry cream to make a total of 3 layers, reserving ¼ cup raspberries, ¼ cup strawberries, ¼ cup blueberries, and a quarter of the kiwi slices for garnish. Cover the bowl with plastic wrap and refrigerate for at least 6 hours but no more than 36 hours.

3. FOR THE WHIPPED CREAM: When ready to serve, beat the cream and sugar in the chilled bowl of a standing mixer at medium speed to soft peaks; add the vanilla. Continue to beat to barely stiff

peaks. Using a pastry bag, pipe the whipped cream over the top of the trifle. (Or, simply spread the whipped cream with a spoon.) Garnish with the reserved fruit and serve immediately.

SACHER TORTE

A CREATION OF EARLY 19TH-CENTURY Vienna, the Sacher torte is a chocolate cake flavored with apricot jam or glaze and coated with a thin, rich layer of chocolate. Despite the dessert's simplicity, we found countless different recipes— everything from the cake to the filling and icing was called into question. With our heads spinning with the different avenues to explore, we went into the test kitchen determined to make this elegant, flavorful dessert live up to its refined reputation.

We began our testing at square one by baking and tasting a variety of chocolate cakes. Devil's food cake and American chocolate butter cakes were quickly ruled out for this dessert as either too sweet or too rich. We tried sponge cakes, some laced with finely ground nuts (a traditional touch we found in several recipes), and compared those against our Chocolate Génoise cake recipe. Tasters much preferred the chocolate génoise. Relatively light in texture, the cake had just the right amount of chocolate flavor and richness. Easy to make, the chocolate génoise delivered a delicate chocolate flavor and light texture that readily absorbed the flavor of the apricot jam and complemented the sleek chocolate glaze. (For more information on génoise, see page 364.)

As for the apricot flavoring, some recipes claim that the cake should simply be coated in an apricot glaze made from apricot jam that has been simmered with additional sugar until syrupy and strained of any chunky pieces. Others claim that a layer of raw apricot jam sandwiched between layers of cake, in addition to the coating of glaze, is the more authentic version. In the test kitchen, we tasted both versions and much preferred the additional layer of jam in the center of the cake. Tasters found the fresher, more pronounced apricot flavor a better accent to the cake's rich chocolate coating. Some testers felt that the chunky bits of fruit marred the cake's texture, so we opted to process the jam in a food processor until relatively smooth. Briefly heating the jam made it easier to spread onto the cake.

For the smooth chocolate topping, we tried a variety of different chocolate glazes. Most were variations on ganache, a mixture of melted chocolate and cream, often with butter added. Although delicious in their own right (we have used ganache in many other applications, such as in Yellow Cupcakes on page 345 and Yule Log Cake on page 386), these coatings were too thick and creamy. They were more akin to frosting than glaze. We then tried adding corn syrup to the chocolate and cream as we had done for our Boston Cream Pie (page 357). The result was just right. Adding the corn syrup gave the glaze a sleek, shiny texture and a smooth pourable consistency.

Its long and famous history would suggest that this cake is for adventurous pastry experts alone. But in reality the cake requires few ingredients and, with our Chocolate Génoise, store-bought apricot jam, and our chocolate glaze, is simple to make, too.

Sacher Torte

SERVES 8 TO 10

This cake stores very well in an airtight container or under a glass cake dome in the refrigerator for up to 48 hours. The cake texture becomes slightly more dense and the overall flavor more intense after at least 6 hours in the refrigerator. Bring the cake to room temperature before serving with whipped cream (see page 500) and, according to tradition, a cup of strong coffee.

APRICOT FILLING

1 (18-ounce) jar apricot jam (about 1 1/3 cups)

CHOCOLATE GLAZE

1/2 cup heavy cream

2 tablespoons light corn syrup

4 ounces semisweet or bittersweet chocolate, chopped

1/2 teaspoon vanilla extract

1 recipe Chocolate Génoise (page 367), cooled and split in half following instructions on page 368

1. FOR THE FILLING: Process the apricot jam in a food processor until smooth, about 10 seconds. Transfer to a small saucepan and bring to a simmer, stirring constantly, over medium heat. Remove from the heat and set aside.

2. FOR THE GLAZE: Bring the cream and corn syrup to a full simmer over medium heat in a medium saucepan. Off heat, add the chocolate; cover and let stand for 8 minutes. (If the chocolate has not completely melted, return the saucepan to low heat and stir constantly until melted.) Add the vanilla; stir very gently until the mixture is smooth. Cool until tepid so that a spoonful drizzled back into the pan mounds slightly. (The glaze can be refrigerated to speed up the cooling process, stirring every few minutes to ensure even cooling.)

3. TO ASSEMBLE THE TORTE: Invert the top layer of the cake onto a cardboard round cut just larger than the diameter of the cake. Using an offset spatula, spread ½ cup of the apricot jam evenly over the cake. Invert the second layer of cake over the first. Place the cake and cardboard round on a wire rack that has been set on a large rimmed baking sheet. Pour the remaining apricot jam on the top of the cake and, using an offset spatula, spread the jam over the edges and along the sides of the cake. Allow the excess jam to fall off the sides of the cake onto the baking sheet. Refrigerate the cake on the wire rack set on the baking sheet until the apricot jam is set, about 30 minutes.

4. Pour the chocolate glaze on top of the cake. Using an offset spatula, spread the glaze evenly over the top of the cake and spread it along the sides of the cake. Refrigerate the cake, still on the rack set over the baking sheet, until set, at least 1 hour and up to 48 hours. Transfer the cake to a large platter and serve.

BLACK FOREST CAKE

A CLASSIC CAKE FROM SWABIA IN THE BLACK Forest region of Germany, Black Forest cake is an architectural masterpiece that combines layers of kirsch-soaked (cherry-flavored brandy) chocolate cake with marinated cherries and thick drifts of sweetened whipped cream. Finished with a garnish of chocolate shavings and additional cherries, it's one of those over-the-top cakes that children dream of and adults find irresistible. While we found recipes of all stripes, from simple to incredibly complex, we chose to develop a recipe as streamlined as possible that focused on the dessert's key components—cherries, chocolate, and whipped cream.

First things first: We tested several different kinds of chocolate cake. Tasters found American-style chocolate cakes inappropriate for this dessert, as they were too rich to absorb the flavors of the cherries and the soaking syrup. We guessed a chocolate sponge cake, with its lighter texture, would be the best option (and closer to the original recipe). After comparing different types of sponge cake, tasters preferred a chocolate génoise (the recipe for which is found on page 367) because the cake's light, airy texture perfectly absorbed the cherry juices and kirsch soaking syrup.

Cake in hand, we tackled the cherry filling and whipped cream. Tart sour cherries are the best type for Black Forest cake, as their acidity accents the richness of the chocolate and whipped cream. Sweet cherries, while good eaten out of hand, lack the necessary tartness. Fresh sour cherries, however, can be nearly impossible to find, due to their brief season and sparse availability. Most canned cherries, aka pie filling, leave us disappointed by their bland flavor and mushy texture. Jarred cherries, however, are altogether different. These cherries taste bright and fruity, and they are firm textured. They are ideal for the filling, especially when galvanized by a shot of kirsch.

As for the whipped cream filling and topping, we found ourselves in a bit of a quandary. We knew that the cake would best absorb the flavors of the soaking syrup and cherries if it were refrigerated for at least several hours. Yet, our basic whipped cream recipe (page 500) was too delicate to withstand such a lengthy stay in the refrigerator. We considered ways of stabilizing the whipped cream. Adding gelatin is a traditional method used to prolong the life of whipped cream and prevent it from "weeping," or exuding liquid. Working with gelatin, however, can be fussy—proper temperature and exacting measuring are crucial to success—so it is something we generally like to avoid. We then considered adding cornstarch to the whipped cream. We knew from previous savory and sweet applications that cornstarch absorbs liquid and helps thicken sauces, custards, puddings, and the like. But adding the starch directly to the whipped cream imparted an unpleasant chalky texture to the whipped cream. We then considered cooking the starch with the sugar and a small amount of the cream and then adding it to the whipping cream. The results were excellent. Cooking the starch got rid of the chalky texture. Yet, the starch continued to work its magic and stiffen the cream, and help retain liquid, preventing the cream from weeping as it chilled in the refrigerator for up to 48 hours.

Coating the sides of the frosted cake in chocolate shavings heightens the chocolate flavor and adds a festive element to the cake. We wanted to avoid techniques that required tempering, the process of heating and cooling chocolate to specific temperatures to ensure a smooth and shiny appearance and firm texture. Large chocolate curls were too heavy for the sides of this cake. After several experiments, we found that simply drawing a paring knife across a block of chocolate produced small curls that were the right size for our cake. The technique works best when the chocolate is at warm room temperature, about 80 degrees. Once the curls have been made, avoid touching them with your hands to prevent the chocolate from melting. The shavings are best applied to the frosted cake with an icing spatula.

Black Forest Cake

SERVES 8 TO 10

Do not overbeat the stabilized whipped cream. Beat the cream just until soft peaks begin to form. The movement of the metal spatula when filling and frosting the cake with the cream will cause the cream to thicken and stiffen

further. Also, be sure to add the cream and cornstarch mixture when it has cooled to room temperature. If you can find only cherries packed in water, skip step 2 and use the soaking syrup from the génoise cake found on page 367.

CHERRY FILLING AND DECORATION

2 cups jarred sour cherries in light syrup, drained, 1 cup syrup reserved (or high-quality canned sour cherries, drained)
½ cup kirsch or other cherry-flavored liqueur
½ cup (3½ ounces) sugar

WHIPPED CREAM FILLING AND FROSTING

¼ cup (1¾ ounces) sugar
1 tablespoon cornstarch
3 cups heavy cream, chilled
1½ teaspoons vanilla extract

CHOCOLATE SHAVINGS

7 ounces bittersweet chocolate

1 recipe Chocolate Génoise (page 367), cooled and split into 3 layers following instructions on page 368

1. FOR THE CHERRIES: Combine the cherries and kirsch in a bowl, cover, and set aside.

2. Bring the reserved cherry juice and the sugar to a simmer in a medium saucepan over medium heat and cook until the mixture is reduced to ½ cup, 8 to 10 minutes. Transfer the liquid to the bowl with the reserved cherry mixture, cover with plastic wrap, and set aside.

3. FOR THE WHIPPED CREAM: Place the sugar and cornstarch in a small saucepan. Stirring constantly, slowly add ½ cup of the cream. Bring the cream mixture to a boil over medium heat, stirring constantly, until the mixture simmers briefly and thickens, 2 to 3 minutes. Transfer the mixture to a small bowl and set aside to cool to room temperature.

4. Chill a nonreactive, deep bowl and the beaters of a standing mixer in the freezer for at least 20 minutes. (If the freezer is too crowded to accommodate the bowl, place the beaters in the bowl, fill

it with ice water, and chill on the counter. When the bowl and beaters are well chilled, dump out the ice water and dry thoroughly.)

5. Add the remaining 2½ cups cream and vanilla to the chilled bowl and beat on low speed until small bubbles form, about 30 seconds. Increase the speed to medium and continue beating until the beaters leave a trail, about 30 seconds. Slowly add the cooled cornstarch mixture and continue beating until the cream is smooth, thick, and forms soft peaks, 30 to 60 seconds. If necessary, finish beating with a whisk to adjust consistency. Cover and refrigerate until ready to use, up to 8 hours.

6. FOR THE CHOCOLATE SHAVINGS: Following illustration 1 on page 349, use a paring knife to scrape chocolate shavings from the block of chocolate. Transfer to a plate with a frosting spatula and set aside in a cool, dry place.

7. TO ASSEMBLE THE CAKE: Using a slotted spoon, remove 8 cherries from the syrup and reserve for the garnish. Remove the remaining cherries from the syrup with the slotted spoon, transfer to a cutting board, and slice in half. Set aside.

8. Place a cardboard round in the bottom of a 9-inch springform pan. Invert the top layer of cake onto the cardboard round. Using a pastry brush, brush about ¼ cup of the cherry syrup over the cake layer. Using an offset spatula, spread ½ cup of the whipped cream over the cake. Dot the whipped cream with half of the sliced cherries. Brush another ¼ cup of the syrup over the middle cake layer and invert this layer over the filled layer, pressing down gently. Brush the middle layer with another ¼ cup of the syrup. Spread another ½ cup of the whipped cream over the cake. Dot the whipped cream with the remaining sliced cherries. Brush the remaining cherry syrup over the final cake layer and invert the layer onto the cake, again pressing down gently. Remove the springform ring and lift the cake and cardboard round off the pan bottom. Using an offset spatula, coat the sides and top of the cake with the remaining whipped cream. Refrigerate the cake for a minimum of 2 hours before serving, or up to 24 hours.

9. When ready to serve, coat the sides of the cake with the chocolate shavings by using the frosting spatula to lift the shavings and gently touch them to the sides of the cake, reserving about ½ cup of the shavings for the top of the cake. Evenly space 8 piles of chocolate shavings (1 tablespoon each) around the top perimeter of the cake. Top each pile of chocolate shavings with a reserved cherry. Serve.

FLOURLESS CHOCOLATE CAKE

TO OUR KNOWLEDGE, FLOURLESS CHOCOLATE cake is the only dessert that is named for a missing ingredient. Besides this, using the word "cake" for this very popular dessert is a stretch. Although some recipes replace flour or crumbs with ground nuts, the quintessence of the genre contains only chocolate, butter, and eggs—nothing that could conceivably be called a dry ingredient. The result is moist and fudgy, more confection than cake.

Although the ingredient choices are limited—chocolate, butter, and eggs, sometimes sugar, and sometimes liquid such as water, coffee, or liqueur—the proportions as well as mixing and baking methods differed considerably in the recipes we researched.

We selected and baked six recipes that represented the array of choices. The results were staggering in their variety. One resembled a flourless fudge brownie, one was more like an ultra-dense, creamy custard, and one was a pouffy, fallen soufflé-like affair. Some were very bittersweet, others quite sweet. All, however, had the richness and intensity of a confection.

Although almost all the desserts were very enticing, we were quickly able to define our criteria for the ultimate flourless chocolate cake. We wanted something dense, moist, and ultra-chocolatey, but with some textural finesse. We wanted a mouthfeel and texture somewhere between a substantial *marquis au chocolat*—that dense, buttery, and just slightly aerated chocolate mousse with a characteristic dry but creamy texture—and a heavy New York–style cheesecake, which requires the mouth to work for just a second before it melts and dissolves with sublime flavor. We wanted the flavor and character of good, eating-quality chocolate to reign supreme, with no unnecessary sweetness and not even the slightest grain of sugar on the palate. In short, we wanted an intense bittersweet "adult" dessert, not a piece of fudge or a brownie or a thick chocolate pudding—and certainly nothing fluffy.

Some recipes used unsweetened chocolate instead of semisweet or bittersweet, but we rejected this idea after tasting just one cake made with unsweetened chocolate. Neither flavor nor texture was smooth or silky enough for this type of dessert, and there was a slight chalky sensation on the palate. This made sense. Unsweetened chocolate is coarse and needs high heat to blend with the sugar required to sweeten it. It is most successful in desserts with a cakey or fudgy texture, when perfect smoothness is unnecessary. Hot fudge sauce made with unsweetened chocolate is smooth because it is cooked to a temperature high enough to melt the sugar and change the physical properties of the chocolate. But our flourless chocolate cake is more like chocolate mousse, chocolate truffles, or ganache; the ingredients are few, cooked very gently, and the results must be perfectly smooth. Made to be nibbled, semisweet and bittersweet chocolates are incomparably smooth, refined so that chocolate and sugar are intimately married and every particle is smaller than the human palate can detect.

The next decision had to do with the baking temperature and whether or not a water bath was indicated. The original recipe for this now-popular dessert was flawed by hard, crumbly edges—surely caused by baking for a short time at a high temperature without a water bath. We tried a similar recipe baked at a high temperature for a short time but in a water bath. It was creamier by far, but we could taste raw egg. We guessed that, like cheesecake, this dessert required a longer baking time at a lower temperature in a water bath to allow the interior to reach a safe temperature without overcooking the edges. We found that 325 degrees in a water bath produced a successful sample.

The trick in baking this cake, however, is knowing when to stop. Just like cheesecake, our flourless chocolate cake must be taken from the oven when the center still jiggles and looks quite underdone, as it continues to cook after it comes out of the oven.

At first we used a thermometer to make sure that the center of the cake had reached the safe temperature of 160 degrees (so that any salmonella bacteria present in the eggs would be killed). But this cake was clearly overbaked; the texture was dryish and chalky. Knowing that a temperature of at least 140 degrees held for five minutes also kills salmonella bacteria, we let the cake reach 140 degrees and then left it in the oven for five more minutes. It was overbaked as well. After trying four, three, and two extra minutes in the oven, we finally realized that if we removed the cake at 140 degrees it would stay at or even above 140 degrees for at least five minutes (thus killing off salmonella) as the heat from the edges of the cake penetrated the center. The results were perfect.

Before determining the proper quantities of butter and eggs for a pound of chocolate, we decided to test textures. We were pretty sure that the ultimate cake would need some form of aeration from beaten eggs to achieve the texture that we wanted. In the first test, we whisked the eggs over gentle heat to warm them (as for a génoise) and then beat them until they had about tripled in volume and were the consistency of soft whipped cream. We then folded the whipped eggs into the warm chocolate and butter in three parts. In the second test, we separated the eggs, whisked the yolks into the warm chocolate and butter and then beat the whites to a meringue before folding them in. In the third test, we simply whisked the eggs, one by one, into the warm chocolate and butter, as though making a custard.

The sample made with eggs simply whisked into the melted chocolate and butter was dense and smooth like a very rich custard or crème brûlée. Our definition of the ultimate flourless chocolate cake ruled this version out. The cake with beaten whole eggs differed from the one with yolks and meringue more than we expected. Surprisingly, the difference in flavor was greater than the difference in texture. Whole beaten eggs produced a dessert with nicely blended flavors, while the cake with separated eggs tasted as though the ingredients had not been completely integrated. Along the way, we realized that we could eliminate the step of warming the eggs before beating them, since cold eggs produce a denser foam with smaller bubbles, which in turn gave the cake a more velvety texture.

Flourless Chocolate Cake

SERVES 12 TO 16

Even though the cake may not look done, pull it from the oven when an instant-read thermometer registers 140 degrees. (Make sure not to let the tip of the thermometer hit the bottom of the pan.) It will continue to firm up as it cools. If you use a 9-inch springform pan instead of the preferred 8-inch, reduce the baking time to 18 to 20 minutes. See page 9 for more information about choosing a particular brand of chocolate for this recipe. We like the pure flavor of chocolate; however, coffee or liqueur (choose something that tastes like nuts, coffee, or oranges) can be added if desired.

- 8 large eggs, cold
- 1 pound bittersweet or semisweet chocolate, chopped coarse
- 16 tablespoons (2 sticks) unsalted butter, cut into 16 pieces
- 1/4 cup strong coffee or liqueur (optional)
  Confectioners' sugar or cocoa powder for dusting on the cake

1. Adjust an oven rack to the lower-middle position and heat the oven to 325 degrees. Line the bottom of an 8-inch springform pan with parchment paper or waxed paper and grease the sides of the pan. Wrap the outside of the pan with 2 sheets of heavy-duty foil and set in a large roasting pan. Bring a kettle of water to a boil.

2. Beat the eggs in the bowl of a standing mixer at high speed until the volume doubles (to approximately 1 quart), about 5 minutes.

3. Meanwhile, melt the chocolate and butter (adding the coffee, if using) in a large heatproof bowl set over a pan of almost simmering water, until smooth and very warm (about 115 degrees on an instant-read thermometer), stirring once or twice. (To melt in a microwave, heat the chocolate in a microwave-safe bowl at 50 percent power for 2 minutes, stir, add the butter and coffee, if using, and continue heating at 50 percent power, stirring

every minute, until the chocolate and butter have melted and are smooth, another 2 to 3 minutes total.) Fold a third of the egg foam into the chocolate mixture using a large rubber spatula until only a few streaks of egg are visible; fold in half of the remaining foam, then the last of the foam, until the mixture is totally homogenous.

4. Scrape the batter into the prepared springform pan and smooth the surface with a rubber spatula. Set the roasting pan on the oven rack and pour in enough boiling water to come about halfway up the sides of the springform pan. Bake until the cake has risen slightly, the edges are just beginning to set, a thin glazed crust (like a brownie) has formed on the surface, and an instant-read thermometer inserted halfway into the center reads 140 degrees, 22 to 25 minutes. Remove the cake pan from the water bath and set on a wire rack; cool to room temperature. Cover and refrigerate overnight to mellow. (The cake can be covered and refrigerated for up to 4 days.)

5. About 30 minutes before serving, remove the sides of the pan, invert the cake onto a sheet of waxed paper, peel off the parchment paper, and reinvert the cake onto a serving platter. Sieve a light sprinkling of confectioners' sugar or unsweetened cocoa powder over the cake to decorate, if desired. To serve, use a sharp, thin-bladed knife, dipping the knife into a pitcher of hot water and wiping the blade before each cut.

FALLEN CHOCOLATE CAKE

FALLEN CHOCOLATE CAKE IS AN UNDERCOOKED-in-the-center mound of intense, buttery chocolate cake, which ranges from a dense, brownie-like consistency to something altogether more ethereal. Sometimes referred to as "molten chocolate cake," fallen chocolate cake appeared first on restaurant menus, and thus its popularity grew. (International chef Jean-Georges Vongerichten serves several hundred of these desserts every night in his restaurants.)

Having tasted Vongerichten's recipe on a number of occasions and having also tried this dessert at other trendy eateries, we became intrigued with the notion of turning a restaurant showstopper into a practical recipe for home cooks. We knew that the ingredient list was short and suspected that the techniques would be relatively simple, but, since restaurant recipes rarely work at home, it was clear that a great deal of culinary translation awaited us.

The first step, since this recipe concept encompasses a wide range of styles from half-cooked batter to a chocolate sponge cake, was to organize a tasting in the test kitchen to decide exactly what we were looking for. We made three variations: Warm, Soft Chocolate Cake, from Vongerichten; Fallen Chocolate Cake from the restaurant Olives, created by chef-owner Todd English; and an old favorite called Fallen Chocolate Soufflé Cake, published by the late Richard Sax, a well-known food writer.

Sax's recipe, which is baked in a tube pan rather than in a ramekin, was quite delicious and soufflé-like in texture. However, it lacked the intense whack of chocolate and the rich, buttery texture of the other two desserts. The recipe from Olives was the heaviest of the lot, very good but quite similar to an undercooked brownie. Jean-Georges' cake was the tasting panel's favorite, with the most intense chocolate flavor, a relatively light texture, and a very runny center. We then wondered if we might be able to capture some of the ethereal lightness of Sax's cake, along with the rich taste and buttery mouthfeel of Jean-Georges' dessert.

First we had to decide on the basic preparation method. There were two choices. We could beat the egg yolks and whites separately and then fold them together, or we could beat whole eggs and sugar to create a thick foam. The latter method proved superior, as it delivered the rich, moist texture we were looking for as well as making the recipe simpler. That left us with a recipe that consisted of melting chocolate; beating whole eggs, sugar, and flavorings into a foam; and then folding the two together, perhaps with a little flour or ground nuts for extra body.

Our next step was to determine what amounts of each ingredient made the best cake. After considerable testing, we decided that ½ cup of melted butter made the dessert considerably more moist.

Some recipes use no flour or very little (Jean-Georges, for instance, uses only 4 teaspoons), but we finally settled on 2 tablespoons. The amount of chocolate, a key factor, was highly variable, running from a mere 4 ounces to a high of 12 ounces in English's recipe. Eight ounces provided a good jolt of chocolate without being overbearing.

The eggs, however, were perhaps the most crucial element. We tested six whole eggs (light and airy sponge-cake texture), four whole eggs plus four yolks (moist and dark), and the winning combination of four whole eggs plus one yolk (rich but light, moist, intense, and dark).

When baking these desserts in ramekins at 450 degrees, as called for in the Jean-Georges recipe, we found that the tops were slightly burned and the center was a bit too runny. At 350 degrees, the dessert took on a more cake-like quality and was also drier. Four hundred degrees was best, yielding a light, cake-like perimeter around a moist well of intense chocolate. (When using a cake pan rather than ramekins, though, we found it best to set the oven at 375 degrees.)

At this point, we had the recipe pretty well in order. To finish the translation from restaurant to home kitchen, however, we still had some work to do. The biggest obstacle was the amount of last-minute cooking. No one wants to run out to the kitchen during dinner and whip up an egg foam. Having had some experience with preparing chocolate soufflés ahead of time, we tested pouring the batter into the ramekins, refrigerating them, and then baking them during dinner. This worked, the batter holding for up to eight hours. Although the filled ramekins can be taken directly from the refrigerator to the oven with reasonably good results, they rise better if allowed to sit at room temperature for 30 minutes before baking.

We also wondered if most folks have eight ramekins at home. Therefore, we developed a variation that uses either an 8- or 9-inch springform pan. As an added benefit for the home cook, we discovered that, in cake form, this dessert can be baked up to one hour before serving, remaining warm right in the pan. (In a pinch, this dessert can be held up to two hours in the pan, but it will become slightly denser as it cools.)

Individual
Fallen Chocolate Cakes

SERVES 8

To melt the chocolate and butter in a microwave oven, heat the chocolate alone at 50 percent power for 2 minutes; stir the chocolate, add the butter, and continue heating at 50 percent for another 2 minutes, stopping to stir after 1 minute. If the chocolate is not yet entirely melted, heat an additional 30 seconds at 50 percent power.

2	tablespoons unbleached all-purpose flour, plus more for dusting the ramekins
8	tablespoons (I stick) unsalted butter, cut into 4 pieces
8	ounces bittersweet or semisweet chocolate, chopped coarse
4	large eggs plus I large yolk, at room temperature
I	teaspoon vanilla extract
1/4	teaspoon salt
1/2	cup (3 1/2 ounces) granulated sugar
	Confectioners' sugar or unsweetened cocoa powder for decoration (optional)
	Whipped cream for serving (optional)

1. Adjust an oven rack to the middle position and heat the oven to 400 degrees. Generously grease and flour eight 6-ounce ramekins or heatproof glass baking cups; tap out the excess flour and position the ramekins on a shallow roasting pan or rimmed baking sheet. Meanwhile, melt the butter and chocolate in a medium heatproof bowl set over a pan of almost-simmering water, stirring once or twice, until smooth; remove from the heat.

2. Beat the eggs, yolk, vanilla, salt, and sugar in the bowl of a standing mixer set at the highest speed until the volume nearly triples, the color is very light, and the mixture drops from the beaters in a smooth, thick stream, about 5 minutes. Scrape the egg mixture over the melted chocolate and butter; sprinkle the flour over the egg mixture. Gently fold the egg and flour into the chocolate until the mixture is a uniform color. Ladle or pour the batter into the prepared ramekins. (The ramekins can be covered lightly with plastic wrap and refrigerated up to 8 hours. Return to room temperature for 30 minutes before baking.)

3. Bake until the cakes have puffed about 1/2 inch above the rims of the ramekins, have a thin crust on top, and jiggle slightly at the center when the ramekins are shaken very gently, 12 to 13 minutes. Run a paring knife around the inside edges of the ramekins to loosen the cakes and invert onto serving plates; cool for 1 minute and lift off the ramekins. Sieve a light sprinkling of confectioners' sugar or cocoa powder over the cakes to decorate, if desired, and serve immediately with whipped cream, if using.

> VARIATIONS

Large Fallen Chocolate Cake

SERVES 8 TO 10

One large chocolate cake can be prepared in a springform pan. Do not use a regular cake pan, as the cake will be impossible to remove once baked. Though the cake is best when served warm, within about 30 minutes of being unmolded, it can also be held in the pan for up to 2 hours.

Follow the recipe for Individual Fallen Chocolate Cakes, substituting an 8- or 9-inch springform pan for the ramekins. Decrease the baking temperature to 375 degrees and bake until the cake looks puffed, a thin top crust has formed, and the center jiggles slightly when the pan is shaken gently, 22 to 25 minutes for a 9-inch pan or 27 to 30 minutes for an 8-inch pan. Cool the cake for 15 minutes, run a paring knife around the inside edge of the pan, and remove the pan sides. Sieve a light sprinkling of confectioners' sugar or unsweetened cocoa powder over the cake to decorate, if desired, just before serving and serve warm, with optional whipped cream.

Orange Chocolate Cakes

Follow the recipe for Individual Fallen Chocolate Cakes or Large Fallen Chocolate Cake, folding 1 tablespoon finely grated zest from 2 medium oranges and 2 tablespoons orange liqueur (such as Grand Marnier or Triple Sec) into the beaten egg and melted chocolate mixture.

CHOCOLATE-HAZELNUT CAKE

CHOCOLATE AND HAZELNUTS ARE A CLASSIC combination. In Italy, this flavor pairing is called gianduja. For this recipe, we focused on developing a cake that forms a crackly, crisp, meringue-like top when baked; the inside is dense and slightly coarse, yet very moist. This cake is rich enough that it does not need a glaze or frosting, just a light dusting of confectioners' sugar to dress up its appearance.

The taste and texture of the cake are based on a delicate balance of eggs, butter, sugar, bittersweet chocolate, ground nuts, and, possibly, a small amount of flour. The eggs are separated; the yolks are added to the batter, and the whites are whipped to stiff peaks and folded in at the end. There are no chemical leaveners; the whipped whites are the sole means of leavening the cake.

Because eggs are crucial to this recipe, we decided to begin our tests with this ingredient. We first tried the cake with six eggs. The inside of the cake was very dense, moist, and cakey. However, the top expanded a bit too much and formed a gap between the surface and the rest of the cake. Five eggs produced good results, but we found that using six yolks and five whites produced a cake with a slightly firmer and denser center. The surface of the cake was crisp and crackly but did not expand too much.

The texture and crumb of this cake are established largely by the quantity and texture of the nuts. The coarser the nuts, the coarser the crumb. Some recipes call for finely chopped hazelnuts. We found that grinding the nuts in the food processor was much easier and produced a finer consistency than hand chopping. In addition, we found that grinding the nuts with a small amount of sugar helps prevent them from clumping in the batter. The quantity of nuts affects the flavor as well as the texture. The flavor of the hazelnuts is quite mild compared with the bold, assertive flavor of chocolate. We tested 6 ounces of chocolate with 1 cup of nuts and found the chocolate overpowering and the texture extremely moist and fudgy—overly so, in our opinion. We got better results from 1½

cups of nuts, but we still felt the cake could be lighter. We tried replacing a bit of the nuts with 2 tablespoons of flour. This hit the mark; the cake retained a moist, rich, melt-in-the-mouth quality but was less dense, with a lighter, cakier texture.

We began our testing using a standard 9-inch cake pan, as most recipes suggest. It became apparent that, due to the fragile nature of the cake's surface, removing the cake from the pan was problematic, and we often shattered the crisp crust in the process. We switched to a 9-inch springform pan, which eliminated the need to invert the cake in order to remove it from the pan.

Some recipes suggest finishing this cake with a chocolate glaze or ganache to dress it up and cover the imperfections of the crackle surface. We preferred the cake simply sprinkled with powdered sugar, as it gave the cake a certain rustic charm. Furthermore, the cake is super-rich and intensely chocolate as is, and tasters felt that the extra chocolate was overkill.

Chocolate-Hazelnut Cake
SERVES 8
See page 239 for information about handling the hazelnuts for this recipe.

6	ounces semisweet or bittersweet chocolate, chopped
1⅓	cups hazelnuts, toasted, skinned, and toasted again
1	cup (7 ounces) sugar
2	tablespoons unbleached all-purpose flour
8	tablespoons (1 stick) unsalted butter, softened but still cool
5	large eggs, separated, plus 1 large egg yolk
¼	teaspoon salt
	Confectioners' sugar for dusting the cake
	Lightly sweetened whipped cream (optional)

1. Adjust an oven rack to the middle position and heat the oven to 350 degrees. Generously grease a 9-inch springform pan.

2. Place the chocolate in a medium heatproof bowl set over a pan of simmering water. Melt the chocolate, stirring occasionally to speed the

process. Remove the bowl from the heat and cool to room temperature.

3. Place the hazelnuts, ¼ cup of the sugar, and the flour in a food processor. Process until the nuts are finely ground, 15 to 20 1-second pulses.

4. Beat the butter in the bowl of a standing mixer set at medium speed until fluffy, about 2 minutes. Gradually add the remaining ¾ cup sugar, beating until creamy, 2 to 3 minutes. Add the 6 egg yolks one at a time, beating well after each addition. Add the cooled chocolate and beat just until blended in. Stir in the ground hazelnuts.

5. Put the egg whites and the salt in a large, clean bowl and beat with the mixer until they form stiff peaks. With a rubber spatula, fold in a third of the whites to the chocolate-nut mixture. Carefully fold in the remaining whites in two batches, taking care not to deflate the batter. Pour the batter into the prepared pan.

6. Bake until a toothpick or thin skewer inserted halfway between the center and the outer rim of the cake comes out clean, 45 to 50 minutes. (The center of the cake will still be moist.) Remove the pan from the oven and cool completely on a wire rack, about 3 hours. (The cake can be wrapped in plastic and refrigerated for several days.) Just before serving, dust with confectioners' sugar. Cut the cake into wedges and serve with whipped cream, if desired.

YULE LOG CAKE

CALLED *BÛCHE DE NOËL* IN FRANCE, A YULE log cake is a festive way to celebrate Christmas or other winter holidays. But in a recent discussion of holiday desserts, a few cooks in the test kitchen complained that yule logs have always looked far more impressive than they tasted, so we set out to make the ultimate yule log cake—something that was more than a fancy jelly roll with a few meringue mushrooms. From start to finish, this cake would pack an indelible flavor punch.

A yule log cake starts with a sponge cake that's soft and moist but sturdy enough to be rolled. A sponge cake roll begins life as a thin sponge cake baked quickly in a rimmed baking sheet, unmolded, and rolled up around a creamy filling. A rich frosting or glaze is often added to complement the cake and soft filling. We wanted our sponge cake to be chocolate.

A sponge cake by definition contains little or no butter, and its (usually) separated eggs are whipped with sugar before the dry ingredients are folded in. Structurally speaking, a sponge cake sheet must be thin, even, and "rollable." Given the demands of its form, this cake cannot be fudgy, buttery, or rich. But it must pack serious chocolate flavor; remain moist, tender, and fine-pored; and refrain from being overly sweet.

To begin, we made five chocolate sponge cake recipes. Several things were immediately evident: Chemical leaveners were superfluous; cakes with more sugar failed to set the filling off to its advantage; and a rich, dark color was important to the cake's overall appeal. Only one of the cakes we baked used chocolate rather than cocoa, and that cake possessed by far the best flavor. Where every last cake fell from grace was in textural terms. We nibbled sheets of thick chocolate felt and soggy chocolate omelets. We wanted a texture that ventured to neither of these extremes.

Having chosen chocolate as the chief flavoring agent in our cake, we needed to determine which kind to use. We rejected unsweetened chocolate as too heavy-handed for this light, airy cake. Anything less than six ounces of semi- or bittersweet chocolate rendered a flavor too mild. One-third cup sugar tasted good with both semi- and bittersweet. We also added 2 tablespoons of butter to the melting chocolate. Though not enough to weigh down the cake, this small amount contributed to flavor and tenderness.

Because eggs are usually the sole liquid ingredient in a sponge cake—crucial for lightness of texture and ease of rolling—their number is key. Too few and our cake was not supple. Too many and we got either a wet chocolate sponge (if there was no flour in the recipe) or dry chocolate matting (if the proportion of eggs was too high). Six eggs provided the support necessary to blend the ingredients, the lift required to rise the cake, and the flexibility needed to roll it.

Still, even with chocolate contributing some

structure, the fragile egg and sugar foam needed more support. We tested ¼ cup flour against the same amount of cocoa and ended up giving them equal partnership. The flour offered structural support, which kept the cake from becoming too moist after it was filled; the cocoa added a chocolatey undercurrent, which dramatically improved the overall flavor of the cake. Because the flavor of cocoa becomes more intense when it is mixed with water, we added 2 tablespoons of water to the recipe. The water helped to deepen the chocolate flavor and made the batter glossy and beautiful.

Recipes offer several techniques for coaxing sheet cakes into their customary cylindrical shape. Our cake responded best when cooled briefly in the pan on a cooling rack and then unmolded onto a kitchen towel rubbed with cocoa to prevent sticking. The cake, still quite warm, was then rolled up, towel and all. Allowed thus to cool briefly, the roll could be unrolled, retain its rolled memory, then be filled and rerolled.

The cake was now delectable, with a yielding, melting texture and intense chocolate flavor. It needed a rich but adaptable filling. Not wanting to crack open the cupboards and make a big mess, we decided to use a modified tiramisu filling made with lightly sweetened mascarpone and some ground espresso.

For frosting our yule log, the choice was unanimous: rich, dark, chocolate ganache. Ganache is made from nothing more than cream, chocolate, butter, and sometimes liqueur—it is rich and luscious and easy to prepare. Rose Levy Beranbaum, author of *The Cake Bible* (William Morrow, 1988), acquainted us with the technique of making ganache in a food processor, a method that beats all others for ease and consistency. A glossy coat of ganache put another flavor layer in place and made the cake look beautiful. As a finishing touch, we added meringue mushrooms to our yule log; they are not essential but are traditional and do make an attractive garnish. At last, we had a yule log that is more than a centerpiece for the holiday table.

Yule Log Cake
SERVES 8 TO 10

This cake is so good, we don't think it should be saved just for winter holidays. Simply skip the meringue mushrooms and call it chocolate roulade. We suggest that you make the filling and ganache first, then make the cake while the ganache is setting up. Or, if you prefer, the cake can be baked, filled, and rolled—but not iced—then wrapped in plastic and refrigerated for up to 24 hours. Rolling a yule log cake is similar to rolling a jelly roll cake; refer to page 370 for instructions.

CHOCOLATE SPONGE CAKE

¼	cup (1¼ ounces) unbleached all-purpose flour, plus more for dusting the baking sheet
6	ounces bittersweet or semisweet chocolate, chopped fine
2	tablespoons cold unsalted butter, cut into 2 pieces
2	tablespoons cold water
¼	cup (¾ ounce) Dutch-processed cocoa, sifted, plus more for unmolding and garnish
⅛	teaspoon salt
6	large eggs, separated, at room temperature
⅓	cup (2⅓ ounces) sugar
1	teaspoon vanilla extract
⅛	teaspoon cream of tartar

1	recipe Espresso-Mascarpone Cream (recipe follows)
1	recipe Dark Chocolate Ganache (recipe follows)
1	recipe Meringue Mushrooms (recipe follows) Confectioners' sugar, for garnish

1. FOR THE CAKE: Adjust an oven rack to the upper-middle position and heat the oven to 400 degrees. Spray an 18 by 12-inch rimmed baking sheet with nonstick cooking spray, cover the pan bottom with parchment paper or waxed paper, and spray the parchment with nonstick cooking spray; dust the baking sheet with flour, tapping out the excess.

2. Bring 2 inches of water to a simmer in a small saucepan over medium heat. Combine the chocolate, butter, and water in a small heatproof bowl and cover tightly with plastic wrap. Set the bowl over

the pan, reduce the heat to medium-low, and heat until the butter is almost completely melted and the chocolate pieces are glossy, have lost definition, and are fully melted around the edges, about 15 minutes. (Do not stir or let the water in the saucepan come to a boil.) Remove the bowl from the heat, unwrap, and stir until smooth and glossy. While the chocolate is melting, sift the ¼ cup cocoa, the flour, and salt together into a small bowl and set aside.

3. In the bowl of a standing mixer, beat the egg yolks at medium-high speed until just combined, about 15 seconds. With the mixer running, add half of the sugar. Continue to beat, scraping down the sides of the bowl as necessary until the yolks are pale yellow and the mixture falls in a thick ribbon when the beaters are lifted, about 8 minutes. Add the vanilla and beat to combine, scraping down the bowl once, about 30 seconds. Turn the mixture into a medium bowl; wash the mixer bowl and beaters and dry with paper towels. (If you have 2 mixer bowls, leave the yolk mixture in the mixer bowl; wash and dry the beaters and use a second bowl in step 4.)

4. In a clean bowl with clean beaters, beat the egg whites and cream of tartar at medium speed until foamy, about 30 seconds. With the mixer running, add about 1 teaspoon of the sugar; continue beating until soft peaks form, about 40 seconds. Gradually add the remaining sugar and beat until the whites are glossy and supple and hold stiff peaks when the whisk is lifted, about 1 minute longer. Do not overbeat (if the whites look dry and granular, they are overbeaten). While the whites are beating, stir the chocolate mixture into the yolks. With a rubber spatula, stir a quarter of the whites into the chocolate mixture to lighten it. Fold in the remaining whites until almost no streaks remain (see the illustrations on page 145). Sprinkle the dry ingredients over the egg and chocolate mixture and fold in quickly but gently.

5. Pour the batter into the prepared pan; using an offset icing spatula and working quickly, smooth the surface and spread the batter into the pan corners. Bake until the center of the cake springs back when touched with a finger, 8 to 10 minutes, rotating the pan halfway through the baking time. Cool the cake in the pan on a wire rack for 5 minutes.

6. While the cake is cooling, lay a clean kitchen towel over a work surface and sift 1 tablespoon cocoa over the towel; with your hands, rub the cocoa into the towel. Run a paring knife around the perimeter of the baking sheet to loosen the cake. Invert the cake onto the towel and peel off the parchment.

7. TO FILL AND FROST: Starting at a long side, roll the cake and towel together into a jelly roll shape (see the illustrations on page 370). Cool for 15 minutes, then unroll the cake and towel. Using an offset spatula, immediately spread the mascarpone cream filling evenly over the surface of the cake, almost to the edges. Reroll the cake gently but snugly around the filling. Set a large sheet of parchment paper on an overturned rimmed baking sheet and set the cake seam-side down on top. Trim both ends of the cake on the diagonal. Reserve ¼ cup of the ganache for attaching the meringue mushrooms. Spread the ganache over the roulade with a small icing spatula. Use a fork to make wood-grain striations on the surface of the ganache before it has set. Refrigerate the cake, uncovered, on the baking sheet to slightly set the icing, about 20 minutes.

8. When ready to serve, carefully slide 2 wide metal spatulas under the cake and transfer the cake to a serving platter. Arrange the meringue mushrooms around the cake, attaching them with dabs of reserved ganache. Sift a light dusting of cocoa over the mushrooms. Sift the yule log with confectioners' sugar. Serve within a few hours.

Espresso-Mascarpone Cream

MAKES ABOUT 2 ½ CUPS,
ENOUGH TO FILL 1 YULE LOG

Mascarpone is a fresh Italian cheese that is supple and spreadable. Its flavor is unique—mildly sweet and refreshing. It is sold in small containers in some supermarkets as well as most gourmet stores, cheese shops, and Italian markets.

½	cup heavy cream
4	teaspoons whole espresso beans, finely ground (about 2 tablespoons ground)
6	tablespoons (1 ½ ounces) confectioners' sugar
16½	ounces (about 2 cups) mascarpone cheese

1. Bring the cream to a simmer in a small saucepan over high heat. Remove from the heat and stir in the espresso and confectioners' sugar; cool slightly.

2. With a rubber spatula, beat the mascarpone in a medium bowl until softened. Gently whisk in the cooled cream mixture until combined. Cover with plastic wrap and refrigerate until ready to use.

Dark Chocolate Ganache

MAKES ABOUT 1 ½ CUPS,
ENOUGH TO COVER 1 FILLED YULE LOG

If your kitchen is cool and the ganache becomes too stiff to spread, set the bowl over a saucepan of simmering water, then stir briefly until smooth and icing-like. We especially like Hershey's Special Dark chocolate for this recipe.

> ¾   **cup heavy cream**
> 2   **tablespoons unsalted butter**
> 6   **ounces high-quality bittersweet or semisweet chocolate, chopped**
> 1   **tablespoon cognac**

Microwave the cream and butter in a microwave-safe measuring cup on high until bubbling, about 1½ minutes. (Alternatively, bring to a simmer in a small saucepan over medium-high heat.) Place the chocolate in a food processor. With the machine running, gradually add the hot cream and cognac through the feed tube and process until smooth and thickened, about 3 minutes. Transfer the ganache to a medium bowl and let stand at room temperature 1 hour, until spreadable (the ganache should have the consistency of soft icing).

Meringue Mushrooms

MAKES ABOUT 30

Meringue mushrooms are a traditional yule log garnish, although the cake will taste just fine without them. If you are inclined to make the mushrooms, they are not difficult, but they do require a stabilized meringue called an Italian meringue. One of the three methods of making meringue (see page 477), Italian meringue involves beating egg whites with a hot sugar syrup, a sugar and water mixture cooked to at least the soft-ball stage. *Although generally simple, the process does involve careful timing and attention to the consistency of the sugar syrup and egg whites. The syrup must be poured in a slow steady stream into beating egg whites that are approaching their maximum volume. Adding the hot sugar syrup to the whites brings the temperature of the whites to 160 degrees, effectively cooking the whites. Properly done, the meringue will not leach water or deflate and will hold up well when piped with a pastry bag. If the caps and stems become soggy during storage, crisp them in a 200-degree oven for 30 minutes before assembling the mushrooms.*

PIPING MERINGUE

1. Holding the pastry bag about ¼ inch above the paper, pipe 30 rounds of varying sizes to form mushroom caps. Keep the tip steady as the meringue flows into a round shape, stopping the pressure when the desired size is reached. To release the meringue without making a point, turn the tip clockwise and lift the bag straight up. If a pointed tip forms, dip your finger into a bowl of cold water and gently smooth the top of the cap to remove the tip.

2. To shape mushroom stems, hold the pastry bag perpendicular to the pan, almost touching the paper. Squeeze the meringue through the tip as you pull up on the bag. The stems should be about 1 inch tall and stand up straight. Pointed ends are desired so stop squeezing the bag as you lift it straight up.

¼ cup water

½ cup (3 ½ ounces) sugar

2 large egg whites, at room temperature

Pinch salt

⅛ teaspoon cream of tartar

½ teaspoon vanilla extract

1. Adjust the oven racks to the middle and lowest positions and heat the oven to 200 degrees. Line 2 rimmed baking sheets with parchment paper.

2. Combine the water and sugar in a small, heavy saucepan. Cover and bring to a boil over medium-high heat. Boil, swirling the pan once or twice, until the sugar has dissolved, 1 to 2 minutes. If necessary, wash down any sugar crystals on the sides of the pan with a damp pastry brush. Cook, uncovered, until the temperature registers 238 degrees on a candy thermometer, about 10 minutes.

FORMING MERINGUE MUSHROOMS

1. Use a small paring knife or skewer to make an indentation in the underside of each mushroom cap.

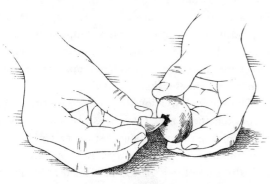

2. Use the tip of a knife or a toothpick to place a small dot of ganache into the hole in each cap and onto the tip of each stem. Gently press the cap onto the end of the stem.

3. While the syrup is cooking, place the egg whites in the bowl of a standing mixer fitted with the whisk. Beat at medium-low speed until frothy, about 1 minute. Add the salt and cream of tartar and beat, gradually increasing the speed to high, until the whites hold soft peaks, about 1 minute.

4. With the mixer at medium speed, slowly pour the hot syrup into the egg whites, avoiding the whisk. Increase the speed to medium-high and continue to beat until the meringue cools to room temperature and becomes very thick and shiny, 5 to 10 minutes. Add the vanilla.

5. Fit a pastry bag with a ¼-inch pastry tip and fill with the meringue. Pipe about 30 caps and an equal number of stems onto the prepared pans (see the illustrations on page 388).

6. Bake the meringue for 2 hours, turn off the oven, and leave the meringue in the oven until very dry and crisp, about 30 minutes longer. Cool the mushroom caps and stems on the baking sheets. (The caps and stems may be stored in an airtight container for up to 1 week.) To assemble the mushrooms, use the ganache to glue the caps and stems together (see the illustrations at left).

NEW YORK CHEESECAKE

AN ORCHESTRATION OF DIFFERENT TEXTURES and an exercise in flavor restraint, New York cheesecake is a tall, bronze-skinned, and dense affair. At the core, it is cool, thick, smooth, satiny, and creamy; radiating outward, the texture goes gradually from velvety to suede-like, until finally becoming cake-like and fine-pored at the edges. The flavor is simple and pure and minimalist, sweet and tangy, and rich to boot. New York cheesecake should not be citrusy, vanilla-scented, fluffy, mousse-like, leaden, gummy, chewy, or starchy. It should not be so dry as to make you gag, and it definitely should not bake up with a fault as large as the San Andreas (we're talking New York, after all).

We decided to start with the crust and work our way up. Some recipes claim that a pastry crust was the crust of choice for the original New York cheesecake. We tried one, but after a lot of expended effort, a pastry crust only became soggy beneath the filling. Cookie and cracker crumbs were tasty and more practical options. Every taster considered a mere dusting of crumbs on the bottom of the cheesecake insufficient. We wanted a crust with more presence.

A graham cracker crust made with a cup of crumbs, some sugar, and melted butter, pressed into the bottom of the springform pan and pre-baked until it was fragrant and brown around the edges, was ideal at a thickness of about ⅜ inch. If served within a day of baking, it retained its crispness. If the cheesecake was held for a couple days, the crust softened, but tasters didn't seem to mind—the graham cracker crumbs still offered their sweet toasty flavor.

A great New York cheesecake should be of great stature. One made with 2 pounds (four bars) of cream cheese was not tall enough. We threw in another half pound—the springform pan reached maximum capacity, but the cheesecake stood tall and looked right. The amount of sugar was quickly settled upon—1½ cups. The cheesecake struck a perfect balance of sweet and tangy.

Cheesecakes always require a dairy supplement to the cream cheese, usually either heavy cream or sour cream, or sometimes both. We made a cheesecake without any additional dairy and found out why this is true. Though the all-cream-cheese cheesecake tasted undeniably like cream cheese, the texture was gluey and pasty, akin to mortar, and much like a bar of cream cheese straight out of its wrapper. Additional dairy loosens up the texture of the cream cheese, giving the cake a smoother, more luxurious feel.

We found that heavy cream, even when used in the smallest amounts, dulled and flattened the flavor of the cream cheese. Sour cream, with a tartness of its own, supplemented the tangy quality of the cream cheese, but an overabundance made the cheesecake taste sour and acidic. What tasters preferred was a relatively small amount of sour cream—⅓ cup. It was enough to offer a touch of tartness and help give the cheesecake a smoother, creamier texture without advertising its presence.

Eggs help bind the cheesecake and give it structure. They also help create a smooth, creamy texture. Whole eggs are often called for in cheesecakes of non–New York persuasions. We tried as few as four and as many as six whole eggs—these cheesecakes had textures that were called "light," "fluffy," and even "whipped." Recipes for New York cheesecake seem to agree that a few yolks in addition to whole eggs help to get the velvety, lush texture of a proper New York cheesecake. Our testing bore this out, and ultimately we concluded that a generous amount of eggs—six whole and two yolks—yield a cheesecake of unparalleled texture: dense but not heavy, firm but not rigid, and perfectly rich.

Some kind of starch—usually either flour or cornstarch—makes a regular appearance in cheesecake recipes. Starch helps to thicken the texture and guard against the cracking that results from overbaking, but as evidenced by the half-dozen or so starch-laced cakes we made, even in small amounts, a gummy, starchy presence can be detected. Tasters noticed a dry, pasty mouthfeel in cheesecakes made with only a tablespoon of flour and cornstarch. They much preferred the meltingly luxurious quality of a completely starch-free cheesecake.

Perfecting the flavor of the cheesecake was easy. Tasters complained that the orange zest that recipes often call for made the cheesecake taste like a Creamsicle, so it was out of there in a New York minute. Next to go was lemon zest because its flavor was distracting. A couple of teaspoons of lemon juice, however, helped to perk up the flavors without adding a lemon-flavored hit. Just a bit of salt (cream cheese already contains a good dose of sodium) and a couple teaspoons of vanilla extract rounded out the flavors. Everyone in the test kitchen appreciated this minimalist cheesecake.

Cheesecake is well loved by cooks for the fact that it goes together easily. However, care must be used when mixing the ingredients lest the batter contain small nodules of unmixed cream cheese that can mar the smoothness of the baked cake. Frequent and thorough scraping of the bowl during mixing is key to ensuring that every spot of cream cheese is incorporated, but starting with semisoftened cream cheese is certainly helpful. Simply cutting it into chunks and letting it stand while the crust is prepared and the other ingredients assembled—30 to 45 minutes—made mixing easier.

There are many ways to bake a cheesecake: in a moderate oven, in a low oven, in a water bath, and in accordance with the New York method—500 degrees for about 10 minutes, then 200 degrees for about an hour—which appears to be a standard technique. We tried them all, but the New York method was the only one that yielded the nut-brown surface that is a distinguishing mark of an exemplary New York cheesecake. This dual-temperature, no-water-bath baking method also produced a lovely graded texture, soft and creamy at the center and firm and dry at the periphery.

The New York baking method was not without flaws, however. After an hour at 200 degrees, the very center of the cheesecake—even after chilling—was loose and slurpy, a result of underbaking. Some recipes leave the cheesecake in the still-warm, turned-off, propped-open oven for about 30 minutes to finish "baking." Handled this way, the cheesecake was marginally better but still insufficiently baked.

We tried extending the hour-long baking time to get the center of the cheesecake to set up to the right consistency. We took it 15 and 30 minutes past an hour. The cheesecake baked for 1½ hours to an internal temperature of about 150 degrees was whisked out of the oven. Chilled, it was cheesecake perfection. It sliced into a neat slab with a cleanly set center texture—not a wet, sloppy one. Each slice kept its shape, and each bite felt satiny on the tongue. Though this prolonged New York baking method was relatively foolproof, we do caution against taking the cheesecake beyond an internal temperature of 160 degrees. The few that we did were hideously and hopelessly cracked. Uptight though it may seem, an instant-read thermometer inserted into the cake is the most reliable means of judging the doneness of the cheesecake.

Cheesecake is also well loved (by the sweet tooth, not the waistline) because it lasts longer in the refrigerator than a dessert should. After a day or two, the crust is a little soggy, but the cake tastes every bit as good.

New York Cheesecake
SERVES 12 TO 16

For the crust, chocolate wafers (such as Nabisco Famous) may be substituted for graham crackers; you will need about 14 wafers. The flavor and texture of the cheesecake are best if the cake is allowed to stand at room temperature for about 30 minutes before serving. When cutting the cake, have a pitcher of hot tap water ready; dipping the blade of the knife into the water and wiping it after each slice helps make clean slices. See the illustrations on page 143 for tips on preparing cheesecake.

GRAHAM CRACKER CRUST

5	tablespoons unsalted butter, melted, plus 1 tablespoon melted unsalted butter for greasing the pan
8	whole graham crackers (4 ounces), broken into rough pieces and processed in a food processor to fine, even crumbs
1	tablespoon sugar

FILLING

2½	pounds (five 8-ounce packages) cream cheese, cut into rough 1-inch chunks, at room temperature
⅛	teaspoon salt
1½	cups (10½ ounces) sugar
⅓	cup sour cream
2	teaspoons juice from 1 lemon
2	teaspoons vanilla extract
2	large egg yolks plus 6 large eggs, at room temperature

1. FOR THE CRUST: Adjust an oven rack to the lower-middle position and heat the oven to 325 degrees. Brush the bottom and sides of a 9-inch springform pan with ½ tablespoon of the melted butter. Combine the graham cracker crumbs and sugar in a medium bowl; add 5 tablespoons of the melted butter and toss with a fork until evenly moistened. Empty the crumbs into the springform pan and, following the illustrations on page 395, press evenly into the pan bottom. Bake until fragrant and beginning to brown around the edges, about 13 minutes. Cool on a wire rack while making the filling.

2. FOR THE CHEESECAKE FILLING: Increase the

oven temperature to 500 degrees. In the bowl of a standing mixer, beat the cream cheese at medium-low speed to break up and soften it slightly, about 1 minute. Scrape the beater and the bottom and sides of the bowl well with a rubber spatula; add the salt and about half of the sugar and beat at medium-low speed until combined, about 1 minute. Scrape the bowl; beat in the remaining sugar until combined, about 1 minute. Scrape the bowl; add the sour cream, lemon juice, and vanilla, and beat at low speed until combined, about 1 minute. Scrape the bowl; add the egg yolks and beat at medium-low speed until thoroughly combined, about 1 minute. Scrape the bowl; add the remaining eggs 2 at a time, beating until thoroughly combined, about 1 minute, scraping the bowl between additions.

3. Brush the sides of the springform pan with the remaining ½ tablespoon melted butter. Set the springform pan on a rimmed baking sheet (to catch any spills if the pan leaks). Pour the filling into the cooled crust and bake 10 minutes; without opening the oven door, reduce the oven temperature to 200 degrees and continue to bake until the cheesecake reads about 150 degrees on an instant-read thermometer inserted in the center, about 1½ hours. Transfer the cake to a wire rack and cool until barely warm, 2½ to 3 hours. Run a paring knife between the cake and the springform pan sides. Wrap tightly in plastic wrap and refrigerate until cold, at least 3 hours. (The cheesecake can be refrigerated up to 4 days.)

4. To unmold the cheesecake, remove the sides of the pan. Slide a thin metal spatula between the crust and the bottom of the pan to loosen, then slide the cake onto a serving plate. Let the cheesecake stand at room temperature about 30 minutes, then cut into wedges (see note) and serve with Fresh Strawberry Topping, if desired.

Fresh Strawberry Topping

MAKES ABOUT 1½ QUARTS

The dense, creamy richness of a New York cheesecake makes it the perfect candidate for some kind of fruity foil. A ruby-colored, glazed strawberry topping is the classic accompaniment to New York cheesecake. This topping is best served the same day it is made.

2 pounds strawberries, cleaned, hulled, and cut lengthwise into ¼- to ⅜-inch wedges
½ cup (3½ ounces) sugar
Pinch salt
1 cup strawberry jam
2 tablespoons juice from 1 lemon

1. Toss the berries, sugar, and salt in a medium bowl; let stand until the berries have released some juice and the sugar has dissolved, about 30 minutes, tossing occasionally to combine.

2. Process the jam in a food processor until smooth, about 8 seconds; transfer to a small saucepan. Bring the jam to a simmer over medium-high heat; simmer, stirring frequently, until dark and no longer frothy, about 3 minutes. Stir in the lemon juice; pour the warm jam over the strawberries and stir to combine. Cover with plastic wrap and refrigerate until cold, at least 2 hours or up to 12. To serve, spoon a portion of sauce over individual slices of cheesecake.

LEMON CHEESECAKE

ALTHOUGH SOME WOULD NEVER DARE TO adulterate plain cheesecake, there are plenty of variations out there: some good, some bad, some ugly. We wanted a variation that serves a function by cutting through the cloying nature of this rich dessert. We found that variation with lemon.

During our initial recipe testing, we discovered a host of different lemon cheesecake styles. One was a towering soufflé made by separating the eggs, whipping the whites, and folding them in at the end. Another had a pasty texture owing to the addition of sweetened condensed milk. And in all cases the lemon flavor was either too fleeting or too harsh. What we wanted was a light, creamy-textured cheesecake, a style that everyone in the test kitchen felt would be a good partner with the flavor of lemon.

We decided to concentrate first on the crust, the foundation of the cheesecake. We liked a graham cracker crust for our New York Cheesecake because it remained crunchy under the weight of the cheese filling, but its sweet and spicy flavor overpowered the lemon. We experimented with several types of crumb crusts and ended up preferring one made with biscuit-type cookies. Of all the brands that we tried, Nabisco's Barnum's Animals Crackers were the surprise favorite (see "Cookies for Crumb Crust," page 395).

For the filling, we started with the filling for our New York Cheesecake. Our first move was to lighten it by reducing the amount of cream cheese from 2½ pounds to 1½. With less cream cheese, we found that we needed less sugar and fewer eggs. Next we eliminated the sour cream, because the addition of lemon provided enough of a tangy counterpoint to the cream cheese. We added some heavy cream for a luscious texture.

As for the lemon flavor, we discovered that one can have too much of a good thing by using too much lemon juice. Zest provided a balanced lemon flavor, but it came with a hitch: The fibrous texture of the zest marred the creamy smoothness of the filling. To solve this problem, we tried processing the zest and sugar together before adding them to the cream cheese. This produced a wonderfully potent lemon flavor by breaking down the zest and releasing its oils, but it also caused the cheesecake to become strangely dense. After many trials, we realized that the food processor was wreaking havoc with the sugar, breaking down its crystalline structure (necessary for the aeration of the cream cheese) as well as melding it with the oils from the lemon zest. By processing only ¼ cup of the sugar with the zest and then stirring in the remaining sugar by hand, we solved the problem.

Baking this cheesecake in a water bath at a low

oven temperature of 325 degrees was also key to achieving a creamy texture. We were surprised to find that when we used hot tap water instead of boiling water (we like shortcuts), the result was a more evenly baked cheesecake (and about 10 minutes of extra baking time). We also discovered that an additional hour in the oven, with the heat off and the door ajar, was crucial to a consistent texture. When we tried to skip this step, the cheesecake set up on the edges but remained gooey in the center.

Our cheesecake was certainly lemony, but we wanted more pizzazz. We found it with a topping of lemon curd. The only problem remaining was the curd's slightly acidic edge. To curb it, we mixed in 1 tablespoon of heavy cream at the end of cooking, along with a dash of vanilla. Cold cubed butter, also added at the end, served both to cool the curd (and prevent overcooking) and to form a smoother emulsion. We found we could make a curd in just five minutes and let it set up in the refrigerator while the cheesecake was baking and cooling. The curd complements the cheesecake perfectly, adding a bit of easy showmanship to this otherwise plain dessert.

Lemon Cheesecake

SERVES 12 TO 16

While this recipe takes several hours from start to finish, the actual preparation is simple, and baking and cooling proceed practically unattended. The cheesecake can be made up to a day in advance; leftovers can be refrigerated for up to 4 days, although the crust will become soggy.

JUDGING WHEN THE CURD IS COOKED

At first, the curd will appear thin and soupy, as shown at left. When the spatula leaves a clear trail in the bottom of the saucepan (which quickly disappears), the curd is ready to come off the heat (center). If the curd continues to cook, it will become too thick and pasty, and a spatula will leave a wide clear trail (right).

COOKIE CRUMB CRUST

5	ounces Nabisco's Barnum's Animals Crackers or Social Tea Biscuits
3	tablespoons sugar
4	tablespoons (1/2 stick) unsalted butter, melted and kept warm

FILLING

1 1/4	cups (8 3/4 ounces) sugar
1	tablespoon grated zest plus 1/4 cup juice from 1 or 2 lemons
1 1/2	pounds (three 8-ounce packages) cream cheese, cut into rough 1-inch chunks, at room temperature
4	large eggs, at room temperature
2	teaspoons vanilla extract
1/4	teaspoon salt
1/2	cup heavy cream

LEMON CURD

1/3	cup juice from 2 lemons
2	large eggs plus 1 large egg yolk
1/2	cup (3 1/2 ounces) sugar
2	tablespoons cold unsalted butter, cut into 1/2-inch cubes
1	tablespoon heavy cream
1/4	teaspoon vanilla extract
	Pinch salt

1. FOR THE CRUST: Adjust an oven rack to the lower-middle position and heat the oven to 325 degrees. In a food processor, process the cookies to fine, even crumbs, about 30 seconds (you should have about 1 cup). Add the sugar and pulse 2 or 3 times to incorporate. Add the warm melted butter in a slow, steady stream while pulsing; pulse until the mixture is evenly moistened and resembles wet sand, about ten 1-second pulses. Transfer the mixture to a 9-inch springform pan and, following the illustrations on page 395, press evenly into the pan bottom. Bake until fragrant and golden brown, 15 to 18 minutes. Cool on a wire rack to room temperature, about 30 minutes. When cool, wrap the outside of the pan with two 18-inch-square pieces of heavy-duty foil; set the springform pan in a roasting pan.

2. FOR THE FILLING: While the crust is cooling, process 1/4 cup of the sugar and the lemon zest in a food processor until the sugar is yellow and the zest is broken down, about 15 seconds, scraping down the bowl if necessary. Transfer the lemon sugar to a small bowl; stir in the remaining 1 cup sugar.

3. In the bowl of a standing mixer set at low speed, beat the cream cheese to break it up and soften it slightly, about 5 seconds. With the machine running, add the sugar mixture in a slow steady stream; increase the speed to medium and continue to beat until the mixture is creamy and smooth, about 3 minutes, scraping down the bowl with a rubber spatula as needed. Reduce the speed to medium-low and add the eggs 2 at a time; beat until incorporated, about 30 seconds, scraping the sides and bottom of the bowl well after each addition. Add the lemon juice, vanilla, and salt and mix until just incorporated, about 5 seconds; add the heavy cream and mix until just incorporated, about 5 seconds longer. Give the batter a final scrape, stir with a rubber spatula, and pour into the prepared springform pan; fill the roasting pan with enough hot tap water to come halfway up the sides of the springform pan. Bake until the center jiggles slightly, the sides just start to puff, the surface is no longer shiny, and an instant-read thermometer inserted in the center of the cake reads 150 degrees, 55 to 60 minutes. Turn off the oven and prop open the oven door with a potholder or wooden spoon handle; allow the cake to cool in the water bath in the oven for

THE IMPORTANCE OF CHILLING CHEESECAKE

CHILLED 2 HOURS   **CHILLED 5 HOURS**

If the cheesecake is not thoroughly chilled, it will not hold its shape when sliced (left). After 5 hours in the refrigerator, the cheesecake has set up and can be sliced neatly (right).

1 hour. Transfer the springform pan without foil to a wire rack; run a small paring knife around the inside edge of the pan to loosen the sides of the cake and cool the cake to room temperature, about 2 hours.

4. FOR THE LEMON CURD: While the cheesecake bakes, heat the lemon juice in a small nonreactive saucepan over medium heat until hot but not boiling. Whisk the eggs and yolk in a medium nonreactive bowl; gradually whisk in the sugar. Whisking constantly, slowly pour the hot lemon juice into the eggs, then return the mixture to the saucepan and cook over medium heat, stirring constantly with a wooden spoon, until the mixture registers 170 degrees on an instant-read thermometer and is thick enough to cling to the spoon, about 3 minutes (see the photos on page 393). Immediately remove the pan from the heat and stir in the cold butter until incorporated; stir in the cream, vanilla, and salt, then pour the curd through a fine-mesh strainer into a small nonreactive bowl. Cover the surface of the curd directly with plastic wrap; refrigerate until needed.

5. TO FINISH THE CAKE: When the cheesecake is cool, scrape the lemon curd onto the cheesecake still in the springform pan; using an offset icing spatula, spread the curd evenly over the top of the cheesecake. Cover tightly with plastic wrap and refrigerate for at least 5 hours or up to 24 hours. To serve, remove the sides of the springform pan and cut the cake into wedges.

INGREDIENTS: Cookies for Crumb Crust

After rejecting graham crackers in favor of something more delicate, we decided to try shortbread cookies in the crust for our Lemon Cheesecake. Walkers Shortbread, Nabisco's Lorna Doones, and Keebler Sandies all produced crusts that were dense and chewy, with a toffee-like flavor that was too rich and sweet. One test cook suggested digestive biscuits. Although this crust was too sweet and a little gritty (these biscuits contain whole-wheat flour), the dryness of the biscuit produced the best-textured crust to complement the creamy cheesecake; it also let us add more butter to the recipe, which resulted in a better flavor. After testing all of the biscuit-type cookies we could find, the surprise favorite was Barnum's Animals Crackers from Nabisco. Nabisco's Social Tea Biscuits were a close second.

PUMPKIN CHEESECAKE

PUMPKIN CHEESECAKE STANDS SECOND TO the traditional pumpkin pie as a holiday dessert. Those who suffer from pumpkin pie ennui embrace pumpkin cheesecake as "a nice change," but the expectations are low. Undoubtedly, pumpkin cheesecake can be good in its own right; though, as proven by a half-dozen recipes, it rarely is. The tendency was for extremes in texture—dry, dense, chalky cakes or wet, soft mousse-like ones. Flavors veered to far too cheesy and tangy, pungently overspiced, noxiously sweet, and totally bland. Merely mixing a can of pumpkin into a standard cheesecake

PRESSING THE CRUMBS INTO THE PAN

1. Use the bottom of a ramekin, 1 cup measuring cup, or drinking glass to press the crumbs into the bottom of a springform pan. Press the crumbs as far as possible into the edges of the pan.

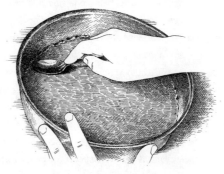

2. Use a teaspoon to neatly press the crumbs into the corners of the pan to create a clean edge.

didn't work; the texture was amiss (leaden and sloppy) and the pumpkin flavor was thwarted. And then there were soggy, grease-leaching crumb crusts. We were prepared to remedy all of this, to make a creamy pumpkin cheesecake with a velvety smooth texture that tasted of sweet, earthy pumpkin as well as tangy cream cheese, that struck a harmonious spicy chord, and, of course, that had a crisp, buttery, cookie-crumb crust.

To make a crumb crust for pumpkin cheesecake, the options were ground-up vanilla wafers, animal crackers (which worked well in our Lemon Cheesecake), gingersnaps, and graham crackers, which we like with our New York Cheesecake. The first two were too mild-flavored for the spicy filling. Gingersnaps were well liked for their spicy bittersweet molasses notes, which balanced well against the pumpkin flavor of the cake, but no matter the brand or the amount of butter and sugar we added—and despite prebaking—they refused to form a crust that retained its crispness.

With graham crackers we had success. Five ounces of crackers (nine whole ones), crushed to crumbs, formed a substantial crust. Too little butter and the crust was not cohesive; 6 tablespoons was just the right amount. Too little sugar and the crust was not adequately sweet; 3 tablespoons was a good amount. Pressed into the bottom of the springform pan and baked until browned about the edges, the graham crackers formed a sturdy, crisp, buttery crust. (Without prebaking, the crust became a pasty, soggy layer beneath the filling.) We then replaced the granulated sugar with dark brown sugar to replicate the molasses flavor of the gingersnaps, but the sugar's moisture caused sogginess, so we went back to granulated. To increase spiciness, we added doses of ground cinnamon and ground ginger.

Anyone who has prepared fresh pumpkin for pumpkin pie can attest to the fact that cutting, seeding, peeling, and cooking fresh pumpkin is not time and effort well spent. Opening a can takes only a few seconds; preparing fresh pumpkin takes a few hours. Moreover, all pumpkin cheesecake recipes call for canned pumpkin; it was a perfectly acceptable ingredient.

With a working recipe pieced together, we found that one can of pumpkin and 1½ pounds of cream cheese made a tall, handsome cake with a balance of tang and earthy pumpkin flavor. We were using granulated sugar to sweeten the cheesecake, but we surmised that brown sugar, with its molasses flavor, would add depth and richness. We were wrong. Substituted for the entire amount of granulated sugar, brown sugar only mucked up and masked the flavor of the pumpkin while giving the cheesecake a dirty brown hue (this was especially true of dark brown sugar).

According to recipes, most pumpkin cheesecakes, unlike plain ones, require neither sour cream nor heavy cream. No matter. We tried them both. Sour

SCIENCE: Is a Water Bath Worth the Trouble?

A water bath is commonly called for in the baking of cheesecakes and custards. The theory is that a water bath moderates the temperature around the perimeter of the pan, preventing overcooking at the edges. To figure out exactly what's happening, we prepared two identical cheesecakes and baked one directly on the oven rack and the other in a water bath. Both were removed from the oven when their centers reached 147 degrees. The cake that had been baked in a water bath was even-colored and smooth; the other cake was browned and cracked. A quick comparison of the temperature at the edges of the cakes confirmed what we suspected. Upon removal from the oven, the cake that had had the benefit of a water bath was 184 degrees at the edge, whereas the cake baked without the water bath had climbed to 213 degrees.

Why was the cheesecake baked in a water bath 30 degrees cooler at the edges than the cake baked without a water bath? Although in both cases the oven had been set to 325 degrees, a water bath cannot exceed 212 degrees, as this is the temperature at which water converts to steam. In fact, the temperature of the water bath was lower than 190 degrees. The oven just wasn't producing enough heat to boil the water.

How did the water bath keep the cheesecake top even and uncracked? More than four cups of water evaporated from the bath during cooking, resulting in quite a humid oven. The moisture in the air reduced the overall loss of moisture from the cake, as the moisture in the air returned to the cake in the form of condensation. This added moisture kept the top flat and prevented cracking.

cream, even in small amounts, was too assertive; its tang eclipsed the delicate flavor of the pumpkin. On the other hand, heavy cream—a cup of it—made the cheesecake feel and taste smooth and lush. It seemed to mitigate the slightly mealy fibrousness of the pumpkin and enrich the cheesecake without obscuring the pumpkin flavor. It did, however, affect the texture, making it loose and soft. Not wanting to compromise the richness, we attempted to remedy the problem by adjusting the eggs, but to no avail. We then tried flour and cornstarch in hopes that one would absorb excess moisture, but both resulted in a starchy, pasty, unappealing texture.

As we were reevaluating heavy cream as an essential ingredient, a colleague suggested cooking the pumpkin before adding it to the cheesecake. It then occurred to us that if we could remove some moisture from the pumpkin, perhaps we could improve the texture. We emptied a can of pumpkin into a nonstick skillet and cooked it until it had lost a surprising amount of moisture—nearly five ounces, or more than half a cup. The cheesecake made with this "dried" pumpkin had a thick, plush, velvety texture to match its rich flavor.

The downside to cooking the pumpkin, which involved frequent stirring and then a cooling period, was the time involved. Draining it simply did not work. In our numerous dealings with canned pumpkin, we noticed that it had cohesion and a nonstick quality. We spread the pumpkin onto a baking sheet lined with paper towels—like spreading frosting on a cake—and then pressed additional paper towels down on its surface to wick away more moisture. In seconds, the pumpkin shed enough liquid (about four ounces) to yield a lovely textured cheesecake, and the paper towels were peeled away almost effortlessly.

With the essential ingredients determined, we turned to eggs. After making some 10 cheesecakes with different amounts of egg in various configurations (whole eggs, egg whites, and egg yolks), we had discovered a surprising range of textures, from stiff and dry to waxy. Five whole eggs produced our favorite cheesecake, one that was satiny, creamy, and unctuous.

Finally, we worked on refining the flavorings. Vanilla and salt were good additions, as was a tablespoon of lemon juice for brightness. Sweet, warm cinnamon was favored at the fore; sharp, spicy ground ginger and small amounts of cloves, nutmeg, and allspice produced, in unison, a deep, resounding flavor but not an overspiced burn.

In its springform pan, a cheesecake can be baked either directly on the oven rack like a regular cake or in a water bath like a delicate custard. The cake baked in a water bath was undeniably better than the version baked without a water bath. (For more information, see "Is a Water Bath Worth the Trouble?", page 396.) We tried a few different oven temperatures, and 325 degrees worked best. At temperatures too high, the water in the bath reached a simmer; too low and the cheesecake took an inordinate amount of time to bake.

Sliced into neat wedges and served with bourbon and brown-sugar-laced whipped cream (many at first decried this as over-the-top, but they were silenced after a single taste), here was a pumpkin cheesecake that pleased the pumpkin pie traditionalists and that for the others was a nice change from "a nice change."

Spiced Pumpkin Cheesecake
SERVES 12 TO 16

Depending on the oven and the temperature of the ingredients, this cheesecake may bake about 15 minutes faster or slower than the instructions indicate; it is therefore best to check the cake 1¼ hours into baking. Although the cheesecake can be made up to 3 days in advance, the crust will begin to lose its crispness after only 1 day. To make slicing the cheesecake easy and neat, use a knife with a narrow blade, such as a carving knife; between cuts, dip the blade into a pitcher of hot water and wipe it clean with paper towels. The cheesecake is good on its own, but the Brown Sugar and Bourbon Cream (recipe follows) is a grand addition.

CRUST

9	whole graham crackers (5 ounces), broken into large pieces
3	tablespoons sugar
½	teaspoon ground ginger
½	teaspoon ground cinnamon
¼	teaspoon ground cloves
6	tablespoons (¾ stick) unsalted butter, melted

FILLING

1 1/3	cups (10 1/3 ounces) sugar
1	teaspoon ground cinnamon
1/2	teaspoon ground ginger
1/4	teaspoon freshly grated nutmeg
1/4	teaspoon ground cloves
1/4	teaspoon ground allspice
1/2	teaspoon salt
1	(15-ounce) can pumpkin puree
1 1/2	pounds (three 8-ounce packages) cream cheese, cut into 1-inch chunks, at room temperature
1	tablespoon vanilla extract
1	tablespoon juice from 1 lemon
5	large eggs, at room temperature
1	cup heavy cream

1. FOR THE CRUST: Adjust an oven rack to the lower-middle position and heat the oven to 325 degrees. Spray the bottom and sides of a 9-inch springform pan evenly with nonstick cooking spray. Place the crackers, sugar, and spices in a food processor and process until evenly and finely ground, about fifteen 2-second pulses. Transfer the crumbs to a medium bowl, drizzle the melted butter over, and mix with a rubber spatula until evenly moistened. Turn the crumbs into the prepared springform pan and spread the crumbs into an even layer, following the illustrations on page 395. Bake until fragrant and browned about the edges, about 15 minutes. Cool on a wire rack to room temperature, about 30 minutes. When cool, wrap the outside of the pan with two 18-inch-square pieces of heavy-duty foil; set the springform pan in a roasting pan.

2. FOR THE FILLING: Bring about 4 quarts water to a simmer in a stockpot. While the crust is cooling, whisk the sugar, spices, and salt in a small bowl; set aside. Line a baking sheet with a triple layer of paper towels. Spread the pumpkin on the towels and cover with a second triple layer of towels. Press firmly until the towels are saturated. Peel back the top layer of towels and discard. Grasp the bottom towels and fold the pumpkin in half; peel back the towels. Repeat and flip the pumpkin onto the baking sheet; discard the towels.

3. Beat the cream cheese in the bowl of a standing mixer set at medium speed to break up and soften slightly, about 1 minute. Scrape the beater and the bottom and sides of the bowl well with a rubber spatula. Add about a third of the sugar mixture and beat at medium-low speed until combined, about 1 minute; scrape the bowl and add the remaining sugar in two additions, scraping the bowl after each addition. Add the pumpkin, vanilla, and lemon juice and beat at medium speed until combined, about 45 seconds; scrape the bowl. Add 3 of the eggs and beat at medium-low speed until incorporated, about 1 minute; scrape the bowl. Add the remaining 2 eggs and beat at medium-low speed until incorporated, about 45 seconds; scrape the bowl. Add the heavy cream and beat at low speed until combined, about 45 seconds. Using a rubber spatula, scrape the bottom and sides of the bowl and give a final stir by hand.

4. Pour the filling into the springform pan and smooth the surface; set the roasting pan in the oven and pour enough boiling water to come about halfway up the sides of the springform pan. Bake until the center of the cake is slightly wobbly when the pan is shaken and the center of the cake reads 150 degrees on an instant-read thermometer, about 1½ hours (see note). Set the roasting pan on a wire rack and cool until the water is just warm, about 45 minutes. Remove the springform pan from the water bath, discard the foil, and set on a wire rack; run a paring knife around the inside edge of the pan to loosen the sides of the cake and cool until barely warm, about 3 hours. Wrap with plastic wrap and refrigerate until chilled, at least 4 hours or up to 3 days.

5. TO SERVE: Remove the sides of the pan. Slide a thin metal spatula between the crust and the pan bottom to loosen, then slide the cake onto a serving platter. Let the cheesecake stand at room temperature about 30 minutes, then cut into wedges (see note) and serve with Brown Sugar and Bourbon Cream, if desired.

➤ VARIATION

Pumpkin-Bourbon Cheesecake with Graham-Pecan Crust

Follow the recipe for Spiced Pumpkin Cheesecake, reducing the graham crackers to 3 ounces (5 whole crackers), processing 2 ounces chopped pecans (about ½ cup) with the crackers, and reducing the butter to 4 tablespoons. Omit the lemon juice from the filling, reduce the vanilla extract to 1 teaspoon, and add ¼ cup bourbon along with the heavy cream.

Brown Sugar and Bourbon Cream

MAKES ABOUT 3 CUPS

1	cup heavy cream
½	cup sour cream
⅓	cup packed (2⅓ ounces) light brown sugar
⅛	teaspoon salt
2	teaspoons bourbon

1. In the bowl of a standing mixer, whisk the heavy cream, sour cream, brown sugar, and salt until combined. Cover with plastic wrap and refrigerate until ready to serve the cheesecake, at least 4 hours or up to 24, stirring once or twice during chilling to ensure that the sugar dissolves.

2. When ready to serve the cheesecake, add the bourbon and beat the mixture at medium speed until small bubbles form around the edges, about 40 seconds; increase the speed to high and continue to beat until fluffy and doubled in volume, about 1 minute longer. Spoon the cream onto individual slices of cheesecake.

RICOTTA CHEESECAKE

UNLESS YOU HAVE AN ITALIAN GRAND-mother who likes to bake or you're lucky enough to live near an Italian-American bakery, you probably haven't had the pleasure of eating ricotta cheesecake. Lighter and softer in texture than a cream cheese–based cheesecake, ricotta cheese-cake is also milder in flavor (enough so that it may make converts of those who insist they don't like cheesecake). Our research identified three styles. The standard ricotta cheesecake is made in a springform pan, which has typically been dusted with bread crumbs. Skillet cheesecake usually has no crust and is cooked on the stovetop until the

bottom begins to set, then it is finished in the oven. A third style of ricotta cheesecake is baked in a pastry crust.

We didn't want to be fussing with pastry dough or negotiating between the stovetop and oven and trying to extract a cheesecake from a skillet. Therefore, we focused our attention on the stan-dard ricotta cheesecake and began our work by sampling a half dozen recipes made in springform pans. The recipes that were most appealing to us were pared down to the basics: ricotta cheese, eggs, and sugar, with minimal additional flavoring. Excessive spices (such as cinnamon and nutmeg) sullied the sweet, dairy-rich taste of the ricotta, while nuts and dried fruits conflicted with the light and creamy texture of the cake.

Because a basic ricotta cheesecake can be made with either whole eggs or separated eggs, we had to narrow the playing field even further. In our test-ing, we much preferred the cheesecakes made with separated eggs. Mixing the yolks with the cheese and sugar and folding in the beaten whites at the end produced a light and airy cake that was still beautifully rich and creamy. Whole eggs produced a heavy cheesecake that was more custard-like and that tasters found less appealing.

We next varied the number of eggs in our recipe, using 2 pounds of ricotta cheese (the right amount for a 9-inch springform pan) in each test. Six eggs produced a cheesecake that was very light and airy but more like a soufflé than a cheesecake. Moreover, the flavor of the eggs overpowered the mild cheese. (We learned that ricotta has a lot less personality than American cream cheese and must be seasoned lightly.) Three eggs produced a cheesecake with a prominent cheesy flavor and a dense creamy texture, but the cake seemed a bit flat. We settled on four eggs, which delivered a slightly more substantial cheesecake with just the right balance of creamy richness and lightness. The resulting cheesecake was a little mousse, a little cake, and a little soufflé all in one.

Fresh ricotta cheese, made in Italian markets, is creamier and less watery than the commer-cial ricotta cheese found in supermarkets. This explains why many recipes we tried tasted grainy and wet. Obviously, these recipe writers were using the higher-quality cheese. However, we wanted to develop a recipe that would work with either creamy fresh ricotta from an Italian market or cheese shop or the lumpy, grainy ricotta sold in plastic containers in supermarkets. We solved the graininess problem by pureeing supermarket ricotta cheese in a food processor until it was smooth and creamy.

Some recipes use flour to make the cheesecake firmer and thicker and, possibly, to compensate for excess liquid in the ricotta cheese. We found that anything more than a tablespoon or two of flour made the cheesecakes taste slightly gummy. A better solution to the water problem was to drain the ricotta cheese in a paper towel–lined strainer overnight. About a quarter cup of water drained from the cheese during this time. The cakes made with the drained cheese were less wet, were a bit creamier, and had a more pronounced cheese flavor. We tried eliminating the flour altogether from our recipe. However, even with drained cheese, we found that 1 tablespoon of flour helped bind the mixture and produced a creamier cake without imparting a starchy flavor.

Orange zest, lemon zest, vanilla, and alcohol (rum, brandy, or Marsala wine) are typical flavorings for ricotta cheesecakes. Our tasters preferred lemon to orange zest. Vanilla was essential; 2 teaspoons enhanced the dairy flavor of the cheese. Rum was our booze of choice. We liked its clean but strong flavor.

Most Italian recipes call for sprinkling bread crumbs in the pan before adding the cheese filling. Our tasters strongly felt that the bread crumbs didn't enhance the cheesecake in any way. They became soggy and marred the surface of the cheesecake with unattractive brown spots. While it is not traditional, we thought that a baked cookie crumb crust (such as you might find in an American cheesecake) might add a nice texture and flavor contrast to the cheesecake. Not wanting to stray too far from the recipe's Italian roots, we used amaretti cookies instead of the classic graham crackers with great success. The almond flavor of the amaretti cookies complemented the flavors of the cheesecake and offered a crunchy counterpoint to the creamy cheese filling.

Ricotta Cheesecake
SERVES 8 TO 10

The ricotta cheese must be drained in the refrigerator for at least 8 hours, or overnight. To drain the cheese, line a fine-mesh sieve with two layers of paper towels, place the cheese in the sieve, place the sieve over a bowl, and refrigerate.

AMARETTI COOKIE CRUST

2   heaping cups (4 ounces) amaretti cookies, processed in a food processor to uniformly fine crumbs

5   tablespoons unsalted butter, melted, plus 1 tablespoon melted butter for greasing the pan

RICOTTA FILLING

2   pounds ricotta cheese, drained

4   large eggs, separated

³⁄₄ cup (5¼ ounces) sugar

¼   cup light rum

1   tablespoon unbleached all-purpose flour
     Grated zest of 1 medium lemon

2   teaspoons vanilla extract

⅛   teaspoon salt

1. FOR THE CRUST: Adjust an oven rack to the lower-middle position and heat the oven to 325 degrees. In a small bowl, combine the amaretti crumbs and 5 tablespoons of the melted butter and toss with a fork until evenly moistened. Brush the bottom and sides of a 9-inch springform pan with most of the remaining 1 tablespoon melted butter, making sure to leave enough to brush the sides of the pan after the crust cools. Empty the crumbs into the springform pan and press them evenly into the pan bottom, following the illustrations on page 395. Bake until fragrant and beginning to brown around the edges, about 13 minutes. Cool on a wire rack to room temperature, about 30 minutes. (Do not turn off the oven.) Brush the sides of the springform pan with the remaining melted butter.

2. FOR THE FILLING: While the crust cools, place the drained ricotta in a food processor and process until very smooth, about 1 minute. Add the egg yolks, sugar, rum, flour, lemon zest, vanilla, and salt and process until blended, about 1 more

minute. Scrape the mixture into a large bowl.

3. In the bowl of a standing mixer, beat the egg whites at high speed until they hold stiff peaks. Fold the whites into the ricotta mixture and pour the mixture evenly into the cooled crust.

4. Bake the cheesecake until the top is lightly browned and an instant-read thermometer inserted into the center reads about 150 degrees, about 1¼ hours. (The perimeter of the cake should be firm, but the center will jiggle slightly. It will solidify further as the cake cools.) Transfer the pan to a wire rack and cool for 5 minutes. Run a paring knife between the cake and the side of the springform pan. Cool until barely warm, 2½ to 3 hours. Wrap the pan tightly in plastic wrap and refrigerate until the cheesecake is cold and set, at least 5 hours or up to 2 days.

5. To unmold the cheesecake, remove the sides of the pan. Let the cheesecake stand at room temperature for about 30 minutes, then cut it into wedges and serve.

HOT FUDGE PUDDING CAKE

HOT FUDGE PUDDING CAKE HAS SEVERAL aliases: Denver pudding cake, chocolate upside-down cake, brownie pudding cake, or sometimes simply chocolate pudding cake. This 1950s community cookbook recipe may be a bit dated, but it's a boon to the cook looking for a simple baked dessert that requires no creaming or whipping. Hot fudge pudding cake is definitely not a dessert for entertaining; it does not impress with its looks. It's a humble, homely dessert with bumps, lumps, and cracks, an easy one to turn up your nose at. But those who have eaten hot fudge pudding cake know its charms: unpretentious, moist, brownie-like chocolate cake sitting on a pool of a chocolate sauce so thick it's reminiscent of pudding, with both miraculously baked at the same time in the same dish. Served warm with vanilla ice cream, this cake more than makes up for its lack of looks.

In the matter of pudding cakes, there are two distinct styles. The fussier version requires beaten egg whites rather than chemical leaveners for lift

and a hot water bath to produce a soufflé-like cake above a custard-like sauce. Then there's the absurdly simple hot fudge pudding cake that resembles a chemically leavened brownie and can be made by a rookie baker equipped with only a few bowls and a whisk. It was the latter style that we were pursuing, so we gathered a few recipes and tried them. All were disappointing. Instead of deep and chocolatey, they tasted dull and mild. Instead of providing enough spoon-coating sauce to accompany the cake, some were dry, with a disproportionate amount of cake, while the others were soupy, with a wet, sticky, underdone cake.

For those who aren't familiar with the magic of pudding cakes, here's how they work. The batter is made in the manner of a brownie batter, but with milk added. After the batter goes into the baking dish, things take an unusual turn. A mixture of sugar and cocoa is sprinkled over the batter, then liquid is poured on top, and the mess goes into the oven. (Depending on the recipe, the cocoa and sugar may first be dissolved in hot water, then poured over.) The step of pouring liquid over the batter is so odd that the cook making a hot fudge pudding cake for the first time quickly becomes skeptical. With baking, however, what looks to be a mistake is transformed into a dessert. The cake rises to the surface, and the liquid that started out on top sinks to the bottom, taking the sugar and cocoa with it, becoming the "hot fudge" part of the dessert.

With a working recipe cobbled together, our first goal was to pump up the chocolate flavor, suspecting that the problem was that most recipes call for cocoa rather than chocolate. In our experience, cocoa alone carries potent—sometimes acrid—chocolate flavor, but it cannot deliver the complexity or richness of chocolate. We tried adding different amounts of bittersweet chocolate to the pudding cake. Two ounces in addition to the ⅓ cup of cocoa was the ideal amount to obtain fuller flavor. More chocolate and the cake was too rich and its texture became sodden.

We also thought to try regular "natural" cocoa versus Dutch-processed cocoa. The former is lighter in color and more acidic than the latter. In a side-by-side tasting, we were stunned by the difference. The "natural" cocoa version tasted sharp and harsh, but the one made with Dutch-processed cocoa (we used Droste, a brand widely available in supermarkets) tasted smooth, round, and full. It was unanimous. Every person who tasted the two cakes vastly preferred the one made with Dutch-processed cocoa. To sweeten the cake and counter the bitterness of even the Dutch-processed cocoa, ⅔ cup of sugar was required. We tried substituting some brown sugar for granulated but found it a nuisance because of the way it clumps (not a problem if the butter and sugar were being creamed together, but this cake was too easy for that). Besides, the brown sugar added no significant flavor benefit.

The next issue to settle was that of eggs, and there seemed to be two choices: recipes that contained an egg and those that didn't. The eggless cakes were mushy and crumbly. Their crumb lacked structural integrity, and because they were soft and mushy, there seemed to be little distinction between what was supposed to be cake and what was supposed to be hot fudge. We tried as many as two whole eggs, but our preference was for a pudding cake made with just one yolk. It was brownie-like, with a nice, tooth-sinking crumb. Cakes made with whole eggs were drier and slightly rubbery.

So far, we had been using 1 cup of unbleached all-purpose flour, but the cake layer was a tad too thick. We tried smaller amounts of flour, hoping that the texture wouldn't suffer as a consequence. We ended up preferring the cake with ¾ cup of flour. It tasted more richly of chocolate and had a moist, brownie-like texture. It had a little less height, but this made it a better match for the amount of sauce.

The butter in hot fudge pudding cake is always melted, never creamed. (This cake requires a heavy-duty leavener, such as baking powder, to force the cake layer up through the sludge that becomes the sauce. Although creaming is one way to provide lift, in this case we found that the contribution made by aerated butter was minimal and not worth the effort.) With only 4 tablespoons of melted butter, the cake tasted lean and dry. With 8, it was leaden and greasy. Six tablespoons was the ideal amount. Like most other cakes, hot fudge pudding cake contains some dairy, usually milk. We tried heavy cream and half-and-half to see if either had desirable effects. Heavy cream made a slick, greasy, fat-laden cake. With half-and-half, the cake was somewhat greasy and a little too rich. Milk was the way to go.

For lift, we relied on baking powder. One recipe called for 2 tablespoons per cup of flour ("chemical warfare" was one taster's term for this mixture). Two teaspoons of baking powder was just fine. To heighten the flavor, we added ¼ teaspoon salt and 1 tablespoon vanilla (there was a lot of chocolate flavor to contend with).

As mentioned above, there are two ways to add the ingredients destined to become the

PUDDING CAKE 1-2-3

1. Pour the batter into the prepared baking dish and spread evenly into the sides and corners with a rubber spatula.

2. Sprinkle the cocoa/sugar mixture evenly over the batter. The mixture should cover the entire surface of the batter.

3. Pour the coffee mixture gently over the cocoa mixture and put the baking dish in the oven.

fudge sauce. A mixture of cocoa and sugar can be sprinkled on the batter and water then poured over it, creating what looks like a panful of river sludge. Alternatively, the cocoa and sugar can first be dissolved in boiling water. We compared two such pudding cakes. The one with the sprinkled cocoa-and-sugar mixture baked up with crisp edges and a faintly crisp crust that we preferred over the uniformly soft, cakey surface of the other. It was as if some of the sugar, moistened by the water, remained at the surface even after the liquid seeped to the bottom, and then caramelized to form a pleasing crust.

We tried different amounts of cocoa in the sauce-to-be and landed at ⅓ cup, the same amount we put in the cake. A mixture made with all granulated sugar resulted in a toffee-like crust, rather sticky and tough, with a one-dimensional sweetness. We preferred a mix of granulated and brown sugar, with the molasses flavor of the latter producing a full, round taste.

The amount of water poured over the cake determines the amount of sauce at the bottom. One and one-half cups—a little more than what most recipes call for—was ideal, yielding an ample amount of sauce with the right consistency. Some hot fudge pudding cake recipes suggest using coffee instead of water. Indeed, we thought the coffee was a nice addition. It didn't interfere with the chocolate flavor but nicely complemented it, cutting through some of the cake's cloying sweet quality and enriching the flavor. For ease, we mixed 2 teaspoons of instant coffee into the water, but cold, brewed coffee cut with a little water works as well.

We tested different oven temperatures and baking times. While most recipes indicated 350 degrees for about 35 minutes, we preferred 325 degrees for 45 minutes. The lower temperature helped keep the sauce from bubbling rapidly, a phenomenon that can cause spillage if left unchecked. In addition, the slightly longer baking time promoted a nicer crust. We noted that this cake combined lots of pleasing textures: a silky sauce; a moist, cakey crumb; and a thin, brittle crust, especially around the edges.

When attacked with a spoon straight from the oven, the hot fudge pudding cake revealed a thin, blistering-hot sauce and a sodden cake. If allowed to cool for 20 to 30 minutes, the sauce became pudding-like and the cake brownie-like. The warm cake cries out to be served with vanilla or coffee ice cream (whipped cream just isn't serious enough). For serving to guests, we adapted the recipe to bake in individual ramekins so that apologies for the cake's dowdy appearance need not be made so profusely. Leftovers reheat well in a microwave, but don't count on having any.

Hot Fudge Pudding Cake

SERVES 8

If you have cold, brewed coffee on hand, it can be used in place of the instant coffee and water, but to make sure it isn't too strong, use 1 cup of cold coffee mixed with ½ cup of water. Serve the cake warm with vanilla or coffee ice cream. Leftovers can be reheated, covered with plastic wrap, in a microwave oven.

2	teaspoons instant coffee
1½	cups water
⅔	cup (2 ounces) Dutch-processed cocoa
⅓	cup packed (2⅓ ounces) brown sugar
1	cup (7 ounces) granulated sugar
6	tablespoons (¾ stick) unsalted butter
2	ounces bittersweet or semisweet chocolate, chopped
¾	cup (3¾ ounces) unbleached all-purpose flour
2	teaspoons baking powder
1	tablespoon vanilla extract
⅓	cup whole milk
¼	teaspoon salt
1	large egg yolk

1. Adjust an oven rack to the lower-middle position and heat the oven to 325 degrees. Lightly spray an 8-inch square glass or ceramic baking dish with nonstick cooking spray. Stir the instant coffee into the water; set aside to dissolve. Stir together ⅓ cup of the cocoa, the brown sugar, and ⅓ cup of the granulated sugar in a small bowl, breaking up any large clumps with your fingers; set aside. Melt the butter, the remaining ⅓ cup cocoa, and the chocolate in a small bowl set over a saucepan

of barely simmering water; whisk until smooth and set aside to cool slightly. Whisk the flour and baking powder in a small bowl to combine; set aside. Whisk the remaining ⅔ cup granulated sugar with the vanilla, milk, and salt in a medium bowl until combined; whisk in the yolk. Add the chocolate mixture and whisk to combine. Add the flour mixture and whisk until the batter is evenly moistened.

2. Pour the batter into the prepared baking dish and spread evenly to the sides and corners. Sprinkle the cocoa mixture evenly over the batter (the cocoa mixture should cover the entire surface of the batter); pour the coffee mixture gently over the cocoa mixture. Bake until the cake is puffed and bubbling and just beginning to pull away from the sides of the baking dish, about 45 minutes. (Do not overbake.) Cool the cake in the dish on a wire rack about 25 minutes before serving.

➤ VARIATION
Individual Hot Fudge Pudding Cakes
Follow the recipe for Hot Fudge Pudding Cake, heating the oven to 400 degrees and lightly spraying eight 6- to 8-ounce ramekins with nonstick cooking spray; set the ramekins on a baking sheet. Divide the batter evenly among the ramekins (about ¼ cup per ramekin) and level with the back of a spoon; sprinkle about 2 tablespoons cocoa mixture over the batter in each ramekin. Pour 3 tablespoons coffee mixture over the cocoa mixture in each ramekin. Bake until puffed and bubbling, about 20 minutes. (Do not overbake.) Cool the ramekins about 15 minutes before serving (the cakes will fall).

STICKY TOFFEE PUDDING CAKE

CLASSICALLY BRITISH, STICKY TOFFEE PUDDING cake is a member of the pudding family, a hodge-podge of steamed and baked desserts, which sport such colorful names as "cabinet pudding," "dock pudding," and "roly-poly." Most "pudds" haven't traveled far beyond Britain's shores, but sticky toffee pudding cake is an exception. Flavored with dates and dark brown sugar, it is a simple, moist cake with a straightforward, earthy flavor. It's unapologetically sweet, and many of the versions we have tried have been sickeningly saccharine—enough to make our teeth ache and make us beg off desserts for days to come. Other versions possessed the bland floury flavor of undercooked pancakes. And as for texture, they ranged from stiff and pound-cakey to completely mushy. Our goal was to make a sticky toffee pudding cake that packed a full date flavor and had a tolerable sweetness level and a moist, tender crumb.

There's nothing complicated about this pudding cake; no separated eggs, sifted flour, or whipped anything. It is a simple batter of flour, butter, sweetener, and eggs to which dates are added. Very few recipes we found varied from a basic mixing technique—dry and wet ingredients are mixed separately and then combined—not dissimilar to the quick bread method. Flavors and baking methods, however, varied greatly. That said, we picked our favorite recipe from our initial survey and commenced testing.

The dates have the largest impact on flavor so we opted to start there. Most recipes call for dried dates, the ones stored next to the raisins; unlike fresh dates, they are inexpensive and available year-round. Traditionally, the dried dates are chopped and soaked in hot water laced with baking soda before mixing them into the batter. The alkalinity of the baking soda softens the dates' tough, papery skins and, as a bonus, helps to darken the pudding's color—more a matter of aesthetics than flavor. Skeptics that we are, we prepared batches of the pudding without soaking the dates and found their skins fibrous enough to detract from the pudding's tender texture. And the color was lighter than we desired. Back to tradition we went.

As far as incorporating the dates into the batter, many recipes recommended coarsely chopping them and stirring them in. This worked, but it produced a mild date flavor, because the dates failed to fully permeate the cake. A better option, we found, was to process a portion of the dates with the sugar and leave the remainder coarsely chopped. The flavor surpassed that of the previous batches, and the texture was better as well—moister and softer.

Traditionally, sticky toffee pudding cake is sweetened with treacle, a syrup byproduct of sugar production. It is similar to molasses in flavor but usually milder and without the bitter bite of most varieties of molasses. We tried molasses in our recipe but found it too assertive, even when cut with granulated sugar. Brown sugar proved a better substitute, buttressing the dates' mild flavor rather than overpowering it. Tasters' reactions were split down the middle between light and dark brown sugar, some appreciating the robustness of the dark, others preferring the subtlety of the light. We leave the decision up to you. As for auxiliary flavors, things are traditionally kept simple. Vanilla was a welcome addition, but tasters deemed everything else superfluous.

Sticky toffee pudding cake can either be baked in a large casserole or baking dish, or divvied up into ramekins for individual servings. In either case, we found a water bath essential to a moist, tender texture. Without the temperature-taming water bath, the cake cooked too quickly and acquired a texture similar to quick bread. It was tasty but not the delicate dessert we sought. Surprisingly, there was a notable difference in texture between cake in individual ramekins and a single cake in a large baking dish. The former had a lighter, more delicate texture than the latter, which was cakier and sturdier. The latter was more convenient, however, so we opted to include it as a variation.

The sugar and dates in the cake itself are only part of the "sticky" in the title; the rest comes from a toffee sauce that coats the cake. In all the recipes we found, the sauce was a simple blend of butter, brown sugar or treacle, and cream simmered until blended. After testing a few versions, we tweaked ratios of sugar and butter for a lighter-tasting, smoother sauce and added a splash of rum, a not uncommon flavoring, which cut through the sticky richness.

Individual Sticky Toffee Pudding Cakes

SERVES 8

While sticky toffee pudding is traditionally served with crème anglaise (page 500), vanilla ice cream also serves as a suitable foil to its sweetness. This pudding is best eaten the same day, but it may be stored for up to 2 days and reheated in the microwave before serving.

PUDDING CAKES

1¼	cups (6¼ ounces) unbleached all-purpose flour, plus more for dusting the ramekins
1¼	cups pitted dates, cut crosswise into ¼-inch slices
½	teaspoon baking soda
¾	cup warm water
½	teaspoon baking powder
½	teaspoon salt
¾	cup packed (5¼ ounces) light or dark brown sugar
2	large eggs
1½	teaspoons vanilla extract
4	tablespoons (½ stick) unsalted butter, melted

TOFFEE SAUCE

8	tablespoons (1 stick) unsalted butter
1	cup packed (7 ounces) light or dark brown sugar
⅔	cup heavy cream
1	tablespoon rum

Crème Anglaise (page 500) or vanilla ice cream

1. FOR THE PUDDING CAKES: Adjust an oven rack to the middle position and heat the oven to 350 degrees. Grease and flour eight 4-ounce ramekins and line the bottom of each with a round of parchment paper cut to fit. Set the prepared ramekins in a large roasting pan lined with a clean dish towel. Bring a kettle or large saucepan of water to a boil over high heat.

2. Combine half the dates with the baking soda and water in a glass measuring cup (the dates should be submerged beneath the water) and set aside for 5 minutes. Drain the dates, reserving the

liquid, and transfer to a medium bowl. Whisk the flour, baking powder, and salt together in another medium bowl.

3. In a food processor, process the remaining dates and brown sugar until just blended, about five 1-second pulses. Add the reserved soaking liquid, eggs, and vanilla and process until smooth, about 5 seconds. With the food processor running, pour the melted butter through the feed tube in a steady stream. Transfer this mixture to the bowl with the softened dates.

4. Gently stir the dry mixture into the wet mixture until just combined and the date pieces are evenly dispersed. Distribute the batter evenly among the prepared ramekins. Fill the roasting pan with enough boiling water to come halfway up the sides of the ramekins, making sure not to splash water into the ramekins. Cover the pan tightly with aluminum foil, crimping the edges to seal. Bake the pudding cakes until puffed and small holes appear on their surface, about 40 minutes. Immediately remove the ramekins from the water bath and cool on a wire rack for 10 minutes.

5. For the toffee sauce: Meanwhile, melt the butter in a medium saucepan over medium heat. Whisk in the brown sugar until smooth. Continue to cook, stirring occasionally, until the sugar is dissolved and the mixture looks puffy, 3 to 4 minutes. Slowly pour in the cream and rum, whisk just to combine, reduce the heat, and simmer until frothy,

about 3 minutes. Remove from the heat, cover to keep warm, and set aside.

6. To serve, invert each ramekin onto a plate or shallow bowl, remove the ramekin, and peel off the parchment paper lining. Divide the toffee sauce evenly among the cakes and serve immediately, accompanied by crème anglaise or vanilla ice cream.

➤ VARIATION
Large Sticky Toffee Pudding Cake
If you don't have individual ramekins, you can bake the pudding in an 8-inch square baking dish. The texture will be cakier.

Grease and flour an 8-inch square baking dish and set it in a large roasting pan lined with a clean towel. Follow the recipe for Individual Sticky Toffee Puddings, pouring the batter into the prepared baking dish. Add enough boiling water to reach halfway up the sides and cover the pan tightly with aluminum foil. Bake until the outer 2 inches develop small holes and the center has puffed and is firm to the touch, about 40 minutes. Immediately remove the dish from the water bath and set on a wire rack. Liberally poke the top of the pudding with a paring knife or wooden skewer; pour the toffee sauce over the pudding and spread evenly with a rubber spatula. Cool for 10 minutes, cut into squares, and serve accompanied by crème anglaise or vanilla ice cream.

CHRISTMAS COOKIES **PAGE 454**

Glazed Butter Cookies, Jam Sandwiches, Lime-Glazed Coconut Snowballs,
and Chocolate-Cherry Bar Cookies with Hazelnuts

NUT CRESCENTS AND SNOWBALLS **PAGE 463**

CHEWY, FUDGY TRIPLE-CHOCOLATE BROWNIES **PAGE 486**

LEMON BARS **PAGE 493**

ROULADE-SHAPED RUGELACH AND CRESCENT-SHAPED RUGELACH **PAGE 467**

PROFITEROLES **PAGE 260**

CHOCOLATE-DIPPED COCONUT MACAROONS **PAGE 476**

PEACH CRISP **PAGE 298**

SUMMER BERRY GRATIN **PAGE 313**

TOMATO AND MOZZARELLA TART **PAGE 247**

CRABMEAT QUICHE **PAGE 245**

CLASSIC APPLE PIE **PAGE 184**

CUSTARD PIE **PAGE 200**

SUMMER BERRY PIE **PAGE 198**

POACHED PEAR AND ALMOND TART **PAGE 232**

421

FLAKY APPLE TURNOVERS **PAGE 276**

8

COOKIES, BROWNIES, AND BAR COOKIES

Cookies, Brownies, and Bar Cookies

MAKING COOKIES AND BROWNIES IS America's favorite kind of baking project. Not only are the results usually quite good, but the time, effort, and skills required are usually minimal. Ingredient lists draw heavily on pantry staples as well as refrigerated items, like butter and eggs, that can be found in most reasonably well stocked kitchens. Nor is expensive equipment necessary.

There are thousands of cookie recipes in circulation. Over the years, we have made many of these recipes in our test kitchen and have come to one startling conclusion. The simplest cookies are usually the best and the ones we make most often. Sugar, chocolate chip, oatmeal, and peanut butter cookies are popular for a reason. They may not be much to look at, but they deliver on flavor with very little effort. We do make slightly more elaborate (but not difficult) cookies for holidays and special occasions. Nothing beats gingerbread people at Christmastime or biscotti served with strong coffee following an Italian-inspired meal.

This chapter also includes brownies and bar cookies. Especially convenient because they bake in just one batch, these cookies are quick to get into the oven since the batter or dough is either poured or pressed into the pan. Once cooled, they are cut into squares and ready to go.

Whether you're making cookies or brownies, there are a few tips you should remember:

CREAMING BUTTER AND SUGAR

The butter is creamed with the sugar until light and fluffy. The butter must be softened in order for it to be creamed properly. At 35 degrees (the temperature of most refrigerators), the butter is too cold to combine with the other ingredients. As a result, we have found that cookies made with cold butter are often flat because not enough air is whipped into the butter during the creaming stage. Ideally, an hour or two before you want to make the cookies, remove the butter from the refrigerator and let it warm to about 65 degrees. Butter starts to lose its shape at 68 degrees, so the stick will still be a bit firm when pressed. Avoid using the microwave to soften butter, because it does so

---

COOKIE STORAGE

IF YOU WANT TO KEEP COOKIES FOR several days, we suggest storing them in an airtight container at room temperature (or, to keep cookies soft and fresh, see our tip on page 430). You can restore just-baked freshness to chewy cookies by wrapping a single cookie in a sheet of paper towel and microwaving it until soft, 15 to 25 seconds. Cool microwaved cookies before serving. This technique works best with oversized cookies that should be chewy and a bit soft, like chewy chocolate chip, chocolate, peanut butter, and oatmeal. Do not try this with cookies that should be crisp.

If you know you can't finish off a batch of cookies within a few days, consider freezing part of the dough. Almost every dough can be frozen either in individual portions (see the illustrations on page 480 for more information) or as a block. If you have frozen the dough in balls, simply transfer them to a baking sheet and bake as directed, extending the time in the oven by a few minutes. If the dough is a solid mass, let it thaw in the refrigerator before shaping and baking it.

---

unevenly. Instead, cut the butter into very small bits so it will warm up quickly. By the time you have preheated the oven and assembled and measured the remaining ingredients, the butter should be close to 65 degrees.

Creaming the butter and mixing the dough for most cookie recipes can be done either by hand or with an electric mixer. The cookie recipes in this chapter include timing guidelines for creaming as well as for mixing with an electric mixer. It's not possible to offer time guidelines for hand mixing (because cooks' strengths vary), but we do offer visual cues, such as "cream until light and fluffy" and "add the dry ingredients just until incorporated," so you'll know how to whip up a batch with just a wooden spoon (and a little elbow grease).

ADDING EGGS After creaming, the eggs and other liquids (vanilla or other extracts) are added. Make sure the eggs are at room temperature before adding them to the creamed mixture because cold eggs have a tendency to curdle the batter. Eggs can be brought to room temperature by letting them sit out on the counter for an hour or two or by placing them in a bowl of hot tap water for just five minutes.

ADDING DRY INGREDIENTS In many old-fashioned recipes, the flour, leavener, and salt are sifted together before being added to the batter. This was necessary when flour was often lumpy straight from the bag. Because modern flour is presifted, we find this step to be unnecessary for making cookies. (Cakes, however, are often a different matter.) We simply mix the dry ingredients together in a bowl (a whisk does this well) to make sure that the leavener and salt will be evenly distributed.

There are two dry ingredients that we like to sift. Cocoa powder and confectioners' sugar often have small lumps. We find that sifting breaks up those lumps and does an excellent job of mixing the cocoa or confectioners' sugar with the other dry ingredients.

ADDING SOLID INGREDIENTS Adding solid ingredients, like chocolate chips and nuts, is the final step in the dough-making process. These ingredients can be stirred in by hand or with an electric mixer. If using the mixer, keep the speed low and beat just long enough (five seconds should be enough time) to incorporate the solid ingredients evenly into the dough.

CHILLING THE DOUGH No matter how the dough is shaped, you can inhibit spreading in the oven—and thus prevent the cookies from becoming too thin—by chilling the dough in the refrigerator for at least one hour.

DROP COOKIES The quickest way to get the dough into the oven is to drop the dough from a spoon directly onto a baking sheet. Because the pieces of dough are not round, they spread unevenly in the oven. The resulting cookies have thin, crisp edges and thicker centers.

MOLDED OR SHAPED COOKIES For molded or shaped cookies, each piece of dough is rolled into a ball or otherwise manipulated by hand before being placed on a baking sheet. When rolled into a ball, the dough is often also rolled in sugar before being baked. Shaping the dough into balls promotes even spreading and thickness in the baked cookies.

ROLLED OR CUT-OUT COOKIES This method is used to guarantee thin, crisp cookies suitable for decoration. Rolled-and-cut cookies have an even thickness from edge to edge and usually snap rather than bend.

TIPS FOR COOKIE-BAKING SUCCESS
➤ Measure the batter so that all of the cookies will be the same size and will bake at the same rate.

➤ Make sure to leave enough room between pieces of dough for cookies to spread in the oven. Two inches is usually a safe distance.

➤ Reverse the top and bottom baking sheets and rotate each sheet from back to front at the halfway point of the baking time to promote even baking.

➤ When making second and third batches, do not place the dough directly onto the hot baking sheets. This causes excess spreading and uneven baking because it takes you a few minutes to get all the dough on the sheet.

➤ For bar cookies, use the pan size specified in the recipe, unless an alternative is offered. Bar cookies baked in a pan larger than the size called for will overbake and their texture will be ruined. Bar cookies baked in a pan smaller than specified will take longer to bake through and the edges may overbake by the time the center is done. Also, to make bar removal easy and quick, line your pan with foil or parchment paper. Place two sheets perpendicular to each other in the pan (see the illustration on page 141). Scrape the batter into the pan, pushing it into the corners. After the bars have baked and cooled, use the foil or paper to transfer them to a cutting board, where they can easily be sliced into individual portions.

➤ For chewy, moist cookies, underbake them by a minute or two. Let individual cookies cool and firm up on the baking sheet for a few minutes and then transfer them to a wire rack to finish cooling. Residual heat means that bar cookies (which must be cooled completely in the pan) will continue to bake (and dry out) as they cool to room temperature. Make sure to remove bar cookies, especially brownies, from the oven when a few moist crumbs cling to a toothpick. Don't expect a toothpick to emerge perfectly clean from bar cookies; if it does, the bar cookies are overcooked.

SOFT AND CHEWY SUGAR COOKIES

SUGAR COOKIES HAVE BECOME THE PLAIN Janes of classic American cookies. How could such a simple cookie compare with the decadence of chocolate chip or the sophistication of biscotti? We wondered if we could develop a rich, buttery sugar cookie with a crackling sugar exterior—a chewy cookie with a big vanilla flavor—good enough to stand up to its cookie-plate counterparts.

Sugar cookies contain the most basic of ingredients: butter or shortening, sugar, eggs, flour, and sometimes vanilla extract. During our initial research, we had come across many recipes that used both shortening and butter. Cookies made using this combination were dry and flavorless; an all-butter cookie was clearly the only way to go. Most baking recipes call for butter and sugar to be creamed together until fluffy. Looking for shortcuts, we tried using melted butter, thinking that the dough would be easier to mix. However, creaming the butter and sugar proved to be key (see "Creaming Butter and Sugar" on page 425, for details).

For flour, we chose our kitchen workhorse flour, unbleached all-purpose. Having a chewy cookie meant having only a small amount of leavener; too much and the cookies turned into fluffy little cakes. One-half teaspoon of baking powder did the trick, giving the cookies just the right amount of lift.

What about eggs? We tried one egg, two eggs, and various yolk-and-white combinations in between. One whole egg plus one yolk made the cookies spongy, two eggs made them even fluffier. Using just one whole egg was the answer. With the addition of a little salt and a healthy dose of vanilla, this recipe was on the right track.

Lastly, we addressed the sugary outer crunch. Simply rolling the dough in sugar wasn't enough. The sugar crystals did not stick readily to the dough, and the cookies weren't nearly as sparkly as we wanted. We tried dipping the balls of dough in beaten egg whites, then rolling them in the sugar. No luck. This process made a huge mess and resulted in cookies with an odd, meringue-like coating. The solution was to form the balls of dough using slightly dampened hands. The small amount of water kept our hands from sticking to the dough and ensured that enough sugar remained on the cookies. Because we wanted a thick, substantial cookie, we rolled the dough into 1½-inch balls and then flattened them slightly with the bottom of a drinking glass.

Now the dough was ready for the oven. Proper baking times and temperatures could make or break these cookies. We tried baking them at 350, 375, and 400 degrees. Cookies baked at 350 degrees never browned enough. Four hundred degrees was more than the cookies could handle, turning them into cookie brûlée on the outside and leaving them pasty and underdone on the inside. A more moderate 375 degrees was just right. The cookies emerged from the oven with pale golden centers and toasty browned edges. The edges tasted as good as they looked, but the centers were disappointingly bland. What were they missing? Was there something else that would enhance the flavor of the cookies without making them taste like some other kind of cookie?

We looked at an ingredient that we had taken for granted: the sugar. We had assumed that granulated white sugar was the obvious choice for this cookie. What would happen if we were to use a different kind? We made a batch of cookies using the same recipe and added 1 tablespoon of light brown sugar to the dough. The resulting cookies were perfect; the brown sugar gave the cookies just a hint of nuttiness and brought out the deep, rich tones of the vanilla.

At last, this was a cookie that would definitely turn a few heads.

Soft and Chewy Sugar Cookies

MAKES ABOUT 24

The cookies are softer and more tender when made with lower-protein unbleached flour like Gold Medal or Pillsbury; King Arthur flour has a higher protein content and will result in slightly drier, cakier cookies. Do not discard the butter wrappers; they have just enough residual butter on them for buttering the bottom of the drinking glass used to flatten the dough balls. To make sure the cookies are flat, choose a glass with a smooth, flat bottom. Rolled into balls, the dough will keep in the freezer for up to 1 week. The baked cookies will keep in an airtight container for up to 5 days.

2	cups (10 ounces) lower-protein unbleached all-purpose flour, such as Pillsbury or Gold Medal
1/2	teaspoon baking powder
1/4	teaspoon salt
16	tablespoons (2 sticks) unsalted butter, softened but still cool
1	cup (7 ounces) granulated sugar, plus 1/2 cup for rolling dough
1	tablespoon light brown sugar
1	large egg
1 1/2	teaspoons vanilla extract

1. Adjust the oven racks to the upper- and lower-middle positions and heat the oven to 375 degrees. Line 2 large baking sheets with parchment paper or spray them with nonstick cooking spray. Whisk the flour, baking powder, and salt together in a medium bowl; set aside.

2. Either by hand or with an electric mixer, cream the butter, the 1 cup granulated sugar, and the brown sugar at medium speed until light and fluffy, about 3 minutes, scraping down the sides of the bowl with a rubber spatula as needed. Add the egg and vanilla; beat at medium speed until combined, about 30 seconds. Add the dry ingredients and beat at low speed until just combined, about 30 seconds, scraping down the bowl as needed.

3. Place the 1/2 cup sugar for rolling in a shallow bowl. Fill a medium bowl halfway with cold tap water. Dip your hands in the water and shake off any excess (this will prevent the dough from sticking to your hands and ensure that the sugar sticks to the dough). Roll a heaping tablespoon of dough into a 1½-inch ball between moistened palms, roll the ball in the sugar, and then place it on the prepared baking sheet. Repeat with the remaining dough, moistening your hands as necessary and spacing the balls about 2 inches apart (you should be able to fit 12 cookies on each sheet). Using the butter wrappers, butter the bottom of a drinking glass and then dip the bottom of the glass in the remaining sugar. Flatten the dough balls with the bottom of the glass until they are about ¾ inch thick, dipping the glass in sugar as necessary to prevent sticking (after every 2 or 3 cookies).

4. Bake until the cookies are golden brown around the edges and their centers are just set and very lightly colored, 15 to 18 minutes, rotating the baking sheets front to back and top to bottom halfway through the baking time. Cool the cookies on the baking sheets about 3 minutes; using a wide metal spatula, transfer the cookies to a wire rack and cool to room temperature.

VARIATIONS

Gingered Sugar Cookies

In a food processor, process the ½ cup sugar for rolling and 1 teaspoon grated fresh ginger until combined, about 10 seconds. Follow the recipe for Soft and Chewy Sugar Cookies, adding 2 tablespoons finely chopped crystallized ginger to the creamed butter and sugars along with the egg and vanilla, and using the ginger sugar for coating the dough balls in step 3.

Sugar Cookies with Lime Essence

In a food processor, process the ½ cup sugar for rolling and 1 teaspoon grated lime zest until the zest is evenly distributed, about 10 seconds. Follow the recipe for Soft and Chewy Sugar Cookies, adding 2 teaspoons grated lime zest to the creamed butter and sugars along with the egg and vanilla, and using the lime sugar for coating the dough balls in step 3.

Lemon–Poppy Seed Sugar Cookies

Follow the recipe for Soft and Chewy Sugar Cookies, whisking 1 tablespoon poppy seeds into the dry ingredients and adding 1 tablespoon grated lemon zest to the creamed butter and sugars along with the egg and vanilla.

SNICKERDOODLES

WITH THEIR CRINKLY TOPS AND LIBERAL dusting of cinnamon sugar, chewy snickerdoodles are a favorite in New England. The name is a corruption of a German word that translates as "crinkly noodles."

Traditionally, a snickerdoodle has a subtle tang or sour undertone that contrasts with the cinnamon sugar coating. Most recipes rely on baking soda and cream of tartar as the leavening agents for two reasons. First, the cream of tartar provides the characteristic tang. Second, the cream of tartar and baking soda cause the cookie to rise very quickly and then collapse somewhat. The result is the characteristic crinkly top.

We tested both baking powder and the baking soda and cream of tartar combination. As we expected, the latter is essential to this cookie. Double-acting baking powder caused the cookies to rise too much in the oven. The leavening power of baking soda and cream of tartar is short-lived by comparison, so the cookies rise and then fall rather quickly. To make the cookies especially tangy, we found it helpful not to add vanilla. The vanilla can take away from the sourness, which is fairly subtle.

We noticed that most of the recipes we tested were not nearly chewy enough. We found that increasing the sugar helped, but we wondered why some traditional snickerdoodle recipes contained vegetable shortening or Crisco. Although we generally don't recommend using shortening in cookies (it does not taste as good as butter), we thought it might be worth trying in this case. Unlike butter, which contains about 18 percent water, shortening is 100 percent fat. The water in butter evaporates in the oven and helps the cookies to spread. Since shortening does not contain water, in theory it should help reduce spread in the oven and keep cookies thick and chewy.

Our tests revealed that this bit of common culinary wisdom is in fact true. However, you don't need to use all or even half shortening for the desired effect. When we used 1 part shortening to 1 part butter, we felt the flavor of the cookie was lacking. After several attempts, we discovered that just 1 part shortening for every 3 parts butter is enough to keep the cookies chewy. At this level, the butter flavor still dominates.

SHAPING SUGAR COOKIES

1. Take a heaping spoonful (about 1 1/2 tablespoons) of dough and roll it between your palms into a ball that measures 1 1/2 inches in diameter. Roll the ball of dough in sugar and then place it on the prepared baking sheet.

2. Use a drinking glass with a flat bottom that measures about 2 inches across to flatten the balls of dough to a 3/4-inch thickness right on the cookie sheet. Butter the bottom of the glass before starting and dip it in sugar every two or three cookies.

Snickerdoodles

MAKES ABOUT 30

These old-fashioned cookies are dusted with cinnamon sugar and have a good contrast between crisp exterior and soft, chewy interior.

2¼	cups (11¼ ounces) unbleached all-purpose flour
2	teaspoons cream of tartar
1	teaspoon baking soda
½	teaspoon salt
12	tablespoons (1½ sticks) unsalted butter, softened but still cool
¼	cup vegetable shortening
1½	cups (10½ ounces) granulated sugar, plus 3 tablespoons for rolling dough
2	large eggs
1	tablespoon ground cinnamon for rolling dough

1. Adjust the oven racks to the upper- and lower-middle positions and heat the oven to 400 degrees. Line 2 large baking sheets with parchment paper or spray them with nonstick cooking spray.

2. Whisk the flour, cream of tartar, baking soda, and salt together in a medium bowl; set aside.

3. Either by hand or with an electric mixer, cream the butter, shortening, and the 1½ cups sugar at medium speed until combined, 1 to 1½ minutes. Scrape down the sides of the bowl with a rubber spatula. Add the eggs. Beat until combined, about 30 seconds.

4. Add the dry ingredients and beat at low speed until just combined, about 20 seconds.

5. Mix the 3 tablespoons sugar for rolling and the cinnamon in a shallow bowl. Working with a heaping tablespoon of dough each time, roll the dough into 1½-inch balls (see illustration 1 on page 429). Roll the balls in the cinnamon sugar and place them on the prepared baking sheets, spacing them about 2 inches apart.

6. Bake until the edges of the cookies are beginning to set and the centers are soft and puffy, 9 to 11 minutes, rotating the baking sheets front to back and top to bottom halfway through the baking time. Let the cookies cool on the baking sheets 2 to 3 minutes before transferring them with a wide metal spatula to a wire rack.

CRISP CHOCOLATE CHIP COOKIES

RICH AND BUTTERY, WITH SOFT, TENDER cores and crisp edges, Toll House cookies are the American cookie jar standard. As such, they serve as the springboard for all other versions of the chocolate chip cookie. The two most popular variations, thick and chewy and thin and crisp, embody the Toll House cookie's textural extremes. Given the popularity of chocolate chip cookies in America (and the number of partisans of each style), we decided to develop recipes for cookies at both ends of the textural spectrum.

We could see the thin, crisp cookies clearly. They would be very flat, almost praline in appearance, and would pack a big crunch. They'd have the simple, gratifying flavors of deeply caramelized sugar and rich butter. The chips, tender and super-chocolatey, would not overwhelm but leave plenty of room for enjoyment of the surrounding cookie. Finally, these cookies would be resilient enough for pantry storage and worthy of five consecutive appearances in a school lunchbox.

To get our bearings, we first surveyed a handful of recipes for thin and crisp chocolate chip cookies, taking inventory of the ingredient lists and ratios. We were hoping to find the key to what might make these cookies thinner and crisper than

STORING COOKIES

To ensure that cookies stay soft and fresh, place a small piece of bread along with the cookies in a zipper-lock bag.

the classic Toll House. Our collection of test recipes featured the same basic ingredients—butter, flour, sugar, flavorings, and chocolate chips—but with widely varying ratios and yields. As a result, the cookies were all quite different when baked. While all of the cookies tasted good, tasters were dissatisfied with the various textures, which they found too brittle, too crumbly, too dense, or too greasy. Believe it or not, we were pleased with the mixed reactions. The ingredients we had to work with held promise; we just needed to understand the role of each one and tweak the proportions to arrive at a cookie with the texture we wanted.

Whether chewy or crisp, nearly all chocolate chip cookies contain a mixture of granulated and brown sugars. Aside from contributing sweetness, sugar also affects the texture, flavor, and color of the cookies. Doughs high in granulated sugar yield crisp cookies. As the cookies cool, the sugar crystallizes and the cookies harden. Brown sugar is quite different from granulated. It contains 35 percent more moisture and is also more hygroscopic (that is, it more readily absorbs moisture from the atmosphere). Consequently, cookies made with brown sugar come out of the oven tender and pliable and often soften further as they stand. These characteristics were the opposite of what we were looking for. Nevertheless, we knew the recipe had to include some brown sugar, because it alone is responsible for the irresistible butterscotch flavor we associate with chocolate chip cookies.

With this understanding, we went on to test various proportions of sugar. Too much granulated sugar produced cookies with no butterscotch flavor. Too much brown sugar produced cookies that were delicious but too soft. Desperate to retain the flavor of the brown sugar, we shifted from dark brown to light brown. Light brown sugar, we knew, had the potential to crisp the cookies because it contains half the molasses that dark brown sugar does and, therefore, less moisture. But we were skeptical because its flavor is weaker. We needn't have worried; the cookies were much improved, producing a flavor that fully satisfied tasters. After a little more tinkering, we settled on ⅓ cup light brown sugar and ½ cup granulated sugar, yielding cookies with a notable butterscotch

flavor and sufficient crunch.

Satisfied with the crispness of the cookies, we turned our attention to their thickness. Throughout earlier testing, we hadn't been totally happy with the cookies' spread in the oven—they never became thin enough to achieve the praline-like look we were after. This was important not just for appearance's sake but because we had noticed that the flatter the cookies were, the more delicate and tender they became; we wanted them crisp, without being tough.

After some research, we returned to the kitchen armed with the understanding that a cookie's spread is determined largely by the type, treatment, and melting properties of the fat in the dough. Butter, which is key in this recipe, has both a low melting point and an outstanding flavor. Initial test recipes advised creaming the butter and sugar, but we noticed that cookies made with this technique came out of the oven with a slight lift. We were certain that creaming was the culprit.

When butter and sugar are creamed, rigid sugar crystals cut into the butterfat and create air cells. As the remaining ingredients are incorporated into the airy mixture, the air cells get locked up in the dough and capture moisture from the butter (and other ingredients) as it vaporizes in the oven. The cells expand and the cookies rise. Our other option, melting the butter, was much more successful. Because melted butter, unlike creamed butter, does not accommodate air cells, the moisture from various ingredients has nowhere to go except out. Working our way down from 12 tablespoons, we found that the cookies spread evenly and effortlessly at 8 tablespoons (one stick) of melted butter. To get them thinner still, we added a couple tablespoons of milk. Adding a small amount of liquid to a low-moisture dough thins the dough and enhances its spread. The cookies were flatter than pancakes.

Having spent all of our time thus far perfecting the cookies' texture and spread, we were surprised to notice that they were looking slightly pallid and dull. The light brown sugar we had introduced to the recipe was the problem (it has less browning power than dark brown sugar). Knowing that corn syrup browns at a lower temperature than sugar, we tried adding a few tablespoons. As it happened, the corn syrup made the surface of the cookies shiny and crackly. Despite their new spiffy, dressed-up look, though, they remained a little on the pale side. We rectified the situation by adding a bit of baking soda, which enhances browning reactions in doughs. The cookies went from washed-out to a beautiful deep golden brown.

Finally, after a few last-minute adjustments to the amount of salt and vanilla, we spooned a full recipe of the dough onto two parchment-lined baking sheets and tested baking times and temperatures. Much to our disappointment, these cookies were slightly chewy, because they did not spread properly. After a few batches, we found that these cookies needed to be baked one sheet at a time. In 12 minutes at 375 degrees, they spread, flattened, caramelized, and came out to cool into thin, crisp, and delicious chocolate chip cookies.

Now we just had to find out if these cookies had staying power. We stored a batch of the finished cookies in an airtight container for a week to test their longevity. After the wait, tasters gathered to give them a final critique. The cookies were still a hit, as crisp and flavorful as they had been on day one.

Thin, Crisp Chocolate Chip Cookies

MAKES ABOUT 40

The dough, en masse or shaped into balls and wrapped well, can be refrigerated up to 2 days or frozen up to 1 month. Be sure to bring it to room temperature before baking.

1 1/2	cups (7 1/2 ounces) unbleached all-purpose flour
3/4	teaspoon baking soda
1/4	teaspoon salt
8	tablespoons (1 stick) unsalted butter, melted and cooled
1/2	cup (3 1/2 ounces) granulated sugar
1/3	cup packed (2 1/3 ounces) light brown sugar
2	tablespoons light corn syrup
1	large egg yolk
2	tablespoons milk
1	tablespoon vanilla extract
3/4	cup semisweet chocolate chips

1. Adjust an oven rack to the middle position and heat the oven to 375 degrees. Line 2 large baking sheets with parchment paper or spray them with nonstick cooking spray.

2. Whisk the flour, baking soda, and salt together in a medium bowl until thoroughly combined; set aside.

3. Either by hand or with an electric mixer, beat the melted butter, both sugars, and corn syrup at low speed until thoroughly blended, about 1 minute. Add the yolk, milk, and vanilla; mix until fully incorporated and smooth, about 1 minute, scraping the bottom and sides of the bowl with a rubber spatula as necessary. With the mixer running on low speed, slowly add the dry ingredients and mix until just combined. Do not overbeat. Add the chocolate chips and mix on low speed until distributed evenly throughout the batter, about 5 seconds.

4. Working with a scant tablespoon of dough each time, roll the dough into 1 1/4-inch balls and place them on the prepared baking sheets, spacing them about 2 inches apart. Bake, one sheet at a time, until the cookies are deep golden brown and flat, about 12 minutes, rotating the sheet from front to back halfway through the baking time.

5. Cool the cookies on the baking sheet for 3 minutes. Using a wide metal spatula, transfer the cookies to a wire rack and let sit until crisped and cooled to room temperature.

CHEWY CHOCOLATE CHIP COOKIES

AN ATTRACTIVE VARIATION ON THE TRADITIONAL chocolate chip cookie that some bake shops and cookie stores have recently made their reputations on—not to mention a lot of money—is the oversized cookie. Unlike cookies made at home, these cookies are thick right from the edge to the center. They are also chewy, even a bit soft. Although we knew at the outset that molding the dough rather than dropping it into uneven blobs would be essential to achieving an even thickness, we didn't realize how much of a challenge making a truly chewy cookie would be.

We added more flour or ground oats (as some recipes suggest), which helped the cookies hold their shape and remain thick but also made the texture cakey and dry rather than chewy. When we tried liquid sweeteners, such as molasses and corn syrup, the dough spread too much in the oven, and the cookies baked up thin.

At this point in our testing, we decided to experiment with the butter. Some chewy cookies start with melted rather than creamed butter. In its solid state, butter is an emulsion of butter and water. When butter is melted, the fat and water molecules separate. When melted butter is added to a dough, the proteins in the flour immediately grab onto the freed water molecules to form elastic strands of gluten. The gluten makes a cookie chewy.

Our first attempt with melted butter was disappointing. The dough was very soft from all the liquid, and the cookies baked up greasy. Because the dough was having a hard time absorbing the liquid fat, we reduced the amount of butter from 16 to 12 tablespoons. We also reduced the number of eggs from two to one to stiffen the dough.

The cookies were chewy at this point, but they became somewhat tough as they cooled, and after a few hours, they were hard. Fat acts as a tenderizer, and by reducing the amount of butter in the recipe, we had limited its ability to keep the cookies soft. The only other source of fat is the egg. Since our dough was already soft enough and probably could not stand the addition of too much more liquid, we decided to add another yolk (which contains all the fat) and leave out the white. This dough was still stiff enough to shape, and when baked, the cookies were thick and chewy, and they remained that way when they cooled. Finally, we had the perfect recipe.

SHAPING THICK CHOCOLATE CHIP COOKIES

1. Creating a jagged surface on each dough ball gives the finished cookies an attractive appearance. Start by rolling a scant ¼ cup of dough into a smooth ball.

2. Holding the dough ball in the fingertips of both hands, pull the dough apart into two equal halves.

3. Each half will have a jagged surface where it was ripped from the other. Rotate each piece 90 degrees so that the jagged surface faces up.

4. Jam the halves back together into one ball so that the top surface remains jagged.

Thick and Chewy Chocolate Chip Cookies

MAKES ABOUT 18 LARGE

These oversized cookies are chewy and thick, like many of the chocolate chip cookies sold in gourmet shops and cookie stores. They rely on melted butter and an extra egg yolk to keep their texture soft. These cookies are best served warm from the oven but will retain their texture even when cooled. To ensure the proper texture, cool the cookies on the baking sheet. Oversized baking sheets allow you to get all the dough into the oven at one time. If you're using smaller baking sheets, put fewer cookies on each sheet and bake them in batches. See the illustrations on page 433 for tips on shaping these cookies.

2	cups plus 2 tablespoons (10 $^5/_8$ ounces) unbleached all-purpose flour
$^1/_2$	teaspoon baking soda
$^1/_2$	teaspoon salt
12	tablespoons (1 $^1/_2$ sticks) unsalted butter, melted and cooled until warm
1	cup packed (7 ounces) light or dark brown sugar
$^1/_2$	cup (3 $^1/_2$ ounces) granulated sugar
1	large egg plus 1 egg yolk
2	teaspoons vanilla extract
1–1 $^1/_2$	cups semisweet chocolate chips

1. Adjust the oven racks to the upper- and lower-middle positions and heat the oven to 325 degrees. Line 2 large baking sheets with parchment paper or spray them with nonstick cooking spray.

2. Whisk the flour, baking soda, and salt together in a medium bowl; set aside.

3. Either by hand or with an electric mixer, mix the butter and sugars until thoroughly blended. Beat in the egg, yolk, and vanilla until combined. Add the dry ingredients and beat at low speed just until combined. Stir in the chips to taste.

4. Roll a scant ¼ cup of the dough into a ball. Following the illustrations on page 433, hold the dough ball with the fingertips of both hands and pull into 2 equal halves. Rotate the halves 90 degrees and, with jagged surfaces facing up, join the halves together at their base, again forming a single ball, being careful not to smooth the dough's uneven surface. Place the formed dough balls on the prepared baking sheets, jagged surface up, spacing them 2½ inches apart.

5. Bake until the cookies are light golden brown and the outer edges start to harden yet the centers are still soft and puffy, 15 to 18 minutes, rotating the baking sheets front to back and top to bottom halfway through the baking time. Cool the cookies on the sheets. Remove the cooled cookies from the baking sheets with a wide metal spatula.

➤ VARIATIONS

Chocolate Chip Cookies with Coconut and Toasted Almonds

Follow the recipe for Thick and Chewy Chocolate Chip Cookies, adding 1½ cups sweetened dried coconut and 1 cup toasted sliced almonds along with the chips.

Black and White Chocolate Chip Cookies with Pecans

Follow the recipe for Thick and Chewy Chocolate Chip Cookies, substituting ½ cup white chocolate chips for ½ cup of the semisweet chips. Add 1 cup chopped pecans with the chips.

THICK AND CHEWY DOUBLE-CHOCOLATE COOKIES

ONE OF OUR GREATEST OBSESSIONS IN BAKING has been the first transcendent bite of the perfect chocolate cookie, still warm out of the oven. That first bite would reveal a center of hot fudge sauce, and the texture would call to mind chocolate bread pudding with a deep, complex chocolate flavor. This would be the sort of confection that creates intense focus while it is consumed, sight and sound subordinate to taste, overshadowing the other senses to the point of dysfunction.

The problem is that we have, for years, been trying to perfect this cookie. We have created large, dense cookies that were rich and decadent, but the chocolate flavor was dull. We have also experimented with thin, crisp cookies (nice but not intense), chewy cookies (good but not showstoppers), and cake-like chocolate cookies, which tend to be dry and uninspiring. The test kitchen also made a half-dozen recipes from various cookbooks and discovered a world of difference in texture, flavor, and appearance, from soft mocha-colored disks to thick mounds of pure fudge. This panoply of outcomes gave us pause, since the ingredient lists seemed to have more in common than the cookies themselves. Figuring out what makes a chocolate cookie tick was going to require weeks of testing and a great deal of detective work.

Our first step was to strip the recipes down to their basics to understand the fundamentals. A chocolate cookie is a mixture of melted chocolate, sugar, eggs, butter, flour, baking soda or powder, and salt. Vanilla, coffee, and nuts are extras.

The key issues were how to handle the butter and eggs. The butter can be melted or creamed, and the eggs can be beaten or just whisked into the batter. For the first test batch, we melted the butter and whipped the eggs. The results were good, but the cookies were a bit cakey and loose, without any chew. For the next batch we melted the butter and did not beat the eggs. These cookies were a bit dry and still cakey. When we started creaming the butter and beating the eggs into it after creaming, we noticed an immediate improvement. However, we finally settled on a modified creaming method with minimal beating to produce moist cookies that were not cakey.

The next issue was one of proportions; that is, the ratio of flour to butter to eggs to sugar to chocolate. This was going to be crucial to the thickness of the cookie, its texture, and the degree to which the taste of chocolate would dominate. Looking over the recipes we had tested, we saw so many permutations that we felt like the British trying to crack the German secret code in World War II.

To organize the facts, we made a chart of the various ratios of eggs, sugar, chocolate, and butter to flour, with related comments on the taste, texture, and shape of each cookie we had tested. We quickly noted that the ratio of eggs and butter to flour was less important than the ratio of sugar and chocolate to flour. The driest cookie used less than ½ cup of sugar per cup of flour; the richest,

wettest cookie used 3 cups. The cookie with the faintest chocolate flavor and a relatively firm, dry texture used only 2 ounces of chocolate per cup of flour, whereas other recipes used up to a pound of chocolate with only ½ cup of flour. After many tests designed to balance sweetness and moisture, we settled on 1 cup of sugar and 8 ounces of chocolate to 1 cup of flour. Finally, we had a moist cookie with good chocolate flavor. Nonetheless, we thought the flavor and texture could be still better, so we moved on to other ingredients.

We started with all granulated sugar and then tested a mixture of brown sugar and granulated, which seemed to improve the flavor and added just a bit more moisture. We also tried corn syrup, which had little effect. A small amount of vanilla extract and instant coffee powder rounded out the flavors. Throughout the testing, we had been using all-purpose flour. We decided to try cake flour, but the resulting cookies were a bit too delicate. We also varied the quantity of flour throughout the testing process, starting at 3 cups and eventually working our way down to 2 cups. To create a thicker, more stable cookie, we tried replacing some of the butter with vegetable shortening (Crisco), but this created an unattractive, greasy-looking cookie with a pale white sheen. We thought that the choice of leavener might be important, so we tested baking powder against baking soda and found that the cookies with the powder were slightly thicker.

At this point, our cookie was thick and very good but still not the sort of thing that would reduce the average adult to tears of joy. The flavor remained a bit dull, and the texture was moist but monochromatic. We wondered if we could solve this problem by varying the type of chocolate. We found that unsweetened chocolate, an ingredient often called for in chocolate cookie recipes, added intensity to the flavor. Unfortunately, we also discovered an aggressive sour note in these cookies, even when the sugar level was adjusted for the bitterness of the chocolate. Semisweet and bittersweet chocolate turned out to be better choices owing to their rounder, less potent flavors. These chocolates undergo more processing than unsweetened, and they also get other flavorings; this no doubt gives them a smoother, richer flavor overall.

Our hunt was almost over, but now we wondered if a bit of cocoa powder might add more depth of flavor to our cookie. One-half cup of Dutch-processed cocoa was substituted for the same amount of flour, and the chocolate flavor became both smoother and deeper. (We also tried a batch of cookies made with only cocoa powder and no chocolate, and they were disappointing, having just a faint chocolate flavor.) At last, we had brought our fantasy to life: a double-chocolate cookie that was both rich and soft, with an intense chocolatey center that would drive anyone to distraction.

Thick and Chewy Double-Chocolate Cookies

MAKES ABOUT 42

It is worth buying parchment paper for this recipe because the undersides of the cookies are soft and the parchment makes for easy transfer, removal, and cleanup. We also recommend using a spring-loaded ice cream scoop to scoop the soft dough. Resist the urge to bake the cookies longer than indicated; they may appear underbaked at first but will firm up as they cool.

2	cups (10 ounces) unbleached all-purpose flour
1/2	cup (1 1/2 ounces) Dutch-processed cocoa powder
2	teaspoons baking powder
1/2	teaspoon salt
16	ounces semisweet chocolate, chopped
4	large eggs
2	teaspoons vanilla extract
2	teaspoons instant coffee or espresso powder
10	tablespoons (1 1/4 sticks) unsalted butter, softened but still cool
1 1/2	cups packed (10 1/2 ounces) light brown sugar
1/2	cup (3 1/2 ounces) granulated sugar

1. Sift together the flour, cocoa, baking powder, and salt in a medium bowl; set aside.

2. Melt the chocolate in a medium heatproof bowl set over a pan of almost-simmering water, stirring once or twice, until smooth; remove from the heat. (To melt the chocolate in a microwave oven, see the note on page 383.) In a small bowl,

beat the eggs and vanilla lightly with a fork, sprinkle the coffee powder over to dissolve, and set aside.

3. Either by hand or with an electric mixer, beat the butter at medium speed until smooth and creamy, about 5 seconds. Beat in the sugars until combined, about 45 seconds; the mixture will look granular. Reduce the speed to low and gradually beat in the egg mixture until incorporated, about 45 seconds. Add the chocolate in a steady stream and beat until combined, about 40 seconds. Scrape the bottom and sides of the bowl with a rubber spatula. With the mixer at low speed, add the dry ingredients and mix until just combined. Do not overbeat. Cover with plastic wrap and let stand at room temperature until the consistency is scoopable and fudge-like, about 30 minutes.

4. Meanwhile, adjust the oven racks to the upper- and lower-middle positions and heat the oven to 350 degrees. Line 2 baking sheets with parchment paper. Scoop the dough onto the prepared baking sheets with a 1¾-inch ice cream scoop, spacing the mounds of dough about 1½ inches apart.

5. Bake until the edges of the cookies have just begun to set but the centers are still very soft, about 10 minutes, rotating the baking sheets front to back and top to bottom halfway through the baking time. Cool the cookies on the sheets about 10 minutes, slide the parchment with cookies onto wire racks, and cool to room temperature. Cover one cooled baking sheet with a new piece of parchment paper. Scoop the remaining dough onto the parchment-lined sheet, bake, and cool as directed. Remove cooled cookies from the parchment with a wide metal spatula.

➤ VARIATION

Thick and Chewy Triple-Chocolate Cookies

If you like bursts of warm melted chocolate in your cookies, include chocolate chips in the batter. The addition of chips will slightly increase the yield of the recipe.

Follow the recipe for Thick and Chewy Double-Chocolate Cookies, adding 12 ounces (about 2 cups) semisweet chocolate chips to the batter after the dry ingredients are incorporated in step 3.

PEANUT BUTTER COOKIES

THERE ARE SEVERAL STYLES OF PEANUT butter cookie. Some are thin and candy-like; others are dry and crumbly. For us, the best peanut butter cookie is crisp around the edges, chewy in the center, and slightly puffed. The flavor is buttery and sweet, with a strong hit of peanuts.

We started our tests by focusing on the fat. We quickly determined that butter accentuated the peanut flavor, while margarine and Crisco diminished it. Crisco did make the cookie chewier in the center, but we felt the added chewiness was not worth the loss of peanut flavor. We tried peanut oil (thinking this might boost the overall peanut flavor), but the resulting texture was dry and sandy.

From these early tests, we also noticed that peanut butter types replicated the results we found with fats. Natural peanut butters, with a layer of oil on top, made the cookies sandy. Commercial brands, which contain partially hydrogenated vegetable oils that are similar to Crisco, helped the cookies rise and achieve a crisper edge and chewier center. We tested both smooth and chunky peanut butter and felt that the chunky style contributed more peanut flavor.

We tried using more peanut butter to boost the peanut flavor (we even used all peanut butter

and no butter), but we still could not get a strong enough peanut flavor. Also, the texture suffered as we removed the butter from our working recipe. The cookies were sandy and almost like shortbread. Butter was crucial for lightness and a chewy texture. Clearly, we would need peanuts as well as peanut butter. We found that chopped peanuts tend to slip out of the dough. We then ground them in the food processor and worked them directly into the dough, which greatly improved the peanut flavor.

Salt brings out the flavor of peanuts (salted roasted peanuts taste better than unsalted nuts), and we found that salt also helped bring out the flavor of the peanuts in the cookies. In fact, we found it best to use both salted nuts in addition to salt for the strongest peanut flavor.

At this point, we focused our attention on the sweetener. We had been using granulated sugar and now began to wonder if a liquid sweetener might make the cookies chewier. We tried molasses and corn syrup, but they could not beat granulated sugar. We tried brown sugar but found the resulting cookies to be too sweet and candy-like. However, because the brown sugar did make the cookies taste nuttier, we decided to test half brown sugar and half granulated sugar. This turned out to be ideal, giving the cookies a mild praline flavor that highlighted the flavor of the peanuts.

We found that the amount of flour in the dough also affected the peanut flavor. Too little flour made the cookies taste greasy and not very peanutty. As we increased the flour, the peanut flavor intensified. Too much flour, however, and the cookies became dry. Slightly more flour than butter and peanut butter combined proved to be the right amount.

CROSSHATCHING PEANUT BUTTER COOKIES

To make a crisscross design, dip a dinner fork into a small bowl of cold water and then press the fork into the dough ball. Rotate the fork 90 degrees and press it into the dough ball a second time.

~≈~

Peanut Butter Cookies

MAKES ABOUT 36

These cookies have a strong peanut flavor that comes from extra-crunchy peanut butter (in our taste test, we preferred Jif) as well as from roasted salted peanuts that are ground in a food processor and worked into the dough.

2 1/2 cups (12 1/2 ounces) unbleached all-purpose flour
1/2 teaspoon baking soda
1/2 teaspoon baking powder
1 teaspoon salt
16 tablespoons (2 sticks) unsalted butter, softened but still cool
1 cup packed (7 ounces) light brown sugar
1 cup (7 ounces) granulated sugar
1 cup extra-crunchy peanut butter
2 large eggs
2 teaspoons vanilla extract
1 cup dry-roasted salted peanuts, ground in a food processor to resemble bread crumbs, about 14 pulses

1. Adjust the ovens racks to the upper- and lower-middle positions and heat the oven to 350 degrees. Line 2 large baking sheets with parchment paper or spray them with nonstick cooking spray.

2. Whisk the flour, baking soda, baking powder, and salt together in a medium bowl; set aside.

3. Either by hand or with an electric mixer, beat the butter until creamy. Add the sugars; beat until fluffy, about 3 minutes with an electric mixer, stopping to scrape down the bowl as necessary. Beat in the peanut butter until fully incorporated, then the eggs, 1 at a time, then the vanilla. Gently stir the dry ingredients into the peanut butter mixture. Add the ground peanuts and stir gently until just incorporated.

4. Working with a generous 2 tablespoons each time, roll the dough into 2-inch balls. Place the balls on the prepared baking sheets, spacing them 2 1/2 inches apart. Following the illustration on page 437, press each dough ball twice with a dinner fork dipped in cold water to make a crisscross design.

5. Bake until the cookies are puffed and slightly brown around the edges but not on top, 10 to 12 minutes, rotating the baking sheets front to back and top to bottom halfway through the baking time. (The cookies will not look fully baked.) Cool the cookies on the baking sheets until set, about 4 minutes, then transfer to a wire rack with a wide metal spatula to cool completely.

➤ VARIATION
Peanut Butter Chocolate Chip Cookies
Follow the recipe for Peanut Butter Cookies, adding 1 1/2 cups semisweet chocolate chips with the ground nuts.

OATMEAL COOKIES

WHEN DEVELOPING THIS RECIPE, WE wanted an oversized cookie that was chewy and moist. Most oatmeal cookies seem dry to us, and the flavor of the oats seems too weak. Many recipes don't call for enough oats, and spices often overwhelm the flavor of the oats that are there.

The flavor issues were easily solved with some testing. We experimented with various amounts of oats and found that in order to have a real oat flavor, we needed 2 cups of oats for every cup of flour—far more oats than in most recipes. We also preferred old-fashioned rolled oats to quick oats; the old-fashioned had better texture and flavor. For more about oats, see page 3.

To keep the focus on the oats, we decided to eliminate cinnamon, a common ingredient in these cookies, because it was overpowering the oats. We wanted some spice, however, and chose nutmeg, which has a cleaner, subtler flavor that we liked with the oats.

Our cookies tasted good at this point, but we needed to work on the texture. In our tests, we found that a high proportion of butter to flour helped to keep the cookies moist. We settled on 2 parts butter to 3 parts flour.

We found that shaping the dough into 2-inch balls (rather than dropping the meager rounded tablespoon called for in most recipes) helped keep the cookies more moist and chewy, especially in the center, which remains a bit underbaked in an oversized cookie. Smaller cookies are considerably drier and more cake-like, something we did not want in an oatmeal cookie.

Our final tests involved the sugar. We experimented with various amounts and found that adding a full cup each of brown and granulated sugar delivered the best results, giving us a cookie that was especially moist and rich. Sugar makes baked goods more moist and tender because it helps them hold onto water during the baking process. In addition, sugar encourages exterior browning, which promotes crispness.

Chewy Oatmeal-Raisin Cookies

MAKES ABOUT 18 LARGE

If you prefer a less sweet cookie, you can reduce the granulated sugar by ¼ cup, but you will lose some crispness. Do not overbake these cookies. The edges should be brown, but the rest of the cookie should be very light in color.

- 1½ cups (7½ ounces) unbleached all-purpose flour
- ½ teaspoon baking powder
- ¼ teaspoon freshly grated nutmeg
- ½ teaspoon salt
- 16 tablespoons (2 sticks) unsalted butter, softened but still cool
- 1 cup packed (7 ounces) light brown sugar
- 1 cup (7 ounces) granulated sugar
- 2 large eggs
- 3 cups old-fashioned rolled oats
- 1½ cups raisins (optional)

1. Adjust the oven racks to the low and middle positions and heat the oven to 350 degrees. Line 2 large baking sheets with parchment paper or spray them with nonstick cooking spray.

2. Whisk the flour, baking powder, nutmeg, and salt together in a medium bowl.

3. Either by hand or with an electric mixer, beat the butter on medium speed until creamy. Add the sugars; beat until fluffy, about 3 minutes. Beat in the eggs, 1 at a time.

4. Stir the dry ingredients into the butter-sugar mixture with a wooden spoon or large rubber spatula. Stir in the oats and raisins (if using).

5. Working with a generous 2 tablespoons of dough each time, roll the dough into 2-inch balls. Place the balls on the prepared baking sheets, spacing them at least 2 inches apart.

6. Bake until the cookie edges turn golden brown, 22 to 25 minutes, rotating the baking sheets front to back and top to bottom halfway through the baking time. Let the cookies cool on the baking sheets for 2 minutes. Transfer the cookies with a wide metal spatula to a wire rack. Let cool at least 30 minutes.

➤ VARIATIONS

Date Oatmeal Cookies

Follow the recipe for Chewy Oatmeal-Raisin Cookies, substituting 1½ cups chopped dates for the raisins.

Ginger Oatmeal Cookies

Follow the recipe for Chewy Oatmeal-Raisin Cookies, adding ¾ teaspoon ground ginger to the flour and other dry ingredients and omitting the raisins.

Chocolate Chip Oatmeal Cookies

Follow the recipe for Chewy Oatmeal-Raisin Cookies, omitting the nutmeg and substituting 1½ cups semisweet chocolate chips for the raisins.

Nut Oatmeal Cookies

Follow the recipe for Chewy Oatmeal-Raisin Cookies, decreasing the flour to 1⅓ cups and adding ¼ cup ground almonds and 1 cup chopped walnut pieces along with the oats. (Almonds can be ground in a food processor or blender.) Omit the raisins.

Orange and Almond Oatmeal Cookies

Follow the recipe for Chewy Oatmeal-Raisin Cookies, omitting the raisins and adding 2 tablespoons minced orange zest and 1 cup toasted chopped almonds (toast nuts in a 350-degree oven for 5 minutes) along with the oats.

PECAN SANDIES

TAKE SHORTBREAD, A SCOTTISH COOKIE, and give it a dose of Americana—namely pecans and brown sugar—and it is transformed into a nutty, buttery cookie with a hint of caramel flavor. The texture: tender but crisp and sandy with a slow melt-in-your-mouth character. Call it a "pecan sandy," after its noteworthy texture. Indeed, pecan sandies can be purchased in any grocery store cookie aisle, but for the richest, purest butter, pecan, and brown sugar flavors, they are best (and easily) made at home.

Recipes for pecan sandies run the gamut. Sometimes called pecan or brown sugar pecan shortbread, pecan sandies are rich in butter like shortbread. And because a crisp, sandy texture—not a puffy or cakey crumb—is the goal, they do not contain chemical leaveners for lift (also like shortbread). We made cookies similar to simple sugar cookies that are dropped onto a baking sheet; we baked basic roll-and-cut cookies made with cake flour; we sampled cookies made with vegetable oil and a duo of ground nuts and chopped nuts; we sliced cookies from a refrigerator cookie log. We concluded quickly that cake flour is unnecessary. A tender cookie could be made with unbleached all-purpose flour, our kitchen standard. We found that oil does make for a sandy texture, but it falls pitifully short in flavor—the rich, sweet flavor of pure butter is paramount. Last, we learned that a dropped cookie doesn't have the neat, clean edges that pecan sandies should have. Rolling and cutting the dough or forming it into a sliceable log would be the way to create a perfect-looking pecan sandy.

The type and amount of sugar best for pecan sandies needed to be determined. In a working recipe that we assembled, we tried light brown sugar, dark brown sugar, granulated sugar, confectioners' sugar, and different combinations of each. Confectioners' sugar, with its small amount of cornstarch, had a noticeable tenderizing effect on the cookies. Too much, however, and the cookies turned pasty and gummy; a quarter-cup was all that was needed. Granulated sugar had little to offer in the way of flavor, while dark brown sugar offered too much. Light brown sugar, tinged with molasses, gave the cookies a gentle caramel flavor that complemented, not overwhelmed, the nuttiness of the pecans and richness of the butter.

Next, we made batches of pecan sandies with a whole egg and without. A whole egg was excessive—the dough was sticky and difficult to work with. Without an egg, however, the cookies baked up with a texture more like pie pastry, and they lost their attractive sharp edges in the oven. A single yolk was what the dough needed. By comparison, these cookies were fine-pored and stalwart, keeping their crisp, clean look even after baking.

So far, we had been using a good amount of finely chopped nuts for flavor. We tried grinding a portion of those nuts, leaving the other portion chopped, and found the cookies made with ground nuts to be finer-textured, more tender, and nuttier than those made exclusively with chopped nuts. The oils in the nuts released during grinding contributed to the tenderness and flavor of the cookies. But tasters demanded an even finer cookie, one in which chopped nuts didn't mar the delicate sandy texture, so we ground all of the pecans. Tasters were pleased.

As for flavor refinements, a bit of salt helped to boost flavor. Vanilla extract, even the smallest amount of it, was too perfumed and distracting. Tasters did like a hint of cinnamon, however; its flavor could not be singled out, but it added nuance and a layer of warmth.

A matter of mechanics: We were grinding the pecans in a food processor, but we were making the cookie dough using the typical creamed butter method in an electric mixer. It occurred to us that these cookies were not a far cry from *pâte sucrée*, or French tart pastry, which is made entirely in the food processor, so we gave it a whirl, taking it from start to finish in the processor. We ground the nuts with the sugars to help prevent the nuts from going greasy and clumpy as they broke down, added the flour, cut in the butter, and finally added the egg. The dough quantity was large and resisted being perfectly combined, so we emptied it onto the counter and kneaded it gently until it came together into an even, cohesive dough. It worked faster and more cleanly than we could have hoped—and now we didn't have to take out the butter ahead of time to soften it for creaming or haul out and dirty the electric mixer.

Rolling out the dough into sheets and stamping out cookies with a cutter was one shaping option, but this technique generates scraps, which we preferred to do without. Instead, we treated the dough as we would for refrigerator cookies, shaping the just-made dough into one 12-inch log, cutting it in half, wrapping each half in plastic wrap, and putting them in the freezer just long enough to firm up their exteriors. At this point, we took them out, rolled them along the counter surface to round out the flat side they had rested on while soft, then put them in the refrigerator until thoroughly chilled. After a couple of hours, we sliced the logs into ¼-inch coins and accessorized them with a pecan half pressed into each slice (for presentation; otherwise the cookies look homely), and they were ready to bake.

Pecan sandies should become only modestly brown with baking—the edges should begin to deepen to golden brown, but the bulk of each cookie should be blond. They need to be thoroughly baked, however, even under the pecan adornment, to obtain their characteristic crisp, sandy texture. A 325-degree oven was ideal—a cooler oven took longer than necessary, and a hotter one gave the cookies too much color. Once on the wire rack, pecan sandies must cool completely before being eaten, lest their texture fail to live up to their name.

Pecan Sandies

MAKES ABOUT 32

Once the dough is shaped into logs, it should be frozen for 30 minutes (to speed chilling), and then refrigerated for at least 2 hours. The chilled dough can be refrigerated for up to 3 days before being sliced and baked.

1½	cups pecan halves, plus about 32 pecan halves for pressing onto unbaked cookies
¼	cup (1 ounce) confectioners' sugar
½	cup packed (3½ ounces) light brown sugar
1½	cups (7½ ounces) unbleached all-purpose flour
¼	teaspoon salt
12	tablespoons (1½ sticks) cold unsalted butter, cut into ½-inch cubes
1	large egg yolk

1. In a food processor, process 1½ cups pecans with both sugars until the nuts are ground, about twenty 1-second pulses. Add the flour and salt and process to combine, about twelve 1-second pulses. Scatter the butter pieces over the dry ingredients and process until the mixture resembles damp sand

and rides up the sides of the bowl, about eighteen 1-second pulses. With the machine running, add the yolk and process until the dough comes together into a rough ball, about 20 seconds.

2. Turn the dough (it will look scrappy and uneven) onto a clean, dry work surface and gently knead until it is evenly moistened and cohesive. Using the palms of your hands, roll the dough into an even 12-inch log, cut the log in half with a chef's knife, and wrap each half in plastic wrap. Freeze the dough logs until very cold but still malleable, about 30 minutes. Remove them from the freezer, unwrap them, and roll them on the work surface to round off the flat sides. Rewrap the logs in plastic wrap and refrigerate them until thoroughly chilled and completely firm, about 2 hours.

3. Adjust the oven racks to the upper- and lower-middle positions and heat the oven to 325 degrees. Line 2 large baking sheets with parchment paper or spray them with nonstick cooking spray. Unwrap the dough logs and, using a sharp chef's knife, slice the logs into coins ¼ inch thick, slightly rotating the logs after each slice so that they do not develop a markedly flat side. Place the slices on the prepared baking sheets, spacing them about ¾ inch apart. Press a pecan half in the center of each slice.

4. Bake until the edges of the cookies are golden brown, about 24 minutes, rotating the baking sheets front to back and top to bottom halfway through the baking time. Cool the cookies 3 minutes on the baking sheets, then transfer them to a wire rack with a wide metal spatula and let them cool to room temperature.

➤ VARIATION

Almond Sandies

Follow the recipe for Pecan Sandies, replacing the pecans with an equal amount of whole blanched almonds that have been toasted in a 350-degree oven for 8 minutes, cooled, and then chopped. Add ¼ teaspoon almond extract with the egg yolk.

MOLASSES SPICE COOKIES

WE'VE COME TO APPRECIATE GOOD MOLASSES cookies for their honesty and simplicity. On the outside, their cracks and crinkles give them a humble, charming countenance. Inside, an uncommonly moist, soft yet chewy, tooth-sinking texture is half the appeal; the other half is a warm, tingling spiciness paired with the dark, bittersweet flavor of molasses. Unfortunately, molasses spice cookies are often no more than flat, tasteless cardboard rounds of gingerbread. Some are dry and cakey without the requisite chew; others are timidly flavored with molasses and are either recklessly or vacantly spiced.

We started by testing a half-dozen different recipes, using a variety of fats, flours, and mixing methods. Although these early experiments yielded vastly different cookies in terms of flavor and appearance, a few things were clear. The full, rich flavor of butter was in; flat-tasting shortening was out. We found that a lower-protein unbleached all-purpose flour such as Gold Medal or Pillsbury gave us a more tender cookie. The mixing technique was a standard one: Cream the butter and sugar; add the eggs, then the molasses; and, finally, stir in the dry ingredients.

Molasses is at the core of these cookies. Enough must be used to give them a dark, smoky, bittersweet flavor, but we found that a surfeit of molasses creates a sticky, unworkable dough. For the amount of butter (12 tablespoons) and flour (2½ cups) we were using, the molasses ceiling was ½ cup. We had been using mild (also called light) molasses up to this point, but in an attempt to boost flavor, we baked batches with dark and blackstrap molasses. Cookies made with dark molasses were filled with bold flavor and rich color, and they garnered much praise. Those made with blackstrap molasses had a few fans, but, for most of us, the wicked brew overtook the spices and made the cookies too bitter.

Molasses alone cannot supply the cookies with enough sweetness, so either granulated or brown sugar is required. Dark brown sugar (we chose dark over light for its stronger molasses flavor)

yielded cookies that were surprisingly puffy and cakey, and they spread too little on the baking sheet. Granulated sugar yielded cookies that were pale both in color and flavor. A combination of granulated and brown sugars was the ticket. The brown sugar fortified the molasses flavor, while granulated sugar, a spreading agent, allowed the cookies to attain a good, even thickness in the oven without much puff. After some fiddling, we found equal amounts of brown and granulated sugar to be ideal.

Most molasses cookie recipes call for no more than a single egg to bind things together. However, the white of the egg—harmless as it may seem—made the dough sticky. The difference was subtle, but the white also caused the baked cookies to have a slightly cake-like crumb and a firmer, drier feel than we cared for. A lone yolk was all the cookies needed.

Molasses is a mildly acidic ingredient, so baking soda, an alkali that reacts with the acidity of the molasses to provide lift, is the logical leavener for these cookies. In our testing, cookies with too little baking soda were flat and failed to develop those attractive fault lines. The proper amount of baking soda (1 teaspoon) gave the cookies nice height—a pleasure to sink your teeth into—and a winsome appearance, with large, meandering fissures.

It was time to refine the flavor of the cookies. A teaspoon of vanilla extract complemented generous amounts of sharp, spicy ground ginger and warm, soothing cinnamon. Cloves, rich and fragrant, and allspice, sweet and mysterious, were added, but in more judicious quantities. Nutmeg was pedestrian and had little to offer. Finely and freshly ground black pepper, however, added some intrigue—a *soupçon* of heat against the deep, bittersweet flavor of the molasses.

To shape the molasses cookies, we rolled generous heaping tablespoons of dough into balls and coated them with granulated sugar, which, after baking, gave the cookies a frosted sparkle. Out of a 375-degree oven, the cookies were perfect—the edges were slightly crisped and the interiors soft and chewy. We determined that the cookies must be baked one sheet at a time since cookies baked on the lower rack inevitably puffed and turned out smooth rather than craggy and cracked.

Most important, we noted that the cookies must come out of the oven when they appear substantially underdone; otherwise their soft, moist, chewy texture will harden upon cooling. Whisk them out when the edges are hardly set, the centers are still soft and puffy, and the dough looks shiny and raw between the cracks. The cookies finish baking with residual heat, so don't shortchange them of a five-minute repose on the baking sheet before removal to a wire rack.

Molasses Spice Cookies

MAKES ABOUT 22

For the best flavor, make sure that your spices are fresh. Light or mild molasses gives the cookies a milder flavor; for a stronger flavor, use dark molasses. (See page 4 for more information about molasses.) Either way, measure molasses in a liquid measuring cup. For the best texture and spread, the flour in these cookies should be weighed. Bake the cookies 1 sheet at a time; if baked 2 at a time, the cookies started on the bottom rack won't develop attractive cracks. Remove the cookies from the oven when they still look slightly raw and underbaked. If you plan to glaze the cookies (see the illustration on page 444), save the parchment paper that they were baked on.

2¼	cups (11¼ ounces) lower-protein unbleached all-purpose flour, such as Gold Medal or Pillsbury
1	teaspoon baking soda
1½	teaspoons ground cinnamon
1½	teaspoons ground ginger
½	teaspoon ground cloves
¼	teaspoon ground allspice
¼	teaspoon finely ground black pepper
¼	teaspoon salt
12	tablespoons (1½ sticks) unsalted butter, softened but still cool
⅓	cup packed (2⅓ ounces) dark brown sugar
⅓	cup (2⅓ ounces) granulated sugar, plus ½ cup for rolling the dough
1	large egg yolk
1	teaspoon vanilla extract
½	cup light or dark molasses

1. Adjust an oven rack to the middle position and heat the oven to 375 degrees. Line a large baking sheet with parchment paper or spray it with nonstick cooking spray.

2. Whisk the flour, baking soda, spices, and salt in a medium bowl until thoroughly combined; set aside.

3. Either by hand or with an electric mixer, beat the butter with the brown sugar and the ⅓ cup granulated sugar at medium-high speed until light and fluffy, about 3 minutes. Reduce the speed to medium-low and add the yolk and vanilla; increase the speed to medium and beat until incorporated, about 20 seconds. Reduce the speed to medium-low and add the molasses; beat until fully incorporated, about 20 seconds, scraping the bottom and sides of the bowl once with a rubber spatula. Reduce the speed to the lowest setting; add the flour mixture and beat until just incorporated, about 30 seconds, scraping the bowl down once. Give the dough a final stir by hand to ensure that no pockets of flour remain at the bottom. The dough will be soft.

4. Place the ½ cup sugar for rolling in a shallow bowl. Fill a medium bowl halfway with cold tap water. Dip your hands into the water and shake off the excess (this will prevent the dough from sticking to your hands and ensure that the sugar sticks to the dough). Using a tablespoon measure, scoop a heaping tablespoon of dough and roll it between your moistened palms into a 1¼- to 1½-inch ball; drop the ball into the sugar and repeat to form about 4 balls. Toss the balls in sugar to coat and set them on the prepared baking sheet, spacing them about 2 inches apart. Repeat with the remaining dough, moistening your hands as necessary with the water.

5. Bake until the cookies are browned, still puffy, and the edges have begun to set, but the centers are still soft (the cookies will look raw between the cracks and seem underdone), about 11 minutes, rotating the sheet from front to back halfway through the baking time. Do not overbake.

6. Cool the cookies on the baking sheet for 5 minutes, then use a wide metal spatula to transfer the cookies to a wire rack; cool the cookies to room temperature.

➤ VARIATIONS
Molasses Spice Cookies with Dark Rum Glaze

For the glaze, start by adding the smaller amount of rum; if the glaze is too thick to drizzle, whisk in up to an additional ½ tablespoon rum.

Follow the recipe for Molasses Spice Cookies. When the cookies are completely cool, return them to the cooled parchment-lined baking sheets. Whisk 1 cup confectioners' sugar (about 4 ounces) and 2½ to 3 tablespoons dark rum in a medium bowl until smooth. Drizzle the glaze over the cookies with a soupspoon (see the illustration below), dipping the spoon into the glaze as necessary. Transfer the cookies to a wire rack and allow the glaze to dry, 10 to 15 minutes.

Molasses Spice Cookies with Orange Essence

The orange zest in the sugar coating causes the sugar to become sticky and take on a light orange hue, giving the baked cookies a unique, frosty look.

In the workbowl of a food processor, process ⅔ cup granulated sugar and 2 teaspoons grated orange zest until pale orange, about 10 seconds; transfer the sugar to a shallow bowl and set aside. Follow the recipe for Molasses Spice Cookies, adding 1 teaspoon grated orange zest to the butter and sugar along with the molasses and substituting the orange sugar for granulated sugar when coating the dough balls in step 4.

GLAZING MOLASSES COOKIES

To speed cleanup, line the baking sheet with parchment paper. Dip a spoon into the glaze and move the spoon over the cookies so that the glaze drizzles down onto them. Dip the spoon into the glaze as needed.

GLAZED LEMON COOKIES

LEMON-FLAVORED DESSERTS RUN THE GAMUT from bright and tangy to saccharine-sweet and artificial. Store-bought lemon cookies lean toward the latter, with their thin veneer of frosting and a barely detectable lemon flavor that's more reminiscent of furniture polish than fruit. Cookies made at home can be disappointing as well, with recipes often calling for minuscule amounts of lemon or even ingredients like lemon extract or lemon-flavored cake mix. We thought it was surely possible to make a glazed lemon cookie that was both tart and sweet and tasted like fresh lemons. Our goal was to make a cookie with the perfect balance of lemony zing and rich, buttery sweetness that would be a natural accompaniment to a cup of hot tea.

Looking through various cookbooks, we found that lemon cookies come in all shapes and sizes, from chewy drop cookies to thin and crisp rolled ones. We tried both versions. When baked, the drop cookies remained thick in the middle—great for a heartier cookie like oatmeal or molasses but not right for a lemon cookie. The thinner, more delicate rolled cookies were preferred, but some of these cookies were tough, a result of the dough being overworked by rolling and then rerolling scraps. Was there a way to shape the cookies that would preserve their delicate texture? Refrigerator cookies, with dough that is rolled into a cylinder, chilled, and sliced just before baking, produced the results we were looking for. This process allows the cookies to be sliced thinly and evenly, giving them a uniform shape, thickness, and texture.

Now that we had found the shaping method, it was time to look at the ingredients. For flour, we found that all-purpose was the best choice, making a cookie that was both tender and toothsome. Using one egg yolk instead of a whole egg made the cookies even more tender, and leaving out the egg white also kept the dough from getting too sticky. What about baking powder and baking soda? Cookies made without any leavener were too dense, and even a tiny amount of baking soda (which promotes browning as well as leavening) made them too brittle and brown. One-quarter teaspoon of baking powder gave the cookies the perfect amount of airy crispness.

To get a rich, tender texture, we needed just the right amount of butter. Cookies made with 8 tablespoons were too lean, but 16 tablespoons was too much. Splitting the difference and using 12 tablespoons was the answer. We tried four types of sugar: confectioners', light brown, dark brown, and granulated. Granulated sugar made a cookie with the best texture and balance of flavors.

We wanted to avoid lemon extract, knowing that only fresh lemon (zest or juice) could provide the big, bright flavor we wanted for our cookies. We tried varying amounts of juice, from 1 teaspoon (could hardly taste it) to ¼ cup (very acidic). We tried leaving out the lemon juice altogether and using only zest instead. The resulting cookies were lemony but lacked the zip provided by the juice. The solution? A combination of 2 tablespoons each of zest and juice. A small amount of vanilla rounded out the lemon flavors without detracting from their brightness.

We were almost there, but not entirely satisfied; we wanted more lemon flavor. We'd heard about a technique for grinding the sugar and zest together in a food processor to release even more lemon flavor. This produced exactly the cookie we were looking for: bright, bold lemon flavor without harshness. But now we had a preparation problem, as we needed a food processor for the sugar and zest and an electric mixer for the dough. (The mixer creams softened butter with the blended sugar and zest, and then the yolk and dry ingredients are added.) We tried mixing the dough in the food processor, but the softened butter turned into a greasy mess. We tried it once again, this time with cold butter cut into small pieces. The dough came together easily, and the baked cookies were fragrant and just as tender as the version made with the electric mixer. In the end, the processor not only heightened the lemon flavor but also provided the bonus of speeding up the mixing. (We no longer had to wait for the butter to soften.) As for oven temperatures, 375 degrees worked best. The cookies emerged from the oven thin and crisp, with golden brown edges.

For the glaze, we focused on using confectioners' sugar. It would be impossible to make a quick and easy glaze that would harden without it, but a combination of lemon juice and confectioners' sugar was astringent and harsh. Adding zest only made the glaze unappealingly lumpy. It needed an additional ingredient to temper the acidity. Heavy cream did just that, but it dulled the brightness of the lemon juice, making the glaze taste flat. Both sour cream and yogurt had the opposite effect, heightening the acidity and turning the glaze even more sour. Cream cheese did the trick. Its rich creaminess toned down the lemon's harshness but offered just enough of its own tang to keep the flavors bright. Together with the lemony cookie, the glaze had just the right balance of sweetness and sharpness.

SHAPING THE DOUGH FOR GLAZED LEMON COOKIES

1. Roll the dough into a cylinder approximately 10 inches long and 2 inches in diameter. Center the dough on a piece of parchment. Fold the paper over the dough.

2. Grasp one end of the parchment. With the other hand, use a bench scraper to firmly press the parchment against the dough to form a uniform cylinder.

3. Roll the parchment and twist the ends together to form a tight seal.

Glazed Lemon Cookies

MAKES ABOUT 30

You will need a food processor to make these cookies. The dough, formed into a log and wrapped in parchment paper and then plastic wrap, will keep in the refrigerator for up to 3 days or in the freezer for up to 2 weeks. The cookies are best eaten the day they are glazed.

LEMON COOKIES

³/₄	cup (5 ¹/₄ ounces) granulated sugar
2	tablespoons grated zest plus 2 tablespoons juice from 2 lemons
1 ³/₄	cups (8 ³/₄ ounces) unbleached all-purpose flour
¹/₄	teaspoon baking powder
¹/₄	teaspoon salt
12	tablespoons (1 ¹/₂ sticks) cold unsalted butter, cut into ¹/₂-inch cubes
1	large egg yolk
¹/₂	teaspoon vanilla extract

LEMON GLAZE

1	tablespoon cream cheese, softened
2	tablespoons juice from 1 lemon
1 ¹/₂	cups (6 ounces) confectioners' sugar

1. FOR THE COOKIES: In a food processor, process the granulated sugar and lemon zest until the sugar looks damp and the zest is thoroughly incorporated, about 30 seconds. Add the flour, baking powder, and salt; pulse to combine, about ten 1-second pulses. Scatter the butter pieces over; pulse until the mixture resembles fine cornmeal, about fifteen 1-second pulses. In a measuring cup or small bowl, beat together the lemon juice, egg yolk, and vanilla with a fork to combine. With the machine running, add the juice mixture in a slow, steady stream (the process should take about 10 seconds); continue processing until the dough begins to form into a ball, 10 to 15 seconds longer.

2. Turn the dough and any dry bits onto a clean work surface; working quickly, gently knead together to ensure that no dry bits remain and the dough is homogenous. Following the illustrations on page 445, shape the dough into a log about 10 inches long and 2 inches in diameter, wrap the dough in parchment or plastic wrap, and twist to seal. Chill the dough until firm and cold, about 45 minutes in the freezer or 2 hours in the refrigerator.

3. Meanwhile, adjust the oven racks to the upper- and lower-middle positions; heat the oven to 375 degrees.

4. Line 2 large baking sheets with parchment paper or spray them with nonstick cooking spray. Remove the dough log from its wrapper and, using a sharp chef's knife, slice the dough into rounds ³/₈ inch thick; place the rounds on the prepared baking sheets, spacing them about 1 inch apart. Bake until the centers of the cookies just begin to color and the edges are golden brown, 14 to 16 minutes, rotating the baking sheets front to back and top to bottom halfway through the baking time. Cool the cookies on the baking sheets about 5 minutes; using a wide metal spatula, transfer the cookies to a wire rack and cool to room temperature before glazing.

5. FOR THE GLAZE: Whisk the cream cheese and lemon juice in a medium nonreactive bowl until no lumps remain. Add the confectioners' sugar and whisk until smooth.

6. TO GLAZE THE COOKIES: When the cookies have cooled, working 1 at a time, spoon a scant teaspoon of glaze onto each cookie and spread evenly with the back of the spoon. Let the cookies stand on a wire rack until the glaze is set and dry, about 1 hour.

➤ VARIATIONS

Glazed Lemon–Orange Cornmeal Cookies

Follow the recipe for Glazed Lemon Cookies, substituting 1 tablespoon grated orange zest for an equal amount of lemon zest and ¹/₄ cup cornmeal for an equal amount of flour.

Glazed Lemon and Crystallized Ginger Cookies

Follow the recipe for Glazed Lemon Cookies, processing 3 tablespoons finely chopped crystallized ginger along with the sugar and lemon zest.

NEW YORK BLACK AND WHITE COOKIES

A TREAT FOUND IN NEARLY EVERY NEW York City deli, the black and white cookie is made from butter, sugar, eggs, milk, flour, and a touch of lemon and painted with side-by-side coats of chocolate and vanilla icing. Too often doughy and bland or dry and sweet, contemporary deli versions of the cookie evoke nostalgia for simpler times but offer little present-day gastronomic pleasure. We wanted a delicate, lightly lemon-flavored cookie that was cake-like without being cakey, tender without being too sweet. We wanted a cookie with a low, even rise and smooth, flavorful chocolate and vanilla icings.

Our testing began with a range of black and white cookie recipes. Some were sweet and slightly crisp, others buttery and rich, and still others thick and cakey. Some of the recipes made good cookies but not good New York black and white cookies. We knew we did not want the dense richness of a butter cookie or the sweet crunch of a sugar cookie, so the recipes that fell into these categories were summarily rejected. We focused our testing instead on a widely circulated recipe claiming to be the authentic black and white cookie recipe. In the test kitchen, however, we take claims to authenticity with the proverbial grain of salt. After all, exchanging recipes is a bit like playing the telephone game. As the recipe changes hands, inevitable omissions and substitutions produce a recipe that bears little resemblance to its original version. Additionally, tasters in the test kitchen were wary of "authentic" New York black and white cookies since so few of the cookies found in the city's delis actually taste good.

Nevertheless, we tried the authentic recipe and, not surprisingly, found it wanting. Neither crisp like sugar cookies nor rich like shortbread, these cookies did approximate the distinctive black and white cookie cake-like texture. But they needed a lot of work. Doughy and thick, the cookies had a texture that lay somewhere between a scone and an eggy cake. The cookies had thin edges but mottled and bumpy centers; not the smooth-surfaced, perfectly round cookies we had imagined. Although

it fell short, we sensed that this recipe had the very rough-hewn makings of an ideal New York black and white cookie. We knew we wanted to get rid of the eggy flavor and texture, give the cookie a lower, more even rise, keep a slight cake-like texture but get rid of the doughiness, and make the cookie more tender and delicate.

We followed the traditional creaming method, using two sticks of butter. Then we turned to the eggs and flour. We knew we wanted to reduce both. The original recipe called for 2½ cups all-purpose flour and 2½ cups cake flour. We tried reducing the total flour to 4 cups, 2 cups of each type. The reduction of flour improved the texture of the cookies dramatically, but we still found them somewhat tough. Because all-purpose flour is significantly higher in protein than cake flour (10 to 11 percent versus 6 percent), we knew that using all-purpose flour alone would give the cookies a firmer texture. We experimented with different combinations of all-purpose and cake and finally settled on using cake flour alone. The resulting cookies had a delicate, cake-like texture and very fine crumb.

A reduction in the percentage of total flour in the recipe as well as a reduction in the protein level required a comparative reduction of the liquid ingredients, the eggs and milk. We tried using two eggs and two egg yolks, three whole eggs, and four yolks, among other variations, and found that two large whole eggs worked perfectly in combination with 4 cups, instead of 5 cups, of flour. Surprisingly, we found that the original 1 cup of milk was just right.

The original recipe called for 1¾ cups sugar. We tried altering this amount, testing amounts ranging from 1 cup to 2½ cups sugar and found that 1¾ cups did add the right amount of sweetness while keeping the cookies tender. Any more produced crisper cookies, giving them a texture and flavor more akin to a sugar cookie. Any less and the cookies were not tender and sweet enough.

Our cookies still had a very misshapen appearance. The edges were much thinner than the centers, which were lumpy and thick. After numerous tests, we discovered that just ½ teaspoon of baking powder gave our cookies a thin, even rise. They were almost perfect. Then we found that if we gently pressed the shaped dough with dampened fingers so that the cookies were ⅜ inch thick and 2½ inches in diameter before they went into the oven, the result was perfect.

To give the cookies their traditional subtle lemon flavor, we tried lemon juice, lemon zest, and lemon extract and found that just ¼ teaspoon lemon extract did the job right. The lemon zest was too overpowering even in small amounts and was visually out of place in the cookies. While 1 tablespoon lemon juice is an acceptable substitution if lemon extract is unavailable, tasters preferred the cookies made with lemon extract. Avoid buying lemon flavor (usually lemon oil diluted with canola or other flavorless oil) and look for pure lemon extract. We also preferred a small amount of vanilla extract—½ teaspoon did the job—which gave the subtle, higher lemon notes some depth and rounded out the flavor.

Black and white cookies derive their name from their characteristic icing: Half of the cookie is covered in chocolate icing and the other half in vanilla. We came up with numerous versions of the icing recipe, all calling for confectioners' sugar, some with milk or cream, some with water, boiling water, or corn syrup. Most recipes combined some of the vanilla icing with melted chocolate; others used melted chocolate and cream alone for the chocolate icing. We wanted an icing that would be easy to spread and would coat the cookie in a smooth, even layer. We also wanted the icing to have a bit of a shine and to harden so that our fingers wouldn't be covered in frosting. We wanted our vanilla icing to have a subtle vanilla flavor and our chocolate icing to taste of chocolate, not of brown-colored confectioners' sugar. After numerous tests, we discovered that confectioners' sugar in combination with corn syrup had the best consistency and appearance. Unsweetened chocolate gave the icing a richer, darker color than bittersweet, semisweet, or milk chocolate. If the icings become too stiff as you are coating the cookies, simply add more hot water, teaspoon by teaspoon, until the proper, fluid consistency is achieved. Add more confectioners' sugar if the icing is too thin.

Black and White Cookies

MAKES 26 LARGE COOKIES,
ABOUT 3½ INCHES IN DIAMETER

Use lemon extract, or, in a pinch, fresh lemon juice, to flavor these cookies. Avoid buying "lemon flavor," which is lemon oil diluted in canola oil.

COOKIES

4	cups (16 ounces) plain cake flour
½	teaspoon baking powder
½	teaspoon salt
16	tablespoons (2 sticks) unsalted butter, softened but still cool
1¾	cups (12¼ ounces) granulated sugar
2	large eggs, at room temperature
½	teaspoon vanilla extract
¼	teaspoon lemon extract
1	cup milk

ICINGS

2	ounces unsweetened chocolate, chopped fine
¼	cup light corn syrup
⅓	cup water
5	cups (20 ounces) confectioners' sugar
½	teaspoon vanilla extract

1. FOR THE COOKIES: Adjust the oven racks to the lower- and upper-middle positions and heat the oven to 375 degrees. Line 2 large baking sheets with parchment paper or spray them with nonstick cooking spray.

2. Whisk together the flour, baking powder, and salt in a large bowl; set aside.

3. Either by hand or with an electric mixer, beat the butter at medium speed until creamy, about 30 seconds. Gradually beat in the sugar, increasing the speed to medium high, until light and fluffy, about 3 minutes. Scrape down the sides and bottom of the bowl. Add the eggs, vanilla, and lemon extract and beat at medium speed until combined, about 30 seconds. Again, scrape down the sides and bottom of the bowl. Beginning and ending with the flour mixture, alternately add the flour mixture in 4 additions and the milk in 3 additions at low speed until just combined.

4. Using a ¼-cup dry measure and a soupspoon,

place six ¼ cup-mounds of dough a generous 2 inches apart on each baking sheet. With moistened fingers, gently press each mound of dough into a disk 2½ inches wide and ⅜ inch thick. Bake until the centers of the cookies are firm and the edges are just beginning to turn light golden brown, about 20 minutes, rotating the baking sheets front to back and top to bottom halfway through the baking time. Cool the cookies on the baking sheets for 2 minutes. Using a wide metal spatula, transfer the cookies to a wire rack to cool completely. Repeat with the remaining dough.

5. FOR THE ICINGS: Melt the chocolate in a medium bowl set over a saucepan of almost-simmering water. Remove from the heat and set aside. Bring the corn syrup and the water to a boil in a medium saucepan. Remove the pan from the heat and stir in the confectioners' sugar and vanilla until combined. Transfer ¾ cup of the vanilla icing to the bowl with the melted chocolate and stir to combine.

6. TO GLAZE THE COOKIES: Place 2 or 3 large wire racks on top of parchment or waxed paper. Using a small offset metal spatula, spread about 2 tablespoons of the vanilla icing on half of each cookie. Tilt the cookie and run the spatula around the edge of the cookie to scrape off excess icing. Place the cookies on the wire rack and allow the icing to harden, about 15 minutes. If the vanilla icing begins to thicken, stir in hot water, teaspoon by teaspoon, until the icing is fluid enough to coat the cookies. Alternatively, if the icing is too thin and runny, whisk in additional confectioners' sugar, teaspoon by teaspoon, until the proper consistency is attained. Using the spatula, spread the chocolate icing on the other half of each cookie, tilting the cookie downward and scraping away excess icing. If the chocolate icing thickens and cools, reheat it over a water bath until it is fluid enough to coat the cookies. If the icing is still too thick, stir in hot water, teaspoon by teaspoon, until the proper fluidity is reached. Place the cookies on the wire rack and allow the icings to harden, at least 1 hour. The cookies may be stored at room temperature in an airtight container, layered between sheets of parchment paper, for up to 3 days.

ICEBOX COOKIES

ICEBOX COOKIES, ALSO CALLED REFRIGERATOR or slice-and-bake cookies, are an American invention. Buttery cookie dough is rolled into a log, chilled until firm, and then sliced and baked. The result is a thin, flat cookie. If you like moist, chewy cookies, look elsewhere.

When developing our master recipe for icebox cookies, we had several goals. We wanted these wafer-like cookies to have a crumbly, sandy texture that was tender, not crisp or hard. We also wanted the flavor to be as rich and buttery as possible. Finally, we did not want the dough to be sticky or temperamental. Chilling will make almost any dough firm enough to slice. However, the dough for an icebox cookie must be manipulated right from the mixer. An overly soft or tacky dough would prove problematic.

Our first goal was to make the cookie thin and flat. Some recipes contain baking powder, and others do not. We found that cookies made with baking powder were either too soft or too cakey. Since an icebox cookie is by definition thin, we did not want any lift from a leavener and eliminated it from our working recipe.

Although the cookies made without leavener were thin, we found that they often had bubbles in them. We wanted an even crumb that was dense and tender. Something was still causing the cookies to rise. We tried creaming the butter less and found that reducing the beating time from our standard three minutes to just one minute was the trick. Extensive creaming of the butter beats in too much air. The result is tiny air pockets that prevent the cookies from baking up perfectly flat.

We next focused on the sugar. Granulated sugar is used in recipes where sturdiness is a must, like in rolled sugar cookies. However, we wanted cookies that were finer-textured and a bit crumbly. Confectioners' sugar is used in many cookie recipes to lend a melt-in-the-mouth texture, but we found that using all confectioners' sugar made icebox cookies with a texture that was too crumbly. After several tests, we settled on a ratio of 3 parts granulated sugar to 2 parts confectioners' sugar.

Most icebox cookie recipes rely on whole eggs, and in our testing, we found that they were often quite pale and not very attractive. Using two yolks (rather than one whole egg) solved this problem and also added some more fat. The whites make the dough sticky and should be discarded or saved for another recipe.

Finally, we tested various oven temperatures. We found that a low oven temperature of 325 degrees helps the cookies hold their shape in the oven. At this temperature they also brown more evenly (at higher temperatures the edges burn before the center cooks through), and their texture is more delicate and fragile.

Vanilla Icebox Cookies

MAKES ABOUT 45

These wafer-like cookies bake up fairly thin with a crumbly, sandy texture.

2¹/₄	cups (11¹/₄ ounces) unbleached all-purpose flour
¹/₂	teaspoon salt
16	tablespoons (2 sticks) unsalted butter, softened but still cool
³/₄	cup (5¹/₄ ounces) granulated sugar
¹/₂	cup (2 ounces) confectioners' sugar
2	large egg yolks
2	teaspoons vanilla extract

1. Whisk together the flour and salt in a medium bowl; set aside.

2. Either by hand or with an electric mixer, beat the butter and sugars at medium speed until light and fluffy, 1 to 1½ minutes. Scrape the sides of the bowl with a rubber spatula. Add the yolks and vanilla and beat until incorporated, 15 to 20 seconds. Scrape the bowl with a rubber spatula. Add the dry ingredients and mix at low speed until a dough forms and is thoroughly mixed, about 25 to 30 seconds.

3. The dough will be soft but should not be sticky. If the dough is sticky, chill it for 10 to 15 minutes. Divide the dough in half. Working with one half at a time, roll the dough on a clean work surface into a log measuring about 6 inches long and 2 inches thick (see illustration 1 below). Wrap each log in plastic and refrigerate at least 2 hours or up to 3 days. (Dough can be frozen up to 1 month. Wrap the logs in plastic and then foil before freezing.)

4. Adjust the oven racks to the upper- and lower-middle positions. Heat the oven to 325 degrees. Line 2 large baking sheets with parchment paper or spray them with nonstick cooking spray.

5. Unwrap the dough logs one at a time and with a sharp knife, cut the dough into ¼-inch-thick slices (see illustration 3 below). Place the slices on the prepared baking sheets, spacing them ½ to 1 inch apart.

ROLLING AND SLICING ICEBOX COOKIE DOUGH

1. Pat half of the dough into a rough log shape, then roll with your hands to make a smooth log about 6 inches long and 2 inches thick. Lift the dough log onto a piece of plastic wrap and roll to seal. Chill the dough before baking.

2. The chilled dough can soften by the time you cut an entire 6-inch log into slices. Cut the unwrapped log in half and place one half back in the refrigerator while you slice the other half.

3. Using a very sharp chef's knife, slice the log of dough into thin rounds. To prevent one side from flattening, roll the dough an eighth of a turn after every slice.

6. Bake until the edges begin to brown, about 14 minutes, rotating the baking sheets front to back and top to bottom halfway through the baking time. Cool the cookies on the baking sheets for 2 minutes, then transfer to a wire rack with a wide metal spatula.

➤ VARIATIONS

Chocolate Icebox Cookies

Follow the recipe for Vanilla Icebox Cookies, reducing the flour to 2 cups and whisking the flour and salt with ¼ cup sifted Dutch-processed cocoa. Add 2 ounces melted and cooled semisweet chocolate to the batter along with the yolks and vanilla.

Marble Icebox Cookies

Make a half recipe of both the Vanilla and the Chocolate Icebox Cookies. Combine the doughs as directed in the illustrations below.

Cinnamon-Sugar Icebox Cookies

Save the egg whites when separating the yolks for the dough.

Follow the recipe for Vanilla Icebox Cookies, brushing the chilled logs with the beaten egg whites. Roll the logs in a mixture of 3 tablespoons sugar and 2 teaspoons ground cinnamon.

Ginger Icebox Cookies

Follow the recipe for Vanilla Icebox Cookies, whisking 2 teaspoons ground ginger with the flour and salt.

Butterscotch Icebox Cookies

A maple glaze is especially good with these cookies. Sift 1 cup confectioners' sugar and then whisk with 3 tablespoons maple syrup and 1 tablespoon milk until smooth. See page 444 for information on using a spoon to drizzle cooled cookies with glaze.

Follow the recipe for Vanilla Icebox Cookies, replacing the granulated sugar with an equal amount of brown sugar.

SANDWICH COOKIES

SANDWICH COOKIES LOOK IMPRESSIVE but are actually very simple to make: Two thin, crisp cookies are sandwiched together with a little filling. Sandwich cookies are made from an icebox cookie dough that is sliced very thin. We found it necessary to reduce the baking time for these thinner cookies, but otherwise the cookie part of the recipe is the same.

We tested three chocolate fillings. Plain melted chocolate was too runny to use. A chocolate buttercream frosting, made with butter, milk, and confectioners' sugar, was too creamy and soft. A ganache, which is made by stirring chopped chocolate into hot cream, is much simpler to prepare than buttercream and holds its shape better. It also has a very strong chocolate flavor. The ganache will firm up as it cools, so wait until it reaches room temperature before using it to make the sandwich cookies.

TO MAKE MARBLED DOUGH

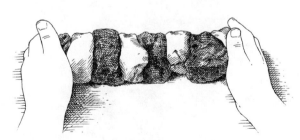

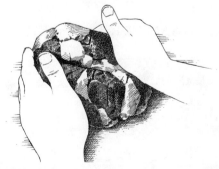

1. To make marble cookies, divide the vanilla and chocolate doughs each into 4 pieces. Lay the pieces next to each other on a clean counter, alternating pieces of vanilla and chocolate dough. Press the pieces together to form a single mass.

2. Lightly knead the dough 3 or 4 times so that it becomes marbled. Do not overwork the dough or you will lose the marbling effect. Form the dough into logs as directed in illustration 1 on page 450.

Next, we moved on to flavor variations for the filling. The addition of mint extract to the ganache gave us a mint-chocolate filling. To mimic the "white" filling of an Oreo (but with improved flavor), we substituted white chocolate for the bittersweet, but tasters felt that the combination of white chocolate and heavy cream was far too rich and cloying. Looking to other dairy solutions, tasters found favor with sour cream, which contains just the right amount of tang to balance sweet white chocolate. For our peanut butter filling, we found that simply adding softened butter and confectioners' sugar to peanut butter gave us a creamy filling with a sweet nutty flavor.

Be stingy with the filling so it doesn't ooze out. Also, we found that cookies should not be filled very far in advance. At most, filled sandwich cookies can be stored for two hours; otherwise they become soggy. If you like, bake the cookies and keep them in an airtight container for two days before adding the filling.

Chocolate Sandwich Cookies

MAKES ABOUT 30

The ganache filling has a good chocolate flavor and will hold its shape once cooled to room temperature.

I	recipe Chocolate Icebox Cookies (page 451)
1/2	cup heavy cream
12	ounces bittersweet or semisweet chocolate, chopped

1. Prepare the dough for Chocolate Icebox Cookies as directed. Cut the cookies into ⅛-inch-thick rounds and reduce baking time by a minute or two. Cool the cookies completely. (The cookies can be stored in an airtight container for up to 2 days.)

2. Place the cream in a small saucepan and bring to a simmer. Turn off the heat and add the chocolate. Wait 3 minutes, then whisk until smooth. Let the mixture cool to room temperature, at least 30 minutes.

3. Following the illustrations below, fill the cookies with the chocolate mixture. Serve within 2 hours.

➤ VARIATIONS

Mint Chocolate Sandwich Cookies

Follow the recipe for Chocolate Sandwich Cookies, adding 1 teaspoon mint extract to the cooled chocolate filling.

"Oreo" Cookies

Follow the recipe for Chocolate Sandwich Cookies, omitting the cream and replacing the bittersweet or semisweet chocolate with an equal amount of white chocolate. Melt the white chocolate in a double boiler. Stir in ½ cup sour cream and cool to room temperature, about 15 minutes. Use the filling as directed.

Chocolate–Peanut Butter Sandwich Cookies

Follow the recipe for Chocolate Sandwich Cookies, replacing the chocolate filling with 1 cup smooth peanut butter that has been beaten with 4 tablespoons softened butter and 1 cup confectioners' sugar, sifted, until fluffy.

FILLING SANDWICH COOKIES

1. Place half of the baked cookies, flat undersides facing up, on a cool baking sheet. Place a small mound of filling in the center of each cookie.

2. One at a time, place the plain baked cookies, flat undersides facing down, on top of the filled cookies. Press gently to spread the filling between the two cookies.

CHRISTMAS COOKIES

ALTHOUGH HOLIDAYS ARE FULL OF GOOD cheer and joyous celebration, they are also fraught with endless preparation and, often, a lack of time. We wanted to create a holiday cookie that was almost as easy as the slice-and-bake tubes of cookie dough in the supermarket but without the glue-like flavor. We wanted a buttery cookie dough that doesn't cling to the rolling pin or rip and tear. We wanted a simple one-hour process, not a half-day project. We wanted to develop a simple recipe that would yield a forgiving, workable dough, producing cookies that would be sturdy enough to decorate yet tender enough to be worth eating. And, to save even more time, we wanted a chameleon-like dough that could be transformed into distinctly different cookies with just a few additional ingredients.

We started our investigation by testing five recipes that called for similar ratios of flour to fat and followed the standard butter-and-sugar creaming method of cookie making. These recipes did vary slightly in their choice of ingredients. One used a combination of shortening and butter, one called for all confectioners' sugar, and another used all light brown sugar. Some added an egg or dairy component, while others utilized a leavener. Although these cookies were certainly edible, we still found ourselves in a sticky situation. Only one batch had been easy to handle, but that batch also tasted like powdery cardboard because it used so much confectioners' sugar. We realized that if we wanted the perfect holiday cookie dough, we would have to go back to basics.

The most important issue was the ratio of flour to butter. After extensive testing, we ended up with 2½ cups of flour to 2 sticks of butter. (Shortening adds no flavor to cookies and is not an option.) This was just enough butter to stay true to the nature of a butter cookie but not so much that the dough would be greasy. Although the dough was not perfect (it still had a tendency to stick when rolling), we at least had a good jumping-off point for our master recipe.

Next we experimented with flour, first testing cake flour, which produced delicate cookies with a chalky texture. We got similar results when we tried replacing different amounts of all-purpose flour with equal parts of cornstarch, another common tenderizing technique. These cookies were also very fragile—not ideal when it's time to decorate. We came to the conclusion that a little bit of structure-providing gluten (the combination of proteins found in greater amounts in all-purpose flour than in cake flour or cornstarch) wasn't necessarily a bad thing.

SCIENCE: Why Does Mixing Method Matter?

Creaming is a common method used in baking. Butter and sugar are whipped until light and fluffy, eggs are added, and then dry ingredients are incorporated gradually. This method delivers good results when making most cookies, but we found that it did not work well for rolled butter cookies, and we wondered why.

Our recipe has two striking features: It contains no leavener (we did not want the cookies to puff) and no liquid. Because the dough is somewhat dry, the flour did not incorporate well when added at the end of the mixing process. As a result, the dough was unevenly mixed, with streaks of butter, which became sticky when handled. This streaking also had negative effects on the final baked product, as the pockets of butter led to puffed, uneven cookies. Butter is about 18 percent water, and when its temperature reaches 212 degrees Fahrenheit, this water turns to steam and expands dramatically, producing bubbles.

When we reversed the order of mixing and added the butter to the flour, the dough was much more uniform. There were no streaks of butter in the dough, so it did not stick when rolled. In addition, because the dough did not contain pockets of butter, the cookies did not puff in the oven, and the baked cookies had flat tops, ready for decorating.

An examination of the interior of two cookies was all the proof we needed. The cookie on the left was mixed using a creaming method. An enormous bubble formed where the butter had not been mixed in completely. The cookie on the right, created using our "reverse" mixing method, looks uniform throughout, indicating that the butter has been evenly distributed.

Because these cookies would play host to glazes or sweet fillings, we did not want to add too much sugar to the dough—just enough to enhance their flavor. Confectioners' sugar was out because of its bland flavor and powdery texture, while brown sugar made the cookies too soft and chewy. But when we tried superfine sugar, we were surprised at the difference it made. Cookies made with regular granulated sugar had a crumb with larger holes and a flaky texture. The cookies made with superfine sugar, on the other hand, had a fine, even crumb and were compact and crisp—very definitely positive attributes. Liking these thin and crisp cookies, we ruled out the use of a leavener (which would make them puff in the oven) and eggs (which would add both moisture and chewiness). But we still needed to enrich the flavor of the cookies, so we tried adding flavorful dairy components to the dough: buttermilk, sour cream, and cream cheese. The buttermilk produced a crisp yet overly tangy cookie, and the sour cream made the dough far too wet. But the cream cheese—a surprise ingredient to be sure—was just right. It gave the cookies flavor and richness without altering their texture. With a pinch of salt and a dash of vanilla, we had obtained a simple but top-notch flavor for our holiday cookies.

We had come a long way in terms of improving the flavor (rich but direct) and texture (fine and crisp) of the baked cookies, but we were still having trouble rolling out the dough. It was less sticky than the doughs we had made from other recipes, but we wanted a dough that was even easier to work with—something foolproof. All the recipes we had tested called for the creaming method, wherein butter and sugar are beaten into a fluffy union. What if we creamed the butter with the sugar *and* the flour? The dough came together in two minutes and was incredibly easy to handle: soft, pliable, and easy to roll. Even with less chilling time than before, the dough was easily rolled to a slight thickness of ⅛ inch, cut out into different shapes, and maneuvered to a baking sheet. (For more on why this technique works well so, see "Why Does Mixing Method Matter?" on page 453.)

As far as oven temperature goes, 375 degrees

was best, as was using only one rack placed in the center of the oven. In the amount of time it took to cut out a second sheet of cookies, the first sheet was finished. But the final selling point was the baked result: thin, flat cookies that were both crisp and sturdy. They tasted great and were foolproof—what more could a holiday baker want?

Glazed Butter Cookies

MAKES ABOUT 38

If you cannot find superfine sugar, you can obtain a close approximation by processing regular granulated sugar in a food processor for about 30 seconds. If desired, the cookies can be finished with sprinkles or other decorations immediately after glazing.

BUTTER COOKIE DOUGH

2½ cups (12½ ounces) unbleached all-purpose flour
¾ cup (5½ ounces) superfine sugar (see note)
¼ teaspoon salt
16 tablespoons (2 sticks) unsalted butter, softened but still cool, cut into sixteen ½-inch pieces
2 teaspoons vanilla extract
2 tablespoons cream cheese, at room temperature

GLAZE

1 tablespoon cream cheese, at room temperature
3 tablespoons milk
1½ cups (6 ounces) confectioners' sugar

1. FOR THE COOKIES: In the bowl of an electric mixer, mix the flour, sugar, and salt at low speed until combined, about 5 seconds. With the mixer running on low, add the butter 1 piece at a time; continue to mix until the mixture looks crumbly and slightly wet, about 1 minute longer. Add the vanilla and cream cheese and mix on low until the dough just begins to form large clumps, about 30 seconds.

2. Knead the dough by hand in the bowl for 2 to 3 turns to form a large, cohesive mass. Turn the dough out onto the countertop; divide it in half, pat each half into a 4-inch disk, wrap the disks in plastic, and refrigerate until they begin to firm up,

ONE DOUGH, MANY COOKIES

Our butter cookie dough is not only foolproof but also the perfect vehicle for a number of different flavorings, shapes, and sizes. One easy-to-handle dough can be the basis for a wide assortment of holiday cookies. Here are 3 of our favorite cookies made with this dough.

JAM SANDWICHES

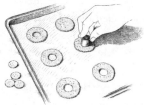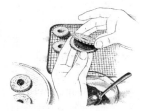

1. Using a 2-inch fluted round cookie cutter, cut rounds from one piece of dough and bake on a parchment-lined baking sheet in a 375-degree oven until light golden brown, 8 to 10 minutes.

2. Sprinkle the second piece of rolled dough evenly with the sugar.

3. Using a 2-inch fluted round cookie cutter, cut out rounds of sugar-sprinkled dough and place on a parchment-lined baking sheet. Using a $^3/_4$-inch round cookie cutter, cut out the centers of the rounds and bake until light golden brown, about 8 minutes.

4. When the cookies have cooled, spread 1 teaspoon jam on the solid cookies, then place the cut-out cookies on top. Let the filled cookies stand until set, about 30 minutes.

CHOCOLATE-CHERRY BAR COOKIES WITH HAZELNUTS

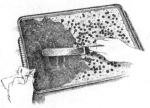

1. Press the dough in an even layer into a parchment-lined 18 by 12-inch baking sheet. Bake the cookies on the lower-middle rack in a 375-degree oven until golden brown, about 20 minutes.

2. Immediately after removing the baking sheet from the oven, sprinkle evenly with the chocolate chips; let stand to melt, about 3 minutes.

3. Use an offset icing spatula to spread the chocolate into an even layer, then sprinkle evenly with the chopped hazelnuts. Cool on a wire rack until just warm, 15 to 20 minutes.

4. Use a pizza wheel to cut the cookies into 1$^1/_4$-inch diamonds. Transfer the cookies to a wire rack to cool completely.

LIME-GLAZED COCONUT SNOWBALLS

1. Use your hands to roll the dough into 1-inch balls. Place on parchment-lined baking sheets, spacing about 1$^1/_2$ inches apart. Bake one batch at a time in a 375-degree oven until lightly browned, about 12 minutes. Cool to room temperature.

2. Dip the tops of the cookies into the glaze and scrape away the excess, then dip into coconut. Set the cookies on a parchment-lined baking sheet; let stand until the glaze dries and sets, about 20 minutes.

20 to 30 minutes. (Disks can be refrigerated up to 3 days or frozen up to 2 weeks; defrost in the refrigerator before using.)

3. Adjust an oven rack to the middle position; heat the oven to 375 degrees. Roll out 1 dough disk to an even ⅛-inch thickness between 2 large sheets of parchment paper; slide the rolled dough, still on the parchment, onto a baking sheet and refrigerate until firm, about 10 minutes. Meanwhile, repeat with the second disk.

4. Working with the first portion of rolled dough, cut into desired shapes using cookie cutters and place the shapes on a parchment-lined baking sheet, spacing them about 1½ inches apart. Bake until the cookies are light golden brown, about 10 minutes, rotating the baking sheet halfway through the baking time. Repeat with the second portion of rolled dough. (The dough scraps can be patted together, chilled, and rerolled once.) Cool the cookies to room temperature on a wire rack.

5. FOR THE GLAZE: Whisk the cream cheese and 2 tablespoons of the milk in a medium bowl until combined and no lumps remain. Whisk in the confectioners' sugar until smooth, adding the remaining milk as needed until the glaze is thin enough to spread easily. Drizzle or spread a scant teaspoon glaze with the back of a spoon onto each cooled cookie, as desired.

➤ VARIATIONS
Jam Sandwiches
MAKES ABOUT 30

1	recipe Butter Cookie Dough (page 454), prepared through step 3
2	tablespoons turbinado, Demerara, or white decorating sugar
1¼	cups (12 ounces) raspberry jam, strained, simmered until reduced to 1 cup, and cooled to room temperature

Follow the illustrations on page 455.

Chocolate–Cherry Bar Cookies with Hazelnuts
MAKES ABOUT 50

1	recipe Butter Cookie Dough (page 454), with 1 cup chopped dried cherries added with dry ingredients, and prepared through step 1
1½	cups (9 ounces) semisweet chocolate chips
1½	cups (7 ounces) hazelnuts, toasted, skinned, and chopped (see page 239)

Follow the illustrations on page 455.

Lime-Glazed Coconut Snowballs
MAKES ABOUT 40

1	recipe Butter Cookie Dough (page 454), with 1 teaspoon grated lime zest added with dry ingredients, and prepared through step 1
1	recipe Glaze, with 3 tablespoons lime juice substituted for milk
1½	cups sweetened shredded coconut, pulsed in a food processor until finely chopped, about fifteen 1-second pulses

Follow the illustrations on page 455.

GINGERBREAD COOKIES

GINGERBREAD COOKIES ARE UBIQUITOUS AT holiday time—stuffed into stockings, propped up around candles to make centerpieces, and hung in windows and on Christmas trees. Only rarely, though, do gingerbread cookies appear on cookie trays, and when they do most people pass them by. People know from experience that gingerbread cookies, no matter how pretty they may be, are usually hard and dry. But this outcome is not inevitable. We have discovered that by using the right proportions of ingredients, it is possible to produce gingerbread cookies that are a pleasure to eat.

There are actually two types of gingerbread cookies. When you roll the dough thick and bake the cookies only briefly, you get soft, moist, gently chewy cookies—or at least that is what you want to end up with. If you roll the dough thin and bake the cookies somewhat longer, you get buttery-tasting, snapping-crisp cookies; a type of gingersnap, really. Thick gingerbread cookies are primarily suitable for the cookie tray. Thin gingerbread cookies also make delicious tray cookies, but, because they are sturdy and keep well, they are also the cookies you want to use to decorate the tree. In setting out to develop a perfect recipe for gingerbread cookies, we focused on the thick ones, which are more difficult to produce. In our experience, any dough that will make good thick gingerbread cookies can be adapted to make delicious thin ones.

A review of the recipes in contemporary cookbooks quickly revealed the root of the problem with most gingerbread cookies. Any experienced cookie baker knows that cookies made with less than four tablespoons of fat to a cup of flour will be dry. Yet many of the recipes we examined called for as little as two or three tablespoons of butter or shortening to a cup of flour. The writers of these recipes were not concerned with holiday waistlines. Rather, they wanted to make sure the dough would be firm enough to handle and then cut into intricate shapes. Fat makes dough soft. From the standpoint of convenience, the less fat in a gingerbread cookie dough, the better.

But what about taste? Surely there was a middle ground. After a little searching, we discovered several recipes that called for the requisite ¼ cup of fat to 1 cup of flour. We made one of these. The cookies turned out soft and fairly moist, but they were pale, bland, and generally uninteresting. After doing some thinking and calculating, we added 50 percent more brown sugar and molasses. The resulting cookies were delicious: flavorful, pleasantly sweet, and moist and chewy.

But they still were not perfect. Instead of rising flat and level, they looked a little bumpy. This would not be a problem if the cookies were presented plain, but any decorations would be marred by the cookies' uneven surface. We knew where the problem lay. The extra sugar we had added to the dough was absorbing too much of the available liquid. Sugar is hygroscopic; that is, it soaks up liquid. This is why very sugary cookies, such as wafers and tuiles, bake up so crisp and dry and also

why the same cookies, unless very tightly covered, tend to go soft and tacky again after just a few days' keeping. The sugar absorbs moisture from the air. The extra sugar we had added to the dough was not quite sufficient to make the cookies hard and dry, thank goodness, but it was still having an effect.

By absorbing the liquid in the dough, the sugar, evidently, was preventing the formation of gluten, which develops when flour proteins are moistened and kneaded. Gluten creates a network of air spaces in dough that bakers refer to as structure. When doughs have a great deal of structure, they puff dramatically. When they have none, they do not puff at all. And when they have just a little, as was the case with our gingerbread cookies, they tend to puff a little but then deflate, the dough being too "weak" to hold its form after it has risen.

What we needed to do was make our gingerbread, which was close to becoming a crisp, flat cookie, slightly more akin to a cake. The obvious solution was to add a couple of tablespoons of milk. We feared, however, that the dough, already chock-full of butter, brown sugar, and molasses, would surely be too soft to handle if we tried to sneak in some liquid.

We tried the dough as before, with the full complement of all the good stuff, plus two tablespoons of milk. To our delight, the dough proved quite manageable when handled in the usual way—chilled, then rolled on a lightly floured surface—and downright obliging when rolled between sheets of parchment. And the cookies were perfect: smooth, even, and delightful to eat, whether rolled thick or thin.

To make the process of rolling out the cookies even easier, we also altered the usual mixing method. Most recipes for gingerbread cookies call for making the dough by creaming softened butter and sugar, then adding the dry and liquid ingredients, as if making a cake. When mixed in this manner, the dough is inevitably quite soft and must be refrigerated for several hours, even overnight, before being rolled and cut. We prefer instead to mix the dough in the food processor, first blending the dry ingredients, then cutting in slightly softened butter, and, finally, adding the molasses and other liquid ingredients, as if making a pie crust. When mixed in this way, the dough is firm enough to be used at once, though we prefer to roll it between sheets of parchment paper and then chill it briefly before cutting to make sure the cookies will maintain a perfect shape when transferred to the baking sheets. Even assuming that you do take the time to chill the dough before cutting, you will still save some time by using the food processor to mix the gingerbread—a welcome convenience during the hectic holiday season.

Thick and Chewy Gingerbread Cookies

MAKES ABOUT TWENTY 5-INCH GINGERBREAD PEOPLE OR 30 COOKIES

If you plan to decorate your gingerbread cookies and make ornaments out of them, follow the directions for Thin, Crisp Gingerbread Cookies. Because flour is not added during rolling, dough scraps can be rolled and cut as many times as necessary. Don't overbake the cookies or they will be dry. Store soft gingerbread in a wide, shallow airtight container or tin with a sheet of parchment or waxed paper between the cookie layers. These cookies are best eaten within 1 week.

3	cups (15 ounces) unbleached all-purpose flour
3/4	cup packed (5 1/4 ounces) dark brown sugar
3/4	teaspoon baking soda
1	tablespoon ground cinnamon
1	tablespoon ground ginger
1/2	teaspoon ground cloves
1/2	teaspoon salt
12	tablespoons (1 1/2 sticks) unsalted butter, softened but still cool, cut into 12 pieces
3/4	cup molasses
2	tablespoons milk

1. In a food processor, process the flour, brown sugar, baking soda, cinnamon, ginger, cloves, and salt until combined, about 10 seconds. Scatter the butter pieces over the flour mixture and process until the mixture is sandy and resembles very fine meal, about 15 seconds. With the machine running, gradually add the molasses and milk; process until the dough is evenly moistened and forms a

INGREDIENTS: Fresh or Candied Ginger

People like to add crystallized and fresh ginger to gingerbread, and we were curious to know if there was any point in using either in gingerbread cookies. The answer is yes—but with qualifications.

Candied ginger gives gingerbread cookies a nice pungency without imparting a harsh bite. We found that a full half cup, or about 2 1/2 ounces, was required to make a difference in flavor. The ginger must be ground very fine, or the dough will be difficult to cut into neat shapes. First, slice it into thin flakes with a knife. Then combine the ginger and the brown sugar called for in the recipe in the food processor and process until the ginger practically disappears, about two minutes. Add the remaining dry ingredients, process to blend, and proceed with the recipe. Do not decrease the ground ginger; the cookies will be bland if you do.

Fresh ginger proved to be more problematic. We really liked the lively, almost tingly flavor that it imparted, but we would not use it in thick gingerbread cookies that we intended to decorate. Perhaps because it is moister than candied ginger, fresh ginger makes thick gingerbread cookies puffy and wrinkly. (Thin gingerbread cookies made with fresh ginger looked fine, and their flavor was altered, though only marginally.) You will need a lot of ginger to make an impact—a good three ounces, or a piece roughly six inches long and one inch wide. Peel the ginger and grate it to a pulp. You should have 1/4 cup of pulp. Add the pulp with the molasses to the batter and omit the milk. Again, do not decrease the amount of ground ginger.

Of course, the easiest way to make your gingerbread cookies more gingery is simply to add more ground ginger. If you want really hot, spicy gingerbread cookies, you will want to add a full ounce, or about a quarter cup.

soft mass, about 10 seconds. Alternatively, with an electric mixer, stir together the flour, sugar, baking soda, cinnamon, ginger, cloves, and salt at low speed until combined, about 30 seconds. Stop the mixer and add the butter pieces; mix at medium-low speed until the mixture is sandy and resembles fine meal, about 1½ minutes. Reduce the speed to low and, with the mixer running, gradually add the molasses and milk; mix until the dough is evenly moistened, about 20 seconds. Increase the speed to medium and mix until thoroughly combined, about 10 seconds.

2. Scrape the dough onto a work surface; divide it in half. Working with one portion at a time, roll

the dough ¼ inch thick between 2 large sheets of parchment paper. Leaving the dough sandwiched between the parchment layers, stack on a baking sheet and freeze until firm, 15 to 20 minutes. (Alternatively, refrigerate the dough 2 hours or overnight.)

3. Adjust the oven racks to the upper- and lower-middle positions and heat the oven to 350 degrees. Line 2 baking sheets with parchment paper or spray them with nonstick cooking spray.

4. Remove 1 dough sheet from the freezer; place on the work surface. Peel off the top parchment sheet and gently lay it back in place. Flip the dough over; peel off and discard second parchment layer. Cut the dough into 5-inch gingerbread people or 3-inch gingerbread cookies, transferring shapes to prepared baking sheets with a wide metal spatula, spacing them ¾ inch apart; set the scraps aside. Repeat with the remaining dough until the baking sheets are full. Bake the cookies until set in the centers and the dough barely retains an imprint when touched very gently with a fingertip, 8 to 11 minutes, rotating the baking sheets front to back and switching positions top to bottom halfway through the baking time. Do not overbake. Cool the cookies on the sheets 2 minutes, then remove the cookies with a wide metal spatula to a wire rack; cool to room temperature.

5. Gather the scraps; repeat rolling, cutting, and baking in steps 2 and 4.

➤ VARIATION
Thin, Crisp Gingerbread Cookies
MAKES ABOUT 34 GINGERBREAD PEOPLE OR 54 COOKIES

These gingersnap-like cookies are sturdy and therefore suitable for making ornaments. If you wish to thread the cookies, snip wooden skewers to ½-inch lengths and press them into the cookies just before they go into the oven; remove the skewers immediately after baking. Or, use a drinking straw to punch holes in the cookies when they're just out of the oven and still soft. Store in an airtight container. In dry climates, the cookies should keep about a month.

Follow the recipe for Thick and Chewy Gingerbread Cookies, quartering rather than halving the dough, rolling each dough quarter ⅛ inch thick, reducing the oven temperature to 325 degrees, and baking the cookies until slightly darkened and firm in the center when pressed with a finger, 15 to 20 minutes.

HERMITS

THE HERMIT IS A COOKIE CERTAINLY WORTHY of its eccentric name. Depending on who you ask, it can be a bar or drop cookie; soft and spongy or dry and biscuit-like; packed with dried fruit and nuts or free of both; and heavily seasoned with warm spices like ginger, cloves, and nutmeg or flavored only with molasses. Whatever the particular recipe, most sources trace the hermit's origin to colonial New England. The name is supposedly derived from the fact that the cookies were better after several days hidden away, which allowed the flavors to blend and intensify.

After a taste test that included cookies we baked in-house and commercially produced hermits from local and national bakeries, tasters agreed that an ideal hermit should have a texture in between a cake and a brownie—that is, it should be soft, moist, and dense. We decided that hermits should be studded with raisins and taste predominantly of molasses, but with warm spices lingering in the background. And tasters favored thick-sliced biscotti-like cookies over both bar and drop cookies because they had more crust than bar cookies and a softer crumb than either bar or drop cookies.

From the outset, we knew that attaining the right texture would be tricky. Most hermit recipes we tried relied on two eggs as well as some baking soda and baking powder for their rise. The result is a puffy cookie that is dry and too cakey for our taste. We found that omitting baking powder from the batter limited the cookies' spread and height, but they were still too loose-crumbed and fluffy. Leaving out one of the two eggs made them too dense, but we realized we were on the right track. In the next batch, we omitted the white of one of the eggs, and the resulting cookies were everything we wanted—soft and rich but with a slightly cakey crumb. The cakey crumb is the secret to their longevity. We enjoyed these cookies up to a week after baking them. And, as the story of how they got their name suggests, the flavors were better after a couple of days of storage.

For both sweetening and flavor, hermits depend on molasses. We tried mild, dark, and blackstrap molasses and found that most tasters favored mild, although some liked the stronger-flavored dark molasses. Molasses alone was not enough to fully sweeten the cookies, so we included light brown sugar. Dark brown pushed the bittersweet flavor of the molasses over the edge, while granulated sugar seemed a bit dull.

A healthy amount of raisins also helped sweeten the cookies and rounded out the flavors. Raisins also lent the cookies a pleasing toothsome quality that contrasted nicely with the crisp crust and soft crumb.

Since the hermit is a not-very-distant relation of the spice cookie, we felt it appropriate to borrow the spice mixture from our favorite molasses spice cookie (page 443) and revise it to best suit the hermits. We decided to keep the unlikely spice black pepper, which contributes a kick that heightens the piquancy of the other spices. Tasters agreed that it significantly improved the flavor of our hermits.

Hermits

MAKES ABOUT 16

The dusting of confectioners' sugar is optional, but it does improve the cookies' appearance. It is important to wait until the cookies are completely cooled before dusting them, otherwise the sugar can melt and turn gummy. We like to keep hermits around during the holidays because they store well, and the flavors work well with both eggnog and mulled cider.

2	cups (about 10 ounces) unbleached all-purpose flour
1/2	teaspoon baking soda
1/2	teaspoon ground cinnamon
1/2	teaspoon ground cloves
1/4	teaspoon ground allspice
1/4	teaspoon ground ginger
1/8	teaspoon finely ground black pepper
1/2	teaspoon salt
8	tablespoons (1 stick) unsalted butter, melted and cooled
1/2	cup packed (3 1/2 ounces) light brown sugar
2	large eggs, 1 whole and 1 separated, white lightly beaten
1/2	cup light or dark molasses
1 1/2	cups raisins
2	tablespoons confectioners' sugar (optional)

1. Whisk the flour, baking soda, spices, and salt together in a medium bowl; set aside.

2. Whisk the melted butter and brown sugar together in another medium bowl until just combined. Add the whole egg, egg yolk, and molasses and whisk thoroughly. Using a rubber spatula, fold the dry ingredients into the molasses mixture until

SHAPING HERMITS

1. Divide the dough in half and shape each half on a parchment-lined baking sheet into a log that measures 14 inches long, 2 inches across, and 2 inches high. The logs should be at least 4 inches apart because they will spread during baking.

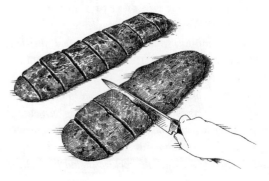

2. Cool the baked logs (still on the pan) on a wire rack for 15 minutes. Using 2 wide metal spatulas, transfer the logs to a cutting board. With a sharp chef's knife or serrated bread knife, cut the logs crosswise into cookies about 2 inches thick.

combined. Stir in the raisins. Cover the bowl with plastic wrap and refrigerate for at least 1 hour.

3. Adjust an oven rack to the middle position and heat the oven to 350 degrees. Line a baking sheet with parchment paper or spray it with non-stick cooking spray.

4. Using a rubber spatula, form the dough into two logs on the prepared baking sheet, as shown in illustration 1 on page 460. Brush the logs with the beaten egg white.

5. Bake until the tops of the logs have browned and spring back when touched, rotating the baking sheet front to back halfway through the baking time, 20 to 25 minutes. Set the sheet on a cooling rack and cool for 15 minutes. Using 2 wide metal spatulas, transfer the logs to a cutting board, and follow the directions in illustration 2 on page 460 to slice. When the cookies have completely cooled, dust them with confectioners' sugar if desired.

NUT CRESCENT COOKIES

NUT CRESCENTS, COATED IN A PASTY LAYER of melting confectioners' sugar, can taste like stale, dry, floury, flavorless little chokeballs. They often fall short of the buttery, nutty, slightly crisp, slightly crumbly, melt-in-your-mouth nuggets they should be.

But that is a shame. When they are well made, they are delicious. Nut crescents are very much an "adult" cookie, low on sweetness, simple in flavor, and the perfect accompaniment to a cup of coffee or tea. Their snowy white appearance also makes them festive enough for the holiday cookie platter.

We gathered recipe after recipe from large, authoritative books and small, pamphlet-sized publications in our quest for the best nut crescent cookies. These cookies, round or crescent-shaped, go by different names: Viennese crescents, butterballs, and Mexican wedding cakes, as well as almond, pecan, or walnut crescents. All the recipes are surprisingly similar, differing mainly in the amount and type of sugar and nuts. The standard ratio of butter to flour is 1 cup to 2 cups, with the amount of flour in a few instances going as low as

1¾ cup or as high as 2½ cups. Across the board, the ingredients are simple: flour, sugar, butter, and nuts. Some add vanilla extract and salt. We chose four recipes and, with the input of a few tasters, formed a composite recipe to serve as the springboard for our testing.

Flour was our starting point. We certainly didn't need to go very far. Cookies made with 2 cups of all-purpose flour to 1 cup of butter were right on. The dough was easy to shape and handle, and the baked cookies were tender, delicate, and shapely. Any less flour and the rich cookies spread and lost some form in the oven; any more and they were dry and floury. We tried cake flour and cornstarch in place of some of the all-purpose flour, thinking that one or another would provide extra tenderness. Both were failures. The resulting cookies lacked body and structure and disintegrated unpleasantly in the mouth.

Next we zeroed in on sugar. We liked the sweetness of the cookies already but needed to discover the effects of granulated, confectioners', and superfine sugar. Granulated sugar yielded a cookie that was tasty but coarse in both texture and appearance. Cookies made with confectioners' sugar were very tender, light, and fine-textured. Superfine sugar, however, proved superior, producing cookies that were delicate, lightly crisp, and superbly tender, with a true melt-in-your-mouth quality. In a side-by-side tasting, the cookies made with superfine sugar were nuttier and purer in flavor, while the cornstarch in the confectioners' sugar bogged down the flavor and left a faint pastiness in the mouth.

As we tinkered with the amount of sugar, we had to keep in mind that these cookies are coated in confectioners' sugar after they are baked. One-third cup gives them a mildly sweet edge when they're eaten plain, but it's the roll in confectioners' sugar that gives them their finished look and just the right amount of extra sweetness.

When to give the baked cookies their coat of confectioners' sugar is a matter of some debate. Some recipes say to dust or dip them while they're still hot or warm. The sugar melts a bit, and then they're usually given a second coat to even out their appearance and form a thicker coating. But we didn't like the layer of melting moistened confectioners' sugar, concealed or not. It formed a thin skin that was pasty and gummy and didn't dissolve on the tongue with the same finesse as a fine, powdery coat. We found it better to wait until the cookies had cooled to room temperature before coating them with confectioners' sugar.

Sifting sugar over the cooled cookies was tedious, and we weren't able to achieve a heavy enough coating on the tops, or any at all on the bottoms. What worked much better was simply rolling them in confectioners' sugar. One roll resulted in a rather thin layer that was a bit spotty, but a second coat covered any blemishes, giving them an attractive, thick, powdery white coating. If not served immediately, the cookies may lose a little in looks due to handling and storage. This problem can be easily solved by reserving the second coat of confectioners' sugar until just before serving.

While testing the nuts, we concluded that what affected the cookies most was not the taste of the nuts but whether they were oily or dry. We found that when they were ground, the two types of nuts affected the cookies in different ways.

The flavor of oily nuts like walnuts and pecans is strong and distinct. These nuts are easier to chop and grind and, when finely ground, become quite oily. This is a definite advantage when making nut crescents, because the dough becomes softer and

the resulting cookies are incredibly tender and delicate. Dry nuts like almonds and hazelnuts taste rather subdued by comparison. Toasting brings out their maximum flavor and crunchiness. Although nut crescents made with almonds or hazelnuts are delicious, they just don't melt in your mouth with the same abandon as the pecan and walnut ones.

In a recipe using 1 cup of butter and 2 cups of flour, various bakers called for anywhere from ½ cup to a hefty 2 cups of nuts, either roughly chopped, finely chopped, or ground. We wanted to cram as much nut flavor as we could into these cookies, but we found that 2 cups of ground nuts made them a tad greasy, while 1½ cups didn't give as much flavor as we were hoping for, so 1¾ cups was a happy compromise.

Chopped nuts were too coarse for the fine texture of the crescents and were quickly dismissed. Ground nuts, on the other hand, warranted further investigation. Ground nuts were flavorful, and because grinding really brought out the oils, they actually tenderized the cookies. We thought, though, that using a combination of ground and finely chopped nuts might tenderize, be flavorful, and add a pleasant crunch. Hands down, a combination of 1 cup of finely chopped and ¾ cup of ground nuts was the tasters' choice.

Up to this point, we had baked over 30 batches of cookies. We pressed on, however, knowing that we were very close. Recipes suggested baking

FORMING NUT CRESCENTS

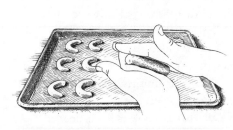

1. Working with 1 tablespoon of dough each time, roll the dough into 1¼-inch balls. Roll each ball between your palms into a rope that measures 3 inches long.

2. Place the ropes on an ungreased baking sheet and turn up the ends to form a crescent shape.

3. Rolling the cooled crescents in a bowl of confectioners' sugar creates a thicker, more attractive coating than sifting the sugar over the cookies.

temperatures ranging from a ridiculously low 300 degrees to a hot 400. At 400 degrees, the cookies browned too quickly, while at 300, they never achieved a nice golden hue, even after nearly half an hour of baking. Cookies baked at 350 degrees were good, but those baked at 325 degrees had a smoother, finer appearance and were more tender and evenly textured and colored.

Pecan or Walnut Crescent Cookies

MAKES ABOUT 48

You can buy superfine sugar in most grocery stores. You can also process regular granulated sugar to superfine consistency in about 30 seconds in a food processor. To shape the dough into snowballs rather than crescents, simply roll 1 tablespoon dough between the palms of your hands into a ball.

2	cups whole pecans or walnuts, chopped fine
2	cups (10 ounces) unbleached all-purpose flour
³/₄	teaspoon salt
16	tablespoons (2 sticks) unsalted butter, softened but still cool
¹/₃	cup (2¹/₂ ounces) superfine sugar
1¹/₂	teaspoons vanilla extract
1¹/₂	cups (6 ounces) confectioners' sugar for rolling cooled cookies

1. Adjust the oven racks to the upper- and lower-middle positions and heat the oven to 325 degrees. Line 2 large baking sheets with parchment paper or spray them with nonstick cooking spray.

2. Mix 1 cup of the chopped nuts, the flour, and salt in a medium bowl; set aside. Place the remaining chopped nuts in a food processor and process until they are the texture of coarse cornmeal, 10 to 15 seconds (do not overprocess); stir into the flour mixture and set aside. (To finely grind chopped nuts by hand, roll them between 2 large sheets of plastic wrap with a rolling pin, applying moderate pressure, until broken down to a coarse cornmeal–like texture.)

3. Either by hand or with an electric mixer, cream the butter and superfine sugar until light and fluffy, about 1½ minutes; beat in the vanilla.

Scrape the sides and bottom of the bowl with a rubber spatula; add the flour mixture and beat at low speed until the dough just begins to come together but still looks scrappy, about 15 seconds. Scrape the sides and bottom of the bowl again with the rubber spatula; continue beating at low speed until the dough is cohesive, 6 to 9 seconds longer. Do not overbeat.

4. Working with about 1 tablespoon dough at a time and following illustrations 1 and 2 on page 462, roll and shape the cookies into crescents. Bake until the tops are pale golden and the bottoms are just beginning to brown, 17 to 19 minutes, rotating the baking sheets front to back and top to bottom halfway through the baking time.

5. Cool the cookies on the baking sheets about 2 minutes; remove with a wide metal spatula to a wire rack and cool to room temperature, about 30 minutes. Working with 3 or 4 cookies at a time and referring to illustration 3 on page 462, roll the cookies in the confectioners' sugar to coat them thoroughly. Gently shake off excess. (They can be stored in an airtight container up to 5 days.) Before serving, roll the cookies in the confectioners' sugar a second time to ensure a thick coating and tap off the excess.

> VARIATION

Almond or Hazelnut Crescent Cookies

Choosing almonds for your cookies automatically presents you with a second choice: whether to use them raw for traditional almond crescent cookies that are light in both color and flavor or to toast them to enhance the almond flavor and darken the crescent. Toast almonds or hazelnuts in a preheated 350-degree oven until very lightly browned, stirring twice during baking, 12 to 14 minutes. The hazelnuts should be skinned after they are toasted; see the illustrations on page 239.

Follow the recipe for Pecan or Walnut Crescent Cookies, substituting a scant 1¾ cups whole blanched almonds (toasted or not) or 2 cups toasted, skinned hazelnuts for the pecans or walnuts. If using almonds, add ½ teaspoon almond extract along with the vanilla extract.

BUTTERY SHORTBREAD

THICK, GOLDEN SHORTBREAD WEDGES, pierced by the tines of a fork and twinkling with fine sugar, are a tribute to Scottish frugality. A stout, plain, unfilled cookie, shortbread is sandy, sweet, and buttery-rich and crumbles easily. At the cookie's edge, the fine crumb opens slightly and goes tawny and crisp.

If this description sounds unfamiliar, that is because commercial shortbreads are too often stubbornly rigid (when a dough is too lean) or crumbly soft (when vegetable shortening edges out butter). Good homemade shortbread is a transcendent cookie, and its success depends on finesse and a keen eye for proportion.

Making our way through a host of shortbread recipes, we quickly came to the conclusion that an authentic shortbread should have but four ingredients: butter, sugar, flour, and salt. Shortbreads made with vanilla, cream, or eggs invariably signaled the work of an interloper, one that lured the shortbread down the tawdry path of sugar cookies or sweet pie dough.

Because shortbread recipes contain no liquid (other than the water in the butter), the means of transforming the four ingredients into a dough is paramount. Our first order of business, therefore, would be to develop a reliable mixing method. The creaming method—in which softened butter and sugar are beaten and the flour is folded in—is a standard butter cookie technique. It adapts nicely to shortbread: The butter becomes aerated, the sugar partially melts, and the flour folds in comfortably at the end. The shortbreads we made this way were fine-pored and fairly delicate.

The biscuit method, in which cold butter and dry ingredients are rubbed together with a pastry cutter or fingertips, is esteemed for delicate biscuits and scones. Even quicker is the food processor (cold butter and a whirring blade). Both the creaming and the biscuit methods, however, resulted in loose, feathery crumbs that required light kneading. Even after this extra step, the resulting shortbread was less than spectacular.

In the end, we chose an electric mixer, using chilled butter and a low speed, and reproduced the biscuit method by "rubbing" the butter into the dry ingredients without softening it unduly. Then, rather than manipulating the crumbs any further, we simply patted them into a disk and baked it. These shortbreads were the best of the lot—fine-pored, tender, and buttery.

Though shortbread cookies want some structure, their delicate texture calls for a softer, lower-protein flour. Among unbleached all-purpose flours, we prefer Pillsbury and Gold Medal, which have a moderate protein content of just above 10 percent. (Some all-purpose flours go above 11 percent.)

We were curious to see if a small percentage of rice flour or cornstarch might effect a more tender cookie (many Scottish recipes feature these). Because these starches have virtually no protein and so do not form gluten (the protein that gives structure to baked goods made with wheat flour), we hoped they would hold the shape of the dough, keep the crumb fine, and make the cookies even more tender. Replacing ¼ cup of the flour with an equal amount of either cornstarch or rice flour did the trick; it was just enough to make the shortbread meltingly tender but not too soft.

What would a baking recipe from Great Britain be without castor sugar? In American parlance, that is superfine sugar, and it was the clear winner in our tests. Regular granulated sugar produced cookies that were too coarse, and confectioners' sugar had a powdery, drying effect on the crumb. Two-thirds cup superfine sugar was ideal. As insignificant as ¼ teaspoon salt might seem, it is in many ways a crucial ingredient. The shortbread was flavor-deprived and one-dimensional without it.

Butter is definitely the key player here, giving shortbread its rich, nutty flavor and crumbly texture. We wanted to use as much as possible to add flavor and to help hold the dough together. Tests showed that two sticks were just right. Less butter produced doughs that fell apart easily and were slightly dry when baked. More butter made the shortbread lose its shape in the oven.

From the beginning, we had been taken with traditional round, free-form shortbread scored into portions and pierced with a fork. Baking shortbread in a cake pan made sense at first, but the better approach turned out to be using the pan to mold the dough and then unmolding it before baking. This produced a perfectly flat top and crisp, well-defined edges while avoiding the problem of having to unmold the delicate baked disk and then turn it over to expose the fork pattern. The free-form dough also baked better around the edges than the dough baked in a pan.

Thinking shortbread should be a full ¾ inch thick, we began our baking tests using an 8-inch cake pan and a 300-degree oven. But even after as much as an hour and 15 minutes, the shortbread remained soft in the center. Reducing the oven temperature caused the cookies to lose definition; raising it made them too brown. When we traded in our 8-inch cake pan for a 9-inch, the slightly thinner shortbreads baked better in the middle, although the centers were still a bit underdone. To solve this problem, we tried stamping a small round of dough from the center with a biscuit cutter, replacing the cutter in the center of the shortbread, and baking the stamped-out round to the

side. This accomplished a number of things: The shortbread baked evenly without overbrowning, the metal cutter conducted heat to the center of the dough, and we had one wayward cookie to eat right away before the larger disk had cooled.

We also noticed that the shortbread spread a bit in such a low oven, so we tried preheating the oven to 425 degrees to set the dough quickly and turning it down to 300 degrees as soon as the shortbread went in. One hour later, the shortbread was golden and done, and it had not spread.

In the course of testing, one is bound to pick up tips, some of which are simply flukes. Though we had been scoring the shortbread into 16 slender wedges and piercing them through before baking, on one occasion we forgot. When we pulled the shortbread out after 20 minutes to score and pierce it, the design was easier to execute and prettier than it had been in the raw dough. We also found that a wooden skewer did the piercing more neatly than a fork. (Though

SHAPING SHORTBREAD

1. Turn half of the crumbs into a 9-inch parchment-lined cake pan and even lightly with the fingers. Press heavily with a second cake pan.

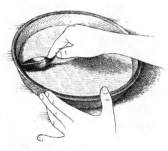

2. Add the remaining crumbs and press as in step 1. Working quickly, smooth the top of the dough with the back of a spoon.

3. Insert a paring knife between the dough and the pan. Leaving the knife stationary, rotate the pan counterclockwise to free the edges of the dough.

4. Unmold the dough onto a rimless or inverted baking sheet lined with parchment. Peel the parchment round from the dough; smooth the edges if necessary.

5. Place a 2-inch biscuit cutter in the center of the dough and cut out the center. Place the extruded round to the side, then replace the biscuit cutter.

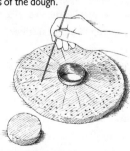

6. After baking 20 minutes, score the top surface of the shortbread into 16 even wedges with a thin knife, then pierce a design with a skewer.

465

tests revealed that this design has no function beyond aesthetics, piercing is both attractive and traditional.) Shortbread is traditionally sprinkled with superfine sugar. The light dusting of sugar is best left until the shortbread comes out of the oven and best kept to a minimum. Early sprinkling mars the design, and too much sugar creates a pasty, suede-like surface. One tablespoon of sugar reserved from the original two-thirds cup was ideal. Finally, the shortbread cuts nicely right out of the oven.

Perhaps the best news is this: Shortbread improves with age (to a point). Taking far longer to cool than other cookies, shortbread left out on a rack the first night (another oversight) actually improved in texture. A week in a tin or even well covered on a plate will not dim its greatness.

Buttery Shortbread

MAKES 16 WEDGES

Rice flour can be found in some supermarkets and many natural food stores. If you are unable to find it locally, order it from The Baker's Catalogue; www.kingarthurflour.com. An equal amount of cornstarch may be substituted for the rice flour. Superfine sugar, if not available, can be made by processing granulated sugar in a food processor for about 30 seconds. When cutting the butter into cubes, work quickly so that the butter stays cold, and when molding the shortbread, form, press, and unmold it without delay. Be sure to use a plain round biscuit cutter to stamp out the center, not a fluted cutter.

1 3/4	cups (8 3/4 ounces) unbleached all-purpose flour, preferably lower-protein flour like Gold Medal or Pillsbury
1/4	cup (1 1/3 ounces) rice flour
2/3	cup (5 ounces) superfine sugar (see note)
1/4	teaspoon salt
16	tablespoons (2 sticks) cold unsalted butter

1. Adjust an oven rack to the middle position and heat the oven to 425 degrees. Line an ungreased 9-inch round cake pan with a round piece of parchment paper and line a large baking sheet with parchment paper; set both aside.

2. In the bowl of an electric mixer, mix the flours, all but 1 tablespoon of the sugar (reserve for sprinkling), and salt at low speed until combined, about 5 seconds. Cut the butter into 1/2-inch cubes and toss with 1/4 cup of the flour mixture in a small bowl. Add the butter and any flour remaining to the flour mixture in the bowl. Mix at low speed until the dough is pale yellow and resembles damp crumbs, about 4 minutes.

3. Remove the bowl from the mixer and toss the mixture lightly with your fingers to fluff and loosen; rub any remaining butter bits into the flour mixture with your fingertips. Follow the illustrations on page 465 to form and unmold the shortbread onto the prepared baking sheet. Place the shortbread in the oven; immediately reduce the temperature to 300 degrees. Bake 20 minutes; remove the baking sheet from the oven and follow illustration 6 to score and pierce the shortbread. Return the shortbread to the oven and continue to bake until pale golden, about 40 minutes longer. Slide the parchment with the shortbread onto a cutting board, remove the cutter from the center, sprinkle the shortbread evenly with the reserved 1 tablespoon sugar, and cut at the scored marks into wedges. Slide the parchment with the shortbread onto a wire rack and cool to room temperature, at least 3 hours. (The shortbread can be wrapped well and stored at room temperature up to 7 days.)

RUGELACH

RUGELACH ARE A TRADITIONAL JEWISH PASTRY snack, often seasoned with a sweep of apricot preserves and cinnamon sugar and laced with raisins and walnuts. Part cookie, part pastry, rugelach are also a little bit like a sweetmeat.

We started by creating a "wish list" for making memorable rugelach. First, they should be made out of a meltingly tender, delicate dough with a slightly acidic tang. Second, the dough should bake to a stable (but not rigid) pastry. And finally, the filling should be a bounteous combination of preserves, fruit, and nuts, plus a spice-spiked sugar.

We began with the most crucial element, the dough. We started with a traditional rugelach dough recipe as the launching point but quickly found that it was much too sticky. As we attempted to fill and roll the cookies, the fully chilled dough adhered to the bottom sheet of waxed paper. We placed the rounds in the freezer and, 30 minutes later, worked with the frozen rounds of dough. Eventually, we could fill and roll the rugelach, but at that point our exchange with the dough seemed endless and too much of a hassle. Then the rugelach collapsed as they baked.

Eventually, through many trials and errors, we found that by increasing the amount of flour, adding two tablespoons of sour cream, and freezing the circles of rolled-out dough before applying the filling, we could create a dough with a silky, flaky quality and a light, creamy crumb. The addition of 1½ tablespoons of granulated sugar gave it depth and helped deepen the final color. This was a dreamy, supple dough; the best of them all.

Next came the issue of assembling the filling and dealing with its tendency to leak out as the cookies baked. After several more batches of rugelach, we found two techniques that helped control excessive leaking. First, we chopped the nuts very fine and added them to the filling last, so they would block seepage. Second, we processed the preserves briefly in the food processor to break up larger pieces of fruit, which tend to spill out during baking. A little of the preserves still puddled around the baked rugelach, though, so we resigned ourselves to the fact that our rugelach would have a somewhat rustic appearance. Because the preserves leak slightly, it's important to remove the cookies from the pans as soon as they are baked. If you leave them a little longer, the preserves will form a lacy edge on the cookies; simply cut away this border with a small paring knife.

Once we had filled and rolled the rugelach (see the illustrations on page 468), we placed them on heavy rimmed baking pans lined with parchment paper. If you don't have any of these rimmed pans, use the heaviest baking sheets you have in order to avoid scorching and possibly overcaramelizing the bottoms of the rugelach as they bake. Alternatively, you can double up lightweight baking sheets by stacking one directly on top of another.

Crescent-Shaped Rugelach with Raisin-Walnut Filling
MAKES 32

If the dough gathers into a cohesive mass around the blade in the food processor, you have overprocessed it. Make sure to stop processing when the mixture is separate and pebbly. If at any point during the cutting and rolling of the crescents the sheet of dough softens and becomes impossible to roll, slide it onto a baking pan and freeze it until it is firm enough to handle. Once the crescents are baking in the oven, start checking them for doneness at 18 or 19 minutes, especially those on the higher rack. Feel free to substitute an equal quantity of chopped pitted prunes, chopped dried apricots, dried currants, dried cherries, or dried cranberries for the raisins in the filling.

CREAM CHEESE AND SOUR CREAM DOUGH

- 2¼ cups (11¼ ounces) unbleached all-purpose flour
- 1½ tablespoons sugar
- ¼ teaspoon salt
- 16 tablespoons (2 sticks) cold unsalted butter, cut into ¼-inch pieces
- 8 ounces cold cream cheese, cut into ½-inch chunks
- 2 tablespoons sour cream

FILLING

- 1 cup (7 ounces) sugar
- 1 tablespoon ground cinnamon
- ⅔ cup apricot preserves, processed briefly in a food processor to break up large chunks
- 1 cup raisins, preferably golden
- 2¼ cups walnuts, chopped fine

EGG YOLK AND MILK GLAZE

- 2 large egg yolks
- 2 tablespoons milk

1. FOR THE DOUGH: Place the flour, sugar, and salt in a food processor and pulse to combine. Add the butter, cream cheese, and sour cream; process until the dough comes together in small, uneven pebbles the size of cottage cheese curds, about sixteen 1-second pulses. Turn the mixture onto a work surface, press into a 9 by 6-inch log,

divide the log into 4 equal portions (see illustration 1, below), and press each portion into a 4½ by ¾-inch disk. Place each disk between two sheets of plastic wrap and roll it out to form an 8½-inch circle (illustration 2). Stack the dough circles on a plate; freeze 30 minutes (or up to 1 month, stored in a zipper-lock freezer bag).

2. FOR THE FILLING: Meanwhile, mix the sugar and cinnamon in a small bowl; set aside with the other filling ingredients. Line 2 large, heavy rimmed baking sheets with parchment paper. Working with one round at a time, remove the dough from the freezer and spread 2½ tablespoons preserves, ¼ cup raisins, 2 tablespoons cinnamon sugar, and ½ cup walnuts, in that order, over the dough; pat down gently with your fingers (illustration 3). Cut the dough round into 8 wedges. Roll each wedge into a crescent shape and place the crescents 2 inches apart on prepared sheets (see the illustration below). Freeze the crescents at least 15 minutes.

3. TO GLAZE AND BAKE: Adjust the oven racks to the upper- and lower-middle positions and heat the oven to 375 degrees. Whisk the egg yolks and milk in a small bowl until smooth. Brush the tops and sides of the frozen crescents with the egg-and-milk mixture. Bake the crescents until pale gold and slightly puffy, 21 to 23 minutes, rotating the baking sheets front to back and top to bottom halfway through the baking time. Immediately sprinkle each cookie with a scant teaspoon cinnamon sugar; carefully transfer the hot, fragile cookies to a wire rack using a wide metal spatula. (The rugelach can be stored in an airtight container up to 4 days.)

➤ VARIATIONS
Roulade-Shaped Rugelach
Follow the recipe for Crescent-Shaped Rugelach with Raisin-Walnut Filling, rolling the dough to an 11 by 7-inch rectangle. Follow the illustrations below to roll the dough and form roulades.

FILLING AND FORMING RUGELACH

1. Cut the dough into even quarters. Press each quarter into a round, flat disk about 4½ inches in diameter for crescents; or an 8 by 4-inch rectangle for roulades.

2. Place each disk between 2 pieces of plastic wrap and roll it into an 8½-inch disk for crescents or an 11 by 7-inch rectangle for roulades. Leave in the plastic wrap and stack on top of each other on a large plate and place in the freezer.

3. Remove the dough from the freezer, place it on a work surface, peel off the top layer of plastic wrap, and cover the dough with preserves, raisins, cinnamon sugar, and walnuts.

FOR CRESCENTS
Cut the dough into 8 pie-shaped wedges. Starting with the wide side opposite the point, roll up the wedges to form crescents. Freeze them for 15 minutes, then bake as directed.

FOR ROULADES
1. Starting from the long side, roll the dough tightly into a cylinder, taking care not to squeeze any filling out the sides as you roll.

2. Cut off a ¼-inch section from each end of the cylinder and discard it. Cut the roll into 1-inch pieces. Place them seam-side down on parchment paper-lined baking sheets. Freeze them for 15 minutes, then bake as directed.

ONCE YOU HAVE ASSEMBLED THEM, YOU can freeze rugelach for up to six weeks before baking. When they come out of the oven, they will taste every bit as good as rugelach assembled and baked the same day.

Roll, fill, and form the rugelach according to the directions. Place them ½ inch apart on a large baking sheet lined with parchment or waxed paper. Cover the pan loosely with plastic wrap and freeze until the cookies are firm, about 1¼ hours. Transfer the frozen cookies to a sturdy, airtight, food-safe storage container and cover it tightly. Or enclose the cookies in plastic wrap in bundles of two or three, then slip them into zipper-lock freezer storage bags. Freeze on a jostle-free shelf.

To bake frozen rugelach, place them on parchment paper–lined baking pans, glaze and bake immediately, increasing the baking time by about six to seven minutes.

Rugelach with Chocolate-Walnut Filling

Chocolate-and-walnut rugelach are excellent without preserves altogether or with seedless raspberry preserves in place of the apricot.

Follow the recipe for either Crescent- or Roulade-Shaped Rugelach, omitting the apricot preserves (or substituting raspberry) and substituting 1 cup semisweet chocolate minichips for the raisins.

BISCOTTI

DESPITE THEIR ELEGANT APPEARANCE, THE twice-baked Italian cookies known as biscotti are easy to make. A longer-than-average baking time yields a uniquely crunchy texture and also gives them an unusually long shelf life. Together, these factors make biscotti an excellent choice for home bakers. To find out how to make the very best biscotti, we decided to test and compare the dozens of traditional recipes that are out there. The results were surprising.

Most recipes have a fairly constant ratio of sugar to flour to flavorings. The major difference in the recipes is the type and quantity of fat used, which varied dramatically. It is this "fat factor," we discovered, that has the most dramatic effect on the taste, texture, and shelf life of the resulting biscotti.

There are three styles of biscotti, based on their fat content. The richest variety contains butter and eggs. The most traditional recipes contain whole eggs, sometimes supplemented by additional yolks, but no butter. The leanest biscotti contain just egg whites—no yolks or butter. We tested all three varieties and found differences in texture and taste.

In the matter of texture, we found that recipes containing butter produced satisfyingly crunchy biscuits that were nonetheless somewhat softer and richer—more cookie-like—than those not containing butter. We also discovered that recipes using whole eggs only, without additional yolks, were noticeably less cake-like, with a more straightforward crunch. (Biscotti with whole eggs and additional yolks were more like those with butter.) On the other end of the scale, the biscotti made with egg whites only—no butter or yolks—produced the driest and crispest cookies, reminiscent of hard candy. In fact, these cookies were so hard that they might present the risk of cracking a tooth if eaten without dunking in milk or coffee first. We liked biscotti made with butter and with whole eggs but rejected those made with just whites.

In the matter of taste, the fresh-baked biscotti containing butter provided a superior and irresistibly rich flavor. On the other hand, the biscotti made with whole eggs but no additional yolks or butter resulted in the cleanest delivery of the flavorings in these cookies. Because both styles of biscotti had their merits, we decided to include recipes for both.

We found that storage and shelf life were also directly affected by fat content. As we experimented with different doughs, we noticed that recipes using butter initially had the best taste and texture but lost their full flavor and satisfying crunch after only one day, as the butter baked into the cookies began to go stale. Recipes with eggs but no butter held up better in both categories as the days went by. They seemed to get even better with time; they tasted great and remained very crisp after a week, and if stored properly, they kept for several weeks.

Whatever the amount and type of fat they contain, all biscotti recipes share the common characteristics of quick preparation time and a relatively long baking time. For most recipes, preparation involves simply mixing the wet ingredients with a whisk in one bowl, whisking the dry ingredients together in another bowl, then folding the dry into the wet, along with flavorings. Because they are baked twice, however, the total baking time for biscotti is longer than for regular cookies; first they are baked in flat loaves for 30 to 40 minutes, then they are sliced and baked again for an additional 10 to 15 minutes. This double-baking technique ensures a very low moisture content, contributing enormously to this cookie's great potential for storage.

Biscotti's plain dough adapts beautifully to literally dozens of flavor combinations. Citrus fruit zests such as lemon and orange and dry spices such as cinnamon, cloves, and ginger work well in the dough. Likewise, dried and candied fruits and nuts such as walnuts, hazelnuts, almonds, pistachios, and sesame seeds not only lend biscotti flavor and texture but contribute to their appearance as well.

The batter may at first appear rather sticky, but resist the urge to dust with flour: too much and the biscotti will become heavy and dense. It is preferable to use a rubber spatula, waxed paper, or plastic wrap if you have trouble handling the dough. One final note: Biscotti must be completely cooled before storage to ensure that all the moisture has escaped.

Lemon-Anise Biscotti

MAKES ABOUT 42

Anise seed, which lends these biscotti their licorice-like flavor, is found in the spice section of most supermarkets (fennel seed is an acceptable substitute). A Sicilian specialty, this recipe (without butter) produces a relatively hard biscuit—perfect with an afternoon cup of coffee. The cookies are also delicious dunked in a glass of sherry, Marsala, or Vin Santo. See the illustrations on page 471 for tips on shaping and cutting biscotti dough.

2	cups (10 ounces) unbleached all-purpose flour
1	teaspoon baking powder
1/4	teaspoon salt
1	cup (7 ounces) sugar
2	large eggs
1/4	teaspoon vanilla extract
1	tablespoon minced zest from 1 lemon
1	tablespoon anise seed

1. Adjust an oven rack to the middle position and heat the oven to 350 degrees. Line a large baking sheet with parchment paper or spray it with non-stick cooking spray. Whisk the flour, baking powder, and salt together in a medium bowl; set aside.

2. Whisk the sugar and eggs in a large bowl to a light lemon color; stir in the vanilla, lemon zest, and anise seed. Sprinkle the dry ingredients over the egg mixture, then fold in until the dough is just combined.

3. Halve the dough and turn both portions onto the prepared baking sheet. Using floured hands, quickly stretch each portion of dough into a rough 13 by 2-inch loaf. Place the loaves about 3 inches apart on the baking sheet; pat each one smooth. Bake until the loaves are golden and just beginning to crack on top, about 35 minutes, rotating the pan halfway through the baking time. Remove the baking sheet from the oven and place it on a wire rack.

4. Cool the loaves for 10 minutes; lower the oven temperature to 325 degrees. Use a wide metal spatula to transfer the loaves to a cutting board. With a serrated knife, cut each loaf diagonally into 3/8-inch-thick slices. Lay the slices about 1/2 inch apart on the baking sheet, cut-side up, and return them to the oven. Bake, turning over each cookie halfway through baking, until crisp and golden brown on both sides, about 15 minutes. Transfer the biscotti to a wire rack and cool completely. (Biscotti can be stored in an airtight container for up to 1 month.)

Honey-Lavender Biscotti

MAKES ABOUT 54

These biscotti are best made with an assertive honey, such as spicy clover. Dried lavender blossoms can be found in spice shops and natural food stores. These biscotti are delicious even without the lavender. See the illustrations below for tips on shaping and cutting biscotti dough.

2¼	cups (11¼ ounces) unbleached all-purpose flour
1	teaspoon baking powder
½	teaspoon baking soda
¼	teaspoon salt
⅔	cup (4⅔ ounces) sugar
3	large eggs
3	tablespoons honey
½	teaspoon vanilla extract
2	tablespoons minced zest from 1 orange
1	tablespoon dried lavender blossoms (optional)

1. Adjust an oven rack to the middle position and heat the oven to 350 degrees. Line a large baking sheet with parchment paper or spray it with nonstick cooking spray. Whisk the flour, baking powder, baking soda, and salt in a medium bowl; set aside.

2. Whisk the sugar and eggs in a large bowl to a light lemon color; stir in the honey, vanilla, orange zest, and lavender, if using. Sprinkle the dry ingredients over the egg mixture, then fold in until the dough is just combined.

3. Halve the dough and turn both portions onto the prepared baking sheet. Using floured hands, quickly stretch each portion of dough into a rough 13 by 2-inch loaf. Place the loaves about 3 inches apart on the baking sheet; pat each one smooth. Bake until the loaves are golden and just beginning to crack on top, about 35 minutes, rotating the pan halfway through the baking time. Remove the baking sheet from the oven and place it on a wire rack.

4. Cool the loaves for 10 minutes; lower the oven temperature to 325 degrees. Use a wide metal spatula to transfer the loaves to a cutting board. With a serrated knife, cut each loaf diagonally into ⅜-inch-thick slices. Lay the slices about ½ inch apart on the baking sheet, cut-side up, and return them to the oven. Bake, turning over each cookie halfway through baking, until crisp and golden brown on both sides, about 15 minutes. Transfer the biscotti to a wire rack and cool completely. (Biscotti can be stored in an airtight container for up to 1 month.)

Spiced Biscotti

MAKES ABOUT 54

If you like, macerate ¾ cup currants, chopped raisins, or dates in ¼ cup brandy or Marsala for about 1 hour. Drain and fold into the dough in step 2, adding a teaspoon or so of the macerating liquid. This recipe contains additional yolks and is a bit richer than the preceding biscotti. See the illustrations below for tips on shaping and cutting biscotti dough.

MAKING BISCOTTI

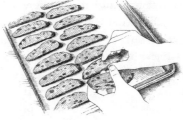

1. Divide the dough in half. Using floured hands, quickly stretch each portion of dough into a rough 13 by 2-inch loaf. Place the loaves about 3 inches apart on the baking sheet; pat each one smooth.

2. Bake the dough loaves for 35 minutes at 350 degrees, remove them from the oven, and cool for 10 minutes. With a serrated knife, cut each loaf on the diagonal into ³⁄₈-inch-thick slices.

3. Lay the slices about ½ inch apart on the baking sheet, cut-side up, and return them to a 325-degree oven. Bake, turning once, until crisp, about 15 minutes.

2¼ cups (11¼ ounces) unbleached all-purpose flour
1 teaspoon baking powder
½ teaspoon baking soda
¼ teaspoon ground white or black pepper
½ teaspoon ground cloves
½ teaspoon ground cinnamon
¼ teaspoon ground ginger
¼ teaspoon salt
1 cup (7 ounces) sugar
2 large eggs plus 2 large egg yolks
½ teaspoon vanilla extract

1. Adjust an oven rack to the middle position and heat the oven to 350 degrees. Line a large baking sheet with parchment paper or spray it with nonstick cooking spray. Whisk the flour, baking powder, baking soda, spices, and salt together in a medium bowl; set aside.

2. Whisk the sugar, eggs, and yolks in a large bowl to a light lemon color; stir in the vanilla extract. Sprinkle the dry ingredients over the egg mixture, then fold in until the dough is just combined.

3. Halve the dough and turn each portion onto the prepared baking sheet. Using floured hands, quickly stretch each portion of dough into a rough 13 by 2-inch loaf. Place the loaves about 3 inches apart on the baking sheet; pat each one smooth. Bake until the loaves are golden and just beginning to crack on top, about 35 minutes, rotating the pan halfway through the baking time. Remove the baking sheet from the oven and place it on a wire rack.

4. Cool the loaves for 10 minutes; lower the oven temperature to 325 degrees. Use a wide metal spatula to transfer the loaves to a cutting board. With a serrated knife, cut each loaf diagonally into ⅜-inch-thick slices. Lay the slices about ½ inch apart on the baking sheet, cut-side up, and return them to the oven. Bake, turning over each cookie halfway through baking, until crisp and golden brown on both sides, about 15 minutes. Transfer the biscotti to a wire rack and cool completely. (Biscotti can be stored in an airtight container for up to 1 month.)

⊁

Orange–Almond Biscotti
MAKES ABOUT 42

The addition of a small amount of butter produces a richer, more cookie-like texture. Although they will keep for 2 weeks in an airtight container, these biscotti are best eaten the same day they are baked. You can substitute toasted hazelnuts for the almonds in this recipe. A combination of hazelnuts and almonds also works well. See the illustrations on page 471 for tips on shaping and cutting biscotti dough.

2 cups (10 ounces) unbleached all-purpose flour
1 teaspoon baking powder
¼ teaspoon salt
4 tablespoons (½ stick) unsalted butter, softened but still cool
1 cup (7 ounces) sugar
2 large eggs
½ teaspoon vanilla extract
¼ teaspoon almond extract
¾ cup whole almonds with skins, toasted, cooled, and chopped coarse
2 tablespoons minced zest from 1 orange

1. Adjust an oven rack to the middle position and heat the oven to 350 degrees. Line a large baking sheet with parchment paper or spray it with nonstick cooking spray. Whisk the flour, baking powder, and salt together in a medium bowl; set aside.

2. By hand or with an electric mixer, cream the butter and sugar until light and smooth, about 2 minutes. Beat in the eggs 1 at a time, then the extracts. Stir in the almonds and zest. Sprinkle the dry ingredients over the egg mixture, then fold in until the dough is just mixed.

3. Halve the dough and turn both portions onto the prepared baking sheet. Using floured hands, quickly stretch each portion of dough into a rough 13 by 2-inch loaf. Place the loaves about 3 inches apart on the baking sheet; pat each one smooth. Bake until the loaves are golden and just beginning to crack on top, about 35 minutes, rotating the pan halfway through the baking time. Remove the baking sheet from the oven and place it on a wire rack.

4. Cool the loaves for 10 minutes; lower the oven temperature to 325 degrees. Use a wide metal spatula to transfer the loaves to a cutting board. With a serrated knife, cut each loaf diagonally into ⅜-inch-thick slices. Lay the slices about ½ inch apart on the baking sheet, cut-side up, and return them to the oven. Bake, turning over each cookie halfway through baking, until crisp and golden brown on both sides, about 15 minutes. Transfer the biscotti to a wire rack and cool completely. (Biscotti can be stored in an airtight container for up to 2 weeks.)

ALMOND MACAROONS

ENTER MOST ITALIAN-AMERICAN BAKERIES and you might be tempted to pass by the unassuming almond macaroon, in favor of the more glamorous biscotti. From the outside, almond macaroons look like almost any other cookie, but take a bite and you'll be pleasantly surprised. The exterior of the cookie features a thin toasty, chewy crust, encasing a sweet moist center—more in line with candy than a cakey cookie. Distinctly sweet, the almond flavor of macaroons should be notable but not bitter or overpowering.

We started our testing with the traditional recipes used by seventeenth-century bakers. Almond macaroons at this time were made with a third less sugar than we use today, and because contemporary taste seems to be running toward less sweet desserts, we decided to test this version. The resulting macaroons were surprisingly different from the usual modern kind, not only less sweet but also harder, drier, and crunchier, with a solid, heavy feel in the hand. Actually, we liked these cookies, but they were not macaroons as we know them.

We then tried a recipe based on commercial almond paste rather than almonds. The cookies were gummy and lifeless, lacking both crunch and nuttiness. Clearly, starting with almonds that we ground ourselves with sugar would be key for maximum flavor.

We decided to return to the older recipe, guessing that tweaking the sugar could get us the macaroon we were looking for. We were right. After much testing, we found that 3 cups of blanched slivered almonds ground with 1½ cups of sugar were the perfect proportions. Three egg whites bound this mixture together, and a little almond extract heightened the nut flavor. You can purchase almonds already blanched and slivered in most supermarkets. Blanching removes the almond skins, which if left on would give the delicate macaroon a bitter aftertaste, speckled appearance, and grainy texture. Avoid using whole blanched almonds, which turn greasy by the time they break down in the food processor.

To make the cookies, you simply grind the almonds and sugar in a food processor, add the egg whites and extract, and process until the mixture binds into a stiff but cohesive dough. Next, you drop or pipe the paste onto a parchment-lined sheet and bake. (We found out the hard way that parchment paper is essential; cookies made without parchment spread and fused together.) The result: perfect macaroons that were moist and soft on the inside, crunchy-chewy on the outside.

We then moved on to explore variations of the almond macaroon. We began with a variation that simply adds another flavor to the almond; in this case, chocolate. Our first few batches proved similar to previous efforts of trying to add chocolate to cookies—disappointingly pale and bland. Eventually, though, we realized that by simply adding a lot more cocoa than other recipes suggested (we ended up using a full cup), we could produce cookies with the black sheen and deep fudginess that we were after.

Next we moved on to the nut-flavored variations, substituting hazelnuts for the almonds. Despite toasting and skinning the nuts (a process that took some time), our hazelnut macaroons turned out tasting very much like almond macaroons. In short, we decided hazelnut macaroons are pointless.

In our visits to bakeries, we would sometimes see almond macaroons studded with pine nuts. We found that simply rolling the macaroon dough first in beaten egg white and then in pine nuts just before baking gave us this popular variation. One of our test cooks who loves all things lemon developed a version where grated lemon zest is added to the dough to yield a macaroon with a citrus kick.

Almond Macaroons

MAKES ABOUT 24

Macaroons must be baked on parchment paper. They will stick to an ungreased sheet and spread on a greased one. You need a slightly less stiff dough if piping the macaroons, so add water, as needed, to make a softer paste. These cookies can be stored in an airtight container for at least 4 days or frozen up to 1 month.

3	cups blanched slivered almonds (measure without packing or shaking the cup)
1 1/2	cups (10 1/2 ounces) sugar
3	large egg whites
1	teaspoon almond extract

1. Adjust the oven racks to the upper- and lower-middle positions and heat the oven to 325 degrees. Line 2 large baking sheets with parchment paper.

2. Place the almonds in a food processor; process 1 minute. Add the sugar; process 15 seconds longer. Add the whites and almond extract; process until the paste wads around the blade. Scrape the sides and bottom of the workbowl with a spatula; process until the mixture turns into a stiff but cohesive, malleable paste (similar in consistency to marzipan or pasta dough), about 5 seconds longer. If the mixture is crumbly or dry, turn the machine back on and add water drop by drop through the feeder tube until the proper consistency is reached.

3. Allowing a scant 2 tablespoons of paste for each macaroon, form a dozen cookies on each parchment-lined sheet, spacing the cookies 1½ inches apart. You can drop the paste from a spoon or, for a neater look, roll it into 1-inch balls between your palms. (Rinse and dry your hands if they become too sticky.)

4. Bake the macaroons until golden brown, 20 to 25 minutes, rotating the baking sheets front to back and top to bottom halfway through the baking time. If overbaked, the macaroons will dry out rather quickly when stored. Leave the macaroons on papers until completely cooled or they may tear.

> VARIATIONS

Fudge-Almond Macaroons

If you wish, press a candied cherry half or a dime-size piece of candied ginger onto the top of each cookie before baking.

Follow the recipe for Almond Macaroons, decreasing the almonds to 1½ cups and adding 1 cup (3 ounces) Dutch-processed cocoa and ¼ teaspoon salt along with the sugar. The macaroons are done when they have cracked lightly across the top.

Pine Nut–Crusted Almond Macaroons

Follow the recipe for Almond Macaroons, rolling the paste into balls between your palms. Dip each ball into beaten egg white, then roll in pine nuts, lightly pressing with your fingertips. You will need 2 to 3 egg whites and 2½ to 3 cups pine nuts altogether. Transfer the cookies to the baking sheets and flatten slightly with your fingers, making 1-inch-wide buttons.

Lemon-Almond Macaroons

Follow the recipe for Almond Macaroons, making the paste without water in step 2. Add 2 tablespoons grated lemon zest (from 2 large lemons) and process 10 seconds longer.

COCONUT MACAROONS

WHEN WE BEGAN LOOKING AT RECIPES for modern coconut macaroons, we found many versions. In addition to different kinds of coconut and sweeteners, they often called for one or more of a wide range of ingredients, including extracts such as vanilla or almond, salt, flour, sugar, sweetened condensed milk, and even an egg or two in extreme variations. When tested, we found that most were lackluster mounds of beaten egg whites and coconut shreds or, at their worst, nothing more than a baked mixture of condensed milk and sweetened coconut. We were sure that somewhere among these second-rate cookies was a great coconut macaroon waiting to be found, with a pleasing texture and real, honest coconut flavor.

The initial recipe testing included five recipes.

What came out of the oven that day ranged from dense, wet cookies to light, if not dry, mounds of coconut. In the former category were recipes that used unbeaten egg whites mixed with sweetened coconut and sugar. (One of them, a Brazilian macaroon, included whole eggs and produced a gooey, cavity-inducing cookie with a strong caramel flavor but nary a hint of coconut.) A recipe calling for beaten egg whites resulted in a light, airy, meringue-style cookie, pleasantly delicate but totally lacking in coconut flavor or chew. The test winners were simple enough: unbeaten egg whites mixed with sugar, unsweetened coconut, salt, and vanilla. But even these lacked coconut flavor and were a bit on the dry side, not sufficiently chewy or moist. We set out to find a happy medium among our test recipes.

Our testing had shown us that the choice of sweetened versus unsweetened coconut had a major effect on texture. The unsweetened variety resulted in a less sticky, more appealing texture, but it made the cookies just a bit too dry. Flour—we tried both cake and all-purpose—was helpful in eliminating the stickiness of cookies made entirely with sweetened coconut, but it also made the cookies a bit too dense. Looking for a way past this roadblock, we decided to test a combination of sweetened and unsweetened coconut. This worked very well, giving the cookies a somewhat more luxurious texture without making them wet or heavy.

We also found, to our surprise, that the sweetened coconut had more flavor than unsweetened, so the coconut flavor was turned up a notch. A scientist who works with the Baker's brand of coconut, which is sweetened and flaked, explained this phenomenon. He said that fresh coconut is 53 percent moisture; unsweetened dried coconut is 3 to 5 percent moisture; and sweetened and flaked coconut (which is dried before being flaked and then rehydrated) is 9 to 25 percent moisture. Coconuts are mostly fat and not very sweet, so they are rather tasteless when dried, unlike sweet fruits such as apples or apricots. Hydrating dried coconut therefore adds flavor, as does the addition of sugar. Although one could add both more moisture and more sweetness to a macaroon batter and then use dried, unsweetened coconut, the coconut

itself would still be less flavorful than sweetened coconut flakes.

Another key issue was the ratio of coconut to unbeaten egg whites. Testing showed that cookies made with 3½ cups of coconut and only one egg white were dense and heavy; 3 cups of coconut to four egg whites seemed a better ratio.

To add still a bit more moisture to the cookies, we tried using corn syrup instead of sugar as a sweetener and found that the cookies were slightly more moist, held together a bit better, and were pleasantly chewy. Melted butter was tried but discarded since it masked the flavor of the coconut, as did sweetened condensed milk.

We still felt that the cookies were a bit light in coconut flavor. To remedy this, we tried adding cream of coconut, and we hit the jackpot. The coconut flavor was superior to any of the cookies we had made to date. Finally, we had a coconut macaroon with real coconut flavor. (Since cream of coconut is sweetened, we did have to decrease the amount of corn syrup.) Putting these cookies together is easy: no need even to whip the egg whites. The liquid ingredients are whisked together, the dry ingredients are mixed, and then the two are combined. We found it best to refrigerate this dough for 15 minutes to make it easier to work with, but in a pinch you can skip this step. In an effort to produce a nicely browned, crisp exterior, we experimented with oven temperatures and finally settled on 375 degrees; the bottoms tended to overcook at 400 degrees, and lower temperatures never produced the sort of browning we were after.

Most of our test cooks prefer a slightly dainty confection, so our final recipe calls for a smaller cookie—not the two-fisted size you often see in bakeries and delis. We also found that these cookies are great when the bottom third is dipped in chocolate. Since the cookie is not overly sweet, the chocolate is a nice complement, not a case of gilding the lily.

Coconut Macaroons

MAKES ABOUT 48

Cream of coconut, available canned, is sweetened coconut juice commonly used in piña colada cocktails. Be sure to mix the can's contents thoroughly before using since the mixture separates upon standing. Unsweetened desiccated coconut is commonly sold in natural food stores or Asian markets. If you are unable to find any, use all sweetened flaked or shredded coconut, but reduce the amount of cream of coconut to ½ cup, omit the corn syrup, and toss 2 tablespoons cake flour into the coconut before adding the liquid ingredients. For larger macaroons, shape haystacks from generous quarter cups of batter and up the baking time to 20 minutes.

I	cup cream of coconut
2	tablespoons light corn syrup
4	large egg whites
2	teaspoons vanilla extract
½	teaspoon salt
3	cups unsweetened shredded coconut
3	cups sweetened flaked or shredded coconut

1. Adjust the oven racks to the upper- and lower-middle positions and heat the oven to 375 degrees. Line 2 baking sheets with parchment paper and lightly spray the parchment with non-stick cooking spray.

2. Whisk together the cream of coconut, corn syrup, egg whites, vanilla, and salt in a small bowl; set aside. Combine the unsweetened and sweetened coconut in a large bowl; toss together, breaking up clumps with your fingertips. Pour the liquid ingredients into the coconut and mix with a rubber spatula until evenly moistened.

3. Drop heaping tablespoons of the batter onto the prepared sheets, spacing them about 1 inch apart. Form the cookies into loose haystacks with your fingertips, moistening your hands with water as necessary to prevent sticking. Bake until the cookies are light golden brown, about 15 minutes, rotating the baking sheets front to back and top to bottom halfway through the baking time.

4. Cool the cookies on the baking sheets until slightly set, about 2 minutes; remove to a wire rack with a wide metal spatula.

➤ VARIATION

Chocolate-Dipped Coconut Macaroons

The two-stage melting process for the chocolate helps ensure that it is the proper consistency for dipping the cookies.

Follow the recipe for Coconut Macaroons. Cool the baked macaroons to room temperature,

SHAPING COCONUT MACAROONS

1. Using your fingers, form the cookies into loose haystacks. Moisten your fingers with water if needed to prevent sticking.

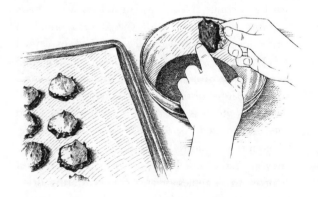

2. If desired, dip the bottom half inch of the baked cookies into melted chocolate, tapping off excess chocolate with your finger.

about 30 minutes. Line 2 baking sheets with parchment paper. Chop 10 ounces semisweet chocolate; melt 8 ounces in a small heatproof bowl set over a pan of almost-simmering water, stirring once or twice, until smooth. (To melt the chocolate in a microwave, heat at 50 percent power for 3 minutes and stir. If the chocolate is not yet entirely melted, heat an additional 30 seconds at 50 percent power.) Remove from the heat; stir in the remaining 2 ounces chocolate until smooth. Holding a macaroon by its pointed top, dip the bottom and ½ inch up the sides in the chocolate; scrape off the excess chocolate with your finger and place the macaroon on a prepared baking sheet. Repeat with the remaining macaroons. Refrigerate the macaroons until the chocolate sets, about 15 minutes.

MERINGUE COOKIES

MERINGUE COOKIES ARE A SIMPLE TREAT made by beating egg whites and sugar; they should be lightly sweet with a delicate texture. After the first bite through the thin, crisp exterior, meringues should have just a hint of chew before dissolving on the tongue. Too often, however, we find meringues to be so cloyingly sweet and sticky that we can virtually feel the sugar eating away at our tooth enamel. Other times, the cookies are so hard, bland, and crumbly that they look—and taste—like Styrofoam. Why does such a simple cookie, with so few ingredients, produce unreliable and disappointing results? In the test kitchen, we set out to uncover the secrets to perfect meringues.

In its broadest sense, meringue refers to a voluminous mixture of beaten egg whites and sugar. Depending upon how it is made and baked, meringue can be used to make buttercream frosting, top pies, and lighten soufflés, among dozens of other applications. It can also be shaped and baked into cookies. Our research identified three different methods for preparing the meringue batter. The most basic version—often called French, simple, or plain meringue—involves beating egg whites with sugar until stiff peaks form. In the second method—called cooked or Swiss meringue—the egg whites and sugar are heated

over a water bath before being beaten to stiff peaks. A third method—generally called Italian meringue—involves beating the egg whites with a hot sugar syrup, a sugar and water mixture cooked to the soft-ball stage (about 239 degrees).

We began our testing by making each of these versions of meringue and found that the basic meringue method was not only the simplest of the three but also produced cookies with the most delicate texture. Pale white in color, these cookies were crisp on the outside and had a light, open, and airy crumb with just a hint of chew. Both the Swiss and the Italian meringue methods produced bright white cookies with a glossy sheen, firmer texture, and denser crumb that tasters found too compact and tough. However, heating the egg whites and sugar creates a more stable meringue that holds its shape well. We were willing to trade more durability for a chewier (and more appealing) texture and decided to stick with the basic uncooked meringue.

Since by their very definition meringues are made from egg whites and sugar, recipes for basic meringue do not vary widely. A significant variation we discovered in our research was the type of sugar used. Some recipes called for confectioners' sugar alone, others for a combination of confectioners' sugar and granulated sugar, and still others for granulated sugar alone. We tried these three approaches and found that granulated sugar alone produced the texture and flavor we were looking for. Some recipes claim that the cornstarch in confectioners' sugar—added to prevent the pulverized sugar granules from clumping together—has the further benefit of stabilizing the meringue. In the test kitchen, however, we found that meringue made with confectioners' sugar was no more stable than meringue made from granulated sugar alone. Furthermore, tasters preferred the clean flavor of the meringues made with granulated sugar alone to the subtle starchy residue left in the cookies made with even a small amount of confectioners' sugar. After testing different amounts of sugar, we found that ¼ cup granulated sugar per egg white produced the optimum flavor and texture. The only other variation among recipes was the use of vanilla extract. In the test kitchen, tasters preferred meringues with a touch of vanilla extract. We found that ¾ tea-spoon for four egg whites added the right amount of vanilla without weighing down these ethereal creations with a strong, earthy vanilla flavor.

The transformation of an egg white—with a little mechanical action and the addition of sugar—into a light and airy meringue is a remarkable feat explained by food science and learned by experience. Meringue recipes typically include numerous warnings and caveats about egg whites and sugar but few clear explanations and descriptive cues. Once we determined our preparation method and selected the type of sugar to use, we tested every recipe admonition we could find in order to understand what scientific principles are at work in a meringue. We did not want simply to assemble a list of strongly worded dos and don'ts. Instead we wanted to understand the conditions necessary to make perfect meringues (and to deflate the aura of intimidation that surrounds this simple preparation) at the same time as we whipped the whites into voluminous cloud-like cookies.

We found that there is no need to rush out and buy fresh eggs to make meringue. Meringue is an excellent way to use the whites from eggs that have been hidden in the back of the refrigerator for some time (but not past the carton's expiration date). Egg whites become less viscous as they age and will attain a greater volume if they are not fresh. If you have only fresh eggs on hand—not much of a concern if you are buying supermarket eggs these days—you may separate the eggs and refrigerate the whites in an airtight container overnight. The next day, they will be slightly more liquid and will produce a more voluminous meringue. Since eggs separate most easily when cold, this approach allows you to take advantage of the ease of separating cold eggs and the increased volume and height of aged eggs. Simply allow the previously separated, chilled whites to come to room temperature or submerge the sealed container in warm water to elevate the temperature of the egg whites quickly—room temperature whites will attain significantly greater volume than cold whites. See the photographs on page 145 for more information about beating egg whites. Regardless of whether you use fresh or aged eggs, be sure to bring the whites to room temperature.

Claiming that fat inhibits the ability of egg whites to trap air, most meringue recipes warn against dropping even a speck of yolk into the whites. While we found that in significant quantities the fat from egg yolks interferes with the ability of the proteins in the egg white to coagulate and trap bubbles of air, small specks of yolk floating in a bowl of whites did not inhibit the whites from achieving voluminous peaks. It is wise to use a clean bowl and beater free from any fatty residue. But don't toss out an entire batch of egg whites simply because a drop of egg yolk slipped in. If you would like to remove the egg yolk, simply use a clean, half eggshell to scoop it up. The yolk will be drawn to the shell. The same is true of small bits of eggshell that fall into the whites and are virtually impossible to snare with a spoon or fingertips. Use the clean broken half shell to scoop up any wayward broken shell pieces. Of course, to avoid accidentally dropping any egg yolk into the bowl of egg whites, you should crack each egg individually over a bowl, allowing the white to fall into the bowl, and place the yolk in another bowl. Then pour the white into the mixing bowl of egg whites.

Adding ¼ teaspoon cream of tartar to four egg whites once they have started foaming helps stabilize the protein bonds and prevent the whites from breaking. (If you find that you have no cream of tartar, you may use the same amount of another acid, such as lemon juice or vinegar.) Place the whites in the clean bowl of an electric mixer fitted with a clean whisk attachment and begin beating them at medium-low speed until the yellowish, gelatinous whites begin to produce large, fragile bubbles that look like sea foam, about 30 seconds. Add the cream of tartar and raise the speed to medium-high. At this point, you will need to watch the whites carefully and observe subtle changes in their texture and volume. As the whisk denatures (relaxes and unravels) the individual knotted proteins in the egg whites, the proteins connect with each other and form a network of bonds that trap air. As more air is trapped in the whites, smaller and more numerous bubbles appear. The whites become opaque and frothy and then pale white in color with tiny bubbles. The whisk creates tracks in the increasingly voluminous whites, and the consistency of the whites becomes less fluid and more stiff as the beating continues.

When the whites look like shaving cream—white, thick, and billowy with a matte finish—gradually sprinkle in half of the sugar and add the vanilla extract. Once the first half of the sugar is completely incorporated, reduce the speed to the lowest possible setting and quickly sprinkle in the remaining sugar. Alternatively, you may remove the bowl from the mixer and fold in the remaining sugar with a rubber spatula. At this point, we found that it is important to stop beating the whites. If the whites are beaten much further, the sugar dissolves into the whites, reducing their volume and giving them a thick and syrupy consistency. Adding half the sugar once the whites have attained their maximum volume—but before protein bonds begin to rupture and form curd-like chunks of egg whites—stabilizes the protein bonds and prevents the whites from breaking. Adding the sugar any earlier stabilizes the whites but interferes with the ability of the proteins in the whites to form the bonds that trap air. The resulting meringue is less voluminous.

Because basic meringue does not keep well until it is baked, it is important to stop the mixer once the last of the sugar has been incorporated and to shape and bake the cookies immediately. While you may use a pastry bag and tip to create any number of shapes, we prefer using two soupspoons to drop small, free-form, cloud-like cookies on a baking sheet lined with parchment paper. After numerous tests, we found that meringues bake best at 200 degrees. If the oven is any warmer, the sugar in the meringue will caramelize and give the cookies a light golden color. The goal is to retain the white color while baking the cookies until they are crisp on the outside and ever-so-slightly soft and chewy in the center.

Getting the timing right can be a bit tricky. On humid days, it is often impossible. Check the meringues after 1½ hours. If they are still soft on the outside and somewhat sticky, keep them in the oven another half hour and check again. If the meringues feel firm to the touch and dry, turn off the oven and allow them to cool for several hours.

Meringues store quite well if thoroughly dried, cooled, and covered in an airtight container and will keep for up to two weeks.

Meringue Cookies
MAKES ABOUT 30

Avoid making meringues on humid days, when preventing the cookies from becoming sticky and soft will be nearly impossible.

4	large egg whites, at room temperature
¼	teaspoon cream of tartar
1	cup (7 ounces) sugar
¾	teaspoon vanilla extract

1. Adjust the oven racks to the upper- and lower-middle positions and heat the oven to 200 degrees. Line 2 large baking sheets with parchment paper.

2. With an electric mixer, beat the egg whites at medium-low speed until they are opaque and frothy, about 30 seconds. Add the cream of tartar, increase the speed to medium-high, and, watching carefully, beat the egg whites until they are white, thick, voluminous, and the consistency of shaving cream, about 90 seconds. Slowly sprinkle in half of the sugar and continue to beat until incorporated, about 60 seconds. Add the vanilla. Reduce the

SHAPING MERINGUES

Use 2 soupspoons to drop 2-tablespoon dollops on 2 parchment-lined baking sheets. Place 3 rows of 5 cookies on each sheet.

479

Better Cookies and Brownies

DISTRIBUTING GOODIES EVENLY IN THE DOUGH

The last few cookies from a batch of chocolate chip cookie dough never seem to have as many chips as the first few cookies. The same thing happens with nuts and raisins. You can avoid this problem by reserving some of the chips and other goodies and then mixing them into the dough after about half of it has been scooped out for cookies.

MEASURING OUT STICKY DOUGH

Some cookie dough can be so sticky that your hands become a mess in no time. To prevent this problem, use a small ice cream scoop to measure the dough. Dip the scoop into cold water between scoopings to ensure that the dough releases every time.

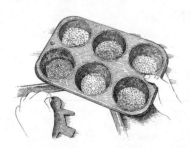

ORGANIZING COOKIE DECORATIONS

During the holiday season, you may be decorating cookies several times. Here's a good way to organize your favorite decorations. Place a different decoration in each cup of a muffin tin, which is easy to move around the kitchen and store for next time.

FREEZING DOUGH

Sometimes you don't want to bake a whole batch of cookie dough. Freezing individual balls of dough allows you to bake as many cookies as you like—even just 1 or 2—when a craving strikes. Best of all, you can enjoy warm cookies whenever you like.

1. Scoop out or roll individual balls of cookie dough and place them on a baking sheet lined with parchment or waxed paper. Place the baking sheet in the freezer for 1 to 2 hours, until the dough balls are completely frozen.

DRYING FROSTED COOKIES

Finding space to let frosted cookies dry can be a challenge. Here's how to handle this task in a cramped kitchen.

Coat the rim of a small paper cup with frosting and invert it onto the middle of a paper plate. Arrange as many drying cookies around the cup as will fit comfortably on the plate. Dab the exposed rim of the cup with frosting, then make another plate in the same manner and stack it on top of the first. Repeat until you have a stack of 4 or 5 cookie-laden plates.

INDIVIDUAL BROWNIES

To make individual brownies that are perfect for lunchboxes or picnics, pour the batter into a greased muffin tin. Fill a regular muffin tin to a depth of about 1 inch, or $^2/_3$ full. Portioned this way, our Chewy, Fudgy Triple-Chocolate Brownies (page 486) will bake in just 15 minutes, about half the usual time.

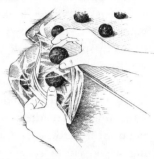

2. Once the dough balls are frozen hard, transfer them to a zipper-lock bag for storage in the freezer. There is no need to defrost the dough balls before baking them; just increase the baking time by 1 or 2 minutes.

KEEPING COOKIES FRESH

Decorative cookie jars are often not airtight, and cookies stored in them can become stale very quickly. To preserve the freshness of just-baked cookies, line the jar with a large plastic zipper-lock bag, place the cooled cookies inside the bag, and seal tightly.

speed to the lowest possible setting, sprinkle in the remaining sugar, and mix just until incorporated.

3. Using 2 soupspoons, place dollops of meringue, 2 tablespoons each (about the size of a walnut), 1 inch apart, fitting 3 rows of 5 cookies on each sheet. Bake for 1½ hours or until the cookies have smooth, dry, and firm exteriors. Turn the oven off and allow the cookies to cool in the oven for several hours. Once cool, store the cookies in an airtight container, where they will keep for a couple of weeks.

➤ VARIATIONS

Chocolate Chip Meringues

Follow the recipe for Meringue Cookies. Fold 1 cup chocolate chips into the meringues after all the sugar has been added and before shaping. Shape and bake according to the instructions above.

Almond Meringues

Finely grind 1 cup toasted almonds and ½ cup of the sugar in a food processor, about ten 1-second pulses. Set aside. Follow the recipe for Meringue Cookies, adding the first half of the sugar to the whites as directed. Sprinkle the almond mixture over the whites and mix on low speed. Shape and bake according to the instructions above.

LACE COOKIES

MADE FROM A DROPPED BATTER THAT spreads and separates as it bakes into lacy, brittle, see-through wafers, these fancy-looking cookies crunch when you bite into them and immediately melt in your mouth with the rich taste of butter and brown sugar. They look and taste so complicated that you might assume they took hours to make.

After making countless batches, we are happy to report that these cookies are actually easy to make, using ingredients that you probably have in your cupboard right now. Because there is no rolling or cutting of dough, they are also fast.

But despite their simplicity, we found a number of issues to resolve when making lace cookies. Getting the texture of the batter just right was important for controlling the spread of the cookies during baking, and thus the shape of the finished cookie. We also wanted to temper the sweetness a bit in order to bring out the flavor of the nuts or oats included as an ingredient. In addition, because the 30 recipes we tested included different sweeteners, we needed to settle on which sweetener tasted best and how it would affect the texture of the batter. Finally, we needed to resolve the most widely recognized difficulty with these cookies (and the actual reason why our mothers made them so rarely): their tendency to stick to the pan, bunching and tearing when you remove them.

Because we were looking for a gossamer-thin cookie with a brittle texture, we quickly eliminated all recipes that included eggs and chemical leaveners because these additions produced flat yet vaguely puffy cookies.

We then moved on to considering sweeteners. After toying with every combination we could think of—from all white or all brown sugar to mixtures that included molasses and light or dark corn syrup—we ended up being happiest with ½ cup light corn syrup mixed with ¾ cup dark brown sugar. The brown sugar contributed not only an appealing deep brown color but also a wonderful praline flavor; the corn syrup added a more subtle sweetness and also gave the cookies a less crumbly consistency. The flour-to-butter ratio was the second key to the texture of the batter and therefore to its spreading behavior. In our research, we had found recipes with ratios ranging from 1½ tablespoons to 2 cups of flour per stick of butter. We tested them all and had the most success with 6 tablespoons of flour per stick of butter. Less flour made greasy cookies that flowed right off the pan; more flour destroyed the lacy quality we wanted, giving us a compact cookie. Had corn syrup not been part of our formula, we could have gotten away with as little as 4 tablespoons of flour. But in our recipe, we needed the extra 2 tablespoons to compensate for the moisture in the corn syrup.

Finally, we tested the effects of heavy cream and milk. It turned out that adding a tablespoon of heavy cream to the batter made the baked cookies easier to shape because the added fat and emulsifiers in the batter helped keep the cookies soft for a little extra time just out of the oven. And because the cream imparted richness to the flavor as well, we decided to include it in our master recipe.

The sticking problem turned out to have a three-part, yet very straightforward, solution.

First, it serendipitously turned out that eliminating eggs from the batter helped reduce sticking because the liquid protein in eggs can get into even the most minute holes in the surface of a baking sheet, even a nonstick one, and make the cookies stick like crazy.

Second, we found that using a reusable nonstick baking sheet liner made a tremendous difference in how well the cookies came off the sheets. The performance differences between different types of liners were subtle, but whichever you choose, we definitely recommend using one. Silpat, which is quite durable, is a commonly available brand carried by many kitchenware stores. Parchment paper also worked, although it did not offer the same degree of easy release as the nonstick liners.

Careful timing once the cookies emerged from the oven was the final part of the solution. After cooling on the baking sheet for one to two minutes, the cookies were just starting to firm up, and we could handle them comfortably. If you are going to shape the cookies, you must work within this limited time frame, for even one extra minute renders them too firm to work with.

Lace Cookies
MAKES ABOUT 36

Using a nonstick baking sheet liner completely prevents the cookies from sticking. Parchment paper, though a little less effective, can also be used. Our recipe (and the walnut variation on page 484) contain nuts for flavor, but oats are traditional as well (see our variation for Orange-Oatmeal Lace Cookies on page 484). Humidity is the archenemy of lace cookies, so try to make them on a dry day. Otherwise, they will absorb too much moisture and be chewy instead of caramelized and brittle. If the cookies cool too much on the pan, return them to the oven to resoften them, about 1 minute.

4	tablespoons ($\frac{1}{2}$ stick) unsalted butter
6	tablespoons packed ($2\frac{5}{8}$ ounces) dark brown sugar
$\frac{1}{4}$	cup light corn syrup
$\frac{1}{2}$	teaspoon vanilla extract
$\frac{1}{8}$	teaspoon salt
3	tablespoons unbleached all-purpose flour, sifted
$\frac{1}{2}$	cup pecans or almonds, chopped fine
$1\frac{1}{2}$	teaspoons heavy cream

1. Adjust an oven rack to the middle position and heat the oven to 350 degrees. Line a large

DECORATING LACE COOKIES WITH CHOCOLATE

You can melt about 6 ounces of semisweet chocolate over simmering water. Lay the cookies on waxed paper to set.

A. Flat cookies may be painted with a pastry brush or a spoon or you may dip the bottom into the glaze.

B. Another option for flat cookies is to place them on a sheet of waxed paper, then use a pastry bag or a fork dipped into the chocolate to drizzle the chocolate over the cookies.

C. Cigarette shapes or flat cookies may be dipped halfway into the glaze.

baking sheet with a nonstick baking sheet liner or parchment paper. Bring the butter, brown sugar, and corn syrup just to a boil in a medium saucepan over medium heat, stirring frequently. Turn off the heat; beat in the vanilla, salt, flour, nuts, and cream until smooth.

2. Drop 6 rounded teaspoons of batter at 3-inch intervals onto the prepared baking sheet. For larger cookies, substitute a tablespoon for the teaspoon and estimate 5 cookies per sheet. Bake the cookies until they are spread thin, deep golden brown, and no longer bubbling, 6 to 7 minutes.

3. Let the cookies cool and firm up slightly on the baking sheet, 1 to 2 minutes. Following the illustrations below, transfer the cookies to a wire rack with a wide metal spatula or shape as desired. If you like, follow the illustrations on page 482 to decorate the cookies. Repeat with the remaining batter without cooling the baking sheet. (The cookies can be stored in an airtight container up to 1 month.)

SHAPING LACE COOKIES

Until you get the hang of shaping these cookies, we recommend baking only 2 or 3 at a time. If the cookies cool on the baking sheet too long and become too brittle to shape, place the entire sheet back in the oven for a minute or two until the cookies are soft again. If any of the cookies shatter after you have shaped them, save the crumbs to sprinkle on ice cream sundaes.

Let the baked cookies cool for 1 to 2 minutes, then try to slide a wide metal spatula under 1 cookie. If you can do so without disturbing the shape of the cookie, it is ready to remove. If the cookie bunches or tears when you try to remove it, let it cool for another 30 seconds.

"CIGARETTES"

Hold one edge of the cookie against the handle of a wooden spoon and roll the cookie over itself as quickly as possible. Hold the cookie in place gently until it is set, about 10 seconds, then let it cool on a wire rack.

TUILES

Lay the cookie over a rolling pin or a wine bottle set on its side so that the cookie forms a gentle curve. Hold the cookie in place until it is set, about 10 seconds, then let it cool on a wire rack.

CONES

Cones are best shaped by hand. Holding both sides of the cookie, wrap one side over the other, overlapping about an inch or so. Hold the cookie until it is set, about 10 seconds, and let it cool on a wire rack

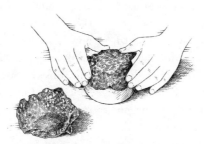

BOWLS

Choose a small bowl or cup that has a flattish bottom. Turn the bowl upside down and lay the cookie over the bottom. Gently form the cookie over the bowl. Hold the cookie until it is set, about 10 seconds, remove from the bowl, and let it cool on a wire rack.

TRICORNERED HAT

Mold the cookie over the opening of a wine bottle or other bottle of similar shape, then flute the edges to form a tricornered hat shape. Hold the cookie until it is set, about 10 seconds, remove from the bottle, and let it cool on a wire rack.

Orange-Oatmeal Lace Cookies

Follow the recipe for Lace Cookies, substituting 1 cup quick-cooking oats for the nuts and adding 1 tablespoon finely grated zest from 1 large orange with the vanilla.

Spiced Walnut Lace Cookies

Follow the recipe for Lace Cookies, substituting 1 cup finely chopped walnuts for the pecans or almonds and adding ½ teaspoon each nutmeg and cinnamon and ¼ teaspoon each allspice, ground cloves, and ground ginger with the vanilla.

BROWNIES

MOST AMERICANS ARE PASSIONATE ABOUT brownies. Some are passionate about eating them, indulging in a brownie's rich, chocolatey decadence. Others are passionate about a recipe scrawled on a stained index card, bequeathed to them by their mother, guaranteeing everyone they meet that this family heirloom produces the best brownie of all.

We've sampled good brownies, but never have we encountered our perfect brownie. So many brownies are light and cakey versions—not for us. We imagine a moist, dark, luscious interior with a firm, smooth, velvety texture that your teeth glide through easily, meeting just a little resistance in chewing. Our perfect brownie must pack an intense chocolate punch and have deep, resonant chocolate flavor, but it must fall just short of overwhelming the palate. It must not be so sweet as to make your teeth ache, and it must certainly have a thin, shiny, papery crust and edges that crisp during baking, offering a contrast with the brownie's moist center. With all of this in mind, we began our quest, determined to meet our brownie ideal.

Our baking sense told us that the taste and texture of the brownie we sought lay in a delicate balance of the five ingredients basic to all brownie recipes: chocolate, flour, sugar, butter, and eggs. After gathering a number of recipes that promised to deliver a fudgy brownie, we made a select six recipes. The varying proportions of these five ingredients

produced batches of brownies that were soft and pasty; dry and cakey; or chewy, like a Tootsie Roll. Chocolate flavor was divergent, too, ranging from intense but one-dimensional jolts to weak, muted touches on the palate. Our next step was to cobble together a composite recipe that would incorporate the best traits of these six recipes. It would serve as the foundation for all of our testing.

The two essential qualities we were looking for in these brownies were a chewy, fudgy texture and a rich chocolate flavor. We went to work on flavor first. After making the six initial test recipes, we knew that unsweetened chocolate was a good source of assertive chocolate flavor. Semisweet and bittersweet chocolates don't have as much chocolate punch because of the large amount of sugar they contain. But this is also why they are smoother and milder. One of our favorite recipes from the initial test yielded a brownie with exceptional chocolate flavor. This recipe combined unsweetened and bittersweet chocolates, so to the composite recipe we tried adding varying amounts of the two chocolates. (Semisweet and bittersweet chocolates are not identical but can be exchanged for one another in many recipes, depending on what's available at the supermarket. We'll refer to semisweet from here on because it's what we used when testing the recipes.)

Too much unsweetened chocolate and the brownies were sour and acrid; too much semisweet chocolate and they were one-dimensional and boring. We found that 5 ounces of semisweet and 2 ounces of unsweetened created just the right flavor balance. Next we thought to add some cocoa powder, which typically contributes flavor but no harshness. We were pleased with this combination. The unsweetened chocolate laid a solid, intense chocolate foundation; the semisweet provided a mellow, even, sweet flavor; and the cocoa smoothed any rough edges and added depth and complexity. We tried both Dutch-processed cocoa and natural cocoa and found them to work equally well.

We then fiddled with the type and quantity of sugar needed to sweeten the brownies, given the amount and types of chocolate and cocoa they contained. In addition to granulated sugar, we tried brown sugar to see if it might add flavor, but

One of the more interesting ideas we heard about the dos and don'ts of working with chocolate desserts was proposed to us by famed New York chef Jean-Georges Vongerichten, who stated that the less one cooks chocolate, the better it tastes. We decided to check this out with Tom Lehmann, director of bakery assistance at the American Institute of Baking. He agreed.

Chocolate, Lehmann explained, is a very delicate substance, full of highly sensitive, volatile compounds that give chocolate much of its flavor. When chocolate is heated, the liquids in it turn to steam and carry away these volatile compounds. That's what makes the kitchen smell so good when brownies are in the oven. The bad news is that these volatile compounds are no longer in the brownies—which is where you really want them to be. This situation is made even more acute by the fact that unwanted volatile compounds have already been driven off during the processes of roasting and conching (kneading, grinding, and smoothing the chocolate). Additional exposure to heat, therefore, has no benefits; it simply makes the chocolate more bitter and less complex tasting.

So, what are the lessons to be learned for home cooks who bake with chocolate? First, underbaking is always better than overbaking. Dry chocolate desserts will have much less flavor and tend to be bitter. Second, use as much fat as possible. Fat increases the retention of volatile compounds. That's why low-fat chocolate desserts usually taste like sugar but not chocolate.

it didn't. We also tried a bit of corn syrup, thinking it might add moistness and chew, but it only made the brownies wet and gummy and the crust dull. Satisfied that granulated sugar was the best sweetener for the job, we tested varying amounts. We knew we didn't want overly sweet brownies. Too little sugar, though, left the brownies with a chocolate flavor that was dull, muted, and flat, much like mashed potatoes without salt. Just the right degree of sweetness was provided by 1¼ cups sugar; the flavor of the brownies was perfect.

Satisfied with the flavor of the brownies, we moved on to refining the texture, starting with flour. Our composite recipe contained ¾ cup flour, but wanting to exhaust all reasonable quantities, we baked brownies with as little as ¼ cup and up to 1¼ cups, increasing the quantity in quarter-cup increments. The batch with the smallest amount of flour was like goopy, sticky, chocolate-flavored

Spackle, so pasty it cemented your mouth shut. The one with 1¼ cups flour had good chew, but it verged on dry, and the chocolate flavor was light and muted. One cup was perfect. The chocolate flavor remained deep and rich, and the texture was fudgy, smooth, and dense, the moist crumb putting up a gentle resistance when chewed.

Butter was up next. Melting butter, rather than creaming it with sugar and eggs, makes for a dense, fudgy texture. Creaming produces an aerated batter, which bakes into lighter, cakier brownies. Had we questioned this baker's axiom, our initial test, in which all of the six recipes employ the melted butter technique, would have dispelled any doubts. But now the question of how much butter remained.

Semisweet chocolate contains less fat than unsweetened chocolate, yet many recipes that call exclusively for one type of chocolate frequently call for the same amount of butter (some 16 tablespoons) per cup of flour. As it stood, our working recipe used semisweet and unsweetened chocolate, cocoa, 1 cup flour, and 10 tablespoons butter. The texture of the brownies this recipe produced was moist and dense, albeit a bit sodden and pasty. Improvement came with less butter. Minus 2 tablespoons, the brownies shed their soggy, sodden quality but still remained moist and velvety.

With butter and flour set, we went to work on eggs. We tried as few as two and as many as six. Two eggs left the brownies dry and gritty and compromised the chocolate flavor. With four or more eggs, the brownies baked into cakey rubber erasers with an unattractive, high-domed, matte crust. Three was the magic number—the brownies were moist and smooth, with great flavor and delicate chew.

We finalized the recipe by making adjustments to vanilla and salt and then began to examine other factors that might have an impact on the brownies. First we tried baking in a water bath, a technique used for delicate custards, reasoning that gentle heat might somehow improve texture. Not so. We got a grainy, sticky, pudding-like brownie.

We experimented with midrange oven temperatures. A 350-degree oven did the job and did it relatively quickly, in about 35 minutes (many brownies bake for nearly an hour). As is the case with most other brownies, these brownies run the risk of drying out if baked too long; they must be pulled from the oven when a toothpick inserted into the center comes out with some sticky crumbs clinging to it. To read more about the effects of chocolate diffusion, see page 485.

After making more than 50 batches, we really began to appreciate an aspect of brownies quite beside their rich flavor and texture: with only a couple of bowls, a whisk, and a spatula, the batter can be mixed and in the oven in 10 minutes.

Chewy, Fudgy Triple-Chocolate Brownies

MAKES SIXTY-FOUR 1-INCH BROWNIES

Either Dutch-processed or natural cocoa works well in this recipe. These brownies are very rich, so we prefer to cut them into small squares for serving. To melt the chocolate and butter in a microwave oven, microwave the chocolate alone at 50 percent power for 2 minutes. Stir the chocolate; add the butter; and continue microwaving at 50 percent for another 2 minutes, stopping to stir the mixture after 1 minute. If the chocolate is not entirely melted, microwave an additional 30 seconds at 50 percent power.

5	ounces semisweet or bittersweet chocolate, chopped
2	ounces unsweetened chocolate, chopped
8	tablespoons (1 stick) unsalted butter, cut into quarters
3	tablespoons cocoa powder
3	large eggs
1 1/4	cups (8 3/4 ounces) sugar
2	teaspoons vanilla extract
1/2	teaspoon salt
1	cup (5 ounces) unbleached all-purpose flour

1. Adjust an oven rack to the lower-middle position and heat the oven to 350 degrees. Spray an 8-inch square baking pan with nonstick cooking spray. Fold two 16-inch pieces of foil or parchment paper lengthwise to measure 8 inches wide. Following the illustration on page 141, fit 1 sheet in the bottom of the greased pan, pushing it into the corners and up the sides of the pan (overhang will help in removal of baked brownies). Fit the second sheet in the pan in the same manner, perpendicular to the first sheet. Spray the sheets with nonstick cooking spray.

2. In a medium heatproof bowl set over a pan of almost-simmering water, melt the chocolates and butter, stirring occasionally until smooth. Whisk in the cocoa until smooth. Set aside to cool.

3. Whisk together the eggs, sugar, vanilla, and salt in a medium bowl until combined, about 15 seconds. Whisk the warm chocolate mixture into the egg mixture; then stir in the flour with a wooden spoon until just combined. Pour the mixture into the prepared pan, spread into the corners, and level the surface with a rubber spatula. Bake until slightly puffed and a toothpick inserted in the center comes out with a small amount of sticky crumbs clinging to it, 35 to 40 minutes. Cool on a wire rack to room temperature, about 2 hours. Remove the brownies from the pan using the foil or parchment handles and transfer to a cutting board. Cut into 1-inch squares. (Do not cut brownies until ready to serve; uncut brownies can be wrapped in plastic and refrigerated up to 5 days.)

> VARIATION

Triple-Chocolate Espresso Brownies

Follow the recipe for Chewy, Fudgy Triple-Chocolate Brownies, whisking in 1½ tablespoons instant espresso or coffee powder along with the cocoa in step 2.

CREAM CHEESE BROWNIES

FOR MANY DESSERT LOVERS, NOTHING could be better than a rich, fudgy brownie with generous dollops of cheesecake baked inside. The ideal cream cheese brownie should be distinctly a brownie, but with a swirl of cream cheese filling in every bite. We wanted the brownie portion of the bar to have a rich, soft texture that would complement the lush cream cheese filling, yet at the same time contrast its soft interior with a thin, crisp (but not overbaked) crust. These brownies would taste intensely of chocolate, with a tangy filling that could hold its own against such a dominant partner.

We nixed the idea of adding a cream cheese

filling to our Chewy, Fudgy Triple-Chocolate Brownies, as it would have been gilding the lily. We turned to a basic brownie recipe for thin, moist squares, with a good chocolate flavor and a fine, tender crumb; in other words, classic brownies. Adding cream cheese batter to the equation, however, turned the chief assets of these brownies into liabilities. When paired with dense, tangy cream cheese, the brownies' fine cake-flour crumb did not provide enough structure to suspend the filling; their otherwise pleasant chocolate flavor lacked intensity; and, finally, the amount of batter did not produce a tall enough bar for cream cheese brownies. To make this brownie batter more suitable for its cream cheese partner, we needed to strengthen its structure, infuse it with more chocolate flavor, and give it a bit more height.

To this end, we increased our brownie recipe by half (for added height), used all-purpose flour instead of cake flour (for strengthened structure), and threw in an extra ounce of unsweetened chocolate (for a more intense chocolate flavor). Baking the increased amount of batter in the same size pan solved the height problem. The extra height, however, accentuated the brownie's cakey qualities. Desiring a denser, softer texture, we made the brownies again, this time returning the flour and baking powder to the original amounts but leaving the eggs and vanilla at the increased quantities. This equation created a dense but relatively dry brownie. The increased amount of unsweetened chocolate, while making the brownie more intensely flavored, also caused it to taste bitter.

From previous chocolate experiments, we deduced that the unsweetened chocolate might be at the root of our harsh, bitter brownies. We made three pans of brownies: one with all unsweetened chocolate, another with all bittersweet chocolate, and a third with a combination of the two, adjusting the sugar as necessary. The brownies made with unsweetened chocolate alone were dry and crumbly, with a slightly bitter finish. On the other hand, the brownies created with all bittersweet chocolate were too soft and gooey. A combination of unsweetened and bittersweet chocolate corrected the texture and flavor deficiencies and delivered a perfect cream cheese brownie base—intensely

chocolate, soft, lush, with just a hint of structure.

What's the reason behind this unusual result? Unlike unsweetened chocolate, bittersweet chocolate (or semisweet chocolate, which can be used interchangeably with bittersweet) contains lecithin, an emulsifier that is responsible for chocolate's creamy mouthfeel. It makes sense that these smoother, creamier sweetened varieties would bake into gooier, chewier brownies. Because unsweetened chocolate contains no lecithin, brownies made with this ingredient tend to be drier and more crumbly.

Second, during the manufacture of sweetened chocolates, sugar and chocolate are heated together so that the sugar dissolves and the cocoa butter melts, bonding the two together. Unsweetened chocolate contains no sugar, so larger quantities of granulated sugar must be mixed with the chocolate just before baking. These undissolved sugar granules remain distinct and separate in the batter. Sugar is hygroscopic (that is, it readily takes up and retains moisture), which causes the undissolved granules to absorb moisture during baking, resulting in a drier, more crumbly brownie. Because brownies are so rich in chocolate, the types of chocolate used in the cream cheese brownie batter create dramatic differences in the recipe.

Fortunately, the cream cheese filling was much simpler to develop than the brownie batter. We were looking for an intensely flavored filling, but we found that other common cheesecake ingredients like sour cream, butter, and cream simply diluted the intense cream cheese flavor we were after. As it turned out, we only needed to add an egg yolk, a quarter cup of sugar, and a couple of drops of vanilla extract to an 8-ounce package of cream cheese to achieve the flavor and texture we were seeking.

To determine the best way to incorporate the filling into the batter, we experimented with four options: First we spread a thin layer of cream cheese filling between two layers of brownie batter. Next we sandwiched dollops of the cream cheese filling between the two layers of brownie batter. Then we sandwiched dollops of the cream cheese filling between two layers of brownie batter and then swirled them with a knife. Finally, we alternated two layers of brownie batter with two layers of cream cheese dollops that we then swirled with a knife. The final technique—which created a visible swirl of light on dark and evenly distributed the filling throughout the brownies—was the winner.

This ultra-thick brownie, with its delicate filling, needed to be baked at a relatively low oven temperature. Brownies baked at 350 degrees burned at the edges, requiring the crusts to be trimmed, or turned out hard and inedible. At 325 degrees, however, the problem was solved. By putting a foil sling coated with cooking spray in the bottom of the pan before we added the batter, we were able to remove the brownies from the pan almost immediately after baking, which made cooling, cutting, and serving the brownies a breeze.

Cream Cheese Brownies

MAKES 16

Knowing when to remove a pan of brownies from the oven is the only difficult part about baking them. If you wait until an inserted toothpick comes out clean, the brownies are overcooked. But if a toothpick inserted in the middle of the pan comes out with fudgy crumbs, remove the pan immediately. To melt the chocolate and butter in a microwave oven, microwave the chocolate alone at 50 percent power for 2 minutes. Stir the chocolate; add the butter; and continue microwaving at 50 percent for another 2 minutes, stopping to stir the mixture after 1 minute. If the chocolate is not entirely melted, microwave an additional 30 seconds at 50 percent power.

BROWNIE BASE

2/3	cup (3 1/3 ounces) unbleached all-purpose flour
1/4	teaspoon salt
1/2	teaspoon baking powder
2	ounces unsweetened chocolate, chopped
4	ounces bittersweet or semisweet chocolate, chopped
8	tablespoons (1 stick) unsalted butter, cut into quarters
1	cup (7 ounces) sugar
2	teaspoons vanilla extract
3	large eggs

CREAM CHEESE FILLING

8	ounces cream cheese, at room temperature
1/4	cup (1 3/4 ounces) sugar
1/2	teaspoon vanilla extract
1	egg yolk

1. FOR THE BROWNIE BASE: Adjust an oven rack to the lower-middle position and heat the oven to 325 degrees. Spray an 8-inch square baking pan with nonstick cooking spray. Fold two 16-inch pieces of foil or parchment paper lengthwise to measure 8 inches wide. Following the illustration on page 141, fit 1 sheet in the bottom of the greased pan, pushing it into the corners and up the sides of the pan (overhang will help in removal of the baked brownies). Fit the second sheet in the pan in the same manner, perpendicular to the first sheet. Spray the sheets with nonstick cooking spray. Whisk the flour, salt, and baking powder together in a small bowl; set aside.

2. In a medium heatproof bowl set over a pan of almost-simmering water, melt the chocolates and butter, stirring occasionally until the mixture is smooth. Remove the melted chocolate mixture from the heat; whisk in the sugar and vanilla; cool slightly. Whisk in the eggs, 1 at a time, fully incorporating each before adding the next. Continue whisking until the mixture is completely smooth. Add the dry ingredients; whisk until just incorporated.

3. FOR THE CREAM CHEESE FILLING: In a small bowl, beat the cream cheese with the sugar, vanilla, and egg yolk until evenly blended.

4. Pour half the brownie batter into the prepared pan. Drop half the cream cheese mixture, by spoonfuls, over the batter. Repeat, layering the remaining brownie batter and cream cheese filling. Use the blade of a table knife or a spoon handle to gently swirl the brownie batter and cream cheese filling, creating a marbled effect.

5. Bake until the edges of the brownies have puffed slightly, the center feels not quite firm when touched lightly, and a toothpick or cake tester inserted into the center comes out with several moist, fudgy crumbs adhering to it, 50 to 60 minutes.

6. Cool the brownies in a pan on a wire rack for 5 minutes. Remove the brownies from the pan using the foil or parchment handles. Place the brownies on a wire rack; allow them to cool to room temperature. Refrigerate until chilled, at least 3 hours. (To hasten cooling, place the brownies in the freezer for about 1½ hours.) Cut into 2-inch squares and serve. (To keep them from drying out, do not cut the brownies until ready to serve. The brownies can be wrapped, uncut, in plastic wrap, then foil, and refrigerated up to 5 days.)

Blondies

BLONDIES ARE FIRST COUSINS TO BOTH brownies and chocolate chip cookies. Although blondies are baked in a pan like brownies, the flavorings are similar to those in chocolate chip cookies—vanilla, butter, and brown sugar, otherwise known as butterscotch. Blondies are sometimes laced with nuts and chocolate chips or butterscotch chips. Most of the time, blondies are pretty bland and need all the help they can get from additional ingredients. Dry, floury, flavorless—we have eaten them all. What does it take to make a good blondie?

The majority of the recipes we found had essentially the same ingredients but in different proportions that yielded blondies with dramatically different textures—from light and cakey to dense and buttery. Tasters preferred the latter, but with reservations. They felt that blondies could be too dense, as were some of the ones we tried. Super-dense blondies tasted of little more than raw flour and butter.

After baking a variety of blondie recipes, we found that the key to dense blondies that did not taste raw lay in how the butter was incorporated into the batter and the amount of flour in the batter. Melted butter produced a much denser blondie than creamed butter because the creaming process incorporates air into the batter. Melting the butter also meant that we could make the batter by hand rather than dirtying a food processor or electric mixer.

While we knew all-purpose flour would give us the chewiest, densest texture, the exact amount of flour was tricky to determine. Too much flour

resulted in a dense, flavorless bar cookie, and too little produced a greasy bar cookie that oozed butter. After a dozen batches with the slightest variations in the amounts of flour, we finally settled on 1½ cups of all-purpose flour leavened with a small amount of baking powder. These blondies were definitely dense and very chewy, but they had risen just enough to prevent them from being gooey.

For sweetening and flavor, tasters favored light brown sugar, which lent the right amount of earthy, molasses flavor; dark brown sugar was overpowering. And combined with a substantial amount of vanilla extract and salt (to sharpen the sweetness), the light brown sugar developed a rich butterscotch flavor.

To add both texture and flavor to the blondies, we included chocolate chips, and pecans. While the chips are traditional, pecans are not. Most recipes suggest walnuts, but tasters thought the pecans better complemented the butterscotch flavor.

We also tried butterscotch chips, but most tasters found that they did little for this recipe. On a whim, we included white chocolate chips with the semisweet chips, and we were surprised that they produced the best blondie yet. While white chocolate does not have cocoa, it does have cocoa butter, which highlighted both the vanilla and caramel flavors. These blondies now had a significantly deeper and richer flavor.

Blondies
MAKES 36

If you have trouble finding white chocolate chips, feel free to chop a bar of white chocolate into small chunks.

1½	cups (7½ ounces) unbleached all-purpose flour
1	teaspoon baking powder
½	teaspoon salt
12	tablespoons (1½ sticks) unsalted butter, melted and cooled
1½	cups packed (10½ ounces) light brown sugar
2	large eggs
1½	teaspoons vanilla extract
½	cup semisweet chocolate chips
½	cup white chocolate chips
1	cup pecans, toasted and chopped coarse

1. Adjust an oven rack to the middle position and heat the oven to 350 degrees. Spray a 13 by 9-inch pan with nonstick cooking spray. Fold two 16-inch pieces of foil or parchment paper lengthwise so that 1 measures 13 inches wide and the other measures 9 inches wide. Following the illustration on page 141, fit one sheet in the bottom of the greased pan, pushing it into the corners and up the sides of the pan (overhang will help in removal of baked bars). Fit the second sheet in the pan in the same manner, perpendicular to the first sheet. Spray the sheets with nonstick cooking spray.

2. Whisk the flour, baking powder, and salt together in a medium bowl; set aside.

3. Whisk the melted butter and brown sugar together in a medium bowl until combined. Add the eggs and vanilla and mix well. Using a rubber spatula, fold the dry ingredients into the egg mixture until just combined. Do not overmix. Fold in the semisweet and white chocolate chips and the nuts and turn the batter into the prepared pan, smoothing the top with a rubber spatula.

4. Bake until the top is shiny and cracked and feels firm to the touch, 22 to 25 minutes. Cool completely on a wire rack. Remove the bars from the pan using the foil or parchment handles and transfer to a cutting board. Cut into 1½ by 2-inch bars and serve.

➤ VARIATION

Congo Bars

MAKES 36

Congo bars are little but blondies enriched with coconut. We tried adding both sweetened, flaked coconut and unsweetened, shredded coconut to our blondies, and tasters unanimously preferred the unsweetened. Sweetened coconut made the bars overly sweet and unpleasantly chewy. We were able to extract a bit more flavor from the unsweetened coconut by toasting it golden brown before adding it to the blondie dough. Unsweetened shredded coconut can be found in natural food stores and Asian markets. Keep a close eye on the coconut when toasting as it can burn quickly.

Toast 1½ cups unsweetened, shredded coconut on a rimmed baking sheet on the middle oven rack at 350 degrees, stirring 2 to 3 times, until light golden, 5 to 7 minutes. Transfer to a small bowl to cool. Follow the recipe for Blondies, adding the toasted coconut with the chocolate chips and nuts in step 3.

SEVEN-LAYER BARS

SEVEN-LAYER BARS, ALSO KNOWN AS MAGIC bars, are indeed made in seven layers and, you could say, come together like magic. Seven-layer bars are a jumble of chips (chocolate and otherwise), nuts, and coconut layered over a crust of crumbled graham crackers. The magic is the sweetened condensed milk, which when poured over these ingredients and baked, brings them together to create a cohesive bar cookie. Seven-layer bars are rich, supremely decadent, and sticky-sweet.

Simplicity in construction aside, seven-layer bars are not without their share of problems. They are most often flavor-related (the medley of chips tends to be mismatched and at times overpowering), but sometimes poor construction can cause problems. Seven-layer bars can be too delicate and fall apart at the first bite, can have too thin a graham cracker crust, or can be insufficiently gooey, so the ingredients won't stay together. We were after a solid bar cookie loaded with sweet, rich flavors and a chewy-crunchy texture.

Starting at the bottom, we tested our graham cracker crust options. Most graham cracker crusts are made by combining graham crumbs with melted butter. This crust would be no exception. Although store-bought crumbs are convenient, the crust they formed was far too delicate to support all the ingredients that would be layered on them. In order to produce a more substantial crust, we found it was necessary to hand-crush whole graham crackers into coarser crumbs. We placed whole crackers in a large zipper-lock bag and pounded them with whatever blunt instrument was handy (the underside of a measuring cup, a rolling pin). The result was a motley crew of crumbs, bits, and chunks. When brought together with the butter and then the condensed milk, these coarse crumbs created a sturdy crust packed with graham cracker flavor.

Next we tested every chip combination imaginable and let our tasters determine which options were worthy and which needed reconsidering. Toffee chips were the biggest loser of the bunch. The small nuggets of toffee melted away into nothing but a thin, sticky, almost flavorless layer and did little to contribute to the structure of the bar. Since bar structure was indeed an important factor, it became clear that we would have to stick to the standard morsel-shaped chips, as they tended to keep their shape better than smaller "bits" or mini-chips. When baked, morsels became soft and luxurious but retained enough shape to help add more bulk to this bar cookie.

The least favorite flavor of chip turned out to be peanut butter. They were salty and somewhat artificial-tasting, and the combination of peanut butter, coconut, and graham crackers seemed to turn tasters off. Chocolate chips—both semi-sweet and white chocolate—were well liked. Butterscotch chips also made the cut. They were buttery, slightly spicy, and a nice flavor change from the chocolate. In the end, we found that two cups of chips was the perfect amount. Tasters liked semisweet chocolate chips more than any of the others, so we settled on one cup of semisweet morsels and split the second cup between the white chocolate and butterscotch chips.

Next it was time to concentrate on the coconut. Some of the recipes we initially tested were overly coconut, and tasters were quite clear that they expected less. When we found the optimum amount—one cup—there was still something missing. The coconut flavor was flat and somewhat uninteresting. So we decided to toast the coconut to enhance its flavor. Fully toasted coconut, which was then baked on top of the seven layers for 25 minutes, came out of the oven in shards, too brown and overly crunchy. But without any toasting, the flavor was insipid. The solution was to toast the coconut ever so slightly. On top of the seven layers, the slightly toasted coconut browned evenly without becoming hard, and its flavor was much improved.

When it came to nuts, we tested all the usual suspects: pecans, walnuts, almonds, and macadamia nuts. Tasters preferred walnuts because of their meaty texture and big flavor. We tried toasting the nuts to enhance their flavor, but the difference was marginal and not worth the extra effort.

Sweetened condensed milk is a mixture of whole milk and sugar (up to 45 percent of its content) that is heated until 60 percent of the water content evaporates. What's left behind is an ooey-gooey, light tan liquid, which acts as the "glue" in seven-layer bars. The technique couldn't be simpler: Just open the can and pour it all over the top, as evenly as possible. We tested several ways of spreading the condensed milk evenly over the layers. Running a spatula over the condensed milk unearthed the layers below and made a mess of the whole thing. In the end, we just poured the condensed milk as evenly as we could over the layers and then let the heat of the oven do the rest.

Seven-Layer Bars
MAKES 18

Place the graham crackers in a large zipper-lock plastic bag and pound them with the bottom of a measuring cup, a rolling pin, or a smooth meat mallet. The result should be an assortment of crumbs, bits, and chunks that measures about 1½ cups.

I	cup sweetened flaked coconut
8	tablespoons (I stick) unsalted butter
9	graham crackers (5 ounces), crushed (see note)
I	cup finely chopped walnuts
I	cup semisweet chocolate chips
½	cup white chocolate chips
½	cup butterscotch-flavored chips
I	(14-ounce) can sweetened condensed milk

1. Adjust an oven rack to the lower-middle position and heat the oven to 350 degrees. Spray a 13 by 9-inch pan with nonstick cooking spray. Fold two 16-inch pieces of foil or parchment paper lengthwise so that 1 measures 13 inches wide and the other measures 9 inches wide. Following the illustration on page 141, fit 1 sheet in the bottom of the greased pan, pushing it into the corners and up the sides of the pan (overhang will help in removal of baked bars). Fit the second sheet in the pan in the same manner, perpendicular to the first sheet. Spray the sheets with nonstick cooking spray.

2. Spread the coconut on a baking sheet and bake until the outer flakes just begin to brown, about 8 minutes; set aside. Meanwhile, place the stick of butter in the prepared baking pan and put it in the oven to melt, about 6 minutes.

3. When the butter has melted, remove the pan from the oven and sprinkle the graham cracker

crumbs over the melted butter. Toss lightly until all the butter is absorbed and the crumbs are evenly distributed. In order, sprinkle the walnuts, chocolate chips, white chocolate chips, butterscotch chips, and coconut over the graham crumbs. Pour the condensed milk evenly over the entire dish.

4. Return the pan to the oven and bake until the top is golden brown, about 25 minutes. Cool on a wire rack to room temperature, about 2 hours. Remove the bars from the pan using the foil or parchment handles and transfer to a cutting board. Using a sharp knife, cut into 2 by 3-inch bars.

Lemon Bars

TO MAKE LEMON BARS, A BOTTOM LAYER, or crust, is pressed into a pan, baked, and then topped with a filling. The filling and crust are baked again and then cut into bars. Lemon bars are pretty easy to make, but that doesn't mean it's easy to get them just the way you want them. Whether from bakeries or home recipes, the crust is often quite soggy, and many versions are too sweet and lack true lemon flavor.

We started with the crust, knowing that flour, butter, and sugar would be the main ingredients. We also knew that since we wanted a cookie or shortbread texture rather than a pastry-type crust, we would need a fair amount of sugar.

Our first challenge was to decide the proportion of flour to butter and the amount, as well as the type, of sugar. We decided, after several taste tests, that a crust made with ½ cup of butter per 1¼ cups of flour was just right—it was neither too greasy nor too dry. Since sugar affects tenderness as well as sweetness, the amount and type of sugar needed to be determined along with the butter. Brown sugar proved too rich for our tasters' palates, while granulated sugar produced a crust that was a bit brittle and gritty. The best, most tender texture came from confectioners' sugar.

Having decided on the basic ingredients, we began to investigate ways to combine and bake them. For most cookies and one type of pastry, the fat and sugar are creamed together in the first step. The alternative is to start by cutting the fat into the flour with your fingertips or a food processor, which is common in most pastry crusts. After testing both methods, we decided that because of the proportion of flour to butter and the absence of liquid, the second method was best suited for this crust. Cutting the butter into the flour created a crumbly mixture that could be pressed into the pan. The standard oven temperature of 350 degrees worked best to produce a golden-brown, crisp crust.

Lemon bars are traditionally made by adding a raw mixture of eggs, sugar, flour, lemon juice, and lemon zest to the prebaked crust and then baking again to set the filling. Once we had settled on our crust, we tried a number of recipes using this technique, and regardless of ingredient portions, we turned out consistently soggy crusts. We wanted a crust that would stay crisp even after it was topped with a filling and concluded that the only way to achieve this would be to abandon tradition and cook a lemon filling (lemon curd) on the stove before adding it to the crust.

For a 9-inch square pan, we estimated that we would need about 3 cups of lemon curd. The traditional lemon curds all contained between 1 and 1½ cups sugar, but the amount of lemon juice varied widely, between ½ and 1½ cups. There was also quite a bit of play between whole eggs and yolks, with the average falling between eight and 10 eggs total. Though the recipes were divided on the matter of using direct heat versus a double boiler, most were quite cavalier about cooking time, with visual descriptions of the desired final texture ranging from "thick" to "very thick" to "like whipped cream." Only two mentioned cooking temperatures: 160 and 180 degrees, a rather wide range when dealing with eggs. Some recipes added butter at the beginning of the cooking time; others specified to whisk it in later.

During our early experiments, certain proportions emerged easily. The balance of sweetness and tartness we sought came in at roughly 2 parts sugar to 1 part lemon juice. Four full tablespoons of finely grated lemon zest (strained out after cooking along with any hardened bits of egg whites from the eggs) packed enough lemon punch without having to linger in the final custard, where it would become bitter or usurp the silky texture.

A pinch of salt brightened the flavor. Four tablespoons of butter were perfect, smoothing taste and refining texture.

Holding the proportions of the above ingredients constant, we made a number of lemon curds testing various combinations of whole eggs and yolks. Somewhat surprisingly, the curds that tasted great in a spoon were not always the ones that tasted best baked. The curd made with whole eggs alone had a light texture in the spoon and a gorgeous sheen, but it had a muted color and a texture most tasters described as "mayonnaise-like" when baked. The curd made with whole eggs and whites had a smooth, translucent surface but firmed up too much, while the curd made with an equal ratio of whole eggs to yolks was faulted for being cloyingly rich. In the end, most tasters preferred a curd made principally with yolks and only a couple of whole eggs for structure. Creamy and dense with a vibrant color, it did not become gelatinous when baked, as did those curds made with whole eggs, but it did set up enough to slice.

But the most interesting discovery was still to come. Remembering a lemon mousse we'd made, we wanted to see what a splash of cream might do to the curd. Adding cream before cooking the curd on the stovetop gave it a cheesy flavor. But 3 tablespoons of cold, raw cream stirred in just before baking proved a winning touch. It cooled the just-cooked curd, blunted its acidity, and lightened its final baked texture to a celestial creaminess.

When added to the crust and baked just to set, the curd maintained its heavenly texture, and the crust stayed perfectly crispy.

Lemon Bars

MAKES 16

The warm filling must be added to a warm crust. Start preparing the filling when the crust goes into the oven. Be sure to cool the bars completely before cutting them.

CRUST

1 1/4	cups (6 1/4 ounces) unbleached all-purpose flour
1/2	cup (2 ounces) confectioners' sugar, plus more to decorate the finished bars
1/2	teaspoon salt
8	tablespoons (1 stick) unsalted butter, softened but still cool, cut into 1-inch pieces

LEMON FILLING

7	large egg yolks, plus 2 large eggs
1	cup plus 2 tablespoons (7 7/8 ounces) granulated sugar
2/3	cup juice from 4 or 5 medium lemons, plus 1/4 cup finely grated zest Pinch salt
4	tablespoons (1/2 stick) unsalted butter, cut into 4 pieces
3	tablespoons heavy cream

1. FOR THE CRUST: Spray a 9-inch square baking pan with nonstick cooking spray. Fold two 16-inch pieces of foil or parchment paper lengthwise to measure 9 inches wide. Following the illustration on page 141, fit 1 sheet in the bottom of the greased pan, pushing it into the corners and up the sides of the pan (overhang will help in removal of baked bars). Fit the second sheet in the pan in the same manner, perpendicular to the first sheet. Spray the sheets with nonstick cooking spray.

2. Place the flour, confectioners' sugar, and salt in a food processor and process briefly. Add the butter and process to blend, 8 to 10 seconds, then process until the mixture is pale yellow and resembles coarse meal, about three 1-second pulses. Sprinkle the mixture into the prepared pan and press firmly with your fingers into an even layer over the entire pan bottom. Refrigerate for 30 minutes.

3. Adjust an oven rack to the middle position and heat the oven to 350 degrees. Bake the crust until golden brown, about 20 minutes.

4. FOR THE FILLING: In a medium nonreactive bowl, whisk together the yolks and whole eggs until combined, about 5 seconds. Add the granulated sugar and whisk until just combined, about 5 seconds. Add the lemon juice, zest, and salt; whisk until combined, about 5 seconds. Transfer the mixture to a medium nonreactive saucepan, add the butter pieces, and cook over medium-low heat, stirring constantly with a wooden spoon, until the curd thickens to a thin sauce-like consistency and registers 170 degrees on an instant-read

thermometer, about 5 minutes. Immediately pour the curd through a single-mesh stainless steel strainer set over a clean nonreactive bowl. Stir in the heavy cream; pour the curd into the warm crust immediately.

5. Bake until the filling is shiny and opaque and the center 3 inches jiggle slightly when shaken, 10 to 15 minutes. Cool on a wire rack to room temperature, about 45 minutes. Remove the bars from the pan using the foil or parchment handles and transfer to a cutting board. Cut into 2¼-inch squares, wiping the knife clean between cuts as necessary. Sieve confectioners' sugar over the bars, if desired.

RASPBERRY SQUARES

RASPBERRY SQUARES ARE ONE OF THE BEST and easiest bar cookies to prepare: The filling is ready-made (it comes straight from a jar of raspberry preserves). And these homey bars also have textural interest created by the layering of filling on crust.

Bar cookies can be loosely divided into two camps. There's the cake-like version, which includes the chocolate brownie, and the cookie-like version, which, stripped down to the basics, is what bakers call a "short" pastry, such as raspberry squares. A short pastry has a tender, almost sandy crumb that it gets by way of the right combination of flour, fat, sugar, and salt—with an emphasis on the fat and the flour. In a short pastry (think of shortbread), a generous amount of fat is required to coat the particles of flour and restrict the flour's access to liquid. Flour contains proteins that when combined with water and kneaded form gluten, which is desirable in bread, where you want chew, but not in a raspberry square, where you want tenderness.

In the many recipes for all manner of "short" bar cookies we looked at, the amount of butter ranged from ½ cup to 1 cup for about 2½ cups of flour. We found that a whole cup of butter made the raspberry squares greasy, whereas ½ cup left them on the dry side; ¾ cup butter was just right.

The sugar in many of the recipes also ranged from ½ cup to 1 cup, with some calling for granulated sugar, some for brown, some for a mix of the two. Here, too, we went for the middle way, deciding on equal amounts of granulated and light brown sugar, which made for a deeper flavor than granulated alone, and on a total of ⅔ cup, which was sweet enough to be pleasing but not cloying.

Although we weren't interested in tampering too much with the flavor of our crust by adding things like vanilla, cinnamon, or lemon zest, as called for in some recipes, we did find it a bit plain as it was. We were attracted by the idea of adding some oats or nuts, which would make a more subtle contribution to flavor while also adding some textural interest. The oats, with their bulk and absorbency, would have to displace some of the flour. After trying various proportions, we found that we liked the combination of 1¼ cups oats and 1½ cups flour. We played around with the nuts and found ourselves preferring a pairing of sweet almonds with nutty pecans (although either also works on its own).

We were now pretty pleased with our crust except for one nagging problem: It was rather pale, not golden brown. We wanted that golden brown color not only for appearance's sake but for flavor; we knew that a deeply colored crust would have a more developed, nutty flavor.

The procedure we had been following to prepare the squares for baking was recommended in a number of recipes. It involved lining the bottom of the pan with most of the dough, spreading the preserves on top, and then covering the preserves with the rest of the dough. One or two recipes had recommended baking the bottom crust alone first to brown it and firm it up, but we had rejected this option as being a bit fussy. Now we tried this procedure and were happy to learn that it effectively colored—and flavored—the crust.

These squares can easily be put together in 15 minutes. The only inconvenience is having to wait for them to bake and cool before digging in.

Raspberry Squares
MAKES 36

For a nice presentation, trim ¼ inch off the outer rim of the uncut baked block. The outside edges of all the cut squares will then be neat.

1 1/2   cups (7 1/2 ounces) unbleached all-purpose flour
1 1/4   cups quick-cooking oats
1/3   cup (2 1/3 ounces) granulated sugar
1/3   cup packed (2 1/3 ounces) light brown sugar
1/4   teaspoon baking soda
1/4   teaspoon salt
1/2   cup finely chopped pecans or almonds, or a combination
12   tablespoons (1 1/2 sticks) unsalted butter, softened but still cool, cut into 12 pieces
1   cup raspberry preserves

1. Adjust an oven rack to the lower-middle position and heat the oven to 350 degrees. Spray a 9-inch square baking pan with nonstick cooking spray. Fold two 16-inch pieces of foil or parchment paper lengthwise to measure 9 inches wide. Following the illustration on page 141, fit 1 sheet in the bottom of the greased pan, pushing it into the corners and up the sides of the pan (overhang will help in removal of baked squares). Fit the second sheet in the pan in the same manner, perpendicular to the first sheet. Spray the sheets with nonstick cooking spray.

2. In a bowl of an electric mixer, mix the flour, oats, sugars, baking soda, salt, and nuts at low speed until combined, about 30 seconds. With the mixer running at low speed, add the butter pieces; continue to beat until the mixture is well blended and resembles wet sand, about 2 minutes.

3. Transfer two thirds of the oat mixture to the prepared pan and use your hands to press the crumbs evenly into the bottom. Bake until the crust starts to brown, about 20 minutes. Using a rubber spatula, spread the preserves evenly over the hot bottom crust; sprinkle the remaining oat mixture evenly over the preserves. Bake until the preserves bubble around the edges and the top is golden brown, about 30 minutes, rotating the pan from front to back halfway through the baking time. Cool on a wire rack to room temperature, about 1½ hours. Remove the squares from the pan using the foil or parchment handles and transfer to a cutting board. Cut into 1½-inch squares.

> VARIATION
Fig Squares
These not-too-sweet squares will remind you of the childhood favorite—Fig Newton cookies.

Combine 1 pound Turkish figs (tough stems trimmed), 3 cups apple juice, and a pinch of salt in a medium saucepan over medium heat and bring to a simmer. Cook, stirring occasionally, until the figs are very soft and the juice is syrupy, 35 to 40 minutes. Transfer to a medium bowl and cool until warm. Puree the figs in a food processor until they are the consistency of thick jam and smooth, scraping down the sides of the workbowl as necessary. Return to the bowl and set aside. Follow the recipe for Raspberry Squares, substituting the fig puree for the jam in step 3.

PECAN BARS
PECAN BARS ARE BASICALLY PECAN PIE baked into small, manageable rectangles or squares. The filling is a bit firmer so that it can be neatly cut. And instead of a pastry crust, most pecan bars call for a cookie-type crust, akin to shortbread.

Starting from the bottom up, we decided on a shortbread-like crust that would be substantial enough to support the filling. But the crust also had to be tender and buttery. In our experience, the crust is usually the fatal flaw of a bar cookie; it is often soggy and undercooked or rock hard and tough.

We tested several shortbread recipes until we found one close to what we wanted—buttery and rich but still strong enough to slice and support the filling—and then hammered out the finer points. We had the best results making the dough in a food processor, which quickly cuts the butter into the flour without overheating it, and is an easy method to boot. It took under two minutes to process the crust and gently pack it into a lined baking pan. We found that a crust baked three quarters of the way or until it was just beginning to brown resulted in the most flavor and best texture.

Although we were pleased with the crust's flavor and texture—buttery and just firm enough—one of the tasters made a suggestion that would change our opinion. She proposed adding ground pecans, bringing it more into "pecan sandy" territory. With a couple of minor adjustments to the flour and butter amounts to accommodate the nuts, the crust was markedly improved. The nuts' sandy texture pleasingly contrasted with the silky filling, and the nuts also prevented the crust from becoming too tough.

As the crust bakes, the filling can be assembled. Since there is less filling in a pecan bar than in a pie, the flavors must be more concentrated. Working with our favorite pecan pie filling recipe, we cut back on both wet and dry ingredients until we hit the delicate balance of sweetness and gooeyness we desired.

To boost the flavor, we added a substantial amount of vanilla extract, along with bourbon or rum—both common to many Southern-style pecan pie recipes. The liquor cut through the sweetness and intensified the flavor of the nuts. We also included a healthy dose of salt, which sharpened the sweetness and also intensified the pecan flavor.

While it may sound like a minor issue, the size of the pecans proved to be important. Tasters definitely had opinions—some favored whole pecans, and some preferred them finely chopped. The whole pecans were attractive, floating on top of the cookie, but they did not cut easily and made the bars hard to eat out of hand. Finely chopped nuts were not as visually appealing but were easier to eat. We decided to chop the pecans coarsely and managed to please everyone.

Pecan Bars

MAKES 24

Assemble the pecan filling while the crust bakes. Once the crust is lightly browned, spread the filling on top and continue baking. Because of their high sugar content, pecan bars store well and taste great up to 5 days after baking. While we liked bourbon the best, dark rum is quite good. For a very boozy tasting bar cookie, add another tablespoon of liquor.

CRUST

1	cup (5 ounces) unbleached all-purpose flour
¼	teaspoon baking powder
1	teaspoon salt
⅓	cup packed (2⅓ ounces) light brown sugar
¼	cup pecans, toasted and chopped coarse
6	tablespoons (¾ stick) cold unsalted butter, cut into small pieces

FILLING

4	tablespoons (½ stick) unsalted butter, melted
½	cup packed (3½ ounces) light brown sugar
⅓	cup light corn syrup
2	teaspoons vanilla extract
1	tablespoon bourbon or dark rum
½	teaspoon salt
1	large egg, lightly beaten
1¾	cups pecans, toasted and chopped coarse

1. FOR THE CRUST: Adjust an oven rack to the middle position and heat the oven to 350 degrees. Spray a 9-inch square baking pan with nonstick cooking spray. Fold two 16-inch pieces of foil or parchment paper lengthwise to measure 9 inches wide. Following the illustration on page 141, fit 1 sheet in the bottom of the greased pan, pushing it into the corners and up the sides of the pan (overhang will help in removal of baked bars). Fit the second sheet in the pan in the same manner, perpendicular to the first sheet. Spray the sheets with nonstick cooking spray.

2. Place the flour, baking powder, salt, brown sugar, and ¼ cup pecans in a food processor. Process the mixture until it resembles coarse cornmeal, about five 1-second pulses. Add the butter and pulse until the mixture resembles sand, about eight 1-second pulses. Pat the mixture evenly into the prepared pan and bake until the crust is light brown and springs back when touched, about 20 minutes.

3. FOR THE FILLING: While the crust is in the oven, whisk together the melted butter, brown sugar, corn syrup, vanilla, bourbon, and salt in a medium bowl until just combined. Add the egg and whisk until incorporated.

4. Pour the filling on top of the hot crust and sprinkle the 1¾ cups pecans evenly over the top. Bake until the top is brown and cracks start to form across the surface, 22 to 25 minutes. Cool on a wire rack for 1 hour. Remove the bars from the pan using the foil or parchment handles and transfer to a cutting board. Cut into bars that measure 1½ inches by 2¼ inches.

GRANOLA BARS

IN ESSENCE, GRANOLA BARS ARE NOTHING but granola cereal bound together and packed into a firm, transportable form. Rock hard, saccharine sweet, and greasy to boot, the average store-bought granola bar provides plenty of calories but little gustatory pleasure. We wanted a great-tasting granola bar with plenty of crunch and fully flavored with toasted oats, nuts, and sometimes dried fruit or spices. As always, we started development by looking for recipes in other cookbooks. We were surprised to find very few, and those we did find were somewhat dubious, employing a wide range of questionable ingredients and odd instructions. That said, we were able to identify the three key issues with granola bars: preparing the oats (toasting), binding the bars together, and adding additional flavors.

Some recipes we found avoided the oats issue altogether by specifying store-bought granola in the ingredient list, a tack we weren't willing to take. Commercial granola is usually highly flavored, fatty, and packed with a variety of ingredients. We wanted to pick our own flavorings and control the amount of oil added. Other recipes skipped toasted oats altogether, yielding bland bars with no discernible flavor. Following the lead of the most promising recipe we found, we started off by making what was essentially a simple granola: old-fashioned rolled oats tossed with vegetable oil to encourage browning and a crisp texture and salt to bring out the oats' flavor. When toasted at too high a temperature, the oats browned too quickly and developed a bitter flavor. When toasted at too low a temperature, it took well over an hour for any browning. After experimenting with a variety of temperatures, we settled on 375 degrees as the perfect temperature, as the oats toasted to an even light gold within 30 minutes.

To bind and sweeten the oats, we turned to honey, a common ingredient in the recipes we found. We tossed the toasted oats with honey and packed the sticky mixture into the rimmed baking sheet in which the oats had been toasted. In the slow, even heat of the oven, the honey's moisture evaporated and the oats were bound firmly together. Once cool, the bars were crunchy, but

the texture was not to last for long. Within a day, they had softened to an unpleasantly stale consistency. Honey is hygroscopic, meaning it attracts and absorbs water, and hence rendered the bars soft. Tasters liked the honey flavor so we didn't want to exclude it altogether, but we clearly needed to replace a portion of the honey with a less hygroscopic sweetener, like granulated or brown sugar. (Fructose, the main component of honey, is more hygroscopic than sucrose, the main component of granulated and brown sugar.) Tasters preferred either light or dark brown sugar to granulated, as it deepened the oat flavor. We experimented with ratios to get the best flavor and texture and found that equal parts honey and brown sugar yielded the most flavorful results. For additional flavor, we added a hefty dose of vanilla extract, which intensified both the oat flavor and the honey's floral tones.

While the bars tasted good, tasters noted that the sugary binder was pooling in the crevices between the oats and hardening to a toffee-like, tooth-pulling texture. The spaces between the oats needed to be filled to prevent the pooling. Grinding a portion of the oats or adding flour was a straightforward option, but neither added any flavor to the bars.

Finely chopped nuts proved a better bet. The sand-size pieces readily filled the spaces between the oats and made for a denser bar without pockets of hard sweetener. Leaving a portion of the nuts only coarsely chopped lent the bars texture and visual definition—tasters liked seeing exactly what sort of nut they were eating. That said, almonds, walnut, and pecans all found fans among tasters. Peanuts were deemed "boring" and pistachios too exotic for such homey fare.

Along with nuts, dried fruit seemed a logical addition but one that proved problematic. We added raisins to the oats mixture and found that during the long baking time, they puffed up, burnt, and turned hard—a true failure. Plumping them in apple juice prior to baking alleviated the latter issue, but they still tasted acrid and burnt. We realized that the raisins' thin skins were burning in the oven's heat (a problem exacerbated by their high sugar content). We didn't want to change our basic technique so we opted to try other dried fruits instead. Chopped apples turned as tough as the raisins and rendered the bars chewy because of their high moisture content. Frustrated, we moved on to dried cranberries, which, once plumped in juice (either apple or orange), worked beautifully. The fruits' thick skins and low-sugar content prevented them from burning and kept them pliant despite the long spell in the oven. Dried sour cherries, coarsely chopped, worked equally well.

Crunchy Granola Bars

MAKES 36

Make sure to press forcefully when packing the granola mixture into the pan; otherwise the bars may be crumbly once cut. If you like, add up to ½ cup of wheat germ and ¾ cup of sunflower seeds to the oats after toasting. And feel free to add your favorite spice: grated nutmeg and ground ginger are pleasant additions to the suggested cinnamon. The bars can be effectively stored in the rimmed baking sheet, wrapped tightly in plastic wrap, or in an airtight plastic container for up to 1 week.

7	cups (21 ounces) old-fashioned rolled oats
½	cup vegetable oil
½	teaspoon salt
1½	cups whole almonds, pecans, or walnuts
¾	cup honey
¾	cup packed (5¼ ounces) light or dark brown sugar
1	tablespoon vanilla extract
2	teaspoons ground cinnamon (optional)

1. Adjust an oven rack to the middle position and heat the oven to 375 degrees. Line an 18 by 12-inch rimmed baking sheet with aluminum foil. Combine the oats, oil, and salt in a large bowl and mix until the oats are evenly coated. Transfer the mixture to the baking sheet (save the mixing bowl for use in step 3) and spread into an even layer. Bake, stirring every 10 minutes, until pale gold, about 30 minutes. Remove the oats and lower the oven temperature to 300 degrees.

2. Place the nuts in a food processor and process until coarsely chopped, about ten 1-second pulses. Place ¾ cup of the nuts in a small bowl and process the remaining nuts until finely ground, 20 to 30 seconds. Add the finely ground nuts to the bowl with the coarsely chopped nuts and set aside. Combine the honey and brown sugar in a small saucepan over medium heat and cook, stirring frequently, until the sugar is fully dissolved, about 5 minutes. Stir in vanilla and cinnamon, if using, and set aside.

3. Combine the oats, nuts, and honey mixture in a large bowl and stir with a large rubber spatula until the oats are evenly coated with the honey mixture. Transfer the mixture to the prepared baking sheet and spread in an even layer. Wet the spatula with water and forcefully pack the mixture into a very flat, tight, even layer. Bake until golden, about 45 to 50 minutes. Cool, in the baking sheet, on a wire rack for 10 minutes and cut into 2 by 3-inch bars with a chef's knife. Remove the foil from each bar before serving. Cool completely before wrapping and storing.

➤ VARIATIONS

Dried Cranberry and Ginger Granola Bars

Dried cherries, coarsely chopped, may be substituted for the cranberries if you prefer.

Bring 1 cup dried cranberries and 1 cup apple or orange juice to a simmer in a small saucepan over medium-low heat and cook until very tender, 10 to 15 minutes. Strain through a fine-meshed strainer, gently pushing on the cranberries to extract excess liquid, and cool. (Discard the soaking liquid.) Follow the recipe for Crunchy Granola Bars, adding the cranberries and ¼ cup chopped crystallized ginger to the oats in step 3 after adding the honey mixture. Stir thoroughly to incorporate evenly.

Coconut and Sesame Granola Bars

Follow the recipe for Crunchy Granola Bars, adding ½ cup each sesame seeds and unsweetened coconut to the oats in step 3.

Sauces and Accompaniments

Berry Coulis

MAKES ABOUT 1 ½ CUPS

Coulis is simply sweetened fruit pureed into a sauce. Because the types of berries used as well as their ripeness will affect the sweetness of the coulis, the amount of sugar is variable. Start with 5 tablespoons, then add more if you prefer a sweeter coulis. Additional sugar should be stirred in immediately after straining, while the coulis is still warm, so that the sugar will readily dissolve. Serve the coulis with Lemon Cheesecake (page 393), Classic Pound Cake (page 329), Angel Food Cake (page 323), Chocolate Truffle Tart (page 229), or ice cream.

12	ounces (2 ½ to 3 cups) fresh or thawed frozen raspberries, blueberries, blackberries, or strawberries (fresh strawberries hulled and sliced, if using)
¼	cup water
5–7	tablespoons sugar
⅛	teaspoon salt
2	teaspoons juice from 1 lemon

1. Bring the berries, water, 5 tablespoons of the sugar, and salt to a bare simmer in a medium saucepan over medium heat. Cook, stirring occasionally, until the sugar is dissolved and the berries are heated through, about 1 minute longer.

2. Transfer the mixture to a blender or food processor; puree until smooth, about 20 seconds. Strain through a fine-mesh strainer into a small bowl, pressing and stirring the puree with a rubber spatula to extract as much seedless puree as possible. Stir in the lemon juice and additional sugar, if desired. Cover with plastic wrap and refrigerate until cold, at least 1 hour. Stir to recombine before serving. (Can be refrigerated in an airtight container for up to 4 days. If too thick after chilling, add 1 to 2 teaspoons water.)

Bittersweet Chocolate Sauce

MAKES ABOUT 1 ½ CUPS

This sauce is served over Profiteroles (page 260) and can be served over Classic Pound Cake (page 329) or ice cream.

¾	cup heavy cream
3	tablespoons light corn syrup
3	tablespoons unsalted butter, cut into 3 pieces
	Pinch salt
6	ounces bittersweet chocolate, chopped fine

Bring the heavy cream, corn syrup, butter, and salt to a boil in a small nonreactive saucepan over medium-high heat. Off the heat, add the chocolate while gently swirling the saucepan. Cover the pan and let stand until the chocolate is melted, about 5 minutes. Uncover and whisk gently until combined. (The sauce can be cooled to room temperature, placed in an airtight container, and refrigerated for up to 3 weeks. To reheat, transfer the sauce to a heatproof bowl set over a saucepan of simmering water. Alternatively, microwave at 50 percent power, stirring once or twice, 1 to 3 minutes.)

Caramel Sauce

MAKES ABOUT 1 ½ CUPS

This sauce is a component in Caramel Chocolate Truffle Tart (page 229) as well as an accompaniment to German Apple Pancake (page 302) or ice cream. When the hot cream mixture is added in step 3, the hot sugar syrup will bubble vigorously (and dangerously), so don't use a smaller saucepan.

½	cup water
1	cup (7 ounces) sugar
1	cup heavy cream
⅛	teaspoon salt
½	teaspoon vanilla extract
½	teaspoon juice from 1 lemon

1. Place the water in a heavy-bottomed 2-quart saucepan; pour the sugar in the center of the pan, taking care not to let the sugar crystals adhere to the sides of the pan. Cover and bring the mixture to a boil over high heat; once boiling, uncover and continue to boil until the syrup is thick and straw-colored (the syrup should register 300 degrees on a candy thermometer), about 7 minutes. Reduce the heat to medium and continue to cook until the syrup is a deep amber (350 degrees), about 1 to 2 minutes.

2. Meanwhile, bring the cream and salt to a simmer in a small saucepan over high heat (if the cream boils before the sugar reaches a deep amber color, remove the cream from the heat and cover to keep warm).

3. Remove the sugar syrup from the heat; very carefully pour about one quarter of the hot cream into it (the mixture will bubble vigorously) and let the bubbling subside. Add the remaining cream, vanilla, and lemon juice; whisk until the sauce is smooth. (The sauce can be cooled and refrigerated in an airtight container for up to 2 weeks. Reheat it in the microwave or a small saucepan over low heat until warm and fluid.)

Whipped Cream
MAKES ABOUT 2 CUPS

We prefer pasteurized heavy cream to ultra-pasteurized for whipped cream. Whipped cream can be refrigerated in a fine-mesh sieve set over a measuring cup for up to 8 hours.

1	cup heavy cream, cold
1	tablespoon sugar
1	teaspoon vanilla extract

1. Chill a nonreactive, deep 1- to 1½-quart bowl and beaters for an electric mixer in the freezer for at least 20 minutes.

2. Add the cream, sugar, and vanilla to the chilled bowl. Beat at low speed until small bubbles form, about 30 seconds. Increase the speed to medium and continue beating until the beaters leave a trail, about 30 seconds. Increase the speed to high and continue beating until the cream is smooth, thick, and nearly doubled in volume, about 20 seconds for soft peaks or about 30 seconds for stiff peaks. If necessary, finish beating by hand to adjust the consistency.

Crème Anglaise
MAKES ABOUT 2 CUPS

This simple stirred custard sauce elevates almost any dessert to a more sophisticated level. We especially like crème anglaise with rich desserts such as Individual Sticky Toffee Pudding Cakes (page 405) and Hot Fudge Pudding Cake (page 403). If you cannot find a vanilla bean, 1 teaspoon vanilla extract is a suitable substitution. Be sure to heat the custard slowly, stirring continuously, over low heat. When stirring, run the spoon along the sides and bottom of the saucepan to prevent the yolks from curdling.

½	vanilla bean, halved lengthwise
1½	cups whole milk
5	large egg yolks
¼	cup sugar
	Pinch salt

1. With a paring knife, scrape the vanilla seeds free from the pod. Place the seeds, bean pod, and milk in a medium saucepan and heat the mixture over medium heat until steaming, about 3 minutes. Remove from the heat, cover, and steep for 20 minutes. Uncover, return the mixture to medium heat, and heat until steaming, about 1 minute.

2. Meanwhile, whisk the yolks, sugar, and salt together in a medium bowl until pale yellow in color, about 1 minute. Slowly pour the hot milk into the yolk mixture to temper, whisking constantly. Return the mixture to the saucepan and cook over low heat, stirring constantly with a wooden spoon, until the mixture thickens slightly, coats the back of the spoon with a thin film, and registers 175 to 180 degrees on an instant-read thermometer, 5 to 8 minutes. Immediately pour the mixture through a fine-mesh strainer into a medium bowl set in an ice water bath and cool. Transfer to a clean, airtight container, pressing a piece of plastic wrap flush against the surface to prevent the sauce from forming a skin. Cover and refrigerate until ready to use, up to 2 days.

INDEX